Mining of Massive Datasets

Third Edition

The Web, social media, mobile activity, sensors, Internet commerce, and many other modern applications provide many extremely large datasets from which information can be gleaned by data mining. This book focuses on practical algorithms that have been used to solve key problems in data mining and can be used on even the largest datasets.

It begins with a discussion of the MapReduce framework and related techniques for efficient parallel programming. The tricks of locality-sensitive hashing are explained. This body of knowledge, which deserves to be more widely known, is essential when seeking similar objects in a very large collection without having to compare each pair of objects. Stream-processing algorithms for mining data that arrives too fast for exhaustive processing are also explained. The PageRank idea and related tricks for organizing the Web are covered next. Other chapters cover the problems of finding frequent itemsets and clustering, each from the point of view that the data is too large to fit in main memory. Two applications: recommendation systems and Web advertising, each vital in e-commerce, are treated in detail. Later chapters cover algorithms for analyzing social-network graphs, compressing large-scale data, and machine learning.

This third edition includes new and extended coverage on decision trees, deep learning, and mining social-network graphs. Written by leading authorities in database and Web technologies, it is essential reading for students and practitioners alike.

Mining of Massive Datasets

Third Edition

JURE LESKOVEC

Stanford University

ANAND RAJARAMAN

Rocketship VC

JEFFREY DAVID ULLMAN

Stanford University

CAMBRIDGE
UNIVERSITY PRESS

CAMBRIDGE
UNIVERSITY PRESS

University Printing House, Cambridge CB2 8BS, United Kingdom

One Liberty Plaza, 20th Floor, New York, NY 10006, USA

477 Williamstown Road, Port Melbourne, VIC 3207, Australia

314–321, 3rd Floor, Plot 3, Splendor Forum, Jasola District Centre,
New Delhi – 110025, India

79 Anson Road, #06-04/06, Singapore 079906

Cambridge University Press is part of the University of Cambridge.

It furthers the University's mission by disseminating knowledge in the pursuit of
education, learning, and research at the highest international levels of excellence.

www.cambridge.org
Information on this title: www.cambridge.org/9781108476348
DOI: 10.1017/9781108684163

First edition © A. Rajaraman and J. D. Ullman 2012
Second and Third editions © J. Leskovec, A. Rajaraman, and J. D. Ullman 2014, 2020

First published 2012
Second edition 2014
Third edition 2020

A catalogue record for this publication is available from the British Library

ISBN 978-1-108-47634-8 Hardback

Contents

Preface

This book evolved from material developed over several years by Anand Raja-raman and Jeff Ullman for a one-quarter course at Stanford. The course CS345A, titled "Web Mining," was designed as an advanced graduate course, although it has become accessible and interesting to advanced undergraduates. When Jure Leskovec joined the Stanford faculty, we reorganized the material considerably. He introduced a new course CS224W on network analysis and added material to CS345A, which was renumbered CS246. The three authors also introduced a large-scale data-mining project course, CS341. The book now contains material taught in all three courses.

What the Book Is About

At the highest level of description, this book is about data mining. However, it focuses on data mining of very large amounts of data, that is, data so large it does not fit in main memory. Because of the emphasis on size, many of our examples are about the Web or data derived from the Web. Further, the book takes an algorithmic point of view: data mining is about applying algorithms to data, rather than using data to "train" a machine-learning engine of some sort. The principal topics covered are:

(1) Distributed file systems and map-reduce as a tool for creating parallel algorithms that succeed on very large amounts of data.

(2) Similarity search, including the key techniques of minhashing and locality-sensitive hashing.

(3) Data-stream processing and specialized algorithms for dealing with data that arrives so fast it must be processed immediately or lost.

(4) The technology of search engines, including Google's PageRank, link-spam detection, and the hubs-and-authorities approach.

(5) Frequent-itemset mining, including association rules, market-baskets, the A-Priori Algorithm and its improvements.

(6) Algorithms for clustering very large, high-dimensional datasets.

(7) Two key problems for Web applications: managing advertising and recommendation systems.

(8) Algorithms for analyzing and mining the structure of very large graphs, especially social-network graphs.

(9) Techniques for obtaining the important properties of a large dataset by dimensionality reduction, including singular-value decomposition and latent semantic indexing.

(10) Machine-learning algorithms that can be applied to very large data, such as perceptrons, support-vector machines, gradient descent, decision trees, and neural nets.

(11) Neural nets and deep learning, including the most important special cases: convolutional and recurrent neural networks, and long short-term memory networks.

Prerequisites

To appreciate fully the material in this book, we recommend the following prerequisites:

(1) An introduction to database systems, covering SQL and related programming systems.

(2) A sophomore-level course in data structures, algorithms, and discrete math.

(3) A sophomore-level course in software systems, software engineering, and programming languages.

Exercises

The book contains extensive exercises, with some for almost every section. We indicate harder exercises or parts of exercises with an exclamation point. The hardest exercises have a double exclamation point.

Support on the Web

Go to http://www.mmds.org for slides, homework assignments, project requirements, and exams from courses related to this book.

Gradiance Automated Homework

There are automated exercises based on this book, using the Gradiance root-question technology, available at www.gradiance.com/services. Students may enter a public class by creating an account at that site and entering the class with code 1EDD8A1D. Instructors may use the site by making an account there and then emailing `support at gradiance dot com` with their login name, the name of their school, and a request to use the MMDS materials.

Acknowledgements

Cover art is by Scott Ullman.

We would like to thank Foto Afrati, Arun Marathe, and Rok Sosic for critical readings of a draft of this manuscript.

Errors were also reported by Rajiv Abraham, Ruslan Aduk, Apoorv Agarwal, Aris Anagnostopoulos, Yokila Arora, Stefanie Anna Baby, Atilla Soner Balkir, Arnaud Belletoile, Robin Bennett, Susan Biancani, Richard Boyd, Amitabh Chaudhary, Leland Chen, Hua Feng, Marcus Gemeinder, Anastasios Gounaris, Clark Grubb, Shrey Gupta, Waleed Hameid, Saman Haratizadeh, Julien Hoachuck, Przemyslaw Horban, Hsiu-Hsuan Huang, Jeff Hwang, Rafi Kamal, Lachlan Kang, Ed Knorr, Haewoon Kwak, Ellis Lau, Greg Lee, David Z. Liu, Ethan Lozano, Yunan Luo, Michael Mahoney, Sergio Matos, Justin Meyer, Bryant Moscon, Brad Penoff, John Phillips, Philips Kokoh Prasetyo, Qi Ge, Harizo Rajaona, Timon Ruban, Rich Seiter, Hitesh Shetty, Angad Singh, Sandeep Sripada, Dennis Sidharta, Krzysztof Stencel, Mark Storus, Roshan Sumbaly, Zack Taylor, Tim Triche Jr., Wang Bin, Weng Zhen-Bin, Robert West, Steven Euijong Whang, Oscar Wu, Xie Ke, Christopher T.-R. Yeh, Nicolas Zhao, and Zhou Jingbo, The remaining errors are ours, of course.

J. L.
A. R.
J. D. U.
Palo Alto, CA
July, 2019

1   Data Mining

In this introductory chapter we begin with the essence of data mining and a discussion of how data mining is treated by the various disciplines that contribute to this field. We cover "Bonferroni's Principle," which is really a warning about overusing the ability to mine data. This chapter is also the place where we summarize a few useful ideas that are not data mining *per se*, but are useful in understanding some important data-mining concepts. These include the TF.IDF measure of word importance, behavior of hash functions and indexes, and identities involving e, the base of natural logarithms. Finally, we give an outline of the topics covered in the balance of the book.

1.1   What is Data Mining?

In the 1990s "data mining" was an exciting and popular new concept. Around 2010, people instead started to speak of "big data." Today, the popular term is "data science." However, during all this time, the concept remained the same: use the most powerful hardware, the most powerful programming systems, and the most efficient algorithms to solve problems in science, commerce, healthcare, government, the humanities, and many other fields of human endeavor.

1.1.1   Modeling

To many, data mining is the process of creating a model from data, often by the process of machine learning, which we mention in Section 1.1.3 and discuss more fully in Chapter 12. However, more generally, the objective of data mining is an algorithm. For instance, we discuss locality-sensitive hashing in Chapter 3 and a number of stream-mining algorithms in Chapter 4, none of which involve a model. Yet in many important applications, the hard part is creating the model, and once the model is available, the algorithm to use the model is straightforward.

EXAMPLE 1.1 Consider the problem of detecting emails that are phishing attacks. The most common approach is to build a model of phishing emails, perhaps by examining emails that people have recently reported as phishing attacks and looking for the words or phrases that appear unusually often in those emails, such as "Nigerian prince" or "verify account." The model could be weights on words, with positive weights for words that appear frequently in phishing emails and negative weights for words that do not. Then the algorithm to detect phishing emails is simple. Apply the model to each email, that is, sum the weights of the words in that email, and say the email is phishing if and only if the sum is positive. Finding the best weights is a difficult problem, one we shall take up in Section 12.2. □

1.1.2   Statistical Modeling

Statisticians were the first to use the term "data mining." Originally, "data mining" or "data dredging" was a derogatory term referring to attempts to extract information that was not supported by the data. Section 1.2 illustrates the sort of errors one can make by trying to extract what really isn't in the data. Today, "data mining" has taken on a positive meaning. Now, statisticians view data mining as the construction of a *statistical model*, that is, an underlying distribution from which the visible data is drawn.

EXAMPLE 1.2 Suppose our data is a set of numbers. This data is much simpler than data that would be data-mined, but it will serve as an example. A statistician might decide that the data comes from a Gaussian distribution and use a formula to compute the most likely parameters of this Gaussian. The mean and standard deviation of this Gaussian distribution completely characterize the distribution and would become the model of the data. □

1.1.3   Machine Learning

There are some who regard data mining as synonymous with machine learning. There is no question that some data mining appropriately uses algorithms from machine learning. Machine-learning practitioners use the data as a training set, to train an algorithm of one of the many types used for machine-learning, such as Bayes nets, support-vector machines, decision trees, hidden Markov models, and a great variety of others.

There are situations where using data in this way makes sense. The typical case where machine learning is a good approach is when we have little idea of what the data says about the problem we are trying to solve. For example, it is rather unclear what it is about movies that makes certain movie-goers like or dislike it. Thus, in answering the "Netflix challenge" to devise an algorithm that predicts the ratings of movies by users, based on a sample of their responses, machine-learning algorithms have proved quite successful. We shall discuss a simple form of this type of algorithm in Section 9.4.

However, machine learning can be uncompetitive in situations where we can describe the goals of the mining more directly. An interesting case in point is the attempt by WhizBang! Labs[1] to use machine learning to locate people's resumes

---

[1] This startup attempted to use machine learning to mine large-scale data, and hired many of the top machine-learning people to do so. Unfortunately, it was not able to survive.

on the Web. It was not able to do better than algorithms designed by hand to look for some of the obvious words and phrases that appear in the typical resume. Since everyone who has looked at or written a resume has a pretty good idea of what resumes contain, there was no mystery about what makes a Web page be a resume. Thus, there was no advantage to machine-learning over the direct design of an algorithm to discover resumes.

Another problem with some machine-learning methods is that they often yield a model that, while it may be quite accurate, is not explainable. In some cases, explainability is not important. For example, if you ask Google why it has classi-fied a gmail as spam, it usually says something like "it looks like other messages that people have identified as spam." That is, the email matches whatever model of spam Google has developed that day, undoubtedly using a technique from the arsenal of machine-learning algorithms. That explanation is probably satisfac-tory. We really don't care what Google does, as long as it makes the correct spam/not-spam decision.

On the other hand, consider an automobile-insurance company that creates a model of the risk associated with each driver and assigns different premiums to each, according to the model. If your premium goes up, you might well want an explanation of what the new model is doing and why it changed the estimate of your risk. Unfortunately, in many machine-learning methods, especially "deep learning," where the model involves layer upon layer of small elements, each of which makes a decision based on inputs from the previous layer, it may not be possible to give a coherent explanation of what the model is doing.

1.1.4 Computational Approaches to Modeling

In contrast to the statisical approach, computer scientists tend to look at data mining as an algorithmic problem. In this case, a model of the data is simply the answer to a complex query about that data. For instance, given the set of numbers of Example 1.2, we might compute their average and standard deviation. Note that these values might not be the parameters of the Gaussian that best fits the data, although they will almost certainly be very close if the size of the data is large, and the source of the data is truly Gaussian.

There are many different approaches to modeling data. We have already men-tioned the possibility of constructing a random process whereby the data could have been generated. Most other approaches to modeling can be described as either

(1) Summarizing the data succinctly and approximately, or

(2) Extracting the most prominent features of the data and ignoring the rest.

We shall explore these two approaches in the following sections.

1.1.5 Summarization

One of the most interesting forms of summarization is the PageRank idea, which made Google successful and which we shall cover in Chapter 5. In this form of Web mining, the entire complex structure of the Web is summarized by a single number for each page. This number, the "PageRank" of the page, is (oversimplifying somewhat) the probability that a random walker on the graph would be at that page at any given time. Remarkably, this ranking reflects very well the "importance" of the page – the degree to which typical searchers would like that page returned as an answer to their search query.

Another important form of summary – clustering – will be covered in Chapter 7. Here, data is viewed as points in a multidimensional space. Points that are "close" in this space are assigned to the same cluster. The clusters themselves are summarized, perhaps by giving the centroid of the cluster and the average distance from the centroid of points in the cluster. These cluster summaries then become the summary of the entire data set.

EXAMPLE 1.3 A famous instance of clustering to solve a problem took place long ago in London, and it was done entirely without computers.[2] The physician John Snow, dealing with a Cholera outbreak plotted the cases on a map of the city. A small illustration suggesting the process is shown in Fig. 1.1.

Figure 1.1 Plotting cholera cases on a map of London

The cases clustered around some of the intersections of roads. These intersections were the locations of wells that had become contaminated; people who lived nearest these wells got sick, while people who lived nearer to wells that had not been contaminated did not get sick. Without the ability to cluster the data, the cause of cholera would not have been discovered. □

[2] See http://en.wikipedia.org/wiki/1854_Broad_Street_cholera_outbreak.

1.1.6   Feature Extraction

The typical feature-based model looks for the most extreme examples of a phenomenon and represents the data by these examples. If you are familiar with Bayes nets, a branch of machine learning and a topic we do not cover in this book, you know how a complex relationship between objects is represented by finding the strongest statistical dependencies among these objects and using only those in representing all statistical connections. Some of the important kinds of feature extraction from large-scale data that we shall study are:

(1) *Frequent Itemsets.* This model makes sense for data that consists of "baskets" of small sets of items, as in the market-basket problem that we shall discuss in Chapter 6. We look for small sets of items that appear together in many baskets, and these "frequent itemsets" are the characterization of the data that we seek. The original application of this sort of mining was true market baskets: the sets of items, such as hamburger and ketchup, that people tend to buy together when checking out at the cash register of a store or super market.

(2) *Similar Items.* Often, your data looks like a collection of sets, and the objective is to find pairs of sets that have a relatively large fraction of their elements in common. An example is treating customers at an on-line store like Amazon as the set of items they have bought. In order for Amazon to recommend something else they might like, Amazon can look for "similar" customers and recommend something many of these customers have bought. This process is called "collaborative filtering." If customers were single-minded – that is, they bought only one kind of thing – then clustering customers might work. However, since customers tend to have interests in many different things, it is more useful to find, for each customer, a small number of other customers who are similar in their tastes, and represent the data by these connections. We discuss similarity in Chapter 3.

1.2   Statistical Limits on Data Mining

A common sort of data-mining problem involves discovering unusual events hidden within massive amounts of data. This section is a discussion of the problem, including "Bonferroni's Principle," a warning against overzealous use of data mining.

1.2.1   Total Information Awareness

Following the terrorist attack of Sept. 11, 2001, it was noticed that there were four people enrolled in different flight schools, learning how to pilot commercial aircraft, although they were not affiliated with any airline. It was conjectured that the information needed to predict and foil the attack was available in data, but that there was then no way to examine the data and detect suspicious events. The response was a program called TIA, or *Total Information Awareness*, which was intended to mine all the data it could find, including credit-card receipts, hotel records, travel data, and many other kinds of information in order to track terrorist activity. Now *information integration* – the idea of relating and combining different data sources to obtain insights that are not available from any one source – is often a key step on the way to solving an important problem.

TIA naturally caused great concern among privacy advocates, and the project was eventually killed by Congress. It is not the purpose of this book to discuss the difficult issue of the privacy-security tradeoff. However, the prospect of TIA or a system like it does raise many technical questions about its feasibility. In this section, we wish to focus on one particular technical problem: if you look in your data for too many things at the same time, you will see things that look interesting, but are in fact simply statistical artifacts and have no significance. That is, if you search your data for activities that look like terrorist behavior, are you not going to find many innocent activities – or even illicit activities that are not terrorism – that will result in visits from the police and maybe worse than just a visit? The answer is that it all depends on how narrowly you define the activities that you look for. Statisticians have seen this problem in many guises and have a theory, which we introduce in the next section, for avoiding this sort of error.

1.2.2 Bonferroni's Principle

Suppose you have a certain amount of data, and you look for events of a certain type within that data. You can expect events of this type to occur, even if the data is completely random, and the number of occurrences of these events will grow as the size of the data grows. These occurrences are "bogus," in the sense that they have no cause other than that random data will always have some number of unusual features that look significant but aren't. A theorem of statistics, known as the *Bonferroni correction* gives a statistically sound way to avoid most of these bogus positive responses to a search through the data. Without going into the statistical details, we offer an informal version, *Bonferroni's principle*, that helps us avoid treating random occurrences as if they were real. Calculate the expected number of occurrences of the events you are looking for, on the assumption that data is random. If this number is significantly larger than the number of real instances you hope to find, then you must expect almost anything you find to be bogus, i.e., a statistical artifact rather than evidence of what you are looking for. This observation is the informal statement of Bonferroni's principle.

In a situation like searching for terrorists, where we expect that there are few terrorists operating at any one time, Bonferroni's principle says that we may only detect terrorists by looking for events that are so rare that they are unlikely to occur in random data. We give an extended example below.

1.2.3   An Example of Bonferroni's Principle

Suppose there are believed to be some "evil-doers" out there, and we want to detect them. Suppose further that we have reason to believe that periodically, evil-doers gather at a hotel to plot their evil. Let us make the following assumptions about the size of the problem:

(1) There are one billion people who might be evil-doers.

(2) Everyone goes to a hotel one day in 100.

(3) A hotel holds 100 people. Hence, there are 100,000 hotels – enough to hold the 1% of a billion people who visit a hotel on any given day.

(4) We shall examine hotel records for 1000 days.

To find evil-doers in this data, we shall look for people who, on two different days, were both at the same hotel. Suppose, however, that there really are no evil-doers. That is, everyone behaves at random, deciding with probability 0.01 to visit a hotel on any given day, and if so, choosing one of the 10^5 hotels at random. Would we find any pairs of people who appear to be evil-doers?

We can do a simple approximate calculation as follows. The probability of any two people both deciding to visit a hotel on any given day is .0001. The chance that they will visit the same hotel is this probability divided by 10^5, the number of hotels. Thus, the chance that they will visit the same hotel on one given day is 10^{-9}. The chance that they will visit the same hotel on two different given days is the square of this number, 10^{-18}. Note that the hotels can be different on the two days.

Now, we must consider how many events will indicate evil-doing. An "event" in this sense is a pair of people and a pair of days, such that the two people were at the same hotel on each of the two days. To simplify the arithmetic, note that for large n, $\binom{n}{2}$ is about $n^2/2$. We shall use this approximation in what follows. Thus, the number of pairs of people is $\binom{10^9}{2} = 5 \times 10^{17}$. The number of pairs of days is $\binom{1000}{2} = 5 \times 10^5$. The expected number of events that look like evil-doing is the product of the number of pairs of people, the number of pairs of days, and the probability that any one pair of people and pair of days is an instance of the behavior we are looking for. That number is

$$5 \times 10^{17} \times 5 \times 10^5 \times 10^{-18} = 250,000$$

That is, there will be a quarter of a million pairs of people who look like evil-doers, even though they are not.

Now, suppose there really are 10 pairs of evil-doers out there. The police will need to investigate a quarter of a million other pairs in order to find the real evil-doers. In addition to the intrusion on the lives of half a million innocent people, the work involved is sufficiently great that this approach to finding evil-doers is probably not feasible.

1.2.4   Exercises for Section 1.2

EXERCISE 1.2.1   Using the information from Section 1.2.3, what would be the number of suspected pairs if the following changes were made to the data (and all other numbers remained as they were in that section)?

(a) The number of days of observation was raised to 2000.
(b) The number of people observed was raised to 2 billion (and there were therefore 200,000 hotels).
(c) We only reported a pair as suspect if they were at the same hotel at the same time on three different days.

! EXERCISE 1.2.2   Suppose we have information about the supermarket purchases of 100 million people. Each person goes to the supermarket 100 times in a year and buys 10 of the 1000 items that the supermarket sells. We believe that a pair of terrorists will buy exactly the same set of 10 items (perhaps the ingredients for a bomb?) at some time during the year. If we search for pairs of people who have bought the same set of items, would we expect that any such people found were truly terrorists?[3]

1.3   Things Useful to Know

In this section, we offer brief introductions to subjects that you may or may not have seen in your study of other courses. Each will be useful in the study of data mining. They include:

(1) The TF.IDF measure of word importance.
(2) Hash functions and their use.
(3) Secondary storage (disk) and its effect on running time of algorithms.
(4) The base e of natural logarithms and identities involving that constant.
(5) Power laws.

1.3.1   Importance of Words in Documents

In several applications of data mining, we shall be faced with the problem of categorizing documents (sequences of words) by their topic. Typically, topics are identified by finding the special words that characterize documents about that topic. For instance, articles about baseball would tend to have many occurrences of words like "ball," "bat," "pitch," "run," and so on. Once we have classified documents to determine they are about baseball, it is not hard to notice that words such as these appear unusually frequently. However, until we have made the classification, it is not possible to identify these words as characteristic.

---

[3] That is, assume our hypothesis that terrorists will surely buy a set of 10 items in common at some time during the year. We don't want to address the matter of whether or not terrorists would necessarily do so.

Thus, classification often starts by looking at documents, and finding the significant words in those documents. Our first guess might be that the words appearing most frequently in a document are the most significant. However, that intuition is exactly opposite of the truth. The most frequent words will most surely be the common words such as "the" or "and," which help build ideas but do not carry any significance themselves. In fact, the several hundred most common words in English (called *stop words*) are often removed from documents before any attempt to classify them.

In fact, the indicators of the topic are relatively rare words. However, not all rare words are equally useful as indicators. There are certain words, for example "notwithstanding" or "albeit," that appear rarely in a collection of documents, yet do not tell us anything useful. On the other hand, a word like "chukker" is probably equally rare, but tips us off that the document is about the sport of polo. The difference between rare words that tell us something and those that do not has to do with the concentration of the useful words in just a few documents. That is, the presence of a word like "albeit" in a document does not make it terribly more likely that it will appear multiple times. However, if an article mentions "chukker" once, it is likely to tell us what happened in the "first chukker," then the "second chukker," and so on. That is, the word is likely to be repeated if it appears at all.

The formal measure of how concentrated into relatively few documents are the occurrences of a given word is called TF.IDF (*Term Frequency times Inverse Document Frequency*). It is normally computed as follows. Suppose we have a collection of N documents. Define f_{ij} to be the *frequency* (number of occurrences) of term (word) i in document j. Then, define the *term frequency* TF_{ij} to be:

$$TF_{ij} = \frac{f_{ij}}{\max_k f_{kj}}$$

That is, the term frequency of term i in document j is f_{ij} normalized by dividing it by the maximum number of occurrences of any term (perhaps excluding stop words) in the same document. Thus, the most frequent term in document j gets a TF of 1, and other terms get fractions as their term frequency for this document.

The IDF for a term is defined as follows. Suppose term i appears in n_i of the N documents in the collection. Then $IDF_i = \log_2(N/n_i)$. The TF.IDF score for term i in document j is then defined to be $TF_{ij} \times IDF_i$. The terms with the highest TF.IDF score are often the terms that best characterize the topic of the document.

EXAMPLE 1.4   Suppose our repository consists of $2^{20} = 1{,}048{,}576$ documents. Suppose word w appears in $2^{10} = 1024$ of these documents. Then $IDF_w = \log_2(2^{20}/2^{10}) = \log 2(2^{10}) = 10$. Consider a document j in which w appears 20 times, and that is the maximum number of times in which any word appears (perhaps after eliminating stop words). Then $TF_{wj} = 1$, and the TF.IDF score for w in document j is 10.

Suppose that in document k, word w appears once, while the maximum number of occurrences of any word in this document is 20. Then $TF_{wk} = 1/20$, and the TF.IDF score for w in document k is $1/2$. $\square$

1.3.2   Hash Functions

The reader has probably heard of hash tables, and perhaps used them in Java classes or similar packages. The hash functions that make hash tables feasible are also essential components in a number of data-mining algorithms, where the hash table takes an unfamiliar form. We shall review the basics here.

First, a hash function h takes a *hash-key* value as an argument and produces a *bucket number* as a result. The bucket number is an integer, normally in the range 0 to $B-1$, where B is the number of buckets. Hash-keys can be of any type. There is an intuitive property of hash functions that they "randomize" hash-keys. To be precise, if hash-keys are drawn randomly from a reasonable population of possible hash-keys, then h will send approximately equal numbers of hash-keys to each of the B buckets. It would be impossible to do so if, for example, the population of possible hash-keys were smaller than B. Such a population would not be "reasonable." However, there can be more subtle reasons why a hash function fails to achieve an approximately uniform distribution into buckets.

EXAMPLE 1.5   Suppose hash-keys are positive integers. A common and simple hash function is to pick $h(x) = x \mod B$, that is, the remainder when x is divided by B. That choice works well if our population of hash-keys is all positive integers. $1/B$th of the integers will be assigned to each of the buckets. However, suppose our population is the even integers, and $B = 10$. Then only buckets 0, 2, 4, 6, and 8 can be the value of $h(x)$, and the hash function is distinctly nonrandom in its behavior. On the other hand, if we picked $B = 11$, then we would find that $1/11$th of the even integers get sent to each of the 11 buckets, so the hash function would work well in this case. $\square$

The generalization of Example 1.5 is that when hash-keys are integers, chosing B so it has any common factor with all (or even most of) the possible hash-keys will result in nonrandom distribution into buckets. Thus, it is normally preferred that we choose B to be a prime. That choice reduces the chance of nonrandom behavior, although we still have to consider the possibility that all hash-keys have B as a factor. Of course there are many other types of hash functions not based on modular arithmetic. We shall not try to summarize the options here, but some sources of information will be mentioned in the bibliographic notes.

What if hash-keys are not integers? In a sense, all data types have values that are composed of bits, and sequences of bits can always be interpreted as integers. However, there are some simple rules that enable us to convert common types to integers. For example, if hash-keys are strings, convert each character to its ASCII or Unicode equivalent, which can be interpreted as a small integer. Sum the integers before dividing by B. As long as B is smaller than the typical sum of character codes for the population of strings, the distribution into buckets will be relatively uniform. If B is larger, then we can partition the characters of a string into groups of several characters each. Treat the concatenation of the codes for the characters of a group as a single integer. Sum the integers associated with all the groups of a string, and divide by B as before. For instance, if B is around a billion, or 2^{30}, then grouping characters four at a time will give us 32-bit integers. The sum of several of these will distribute fairly evenly into a billion buckets.

For more complex data types, we can extend the idea used for converting strings to integers, recursively.

- For a type that is a record, each of whose components has its own type, recursively convert the value of each component to an integer, using the algorithm appropriate for the type of that component. Sum the integers for the components, and convert the integer sum to buckets by dividing by B.
- For a type that is an array, set, or bag of elements of some one type, convert the values of the elements' type to integers, sum the integers, and divide by B.

1.3.3   Indexes

An *index* is a data structure that makes it efficient to retrieve objects given the value of one or more elements of those objects. The most common situation is one where the objects are records, and the index is on one of the fields of that record. Given a value v for that field, the index lets us retrieve all the records with value v in that field, without having to retrieve all the records in the file. For example, we could have a file of (name, address, phone) triples, and an index on the phone field. Given a phone number, the index allows us to find quickly the record or records with that phone number.

There are many ways to implement indexes, and we shall not attempt to survey the matter here. The bibliographic notes give suggestions for further reading. However, a hash table is one simple way to build an index. The field or fields on which the index is based form the hash-key for a hash function. We apply the hash function applied to value of the hash-key for each record, and the record itself is placed in the bucket whose number is determined by the hash function. The bucket could be a list of records in main-memory, or a disk block, for example.

Then, given a hash-key value, we can hash it, find the bucket, and need to search only that bucket to find the records with that value for the hash-key. If we choose the number of buckets B to be comparable to the number of records in the file, then there will be relatively few records in any bucket, and we will find few, if any, records in the bucket with a hash key that is not the one we are looking for. Thus, the search for the desired records is quite efficient, compared with searching the entire file for records with the desired hash key.

EXAMPLE 1.6   Figure 1.2 suggests what a main-memory index of records with name, address, and phone fields might look like. Here, the index is on the phone

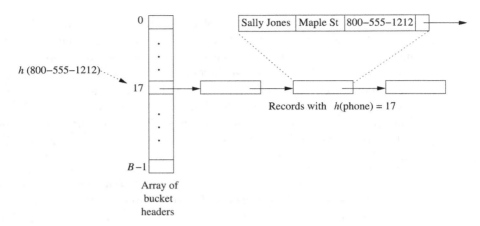

Figure 1.2 A hash table used as an index; phone numbers are hashed to buckets, and the entire record is placed in the bucket whose number is the hash value of the phone

field, and buckets are linked lists. We show the phone 800-555-1212 hashed to bucket number 17. There is an array of *bucket headers*, whose ith element is the head of a linked list for the bucket numbered i. We show, in expanded form, one of the elements of the linked list. It contains a record with name, address, and phone fields. This record is in fact one with the phone number 800-555-1212. Other records in that bucket may or may not have this phone number. We only know that whatever phone number they have is a phone that hashes to 17.   □

1.3.4   Secondary Storage

It is important, when dealing with large-scale data, that we have a good understanding of the difference in time taken to perform computations when the data is initially on disk, as opposed to the time needed if the data is initially in main memory. The physical characteristics of disks is another subject on which we could say much, but shall say only a little and leave the interested reader to follow the bibliographic notes.

Disks are organized into *blocks*, which are the minimum units that the operating system uses to move data between main memory and disk. For example, the Windows operating system uses blocks of 64K bytes (i.e., $2^{16} = 65{,}536$ bytes to be exact). It takes approximately ten milliseconds to *access* (move the disk head to the track of the block and wait for the block to rotate under the head) and read a disk block. That delay is at least five orders of magnitude (a factor of 10^5) slower than the time taken to read a word from main memory, so if all we want to do is access a few bytes, there is an overwhelming benefit to having data in main memory. In fact, if we want to do something simple to every byte of a disk block, e.g., treat the block as a bucket of a hash table and search for a particular value of the hash-key among all the records in that bucket, then the time taken to move the block from disk to main memory will be far larger than the time taken to do the computation.

By organizing our data so that related data is on a single *cylinder* (the collection of blocks reachable at a fixed radius from the center of the disk, and therefore accessible without moving the disk head), we can read all the blocks on the cylinder into main memory in considerably less than 10 milliseconds per block. You can assume that a disk cannot transfer data to main memory at more than a hundred million bytes per second, no matter how that data is organized. That is not a problem when your dataset is a megabyte. But a dataset of a hundred gigabytes or a terabyte presents problems just accessing it, let alone doing anything useful with it.

1.3.5 The Base of Natural Logarithms

The constant $e = 2.7182818\cdots$ has a number of useful special properties. In particular, e is the limit of $(1 + \frac{1}{x})^x$ as x goes to infinity. The values of this expression for $x = 1, 2, 3, 4$ are approximately $2, 2.25, 2.37, 2.44$, so you should find it easy to believe that the limit of this series is around 2.72.

Some algebra lets us obtain approximations to many seemingly complex expressions. Consider $(1 + a)^b$, where a is small. We can rewrite the expression as $(1 + a)^{(1/a)(ab)}$. Then substitute $a = 1/x$ and $1/a = x$, so we have $(1 + \frac{1}{x})^{x(ab)}$, which is

$$\left(\left(1 + \frac{1}{x}\right)^x \right)^{ab}$$

Since a is assumed small, x is large, so the subexpression $(1 + \frac{1}{x})^x$ will be close to the limiting value of e. We can thus approximate $(1 + a)^b$, for small a, as e^{ab}.

Similar identities hold when a is negative. That is, the limit as x goes to infinity of $(1 - \frac{1}{x})^x$ is $1/e$. It follows that the approximation $(1 + a)^b = e^{ab}$ holds even when a is a small negative number. Put another way, $(1 - a)^b$ is approximately e^{-ab} when a is small.

Some other useful approximations follow from the Taylor expansion of e^x. That is, $e^x = \sum_{i=0}^{\infty} x^i/i!$, or $e^x = 1 + x + x^2/2 + x^3/6 + x^4/24 + \cdots$. When x is large, the above series converges slowly, although it does converge because $n!$ grows faster than x^n for any constant x. However, when x is small, either positive or negative, the series converges rapidly, and only a few terms are necessary to get a good approximation.

EXAMPLE 1.7 Let $x = 1/2$. Then

$$e^{1/2} = 1 + \frac{1}{2} + \frac{1}{8} + \frac{1}{48} + \frac{1}{384} + \cdots$$

or approximately $e^{1/2} = 1.64844$.

Let $x = -1$. Then

$$e^{-1} = 1 - 1 + \frac{1}{2} - \frac{1}{6} + \frac{1}{24} - \frac{1}{120} + \frac{1}{720} - \frac{1}{5040} + \cdots$$

or approximately $e^{-1} = 0.36786$.   □

1.3.6   Power Laws

There are many phenomena that relate two variables by a *power law*, that is, a linear relationship between the logarithms of the variables. Figure 1.3 suggests such a relationship. If x is the horizontal axis and y is the vertical axis, then the relationship is $\log_{10} y = 6 - 2 \log_{10} x$.

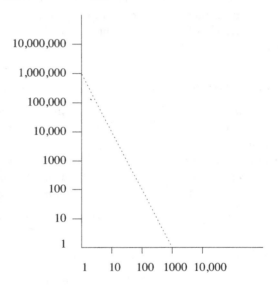

Figure 1.3 A power law with a slope of -2

EXAMPLE 1.8   We might examine book sales at Amazon.com, and let x represent the rank of books by sales. Then y is the number of sales of the xth best-selling book over some period. The implication of the graph of Fig. 1.3 would be that the best-selling book sold 1,000,000 copies, the 10th best-selling book sold 10,000 copies, the 100th best-selling book sold 100 copies, and so on for all ranks between these numbers and beyond. The implication that above rank 1000 the sales are a fraction of a book is too extreme, and we would in fact expect the line to flatten out for ranks much higher than 1000. Moreover, the slope of the line in Fig. 1.3 is probably much too steep for describing book sales, although a line that drops less precipitously would be close to what happens in practice.   □

The general form of a power law relating x and y is $\log y = b + a \log x$. If we raise the base of the logarithm (the base doesn't actually matter in the equation), say e, to the values on both sides of this equation, we get $y = e^b e^{a \log x} = e^b x^a$. Since e^b is just "some constant," let us replace it by constant c. Thus, a power law can be written as $y = c x^a$ for some constants a and c.

The Matthew Effect

Often, the existence of power laws with values of the exponent higher than 1 are explained by the *Matthew effect*. In the biblical *Book of Matthew*, there is a verse about "the rich get richer." Many phenomena exhibit this behavior, where getting a high value of some property causes that very property to increase. For example, if a Web page has many links in, then people are more likely to find the page and may choose to link to it from one of their pages as well. As another example, if a book is selling well on Amazon, then it is likely to be advertised when customers go to the Amazon site. Some of these people will choose to buy the book as well, thus increasing the sales of this book.

EXAMPLE 1.9 In Fig. 1.3 we see that when $x = 1$, $y = 10^6$, and when $x = 1000$, $y = 1$. Making the first substitution, we see $10^6 = c$. The second substitution gives us $1 = c(1000)^a$. Since we now know $c = 10^6$, the second equation gives us $1 = 10^6(1000)^a$, from which we see $a = -2$. That is, the law expressed by Fig. 1.3 is $y = 10^6 x^{-2}$, or $y = 10^6/x^2$. □

We shall meet in this book many ways that power laws govern phenomena. Here are some examples:

(1) *Node Degrees in the Web Graph*: Order all pages by the number of in-links to that page. Let x be the position of a page in this ordering, and let y be the number of in-links to the xth page. Then y as a function of x looks very much like Fig. 1.3. The exponent a is slightly larger than the -2 shown there; it has been found closer to 2.1.

(2) *Sales of Products*: Order products, say books at Amazon.com, by their sales over the past year. Let y be the number of sales of the xth most popular book. Again, the function $y(x)$ will look something like Fig. 1.3. we shall discuss the consequences of this distribution of sales in Section 9.1.2, where we take up the matter of the "long tail."

(3) *Sizes of Web Sites*: Count the number of pages at Web sites, and order sites by the number of their pages. Let y be the number of pages at the xth site. Again, the function $y(x)$ follows a power law.

(4) *Zipf's Law*: This power law originally referred to the frequency of words in a collection of documents. If you order words by frequency, and let y be the number of times the xth word in the order appears, then you get a power law, although with a much shallower slope than that of Fig. 1.3. Zipf's observation was that $y = cx^{-1/2}$. Interestingly, a number of other kinds of data follow this particular power law. For example, if we order states in the US by population and let y be the population of the xth most populous state, then x and y obey Zipf's law approximately.

1.3.7   Exercises for Section 1.3

EXERCISE 1.3.1   Suppose there is a repository of ten million documents. What (to the nearest integer) is the IDF for a word that appears in (a) 40 documents (b) 10,000 documents?

EXERCISE 1.3.2   Suppose there is a repository of ten million documents, and word w appears in 320 of them. In a particular document d, the maximum number of occurrences of a word is 15. Approximately what is the TF.IDF score for w if that word appears (a) once (b) five times?

! EXERCISE 1.3.3   Suppose hash-keys are drawn from the population of all non-negative integers that are multiples of some constant c, and hash function $h(x)$ is x mod 15. For what values of c will h be a suitable hash function, i.e., a large random choice of hash-keys will be divided roughly equally into buckets?

EXERCISE 1.3.4   In terms of e, give approximations to

$$\text{(a) } (1.01)^{500} \text{ (b) } (1.05)^{1000} \text{ (c) } (0.9)^{40}$$

EXERCISE 1.3.5   Use the Taylor expansion of e^x to compute, to three decimal places: (a) $e^{1/10}$ (b) $e^{-1/10}$ (c) e^2.

1.4   Outline of the Book

This section gives brief summaries of the remaining chapters of the book.

Chapter 2 is not about data mining per se. Rather, it introduces us to programming systems that facilitate parallel processing of massive amounts of data. We discuss the cloud-computing architecture, which uses large numbers of connected processors. We discuss in detail programming systems based on MapReduce, and offer MapReduce-based algorithms for a number of common operations using in processing massive datasets.

Chapter 3 is about finding similar items. Our starting point is that items can be represented by sets of elements, and similar sets are those that have a large fraction of their elements in common. The key techniques of minhashing and locality-sensitive hashing are explained. These techniques have numerous applications and often give surprisingly efficient solutions to problems that appear impossible for massive data sets.

In Chapter 4, we consider data in the form of a stream. The difference between a stream and a database is that the data in a stream is lost if you do not do something about it immediately. Important examples of streams are the streams of search queries at a search engine or clicks at a popular Web site. In this chapter, we see several of the surprising applications of hashing that make management of stream data feasible.

Chapter 5 is devoted to a single application: the computation of PageRank. This computation is the idea that made Google stand out from other search engines, and it is still an essential part of how search engines know what pages the user is likely to want to see. Extensions of PageRank are also essential in the fight against spam (euphemistically called "search engine optimization"), and we shall examine the latest extensions of the idea for the purpose of combating spam.

Then, Chapter 6 introduces the market-basket model of data, and its canonical problems of association rules and finding frequent itemsets. In the market-basket model, data consists of a large collection of baskets, each of which contains a small set of items. We give a sequence of algorithms capable of finding all frequent pairs of items, that is pairs of items that appear together in many baskets. Another sequence of algorithms are useful for finding most of the frequent itemsets larger than pairs, with high efficiency.

Chapter 7 examines the problem of clustering. We assume a set of items with a distance measure defining how close or far one item is from another. The goal is to examine a large amount of data and partition it into subsets (clusters), each cluster consisting of items that are all close to one another, yet far from items in the other clusters.

Chapter 8 is devoted to on-line advertising and the computational problems it engenders. We introduce the notion of an on-line algorithm – one where a good response must be given immediately, rather than waiting until we have seen the entire dataset. The idea of competitive ratio is another important concept covered in this chapter; it is the ratio of the guaranteed performance of an on-line algorithm compared with the performance of the optimal algorithm that is allowed to see all the data before making any decisions. These ideas are used to give good algorithms that match bids by advertisers for the right to display their ad in response to a query against the search queries arriving at a search engine.

Chapter 9 is devoted to recommendation systems. Many Web applications involve advising users on what they might like. The Netflix challenge is one example, where it is desired to predict what movies a user would like, or Amazon's problem of pitching a product to a customer based on information about what they might be interested in buying. There are two basic approaches to recommendation. We can characterize items by features, e.g., the stars of a movie, and recommend items with the same features as those the user is known to like. Or, we can look at other users with preferences similar to that of the user in question, and see what they liked (a technique known as collaborative filtering).

In Chapter 10, we study social networks and algorithms for their analysis. The canonical example of a social network is the graph of Facebook friends, where the nodes are people, and edges connect two people if they are friends. Directed graphs, such as followers on Twitter, can also be viewed as social networks. A common example of a problem to be addressed is identifying "communities;" that is, small sets of nodes with an unusually large number of edges among them. Other questions about social networks are general questions about graphs, such as computing the transitive closure or diameter of a graph, but are made more difficult by the size of typical networks.

Chapter 11 looks at dimensionality reduction. We are given a very large matrix, typically sparse. Think of the matrix as representing a relationship between two kinds of entities, e.g., ratings of movies by viewers. Intuitively, there are a small number of concepts, many fewer concepts than there are movies or viewers, that explain why certain viewers like certain movies. We offer several algorithms that simplify matrices by decomposing them into a product of matrices that are much smaller in one of the two dimensions. One matrix relates entities of one kind to the small number of concepts, and another relates the concepts to the other kind of entity. If done correctly, the product of the smaller matrices will be very close to the original matrix.

Chapter 12 discusses algorithms for machine learning from very large datasets. Techniques covered include perceptrons, support-vector machines, finding models by gradient descent, nearest-neighbor models, and decision trees.

Finally, Chapter 13 introduces neural nets and deep learning in particular. In addition to the general idea of a neural network, this chapter covers the important special cases of convolutional neural networks, recurrent neural networks, and long short-term memory networks.

1.5   Summary of Chapter 1

◆ *Data Mining*: This term refers to applying the powerful tools of computer science to solve problems in science, industry, and many other application areas. Frequently, the key to a successful application is building a model of the data, that is, a summary or relatively succinct representation of the most relevant features of the data.

◆ *Bonferroni's Principle*: If we are willing to view as an interesting feature of data something of which many instances can be expected to exist in random data, then we cannot rely on such features being significant. This observation limits our ability to mine data for features that are not sufficiently rare in practice.

◆ *TF.IDF*: The measure called TF.IDF lets us identify words in a collection of documents that are useful for determining the topic of each document. A word has high TF.IDF score in a document if it appears in relatively few documents, but appears in this one, and when it appears in a document it tends to appear many times.

◆ *Hash Functions*: A hash function maps hash-keys of some data type to integer bucket numbers. A good hash function distributes the possible hash-key values approximately evenly among buckets. Any data type can be the domain of a hash function.

◆ *Indexes*: An index is a data structure that allows us to store and retrieve data records efficiently, given the value in one or more of the fields of the record. Hashing is one way to build an index.

✦ *Storage on Disk*: When data must be stored on disk (secondary memory), it takes very much more time to access a desired data item than if the same data were stored in main memory. When data is large, it is important that algorithms strive to keep needed data in main memory.

✦ *Power Laws*: Many phenomena obey a law that can be expressed as $y = cx^a$ for some power a, often around -2. Such phenomena include the sales of the xth most popular book, or the number of in-links to the xth most popular page.

1.6   References for Chapter 1

[8] is a clear introduction to the basics of data mining. [3] covers data mining principally from the point of view of machine learning and statistics. The difference between the statistical approach and the computational approach to data mining is expressed in [1].

For construction of hash functions and hash tables, see [5]. Details of the TF.IDF measure and other matters regarding document processing can be found in [6]. See [4] for more on managing indexes, hash tables, and data on disk.

Power laws pertaining to the Web were explored by [2]. The Matthew effect was first observed in [7].

[1] L. Breiman, "Statistical modeling: the two cultures," *Statistical Science* **16**:3, pp. 199–215, 2001.

[2] A. Broder, R. Kumar, F. Maghoul, P. Raghavan, S. Rajagopalan, R. Stata, A. Tomkins, and J. Weiner, "Graph structure in the web," *Computer Networks* **33**:1–6, pp. 309–320, 2000.

[3] M.M. Gaber, *Scientific Data Mining and Knowledge Discovery – Principles and Foundations*, Springer, New York, 2010.

[4] H. Garcia-Molina, J.D. Ullman, and J. Widom, *Database Systems: The Complete Book* Second Edition, Prentice-Hall, Upper Saddle River, NJ, 2009.

[5] D.E. Knuth, *The Art of Computer Programming* Vol. 3 (*Sorting and Searching*), Second Edition, Addison-Wesley, Upper Saddle River, NJ, 1998.

[6] C.P. Manning, P. Raghavan, and H. Schütze, *Introduction to Information Retrieval*, Cambridge University Press, 2008.

[7] R.K. Merton, "The Matthew effect in science," *Science* **159**:3810, pp. 56–63, Jan. 5, 1968.

[8] P.-N. Tan, M. Steinbach, and V. Kumar, *Introduction to Data Mining*, Addison-Wesley, Upper Saddle River, NJ, 2005.

2 MapReduce and the New Software Stack

Modern data-mining applications, often called "big-data" analysis, require us to manage immense amounts of data quickly. In many of these applications, the data is extremely regular, and there is ample opportunity to exploit parallelism. Important examples are:

(1) The ranking of Web pages by importance, which involves an iterated matrix-vector multiplication where the dimension is many billions. This application, called "PageRank," is the subject of Chapter 5.

(2) Searches in "friends" networks at social-networking sites that involve graphs with hundreds of millions of nodes and many billions of edges. Operations on graphs of this type are covered in Chapter 10.

To deal with applications such as these, a new software stack has evolved. These programming systems are designed to get their parallelism not from a "supercomputer," but from "computing clusters" – large collections of commodity hardware, including conventional processors ("compute nodes") connected by Ethernet cables or inexpensive switches. The software stack begins with a new form of file system, called a "distributed file system," which features much larger units than the disk blocks in a conventional operating system. Distributed file systems also provide replication of data or redundancy to protect against the frequent media failures that occur when data is distributed over thousands of low-cost compute nodes.

On top of these file systems, many different higher-level programming systems have been developed. Central to the new software stack is a programming system called *MapReduce*. Implementations of MapReduce enable many of the most common calculations on large-scale data to be performed on computing clusters efficiently and in a way that is tolerant of hardware failures during the computation.

MapReduce systems are evolving and extending rapidly. Today, it is common for MapReduce programs to be created from still higher-level programming systems, often an implementation of SQL. Further, MapReduce turns out to be a useful, but simple, case of more general and powerful ideas. We include in this chapter a discussion of generalizations of MapReduce, first to systems that support acyclic workflows and then to systems that implement recursive algorithms.

Our last topic for this chapter is the design of good MapReduce algorithms, a subject that often differs significantly from the matter of designing good parallel algorithms to be run on a supercomputer. When designing MapReduce algorithms, we often find that the greatest cost is in the communication. We thus investigate communication cost and what it tells us about the most efficient MapReduce algorithms. For several common applications of MapReduce we are able to give families of algorithms that optimally trade the communication cost against the degree of parallelism.

2.1   Distributed File Systems

Most computing is done on a single processor, with its main memory, cache, and local disk (a *compute node*). In the past, applications that called for parallel processing, such as large scientific calculations, were done on special-purpose parallel computers with many processors and specialized hardware. However, the prevalence of large-scale Web services has caused more and more computing to be done on installations with thousands of compute nodes operating more or less independently. In these installations, the compute nodes are commodity hardware, which greatly reduces the cost compared with special-purpose parallel machines.

These new computing facilities have given rise to a new generation of programming systems. These systems take advantage of the power of parallelism and at the same time avoid the reliability problems that arise when the computing hardware consists of thousands of independent components, any of which could fail at any time. In this section, we discuss both the characteristics of these computing installations and the specialized file systems that have been developed to take advantage of them.

2.1.1   Physical Organization of Compute Nodes

The new parallel-computing architecture, sometimes called *cluster computing*, is organized as follows. Compute nodes are stored on *racks*, perhaps 8–64 on a rack. The nodes on a single rack are connected by a network, typically gigabit Ethernet. There can be many racks of compute nodes, and racks are connected by another level of network or a switch. The bandwidth of inter-rack communication is somewhat greater than the intrarack Ethernet, but given the number of pairs of nodes that might need to communicate between racks, this bandwidth may be essential. Figure 2.1 suggests the architecture of a large-scale computing system. However, there may be many more racks and many more compute nodes per rack.

It is a fact of life that components fail, and the more components, such as compute nodes and communication links, a system has, the more frequently something in the system will not be working at any given time. For systems such as Fig. 2.1, the principal failure modes are the loss of a single node (e.g., the disk

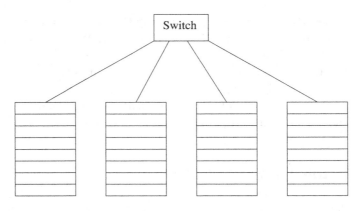

Racks of compute nodes

Figure 2.1 Compute nodes are organized into racks, and racks are interconnected by a switch

at that node crashes) and the loss of an entire rack (e.g., the network connecting its nodes to each other and to the outside world fails).

Some important calculations take minutes or even hours on thousands of compute nodes. If we had to abort and restart the computation every time one component failed, then the computation might never complete successfully. The solution to this problem takes two forms:

(1) Files must be stored redundantly. If we did not duplicate the file at several compute nodes, then if one node failed, all its files would be unavailable until the node is replaced. If we did not back up the files at all, and the disk crashes, the files would be lost forever. We discuss file management in Section 2.1.2.

(2) Computations must be divided into tasks, such that if any one task fails to execute to completion, it can be restarted without affecting other tasks. This strategy is followed by the MapReduce programming system that we introduce in Section 2.2.

2.1.2   Large-Scale File-System Organization

To exploit cluster computing, files must look and behave somewhat differently from the conventional file systems found on single computers. This new file system, often called a *distributed file system* or *DFS* (although this term has had other meanings in the past), is typically used as follows.

- Files can be enormous, possibly a terabyte in size. If you have only small files, there is no point using a DFS for them.
- Files are rarely updated. Rather, they are read as data for some calculation, and possibly additional data is appended to files from time to time. For

---

DFS Implementations

There are several distributed file systems of the type we have described that are used in practice. Among these:

(1) The *Google File System* (GFS), the original of the class.
(2) *Hadoop Distributed File System* (HDFS), an open-source DFS used with Hadoop, an implementation of MapReduce (see Section 2.2) and distributed by the Apache Software Foundation.
(3) *Colossus* is an improved version of GFS, about which little has been published. However, a goal of Colossus is to provide real-time file service.

---

example, an airline reservation system would not be suitable for a DFS, even if the data were very large, because the data is changed so frequently.

Files are divided into *chunks*, which are typically 64 megabytes in size. Chunks are replicated, perhaps three times, at three different compute nodes. Moreover, the nodes holding copies of one chunk should be located on different racks, so we don't lose all copies due to a rack failure. Typically, a rack "fails" because the interconnect among the compute nodes on the rack fails, and the rack can no longer communicate with anything outside itself. Normally, both the chunk size and the degree of replication can be decided by the user.

To find the chunks of a file, there is another small file called the *master node* or *name node* for that file. The master node is itself replicated, and a directory for the file system as a whole knows where to find its copies. The directory itself can be replicated, and all participants using the DFS know where the directory copies are.

2.2   MapReduce

MapReduce is a style of computing that has been implemented in several systems, including Google's internal implementation (simply called MapReduce) and the popular open-source implementation Hadoop which can be obtained, along with the HDFS file system from the Apache Foundation. You can use an implementation of MapReduce to manage many large-scale, parallel computations in a way that is tolerant of hardware faults. All you need to write are two functions, called *Map* and *Reduce*. The system manages the parallel execution and coordination of tasks that execute Map or Reduce. The system also deals with the possibility that one of these tasks will fail to execute. In brief, a MapReduce computation executes as follows:

(1) Some number of Map tasks each are given one or more chunks from a distributed file system. These Map tasks turn the chunk into a sequence of

key-value pairs. The way key-value pairs are produced from the input data is determined by the code written by the user for the Map function.

(2) The key-value pairs from each Map task are collected by a *master controller* and sorted by key. The keys are divided among all the Reduce tasks, so all key-value pairs with the same key wind up at the same Reduce task.

(3) The Reduce tasks work on one key at a time, and combine all the values associated with that key in some way. The manner of combination of values is determined by the code written by the user for the Reduce function.

Figure 2.2 suggests this computation.

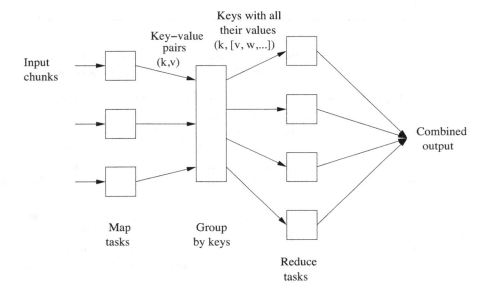

Figure 2.2 Schematic of a MapReduce computation

2.2.1   The Map Tasks

We view input files for a Map task as consisting of *elements*, which can be any type: a tuple or a document, for example. A chunk is a collection of elements, and no element is stored across two chunks. Technically, all inputs to Map tasks and outputs from Reduce tasks are of the key-value-pair form, but normally the keys of input elements are not relevant and we shall tend to ignore them. Insisting on this form for inputs and outputs is motivated by the desire to allow composition of several MapReduce processes.

The Map function takes an input element as its argument and produces zero or more key-value pairs. The types of keys and values are each arbitrary. Further, keys are not "keys" in the usual sense; they do not have to be unique. Rather a Map task can produce several key-value pairs with the same key, even from the same element.

EXAMPLE 2.1   We shall illustrate a MapReduce computation with what has become the standard example application: counting the number of occurrences for each word in a collection of documents. In this example, the input file is a repository of documents, and each document is an element. The Map function for this example uses keys that are of type String (the words) and values that are integers. The Map task reads a document and breaks it into its sequence of words $w_1, w_2, \ldots, w_n$. It then emits a sequence of key-value pairs where the value is always 1. That is, the output of the Map task for this document is the sequence of key-value pairs:

$$(w_1, 1),\ (w_2, 1), \ldots, (w_n, 1)$$

Note that a single Map task will typically process many documents – all the documents in one or more chunks. Thus, its output will be more than the sequence for the one document suggested above. Note also that if a word w appears m times among all the documents assigned to that task, then there will be m key-value pairs $(w, 1)$ among its output. An option, which we discuss in Section 2.2.4, is for this Map task to combine these m pairs into a single pair (w, m), but we can only do that because, as we shall see, the Reduce tasks apply an associative and commutative operation, addition, to the values.   □

2.2.2   Grouping by Key

As soon as the Map tasks have all completed successfully, the key-value pairs are grouped by key, and the values associated with each key are formed into a single list of values for that key. The grouping is performed by the system, regardless of what the Map and Reduce tasks do. The master controller process knows how many Reduce tasks there will be, say r such tasks. The user typically tells the MapReduce system what r should be. Then the master controller picks a hash function that takes a key as argument and produces a bucket number from 0 to $r - 1$. Each key that is output by a Map task is hashed and its key-value pair is put in one of r local files. Each file is destined for one of the r Reduce tasks.[1]

To perform the grouping by key and distribution to the Reduce tasks, the master controller merges the files from each Map task that are destined for a particular Reduce task and feeds the merged file to that process as a sequence of key/list-of-values pairs. That is, for each key k, the input to the Reduce task that handles key k is a pair of the form $(k, [v_1, v_2, \ldots, v_n])$, where $(k, v_1),\ (k, v_2), \ldots, (k, v_n)$ are all the key-value pairs with key k coming from all the Map tasks.

2.2.3   The Reduce Tasks

The Reduce function's argument is a pair consisting of a key and its list of associated values. The output of the Reduce function is a sequence of zero or

---

[1] Optionally, users can specify their own hash function or other method for assigning keys to Reduce tasks. However, whatever algorithm is used, each key is assigned to one and only one Reduce task.

more key-value pairs. These key-value pairs can be of a type different from those sent from Map tasks to Reduce tasks, but often they are the same type. We shall refer to the application of the Reduce function to a single key and its associated list of values as a *reducer*.

A Reduce task receives one or more keys and their associated value lists. That is, a Reduce task executes one or more reducers. The outputs from all the Reduce tasks are merged into a single file.

EXAMPLE 2.2   Let us continue with the word-count example of Example 2.1. The Reduce function simply adds up all the values. The output of a reducer consists of the word and the sum. Thus, the output of all the Reduce tasks is a sequence of (w, m) pairs, where w is a word that appears at least once among all the input documents and m is the total number of occurrences of w among those documents.   □

2.2.4   Combiners

Sometimes, a Reduce function is associative and commutative. That is, the values to be combined can be combined in any order, with the same result. The addition performed in Example 2.2 is an example of an associative and commutative operation. It doesn't matter how we order or group a list of numbers $v_1, v_2, \ldots, v_n$; the sum will be the same.

When the Reduce function is associative and commutative, we can push some of what the reducers do to the Map tasks. For example, instead of each Map task in Example 2.1 producing many pairs $(w, 1)$, $(w, 1), \ldots$, we could apply the Reduce function within each Map task, before the outputs of the Map tasks are subject to grouping and aggregation. These key-value pairs would thus be replaced by one pair with key w and value equal to the sum of all the 1s in all those pairs. That is, the pairs with key w generated by a single Map task would be replaced by a pair (w, m), where m is the number of times that w appears among the documents handled by this Map task. Note that it is still necessary to do grouping and aggregation and to pass the result to the Reduce tasks, since there will typically be one key-value pair with key w coming from each of the Map tasks.

2.2.5   Details of MapReduce Execution

Let us now consider in more detail how a program using MapReduce is executed. Figure 2.3 offers an outline of how processes, tasks, and files interact. Taking advantage of a library provided by a MapReduce system such as Hadoop, the user program forks a Master controller process and some number of Worker processes at different compute nodes. Normally, a Worker handles either Map tasks (a *Map worker*) or Reduce tasks (a *Reduce worker*), but not both.

The Master has many responsibilities. One is to create some number of Map tasks and some number of Reduce tasks, these numbers being selected by the

---

Reducers, Reduce Tasks, Compute Nodes, and Skew

If we want maximum parallelism, then we could use one Reduce task to execute each reducer, i.e., a single key and its associated value list. Further, we could execute each Reduce task at a different compute node, so they would all execute in parallel. This plan is not usually the best. One problem is that there is overhead associated with each task we create, so we might want to keep the number of Reduce tasks lower than the number of different keys. Moreover, often there are far more keys than there are compute nodes available, so we would get no benefit from a huge number of Reduce tasks.

Second, there is often significant variation in the lengths of the value lists for different keys, so different reducers take different amounts of time. If we make each reducer a separate Reduce task, then the tasks themselves will exhibit *skew* – a significant difference in the amount of time each takes. We can reduce the impact of skew by using fewer Reduce tasks than there are reducers. If keys are sent randomly to Reduce tasks, we can expect that there will be some averaging of the total time required by the different Reduce tasks. We can further reduce the skew by using more Reduce tasks than there are compute nodes. In that way, long Reduce tasks might occupy a compute node fully, while several shorter Reduce tasks might run sequentially at a single compute node.

---

user program. These tasks will be assigned to Worker processes by the Master. It is reasonable to create one Map task for every chunk of the input file(s), but we may wish to create fewer Reduce tasks. The reason for limiting the number of Reduce tasks is that it is necessary for each Map task to create an intermediate file for each Reduce task, and if there are too many Reduce tasks the number of intermediate files explodes.

The Master keeps track of the status of each Map and Reduce task (idle, executing at a particular Worker, or completed). A Worker process reports to the Master when it finishes a task, and a new task is scheduled by the Master for that Worker process.

Each Map task is assigned one or more chunks of the input file(s) and executes on it the code written by the user. The Map task creates a file for each Reduce task on the local disk of the Worker that executes the Map task. The Master is informed of the location and sizes of each of these files, and the Reduce task for which each is destined. When a Reduce task is assigned by the Master to a Worker process, that task is given all the files that form its input. The Reduce task executes code written by the user and writes its output to a file that is part of the surrounding distributed file system.

2.2.6 Coping With Node Failures

The worst thing that can happen is that the compute node at which the Master is executing fails. In this case, the entire MapReduce job must be restarted.

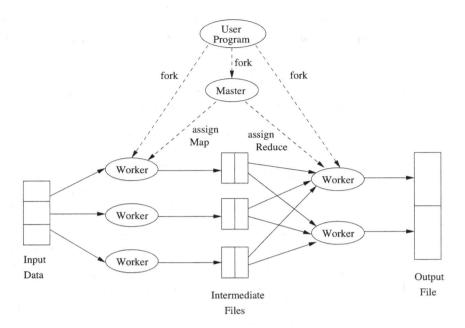

Figure 2.3 Overview of the execution of a MapReduce program

But only this one node can bring the entire process down; other failures will be managed by the Master, and the MapReduce job will complete eventually.

Suppose the compute node at which a Map worker resides fails. This failure will be detected by the Master, because it periodically pings the Worker processes. All the Map tasks that were assigned to this Worker will have to be redone, even if they had completed. The reason for redoing completed Map tasks is that their output destined for the Reduce tasks resides at that compute node, and is now unavailable to the Reduce tasks. The Master sets the status of each of these Map tasks to idle and will schedule them on a Worker when one becomes available. The Master must also inform each Reduce task that the location of its input from that Map task has changed.

Dealing with a failure at the node of a Reduce worker is simpler. The Master simply sets the status of its currently executing Reduce tasks to idle. These will be rescheduled on another Reduce worker later.

2.2.7   Exercises for Section 2.2

EXERCISE 2.2.1   Suppose we execute the word-count MapReduce program described in this section on a large repository such as a copy of the Web. We shall use 100 Map tasks and some number of Reduce tasks.

(a) Suppose we do not use a combiner at the Map tasks. Do you expect there to be significant skew in the times taken by the various reducers to process their value list? Why or why not?

(b) If we combine the reducers into a small number of Reduce tasks, say 10 tasks, at random, do you expect the skew to be significant? What if we instead combine the reducers into 10,000 Reduce tasks?

! (c) Suppose we do use a combiner at the 100 Map tasks. Do you expect skew to be significant? Why or why not?

2.3 Algorithms Using MapReduce

MapReduce is not a solution to every problem, not even every problem that profitably can use many compute nodes operating in parallel. As we mentioned in Section 2.1.2, the entire distributed-file-system milieu makes sense only when files are very large and are rarely updated in place. For instance, we would not expect to use either a DFS or an implementation of MapReduce for managing on-line retail sales, even though a large on-line retailer such as Amazon.com uses thousands of compute nodes when processing requests over the Web. The reason is that the principal operations on Amazon data involve responding to searches for products, recording sales, and so on, processes that involve relatively little calculation and that change the database.[2] On the other hand, Amazon might use MapReduce to perform certain analytic queries on large amounts of data, such as finding for each user those users whose buying patterns were most similar.

The original purpose for which the Google implementation of MapReduce was created was to execute very large matrix-vector multiplications as are needed in the calculation of PageRank (See Chapter 5). We shall see that matrix-vector and matrix-matrix calculations fit nicely into the MapReduce style of computing. Another important class of operations that can use MapReduce effectively are the relational-algebra operations. We shall examine the MapReduce execution of these operations as well.

2.3.1 Matrix-Vector Multiplication by MapReduce

Suppose we have an $n \times n$ matrix M, whose element in row i and column j is denoted m_{ij}. Suppose we also have a vector $\mathbf{v}$ of length n, whose jth element is v_j. Then the matrix-vector product is the vector $\mathbf{x}$ of length n, whose ith element x_i is given by

$$x_i = \sum_{j=1}^{n} m_{ij} v_j$$

If $n = 100$, we do not want to use a DFS or MapReduce for this calculation. But this sort of calculation is at the heart of the ranking of Web pages that goes

---

[2] Recall that even looking at a product you don't buy causes Amazon to remember that you looked at it.

on at search engines, and there, n is on the order of trillions.[3] Let us first assume that n is large, but not so large that vector $\mathbf{v}$ cannot fit in main memory and thus be available to every Map task.

The matrix M and the vector $\mathbf{v}$ each will be stored in a file of the DFS. We assume that the row-column coordinates of each matrix element will be discoverable, either from its position in the file, or because it is stored with explicit coordinates, as a triple (i, j, m_{ij}). We also assume the position of element v_j in the vector $\mathbf{v}$ will be discoverable in the analogous way.

The Map Function The Map function is written to apply to one element of M. However, if $\mathbf{v}$ is not already read into main memory at the compute node executing a Map task, then $\mathbf{v}$ is first read, in its entirety, and subsequently will be available to all applications of the Map function performed at this Map task. Each Map task will operate on a chunk of the matrix M. From each matrix element m_{ij} it produces the key-value pair $(i, m_{ij}v_j)$. Thus, all terms of the sum that make up the component x_i of the matrix-vector product will get the same key, i.

The Reduce Function The Reduce function simply sums all the values associated with a given key i. The result will be a pair (i, x_i).

2.3.2   If the Vector v Cannot Fit in Main Memory

However, it is possible that the vector $\mathbf{v}$ is so large that it will not fit in its entirety in main memory. It is not required that $\mathbf{v}$ fit in main memory at a compute node, but if it does not then there will be a very large number of disk accesses as we move pieces of the vector into main memory to multiply components by elements of the matrix. Thus, as an alternative, we can divide the matrix into vertical *stripes* of equal width and divide the vector into an equal number of horizontal stripes, of the same height. Our goal is to use enough stripes so that the portion of the vector in one stripe can fit conveniently into main memory at a compute node. Figure 2.4 suggests what the partition looks like if the matrix and vector are each divided into five stripes.

The ith stripe of the matrix multiplies only components from the ith stripe of the vector. Thus, we can divide the matrix into one file for each stripe, and do the same for the vector. Each Map task is assigned a chunk from one of the stripes of the matrix and gets the entire corresponding stripe of the vector. The Map and Reduce tasks can then act exactly as was described in Section 2.3.1 for the case where Map tasks get the entire vector.

We shall take up matrix-vector multiplication using MapReduce again in Section 5.2. There, because of the particular application (PageRank calculation),

---

[3] The matrix is sparse, with on the average of 10 to 15 nonzero elements per row, since the matrix represents the links in the Web, with m_{ij} nonzero if and only if there is a link from page j to page i. Note that there is no way we could store a dense matrix whose side was 10^{12}, since it would have 10^{24} elements.

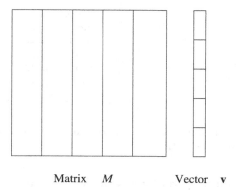

Matrix M Vector $\mathbf{v}$

Figure 2.4 Division of a matrix and vector into five stripes

we have an additional constraint that the result vector should be partitioned in the same way as the input vector, so the output may become the input for another iteration of the matrix-vector multiplication. We shall see there that the best strategy involves partitioning the matrix M into square blocks, rather than stripes.

2.3.3   Relational-Algebra Operations

There are a number of operations on large-scale data that are used in database queries. Many traditional database applications involve retrieval of small amounts of data, even though the database itself may be large. For example, a query may ask for the bank balance of one particular account. Such queries are not useful applications of MapReduce.

However, there are many operations on data that can be described easily in terms of the common database-query primitives, even if the queries themselves are not executed within a database management system. Thus, a good starting point for exploring applications of MapReduce is by considering the standard operations on relations. We assume you are familiar with database systems, the query language SQL, and the relational model, but to review, a *relation* is a table with column headers called *attributes*. Rows of the relation are called *tuples*. The set of attributes of a relation is called its *schema*. We often write an expression like $R(A_1, A_2, \ldots, A_n)$ to say that the relation name is R and its attributes are $A_1, A_2, \ldots, A_n$.

EXAMPLE 2.3   In Fig. 2.5 we see part of the relation *Links* that describes the structure of the Web. There are two attributes, *From* and *To*. A row, or tuple, of the relation is a pair of URLs such that there is at least one link from the first URL to the second. For instance, the first row of Fig. 2.5 is the pair $(url1, url2)$. This tuple says the Web page $url1$ has a link to page $url2$. While we have shown only four tuples, the real relation of the Web, or the portion of it that would be stored by a typical search engine, has trillions of tuples.   □

From	*To*
url1	url2
url1	url3
url2	url3
url2	url4
...	...

Figure 2.5 Relation *Links* consists of the set of pairs of URLs such that the first has one or more links to the second

A relation, however large, can be stored as a file in a distributed file system. The elements of this file are the tuples of the relation.

There are several standard operations on relations, often referred to as *relational algebra*, that are used to implement queries. The queries themselves usually are written in SQL. The relational-algebra operations we shall discuss are:

(1) *Selection*: Apply a condition C to each tuple in the relation and produce as output only those tuples that satisfy C. The result of this selection is denoted $\sigma_C(R)$.

(2) *Projection*: For some subset S of the attributes of the relation, produce from each tuple only the components for the attributes in S. The result of this projection is denoted $\pi_S(R)$.

(3) *Union, Intersection*, and *Difference*: These well-known set operations apply to the sets of tuples in two relations that have the same schema. There are also bag (multiset) versions of the operations in SQL, with somewhat unintuitive definitions, but we shall not go into the bag versions of these operations here.

(4) *Natural Join*: Given two relations, compare each pair of tuples, one from each relation. If the tuples agree on all the attributes that are common to the two schemas, then produce a tuple that has components for each of the attributes in either schema and agrees with the two tuples on each attribute. If the tuples disagree on one or more shared attributes, then produce nothing from this pair of tuples. The natural join of relations R and S is denoted $R \bowtie S$. While we shall discuss executing only the natural join with MapReduce, all *equijoins* (joins where the tuple-agreement condition involves equality of attributes from the two relations that do not necessarily have the same name) can be executed in the same manner. We shall give an illustration in Example 2.4.

(5) *Grouping* and *Aggregation*:[4] Given a relation R, partition its tuples according to their values in one set of attributes G, called the *grouping attributes*. Then,

---

[4] Some descriptions of relational algebra do not include these operations, and indeed they were not part of the original definition of this algebra. However, these operations are so important in SQL, that modern treatments of relational algebra include them.

for each group, aggregate the values in certain other attributes. The normally permitted aggregations are SUM, COUNT, AVG, MIN, and MAX, with the obvious meanings. Note that MIN and MAX require that the aggregated attributes have a type that can be compared, e.g., numbers or strings, while SUM and AVG require that the type allow arithmetic operations, typically only numbers. COUNT can be performed on data of any type. We denote a grouping-and-aggregation operation on a relation R by $\gamma_X(R)$, where X is a list of elements that are each either

(a) A grouping attribute, or

(b) An expression $\theta(A)$, where θ is one of the five aggregation operations such as SUM, and A is an attribute not among the grouping attributes.

The result of this operation is one tuple for each group. That tuple has a component for each of the grouping attributes, with the value common to tuples of that group. It also has a component for each aggregation, with the aggregated value for that group. We shall see an illustration in Example 2.5.

EXAMPLE 2.4   Let us try to find the paths of length two in the Web, using the relation *Links* of Fig. 2.5. That is, we want to find the triples of URLs (u, v, w) such that there is a link from u to v and a link from v to w. We essentially want to take the natural join of *Links* with itself, but we first need to imagine that it is two relations, with different schemas, so we can describe the desired connection as a natural join. Thus, imagine that there are two copies of *Links*, namely $L1(U1, U2)$ and $L2(U2, U3)$. Now, if we compute $L1 \bowtie L2$, we shall have exactly what we want. That is, for each tuple $t1$ of $L1$ (i.e., each tuple of *Links*) and each tuple $t2$ of $L2$ (another tuple of *Links*, possibly even the same tuple), see if their $U2$ components are the same. Note that these components are the second component of $t1$ and the first component of $t2$. If these two components agree, then produce a tuple for the result, with schema $(U1, U2, U3)$. This tuple consists of the first component of $t1$, the second component of $t1$ (which must equal the first component of $t2$), and the second component of $t2$.

We may not want the entire path of length two, but only want the pairs (u, w) of URLs such that there is at least one path from u to w of length two. If so, we can project out the middle components by computing $\pi_{U1,U3}(L1 \bowtie L2)$. □

EXAMPLE 2.5   Imagine that a social-networking site has a relation

$$\text{Friends(User, Friend)}$$

This relation has tuples that are pairs (a, b) such that b is a friend of a. The site might want to develop statistics about the number of friends members have. Their first step would be to compute a count of the number of friends of each user. This operation can be done by grouping and aggregation, specifically

$$\gamma_{\text{User,COUNT(Friend)}}(\text{Friends})$$

This operation groups all the tuples by the value in their first component, so there is one group for each user. Then, for each group the count of the number of friends of that user is made. The result will be one tuple for each group, and a typical tuple would look like (Sally, 300), if user "Sally" has 300 friends.   □

2.3.4   Computing Selections by MapReduce

Selections really do not need the full power of MapReduce. They can be done most conveniently in the map portion alone, although they could also be done in the reduce portion alone. Here is a MapReduce implementation of selection $\sigma_C(R)$.

The Map Function For each tuple t in R, test if it satisfies C. If so, produce the key-value pair (t, t). That is, both the key and value are t. If t does not satisfy C, then the mapper for t produces nothing.

The Reduce Function The Reduce function is the identity. It simply passes each key-value pair to the output.

Note that the output is not exactly a relation, because it has key-value pairs. However, a relation can be obtained by using only the value components (or only the key components) of the output.

2.3.5   Computing Projections by MapReduce

Projection is performed similarly to selection. However, because projection may cause the same tuple to appear several times, the Reduce function must eliminate duplicates. We may compute $\pi_S(R)$ as follows.

The Map Function For each tuple t in R, construct a tuple t' by eliminating from t those components whose attributes are not in S. Output the key-value pair (t', t').

The Reduce Function For each key t' produced by any of the Map tasks, there will be one or more key-value pairs (t', t'). After the system groups key-value pairs by key, the Reduce function turns $(t', [t', t', \ldots, t'])$ into (t', t'), so it produces exactly one pair (t', t') for this key t'.

Observe that the Reduce operation is duplicate elimination. This operation is associative and commutative, so a combiner associated with each Map task can eliminate whatever duplicates are produced locally. However, the Reduce tasks are still needed to eliminate two identical tuples coming from different Map tasks.

2.3.6   Union, Intersection, and Difference by MapReduce

First, consider the union of two relations. Suppose relations R and S have the same schema. Map tasks will be assigned chunks from either R or S; it doesn't matter which. The Map tasks don't really do anything except pass their input tuples as key-value pairs to the Reduce tasks. The latter need only eliminate duplicates as for projection.

The Map Function Turn each input tuple t into a key-value pair (t, t).

The Reduce Function Associated with each key t there will be either one or two values. Produce output (t, t) in either case.

To compute the intersection, we can use the same Map function. However, the Reduce function must produce a tuple only if both relations have the tuple. If the key t has a list of two values $[t, t]$ associated with it, then the Reduce task for t should produce (t, t). However, if the value-list associated with key t is just $[t]$, then one of R and S is missing t, so we don't want to produce a tuple for the intersection.

The Map Function Turn each tuple t into a key-value pair (t, t).

The Reduce Function If key t has value list $[t, t]$, then produce (t, t). Otherwise, produce nothing.

The Difference $R - S$ requires a bit more thought. The only way a tuple t can appear in the output is if it is in R but not in S. The Map function can pass tuples from R and S through, but must inform the Reduce function whether the tuple came from R or S. We shall thus use the relation as the value associated with the key t. Here is a specification for the two functions.

The Map Function For a tuple t in R, produce key-value pair (t, R), and for a tuple t in S, produce key-value pair (t, S). Note that the intent is that the value is the name of R or S (or better, a single bit indicating whether the relation is R or S), not the entire relation.

The Reduce Function For each key t, if the associated value list is $[R]$, then produce (t, t). Otherwise, produce nothing.

2.3.7   Computing Natural Join by MapReduce

The idea behind implementing natural join via MapReduce can be seen if we look at the specific case of joining $R(A, B)$ with $S(B, C)$.[5] We must find tuples that agree on their B components, that is the second component from tuples of R and the first component of tuples of S. We shall use the B-value of tuples from either relation as the key. The value will be the other component and the name of the relation, so the Reduce function can know where each tuple came from.

---

[5] If you are familiar with database implementation, you will recognize the MapReduce implementation of join as the classic parallel hash join.

The Map Function For each tuple (a, b) of R, produce the key-value pair $\big(b, (R, a)\big)$. For each tuple (b, c) of S, produce the key-value pair $\big(b, (S, c)\big)$.

The Reduce Function Each key value b will be associated with a list of pairs that are either of the form (R, a) or (S, c). Construct all pairs consisting of one with first component R and the other with first component S, say (R, a) and (S, c). The output from this key and value list is a sequence of key-value pairs. The key is irrelevant. Each value is one of the triples (a, b, c) such that (R, a) and (S, c) are on the input list of values for key b.

The same algorithm works if the relations have more than two attributes. You can think of A as representing all those attributes in the schema of R but not S. B represents the attributes in both schemas, and C represents attributes only in the schema of S. The key for a tuple of R or S is the list of values in all the attributes that are in the schemas of both R and S. The value for a tuple of R is the name R together with the values of all the attributes belonging to R but not to S, and the value for a tuple of S is the name S together with the values of the attributes belonging to S but not R.

The Reduce function looks at all the key-value pairs with a given key and combines those values from R with those values of S in all possible ways. From each pairing, the tuple produced has the values from R, the key values, and the values from S.

2.3.8   Grouping and Aggregation by MapReduce

As we did for the join, we shall discuss here only the minimal example of grouping and aggregation, where there is one grouping attribute (A), one aggregated attribute (B), and one attribute (C) that is neither grouped nor aggregated. Let $R(A, B, C)$ be a relation to which we apply the operator $\gamma_{A, \theta(B)}(R)$. Map will perform the grouping, while Reduce does the aggregation.

The Map Function For each tuple (a, b, c) produce the key-value pair (a, b).

The Reduce Function Each key a represents a group. Apply the aggregation operator θ to the list $[b_1, b_2, \ldots, b_n]$ of B-values associated with key a. The output is the pair (a, x), where x is the result of applying θ to the list. For example, if θ is SUM, then $x = b_1 + b_2 + \cdots + b_n$, and if θ is MAX, then x is the largest of $b_1, b_2, \ldots, b_n$.

If there are several grouping attributes, then the key is the list of the values of a tuple for all these attributes. If there is more than one aggregation, then the Reduce function applies each of them to the list of values associated with a given key and produces a tuple consisting of the key, including components for all grouping attributes if there is more than one, followed by the results of each of the aggregations.

2.3.9   Matrix Multiplication

If M is a matrix with element m_{ij} in row i and column j, and N is a matrix with element n_{jk} in row j and column k, then the product $P = MN$ is the matrix P with element p_{ik} in row i and column k, where

$$p_{ik} = \sum_j m_{ij} n_{jk}$$

It is required that the number of columns of M equals the number of rows of N, so the sum over j makes sense.

We can think of a matrix as a relation with three attributes: the row number, the column number, and the value in that row and column. Thus, we could view matrix M as a relation $M(I, J, V)$, with tuples (i, j, m_{ij}), and we could view matrix N as a relation $N(J, K, W)$, with tuples (j, k, n_{jk}). As large matrices are often sparse (mostly 0s), and since we can omit the tuples for matrix elements that are 0, this relational representation is often a very good one for a large matrix. However, it is possible that i, j, and k are implicit in the position of a matrix element in the file that represents it, rather than written explicitly with the element itself. In that case, the Map function will have to be designed to construct the I, J, and K components of tuples from the position of the data.

The product MN is almost a natural join followed by grouping and aggregation. That is, the natural join of $M(I, J, V)$ and $N(J, K, W)$, having only attribute J in common, would produce tuples (i, j, k, v, w) from each tuple (i, j, v) in M and tuple (j, k, w) in N. This five-component tuple represents the pair of matrix elements (m_{ij}, n_{jk}). What we want instead is the product of these elements, that is, the four-component tuple $(i, j, k, v \times w)$, because that represents the product $m_{ij} n_{jk}$. Once we have this relation as the result of one MapReduce operation, we can perform grouping and aggregation, with I and K as the grouping attributes and the sum of $V \times W$ as the aggregation. That is, we can implement matrix multiplication as the cascade of two MapReduce operations, as follows. First:

The Map Function For each matrix element m_{ij}, produce the key value pair $\big(j, (M, i, m_{ij})\big)$. Likewise, for each matrix element n_{jk}, produce the key value pair $\big(j, (N, k, n_{jk})\big)$. Note that M and N in the values are not the matrices themselves. Rather they are names of the matrices or, more precisely, a single bit that indicates whether the element comes from M or N (as we mentioned regarding the similar Map function we used for the natural join).

The Reduce Function For each key j, examine its list of associated values. For each value that comes from M, say (M, i, m_{ij}), and each value that comes from N, say (N, k, n_{jk}), produce a key-value pair with key equal to (i, k) and value equal to the product of these elements, $m_{ij} n_{jk}$.

Now, we perform a grouping and aggregation by another MapReduce operation applied to the output of the first MapReduce operation.

The Map Function This function is just the identity. That is, for every input element with key (i, k) and value v, produce exactly this key-value pair.

The Reduce Function For each key (i, k), produce the sum of the list of values associated with this key. The result is a pair $((i, k), v)$, where v is the value of the element in row i and column k of the matrix $P = MN$.

2.3.10   Matrix Multiplication with One MapReduce Step

There often is more than one way to use MapReduce to solve a problem. You may wish to use only a single MapReduce pass to perform matrix multiplication $P = MN$.[6] It is possible to do so if we put more work into the two functions. Start by using the Map function to create the sets of matrix elements that are needed to compute each element of the answer P. Notice that an element of M or N contributes to many elements of the result, so one input element will be turned into many key-value pairs. The keys will be pairs (i, k), where i is a row of M and k is a column of N. Here is a synopsis of the Map and Reduce functions.

The Map Function For each element m_{ij} of M, produce all the key-value pairs $((i, k), (M, j, m_{ij}))$ for $k = 1, 2, \ldots$ up to the number of columns of N. Similarly, for each element n_{jk} of N, produce all the key-value pairs $((i, k), (N, j, n_{jk}))$ for $i = 1, 2, \ldots$ up to the number of rows of M. As before, M and N are really bits to tell which of the two matrices a value comes from.

The Reduce Function Each key (i, k) will have an associated list with all the values (M, j, m_{ij}) and (N, j, n_{jk}), for all possible values of j. The Reduce function needs to connect the two values on the list that have the same value of j, for each j. An easy way to do this step is to sort by j the values that begin with M and sort by j the values that begin with N, in separate lists. The jth values on each list must have their third components, m_{ij} and n_{jk} extracted and multiplied. Then, these products are summed and the result is paired with (i, k) in the output of the Reduce function.

You may notice that if a row of the matrix M or a column of the matrix N is so large that it will not fit in main memory, then the Reduce tasks will be forced to use an external sort to order the values associated with a given key (i, k). However, in that case, the matrices themselves are so large, perhaps 10^{20} elements, that it is unlikely we would attempt this calculation if the matrices were dense. If they are sparse, then we would expect many fewer values to be

---

[6] However, we show in Section 2.6.7 that two passes of MapReduce are usually better than one for matrix multiplication.

associated with any one key, and it would be feasible to do the sum of products in main memory.

2.3.11 Exercises for Section 2.3

EXERCISE 2.3.1 Design MapReduce algorithms to take a very large file of integers and produce as output:

(a) The largest integer.
(b) The average of all the integers.
(c) The same set of integers, but with each integer appearing only once.
! (d) The count of the number of distinct integers in the input.

In each part, you can assume that the key of each output pair will be ignored or dropped.

EXERCISE 2.3.2 Our formulation of matrix-vector multiplication assumed that the matrix M was square. Generalize the algorithm to the case where M is an $r \times c$ matrix for some number of rows r and columns c.

! EXERCISE 2.3.3 In the form of relational algebra implemented in SQL, relations are not sets, but bags; that is, tuples are allowed to appear more than once. There are extended definitions of union, intersection, and difference for bags, which we shall define below. Write MapReduce algorithms for computing the following operations on bags R and S:

(a) *Bag Union*, defined to be the bag of tuples in which tuple t appears the sum of the numbers of times it appears in R and S.
(b) *Bag Intersection*, defined to be the bag of tuples in which tuple t appears the minimum of the numbers of times it appears in R and S.
(c) *Bag Difference*, defined to be the bag of tuples in which the number of times a tuple t appears is equal to the number of times it appears in R minus the number of times it appears in S. A tuple that appears more times in S than in R does not appear in the difference.

! EXERCISE 2.3.4 Selection can also be performed on bags. Give a MapReduce implementation that produces the proper number of copies of each tuple t that passes the selection condition. That is, produce key-value pairs from which the correct result of the selection can be obtained easily from the values.

EXERCISE 2.3.5 The relational-algebra operation $R(A, B) \bowtie_{B<C} S(C, D)$ produces all tuples (a, b, c, d) such that tuple (a, b) is in relation R, tuple (c, d) is in S, and $b < c$. Give a MapReduce implementation of this operation, assuming R and S are sets.

! EXERCISE 2.3.6 In Section 2.3.5 we claimed that duplicate elimination is an associative and commutative operation. Prove this fact.

2.4   Extensions to MapReduce

MapReduce proved so influential that it spawned a number of extensions and modifications. These systems typically share a number of characteristics with MapReduce systems:

(1) They are built on a distributed file system.
(2) They manage very large numbers of tasks that are instantiations of a small number of user-written functions.
(3) They incorporate a method for dealing with most of the failures that occur during the execution of a large job, without having to restart that job from the beginning.

We begin this section with a discussion of "workflow" systems, which extend MapReduce by supporting acyclic networks of functions, each function implemented by a collection of tasks. While many such systems have been implemented (see the bibliographic notes for this chapter), an increasingly popular choice is UC Berkeley's Spark. Also gaining in importance is Google's Tensor-Flow. The latter, while not generally recognized as a workflow system because of its very specific targeting of machine-learning applications, in fact has a workflow architecture at heart.

Another family of systems uses a graph model of data. Computation occurs at the nodes of the graph, and messages are sent from any node to any adjacent node. The original system of this type was Google's Pregel, which has its own unique way of dealing with failures. But it has now become common to implement a graph-model facility on top of a workflow system and use the latter's file system and failure-management facility.

2.4.1   Workflow Systems

Workflow systems extend MapReduce from the simple two-step workflow (the Map function feeds the Reduce function) to any collection of functions, with an acyclic graph representing workflow among the functions. That is, there is an acyclic *flow graph* whose arcs $a \to b$ represent the fact that function as output is an input to function b.

The data passed from one function to the next is a file of elements of one type. If a function has a single input, then that function is applied to each input independently, just as Map and Reduce functions are applied to their input elements individually. The output of the function is a file collected from the result of applying the function to each input. If a function has inputs from more than one file, elements from each of the files can be combined in various ways. But the function itself is applied to combinations of input elements, at most one from each input file. We shall see examples of such combinations when we discuss the implementation of union and the relational join in Section 2.4.2.

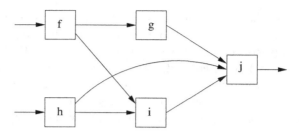

Figure 2.6 An example of a workflow that is more complex than Map feeding Reduce

EXAMPLE 2.6   A suggestion of what a workflow might look like is in Fig. 2.6. There, five functions, f through j, pass data from left to right in specific ways, so the flow of data is acyclic and no task needs to provide data out before its entire input is available. For instance, function h takes its input from a preexisting file of the distributed file system. Each of hs output elements is passed to the functions i and j, while i takes the outputs of both f and h as inputs. The output of j is either stored in the distributed file system or is passed to an application that invoked this dataflow.   □

In analogy to Map and Reduce functions, each function of a workflow can be executed by many tasks, each of which is assigned a portion of the input to the function. A master controller is responsible for dividing the work among the tasks that implement a function, possibly by hashing the input elements to decide on the proper task to receive an element. Thus, like Map tasks, each task implementing a function f has an output file of data destined for each of the tasks that implement the successor function(s) of f. These files are delivered by the master controller at the appropriate time – after the task has completed its work.

The functions of a workflow, and therefore the tasks, share with MapReduce tasks an important property: the *blocking property*, in that they only deliver output after they complete. As a result, if a task fails, it has not delivered output to any of its successors in the flow graph.[7] A master controller can therefore restart the failed task at another compute node, without worrying that the output of the restarted task will duplicate output that previously was passed to some other task.

Some applications of workflow systems are effectively cascades of MapReduce jobs. An example would be the join of three relations, where one MapReduce job joins the first two relations, and a second MapReduce job joins the third relation with the result of joining the first two relations. Both jobs would use an algorithm like that of Section 2.3.7.

There is an advantage to implementing such cascades as a single workflow. For

---

[7] As we shall discuss in Section 2.4.5, the blocking property only holds for acyclic workflows, and systems that support recursion cannot use it to manage failures.

example, the flow of data among tasks, and its replication, can be managed by the master controller, without need to store the temporary file that is output of one MapReduce job in the distributed file system. By locating tasks at compute nodes that have a copy of their input, we can avoid much of the communication that would be necessary if we stored the result of one MapReduce job and then initiated a second MapReduce job (although Hadoop and other MapReduce systems also try to locate Map tasks where a copy of their input is already present).

2.4.2   Spark

Spark is, at its heart, a workflow system. However, it is an advance over the early workflow systems in several ways, including:

(1) A more efficient way of coping with failures.
(2) A more efficient way of grouping tasks among compute nodes and scheduling execution of functions.
(3) Integration of programming language features such as looping (which technically takes it out of the acyclic workflow class of systems) and function libraries.

The central data abstraction of Spark is called the *Resilient Distributed Dataset*, or *RDD*. An RDD is a file of objects of one type. The primary example of an RDD that we have seen so far is the files of key-value pairs that are used in MapReduce systems. They are also the files that get passed among functions that we talked about in connection with Fig. 2.6. RDDs are "distributed" in the sense that an RDD is normally broken into chunks that may be held at different compute nodes. They are "resilient" in the sense that we expect to be able to recover from the loss of any or all chunks of an RDD. However, unlike the key-value-pair abstraction of MapReduce, there is no restriction on the type of the elements that comprise an RDD.

A Spark program consists of a sequence of steps, each of which typically applies some function to an RDD to produce another RDD. Such operations are called *transformations*. It is also possible to take data from the surrounding file system, such as HDFS, and turn it into an RDD, and to take an RDD and return it to the surrounding file system or to produce a result that is passed back to an application that called a Spark program. The latter kinds of operations are called *actions*.

We shall not try to list all the available transformations and actions that are available. Neither shall we fix on the dictions of a particular programming language, since the Spark operations are designed to be expressible in a number of different programming languages. However, here are some of the commonly used operations.

Map, Flatmap, and Filter

The Map transformation takes a parameter that is a function, and it applies that function to every element of an RDD, producing another RDD. This operation should remind us of the Map of MapReduce, but it is not exactly the same. First of all, in MapReduce, a Map function can only apply to a key-value pair. Second, in MapReduce, a Map function produces a set of key-value pairs, and each key-value pair is considered an independent element of the output of the Map function. In Spark, a Map function can apply to any object type, but it produces exactly one object as a result. The type of the resulting object can be a set, but that is not the same as producing many objects from one input object. If you want to produce a set of objects from a single object, Spark provides for you another transformation called *Flatmap*, which is analogous to Map of MapReduce, but without the requirement that all types be key-value pairs.

EXAMPLE 2.7   Suppose our input RDD is a file of documents, as in the "word-count" of Example 2.1. We could write a Spark Map function that takes one document and produces one set of pairs, with each pair of the form $(w, 1)$, where w is one of the words in the document. However, if we do so, then the output RDD is a list of sets, each set consisting of all the words of one document, each word paired with the integer 1. If we want to duplicate the Map function described in Example 2.1, then we need to use Spark's Flatmap transformation. That operation applied to the RDD of documents will produce another RDD, each of whose elements is a single pair $(w, 1)$.   □

Spark also provides an operation similar to a limited form of Map, called *Filter*. Instead of a function as a parameter, the Filter transformation takes a predicate that applies to the type of objects in the input RDD. The predicate returns true or false for each object, and the output RDD of a Filter transformation consists of only those objects in the input RDD for which the filter function returns true.

EXAMPLE 2.8   Continuing Example 2.7, suppose we want to avoid counting stop words: the most common words like "the" or "and." We could write a filter function that has built into it the list of words we want to eliminate. When applied to a pair $(w, 1)$, this function returns true if and only if w is not on the list. We can then write a Spark program that first applies Flatmap to the RDD of documents, producing an RDD R_1 consisting of a pair $(w, 1)$ for each occurrence of the word w in any of the documents. The program then applies the stop-word-eliminating Filter to R_1, producing another RDD, R_2. The latter RDD consists of a pair $(w, 1)$ for each occurrence of word w in any of the documents, but only if w is not a stop word.   □

Reduce

In Spark, the Reduce operation is an action, not a transformation. That is, the operation Reduce applies to an RDD but returns a value and not another RDD. Reduce takes a parameter that is a function which takes two elements of some particular type T and returns another element of the same type T. When applied to an RDD whose elements are of type T, Reduce is applied repeatedly to each pair of consecutive elements, reducing them to a single element. When only one element remains, that becomes the result of the Reduce operation.

For example, if the parameter is the addition function, and this instance of Reduce is applied to an RDD whose elements are integers, then the result will be a single integer that is the sum of all the integers in the RDD. As long as the function parameter is an associative and commutative function, such as addition, it does not matter in which order elements of the input RDD are combined. However, it is also possible to use an arbitrary function, as long as we are satisfied with combination of elements in any order.

Relational Database Operations

There are a number of built-in Spark operations that behave like relational-algebra operators on relations that are represented by RDDs. That is, think of the elements of the RDDs as tuples of a relation. The transformation Join takes two RDDs, each representing one of the relations. The type of each RDD must be a key-value pair, and the key types of both relations must be the same. The Join transformation then looks for two objects, one from each of its input RDDs, such that the key values are the same, say (k, x) and (k, y). For each such pair found, Join produces the key-value pair $(k, (x, y))$, and the output RDD consists of all such objects.

The group-by operation of SQL is also implemented in Spark by the transformation GroupByKey. This transformation takes as input an RDD whose type is key-value pairs. The output RDD is also a set of key-value pairs with the same key type. The value type for the output is a list of values of the input type. GroupByKey sorts its input RDD by key and for each key k produces the pair $(k, [v_1, v_2, \ldots, v_n])$ such that the v_i are all the values associated with key k in the input RDD. Notice that GroupByKey is exactly the operation that is performed behind the scenes by MapReduce in order to group the output of the Map function by key.

2.4.3 Spark Implementation

There are a number of ways that Spark implementation differs from Hadoop or other MapReduce implementations. We shall discuss two important improvements: lazy evaluation of RDDs and lineage for RDDs. Before we do, we should mention one way in which Spark is similar to MapReduce: the way large RDDs are managed.

Recall that when applying Map to a large file, MapReduce divides that file into chunks and creates a Map task for each chunk or group of chunks. The chunks and their tasks are typically distributed among many different compute nodes. Likewise, many Reduce tasks can run in parallel on different compute nodes, and each of these tasks takes a portion of the entire set of key-value pairs that are passed from Map to Reduce. Spark also allows any RDD to be divided into chunks, which it calls *splits*. Each split can be given to a different compute node, and the transformation on that RDD can be performed in parallel on each of the splits.

Lazy Evaluation

As mentioned in Section 2.4.1, it is common for workflow systems to exploit the blocking property for error handling. To do so, a function is applied to a single intermediate file (analogous to an RDD) and the output of that function is made available to consumers of that output only after the function completes. However, Spark does not actually apply transformations to RDDs until it is required to do so, typically because it must apply some action, e.g., storing a computed RDD in the surrounding file system or returning a result to an application.

The benefit of this strategy of *lazy evaluation* is that many RDDs are not constructed all at once. When one split of an RDD is created at a node, it may be used immediately at the same compute node to apply another transformation. The benefit of this startegy is that this RDD is never stored on disk and never transmitted to another compute nodes, thus saving orders of magnitude in running time in some cases.

EXAMPLE 2.9 Consider the situation suggested in Example 2.8, where Flatmap is applied to one RDD, which we shall refer to as R_0. Note that RDD R_0 is created by converting the external file of documents into an RDD. As R_0 is a large file, we shall want to divide it into splits and operate on the splits in parallel.

The first transformation on R_0 applies Flatmap to create a set of pairs $(w, 1)$ for each word. For each split of R_0, a split of the resulting RDD, which we called R_1 in Example 2.8, is created at the same compute node. This split of R_1 is then passed to the transformation Filter, which eliminates pairs whose first component is a stop word. When this Filter is applied to the split, the result is a split of the RDD R_2, located at the same compute node.

However, neither the Flatmap nor Filter transformations occur unless an action is applied to R_2. For example, the Spark program may store R_2 in the surrounding file system or perform a Reduce operation that counts occurrences of the words. Only when the program reaches this action does Spark apply the Flatmap and Filter transformations to R_0, running these transformations at each of the compute nodes that holds a split of R_0, in parallel. Thus, the splits of R_1 and R_2 exist only locally at the compute node that created them, and unless the programmer explicitly calls for them to be maintained, these splits are dropped as soon as they are used locally. □

Resilience of RDDs

One may naturally ask what happens in Example 2.9 if a compute node fails after creating a split of R_1 and before transforming that split into a split of R_2. Since R_1 is not backed up to the file system, is it not lost forever? Spark's substitute for redundant storage of intermediate values is to record the *lineage* of every RDD it creates. The lineage tells the Spark system how to recreate the RDD, or a split of the RDD, if that is needed.

EXAMPLE 2.10   Considering again the situation described in Example 2.9, the lineage for R_2 would say that it is created by applying to R_1 the particular Filter operation that eliminates stop words. In turn, R_1 is created from R_0 by the Flatmap operation that turns words of a document into $(w, 1)$ pairs. And R_0 was created from a particular file of the surrounding file system.

For instance, if we lose a split of R_2, we know we can reconstruct it from the corresponding split of R_1. But since that split exists at the same compute node, we've probably lost that split also. If so, we could reconstruct it from the corresponding split of R_0, which is also probably lost if this compute node has failed. But we know that we can reconstruct the split of R_0 from the surrounding file system, which is presumably redundant and will not be lost. Thus, Spark will find another compute node, reconstruct the lost split of R_0 from the file system there, and then apply the known transformations needed to reconstruct the corresponding splits of R_1 and R_2.   □

As we can see from Example 2.10, recovery from a node failure can be more complex in Spark than in MapReduce or in workflow systems that store intermediate values redundantly. However, the tradeoff of more complex recovery when things go wrong against greater speed when things go right is generally a good one. The faster a Spark program runs, the less chance there is of a node failure while running.

We should contrast Spark's need to be able to execute a program in the face of failures with the need for redundant storage of files that are expected to exist for a long period. Over a long period, failures are almost certain, so we are very likely to lose pieces of a file if we do not store it redundantly. But over a short period – minutes or even hours – there is a good chance of avoiding failures. Thus, it is reasonable to be willing to pay more when there *is* a failure in this case.

2.4.4   TensorFlow

TensorFlow is an open-source system developed initially at Google to support machine-learning applications. Like Spark, TensorFlow provides a programming interface in which one writes a sequence of steps. Programs are typically acyclic, although like Spark it is possible to iterate blocks of code.

One major difference between Spark and TensorFlow is the type of data that is passed between steps of the program. In place of the RDD, TensorFlow uses *tensors*; a tensor is simply a multidimensional matrix.

EXAMPLE 2.11   A constant, e.g. 3.14159, is regarded as a 0-dimensional tensor. A vector is a 1-dimensional tensor. For instance, the vector $(1, 2, 3)$ can be written in tensorFlow as $[1., 2., 3.]$. A matrix is a 2-dimensional tensor. For example, the matrix

$$
\begin{array}{cccc}
1 & 2 & 3 & 4 \\
5 & 6 & 7 & 8 \\
9 & 10 & 11 & 12
\end{array}
$$

is expressed as $[[1., 2., 3., 4.], [5., 6., 7., 8.], [9., 10., 11., 12.]]$.

Higher-dimensional arrays are possible as well. For instance, a $2 \times 2 \times 2$ cube of 0s is represented as $[[[0., 0.], [0., 0.]], [[0., 0.], [0., 0.]]]$. □

Although tensors are in fact a restricted form of RDD, the power of TensorFlow comes from its selection of built-in operations. Linear algebra operations are available as functions. For example, if you want matrix C to be the product of matrices A and B, you can write

```
C = tensorflow.matmul(A,B)
```

Even more powerful are the common approaches to machine learning that are built in as operations. a single statement in the TensorFlow language can cause a model that is a tensor to be constructed from training data, which is also represented as a tensor, using a method like gradient descent. (We discuss gradient descent in Sections 9.4.5 and 12.3.4).

2.4.5 Recursive Extensions to MapReduce

Many large-scale computations are really recursions. An important example is PageRank, which is the subject of Chapter 5. That computation is, in simple terms, the computation of the fixedpoint of a matrix-vector multiplication. It is computed under MapReduce systems by the iterated application of the matrix-vector multiplication algorithm described in Section 2.3.1, or by a more complex strategy that we shall introduce in Section 5.2. The iteration typically continues for an unknown number of steps, each step being a MapReduce job, until the results of two consecutive iterations are sufficiently close that we believe convergence has occurred. A second important example of a recursive algorithm on massive data is gradient descent, which we just mentioned in connection with TensorFlow.

Recursions present a problem for failure recovery. Recursive tasks inherently lack the blocking property necessary for independent restart of failed tasks. It is impossible for a collection of mutually recursive tasks, each of which has an output that is input to at least some of the other tasks, to produce output only at the end of the task. If they all followed that policy, no task would ever receive any input, and nothing could be accomplished. As a result, some mechanism other than simple restart of failed tasks must be implemented in a system that handles recursive workflows (flow graphs that are not acyclic). We shall start by studying an example of a recursion implemented as a workflow, and then discuss approaches to dealing with task failures.

EXAMPLE 2.12 Suppose we have a directed graph whose arcs are represented by the relation $E(X, Y)$, meaning that there is an arc from node X to node Y.

We wish to compute the paths relation $P(X,Y)$, meaning that there is a path of length 1 or more from node X to node Y. That is, P is the *transitive closure* of E. A simple recursive algorithm to do so is:

(1) Start with $P(X,Y) = E(X,Y)$.
(2) While changes to the relation P occur, add to P all tuples in

$$\pi_{X,Y}\big(P(X,Z) \bowtie P(Z,Y)\big)$$

That is, find pairs of nodes X and Y such that for some node Z there is known to be a path from X to Z and also a known path from Z to Y.

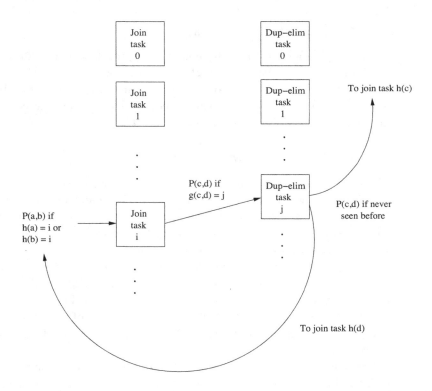

Figure 2.7 Implementation of transitive closure by a collection of recursive tasks

Figure 2.7 suggests how we could organize recursive tasks to perform this computation. There are two kinds of tasks: *Join tasks* and *Dup-elim tasks*. There are n Join tasks, for some n, and each corresponds to a bucket of a hash function h. A path tuple $P(a,b)$, when it is discovered, becomes input to two Join tasks: those numbered $h(a)$ and $h(b)$. The job of the ith Join task, when it receives input tuple $P(a,b)$, is to find certain other tuples seen previously (and stored locally by that task).

(1) Store $P(a,b)$ locally.

(2) If $h(a) = i$ then look for tuples $P(x, a)$ and produce output tuple $P(x, b)$.

(3) If $h(b) = i$ then look for tuples $P(b, y)$ and produce output tuple $P(a, y)$.

Note that in rare cases, we have $h(a) = h(b)$, so both (2) and (3) are executed. But generally, only one of these needs to be executed for a given tuple.

There are also m Dup-elim tasks, and each corresponds to a bucket of a hash function g that takes two arguments. If $P(c, d)$ is an output of some Join task, then it is sent to Dup-elim task $j = g(c, d)$. On receiving this tuple, the jth Dup-elim task checks that it has not received this tuple before, since its job is duplicate elimination. If previously received, the tuple is ignored. But if this tuple is new, it is stored locally and sent to two Join tasks, those numbered $h(c)$ and $h(d)$.

Every Join task has m output files – one for each Dup-elim task – and every Dup-elim task has n output files – one for each Join task. These files may be distributed according to any of several strategies. Initially, the $E(a, b)$ tuples representing the arcs of the graph are distributed to the Dup-elim tasks, with $E(a, b)$ being sent as $P(a, b)$ to Dup-elim task $g(a, b)$. The master controller waits until each Join task has processed its entire input for a round. Then, all output files are distributed to the Dup-elim tasks, which create their own output. That output is distributed to the Join tasks and becomes their input for the next round. □

In Example 2.12 it is not essential to have two kinds of tasks. Rather, Join tasks could eliminate duplicates as they are received, since they must store their previously received inputs anyway. However, this arrangement has an advantage when we must recover from a task failure. If each task stores all the output files it has ever created, and we place Join tasks on different racks from the Dup-elim tasks, then we can deal with any single compute node or single rack failure. That is, a Join task needing to be restarted can get all the previously generated inputs that it needs from the Dup-elim tasks, and vice versa.

In the particular case of computing transitive closure, it is not necessary to prevent a restarted task from generating outputs that the original task generated previously. In the computation of the transitive closure, the rediscovery of a path does not influence the eventual answer. However, many computations cannot tolerate a situation where both the original and restarted versions of a task pass the same output to another task. For example, if the final step of the computation were an aggregation, say a count of the number of nodes reached by each node in the graph, then we would get the wrong answer if we counted a path twice.

There are at least three different approaches that have been used to deal with failures while executing a recursive program.

(1) *Iterated MapReduce*: Write the recursion as repeated execution of a Map-Reduce job or of a sequence of MapReduce jobs. We can then rely on the failure mechanism of the MapReduce implementation to handle failures at

any step. The first example of such a system was HaLoop (see the bibliographic notes for this chapter).

(2) *The Spark Approach*: The Spark language actually includes iterative statements, such as for-loops that allow the implementation of recursions. Here, failure management is implemented using the lazy-evaluation and lineage mechanisms of Spark. In addition, the Spark programmer has options to store intermediate states of the recursion.

(3) *Bulk-Synchronous Systems*: These systems use a graph-based model of computation that we shall describe next. They typically use another resilience approach: periodic checkpointing.

2.4.6   Bulk-Synchronous Systems

Another approach to implementing recursive algorithms on a computing cluster is represented by the Google's Pregel system, which was the first example of a graph-based, bulk-synchronous system for processing massive amounts of data. Such a system views its data as a graph. Each node of the graph corresponds roughly to a task (although in practice many nodes of a large graph would be bundled into a single task, as in the Join tasks of Example 2.12). Each graph node generates output messages that are destined for other nodes of the graph, and each graph node processes the inputs it receives from other nodes.

EXAMPLE 2.13   Suppose our data is a collection of weighted arcs of a graph, and we want to find, for each node of the graph, the length of the shortest path to each of the other nodes. As the algorithm executes, each node a will store a set of pairs (b, w), where w is the length of the shortest path from node a to node b that is currently known.

Initially, each graph node a stores the set of pairs (b, w) such that there is an arc from a to b of weight w. These facts are sent to all other nodes, as triples (a, b, w), with the intended meaning that node a knows about a path of length w to node b.[8] When the node a receives a triple (c, d, w), it must decide whether this fact implies a shorter path than a already knows about from itself to node d. Node a looks up its current distance to c; that is, it finds the pair (c, v) stored locally, if there is one. It also finds the pair (d, u) if there is one. If $w + v < u$, then the pair (d, u) is replaced by $(d, w + v)$, and if there was no pair (d, u), then the pair $(d, w + v)$ is stored at the node a. Also, the other nodes are sent the message $(a, d, w + v)$ in either of these two cases.   □

Computations in Pregel are organized into *supersteps*. In one superstep, all the messages that were received by any of the nodes at the previous superstep (or initially, if it is the first superstep) are processed, and then all the messages generated by those nodes are sent to their destination. It is this packaging of many messages into one that gives this approach the name "bulk-synchronous."

---

[8] This algorithm uses much too much communication, but it will serve as a simple example of the Pregel computation model.

There is a very important advantage to grouping messages in this way. Communication over a network generally requires a large amount of overhead to send any message, however short. Suppose that in Example 2.13 we sent a single new shortest-distance fact to the relevant node every time one was discovered. The number of messages sent would be enormous if the graph was large, and it would not be realistic to implement such an algorithm. However, in a bulk-synchonous system, a task that has the responsibility for managing many nodes of the graph can bundle together all the messages being sent by its nodes to any of the nodes being managed by another task. That choice typically saves orders of magnitude in the time required to send all the needed messages.

Failure Management in Pregel

In case of a compute-node failure, there is no attempt to restart the failed tasks at that compute node. Rather, Pregel *checkpoints* its entire computation after some of the supersteps. A checkpoint consists of making a copy of the entire state of each task, so it can be restarted from that point if necessary. If any compute node fails, the entire job is restarted from the most recent checkpoint.

Although this recovery strategy causes many tasks that have not failed to redo their work, it is satisfactory in many situations. Recall that the reason MapReduce systems support restart of only the failed tasks is that we want assurance that the expected time to complete the entire job in the face of failures is not too much greater than the time to run the job with no failures. Any failure-management system will have that property as long as the time to recover from a failure is much less than the average time between failures. Thus, it is only necessary that Pregel checkpoints its computation after a number of supersteps such that the probability of a failure during that number of supersteps is low.

2.4.7   Exercises for Section 2.4

! EXERCISE 2.4.1   Suppose a job consists of n tasks, each of which takes time t seconds. Thus, if there are no failures, the sum over all compute nodes of the time taken to execute tasks at that node is nt. Suppose also that the probability of a task failing is p per job per second, and when a task fails, the overhead of management of the restart is such that it adds $10t$ seconds to the total execution time of the job. What is the total expected execution time of the job?

! EXERCISE 2.4.2   Suppose a Pregel job has a probability p of a failure during any superstep. Suppose also that the execution time (summed over all compute nodes) of taking a checkpoint is c times the time it takes to execute a superstep. To minimize the expected execution time of the job, how many supersteps should elapse between checkpoints?

2.5   The Communication-Cost Model

In this section we shall introduce a model for measuring the quality of algorithms implemented on a computing cluster of the type so far discussed in this chapter. We assume the computation is described by an acyclic workflow, as discussed in Section 2.4.1. For many applications, the bottleneck is moving data among tasks, such as transporting the outputs of Map tasks to their proper Reduce tasks. As an example, we explore the computation of multiway joins as single MapReduce jobs, and we see that in some situations, this approach is more efficient than the straightforward cascade of 2-way joins.

2.5.1   Communication Cost for Task Networks

Imagine that an algorithm is implemented by an acyclic network of tasks. These tasks could be Map tasks feeding Reduce tasks, as in a standard MapReduce algorithm, or they could be several MapReduce jobs cascaded, or a more general workflow structure, such as a collection of tasks each of which implements the workflow of Fig. 2.6.[9] The *communication cost* of a task is the size of the input to the task. This size can be measured in bytes. However, since we shall be using relational database operations as examples, we shall often use the number of tuples as a measure of size.

The *communication cost of an algorithm* is the sum of the communication cost of all the tasks implementing that algorithm. We shall focus on the communication cost as the way to measure the efficiency of an algorithm. In particular, we do not consider the amount of time it takes each task to execute when estimating the running time of an algorithm. While there are exceptions, where execution time of tasks dominates, these exceptions are rare in practice. We can explain and justify the importance of communication cost as follows.

- The algorithm executed by each task tends to be very simple, often linear in the size of its input.
- The typical interconnect speed for a computing cluster is one gigabit per second. That may seem like a lot, but it is slow compared with the speed at which a processor executes instructions. Moreover, in many cluster architectures, there is competition for the interconnect when several compute nodes need to communicate at the same time. As a result, the compute node can do a lot of work on a received input element in the time it takes to deliver that element.
- Even if a task executes at a compute node that has a copy of the chunk(s) on which the task operates, that chunk normally will be stored on disk, and the time taken to move the data into main memory may exceed the time needed to operate on the data once it is available in memory.

---

[9] Recall that this figure represented functions, not tasks. As a network of tasks, there would be, for example, many tasks implementing function f, each of which feeds data to each of the tasks for function g and each of the tasks for function i.

Assuming that communication cost is the dominant cost, we might still ask why we count only input size, and not output size. The answer to this question involves two points:

(1) If the output of one task τ is input to another task, then the size of τ's output will be accounted for when measuring the input size for the receiving task. Thus, there is no reason to count the size of any output except for those tasks whose output forms the result of the entire algorithm.

(2) But in practice, the algorithm output is rarely large compared with the input or the intermediate data produced by the algorithm. The reason is that massive outputs cannot be used unless they are summarized or aggregated in some way. For example, although we talked in Example 2.12 of computing the entire transitive closure of a graph, in practice we would want something much simpler, such as the count of the number of nodes reachable from each node, or the set of nodes reachable from a single node.

EXAMPLE 2.14   Let us evaluate the communication cost for the join algorithm from Section 2.3.7. Suppose we are joining $R(A, B) \bowtie S(B, C)$, and the sizes of relations R and S are r and s, respectively. Each chunk of the files holding R and S is fed to one Map task, so the sum of the communication costs for all the Map tasks is $r + s$. Note that in a typical execution, the Map tasks will each be executed at a compute node holding a copy of the chunk to which it applies. Thus, no internode communication is needed for the Map tasks, but they still must read their data from disk. Since all the Map tasks do is make a simple transformation of each input tuple into a key-value pair, we expect that the computation cost will be small compared with the communication cost, regardless of whether the input is local to the task or must be transported to its compute node.

The sum of the outputs of the Map tasks is roughly as large as their inputs. Each output key-value pair is sent to exactly one Reduce task, and it is unlikely that this Reduce task will execute at the same compute node. Therefore, communication from Map tasks to Reduce tasks is likely to be across the interconnect of the cluster, rather than memory-to-disk. This communication is $O(r + s)$, so the communication cost of the join algorithm is $O(r + s)$.

The Reduce tasks execute the reducer (application of the Reduce function to a key and its associated value list) for one or more values of attribute B. Each reducer takes the inputs it receives and divides them between tuples that came from R and those that came from S. Each tuple from R pairs with each tuple from S to produce one output. The output size for the join can be either larger or smaller than $r + s$, depending on how likely it is that a given R-tuple joins with a given S-tuple. For example, if there are many different B-values, we would expect the output to be small, while if there are few B-values, a large output is likely.

If the output is large, then the computation cost of generating all the outputs from a reducer could be much larger than $O(r+s)$. However, we shall rely on our supposition that if the output of the join is large, then there is probably some aggregation being done to reduce the size of the output. It will be necessary to communicate the result of the join to another collection of tasks that perform this aggregation, and thus the communication cost will be at least proportional to the computation needed to produce the output of the join.   □

2.5.2   Wall-Clock Time

While communication cost often influences our choice of algorithm to use in a cluster-computing environment, we must also be aware of the importance of *wall-clock time*, the time it takes a parallel algorithm to finish. Using careless reasoning, one could minimize total communication cost by assigning all the work to one task, and thereby minimize total communication. However, the wall-clock time of such an algorithm would be quite high. The algorithms we suggest, or have suggested so far, have the property that the work is divided fairly among the tasks. Therefore, the wall-clock time would be approximately as small as it could be, given the number of compute nodes available.

2.5.3   Multiway Joins

To see how analyzing the communication cost can help us choose an algorithm in the cluster-computing environment, we shall examine carefully the case of a multiway join. There is a general theory in which we:

(1) Select certain attributes of the relations involved in the natural join of three or more relations to have their values hashed, each to some number of buckets.

(2) Select the number of buckets for each of these attributes, subject to the constraint that the product of the numbers of buckets for each attribute is k, the number of reducers that will be used.

(3) Identify each of the k reducers with a vector of bucket numbers. These vectors have one component for each of the attributes selected at step (1).

(4) Send tuples of each relation to all those reducers where it might find tuples to join with. That is, the given tuple t will have values for some of the attributes selected at step (1), so we can apply the hash function(s) to those values to determine certain components of the vector that identifies the reducers. Other components of the vector are unknown, so t must be sent to reducers for all vectors having any value in these unknown components.

Some examples of this general technique appear in the exercises. Here, we shall look only at the join $R(A, B) \bowtie S(B, C) \bowtie T(C, D)$ as an example. Suppose that the relations R, S, and T have sizes r, s, and t, respectively, and for simplicity, suppose p is the probability that

(1) An R-tuple and and S-tuple agree on B, and also the probability that

(2) An S-tuple and a T-tuple agree on C.

If we join R and S first, using the MapReduce algorithm of Section 2.3.7, then the communication cost is $O(r + s)$, and the size of the intermediate join $R \bowtie S$ is prs. When we join this result with T, the communication of this second MapReduce job is $O(t + prs)$. Thus, the entire communication cost of the algorithm consisting of two 2-way joins is $O(r + s + t + prs)$. If we instead join S and T first, and then join R with the result, we get another algorithm whose communication cost is $O(r + s + t + pst)$.

A third way to take this join is to use a single MapReduce job that joins the three relations at once. Suppose that we plan to use k reducers for this job. Pick numbers b and c representing the number of buckets into which we shall hash B- and C-values, respectively. Let h be a hash function that sends B-values into b buckets, and let g be another hash function that sends C-values into c buckets. We require that $bc = k$; that is, each reducer corresponds to a pair of buckets, one for the B-value and one for the C-value. The reducer corresponding to bucket pair (i, j) is responsible for joining the tuples $R(u, v)$, $S(v, w)$, and $T(w, x)$ whenever $h(v) = i$ and $g(w) = j$.

As a result, the Map tasks that send tuples of R, S, and T to the reducers that need them must send R- and T-tuples to more than one reducer. For an S-tuple $S(v, w)$, we know the B- and C-values, so we can send this tuple only to the reducer for $(h(v), g(w))$. However, consider an R-tuple $R(u, v)$. We know it only needs to go to reducers that correspond to $(h(v), y)$, for some y. But we don't know y; the value of C could be anything as far as we know. Thus, we must send $R(u, v)$ to c reducers, since y could be any of the c buckets for C-values. Similarly, we must send the T-tuple $T(w, x)$ to each of the reducers $(z, g(w))$ for any z. There are b such reducers.

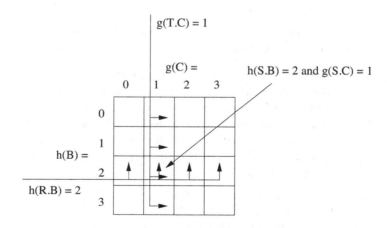

Figure 2.8 Sixteen reducers together perform a 3-way join

EXAMPLE 2.15 Suppose that $b = c = 4$, so $k = 16$. The sixteen reducers can be thought of as arranged in a rectangle, as suggested by Fig. 2.8. There, we see a

---

Computation Cost of the 3-Way Join

Each of the reducers must compute the join of parts of the three relations, and it is reasonable to ask whether this join can be taken in time that is as small as possible: linear in the sum of the sizes of the input and output for that Reduce task. While more complex joins might not be computable in linear time, the join of our running example can be executed at each Reduce process efficiently. First, create an index on $R.B$, to organize the R-tuples received. Likewise, create an index on $T.C$ for the T-tuples. Then, consider each received S-tuple, $S(v,w)$. Use the index on $R.B$ to find all R-tuples with $R.B = v$ and use the index on $T.C$ to find all T-tuples with $T.C = w$.

---

hypothetical S-tuple $S(v,w)$ for which $h(v) = 2$ and $g(w) = 1$. This tuple is sent by its Map task only to the reducer for key $(2,1)$. We also see an R-tuple $R(u,v)$. Since $h(v) = 2$, this tuple is sent to all reducers $(2,y)$, for $y = 1, 2, 3, 4$. Finally, we see a T-tuple $T(w,x)$. Since $g(w) = 1$, this tuple is sent to all reducers $(z,1)$ for $z = 1, 2, 3, 4$. Notice that these three tuples join, and they meet at exactly one reducer, the reducer for key $(2,1)$. □

Now, suppose that the sizes of R, S, and T are different; recall we use r, s, and t, respectively, for those sizes. If we hash B-values to b buckets and C-values to c buckets, where $bc = k$, then the total communication cost for moving the tuples to the proper reducers is the sum of:

(1) s to send each tuple $S(v,w)$ to the reducer $(h(v), g(w))$.

(2) cr to send each tuple $R(u,v)$ to the c reducers $(h(v), y)$ for each of the c possible values of y.

(3) bt to send each tuple $T(w,x)$ to the b reducers $(z, g(w))$ for each of the b possible values of z.

There is also a cost $r + s + t$ to make each tuple of each relation be input to one of the Map tasks. This cost is fixed, independent of b, c, and k.

We must select b and c, subject to the constraint $bc = k$, to minimize $s + cr + bt$. We shall use the technique of Lagrangean multipliers to find the place where the function $s + cr + bt - \lambda(bc - k)$ has its derivatives with respect to b and c equal to 0. That is, we must solve the equations $r - \lambda b = 0$ and $t - \lambda c = 0$. Since $r = \lambda b$ and $t = \lambda c$, we may multiply corresponding sides of these equations to get $rt = \lambda^2 bc$. Since $bc = k$, we get $rt = \lambda^2 k$, or $\lambda = \sqrt{rt/k}$. Thus, the minimum communication cost is obtained when $c = t/\lambda = \sqrt{kt/r}$, and $b = r/\lambda = \sqrt{kr/t}$.

If we substitute these values into the formula $s + cr + bt$, we get $s + 2\sqrt{krt}$. That is the communication cost for the Reduce tasks, to which we must add the cost $s + r + t$ for the communication cost of the Map tasks. The total communication cost is thus $r + 2s + t + 2\sqrt{krt}$. In most circumstances, we can neglect $r + t$, because it will be less than $2\sqrt{krt}$, usually by a factor of $O(\sqrt{k})$.

EXAMPLE 2.16   Let us see under what circumstances the 3-way join has lower communication cost than the cascade of two 2-way joins. To make matters simple, let us assume that R, S, and T are all the same relation R, which represents the "friends" relation in a social network like Facebook. There are roughly a billion subscribers on Facebook, with an average of 300 friends each, so relation R has $r = 3 \times 10^{11}$ tuples. Suppose we want to compute $R \bowtie R \bowtie R$, perhaps as part of a calculation to find the number of friends of friends of friends each subscriber has, or perhaps just the person with the largest number of friends of friends of friends.[10] The communication cost of the 3-way join of R with itself is $4r + 2r\sqrt{k}$; $3r$ represents the cost of the Map tasks, and $r + 2\sqrt{k}r^2$ is the cost of the Reduce tasks. Since we assume $r = 3 \times 10^{11}$, this cost is $1.2 \times 10^{12} + 6 \times 10^{11}\sqrt{k}$.

Now consider the communication cost of joining R with itself, and then joining the result with R again. The Map and Reduce tasks for the first join each have a cost of $2r$, so the first join only has communication cost $4r = 1.2 \times 10^{12}$. But the size of $R \bowtie R$ is large. We cannot say exactly how large, since friends tend to fall into cliques, and therefore a person with 300 friends will have many fewer than the maximum possible number of friends of friends, which is 90,000. Let us estimate conservatively that the size of $R \bowtie R$ is not $300r$, but only $30r$, or 9×10^{12}. The communication cost for the second join of $(R \bowtie R) \bowtie R$ is thus $1.8 \times 10^{13} + 6 \times 10^{11}$. The total cost of the two joins is therefore $1.2 \times 10^{12} + 1.8 \times 10^{13} + 6 \times 10^{11} = 1.98 \times 10^{13}$.

We must ask whether the cost of the 3-way join, which is

$$1.2 \times 10^{12} + 6 \times 10^{11}\sqrt{k}$$

is less than 1.98×10^{13}. That is so, provided $6 \times 10^{11}\sqrt{k} < 1.86 \times 10^{13}$, or $\sqrt{k} < 31$. That is, the 3-way join will be preferable provided we use no more than $31^2 = 961$ reducers. $\square$

2.5.4   Exercises for Section 2.5

EXERCISE 2.5.1   What is the communication cost of each of the following algorithms, as a function of the size of the relations, matrices, or vectors to which they are applied?

(a) The matrix-vector multiplication algorithm of Section 2.3.2.
(b) The union algorithm of Section 2.3.6.
(c) The aggregation algorithm of Section 2.3.8.
(d) The matrix-multiplication algorithm of Section 2.3.10.

! EXERCISE 2.5.2   Suppose relations R, S, and T have sizes r, s, and t, respectively, and we want to take the 3-way join $R(A, B) \bowtie S(B, C) \bowtie T(A, C)$, using k reducers. We shall hash values of attributes A, B, and C to a, b, and c buckets,

---

[10] This person, or more generally, people with large extended circles of friends, are good people to use to start a marketing campaign by giving them free samples.

Star Joins

A common structure for data mining of commercial data is the *star join*. For example, a chain store like Walmart keeps a *fact table* whose tuples each represent a single sale. This relation looks like $F(A_1, A_2, \ldots)$, where each attribute A_i is a key representing one of the important components of the sale, such as the purchaser, the item purchased, the store branch, or the date. For each key attribute there is a *dimension table* giving information about the participant. For instance, the dimension table $D(A_1, B_{11}, B_{12}, \ldots)$ might represent purchasers. A_1 is the purchaser ID, the key for this relation. The B_{1i} might give the purchaser's name, address, phone, and so on. Typically, the fact table is much larger than the dimension tables. For instance, there might be a fact table of a billion tuples and ten dimension tables of a million tuples each.

Analysts mine this data by asking *analytic queries* that typically join the fact table with several of the dimension tables (a "star join") and then aggregate the result into a useful form. For instance, an analyst might ask "give me a table of sales of pants, broken down by region and color, for each month of 2016." Under the communication-cost model of this section, joining the fact table and dimension tables by a multiway join is almost certain to be more efficient than joining the relations in pairs. In fact, it may make sense to store the fact table over however many compute nodes are available, and replicate the dimension tables permanently in exactly the same way as we would replicate them should we take the join of the fact table and all the dimension tables. In this special case, only the key attributes (the *A*s above) are hashed to buckets, and the number of buckets for each key attribute is proportional to the size of its dimension table.

---

respectively, where $abc = k$. Each reducer is associated with a vector of buckets, one for each of the three hash functions. Find, as a function of r, s, t, and k, the values of a, b, and c that minimize the communication cost of the algorithm.

! EXERCISE 2.5.3   Suppose we take a star join of a fact table $F(A_1, A_2, \ldots, A_m)$ with dimension tables $D_i(A_i, B_i)$ for $i = 1, 2, \ldots, m$. Let there be k reducers, each associated with a vector of buckets, one for each of the key attributes $A_1, A_2, \ldots, A_m$. Suppose the number of buckets into which we hash A_i is a_i. Naturally, $a_1 a_2 \cdots a_m = k$. Finally, suppose each dimension table D_i has size d_i, and the size of the fact table is much larger than any of these sizes. Find the values of the a_i that minimize the cost of taking the star join as one MapReduce operation.

2.6   Complexity Theory for MapReduce

Now, we shall explore the design of MapReduce algorithms in more detail. Section 2.5 introduced the idea that communication between the Map and Reduce tasks is often the bottleneck when performing a MapReduce computation. Here, we shall look at how the communication cost relates to other desiderata for

MapReduce algorithms, in particular our desire to shrink the wall-clock time and to execute each reducer in main memory. Recall that a "reducer" is the execution of the Reduce function on a single key and its associated value list. The point of the exploration in this section is that for many problems there is a spectrum of MapReduce algorithms requiring different amounts of communication. Moreover, the less communication an algorithm uses, the worse it may be in other respects, including wall-clock time and the amount of main memory it requires.

2.6.1   Reducer Size and Replication Rate

Let us now introduce the two parameters that characterize families of MapReduce algorithms. The first is the *reducer size*, which we denote by q. This parameter is the upper bound on the number of values that are allowed to appear in the list associated with a single key. Reducer size can be selected with at least two goals in mind.

(1) By making the reducer size small, we can force there to be many reducers, i.e., many different keys according to which the problem input is divided by the Map tasks. If we also create many Reduce tasks – even one for each reducer – then there will be a high degree of parallelism, and we can expect a low wall-clock time.

(2) We can choose a reducer size sufficiently small that we are certain the computation associated with a single reducer can be executed entirely in the main memory of the compute node where its Reduce task is located. Regardless of the computation done by the reducers, the running time will be greatly reduced if we can avoid having to move data repeatedly between main memory and disk.

The second parameter is the *replication rate*, denoted r. We define r to be the number of key-value pairs produced by all the Map tasks on all the inputs, divided by the number of inputs. That is, the replication rate is the average communication from Map tasks to Reduce tasks (measured by counting key-value pairs) per input.

EXAMPLE 2.17   Let us consider the one-pass matrix-multiplication algorithm of Section 2.3.10. Suppose that all the matrices involved are $n \times n$ matrices. Then the replication rate r is equal to n. That fact is easy to see, since for each element m_{ij}, there are n key-value pairs produced; these have all keys of the form (i, k), for $1 \leq k \leq n$. Likewise, for each element of the other matrix, say n_{jk}, we produce n key-value pairs, each having one of the keys (i, k), for $1 \leq i \leq n$. In this case, not only is n the average number of key-value pairs produced for an input element, but each input produces exactly this number of pairs.

We also see that q, the required reducer size, is $2n$. That is, for each key (i, k), there are n key-value pairs representing elements m_{ij} of the first matrix and another n key-value pairs derived from the elements n_{jk} of the second matrix. While this pair of values represents only one particular algorithm for one-pass matrix multiplication, we shall see that it is part of a spectrum of algorithms, and in fact represents an extreme point, where q is as small as can be, and r is at its maximum. More generally, there is a tradeoff between r and q that can be expressed as $qr \geq 2n^2$. $\square$

2.6.2   An Example: Similarity Joins

To see the tradeoff between r and q in a realistic situation, we shall examine a problem known as *similarity join*. In this problem, we are given a large set of elements X and a similarity measure $s(x, y)$ that tells how similar two elements x and y of set X are. In Chapter 3 we shall learn about the most important notions of similarity and also learn some tricks that let us find similar pairs quickly. But here, we shall consider only the raw form of the problem, where we have to look at each pair of elements of X and determine their similarity by applying the function s. We assume that s is symmetric, so $s(x, y) = s(y, x)$, but we assume nothing else about s. The output of the algorithm is those pairs whose similarity exceeds a given threshold t.

For example, let us suppose we have a collection of one million images, each of size one megabyte. Thus, the dataset has size one terabyte. We shall not try to describe the similarity function s, but it might, say, involve giving higher values when images have roughly the same distribution of colors or when images have corresponding regions with the same distribution of colors. The goal would be to discover pairs of images that show the same type of object or scene. This problem is extremely hard, but classifying by color distribution is generally of some help toward that goal.

Let us look at how we might do the computation using MapReduce to exploit the natural parallelism found in this problem. The input is key-value pairs (i, P_i), where i is an ID for the picture and P_i is the picture itself. We want to compare each pair of pictures, so let us use one key for each set of two IDs $\{i, j\}$. There are approximately 5×10^{11} pairs of two IDs. We want each key $\{i, j\}$ to be associated with the two values P_i and P_j, so the input to the corresponding reducer will be $(\{i, j\}, [P_i, P_j])$. Then, the Reduce function can simply apply the similarity function s to the two pictures on its value list; that is, compute $s(P_i, P_j)$, and decide whether the similarity of the two pictures is above threshold. The pair would be output if so.

Alas, this algorithm will fail completely. The reducer size is small, since no list has more than two values, or a total of 2MB of input. Although we don't know exactly how the similarity function s operates, we can reasonably expect that it will not require more than the available main memory. However, the replication rate is 999,999, since for each picture we generate that number of key-value pairs, one for each of the other pictures in the dataset. The total number of bytes communicated from Map tasks to Reduce tasks is 1,000,000 (for the pictures) times 999,999 (for the replication), times 1,000,000 (for the size of each picture). That's approximately 10^{18} bytes, or one exabyte. To communicate this amount of data over gigabit Ethernet would take 10^{10} seconds, or about 300 years.[11]

Fortunately, this algorithm is only the extreme point in a spectrum of possible algorithms. We can characterize these algorithms by grouping pictures into g groups, each of $10^6/g$ pictures.

The Map Function Take an input element (i, P_i) and generate $g - 1$ key-value pairs. For each, the key is one of the sets $\{u, v\}$, where u is the group to which picture i belongs, and v is one of the other groups. The associated value is the pair (i, P_i).

The Reduce Function Consider the key $\{u, v\}$. The associated value list will have the $2 \times 10^6/g$ elements (j, P_j), where j belongs to either group u or group v. The Reduce function takes each (i, P_i) and (j, P_j) on this list, where i and j belong to different groups, and applies the similarity function $s(P_i, P_j)$. In addition, we need to compare the pictures that belong to the same group, but we don't want to do the same comparison at each of the $g - 1$ reducers whose key contains a given group number. There are many ways of handling this problem, but one is as follows. Compare the members of group u at the reducer $\{u, u+1\}$, where the "+1" is taken in the end-around sense. That is, if $u = g$ (i.e., u is the last group), then $u + 1$ is group 1. Otherwise, $u + 1$ is the group whose number is one greater than u.

We can compute the replication rate and reducer size as a function of the number of groups g. Each input element is turned into $g - 1$ key-value pairs. That is, the replication rate is $g - 1$, or approximately $r = g$, since we suppose that the number of groups is still fairly large. The reducer size is $2 \times 10^6/g$, since that is the number of values on the list for each reducer. Each value is about a megabyte, so the number of bytes needed to store the input is $2 \times 10^{12}/g$.

EXAMPLE 2.18   If g is 1000, then the input consumes about 2GB. That's enough to hold everything in a typical main memory. Moreover, the total number of bytes communicated is now $10^6 \times 999 \times 10^6$, or about 10^{15} bytes. While that is still a huge amount of data to communicate, it is 1000 times less than that of the brute-force algorithm discussed first. Moreover, there are still about half a million reducers. Since we are unlikely to have available that many compute nodes, we can divide all the reducers into a smaller number of Reduce tasks and still keep all the compute nodes busy; i.e., we can get as much parallelism as our computing cluster offers us.   □

---

[11] In a typical cluster, there are many switches connecting subsets of the compute nodes, so all the data does not need to go across a single gigabit switch. However, the total available communication is still small enough that it is not feasible to implement this algorithm for the scale of data we have hypothesized.

The computation cost for algorithms in this family is independent of the number of groups g, as long as the input to each reducer fits in main memory. The reason is that the bulk of the computation is the application of function s to the pairs of pictures. No matter what value g has, s is applied to each pair once and only once. Thus, although the work of algorithms in the family may be divided among reducers in widely different ways, all members of the family do the same computation.

2.6.3   A Graph Model for MapReduce Problems

In this section, we begin the study of a technique that will enable us to prove lower bounds on the replication rate, as a function of reducer size, for a number of problems. Our first step is to introduce a graph model of problems. This graph describes how the outputs of the problem depend on the inputs. The key idea to be exploited is that, since reducers operate independently, for each output there must be some reducer that gets all of the inputs needed to compute that output. For each problem solvable by a MapReduce algorithm there is:

(1) A set of inputs.
(2) A set of outputs.
(3) A many–many relationship between the inputs and outputs, which describes which inputs are necessary to produce which outputs.

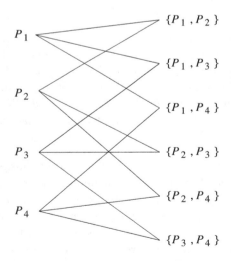

Figure 2.9 Input-output relationship for a similarity join

EXAMPLE 2.19   Figure 2.9 shows the graph for the similarity-join problem discussed in Section 2.6.2, if there were four pictures rather than a million. The inputs are the pictures, and the outputs are the six possible pairs of pictures. Each output is related to the two inputs that are members of its pair. This form of problem, where the outputs are all the pairs of inputs, is common, and we shall refer to it as the *all-pairs* problem. □

EXAMPLE 2.20   Matrix multiplication presents a more complex graph. If we multiply $n \times n$ matrices M and N to get matrix P, then there are $2n^2$ inputs, m_{ij} and n_{jk}, and there are n^2 outputs p_{ik}. Each output p_{ik} is related to $2n$ inputs: $m_{i1}, m_{i2}, \ldots, m_{in}$ and $n_{1k}, n_{2k}, \ldots, n_{nk}$. Moreover, each input is related to n outputs. For example, m_{ij} is related to $p_{i1}, p_{i2}, \ldots, p_{in}$. Figure 2.10 shows the input-output relationship for matrix multiplication for the simple case of 2×2 matrices, specifically

$$\begin{bmatrix} a & b \\ c & d \end{bmatrix} \begin{bmatrix} e & f \\ g & h \end{bmatrix} = \begin{bmatrix} i & j \\ k & l \end{bmatrix}$$ □

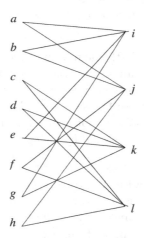

Figure 2.10 Input-output relationship for matrix multiplication

In the problems of Examples 2.19 and 2.20, the inputs and outputs were clearly all present. However, there are other problems where the inputs and/or outputs may not all be present in any instance of the problem. An example of such a problem is the natural join of $R(A, B)$ and $S(B, C)$ discussed in Section 2.3.7. We assume the attributes A, B, and C each have a finite domain, so there are only a finite number of possible inputs and outputs. The inputs are all possible R-tuples, those consisting of a value from the domain of A paired with a value from the domain of B, and all possible S-tuples – pairs from the domains of B and C. The outputs are all possible triples, with components from the domains of A, B, and C in that order. The output (a, b, c) is connected to two inputs, namely $R(a, b)$ and $S(b, c)$.

But in an instance of the join computation, only some of the possible inputs will be present, and therefore only some of the possible outputs will be produced. That fact does not influence the graph for the problem. We still need to know how every possible output relates to inputs, whether or not that output is produced in a given instance.

2.6.4   Mapping Schemas

Now that we see how to represent problems addressable by MapReduce as graphs, we can define the requirements for a MapReduce algorithm to solve a given problem. Each such algorithm must have a *mapping schema*, which expresses how outputs are produced by the various reducers used by the algorithm. That is, a mapping schema for a given problem with a given reducer size q is an assignment of inputs to one or more reducers, such that:

(1) No reducer is assigned more than q inputs.
(2) For every output of the problem, there is at least one reducer that is assigned all the inputs that are related to that output. We say this reducer *covers* the output.

Point (1) is simply the definition of "reducer size." Point (2) is justified by the fact that reducers can only see the inputs they are given. If no reducer sees all the inputs that an output depends upon, then no reducer can correctly produce that output, and therefore the supposed algorithm will not work. It can be argued that the existence of a mapping schema for any reducer size is what distinguishes problems that can be solved by a single MapReduce job from those that cannot.

EXAMPLE 2.21   Let us reconsider the "grouping" strategy we discussed in connection with the all-pairs problem in Section 2.6.2. To generalize the problem, suppose the input is p pictures, which we place in g equal-sized groups of p/g inputs each. The number of outputs is $\binom{p}{2}$, or approximately $p^2/2$ outputs. A reducer will get the inputs from two groups – that is, $2p/g$ inputs – so the reducer size we need is $q = 2p/g$. Each picture is sent to the reducers corresponding to the pairs consisting of its group and any of the $g - 1$ other groups. Thus, the replication rate is $g - 1$, or approximately g. If we replace g by the replication rate r in $q = 2p/g$, we conclude that $r = 2p/q$. That is, the replication rate is inversely proportional to the reducer size. That relationship is common; the smaller the reducer size, the larger the replication rate, and therefore the higher the communication.

This family of algorithms is described by a family of mapping schemas, one for each possible q. In the mapping schema for $q = 2p/g$, there are $\binom{g}{2}$, or approximately $g^2/2$ reducers. Each reducer corresponds to a pair of groups, and an input P is assigned to all the reducers whose pair includes the group of P. Thus, no reducer is assigned more than $2p/g$ inputs; in fact each reducer is assigned exactly that number. Moreover, every output is covered by some reducer. Specifically, if the output is a pair from two different groups u and v, then this output is covered by the reducer for the pair of groups $\{u, v\}$. If the output corresponds to inputs from only one group u, then the output is covered by several reducers – those corresponding to the set of groups $\{u, v\}$ for any $v \neq u$. Note that the algorithm we described has only one of these reducers computing the output, but any of them *could* compute it. □

The fact that an output depends on a certain input means that when that input is processed at the Map task, there will be at least one key-value pair generated to be used when computing that output. The value might not be exactly the input (as was the case in Example 2.21), but it is derived from that input. What is important is that for every related input and output there is a key-value pair that must be communicated. Note that there is technically never a need for more than one key-value pair for a given input and output, because the input could be transmitted to the reducer as itself, and whatever transformations on the input were applied by the Map function could instead be applied by the Reduce function at the reducer for that output.

2.6.5 When Not All Inputs Are Present

Example 2.21 describes a problem where we know every possible input is present, because we can define the input set to be those pictures that actually exist in the dataset. However, as discussed at the end of Section 2.6.3, there are problems like computing the join, where the graph of inputs and outputs describes inputs that might exist, and outputs that are only made when at least one of the inputs exists in the dataset. In fact, for the join, both inputs related to an output must exist if we are to make that output.

An algorithm for a problem where outputs can be missing still needs a mapping schema. The justification is that all inputs, or any subset of them, *might* be present, so an algorithm without a mapping schema would not be able to produce every possible output if all the inputs related to that output happened to be present, and yet no reducer covered that output.

The only way the absence of some inputs makes a difference is that we may wish to rethink the desired value of the reducer size q when we select an algorithm from the family of possible algorithms. Especially, if the value of q we select is that number such that we can be sure the input will just fit in main memory, then we may wish to increase q to take into account that some fraction of the inputs are not really there.

EXAMPLE 2.22 Suppose that we know we can execute the Reduce function in main memory on a key and its associated list of q values. However, we also know that only 5% of the possible inputs are really present in the data set. Then a mapping schema for reducer size q will really send about $q/20$ of the inputs that exist to each reducer. Put another way, we could use the algorithm for reducer size $20q$ and expect that an average of q inputs will actually appear on the list for each reducer. We can thus choose $20q$ as the reducer size, or since there will be some randomness in the number of inputs actually appearing at each reducer, we might wish to pick a slightly smaller value of reducer size, such as $18q$. □

2.6.6   Lower Bounds on Replication Rate

The family of similarity-join algorithms described in Example 2.21 lets us trade off communication against the reducer size, and through reducer size to trade communication against parallelism or against the ability to execute the Reduce function in main memory. How do we know we are getting the best possible tradeoff? We can only know we have the minimum possible communication if we can prove a matching lower bound. Using existence of a mapping schema as the starting point, we can often prove such a lower bound. Here is an outline of the technique.

(1) Prove an upper bound on how many outputs a reducer with q inputs can cover. Call this bound $g(q)$. This step can be difficult, but for examples like the all-pairs problem, it is actually quite simple.

(2) Determine the total number of outputs produced by the problem.

(3) Suppose that there are k reducers, and the ith reducer has $q_i < q$ inputs. Observe that $\sum_{i=1}^{k} g(q_i)$ must be no less than the number of outputs computed in step (2).

(4) Manipulate the inequality from (3) to get a lower bound on $\sum_{i=1}^{k} q_i$. Often, the trick used at this step is to replace some factors of q_i by their upper bound q, but leave a single factor of q_i in the term for i.

(5) Since $\sum_{i=1}^{k} q_i$ is the total communication from Map tasks to Reduce tasks, divide the lower bound from (4) on this quantity by the number of inputs. The result is a lower bound on the replication rate.

EXAMPLE 2.23   This sequence of steps may seem mysterious, but let us consider the all-pairs problem as an example that we hope will make things clear. Recall that in Example 2.21 we gave an upper bound on the replication rate r of $r \leq 2p/q$, where p was the number of inputs and q was the reducer size. We shall show a lower bound on r that is half that amount, which implies that, although improvements to the algorithm are possible,[12] any reduction in communication for a given reducer size will be by a factor of 2 at most.

For step (1), observe that if a reducer gets q inputs, it cannot cover more than $\binom{q}{2}$, or approximately $q^2/2$ outputs. For step (2), we know there are a total of $\binom{p}{2}$, or approximately $p^2/2$ outputs that each must be covered. The inequality constructed at step (3) is thus

$$\sum_{i=1}^{k} q_i^2/2 \geq p^2/2$$

or, multiplying both sides by 2,

$$\sum_{i=1}^{k} q_i^2 \geq p^2 \tag{2.1}$$

---

[12] In fact, an algorithm with r very close to p/q exists, for at least some values of p.

Now, we must do the manipulation of step (4). Following the hint, we note that there are two factors of q_i in each term on the left of Equation (2.1), so we replace one factor by q and leave the other as q_i. Since $q \geq q_i$, we can only increase the left side by doing so, and thus the inequality continues to hold:

$$q \sum_{i=1}^{k} q_i \geq p^2$$

or, dividing by q:

$$\sum_{i=1}^{k} q_i \geq p^2/q \qquad (2.2)$$

The final step, which is step (5), is to divide both sides of Equation 2.2 by p, the number of inputs. As a result, the left side, which is $(\sum_{i=1}^{k} q_i)/p$, is equal to the replication rate, and the right side becomes p/q. That is, we have proved the lower bound on r:

$$r \geq p/q$$

As claimed, this shows that the family of algorithms from Example 2.21 all have a replication rate that is at most twice the lowest possible replication rate.   □

2.6.7   Case Study: Matrix Multiplication

In this section we shall apply the lower-bound technique to one-pass matrix-multiplication algorithms. We saw one such algorithm in Section 2.3.10, but that is only an extreme case of a family of possible algorithms. In particular, for that algorithm, a reducer corresponds to a single element of the output matrix. Just as we grouped inputs in the all-pairs problem to reduce the communication at the expense of a larger reducer size, we can group rows and columns of the two input matrices into bands. Each pair consisting of a band of rows of the first matrix and a band of columns of the second matrix is used by one reducer to produce a square of elements of the output matrix. An example is suggested by Fig. 2.11.

In more detail, suppose we want to compute $MN = P$, and all three matrices are $n \times n$. Group the rows of M into g bands of n/g rows each, and group the columns of N into g bands of n/g columns each. This grouping is as suggested by Fig. 2.11. Keys correspond to two groups (bands), one from M and one from N.

The Map Function For each element of M, the Map function generates g key-value pairs. The value in each case is the element itself, together with its row and column number so it can be identified by the Reduce function. The key is the group to which the element belongs, paired with any of the groups of the matrix N. Similarly, for each element of N, the Map function generates

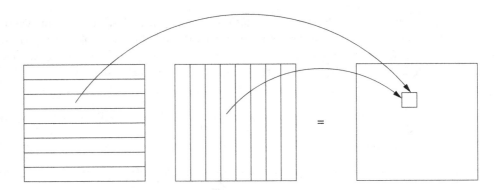

Figure 2.11 Dividing matrices into bands to reduce communication

g key-value pairs. The key is the group of that element paired with any of the groups of M, and the value is the element itself plus its row and column.

The Reduce Function The reducer corresponding to the key (i, j), where i is a group of M and j is a group of N, gets a value list consisting of all the elements in the ith band of M and the jth band of N. It thus has all the values it needs to compute the elements of P whose row is one of those rows comprising the ith band of M and whose column is one of those comprising the jth band of N. For instance, Fig. 2.11 suggests the third group of M and the fourth group of N, combining to compute a square of P at the reducer $(3, 4)$.

Each reducer gets $n(n/g)$ elements from each of the two matrices, so $q = 2n^2/g$. The replication rate is g, since each element of each matrix is sent to g reducers. That is, $r = g$. Combining $r = g$ with $q = 2n^2/g$ we can conclude that $r = 2n^2/q$. That is, just as for similarity join, the replication rate varies inversely with the reducer size.

It turns out that this upper bound on replication rate is also a lower bound. That is, we cannot do better than the family of algorithms we described above in a single round of MapReduce. Interestingly, we shall see that we can get a lower total communication for the same reducer size, if we use two passes of MapReduce as we discussed in Section 2.3.9. We shall not give the complete proof of the lower bound, but will suggest the important elements.

For step (1) we need to get an upper bound on how many outputs a reducer of size q can cover. First, notice that if a reducer gets some of the elements in a row of M, but not all of them, then the elements of that row are useless; the reducer cannot produce any output in that row of P. Similarly, if a reducer receives some but not all of a column of N, these inputs are also useless. Thus, we may assume that the best mapping schema will send to each reducer some number of full rows of M and some number of full columns of N. This reducer is then capable of producing output element p_{ik} if and only if it has received the entire ith row of M and the entire kth column of N. The remainder of the argument for step (1) is to prove that the largest number of outputs are covered when the reducer receives the same number of rows as columns. We leave this part as an exercise.

However, assuming a reducer receives k rows of M and k columns of N, then $q = 2nk$, and k^2 outputs are covered. That is, $g(q)$, the maximum number of outputs covered by a reducer that receives q inputs, is $q^2/4n^2$.

For step (2), we know the number of outputs is n^2. In step (3) we observe that if there are k reducers, with the ith reducer receiving $q_i \leq q$ inputs, then

$$\sum_{i=1}^{k} q_i^2/4n^2 \geq n^2$$

or

$$\sum_{i=1}^{k} q_i^2 \geq 4n^4$$

From this inequality, you can derive

$$r \geq 2n^2/q$$

We leave the algebraic manipulation, which is similar to that in Example 2.23, as an exercise.

Now, let us consider the generalization of the two-pass matrix-multiplication algorithm that we described in Section 2.3.9. First, notice that we could have designed the first pass to use one reducer for each triple (i, j, k). This reducer would get only the two elements m_{ij} and n_{jk}. We can generalize this idea to use reducers that get larger sets of elements from each matrix; these sets of elements form squares within their respective matrices. The idea is suggested by Fig. 2.12. We may divide the rows and columns of both input matrices M and N into g groups of n/g rows or columns each. The intersections of the groups partition each matrix into g^2 squares of n^2/g^2 elements each.

The square of M corresponding to set of rows I and set of columns J combines with the square of N corresponding to set of rows J and set of columns K. These two squares compute some of the terms that are needed to produce the square of the output matrix P that has set of rows I and set of columns K. However, these two squares do not compute the full value of these elements of P; rather they produce a contribution to the sum. Other pairs of squares, one from M and one from N, contribute to the same square of P. These contributions are suggested in Fig. 2.12. There, we see how all the squares of M with a fixed value for set of rows I pair with all the squares of N that have a fixed value for the set of columns K by letting the set J vary.

So in the first pass, we compute the products of the square (I, J) of M with the square (J, K) of N, for all I, J, and K. Then, in the second pass, for each I and K we sum the products over all possible sets J. In more detail, the first MapReduce job does the following.

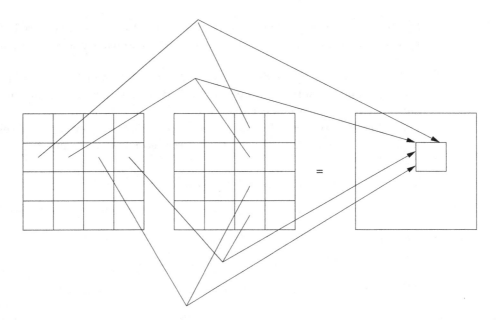

Figure 2.12 Partitioning matrices into squares for a two-pass MapReduce algorithm

The Map Function The keys are triples of sets of rows and/or column numbers (I, J, K). Suppose the element m_{ij} belongs to group of rows I and group of columns J. Then from m_{ij} we generate g key-value pairs with value equal to m_{ij}, together with its row and column numbers, i and j, to identify the matrix element. There is one key-value pair for each key (I, J, K), where K can be any of the g groups of columns of N. Similarly, from element n_{jk} of N, if j belongs to group J and k to group K, the Map function generates g key-value pairs with value consisting of n_{jk}, j, and k, and with keys (I, J, K) for any group I.

The Reduce Function The reducer corresponding to (I, J, K) receives as input all the elements m_{ij} where i is in I and j is in J, and it also receives all the elements n_{jk}, where j is in J and k is in K. It computes

$$x_{iJk} = \sum_{j \text{ in } J} m_{ij} n_{jk}$$

for all i in I and k in K.

Notice that the replication rate for the first MapReduce job is g, and the total communication is therefore $2gn^2$. Also notice that each reducer gets $2n^2/g^2$ inputs, so $q = 2n^2/g^2$. Equivalently, $g = n\sqrt{2/q}$. Thus, the total communication $2gn^2$ can be written in terms of q as $2\sqrt{2}n^3/\sqrt{q}$.

The second MapReduce job is simple; it sums up the x_{iJk}s over all sets J.

The Map Function We assume that the Map tasks execute at whatever compute nodes executed the Reduce tasks of the previous job. Thus, no communication is needed between the jobs. The Map function takes as input one element x_{iJk}, which we assume the previous reducers have left labeled with i and k so we know to what element of matrix P this term contributes. One key-value pair is generated. The key is (i, k) and the value is x_{iJk}.

The Reduce Function The Reduce function simply sums the values associated with key (i, k) to compute the output element P_{ik}.

The communication between the Map and Reduce tasks of the second job is gn^2, since there are n possible values of i, n possible values of k, and g possible values of the set J, and each x_{iJk} is communicated only once. If we recall from our analysis of the first MapReduce job that $g = n\sqrt{2/q}$, we can write the communication for the second job as $n^2 g = \sqrt{2}n^3/\sqrt{q}$. This amount is exactly half the communication for the first job, so the total communication for the two-pass algorithm is $3\sqrt{2}n^3/\sqrt{q}$. Although we shall not examine this point here, it turns out that we can do slightly better if we divide the matrices M and N not into squares but into rectangles that are twice as long on one side as on the other. In that case, we get the slightly smaller constant 4 in place of $3\sqrt{2} = 4.24$, and we get a two-pass algorithm with communication equal to $4n^3/\sqrt{q}$.

Now, recall that the communication cost we computed for the one-pass algorithm is $4n^4/q$. We may as well assume q is less than n^2, or else we can just use a serial algorithm at one compute node and not use MapReduce at all. Thus, $n^3/\sqrt{q}$ is smaller than n^4/q, and if q is close to its minimum possible value of $2n$,[13] then the two-pass algorithm beats the one-pass algorithm by a factor of $O(\sqrt{n})$ in communication. Moreover, we can expect the difference in communication to be the significant cost difference. Both algorithms do the same $O(n^3)$ arithmetic operations. The two-pass method naturally has more overhead managing tasks than does the one-job method. On the other hand, the second pass of the two-pass algorithm applies a Reduce function that is associative and commutative. Thus, it might be possible to save some communication cost by using a combiner on that pass.

2.6.8   Exercises for Section 2.6

EXERCISE 2.6.1   Describe the graphs that model the following problems.

(a) The multiplication of an $n \times n$ matrix by a vector of length n.
(b) The natural join of $R(A, B)$ and $S(B, C)$, where A, B, and C have domains of sizes a, b, and c, respectively.

---

[13] If q is less than $2n$, then a reducer cannot get even one row and one column, and therefore cannot compute any outputs at all.

(c) The grouping and aggregation on the relation $R(A, B)$, where A is the grouping attribute and B is aggregated by the MAX operation. Assume A and B have domains of size a and b, respectively.

! EXERCISE 2.6.2 Provide the details of the proof that a one-pass matrix-multiplication algorithm requires replication rate at least $r \geq 2n^2/q$, including:

(a) The proof that, for a fixed reducer size, the maximum number of outputs are covered by a reducer when that reducer receives an equal number of rows of M and columns of N.

(b) The algebraic manipulation needed, starting with $\sum_{i=1}^{k} q_i^2 \geq 4n^4$.

!! EXERCISE 2.6.3 Suppose our inputs are bit strings of length b, and the outputs correspond to pairs of strings at Hamming distance 1.[14]

(a) Prove that a reducer of size q can cover at most $(q/2) \log_2 q$ outputs.

(b) Use part (a) to show the lower bound on replication rate: $r \geq b/\log_2 q$.

(c) Show that there are algorithms with replication rate as given by part (b) for the cases $q = 2$, $q = 2^b$, and $q = 2^{b/2}$.

!! EXERCISE 2.6.4 For p that is the square of a prime, show that there is a mapping schema for the all-pairs problem that has $r \leq 1 + p/q$.

2.7   Summary of Chapter 2

◆ *Cluster Computing*: A common architecture for very large-scale applications is a cluster of compute nodes (processor chip, main memory, and disk). Compute nodes are mounted in racks, and the nodes on a rack are connected, typically by gigabit Ethernet. Racks are also connected by a high-speed network or switch.

◆ *Distributed File Systems*: An architecture for very large-scale file systems has developed recently. Files are composed of chunks of about 64 megabytes, and each chunk is replicated several times, on different compute nodes or racks.

◆ *MapReduce*: This programming system allows one to exploit parallelism inherent in cluster computing, and manages the hardware failures that can occur during a long computation on many nodes. Many Map tasks and many Reduce tasks are managed by a Master process. Tasks on a failed compute node are rerun by the Master.

◆ *The Map Function*: This function is written by the user. It takes a collection of input objects and turns each into zero or more key-value pairs. Keys are not necessarily unique.

---

[14] Bit strings have *Hamming distance 1* if they differ in exactly one bit position. You may look ahead to Section 3.5.6 for the general definition.

✦ *The Reduce Function*: A MapReduce programming system sorts all the key-value pairs produced by all the Map tasks, forms all the values associated with a given key into a list and distributes key-list pairs to Reduce tasks. Each Reduce task combines the elements on each list, by applying the function written by the user. The results produced by all the Reduce tasks form the output of the MapReduce process.

✦ *Reducers*: It is often convenient to refer to the application of the Reduce function to a single key and its associated value list as a "reducer."

✦ *Hadoop*: This programming system is an open-source implementation of a distributed file system (HDFS, the Hadoop Distributed File System) and MapReduce (Hadoop itself). It is available through the Apache Foundation.

✦ *Managing Compute-Node Failures*: MapReduce systems support restart of tasks that fail because their compute node, or the rack containing that node, fail. Because Map and Reduce tasks deliver their output only after they finish (the blocking property), it is possible to restart a failed task without concern for possible repetition of the effects of that task. It is necessary to restart the entire job only if the node at which the Master executes fails.

✦ *Applications of MapReduce*: While not all parallel algorithms are suitable for implementation in the MapReduce framework, there are simple implementations of matrix–vector and matrix–matrix multiplication. Also, the principal operators of relational algebra are easily implemented in MapReduce.

✦ *Workflow Systems*: MapReduce has been generalized to systems that support any acyclic collection of functions, each of which can be instantiated by any number of tasks, each responsible for executing that function on a portion of the data.

✦ *Spark*: This popular workflow system introduces Resilient Distributed Data-sets (RDDs) and a language in which many common operations on RDDs can be written. Spark has a number of efficiencies, including lazy evaluation of RDDs to avoid secondary storage of intermediate results and the recording of lineage for RDDs so they can be reconstructed as needed.

✦ *TensorFlow*: This workflow system is specifically designed to support machine-learning. Data is represented as multidimensional arrays, or tensors, and built-in operations perform many powerful operations, such as linear algebra and model training.

✦ *Recursive Workflows*: When implementing a recursive collection of functions, it is not always possible to preserve the ability to restart any failed task, because recursive tasks may have produced output that was consumed by another task before the failure. A number of schemes for checkpointing parts of the computation to allow restart of single tasks, or restart all tasks from a recent point, have been proposed.

✦ *Communication-Cost*: Many applications of MapReduce or similar systems do very simple things for each task. Then, the dominant cost is usually the cost of transporting data from where it is created to where it is used. In these cases, efficiency of a MapReduce algorithm can be estimated by calculating the sum of the sizes of the inputs to all the tasks.

✦ *Multiway Joins*: It is sometimes more efficient to replicate tuples of the relations involved in a join and have the join of three or more relations computed as a single MapReduce job. The technique of Lagrangean multipliers can be used to optimize the degree of replication for each of the participating relations.

✦ *Star Joins*: Analytic queries often involve a very large fact table joined with smaller dimension tables. These joins can always be done efficiently by the multiway-join technique. An alternative is to distribute the fact table and replicate the dimension tables permanently, using the same strategy as would be used if we were taking the multiway join of the fact table and every dimension table.

✦ *Replication Rate and Reducer Size*: It is often convenient to measure communication by the replication rate, which is the communication per input. Also, the reducer size is the maximum number of inputs associated with any reducer. For many problems, it is possible to derive a lower bound on replication rate as a function of the reducer size.

✦ *Representing Problems as Graphs*: It is possible to represent many problems that are amenable to MapReduce computation by a graph in which nodes represent inputs and outputs. An output is connected to all the inputs that are needed to compute that output.

✦ *Mapping Schemas*: Given the graph of a problem, and given a reducer size, a mapping schema is an assignment of the inputs to one or more reducers so that no reducer is assigned more inputs than the reducer size permits, and yet for every output there is some reducer that gets all the inputs needed to compute that output. The requirement that there be a mapping schema for any MapReduce algorithm is a good expression of what makes MapReduce algorithms different from general parallel computations.

✦ *Matrix Multiplication by MapReduce*: There is a family of one-pass Map-Reduce algorithms that performs multiplication of $n \times n$ matrices with the minimum possible replication rate $r = 2n^2/q$, where q is the reducer size. On the other hand, a two-pass MapReduce algorithm for the same problem with the same reducer size can use up to a factor of n less communication.

2.8   References for Chapter 2

GFS, the Google File System, was described in [13]. The paper on Google's MapReduce is [10]. Information about Hadoop and HDFS can be found at [15]. More detail on relations and relational algebra can be found in [25].

Several of the earliest workflow systems were Clustera [11] at the University of Wisconsin, and Hyracks (previously called Hyrax) [6], from UC Irvine, and Microsoft's Dryad [17] and later DryadLINQ [26].

Flink is an open-source workflow system designed to handle streaming data [12]. It was originally developed in the Stratosphere project [5] at TU Berlin. Many of the innovations in Spark are described in [27]. The open-source implementation of Spark is at [21]. The information page about TensorFlow is [24].

The iterated-MapReduce approach to implementing recursion is from Haloop [7]. For a discussion of cluster implementation of recursion, see [1].

Pregel is from [19]. There is an open-source version of Pregel called Giraph [14]. GraphLab [18] is another notable parallel implementation system for graph algorithms. GraphX [22] is a graph-based front-end for Spark.

There are a number of other systems built on a distributed file system and/or MapReduce, which have not been covered here, but may be worth knowing about. [8] describes *BigTable*, a Google implementation of an object store of very large size. A somewhat different direction was taken at Yahoo! with *Pnuts* [9]. The latter supports a limited form of transaction processing, for example.

PIG [20] is an implementation of relational algebra on top of Hadoop. Similarly, *Hive* [16] implements a restricted form of SQL on top of Hadoop. Spark also provides a SQL-like front end [23].

The communication-cost model for MapReduce algorithms and the optimal implementations of multiway joins is from [3]. The material on replication rate, reducer size, and their relationship is from [2]. Solutions to Exercises 2.6.2 and 2.6.3 can be found there. The solution to Exercise 2.6.4 is in [4].

[1] F.N. Afrati, V. Borkar, M. Carey, A. Polyzotis, and J.D. Ullman, "Cluster computing, recursion, and Datalog," to appear in *Proc. Datalog 2.0 Workshop*, Elsevier, 2011.

[2] F.N. Afrati, A. Das Sarma, S. Salihoglu, and J.D. Ullman, "Upper and lower bounds on the cost of a MapReduce computation." to appear in *Proc. Intl. Conf. on Very Large Databases*, 2013. Also available as CoRR, abs/1206.4377.

[3] F.N. Afrati and J.D. Ullman, "Optimizing joins in a MapReduce environment," *Proc. Thirteenth Intl. Conf. on Extending Database Technology*, 2010.

[4] F.N. Afrati and J.D. Ullman, "Matching bounds for the all-pairs MapReduce problem," *IDEAS* 2013, pp. 3–4.

[5] A. Alexandrov, R. Bergmann, S. Ewen, J.-C. Freytag, F. Hueske, A. Heise O. Kao, M. Leich, U. Leser, V. Markl, F. Naumann, M. Peters, A. Rheinlander, M.J. Sax, S. Schelter, M. Hoger, K. Tzoumas, and D. Warneke, "The Stratosphere platform for big data analytics," *VLDB J.* **23**:6, pp. 939–964, 2014.

[6] V.R. Borkar, M.J. Carey, R, Grover, N. Onose, and R. Vernica, "Hyracks: A flexible and extensible foundation for data-intensive computing," *Intl. Conf. on Data Engineering*, pp. 1151–1162, 2011.

[7] Y. Bu, B. Howe, M. Balazinska, and M. Ernst, "HaLoop: efficient itera-

tive data processing on large clusters," *Proc. Intl. Conf. on Very Large Databases*, 2010.

[8] F. Chang, J. Dean, S. Ghemawat, W.C. Hsieh, D.A. Wallach, M. Burrows, T. Chandra, A. Fikes, and R.E. Gruber, "Bigtable: a distributed storage system for structured data," *ACM Transactions on Computer Systems* **26**:2, pp. 1–26, 2008.

[9] B.F. Cooper, R. Ramakrishnan, U. Srivastava, A. Silberstein, P. Bohannon, H.-A. Jacobsen, N. Puz, D. Weaver, and R. Yerneni, "Pnuts: Yahoo!'s hosted data serving platform," *PVLDB* **1**:2, pp. 1277–1288, 2008.

[10] J. Dean and S. Ghemawat, "Mapreduce: simplified data processing on large clusters," *Comm. ACM* **51**:1, pp. 107–113, 2008.

[11] D.J. DeWitt, E. Paulson, E. Robinson, J.F. Naughton, J. Royalty, S. Shankar, and A. Krioukov, "Clustera: an integrated computation and data management system," *PVLDB* **1**:1, pp. 28–41, 2008.

[12] flink.apache.org, Apache Foundation.

[13] S. Ghemawat, H. Gobioff, and S.-T. Leung, "The Google file system," *19th ACM Symposium on Operating Systems Principles*, 2003.

[14] giraph.apache.org, Apache Foundation.

[15] hadoop.apache.org, Apache Foundation.

[16] hadoop.apache.org/hive, Apache Foundation.

[17] M. Isard, M. Budiu, Y. Yu, A. Birrell, and D. Fetterly. "Dryad: distributed data-parallel programs from sequential building blocks," *Proceedings of the 2nd ACM SIGOPS/EuroSys European Conference on Computer Systems*, pp. 59–72, ACM, 2007.

[18] Y. Low, D. Bickson, J. Gonzalez, C. Guestrin, A. Kyrola, and J.M. Hellerstein, "Distributed GraphLab: a framework for machine learning and data mining in the cloud," —em Proc. VLDB Endowment **5**:8, pp. 716–727, 2012.

[19] G. Malewicz, M.N. Austern, A.J.C. Sik, J.C. Denhert, H. Horn, N. Leiser, and G. Czajkowski, "Pregel: a system for large-scale graph processing," *Proc. ACM SIGMOD Conference*, 2010.

[20] C. Olston, B. Reed, U. Srivastava, R. Kumar, and A. Tomkins, "Pig latin: a not-so-foreign language for data processing," *Proc. ACM SIGMOD Conference*, pp. 1099–1110, 2008.

[21] spark.apache.org, Apache Foundation.

[22] spark.apache.org/graphx, Apache Foundation.

[23] spark.apache.org/sql, Apache Foundation.

[24] www.tensorflow.org.

[25] J.D. Ullman and J. Widom, *A First Course in Database Systems*, Third Edition, Prentice-Hall, Upper Saddle River, NJ, 2008.

[26] Y. Yu, M. Isard, D. Fetterly, M. Budiu, I. Erlingsson, P.K. Gunda, and J. Currey, "DryadLINQ: a system for general-purpose distributed data-parallel computing using a high-level language," *OSDI*, pp. 1–14, USENIX Association, 2008.

[27] M. Zaharia, M. Chowdhury, T. Das, A. Dave, J. Ma, M. McCauley, M.J. Franklin, S. Shenker, and I. Stoica, "Resilient distributed datasets: A fault-tolerant abstraction for in-memory cluster computing," *Proc. 9th USENIX conference on Networked Systems Design and Implementation*, USENIX Association, 2012.

3 Finding Similar Items

A fundamental data-mining problem is to examine data for "similar" items. We shall take up applications in Section 3.1, but an example would be looking at a collection of Web pages and finding near-duplicate pages. These pages could be plagiarisms, for example, or they could be mirrors that have almost the same content but differ in information about the host and about other mirrors.

The naive approach to finding pairs of similar items requires us to look at every pair of items. When we are dealing with a large dataset, looking at all pairs of items may be prohibitive, even given an abundance of hardware resources. For example, even a million items gives us half a trillion pairs to examine, and a million items is considered a "small" dataset by today's standards.

It is therefore a pleasant surprise to learn of a family of techniques called *locality-sensitive hashing*, or *LSH*, that allows us to focus on pairs that are likely to be similar, without having to look at all pairs. Thus, it is possible that we can avoid the quadratic growth in computation time that is required by the naive algorithm. There is usually a downside to locality-sensitive hashing, due to the presence of false negatives, that is, pairs of items that are similar, yet are not included in the set of pairs that we examine, but by careful tuning we can reduce the fraction of false negatives by increasing the number of pairs we consider.

The general idea behind LSH is that we hash items using many different hash functions. These hash functions are not the conventional sort of hash functions. Rather, they are carefully designed to have the property that pairs are much more likely to wind up in the same bucket of a hash function if the items are similar than if they are not similar. We then can examine only the *candidate pairs*, which are pairs of items that wind up in the same bucket for at least one of the hash functions.

We begin our discussion of LSH with an examination of the problem of finding similar documents – those that share a lot of common text. We first show how to convert documents into sets (Section 3.2) in a way that lets us view textual similarity of documents as sets having a large overlap. More precisely, we measure the similarity of sets by their *Jaccard similarity*, the ratio of the sizes of their intersection and union. A second key trick we need is *minhashing* (Section 3.3), which is a way to convert large sets into much smaller representations, called *signatures,* that still enable us to estimate closely the Jaccard similarity of the represented sets. Finally, in Section 3.4 we see how to apply the bucketing idea inherent in LSH to the signatures.

In Section 3.5 we begin our study of how to apply LSH to items other than sets. We consider the general notion of a distance measure that tells to what degree items are similar. Then, in Section 3.6 we consider the general idea of locality-sensitive hashing, and in Section 3.7 we see how to do LSH for some data types other than sets. Then, Section 3.8 examines in detail several applications of the LSH idea. Finally, we consider in Section 3.9 some techniques for finding similar sets that can be more efficient than LSH when the degree of similarity we want is very high.

3.1   Applications of Set Similarity

We shall focus initially on a particular notion of "similarity": the similarity of sets by looking at the relative size of their intersection. This notion of similarity is called Jaccard similarity, which is introduced in Section 3.1.1. We then examine some of the uses of finding similar sets. These include finding textually similar documents and collaborative filtering by finding similar customers and similar products. In order to turn the problem of textual similarity of documents into one of set intersection, we use the technique called shingling, which is the subject of Section 3.2.

3.1.1   Jaccard Similarity of Sets

The *Jaccard similarity* of sets S and T is $|S \cap T|/|S \cup T|$, that is, the ratio of the size of the intersection of S and T to the size of their union. We shall denote the Jaccard similarity of S and T by $\text{SIM}(S, T)$.

EXAMPLE 3.1   In Fig. 3.1 we see two sets S and T. There are three elements in their intersection and a total of eight elements that appear in S or T or both. Thus, $\text{SIM}(S, T) = 3/8$.   □

3.1.2   Similarity of Documents

An important class of problems that Jaccard similarity addresses well is that of finding textually similar documents in a large corpus such as the Web or a collection of news articles. We should understand that the aspect of similarity we are looking at here is character-level similarity, not "similar meaning," which requires us to examine the words in the documents and their uses. That problem is also interesting but is addressed by other techniques, which we hinted at in Section 1.3.1. However, textual similarity also has important uses. Many of these involve finding duplicates or near duplicates. First, let us observe that testing whether two documents are exact duplicates is easy; just compare the

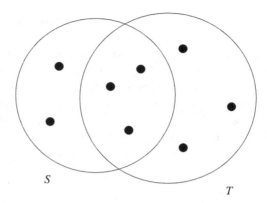

Figure 3.1 Two sets with Jaccard similarity 3/8

two documents character-by-character, and if they ever differ then they are not the same. However, in many applications, the documents are not identical, yet they share large portions of their text. Here are some examples:

Plagiarism

Finding plagiarized documents tests our ability to find textual similarity. The plagiarizer may extract only some parts of a document for his own. He may alter a few words and may alter the order in which sentences of the original appear. Yet the resulting document may still contain much of the original. No simple process of comparing documents character by character will detect a sophisticated plagiarism.

Mirror Pages

It is common for important or popular Web sites to be duplicated at a number of hosts, in order to share the load. The pages of these *mirror* sites will be quite similar, but are rarely identical. For instance, they might each contain information associated with their particular host, and they might each have links to the other mirror sites but not to themselves. A related phenomenon is the reuse of Web pages from one academic class to another. These pages might include class notes, assignments, and lecture slides. Similar pages might change the name of the course, year, and make small changes from year to year. It is important to be able to detect similar pages of these kinds, because search engines produce better results if they avoid showing two pages that are nearly identical within the first page of results.

Articles from the Same Source

It is common for one reporter to write a news article that gets distributed, say through the Associated Press, to many newspapers, which then publish the article on their Web sites. Each newspaper changes the article somewhat. They may cut out paragraphs, or even add material of their own. They most likely will surround the article by their own logo, ads, and links to other articles at their site. However, the core of each newspaper's page will be the original article. News aggregators, such as Google News, try to find all versions of such an article, in order to show only one, and that task requires finding when two Web pages are textually similar, although not identical.[1]

3.1.3 Collaborative Filtering as a Similar-Sets Problem

Another class of applications where similarity of sets is very important is called *collaborative filtering*, a process whereby we recommend to users items that were liked by other users who have exhibited similar tastes. We shall investigate collaborative filtering in detail in Section 9.3, but for the moment let us see some common examples.

On-Line Purchases

Amazon.com has millions of customers and sells millions of items. Its database records which items have been bought by which customers. We can say two customers are similar if their sets of purchased items have a high Jaccard similarity. Likewise, two items that have sets of purchasers with high Jaccard similarity will be deemed similar. Note that, while we might expect mirror sites to have Jaccard similarity above 90%, it is unlikely that any two customers have Jaccard similarity that high (unless they have purchased only one item). Even a Jaccard similarity like 20% might be unusual enough to identify customers with similar tastes. The same observation holds for items; Jaccard similarities need not be very high to be significant.

Collaborative filtering requires several tools, in addition to finding similar customers or items, as we discuss in Chapter 9. For example, two Amazon customers who like science-fiction might each buy many science-fiction books, but only a few of these will be in common. However, by combining similarity-finding with clustering (Chapter 7), we might be able to discover that science-fiction books are mutually similar and put them in one group. Then, we can get a more powerful notion of customer-similarity by asking whether they made purchases within many of the same groups.

Movie Ratings

Netflix records which movies each of its customers rented, and also the ratings assigned to those movies by the customers. We can regard movies as similar if they were rented or rated highly by many of the same customers, and see customers as similar if they rented or rated highly many of the same movies. The same observations that we made for Amazon above apply in this situation: similarities need not be high to be significant, and clustering movies by genre will make things easier.

When our data consists of ratings rather than binary decisions (bought/did

---

[1] News aggregation also involves finding articles that are about the same topic, even though not textually similar. This problem too can yield to a similarity search, but it requires techniques other than Jaccard similarity of sets.

not buy or liked/disliked), we cannot rely simply on sets as representations of customers or items. Some options are:

(1) Ignore low-rated customer/movie pairs; that is, treat these events as if the customer never watched the movie.

(2) When comparing customers, imagine two set elements for each movie, "liked" and "hated." If a customer rated a movie highly, put "liked" for that movie in the customer's set. If they gave a low rating to a movie, put "hated" for that movie in their set. Then, we can look for high Jaccard similarity among these sets. We can use a similar trick when comparing movies.

(3) If ratings are 1-to-5-stars, put a movie in a customer's set n times if they rated the movie n-stars. Then, use *Jaccard similarity for bags* when measuring the similarity of customers. The Jaccard similarity for bags B and C is defined by counting an element n times in the intersection if n is the minimum of the number of times the element appears in B and C. In the union, we count the element the sum of the number of times it appears in B and in C.[2]

EXAMPLE 3.2   The bag-similarity of bags $\{a, a, a, b\}$ and $\{a, a, b, b, c\}$ is 1/3. The intersection counts a twice and b once, so its size is 3. The size of the union of two bags is always the sum of the sizes of the two bags, or 9 in this case. Since the highest possible Jaccard similarity for bags is 1/2, the score of 1/3 indicates the two bags are quite similar, as should be apparent from an examination of their contents.   □

3.1.4   Exercises for Section 3.1

EXERCISE 3.1.1   Compute the Jaccard similarities of each pair of the following three sets: $\{1, 2, 3, 4\}$, $\{2, 3, 5, 7\}$, and $\{2, 4, 6\}$.

EXERCISE 3.1.2   Compute the Jaccard bag similarity of each pair of the following three bags: $\{1, 1, 1, 2\}$, $\{1, 1, 2, 2, 3\}$, and $\{1, 2, 3, 4\}$.

!! EXERCISE 3.1.3   Suppose we have a universal set U of n elements, and we choose two subsets S and T at random, each with m of the n elements. What is the expected value of the Jaccard similarity of S and T?

---

[2] Although the union for bags is normally (e.g., in the SQL standard) defined to have the sum of the number of copies in each of the two bags, this definition causes some inconsistency with the Jaccard similarity for sets. Under this definition of bag union, the maximum Jaccard similarity is 1/2, not 1, since the union of a set with itself has twice as many elements as the intersection of the same set with itself. If we prefer to have the Jaccard similarity of a set with itself be 1, we can redefine the union of bags to have each element appear the maximum number of times it appears in either of the two bags. This change also gives a reasonable measure of bag similarity.

3.2 Shingling of Documents

The most effective way to represent documents as sets, for the purpose of identifying lexically similar documents is to construct from the document the set of
short strings that appear within it. If we do so, then documents that share pieces
as short as sentences or even phrases will have many common elements in their
sets, even if those sentences appear in different orders in the two documents. In
this section, we introduce the simplest and most common approach, shingling,
as well as an interesting variation.

3.2.1 k-Shingles

A document is a string of characters. Define a k-shingle for a document to be
any substring of length k found within the document. Then, we may associate
with each document the set of k-shingles that appear one or more times within
that document.

EXAMPLE 3.3 Suppose our document D is the string abcdabd, and we pick
$k = 2$. Then the set of 2-shingles for D is $\{$ab, bc, cd, da, bd$\}$.
   Note that the substring ab appears twice within D, but appears only once as
a shingle. A variation of shingling produces a bag, rather than a set, so each
shingle would appear in the result as many times as it appears in the document.
However, we shall not use bags of shingles here. □

   There are several options regarding how white space (blank, tab, newline, etc.)
is treated. It probably makes sense to replace any sequence of one or more white-
space characters by a single blank. That way, we distinguish shingles that cover
two or more words from those that do not.

EXAMPLE 3.4 If we use $k = 9$, but eliminate whitespace altogether, then we
would see some lexical similarity in the sentences "The plane was ready for
touch down". and "The quarterback scored a touchdown". However, if we
retain the blanks, then the first has shingles touch dow and ouch down, while
the second has touchdown. If we eliminated the blanks, then both would have
touchdown. □

3.2.2 Choosing the Shingle Size

We can pick k to be any constant we like. However, if we pick k too small, then
we would expect most sequences of k characters to appear in most documents.
If so, then we could have documents whose shingle-sets had high Jaccard similarity, yet the documents had none of the same sentences or even phrases. As
an extreme example, if we use $k = 1$, most Web pages will have most of the
common characters and few other characters, so almost all Web pages will have
high similarity.

How large k should be depends on how long typical documents are and how large the set of typical characters is. The important thing to remember is:

- k should be picked large enough that the probability of any given shingle appearing in any given document is low.

Thus, if our corpus of documents is emails, picking $k = 5$ should be fine. To see why, suppose that only letters and a general white-space character appear in emails (although in practice, most of the printable ASCII characters can be expected to appear occasionally). If so, then there would be $27^5 = 14{,}348{,}907$ possible shingles. Since the typical email is much smaller than 14 million characters long, we would expect $k = 5$ to work well, and indeed it does.

However, the calculation is a bit more subtle. Surely, more than 27 characters appear in emails, However, all characters do not appear with equal probability. Common letters and blanks dominate, while "z" and other letters that have high point-value in Scrabble are rare. Thus, even short emails will have many 5-shingles consisting of common letters, and the chances of unrelated emails sharing these common shingles is greater than would be implied by the calculation in the paragraph above. A good rule of thumb is to imagine that there are only 20 characters and estimate the number of k-shingles as 20^k. For large documents, such as research articles, choice $k = 9$ is considered safe.

3.2.3   Hashing Shingles

Instead of using substrings directly as shingles, we can pick a hash function that maps strings of length k to some number of buckets and treat the resulting bucket number as the shingle. The set representing a document is then the set of integers that are bucket numbers of one or more k-shingles that appear in the document. For instance, we could construct the set of 9-shingles for a document and then map each of those 9-shingles to a bucket number in the range 0 to $2^{32} - 1$. Thus, each shingle is represented by four bytes instead of nine. Not only has the data been compacted, but we can now manipulate (hashed) shingles by single-word machine operations.

Notice that we can differentiate documents better if we use 9-shingles and hash them down to four bytes than to use 4-shingles, even though the space used to represent a shingle is the same. The reason was touched upon in Section 3.2.2. If we use 4-shingles, most sequences of four bytes are unlikely or impossible to find in typical documents. Thus, the effective number of different shingles is much less than $2^{32} - 1$. If, as in Section 3.2.2, we assume only 20 characters are frequent in English text, then the number of different 4-shingles that are likely to occur is only $(20)^4 = 160{,}000$. However, if we use 9-shingles, there are many more than 2^{32} likely shingles. When we hash them down to four bytes, we can expect almost any sequence of four bytes to be possible, as was discussed in Section 1.3.2.

3.2.4 Shingles Built from Words

An alternative form of shingle has proved effective for the problem of identifying similar news articles, mentioned in Section 3.1.2. The exploitable distinction for this problem is that the news articles are written in a rather different style than are other elements that typically appear on the page with the article. News articles, and most prose, have a lot of stop words (see Section 1.3.1), the most common words such as "and," "you," "to," and so on. In many applications, we want to ignore stop words, since they don't tell us anything useful about the article, such as its topic.

However, for the problem of finding similar news articles, it was found that defining a shingle to be a stop word followed by the next two words, regardless of whether or not they were stop words, formed a useful set of shingles. The advantage of this approach is that the news article would then contribute more shingles to the set representing the Web page than would the surrounding elements. Recall that the goal of the exercise is to find pages that had the same articles, regardless of the surrounding elements. By biasing the set of shingles in favor of the article, pages with the same article and different surrounding material have higher Jaccard similarity than pages with the same surrounding material but with a different article.

EXAMPLE 3.5 An ad might have the simple text "Buy Sudzo." However, a news article with the same idea might read something like "*A* spokesperson *for the* Sudzo Corporation revealed today *that* studies *have* shown *it is* good *for* people *to* buy Sudzo products." Here, we have italicized all the likely stop words, although there is no set number of the most frequent words that should be considered stop words. The first three shingles made from a stop word and the next two following are:

```
A spokesperson for
for the Sudzo
the Sudzo Corporation
```

There are nine shingles from the sentence, but none from the "ad." □

3.2.5 Exercises for Section 3.2

EXERCISE 3.2.1 What are the first ten 3-shingles in the first sentence of Section 3.2?

EXERCISE 3.2.2 If we use the stop-word-based shingles of Section 3.2.4, and we take the stop words to be all the words of three or fewer letters, then what are the shingles in the first sentence of Section 3.2?

EXERCISE 3.2.3 What is the largest number of k-shingles a document of n bytes can have? You may assume that the size of the alphabet is large enough that the number of possible strings of length k is at least n.

3.3   Similarity-Preserving Summaries of Sets

Sets of shingles are large. Even if we hash them to four bytes each, the space needed to store a set is still roughly four times the space taken by the document. If we have millions of documents, it may well not be possible to store all the shingle-sets in main memory.[3]

Our goal in this section is to replace large sets by much smaller representations called "signatures." The important property we need for signatures is that we can compare the signatures of two sets and estimate the Jaccard similarity of the underlying sets from the signatures alone. It is not possible that the signatures give the exact similarity of the sets they represent, but the estimates they provide are close, and the larger the signatures the more accurate the estimates. For example, if we replace the 200,000-byte hashed-shingle sets that derive from 50,000-byte documents by signatures of 1000 bytes, we can usually get within a few percent.

3.3.1   Matrix Representation of Sets

Before explaining how it is possible to construct small signatures from large sets, it is helpful to visualize a collection of sets as their *characteristic matrix*. The columns of the matrix correspond to the sets, and the rows correspond to elements of the universal set from which elements of the sets are drawn. There is a 1 in row r and column c if the element for row r is a member of the set for column c. Otherwise the value in position (r, c) is 0.

Element	S_1	S_2	S_3	S_4
a	1	0	0	1
b	0	0	1	0
c	0	1	0	1
d	1	0	1	1
e	0	0	1	0

Figure 3.2 A matrix representing four sets

EXAMPLE 3.6   In Fig. 3.2 is an example of a matrix representing sets chosen from the universal set $\{a, b, c, d, e\}$. Here, $S_1 = \{a, d\}$, $S_2 = \{c\}$, $S_3 = \{b, d, e\}$, and $S_4 = \{a, c, d\}$. The top row and leftmost columns are not part of the matrix, but are present only to remind us what the rows and columns represent.   □

It is important to remember that the characteristic matrix is unlikely to be the way the data is stored, but it is useful as a way to visualize the data. For one

---

[3] There is another serious concern: even if the sets fit in main memory, the number of pairs may be too great for us to evaluate the similarity of each pair. We take up the solution to this problem in Section 3.4.

reason not to store data as a matrix, these matrices are almost always *sparse* (they have many more 0s than 1s) in practice. It saves space to represent a sparse matrix of 0s and 1s by the positions in which the 1s appear. For another reason, the data is usually stored in some other format for other purposes.

As an example, if rows are products, and columns are customers, represented by the set of products they bought, then this data would really appear in a database table of purchases. A tuple in this table would list the item, the purchaser, and probably other details about the purchase, such as the date and the credit card used.

3.3.2 Minhashing

The signatures we desire to construct for sets are composed of the results of a large number of calculations, say several hundred, each of which is a "minhash" of the characteristic matrix. In this section, we shall learn how a minhash is computed in principle, and in later sections we shall see how a good approximation to the minhash is computed in practice.

To *minhash* a set represented by a column of the characteristic matrix, pick a permutation of the rows. The minhash value of any column is the number of the first row, in the permuted order, in which the column has a 1.

EXAMPLE 3.7 Let us suppose we pick the order of rows *beadc* for the matrix of Fig. 3.2. This permutation defines a minhash function h that maps sets to rows. Let us compute the minhash value of set S_1 according to h. The first column, which is the column for set S_1, has 0 in row b, so we proceed to row e, the second in the permuted order. There is again a 0 in the column for S_1, so we proceed to row a, where we find a 1. Thus. $h(S_1) = a$.

Element	S_1	S_2	S_3	S_4
b	0	0	1	0
e	0	0	1	0
a	1	0	0	1
d	1	0	1	1
c	0	1	0	1

Figure 3.3 A permutation of the rows of Fig. 3.2

Although it is not physically possible to permute very large characteristic matrices, the minhash function h implicitly reorders the rows of the matrix of Fig. 3.2 so it becomes the matrix of Fig. 3.3. In this matrix, we can read off the values of h by scanning from the top until we come to a 1. Thus, we see that $h(S_2) = c$, $h(S_3) = b$, and $h(S_4) = a$. □

3.3.3   Minhashing and Jaccard Similarity

There is a remarkable connection between minhashing and Jaccard similarity of the sets that are minhashed.

- The probability that the minhash function for a random permutation of rows produces the same value for two sets equals the Jaccard similarity of those sets.

To see why, we need to picture the columns for those two sets. If we restrict ourselves to the columns for sets S_1 and S_2, then rows can be divided into three classes:

(1) Type X rows have 1 in both columns.
(2) Type Y rows have 1 in one of the columns and 0 in the other.
(3) Type Z rows have 0 in both columns.

Since the matrix is sparse, most rows are of type Z. However, it is the ratio of the numbers of type X and type Y rows that determine both $\text{SIM}(S_1, S_2)$ and the probability that $h(S_1) = h(S_2)$. Let there be x rows of type X and y rows of type Y. Then $\text{SIM}(S_1, S_2) = x/(x+y)$. The reason is that x is the size of $S_1 \cap S_2$ and $x + y$ is the size of $S_1 \cup S_2$.

Now, consider the probability that $h(S_1) = h(S_2)$. If we imagine the rows permuted randomly, and we proceed from the top, the probability that we shall meet a type X row before we meet a type Y row is $x/(x+y)$. But if the first row from the top other than type Z rows is a type X row, then surely $h(S_1) = h(S_2)$. On the other hand, if the first row other than a type Z row that we meet is a type Y row, then the set with a 1 gets that row as its minhash value. However the set with a 0 in that row surely gets some row further down the permuted list. Thus, we know $h(S_1) \neq h(S_2)$ if we first meet a type Y row. We conclude the probability that $h(S_1) = h(S_2)$ is $x/(x+y)$, which is also the Jaccard similarity of S_1 and S_2.

3.3.4   Minhash Signatures

Again think of a collection of sets represented by their characteristic matrix M. To represent sets, we pick at random some number n of permutations of the rows of M. Perhaps 100 permutations or several hundred permutations will do. Call the minhash functions determined by these permutations $h_1, h_2, \ldots, h_n$. From the column representing set S, construct the *minhash signature* for S, the vector $[h_1(S), h_2(S), \ldots, h_n(S)]$. We normally represent this list of hash-values as a column. Thus, we can form from matrix M a *signature matrix*, in which the ith column of M is replaced by the minhash signature for (the set of) the ith column.

Note that the signature matrix has the same number of columns as M but only n rows. Even if M is not represented explicitly, but in some compressed form suitable for a sparse matrix (e.g., by the locations of its 1s), it is normal for the signature matrix to be much smaller than M.

The remarkable thing about signature matrices is that we can use their columns to estimate the Jaccard similarity of the sets that correspond to the columns of signature matrix. By the theorem proved in Section 3.3.3, we know that the probability that two columns have the same value in a given row of the signature matrix equals the Jaccard similarity of the sets corresponding to those columns. Moreover, since the permutations on which the minhash values are based were chosen independently, we can think of each row of the signature matrix as an independent experiment. Thus, the expected number of rows in which two columns agree equals the Jaccard similarity of their corresponding sets. Moreover, the more minhashings we use, i.e., the more rows in the signature matrix, the smaller the expected error in the estimate of the Jaccard similarity will be.

3.3.5 Computing Minhash Signatures in Practice

It is not feasible to permute a large characteristic matrix explicitly. Even picking a random permutation of millions or billions of rows is time-consuming, and the necessary sorting of the rows would take even more time. Thus, permuted matrices like that suggested by Fig. 3.3, while conceptually appealing, are not implementable.

Fortunately, it is possible to simulate the effect of a random permutation by a random hash function that maps row numbers to as many buckets as there are rows. A hash function that maps integers $0, 1, \ldots, k-1$ to bucket numbers 0 through $k-1$ typically will map some pairs of integers to the same bucket and leave other buckets unfilled. However, the difference is unimportant as long as k is large and there are not too many collisions. We can maintain the fiction that our hash function h "permutes" row r to position $h(r)$ in the permuted order.

Thus, instead of picking n random permutations of rows, we pick n randomly chosen hash functions $h_1, h_2, \ldots, h_n$ on the rows. We construct the signature matrix by considering each row in their given order. Let $\text{SIG}(i, c)$ be the element of the signature matrix for the ith hash function and column c. Initially, set $\text{SIG}(i, c)$ to ∞ for all i and c. We handle row r by doing the following:

(1) Compute $h_1(r), h_2(r), \ldots, h_n(r)$.
(2) For each column c do the following:
    (a) If c has 0 in row r, do nothing.
    (b) However, if c has 1 in row r, then for each $i = 1, 2, \ldots, n$ set $\text{SIG}(i, c)$ to the smaller of the current value of $\text{SIG}(i, c)$ and $h_i(r)$.

EXAMPLE 3.8 Let us reconsider the characteristic matrix of Fig. 3.2, which we reproduce with some additional data as Fig. 3.4. We have replaced the letters naming the rows by integers 0 through 4. We have also chosen two hash functions:

Row	S_1	S_2	S_3	S_4	$x+1 \mod 5$	$3x+1 \mod 5$
0	1	0	0	1	1	1
1	0	0	1	0	2	4
2	0	1	0	1	3	2
3	1	0	1	1	4	0
4	0	0	1	0	0	3

Figure 3.4 Hash functions computed for the matrix of Fig. 3.2

$h_1(x) = x + 1 \mod 5$ and $h_2(x) = 3x + 1 \mod 5$. The values of these two functions applied to the row numbers are given in the last two columns of Fig. 3.4. Notice that these simple hash functions are true permutations of the rows, but a true permutation is only possible because the number of rows, 5, is a prime. In general, there will be collisions, where two rows get the same hash value.

Now, let us simulate the algorithm for computing the signature matrix. Initially, this matrix consists of all ∞s:

	S_1	S_2	S_3	S_4
h_1	∞	∞	∞	∞
h_2	∞	∞	∞	∞

First, we consider row 0 of Fig. 3.4. We see that the values of $h_1(0)$ and $h_2(0)$ are both 1. The row numbered 0 has 1s in the columns for sets S_1 and S_4, so only these columns of the signature matrix can change. As 1 is less than ∞, we do in fact change both values in the columns for S_1 and S_4. The current estimate of the signature matrix is thus:

	S_1	S_2	S_3	S_4
h_1	1	∞	∞	1
h_2	1	∞	∞	1

Now, we move to the row numbered 1 in Fig. 3.4. This row has 1 only in S_3, and its hash values are $h_1(1) = 2$ and $h_2(1) = 4$. Thus, we set SIG(1, 3) to 2 and SIG(2, 3) to 4. All other signature entries remain as they are because their columns have 0 in the row numbered 1. The new signature matrix:

	S_1	S_2	S_3	S_4
h_1	1	∞	2	1
h_2	1	∞	4	1

The row of Fig. 3.4 numbered 2 has 1s in the columns for S_2 and S_4, and its hash values are $h_1(2) = 3$ and $h_2(2) = 2$. We could change the values in the signature for S_4, but the values in this column of the signature matrix, $[1, 1]$, are each less than the corresponding hash values $[3, 2]$. However, since the column for S_2 still has ∞s, we replace it by $[3, 2]$, resulting in:

	S_1	S_2	S_3	S_4
h_1	1	3	2	1
h_2	1	2	4	1

Next comes the row numbered 3 in Fig. 3.4. Here, all columns but S_2 have 1, and the hash values are $h_1(3) = 4$ and $h_2(3) = 0$. The value 4 for h_1 exceeds what is already in the signature matrix for all the columns, so we shall not change any values in the first row of the signature matrix. However, the value 0 for h_2 is less than what is already present, so we lower SIG$(2, 1)$, SIG$(2, 3)$ and SIG$(2, 4)$ to 0. Note that we cannot lower SIG$(2, 2)$ because the column for S_2 in Fig. 3.4 has 0 in the row we are currently considering. The resulting signature matrix:

	S_1	S_2	S_3	S_4
h_1	1	3	2	1
h_2	0	2	0	0

Finally, consider the row of Fig. 3.4 numbered 4. $h_1(4) = 0$ and $h_2(4) = 3$. Since row 4 has 1 only in the column for S_3, we only compare the current signature column for that set, $[2, 0]$ with the hash values $[0, 3]$. Since $0 < 2$, we change SIG$(1, 3)$ to 0, but since $3 > 0$ we do not change SIG$(2, 3)$. The final signature matrix is:

	S_1	S_2	S_3	S_4
h_1	1	3	0	1
h_2	0	2	0	0

We can estimate the Jaccard similarities of the underlying sets from this signature matrix. Notice that columns 1 and 4 are identical, so we guess that SIM$(S_1, S_4) = 1.0$. If we look at Fig. 3.4, we see that the true Jaccard similarity of S_1 and S_4 is 2/3. Remember that the fraction of rows that agree in the signature matrix is only an estimate of the true Jaccard similarity, and this example is much too small for the law of large numbers to assure that the estimates are close. For additional examples, the signature columns for S_1 and S_3 agree in half the rows (true similarity 1/4), while the signatures of S_1 and S_2 estimate 0 as their Jaccard similarity (the correct value). □

3.3.6 Speeding Up Minhashing

The process of minhashing is time-consuming, since we need to examine the entire k-row matrix M for each minhash function we want. Let us first return to the model of Section 3.3.2, where we imagine rows are actually permuted. But to compute one minhash function on all the columns, we shall not go all the way to the end of the permutation, but only look at the first m out of k rows. If we make m small compared with k, we reduce the work by a large factor, k/m.

However, there is a downside to making m small. As long as each column has at least one 1 in the first m rows in permuted order, the rows after the mth have no effect on any minhash value and may as well not be looked at. But what if some columns have only 0s in the first m rows? We have no minhash value for those columns, and will instead have to use a special symbol, for which we shall use ∞.

When we examine the minhash signatures of two columns in order to estimate the Jaccard similarity of their underlying sets, as in Section 3.3.4, we have to take into account the possibility that one or both columns have ∞ as their minhash value for some components of the signature. There are three cases:

(1) If neither column has ∞ in a given row, then there is no change needed. Count this row as an example of equal values if the two values are the same, and as an example of unequal values if not.

(2) One column has ∞ and the other does not. In this case, had we used all the rows of the original permuted matrix M, the column that has the ∞ would eventually have been given some row number, and that number will surely not be one of the first m rows in the permuted order. But the other column *does* have a value that is one of the first m rows. Thus, we surely have an example of unequal minhash values, and we count this row of the signature matrix as such an example.

(3) Now, suppose both columns have ∞ in row. Then in the original permuted matrix M, the first m rows of both columns were all 0s. We thus have no information about the Jaccard similarity of the corresponding sets; that similarity is only a function of the last $k - m$ rows, which we have chosen not to look at. We therefore count this row of the signature matrix as neither an example of equal values nor of unequal values.

As long as the third case, where both columns have ∞, is rare, we get almost as many examples to average as there are rows in the signature matrix. That effect will reduce the accuracy of our estimates of the Jaccard distance somewhat, but not much. And since we are now able to compute minhash values for all the columns much faster than if we examined all the rows of M, we can afford the time to apply a few more minhash functions. We get even better accuracy than originally, and we do so faster than before.

3.3.7   Speedup Using Hash Functions

As before, there are reasons not to physically permute rows in the manner assumed in Section 3.3.6. However, the idea of true permutations makes more sense in the context of Section 3.3.6 than it did in Section 3.3.2. The reason is that we do not need to construct a full permutation of k elements, but only pick a small number m out of the k rows and then pick a random permutation of those rows. Depending on the value of m and how the matrix M is stored, it might make sense to follow the algorithm suggested by Section 3.3.6 literally.

However, it is more likely that a strategy akin to Section 3.3.5 is needed. Now, the rows of M are fixed, and not permuted. We choose a hash function that hashes row numbers, and compute hash values for only the first m rows. That is, we follow the algorithm of Section 3.3.5, but only until we reach the mth row, whereupon we stop and, and for each columns, we take the minimum hash value seen so far as the minhash value for that column.

Since some column may have 0 in all m rows, it is possible that some of the minhash values will be ∞. Assuming m is sufficiently large that ∞ minhash values are rare, we still get a good estimate of the Jaccard similarity of sets by comparing columns of the signature matrix. Suppose T is the set of elements of the universal set that are represented by the first m rows of matrix M. Let S_1 and S_2 be the sets represented by two columns of M. Then the first m rows of M represent the sets $S_1 \cap T$ and $S_2 \cap T$. If both these sets are empty (i.e., both columns are all-0 in their first m rows), then this minhash function will be ∞ in both columns and will be ignored when estimating the Jaccard similarity of the columns' underlying sets.

If at least one of the sets $S_1 \cap T$ and $S_2 \cap T$ is nonempty, then the probability of the two columns having equal values for this minhash function is the Jaccard similarity of these two sets, that is

$$\frac{|S_1 \cap S_2 \cap T|}{|(S_1 \cup S_2) \cap T|}$$

As long as T is chosen to be a random subset of the universal set, the expected value of this fraction will be the same as the Jaccard similarity of S_1 and S_2. However, there will be some random variation, since depending on T, we could find more or less than an average number of type X rows (1s in both columns) and/or type Y rows (1 in one column and 0 in the other) among the first m rows of matrix M.

To mitigate this variation, we do not use the same set T for each minhashing that we do. Rather, we divide the rows of M into k/m groups.[4] Then for each hash function, we compute one minhash value by examining only the first m rows of M, a different minhash value by examining only the second m rows, and so on. We thus get k/m minhash values from a single hash function and a single pass over all the rows of M. In fact, if k/m is large enough, we may get all the rows of the signature matrix that we need by a single hash function applied to each of the subsets of rows of M.

Moreover, by using each of the rows of M to compute one of these minhash values, we tend to balance out the errors in estimation of the Jaccard similarity due to any one particular subset of the rows. That is, the Jaccard similarity of S_1 and S_2 determines the ratio of type X and type Y rows. All the type X rows are distributed among the k/m sets of rows, and likewise the type Y rows. Thus, while one set of m rows may have more of one type of row than average, there

---

[4] In what follows, we assume m divides k evenly, for convenience. It is unimportant, as long as k/m is large, if some rows are not included in any group because k is not an integer multiple of m.

must then be some other set of m rows with fewer than average of that same type.

EXAMPLE 3.9   In Fig. 3.5 we see a matrix representing three sets S_1, S_2, and S_3, with a universal set of eight elements; i.e., $k = 8$. Let us pick $m = 4$, so one pass through the rows yields two minhash values, one based on the first four rows and the other on the second four rows.

S_1	S_2	S_3
0	0	0
0	0	0
0	0	1
0	1	1
1	1	1
1	1	0
1	0	0
0	0	0

Figure 3.5 A Boolean matrix representing three sets

First, note that the Jaccard similarities of the three sets are $\text{SIM}(S_1, S_2) = 1/2$, $\text{SIM}(S_1, S_3) = 1/5$, and $\text{SIM}(S_2, S_3) = 1/2$. Now, look at the first four rows only. Whatever hash function we use, the minhash value for S_1 will be ∞, the minhash value for S_2 will be the hash value of the 4th row, and the minhash value for S_3 will be the smaller of the hash values for the third and fourth rows. Thus, the minhash values for S_1 and S_2 will never agree. That makes sense, since if T is the set of elements represented by the first four rows, then $S_1 \cap T = \emptyset$, and therefore $\text{SIM}(S_1 \cap T, S_2 \cap T) = 0$. However, in the second four rows, the Jaccard similarity of S_1 and S_2 restricted to the elements represented by the last four rows is $2/3$.

We conclude that if we generate signatures consisting of two minhash values using this hash function, one based on the first four rows and the second based on the last four rows, the expected number of matches we get between the signatures for S_1 and S_2 is the average of 0 and $2/3$, or $1/3$. Since the actual Jaccard similarity of S_1 and S_2 is $1/2$, there is an error, but not too great an error. In larger examples, where minhash values are based on far more than four rows, the expected error will approach zero.

Similarly, we can see the effect of splitting the rows on the other two pairs of columns. Between S_1 and S_3, the top half represents sets with a Jaccard similarity of 0, while the bottom half represents sets with a Jaccard similarity $1/3$. The expected number of matches in the signatures of S_1 and S_3 is therefore the average of these, or $1/6$. That compares with the true Jaccard similarity $\text{SIM}(S_1, S_3) = 1/5$. Finally, when we compare S_2 and S_3, we note that the Jaccard similarity of these columns in the first four rows is $1/2$, and so is their Jaccard similarity in the bottom four rows. The average, $1/2$, also agrees exactly with $\text{SIM}(S_2, S_3) = 1/2$. □

3.3.8   Exercises for Section 3.3

EXERCISE 3.3.1   Verify the theorem from Section 3.3.3, which relates the Jaccard similarity to the probability of minhashing to equal values, for the particular case of Fig. 3.2.

(a) Compute the Jaccard similarity of each of the pairs of columns in Fig. 3.2.
! (b) Compute, for each pair of columns of that figure, the fraction of the 120 permutations of the rows that make the two columns hash to the same value.

EXERCISE 3.3.2   Using the data from Fig. 3.4, add to the signatures of the columns the values of the following hash functions:

(a) $h_3(x) = 2x + 4 \mod 5$.
(b) $h_4(x) = 3x - 1 \mod 5$.

Element	S_1	S_2	S_3	S_4
0	0	1	0	1
1	0	1	0	0
2	1	0	0	1
3	0	0	1	0
4	0	0	1	1
5	1	0	0	0

Figure 3.6 Matrix for Exercise 3.3.3

EXERCISE 3.3.3   In Fig. 3.6 is a matrix with six rows.

(a) Compute the minhash signature for each column if we use the following three hash functions: $h_1(x) = 2x+1 \mod 6$; $h_2(x) = 3x+2 \mod 6$; $h_3(x) = 5x+2 \mod 6$.
(b) Which of these hash functions are true permutations?
(c) How close are the estimated Jaccard similarities for the six pairs of columns to the true Jaccard similarities?

! EXERCISE 3.3.4   Now that we know Jaccard similarity is related to the probability that two sets minhash to the same value, reconsider Exercise 3.1.3. Can you use this relationship to simplify the problem of computing the expected Jaccard similarity of randomly chosen sets?

! EXERCISE 3.3.5   Prove that if the Jaccard similarity of two columns is 0, then minhashing always gives a correct estimate of the Jaccard similarity.

!! EXERCISE 3.3.6 One might expect that we could estimate the Jaccard similarity of columns without using all possible permutations of rows. For example, we could only allow cyclic permutations; i.e., start at a randomly chosen row r, which becomes the first in the order, followed by rows $r + 1$, $r + 2$, and so on, down to the last row, and then continuing with the first row, second row, and so on, down to row $r - 1$. There are only n such permutations if there are n rows. However, these permutations are not sufficient to estimate the Jaccard similarity correctly. Give an example of a two-column matrix where averaging over all the cyclic permutations does not give the Jaccard similarity.

! EXERCISE 3.3.7 Suppose we want to use a MapReduce framework to compute minhash signatures. If the matrix is stored in chunks that correspond to some columns, then it is quite easy to exploit parallelism. Each Map task gets some of the columns and all the hash functions, and computes the minhash signatures of its given columns. However, suppose the matrix were chunked by rows, so that a Map task is given the hash functions and a set of rows to work on. Design Map and Reduce functions to exploit MapReduce with data in this form.

! EXERCISE 3.3.8 As we noticed in Section 3.3.6, we have problems when a column has only 0s. If we compute a minhash function using entire columns (as in Section 3.3.2), then the only time we get all 0s in a column is if that column represents the empty set. How should we handle the empty set to make sure no errors in Jaccard-similarity estimation are introduced?

!! EXERCISE 3.3.9 In Example 3.9, each of the three estimates of Jaccard similarity we obtained was either smaller than or the same as the true Jaccard similarity. Is it possible that for another pair of columns, the average of the Jaccard similarities of the upper and lower halves will exceed the actual Jaccard similarity of the columns?

3.4   Locality-Sensitive Hashing for Documents

Even though we can use minhashing to compress large documents into small signatures and preserve the expected similarity of any pair of documents, it still may be impossible to find the pairs with greatest similarity efficiently. The reason is that the number of pairs of documents may be too large, even if there are not too many documents.

EXAMPLE 3.10 Suppose we have a million documents, and we use signatures of length 250. Then we use 1000 bytes per document for the signatures, and the entire data fits in a gigabyte – less than a typical main memory of a laptop. However, there are $\binom{1,000,000}{2}$ or half a trillion pairs of documents. If it takes a microsecond to compute the similarity of two signatures, then it takes almost six days to compute all the similarities on that laptop. $\square$

If our goal is to compute the similarity of every pair, there is nothing we can do to reduce the work, although parallelism can reduce the elapsed time. However, often we want only the most similar pairs or all pairs that are above some lower bound in similarity. If so, then we need to focus our attention only on pairs that are likely to be similar, without investigating every pair. There is a general theory of how to provide such focus, called *locality-sensitive hashing* (LSH) or *near-neighbor search*. In this section we shall consider a specific form of LSH, designed for the particular problem we have been studying: documents, represented by shingle-sets, then minhashed to short signatures. In Section 3.6 we present the general theory of locality-sensitive hashing and a number of applications and related techniques.

3.4.1 LSH for Minhash Signatures

One general approach to LSH is to "hash" items several times, in such a way that similar items are more likely to be hashed to the same bucket than dissimilar items are. We then consider any pair that hashed to the same bucket for any of the hashings to be a *candidate pair*. We check only the candidate pairs for similarity. The hope is that most of the dissimilar pairs will never hash to the same bucket, and therefore will never be checked. Those dissimilar pairs that do hash to the same bucket are *false positives*; we hope these will be only a small fraction of all pairs. We also hope that most of the truly similar pairs will hash to the same bucket under at least one of the hash functions. Those that do not are *false negatives*; we hope these will be only a small fraction of the truly similar pairs.

If we have minhash signatures for the items, an effective way to choose the hashings is to divide the signature matrix into b bands consisting of r rows each. For each band, there is a hash function that takes vectors of r integers (the portion of one column within that band) and hashes them to some large number of buckets. We can use the same hash function for all the bands, but we use a separate bucket array for each band, so columns with the same vector in different bands will not hash to the same bucket.

EXAMPLE 3.11   Figure 3.7 shows part of a signature matrix of 12 rows divided into four bands of three rows each. The second and fourth of the explicitly shown columns each have the column vector $[0, 2, 1]$ in the first band, so they will definitely hash to the same bucket in the hashing for the first band. Thus, regardless of what those columns look like in the other three bands, this pair of columns will be a candidate pair. It is possible that other columns, such as the first two shown explicitly, will also hash to the same bucket according to the hashing of the first band. However, since their column vectors are different, $[1, 3, 0]$ and $[0, 2, 1]$, and there are many buckets for each hashing, we expect the chances of an accidental collision to be very small. We shall normally assume that two vectors hash to the same bucket if and only if they are identical.

Two columns that do not agree in band 1 have three other chances to become a

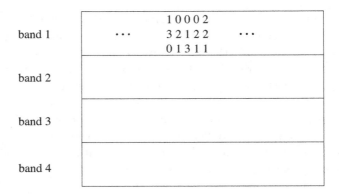

Figure 3.7 Dividing a signature matrix into four bands of three rows per band

candidate pair; they might be identical in any one of these other bands. However, observe that the more similar two columns are, the more likely it is that they will be identical in some band. Thus, intuitively the banding strategy makes similar columns much more likely to be candidate pairs than dissimilar pairs. □

3.4.2 Analysis of the Banding Technique

Suppose we use b bands of r rows each, and suppose that a particular pair of documents have Jaccard similarity s. Recall from Section 3.3.3 that the probability the minhash signatures for these documents agree in any one particular row of the signature matrix is s. We can calculate the probability that these documents (or rather their signatures) become a candidate pair as follows:

(1) The probability that the signatures agree in all rows of one particular band is s^r.

(2) The probability that the signatures disagree in at least one row of a particular band is $1 - s^r$.

(3) The probability that the signatures disagree in at least one row of each of the bands is $(1 - s^r)^b$.

(4) The probability that the signatures agree in all the rows of at least one band, and therefore become a candidate pair, is $1 - (1 - s^r)^b$.

It may not be obvious, but regardless of the chosen constants b and r, this function has the form of an *S-curve*, as suggested in Fig. 3.8. The *threshold*, that is, the value of similarity s at which the probability of becoming a candidate is $1/2$, is a function of b and r. The threshold is roughly where the rise is the steepest, and for large b and r we find that pairs with similarity above the threshold are very likely to become candidates, while those below the threshold are unlikely to become candidates – exactly the situation we want. An approximation to the threshold is $(1/b)^{1/r}$. For example, if $b = 16$ and $r = 4$, then the threshold is approximately at $s = 1/2$, since the 4th root of $1/16$ is $1/2$.

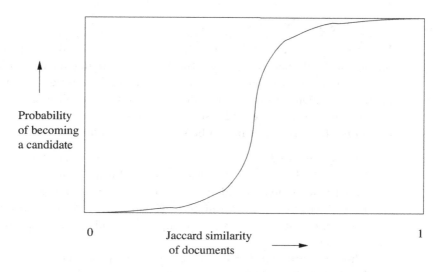

Figure 3.8 The S-curve

EXAMPLE 3.12   Let us consider the case $b = 20$ and $r = 5$. That is, we suppose we have signatures of length 100, divided into twenty bands of five rows each. Figure 3.9 tabulates some of the values of the function $1 - (1 - s^5)^{20}$. Notice that the threshold, the value of s at which the curve has risen halfway, is just slightly more than 0.5. Also notice that the curve is not exactly the ideal step function that jumps from 0 to 1 at the threshold, but the slope of the curve in the middle is significant. For example, it rises by more than 0.6 going from $s = 0.4$ to $s = 0.6$, so the slope in the middle is greater than 3.

s	$1 - (1 - s^r)^b$
.2	.006
.3	.047
.4	.186
.5	.470
.6	.802
.7	.975
.8	.9996

Figure 3.9 Values of the S-curve for $b = 20$ and $r = 5$

For example, at $s = 0.8$, $1 - (0.8)^5$ is about 0.672. If you raise this number to the 20th power, you get about 0.00035. Subtracting this fraction from 1 yields 0.99965. That is, if we consider two documents with 80% similarity, then in any one band, they have only about a 33% chance of agreeing in all five rows and thus becoming a candidate pair. However, there are 20 bands and thus 20 chances to become a candidate. Only roughly one in 3000 pairs that are as high as 80% similar will fail to become a candidate pair and thus be a false negative.   □

3.4.3   Combining the Techniques

We can now give an approach to finding the set of candidate pairs for similar documents and then discovering the truly similar documents among them. It must be emphasized that this approach can produce false negatives – pairs of similar documents that are not identified as such because they never become a candidate pair. There will also be false positives – candidate pairs that are evaluated, but are found not to be sufficiently similar.

(1) Pick a value of k and construct from each document the set of k-shingles. Optionally, hash the k-shingles to shorter bucket numbers.

(2) Sort the document-shingle pairs to order them by shingle.

(3) Pick a length n for the minhash signatures. Feed the sorted list to the algorithm of Section 3.3.5 to compute the minhash signatures for all the documents.

(4) Choose a threshold t that defines how similar documents have to be in order for them to be regarded as a desired "similar pair." Pick a number of bands b and a number of rows r such that $br = n$, and the threshold t is approximately $(1/b)^{1/r}$. If avoidance of false negatives is important, you may wish to select b and r to produce a threshold lower than t; if speed is important and you wish to limit false positives, select b and r to produce a higher threshold.

(5) Construct candidate pairs by applying the LSH technique of Section 3.4.1.

(6) Examine each candidate pair's signatures and determine whether the fraction of components in which they agree is at least t.

(7) Optionally, if the signatures are sufficiently similar, go to the documents themselves and check that they are truly similar, rather than documents that, by luck, had similar signatures.

3.4.4   Exercises for Section 3.4

EXERCISE 3.4.1   Evaluate the S-curve $1 - (1 - s^r)^b$ for $s = 0.1, 0.2, \ldots, 0.9$, for the following values of r and b:

- $r = 3$ and $b = 10$.
- $r = 6$ and $b = 20$.
- $r = 5$ and $b = 50$.

! EXERCISE 3.4.2   For each of the (r, b) pairs in Exercise 3.4.1, compute the threshold, that is, the value of s for which the value of $1 - (1 - s^r)^b$ is exactly $1/2$. How does this value compare with the estimate of $(1/b)^{1/r}$ that was suggested in Section 3.4.2?

! EXERCISE 3.4.3   Use the techniques explained in Section 1.3.5 to approximate the S-curve $1 - (1 - s^r)^b$ when s^r is very small.

! EXERCISE 3.4.4   Suppose we wish to implement LSH by MapReduce. Specifically, assume chunks of the signature matrix consist of columns, and elements are key-value pairs where the key is the column number and the value is the signature itself (i.e., a vector of values).

(a) Show how to produce the buckets for all the bands as output of a single MapReduce process. *Hint*: Remember that a Map function can produce several key-value pairs from a single element.

(b) Show how another MapReduce process can convert the output of (a) to a list of pairs that need to be compared. Specifically, for each column i, there should be a list of those columns $j > i$ with which i needs to be compared.

3.5 Distance Measures

We now take a short detour to study the general notion of distance measures. The Jaccard similarity is a measure of how close sets are, although it is not really a distance measure. That is, the closer sets are, the higher the Jaccard similarity. Rather, 1 minus the Jaccard similarity is a distance measure, as we shall see; it is called the *Jaccard distance*.

However, Jaccard distance is not the only measure of closeness that makes sense. We shall examine in this section some other distance measures that have applications. Then, in Section 3.6 we see how some of these distance measures also have an LSH technique that allows us to focus on nearby points without comparing all points. Other applications of distance measures will appear when we study clustering in Chapter 7.

3.5.1 Definition of a Distance Measure

Suppose we have a set of points, called a *space*. A *distance measure* on this space is a function $d(x, y)$ that takes two points in the space as arguments and produces a real number, and satisfies the following axioms:

(1) $d(x, y) \geq 0$ (no negative distances).

(2) $d(x, y) = 0$ if and only if $x = y$ (distances are positive, except for the distance from a point to itself).

(3) $d(x, y) = d(y, x)$ (distance is symmetric).

(4) $d(x, y) \leq d(x, z) + d(z, y)$ (the *triangle inequality*).

The triangle inequality is the most complex condition. It says, intuitively, that to travel from x to y, we cannot obtain any benefit if we are forced to travel via some particular third point z. The triangle-inequality axiom is what makes all distance measures behave as if distance describes the length of a shortest path from one point to another.

3.5.2   Euclidean Distances

The most familiar distance measure is the one we normally think of as "distance." An *n-dimensional Euclidean space* is one where points are vectors of n real numbers. The conventional distance measure in this space, which we shall refer to as the L_2-*norm*, is defined:

$$d([x_1, x_2, \ldots, x_n], [y_1, y_2, \ldots, y_n]) = \sqrt{\sum_{i=1}^{n}(x_i - y_i)^2}$$

That is, we square the distance in each dimension, sum the squares, and take the positive square root.

It is easy to verify the first three requirements for a distance measure are satisfied. The Euclidean distance between two points cannot be negative, because the positive square root is intended. Since all squares of real numbers are nonnegative, any i such that $x_i \neq y_i$ forces the distance to be strictly positive. On the other hand, if $x_i = y_i$ for all i, then the distance is clearly 0. Symmetry follows because $(x_i - y_i)^2 = (y_i - x_i)^2$. The triangle inequality requires a good deal of algebra to verify. However, it is well understood to be a property of Euclidean space: the sum of the lengths of any two sides of a triangle is no less than the length of the third side.

There are other distance measures that have been used for Euclidean spaces. For any constant r, we can define the L_r-*norm* to be the distance measure d defined by:

$$d([x_1, x_2, \ldots, x_n], [y_1, y_2, \ldots, y_n]) = (\sum_{i=1}^{n}|x_i - y_i|^r)^{1/r}$$

The case $r = 2$ is the usual L_2-norm just mentioned. Another common distance measure is the L_1-norm, or *Manhattan distance*. There, the distance between two points is the sum of the magnitudes of the differences in each dimension. It is called "Manhattan distance" because it is the distance one would have to travel between points if one were constrained to travel along grid lines, as on the streets of a city such as Manhattan.

Another interesting distance measure is the L_∞-norm, which is the limit as r approaches infinity of the L_r-norm. As r gets larger, only the dimension with the largest difference matters, so formally, the L_∞-norm is defined as the maximum of $|x_i - y_i|$ over all dimensions i.

EXAMPLE 3.13   Consider the two-dimensional Euclidean space (the customary plane) and the points $(2, 7)$ and $(6, 4)$. The L_2-norm gives a distance of $\sqrt{(2 - 6)^2 + (7 - 4)^2} = \sqrt{4^2 + 3^2} = 5$. The L_1-norm gives a distance of $|2 - 6| + |7 - 4| = 4 + 3 = 7$. The L_∞-norm gives a distance of

$$\max(|2 - 6|, |7 - 4|) = \max(4, 3) = 4. \qquad \square$$

3.5.3 Jaccard Distance

As mentioned at the beginning of the section, we define the *Jaccard distance* of sets by $d(x, y) = 1 - \text{SIM}(x, y)$. That is, the Jaccard distance is 1 minus the ratio of the sizes of the intersection and union of sets x and y. We must verify that this function is a distance measure.

(1) $d(x, y)$ is nonnegative because the size of the intersection cannot exceed the size of the union.

(2) $d(x, y) = 0$ if $x = y$, because $x \cup x = x \cap x = x$. However, if $x \neq y$, then the size of $x \cap y$ is strictly less than the size of $x \cup y$, so $d(x, y)$ is strictly positive.

(3) $d(x, y) = d(y, x)$ because both union and intersection are symmetric; i.e., $x \cup y = y \cup x$ and $x \cap y = y \cap x$.

(4) For the triangle inequality, recall from Section 3.3.3 that $\text{SIM}(x, y)$ is the probability a random minhash function maps x and y to the same value. Thus, the Jaccard distance $d(x, y)$ is the probability that a random minhash function *does not* send x and y to the same value. We can therefore translate the condition $d(x, y) \leq d(x, z) + d(z, y)$ to the statement that if h is a random minhash function, then the probability that $h(x) \neq h(y)$ is no greater than the sum of the probability that $h(x) \neq h(z)$ and the probability that $h(z) \neq h(y)$. However, this statement is true because whenever $h(x) \neq h(y)$, at least one of $h(x)$ and $h(y)$ must be different from $h(z)$. They could not both be $h(z)$, because then $h(x)$ and $h(y)$ would be the same.

.

3.5.4 Cosine Distance

The *cosine distance* makes sense in spaces that have dimensions, including Euclidean spaces and discrete versions of Euclidean spaces, such as spaces where points are vectors with integer components or Boolean (0 or 1) components. In such a space, points may be thought of as directions. We do not distinguish between a vector and a multiple of that vector. Then the cosine distance between two points is the angle that the vectors to those points make. This angle will be in the range 0 to 180 degrees, regardless of how many dimensions the space has.

We can calculate the cosine distance by first computing the cosine of the angle, and then applying the arc-cosine function to translate to an angle in the 0-180 degree range. Given two vectors x and y, the cosine of the angle between them is the dot product $x.y$ divided by the L_2-norms of x and y (i.e., their Euclidean distances from the origin). Recall that the dot product of vectors $[x_1, x_2, \ldots, x_n].[y_1, y_2, \ldots, y_n]$ is $\sum_{i=1}^{n} x_i y_i$.

EXAMPLE 3.14 Let our two vectors be $x = [1, 2, -1]$ and $= [2, 1, 1]$. The dot product $x.y$ is $1 \times 2 + 2 \times 1 + (-1) \times 1 = 3$. The L_2-norm of both vectors is $\sqrt{6}$. For example, x has L_2-norm $\sqrt{1^2 + 2^2 + (-1)^2} = \sqrt{6}$. Thus, the cosine of the angle between x and y is $3/(\sqrt{6}\sqrt{6})$ or $1/2$. The angle whose cosine is $1/2$ is 60 degrees, so that is the cosine distance between x and y.   □

We must show that the cosine distance is indeed a distance measure. We have defined it so the values are in the range 0 to 180, so no negative distances are possible. Two vectors have angle 0 if and only if they are the same direction.[5] Symmetry is obvious: the angle between x and y is the same as the angle between y and x. The triangle inequality is best argued by physical reasoning. One way to rotate from x to y is to rotate to z and thence to y. The sum of those two rotations cannot be less than the rotation directly from x to y.

3.5.5   Edit Distance

This distance makes sense when points are strings. The distance between two strings $x = x_1x_2\cdots x_n$ and $y = y_1y_2\cdots y_m$ is the smallest number of insertions and deletions of single characters that will convert x to y.

EXAMPLE 3.15   The edit distance between the strings $x =$ abcde and $y =$ acfdeg is 3. To convert x to y:

(1) Delete b.
(2) Insert f after c.
(3) Insert g after e.

No sequence of fewer than three insertions and/or deletions will convert x to y. Thus, $d(x, y) = 3$.   □

Another way to define and calculate the edit distance $d(x, y)$ is to compute a *longest common subsequence* (LCS) of x and y. An LCS of x and y is a string that is constructed by deleting positions from x and y, and that is as long as any string that can be constructed that way. The edit distance $d(x, y)$ can be calculated as the length of x plus the length of y minus twice the length of their LCS.

EXAMPLE 3.16   The strings $x =$ abcde and $y =$ acfdeg from Example 3.15 have a unique LCS, which is acde. We can be sure it is the longest possible, because it contains every symbol appearing in both x and y. Fortunately, these common symbols appear in the same order in both strings, so we are able to use them all in an LCS. Note that the length of x is 5, the length of y is 6, and the length of their LCS is 4. The edit distance is thus $5 + 6 - 2 \times 4 = 3$, which agrees with the direct calculation in Example 3.15.

For another example, consider $x =$ aba and $y =$ bab. Their edit distance is 2. For example, we can convert x to y by deleting the first a and then inserting b

---

[5] Notice that to satisfy the second axiom, we have to treat vectors that are multiples of one another, e.g. $[1, 2]$ and $[3, 6]$, as the same direction, which they are. If we regarded these as different vectors, we would give them distance 0 and thus violate the condition that only $d(x, x)$ is 0.

Non-Euclidean Spaces

Notice that several of the distance measures introduced in this section are not Euclidean spaces. A property of Euclidean spaces that we shall find important when we take up clustering in Chapter 7 is that the average of points in a Euclidean space always exists and is a point in the space. However, consider the space of sets for which we defined the Jaccard distance. The notion of the "average" of two sets makes no sense. Likewise, the space of strings, where we can use the edit distance, does not let us take the "average" of strings.

Vector spaces, for which we suggested the cosine distance, may or may not be Euclidean. If the components of the vectors can be any real numbers, then the space is Euclidean. However, if we restrict components to be integers, then the space is not Euclidean. Notice that, for instance, we cannot find an average of the vectors $[1, 2]$ and $[3, 1]$ in the space of vectors with two integer components, although if we treated them as members of the two-dimensional Euclidean space, then we could say that their average was $[2.0, 1.5]$.

at the end. There are two LCSs: ab and ba. Each can be obtained by deleting one symbol from each string. As must be the case for multiple LCSs of the same pair of strings, both LCSs have the same length. Therefore, we may compute the edit distance as $3 + 3 - 2 \times 2 = 2$. ☐

Edit distance is a distance measure. Surely no edit distance can be negative, and only two identical strings have an edit distance of 0. To see that edit distance is symmetric, note that a sequence of insertions and deletions can be reversed, with each insertion becoming a deletion, and vice versa. The triangle inequality is also straightforward. One way to turn a string s into a string t is to turn s into some string u and then turn u into t. Thus, the number of edits made going from s to u, plus the number of edits made going from u to t cannot be less than the smallest number of edits that will turn s into t.

3.5.6 Hamming Distance

Given a space of vectors, we define the *Hamming distance* between two vectors to be the number of components in which they differ. It should be obvious that Hamming distance is a distance measure. Clearly the Hamming distance cannot be negative, and if it is zero, then the vectors are identical. The distance does not depend on which of two vectors we consider first. The triangle inequality should also be evident. If x and z differ in m components, and z and y differ in n components, then x and y cannot differ in more than $m + n$ components. Most commonly, Hamming distance is used when the vectors are Boolean; they consist of 0s and 1s only. However, in principle, the vectors can have components from any set.

EXAMPLE 3.17   The Hamming distance between the vectors 10101 and 11110 is 3. That is, these vectors differ in the second, fourth, and fifth components, while they agree in the first and third components. ☐

3.5.7   Exercises for Section 3.5

! EXERCISE 3.5.1   On the space of nonnegative integers, which of the following functions are distance measures? If so, prove it; if not, prove that it fails to satisfy one or more of the axioms.

(a) $\max(x, y) =$ the larger of x and y.
(b) $\text{diff}(x, y) = |x - y|$ (the absolute magnitude of the difference between x and y).
(c) $\text{sum}(x, y) = x + y$.

EXERCISE 3.5.2   Find the L_1 and L_2 distances between the points $(5, 6, 7)$ and $(8, 2, 4)$.

!! EXERCISE 3.5.3   Prove that if i and j are any positive integers, and $i < j$, then the L_i norm between any two points is greater than the L_j norm between those same two points.

EXERCISE 3.5.4   Find the Jaccard distances between the following pairs of sets:

(a) $\{1, 2, 3, 4\}$ and $\{2, 3, 4, 5\}$.
(b) $\{1, 2, 3\}$ and $\{4, 5, 6\}$.

EXERCISE 3.5.5   Compute the cosines of the angles between each of the following pairs of vectors.[6]

(a) $(3, -1, 2)$ and $(-2, 3, 1)$.
(b) $(1, 2, 3)$ and $(2, 4, 6)$.
(c) $(5, 0, -4)$ and $(-1, -6, 2)$.
(d) $(0, 1, 1, 0, 1, 1)$ and $(0, 0, 1, 0, 0, 0)$.

! EXERCISE 3.5.6   Prove that the cosine distance between any two vectors of 0s and 1s, of the same length, is at most 90 degrees.

EXERCISE 3.5.7   Find the edit distances (using only insertions and deletions) between the following pairs of strings.

(a) `abcdef` and `bdaefc`.
(b) `abccdabc` and `acbdcab`.
(c) `abcdef` and `baedfc`.

! EXERCISE 3.5.8   There are a number of other notions of edit distance available. For instance, we can allow, in addition to insertions and deletions, the following operations:

[6] Note that what we are asking for is not precisely the cosine distance, but from the cosine of an angle, you can compute the angle itself, perhaps with the aid of a table or library function.

(i) *Mutation*, where one symbol is replaced by another symbol. Note that a mutation can always be performed by an insertion followed by a deletion, but if we allow mutations, then this change counts for only 1, not 2, when computing the edit distance.

(ii) *Transposition*, where two adjacent symbols have their positions swapped. Like a mutation, we can simulate a transposition by one insertion followed by one deletion, but here we count only 1 for these two steps.

Repeat Exercise 3.5.7 if edit distance is defined to be the number of insertions, deletions, mutations, and transpositions needed to transform one string into another.

! EXERCISE 3.5.9 Prove that the edit distance discussed in Exercise 3.5.8 is indeed a distance measure.

EXERCISE 3.5.10 Find the Hamming distances between each pair of the following vectors: 000000, 110011, 010101, and 011100.

3.6 The Theory of Locality-Sensitive Functions

The LSH technique developed in Section 3.4 is one example of a family of functions (the minhash functions) that can be combined (by the banding technique) to distinguish strongly between pairs at a low distance from pairs at a high distance. The steepness of the S-curve in Fig. 3.8 reflects how effectively we can avoid false positives and false negatives among the candidate pairs.

Now, we shall explore other families of functions, besides the minhash functions, that can serve to produce candidate pairs efficiently. These functions can apply to the space of sets and the Jaccard distance, or to another space and/or another distance measure. There are three conditions that we need for a family of functions:

(1) They must be more likely to make close pairs be candidate pairs than distant pairs. We make this notion precise in Section 3.6.1.

(2) They must be statistically independent, in the sense that it is possible to estimate the probability that two or more functions will all give a certain response by the product rule for independent events.

(3) They must be efficient, in two ways:

(a) They must be able to identify candidate pairs in time much less than the time it takes to look at all pairs. For example, minhash functions have this capability, since we can hash sets to minhash values in time proportional to the size of the data, rather than the square of the number of sets in the data. Since sets with common values are colocated in a bucket, we have implicitly produced the candidate pairs for a single minhash function in time much less than the number of pairs of sets.

(b) They must be combinable to build functions that are better at avoiding false positives and negatives, and the combined functions must also take time that is much less than the number of pairs. For example, the banding technique of Section 3.4.1 takes single minhash functions, which satisfy condition (3)(a) but do not, by themselves have the S-curve behavior we want, and produces from a number of minhash functions a combined function that has the S-curve shape.

Our first step is to define "locality-sensitive functions" generally. We then see how the idea can be applied in several applications. Finally, we discuss how to apply the theory to arbitrary data with either a cosine distance or a Euclidean distance measure.

3.6.1   Locality-Sensitive Functions

For the purposes of this section, we shall consider functions that take two items and render a decision about whether these items should be a candidate pair. In many cases, the function f will "hash" items, and the decision will be based on whether or not the result is equal. Because it is convenient to use the notation $f(x) = f(y)$ to mean that $f(x, y)$ is "yes; make x and y a candidate pair," we shall use $f(x) = f(y)$ as a shorthand with this meaning. We also use $f(x) \neq f(y)$ to mean "do not make x and y a candidate pair unless some other function concludes we should do so."

A collection of functions of this form will be called a *family* of functions. For example, the family of minhash functions, each based on one of the possible permutations of rows of a characteristic matrix, form a family.

Let $d_1 < d_2$ be two distances according to some distance measure d. A family **F** of functions is said to be (d_1, d_2, p_1, p_2)-*sensitive* if for every f in **F**:

(1) If $d(x, y) \leq d_1$, then the probability that $f(x) = f(y)$ is at least p_1.
(2) If $d(x, y) \geq d_2$, then the probability that $f(x) = f(y)$ is at most p_2.

Figure 3.10 illustrates what we expect about the probability that a given function in a (d_1, d_2, p_1, p_2)-sensitive family will declare two items to be a candidate pair. Notice that we say nothing about what happens when the distance between the items is strictly between d_1 and d_2, but we can make d_1 and d_2 as close as we wish. The penalty is that typically p_1 and p_2 are then close as well. As we shall see, it is possible to drive p_1 and p_2 apart while keeping d_1 and d_2 fixed.

3.6.2   Locality-Sensitive Families for Jaccard Distance

For the moment, we have only one way to find a family of locality-sensitive functions: use the family of minhash functions, and assume that the distance measure is the Jaccard distance. As before, we interpret a minhash function h to make x and y a candidate pair if and only if $h(x) = h(y)$.

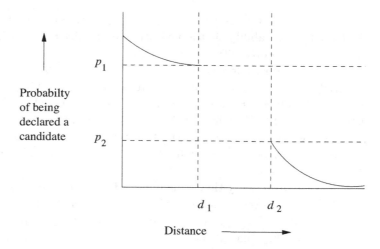

Figure 3.10 Behavior of a (d_1, d_2, p_1, p_2)-sensitive function

- The family of minhash functions is a $(d_1, d_2, 1 - d_1, 1 - d_2)$-sensitive family for any d_1 and d_2, where $0 \leq d_1 < d_2 \leq 1$.

The reason for this is that if $d(x, y) \leq d_1$, where d is the Jaccard distance, then $\text{SIM}(x, y) = 1 - d(x, y) \geq 1 - d_1$. But we know that the Jaccard similarity of x and y is equal to the probability that a minhash function will hash x and y to the same value. A similar argument applies to d_2 or any distance.

EXAMPLE 3.18   We could let $d_1 = 0.3$ and $d_2 = 0.6$. Then we can assert that the family of minhash functions is a $(0.3, 0.6, 0.7, 0.4)$-sensitive family. That is, if the Jaccard distance between x and y is at most 0.3 (i.e., $\text{SIM}(x, y) \geq 0.7$) then there is at least a 0.7 chance that a minhash function will send x and y to the same value, and if the Jaccard distance between x and y is at least 0.6 (i.e., $\text{SIM}(x, y) \leq 0.4$), then there is at most a 0.4 chance that x and y will be sent to the same value. Note that we could make the same assertion with another choice of d_1 and d_2; only $d_1 < d_2$ is required.   □

3.6.3   Amplifying a Locality-Sensitive Family

Suppose we are given a (d_1, d_2, p_1, p_2)-sensitive family **F**. We can construct a new family **F′** by the *AND-construction* on **F**, which is defined as follows. Each member of **F′** consists of r members of **F** for some fixed r. If f is in **F′**, and f is constructed from the set $\{f_1, f_2, \ldots, f_r\}$ of members of **F**, we say $f(x) = f(y)$ if and only if $f_i(x) = f_i(y)$ for all $i = 1, 2, \ldots, r$. Notice that this construction mirrors the effect of the r rows in a single band: the band makes x and y a candidate pair if every one of the r rows in the band say that x and y are equal (and therefore a candidate pair according to that row).

Since the members of **F** are independently chosen to make a member of **F′**, we can assert that $\mathbf{F}'$ is a $(d_1, d_2, (p_1)^r, (p_2)^r)$-sensitive family. That is, for any p, if p is the probability that a member of $\mathbf{F}$ will declare (x, y) to be a candidate pair, then the probability that a member of $\mathbf{F}'$ will so declare is p^r.

There is another construction, which we call the *OR-construction*, that turns a (d_1, d_2, p_1, p_2)-sensitive family $\mathbf{F}$ into a $(d_1, d_2, 1 - (1 - p_1)^b, 1 - (1 - p_2)^b)$-sensitive family $\mathbf{F}'$. Each member f of $\mathbf{F}'$ is constructed from b members of $\mathbf{F}$, say $f_1, f_2, \ldots, f_b$. We define $f(x) = f(y)$ if and only if $f_i(x) = f_i(y)$ for one or more values of i. The OR-construction mirrors the effect of combining several bands: x and y become a candidate pair if any band makes them a candidate pair.

If p is the probability that a member of $\mathbf{F}$ will declare (x, y) to be a candidate pair, then $1 - p$ is the probability it will not so declare. $(1 - p)^b$ is the probability that none of $f_1, f_2, \ldots, f_b$ will declare (x, y) a candidate pair, and $1 - (1 - p)^b$ is the probability that at least one f_i will declare (x, y) a candidate pair, and therefore that f will declare (x, y) to be a candidate pair.

Notice that the AND-construction lowers all probabilities, but if we choose $\mathbf{F}$ and r judiciously, we can make the small probability p_2 get very close to 0, while the higher probability p_1 stays significantly away from 0. Similarly, the OR-construction makes all probabilities rise, but by choosing $\mathbf{F}$ and b judiciously, we can make the larger probability approach 1 while the smaller probability remains bounded away from 1. We can cascade AND- and OR-constructions in any order to make the low probability close to 0 and the high probability close to 1. Of course the more constructions we use, and the higher the values of r and b that we pick, the larger the number of functions from the original family that we are forced to use. Thus, the better the final family of functions is, the longer it takes to apply the functions from this family.

EXAMPLE 3.19   Suppose we start with a family $\mathbf{F}$. We use the AND-construction with $r = 4$ to produce a family $\mathbf{F}_1$. We then apply the OR-construction to $\mathbf{F}_1$ with $b = 4$ to produce a third family $\mathbf{F}_2$. Note that the members of $\mathbf{F}_2$ each are built from 16 members of $\mathbf{F}$, and the situation is analogous to starting with 16 minhash functions and treating them as four bands of four rows each.

p	$1 - (1 - p^4)^4$
0.2	0.0064
0.3	0.0320
0.4	0.0985
0.5	0.2275
0.6	0.4260
0.7	0.6666
0.8	0.8785
0.9	0.9860

Figure 3.11 Effect of the 4-way AND-construction followed by the 4-way OR-construction

The 4-way AND-function converts any probability p into p^4. When we follow it by the 4-way OR-construction, that probability is further converted into $1 - (1 - p^4)^4$. Some values of this transformation are indicated in Fig. 3.11. This function is an S-curve, staying low for a while, then rising steeply (although not too steeply; the slope never gets much higher than 2), and then leveling off at high values. Like any S-curve, it has a *fixedpoint*, the value of p that is left unchanged when we apply the function of the S-curve. In this case, the fixedpoint is the value of p for which $p = 1 - (1 - p^4)^4$. We can see that the fixedpoint is somewhere between 0.7 and 0.8. Below that value, probabilities are decreased, and above it they are increased. Thus, if we pick a high probability above the fixedpoint and a low probability below it, we shall have the desired effect that the low probability is decreased and the high probability is increased.

Suppose $\mathbf{F}$ is the minhash functions, regarded as a $(0.2, 0.6, 0.8, 0.4)$-sensitive family. Then $\mathbf{F}_2$, the family constructed by a 4-way AND followed by a 4-way OR, is a $(0.2, 0.6, 0.8785, 0.0985)$-sensitive family, as we can read from the rows for 0.8 and 0.4 in Fig. 3.11. By replacing $\mathbf{F}$ by $\mathbf{F}_2$, we have reduced both the false-negative and false-positive rates, at the cost of making application of the functions take 16 times as long. □

p	$\left(1 - (1 - p)^4\right)^4$
0.1	0.0140
0.2	0.1215
0.3	0.3334
0.4	0.5740
0.5	0.7725
0.6	0.9015
0.7	0.9680
0.8	0.9936

Figure 3.12 Effect of the 4-way OR-construction followed by the 4-way AND-construction

EXAMPLE 3.20   For the same cost, we can apply a 4-way OR-construction followed by a 4-way AND-construction. Figure 3.12 gives the transformation on probabilities implied by this construction. For instance, suppose that $\mathbf{F}$ is a $(0.2, 0.6, 0.8, 0.4)$-sensitive family. Then the constructed family is a

$$(0.2, 0.6, 0.9936, 0.5740)\text{-sensitive}$$

family. This choice is not necessarily the best. Although the higher probability has moved much closer to 1, the lower probability has also raised, increasing the number of false positives. □

EXAMPLE 3.21   We can cascade constructions as much as we like. For example, we could use the construction of Example 3.19 on the family of minhash functions and then use the construction of Example 3.20 on the resulting family. The constructed family would then have functions each built from 256 minhash functions. It would, for instance transform a $(0.2, 0.8, 0.8, 0.2)$-sensitive family into a $(0.2, 0.8, 0.9991285, 0.0000004)$-sensitive family. □

3.6.4   Exercises for Section 3.6

EXERCISE 3.6.1   What is the effect on probability of starting with the family of minhash functions and applying:

(a) A 2-way AND construction followed by a 3-way OR construction.
(b) A 3-way OR construction followed by a 2-way AND construction.
(c) A 2-way AND construction followed by a 2-way OR construction, followed by a 2-way AND construction.
(d) A 2-way OR construction followed by a 2-way AND construction, followed by a 2-way OR construction followed by a 2-way AND construction.

EXERCISE 3.6.2   Find the fixedpoints for each of the functions constructed in Exercise 3.6.1.

! EXERCISE 3.6.3   Any function of probability p, such as that of Fig. 3.11, has a slope given by the derivative of the function. The maximum slope is where that derivative is a maximum. Find the value of p that gives a maximum slope for the S-curves given by Fig. 3.11 and Fig. 3.12. What are the values of these maximum slopes?

!! EXERCISE 3.6.4   Generalize Exercise 3.6.3 to give, as a function of r and b, the point of maximum slope and the value of that slope, for families of functions defined from the minhash functions by:

(a) An r-way AND construction followed by a b-way OR construction.
(b) A b-way OR construction followed by an r-way AND construction.

3.7   LSH Families for Other Distance Measures

There is no guarantee that a distance measure has a locality-sensitive family of hash functions. So far, we have only seen such families for the Jaccard distance. In this section, we shall show how to construct locality-sensitive families for Hamming distance, the cosine distance and for the normal Euclidean distance.

3.7.1   LSH Families for Hamming Distance

It is quite simple to build a locality-sensitive family of functions for the Hamming distance. Suppose we have a space of d-dimensional vectors, and $h(x, y)$ denotes the Hamming distance between vectors x and y. If we take any one position of the vectors, say the ith position, we can define the function $f_i(x)$ to be the ith bit of vector x. Then $f_i(x) = f_i(y)$ if and only if vectors x and y agree in the ith position. Then the probability that $f_i(x) = f_i(y)$ for a randomly chosen i is exactly $1 - h(x, y)/d$; i.e., it is the fraction of positions in which x and y agree.

This situation is almost exactly like the one we encountered for minhashing. Thus, the family $\mathbf{F}$ consisting of the functions $\{f_1, f_2, \ldots, f_d\}$ is a

$$(d_1, d_2, 1 - d_1/d, 1 - d_2/d)\text{-sensitive}$$

family of hash functions, for any $d_1 < d_2$. There are only two differences between this family and the family of minhash functions.

(1) While Jaccard distance runs from 0 to 1, the Hamming distance on a vector space of dimension d runs from 0 to d. It is therefore necessary to scale the distances by dividing by d, to turn them into probabilities.
(2) While there is essentially an unlimited supply of minhash functions, the size of the family $\mathbf{F}$ for Hamming distance is only d.

The first point is of no consequence; it only requires that we divide by d at appropriate times. The second point is more serious. If d is relatively small, then we are limited in the number of functions that can be composed using the AND and OR constructions, thereby limiting how steep we can make the S-curve be.

3.7.2 Random Hyperplanes and the Cosine Distance

Recall from Section 3.5.4 that the cosine distance between two vectors is the angle between the vectors. For instance, we see in Fig. 3.13 two vectors x and y that make an angle θ between them. Note that these vectors may be in a space of many dimensions, but they always define a plane, and the angle between them is measured in this plane. Figure 3.13 is a "top-view" of the plane containing x and y.

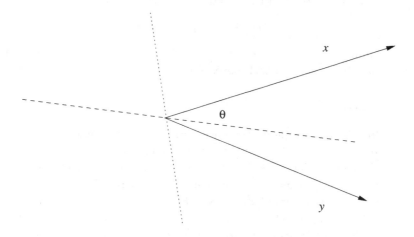

Figure 3.13 Two vectors make an angle θ

Suppose we pick a hyperplane through the origin. This hyperplane intersects the plane of x and y in a line. Figure 3.13 suggests two possible hyperplanes, one whose intersection is the dashed line and the other's intersection is the dotted line. To pick a random hyperplane, we actually pick the normal vector to the hyperplane, say v. The hyperplane is then the set of points whose dot product with v is 0.

First, consider a vector v that is normal to the hyperplane whose projection is represented by the dashed line in Fig. 3.13; that is, x and y are on different sides of the hyperplane. Then the dot products $v.x$ and $v.y$ will have different signs. If we assume, for instance, that v is a vector whose projection onto the plane of x and y is above the dashed line in Fig. 3.13, then $v.x$ is positive, while $v.y$ is negative. The normal vector v instead might extend in the opposite direction, below the dashed line. In that case $v.x$ is negative and $v.y$ is positive, but the signs are still different.

On the other hand, the randomly chosen vector v could be normal to a hyperplane like the dotted line in Fig. 3.13. In that case, both $v.x$ and $v.y$ have the same sign. If the projection of v extends to the right, then both dot products are positive, while if v extends to the left, then both are negative.

What is the probability that the randomly chosen vector is normal to a hyperplane that looks like the dashed line rather than the dotted line? All angles for the line that is the intersection of the random hyperplane and the plane of x and y are equally likely. Thus, the hyperplane will look like the dashed line with probability $\theta/180$ and will look like the dotted line otherwise.

Thus, each hash function f in our locality-sensitive family $\mathbf{F}$ is built from a randomly chosen vector v_f. Given two vectors x and y, say $f(x) = f(y)$ if and only if the dot products $v_f.x$ and $v_f.y$ have the same sign. Then $\mathbf{F}$ is a locality-sensitive family for the cosine distance. The parameters are essentially the same as for the Jaccard-distance family described in Section 3.6.2, except the scale of distances is 0–180 rather than 0–1. That is, $\mathbf{F}$ is a

$$(d_1, d_2, (180 - d_1)/180, (180 - d_2)/180)\text{-sensitive}$$

family of hash functions. From this basis, we can amplify the family as we wish, just as for the minhash-based family.

3.7.3   Sketches

Instead of chosing a random vector from all possible vectors, it turns out to be sufficiently random if we restrict our choice to vectors whose components are $+1$ and -1. The dot product of any vector x with a vector v of $+1$s and -1s is formed by adding the components of x where v is $+1$ and then subtracting the other components of x – those where v is -1.

If we pick a collection of random vectors, say $v_1, v_2, \ldots, v_n$, then we can apply them to an arbitrary vector x by computing $v_1.x, v_2.x, \ldots, v_n.x$ and then replacing any positive value by $+1$ and any negative value by -1. The result is called the *sketch* of x. You can handle 0s arbitrarily, e.g., by chosing a result $+1$ or -1 at random. Since there is only a tiny probability of a zero dot product, the choice has essentially no effect.

EXAMPLE 3.22 Suppose our space consists of 4-dimensional vectors, and we pick three random vectors: $v_1 = [+1, -1, +1, +1]$, $v_2 = [-1, +1, -1, +1]$, and $v_3 = [+1, +1, -1, -1]$. For the vector $x = [3, 4, 5, 6]$, the sketch is $[+1, +1, -1]$. That is, $v_1.x = 3 - 4 + 5 + 6 = 10$. Since the result is positive, the first component of the sketch is $+1$. Similarly, $v_2.x = 2$ and $v_3.x = -4$, so the second component of the sketch is $+1$ and the third component is -1.

Consider the vector $y = [4, 3, 2, 1]$. We can similarly compute its sketch to be $[+1, -1, +1]$. Since the sketches for x and y agree in $1/3$ of the positions, we estimate that the angle between them is 120 degrees. That is, a randomly chosen hyperplane is twice as likely to look like the dashed line in Fig. 3.13 than like the dotted line.

The above conclusion turns out to be quite wrong. We can calculate the cosine of the angle between x and y to be $x.y$, which is

$$6 \times 1 + 5 \times 2 + 4 \times 3 + 3 \times 4 = 40$$

divided by the magnitudes of the two vectors. These magnitudes are

$$\sqrt{6^2 + 5^2 + 4^2 + 3^2} = 9.274$$

and $\sqrt{1^2 + 2^2 + 3^2 + 4^2} = 5.477$. Thus, the cosine of the angle between x and y is 0.7875, and this angle is about 38 degrees. However, if you look at all 16 different vectors v of length 4 that have $+1$ and -1 as components, you find that there are only four of these whose dot products with x and y have a different sign, namely v_2, v_3, and their complements $[+1, -1, +1, -1]$ and $[-1, -1, +1, +1]$. Thus, had we picked all sixteen of these vectors to form a sketch, the estimate of the angle would have been $180/4 = 45$ degrees. □

3.7.4 LSH Families for Euclidean Distance

Now, let us turn to the Euclidean distance (Section 3.5.2), and see if we can develop a locality-sensitive family of hash functions for this distance. We shall start with a 2-dimensional Euclidean space. Each hash function f in our family **F** will be associated with a randomly chosen line in this space. Pick a constant a and divide the line into segments of length a, as suggested by Fig. 3.14, where the "random" line has been oriented to be horizontal.

The segments of the line are the buckets into which function f hashes points. A point is hashed to the bucket in which its projection onto the line lies. If the distance d between two points is small compared with a, then there is a good chance the two points hash to the same bucket, and thus the hash function f will declare the two points equal. For example, if $d = a/2$, then there is at least a 50% chance the two points will fall in the same bucket. In fact, if the angle θ between the randomly chosen line and the line connecting the points is large,

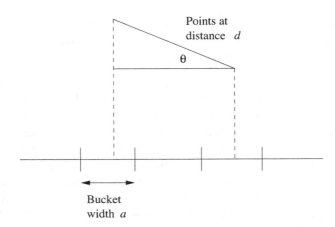

Figure 3.14 Two points at distance $d \gg a$ have a small chance of being hashed to the same bucket

then there is an even greater chance that the two points will fall in the same bucket. For instance, if θ is 90 degrees, then the two points are certain to fall in the same bucket.

However, suppose d is larger than a. In order for there to be any chance of the two points falling in the same bucket, we need $d \cos \theta \leq a$. The diagram of Fig. 3.14 suggests why this requirement holds. Note that even if $d \cos \theta \ll a$ it is still not certain that the two points will fall in the same bucket. However, we can guarantee the following. If $d \geq 2a$, then there is no more than a 1/3 chance the two points fall in the same bucket. The reason is that for $\cos \theta$ to be less than 1/2, we need to have θ in the range 60 to 90 degrees. If θ is in the range 0 to 60 degrees, then $\cos \theta$ is more than 1/2. But since θ is the smaller angle between two randomly chosen lines in the plane, θ is twice as likely to be between 0 and 60 as it is to be between 60 and 90.

We conclude that the family **F** just described forms a $(a/2, 2a, 1/2, 1/3)$-sensitive family of hash functions. That is, for distances up to $a/2$ the probability is at least 1/2 that two points at that distance will fall in the same bucket, while for distances at least $2a$ the probability points at that distance will fall in the same bucket is at most 1/3. We can amplify this family as we like, just as for the other examples of locality-sensitive hash functions we have discussed.

3.7.5   More LSH Families for Euclidean Spaces

There is something unsatisfying about the family of hash functions developed in Section 3.7.4. First, the technique was only described for two-dimensional Euclidean spaces. What happens if our data is points in a space with many dimensions? Second, for Jaccard and cosine distances, we were able to develop locality-sensitive families for any pair of distances d_1 and d_2 as long as $d_1 < d_2$. In Section 3.7.4 we appear to need the stronger condition $d_1 < 4d_2$.

However, we claim that there is a locality-sensitive family of hash functions for any $d_1 < d_2$ and for any number of dimensions. The family's hash functions still derive from random lines through the space and a bucket size a that partitions the line. We still hash points by projecting them onto the line. Given that $d_1 < d_2$, we may not know what the probability p_1 is that two points at distance d_1 hash to the same bucket, but we can be certain that it is greater than p_2, the probability that two points at distance d_2 hash to the same bucket. The reason is that this probability surely grows as the distance shrinks. Thus, even if we cannot calculate p_1 and p_2 easily, we know that there is a (d_1, d_2, p_1, p_2)-sensitive family of hash functions for any $d_1 < d_2$ and any given number of dimensions.

Using the amplification techniques of Section 3.6.3, we can then adjust the two probabilities to surround any particular value we like, and to be as far apart as we like. Of course, the further apart we want the probabilities to be, the larger the number of basic hash functions in **F** we must use.

3.7.6   Exercises for Section 3.7

EXERCISE 3.7.1   Suppose we construct the basic family of six locality-sensitive functions for vectors of length six. For each pair of the vectors 000000, 110011, 010101, and 011100, which of the six functions makes them candidates?

EXERCISE 3.7.2   Let us compute sketches using the following four "random" vectors:

$$v_1 = [+1, +1, +1, -1] \quad v_2 = [+1, +1, -1, +1]$$
$$v_3 = [+1, -1, +1, +1] \quad v_4 = [-1, +1, +1, +1]$$

Compute the sketches of the following vectors.

(a) $[2, 3, 4, 5]$.
(b) $[-2, 3, -4, 5]$.
(c) $[2, -3, 4, -5]$.

For each pair, what is the estimated angle between them, according to the sketches? What are the true angles?

EXERCISE 3.7.3   Suppose we form sketches by using all sixteen of the vectors of length 4, whose components are each $+1$ or -1. Compute the sketches of the three vectors in Exercise 3.7.2. How do the estimates of the angles between each pair compare with the true angles?

EXERCISE 3.7.4   Suppose we form sketches using the four vectors from Exercise 3.7.2.

! (a) What are the constraints on a, b, c, and d that will cause the sketch of the vector $[a, b, c, d]$ to be $[+1, +1, +1, +1]$?

!! (b) Consider two vectors $[a, b, c, d]$ and $[e, f, g, h]$. What are the conditions on $a, b, \ldots, h$ that will make the sketches of these two vectors be the same?

EXERCISE 3.7.5 Suppose we have points in a 3-dimensional Euclidean space: $p_1 = (1, 2, 3)$, $p_2 = (0, 2, 4)$, and $p_3 = (4, 3, 2)$. Consider the three hash functions defined by the three axes (to make our calculations very easy). Let buckets be of length a, with one bucket the interval $[0, a)$ (i.e., the set of points x such that $0 \leq x < a$), the next $[a, 2a)$, the previous one $[-a, 0)$, and so on.

(a) For each of the three lines, assign each of the points to buckets, assuming $a = 1$.

(b) Repeat part (a), assuming $a = 2$.

(c) What are the candidate pairs for the cases $a = 1$ and $a = 2$?

! (d) For each pair of points, for what values of a will that pair be a candidate pair?

3.8   Applications of Locality-Sensitive Hashing

In this section, we shall explore three examples of how LSH is used in practice. In each case, the techniques we have learned must be modified to meet certain constraints of the problem. The three subjects we cover are:

(1) *Entity Resolution*: This term refers to matching data records that refer to the same real-world entity, e.g., the same person. The principal problem addressed here is that the similarity of records does not match exactly either the similar-sets or similar-vectors models of similarity on which the theory is built.

(2) *Matching Fingerprints*: It is possible to represent fingerprints as sets. However, we shall explore a different family of locality-sensitive hash functions from the one we get by minhashing.

(3) *Matching Newspaper Articles*: Here, we consider a different notion of shingling that focuses attention on the core article in an on-line newspaper's Web page, ignoring all the extraneous material such as ads and newspaper-specific material.

3.8.1   Entity Resolution

It is common to have several data sets available, and to know that they refer to some of the same entities. For example, several different bibliographic sources provide information about many of the same books or papers. In the general case, we have records describing entities of some type, such as people or books. The records may all have the same format, or they may have different formats, with different kinds of information.

There are many reasons why information about an entity may vary, even if the field in question is supposed to be the same. For example, names may be expressed differently in different records because of misspellings, absence of a middle initial, use of a nickname, and many other reasons. For example, "Bob S.

Jomes" and "Robert Jones Jr." may or may not be the same person. If records come from different sources, the fields may differ as well. One source's records may have an "age" field, while another does not. The second source might have a "date of birth" field, or it may have no information at all about when a person was born.

3.8.2   An Entity-Resolution Example

We shall examine a real example of how LSH was used to deal with an entity-resolution problem. Company A was engaged by Company B to solicit customers for B. Company B would pay A a yearly fee, as long as the customer maintained their subscription. They later quarreled and disagreed over how many customers A had provided to B. Each had about 1,000,000 records, some of which described the same people; those were the customers A had provided to B. The records had different data fields, but unfortunately none of those fields was "this is a customer that A had provided to B." Thus, the problem was to match records from the two sets to see if a pair represented the same person.

Each record had fields for the name, address, and phone number of the person. However, the values in these fields could differ for many reasons. Not only were there the misspellings and other naming differences mentioned in Section 3.8.1, but there were other opportunities to disagree as well. A customer might give their home phone to A and their cell phone to B. Or they might move, and tell B but not A (because they no longer had need for a relationship with A). Area codes of phones sometimes change.

The strategy for identifying records involved scoring the differences in three fields: name, address, and phone. To create a *score* describing the likelihood that two records, one from A and the other from B, described the same person, 100 points was assigned to each of the three fields, so records with exact matches in all three fields got a score of 300. However, there were deductions for mismatches in each of the three fields. As a first approximation, edit-distance (Section 3.5.5) was used, but the penalty grew quadratically with the distance. Then, certain publicly available tables were used to reduce the penalty in appropriate situations. For example, "Bill" and "William" were treated as if they differed in only one letter, even though their edit-distance is 5.

However, it is not feasible to score all one trillion pairs of records. Thus, a simple LSH was used to focus on likely candidates. Three "hash functions" were used. The first sent records to the same bucket only if they had identical names; the second did the same but for identical addresses, and the third did the same for phone numbers. In practice, there was no hashing; rather the records were sorted by name, so records with identical names would appear consecutively and get scored for overall similarity of the name, address, and phone. Then the records were sorted by address, and those with the same address were scored. Finally, the records were sorted a third time by phone, and records with identical phones were scored.

When Are Record Matches Good Enough?

While every case will be different, it may be of interest to know how the experiment of Section 3.8.3 turned out on the data of Section 3.8.2. For scores down to 185, the value of x was very close to 10; i.e., these scores indicated that the likelihood of the records representing the same person was essentially 1. Note that a score of 185 in this example represents a situation where one field is the same (as would have to be the case, or the records would never even be scored), one field was completely different, and the third field had a small discrepancy. Moreover, for scores as low as 115, the value of x was noticeably less than 45, meaning that some of these pairs did represent the same person. Note that a score of 115 represents a case where one field is the same, but there is only a slight similarity in the other two fields.

This approach missed a record pair that truly represented the same person but none of the three fields matched exactly. Since the goal was to prove in a court of law that the persons were the same, it is unlikely that such a pair would have been accepted by a judge as sufficiently similar anyway.

3.8.3   Validating Record Matches

What remains is to determine how high a score indicates that two records truly represent the same individual. In the example at hand, there was an easy way to make that decision, and the technique can be applied in many similar situations. It was decided to look at the creation-dates for the records at hand, and to assume that 90 days was an absolute maximum delay between the time the service was bought at Company A and registered at B. Thus, a proposed match between two records that were chosen at random, subject only to the constraint that the date on the B-record was between 0 and 90 days after the date on the A-record, would have an average delay of 45 days.

It was found that of the pairs with a perfect 300 score, the average delay was 10 days. If you assume that 300-score pairs are surely correct matches, then you can look at the pool of pairs with any given score s, and compute the average delay of those pairs. Suppose that the average delay is x, and the fraction of true matches among those pairs with score s is f. Then $x = 10f + 45(1 - f)$, or $x = 45 - 35f$. Solving for f, we find that the fraction of the pairs with score s that are truly matches is $(45 - x)/35$.

The same trick can be used whenever:

(1) There is a scoring system used to evaluate the likelihood that two records represent the same entity, and
(2) There is some field, not used in the scoring, from which we can derive a measure that differs, on average, for true pairs and false pairs.

For instance, suppose there were a "height" field recorded by both companies

A and B in our running example. We can compute the average difference in height for pairs of random records, and we can compute the average difference in height for records that have a perfect score (and thus surely represent the same entities). For a given score s, we can evaluate the average height difference of the pairs with that score and estimate the probability of the records representing the same entity. That is, if h_0 is the average height difference for the perfect matches, h_1 is the average height difference for random pairs, and h is the average height difference for pairs of score s, then the fraction of good pairs with score s is $(h_1 - h)/(h_1 - h_0)$.

3.8.4   Matching Fingerprints

When fingerprints are matched by computer, the usual representation is not an image, but a set of locations in which *minutiae* are located. A minutia, in the context of fingerprint descriptions, is a place where something unusual happens, such as two ridges merging or a ridge ending. If we place a grid over a fingerprint, we can represent the fingerprint by the set of grid squares in which minutiae are located.

Ideally, before overlaying the grid, fingerprints are normalized for size and orientation, so that if we took two images of the same finger, we would find minutiae lying in exactly the same grid squares. We shall not consider here the best ways to normalize images. Let us assume that some combination of techniques, including choice of grid size and placing a minutia in several adjacent grid squares if it lies close to the border of the squares enables us to assume that grid squares from two images have a significantly higher probability of agreeing in the presence or absence of a minutia than if they were from images of different fingers.

Thus, fingerprints can be represented by sets of grid squares – those where their minutiae are located – and compared like any sets, using the Jaccard similarity or distance. There are two versions of fingerprint comparison, however.

- The *many–one* problem is the one we typically expect. A fingerprint has been found on a gun, and we want to compare it with all the fingerprints in a large database, to see which one matches.
- The *many–many* version of the problem is to take the entire database, and see if there are any pairs that represent the same individual.

While the many–many version matches the model that we have been following for finding similar items, the same technology can be used to speed up the many-one problem.

3.8.5   A LSH Family for Fingerprint Matching

We could minhash the sets that represent a fingerprint, and use the standard LSH technique from Section 3.4. However, since the sets are chosen from a relatively small set of grid points (perhaps 1000), the need to minhash them into more succinct signatures is not clear. We shall study here another form of locality-sensitive hashing that works well for data of the type we are discussing.

Suppose for an example that the probability of finding a minutia in a random grid square of a random fingerprint is 20%. Also, assume that if two fingerprints come from the same finger, and one has a minutia in a given grid square, then the probability that the other does too is 80%. We can define a locality-sensitive family of hash functions as follows. Each function f in this family $\mathbf{F}$ is defined by three grid squares. Function f says "yes" for two fingerprints if both have minutiae in all three grid squares, and otherwise f says "no." Put another way, we may imagine that f sends to a single bucket all fingerprints that have minutiae in all three of f's grid points, and sends each other fingerprint to a bucket of its own. In what follows, we shall refer to the first of these buckets as "the" bucket for f and ignore the buckets that are required to be singletons.

If we want to solve the many-one problem, we can use many functions from the family $\mathbf{F}$ and precompute their buckets of fingerprints to which they answer "yes." Then, given a new fingerprint that we want to match, we determine which of these buckets it belongs to and compare it with all the fingerprints found in any of those buckets. To solve the many-many problem, we compute the buckets for each of the functions and compare all fingerprints in each of the buckets.

Let us consider how many functions we need to get a reasonable probability of catching a match, without having to compare the fingerprint on the gun with each of the millions of fingerprints in the database. First, the probability that two fingerprints from different fingers would be in the bucket for a function f in $\mathbf{F}$ is $(0.2)^6 = 0.000064$. The reason is that they will both go into the bucket only if they each have a minutia in each of the three grid points associated with f, and the probability of each of those six independent events is 0.2.

Now, consider the probability that two fingerprints from the same finger wind up in the bucket for f. The probability that the first fingerprint has minutiae in each of the three squares belonging to f is $(0.2)^3 = 0.008$. However, if it does, then the probability is $(0.8)^3 = 0.512$ that the other fingerprint will as well. Thus, if the fingerprints are from the same finger, there is a $0.008 \times 0.512 = 0.004096$ probability that they will both be in the bucket of f. That is not much; it is about one in 200. However, if we use many functions from $\mathbf{F}$, but not too many, then we can get a good probability of matching fingerprints from the same finger while not having too many false positives – fingerprints that must be considered but do not match.

EXAMPLE 3.23   For a specific example, let us suppose that we use 1024 functions chosen randomly from $\mathbf{F}$. Next, we shall construct a new family $\mathbf{F}_1$ by performing a 1024-way OR on $\mathbf{F}$. Then the probability that $\mathbf{F}_1$ will put fingerprints from the same finger together in at least one bucket is $1 - (1 - 0.004096)^{1024} = 0.985$. On the other hand, the probability that two fingerprints from different fingers will be placed in the same bucket is $(1 - (1 - 0.000064)^{1024} = 0.063$. That is, we get about 1.5% false negatives and about 6.3% false positives. $\square$

The result of Example 3.23 is not the best we can do. While it offers only a 1.5% chance that we shall fail to identify the fingerprint on the gun, it does force us to look at 6.3% of the entire database. Increasing the number of functions from $\mathbf{F}$ will increase the number of false positives, with only a small benefit of reducing the number of false negatives below 1.5%. On the other hand, we can also use the AND construction, and in so doing, we can greatly reduce the probability of a false positive, while making only a small increase in the false-negative rate. For instance, we could take 2048 functions from $\mathbf{F}$ in two groups of 1024. Construct the buckets for each of the functions. However, given a fingerprint P on the gun:

(1) Find the buckets from the first group in which P belongs, and take the union of these buckets.
(2) Do the same for the second group.
(3) Take the intersection of the two unions.
(4) Compare P only with those fingerprints in the intersection.

Note that we still have to take unions and intersections of large sets of fingerprints, but we compare only a small fraction of those. It is the comparison of fingerprints that takes the bulk of the time; in steps (1) and (2) fingerprints can be represented by their integer indices in the database.

If we use this scheme, the probability of detecting a matching fingerprint is $(0.985)^2 = 0.970$; that is, we get about 3% false negatives. However, the probability of a false positive is $(0.063)^2 = 0.00397$. That is, we only have to examine about 1/250th of the database.

3.8.6 Similar News Articles

Our last case study concerns the problem of organizing a large repository of on-line news articles by grouping together Web pages that were derived from the same basic text. It is common for organizations like The Associated Press to produce a news item and distribute it to many newspapers. Each newspaper puts the story in its on-line edition, but surrounds it by information that is special to that newspaper, such as the name and address of the newspaper, links to related articles, and links to ads. In addition, it is common for the newspaper to modify the article, perhaps by leaving off the last few paragraphs or even deleting text from the middle. As a result, the same news article can appear quite different at the Web sites of different newspapers.

The problem looks very much like the one that was suggested in Section 3.4: find documents whose shingles have a high Jaccard similarity. Note that this problem is different from the problem of finding news articles that tell about the same events. The latter problem requires other techniques, typically examining the set of important words in the documents (a concept we discussed briefly in

Section 1.3.1) and clustering them to group together different articles about the same topic.

However, an interesting variation on the theme of shingling was found to be more effective for data of the type described. The problem is that shingling as we described it in Section 3.2 treats all parts of a document equally. However, we wish to ignore parts of the document, such as ads or the headlines of other articles to which the newspaper added a link, that are not part of the news article. It turns out that there is a noticeable difference between text that appears in prose and text that appears in ads or headlines. Prose has a much greater frequency of stop words, the very frequent words such as "the" or "and." The total number of words that are considered stop words varies with the application, but it is common to use a list of several hundred of the most frequent words.

EXAMPLE 3.24   A typical ad might say simply "Buy Sudzo." On the other hand, a prose version of the same thought that might appear in an article is "I recommend that you buy Sudzo for your laundry." In the latter sentence, it would be normal to treat "I," "that," "you," "for," and "your" as stop words. □

Suppose we define a *shingle* to be a stop word followed by the next two words. Then the ad "Buy Sudzo" from Example 3.24 has no shingles and would not be reflected in the representation of the Web page containing that ad. On the other hand, the sentence from Example 3.24 would be represented by five shingles: "I recommend that," "that you buy," "you buy Sudzo," "for your laundry," and "your laundry x," where x is whatever word follows that sentence.

Suppose we have two Web pages, each of which consists of half news text and half ads or other material that has a low density of stop words. If the news text is the same but the surrounding material is different, then we would expect that a large fraction of the shingles of the two pages would be the same. They might have a Jaccard similarity of 75%. However, if the surrounding material is the same but the news content is different, then the number of common shingles would be small, perhaps 25%. If we were to use the conventional shingling, where shingles are (say) sequences of 10 consecutive characters, we would expect the two documents to share half their shingles (i.e., a Jaccard similarity of $1/3$), regardless of whether it was the news or the surrounding material that they shared.

3.8.7   Exercises for Section 3.8

EXERCISE 3.8.1   Suppose we are trying to perform entity resolution among bibliographic references, and we score pairs of references based on the similarities of their titles, list of authors, and place of publication. Suppose also that all references include a year of publication, and this year is equally likely to be any of the ten most recent years. Further, suppose that we discover that among the pairs of references with a perfect score, there is an average difference in the publication year of $0.1.$[7] Suppose that the pairs of references with a certain score s are found to have an average difference in their publication dates of 2. What is the fraction of pairs with score s that truly represent the same publication? *Note*: Do not make the mistake of assuming the average difference in publication date between random pairs is 5 or 5.5. You need to calculate it exactly, and you have enough information to do so.

EXERCISE 3.8.2 Suppose we use the family $\mathbf{F}$ of functions described in Section 3.8.5, where there is a 20% chance of a minutia in an grid square, an 80% chance of a second copy of a fingerprint having a minutia in a grid square where the first copy does, and each function in $\mathbf{F}$ being formed from three grid squares. In Example 3.23, we constructed family $\mathbf{F}_1$ by using the OR construction on 1024 members of $\mathbf{F}$. Suppose we instead used family $\mathbf{F}_2$ that is a 2048-way OR of members of $\mathbf{F}$.

(a) Compute the rates of false positives and false negatives for $\mathbf{F}_2$.
(b) How do these rates compare with what we get if we organize the same 2048 functions into a 2-way AND of members of $\mathbf{F}_1$, as was discussed at the end of Section 3.8.5?

EXERCISE 3.8.3 Suppose fingerprints have the same statistics outlined in Exercise 3.8.2, but we use a base family of functions $\mathbf{F}'$ defined like $\mathbf{F}$, but using only two randomly chosen grid squares. Construct another set of functions $\mathbf{F}'_1$ from $\mathbf{F}'$ by taking the n-way OR of functions from $\mathbf{F}'$. What, as a function of n, are the false positive and false negative rates for $\mathbf{F}'_1$?

EXERCISE 3.8.4 Suppose we use the functions $\mathbf{F}_1$ from Example 3.23, but we want to solve the many-many problem.

(a) If two fingerprints are from the same finger, what is the probability that they will not be compared (i.e., what is the false negative rate)?
(b) What fraction of the fingerprints from different fingers will be compared (i.e., what is the false positive rate)?

! EXERCISE 3.8.5 Assume we have the set of functions $\mathbf{F}$ as in Exercise 3.8.2, and we construct a new set of functions $\mathbf{F}_3$ by an n-way OR of functions in $\mathbf{F}$. For what value of n is the sum of the false positive and false negative rates minimized?

3.9   Methods for High Degrees of Similarity

LSH-based methods appear most effective when the degree of similarity we accept is relatively low. When we want to find sets that are almost identical, there are other methods that can be faster. Moreover, these methods are exact, in that

---

[7] We might expect the average to be 0, but in practice, errors in publication year do occur.

they find every pair of items with the desired degree of similarity. There are no false negatives, as there can be with LSH.

3.9.1   Finding Identical Items

The extreme case is finding identical items, for example, Web pages that are identical, character-for-character. It is straightforward to compare two documents and tell whether they are identical, but we still must avoid having to compare every pair of documents. Our first thought would be to hash documents based on their first few characters, and compare only those documents that fell into the same bucket. That scheme should work well, unless all the documents begin with the same characters, such as an HTML header.

Our second thought would be to use a hash function that examines the entire document. That would work, and if we use enough buckets, it would be very rare that two documents went into the same bucket, yet were not identical. The downside of this approach is that we must examine every character of every document. If we limit our examination to a small number of characters, then we never have to examine a document that is unique and falls into a bucket of its own.

A better approach is to pick some fixed random positions for all documents, and make the hash function depend only on these. This way, we can avoid a problem where there is a common prefix for all or most documents, yet we need not examine entire documents unless they fall into a bucket with another document. One problem with selecting fixed positions is that if some documents are short, they may not have some of the selected positions. However, if we are looking for highly similar documents, we never need to compare two documents that differ significantly in their length. We exploit this idea in Section 3.9.3.

3.9.2   Representing Sets as Strings

Now, let us focus on the harder problem of finding, in a large collection of sets, all pairs that have a high Jaccard similarity, say at least 0.9. We can represent a set by sorting the elements of the universal set in some fixed order, and representing any set by listing its elements in this order. The list is essentially a string of "characters," where the characters are the elements of the universal set. These strings are unusual, however, in that:

(1) No character appears more than once in a string, and
(2) If two characters appear in two different strings, then they appear in the same order in both strings.

EXAMPLE 3.25   Suppose the universal set consists of the 26 lower-case letters, and we use the normal alphabetical order. Then the set $\{d, a, b\}$ is represented by the string abd. □

In what follows, we shall assume all strings represent sets in the manner just described. Thus, we shall talk about the Jaccard similarity of strings, when strictly speaking we mean the similarity of the sets that the strings represent. Also, we shall talk of the length of a string, as a surrogate for the number of elements in the set that the string represents.

Note that the documents discussed in Section 3.9.1 do not exactly match this model, even though we can see documents as strings. To fit the model, we would shingle the documents, assign an order to the shingles, and represent each document by its list of shingles in the selected order.

3.9.3 Length-Based Filtering

The simplest way to exploit the string representation of Section 3.9.2 is to sort the strings by length. Then, each string s is compared with those strings t that follow s in the list, but are not too long. Suppose the lower bound on Jaccard similarity between two strings is J. For any string x, denote its length by L_x. Note that $L_s \leq L_t$. The intersection of the sets represented by s and t cannot have more than L_s members, while their union has at least L_t members. Thus, the Jaccard similarity of s and t, which we denote $\text{SIM}(s,t)$, is at most L_s/L_t. That is, in order for s and t to require comparison, it must be that $J \leq L_s/L_t$, or equivalently, $L_t \leq L_s/J$.

EXAMPLE 3.26 Suppose that s is a string of length 9, and we are looking for strings with at least 0.9 Jaccard similarity. Then we have only to compare s with strings following it in the length-based sorted order that have length at most $9/0.9 = 10$. That is, we compare s with those strings of length 9 that follow it in order, and all strings of length 10. We have no need to compare s with any other string.

Suppose the length of s were 8 instead. Then s would be compared with following strings of length up to $8/0.9 = 8.89$. That is, a string of length 9 would be too long to have a Jaccard similarity of 0.9 with s, so we only have to compare s with the strings that have length 8 but follow it in the sorted order. □

3.9.4 Prefix Indexing

In addition to length, there are several other features of strings that can be exploited to limit the number of comparisons that must be made to identify all pairs of similar strings. The simplest of these options is to create an index for each symbol; recall a symbol of a string is any one of the elements of the universal set. For each string s, we select a prefix of s consisting of the first p symbols of s. How large p must be depends on L_s and J, the lower bound on Jaccard similarity. We add string s to the index for each of its first p symbols.

In effect, the index for each symbol becomes a bucket of strings that must be compared. We must be certain that any other string t such that $\text{SIM}(s,t) \geq J$ will have at least one symbol in its prefix that also appears in the prefix of s. Suppose not; rather $\text{SIM}(s,t) \geq J$, but t has none of the first p symbols of

---

> ### A Better Ordering for Symbols
>
> Instead of using the obvious order for elements of the universal set, e.g., lexico-graphic order for shingles, we can order symbols rarest first. That is, determine how many times each element appears in the collection of sets, and order them by this count, lowest first. The advantage of doing so is that the symbols in prefixes will tend to be rare. Thus, they will cause that string to be placed in index buckets that have relatively few members. Then, when we need to examine a string for possible matches, we shall find few other strings that are candidates for comparison.

s. Then the highest Jaccard similarity that s and t can have occurs when t is a suffix of s, consisting of everything but the first p symbols of s. The Jaccard similarity of s and t would then be $(L_s - p)/L_s$. To be sure that we do not have to compare s with t, we must be certain that $J > (L_s - p)/L_s$. That is, p must be at least $\lfloor (1-J)L_s \rfloor + 1$. Of course we want p to be as small as possible, so we do not index string s in more buckets than we need to. Thus, we shall hereafter take $p = \lfloor (1-J)L_s \rfloor + 1$ to be the length of the prefix that gets indexed.

EXAMPLE 3.27   Suppose $J = 0.9$. If $L_s = 9$, then $p = \lfloor 0.1 \times 9 \rfloor + 1 = \lfloor 0.9 \rfloor + 1 = 1$. That is, we need to index s under only its first symbol. Any string t that does not have the first symbol of s in a position such that t is indexed by that symbol will have Jaccard similarity with s that is less than 0.9. Suppose s is bcdefghij. Then s is indexed under b only. Suppose t does not begin with b. There are two cases to consider.

(1) If t begins with a, and SIM$(s,t) \geq 0.9$, then t must be abcdefghij. But if that is the case, t will be indexed under both a and b. The reason is that $L_t = 10$, so t will be indexed under the symbols of its prefix of length $\lfloor 0.1 \times 10 \rfloor + 1 = 2$.

(2) If t begins with c or a later letter, then the maximum value of SIM(s,t) occurs when t is cdefghij. But then SIM$(s,t) = 8/9 < 0.9$.

In general, with $J = 0.9$, strings of length up to 9 are indexed by their first symbol, strings of lengths 10–19 are indexed under their first two symbols, strings of length 20–29 are indexed under their first three symbols, and so on.   □

We can use the indexing scheme in two ways, depending on whether we are trying to solve the many-many problem or a many-one problem; recall the distinction was introduced in Section 3.8.4. For the many-one problem, we create the index for the entire database. To query for matches to a new set S, we convert that set to a string s, which we call the *probe* string. Determine the length of the prefix that must be considered, that is, $\lfloor (1-J)L_s \rfloor + 1$. For each symbol appearing in one of the prefix positions of s, we look in the index bucket for that symbol, and we compare s with all the strings appearing in that bucket.

If we want to solve the many-many problem, start with an empty database of strings and indexes. For each set S, we treat S as a new set for the many-one problem. We convert S to a string s, which we treat as a probe string in the many-one problem. However, after we examine an index bucket, we also add s to that bucket, so s will be compared with later strings that could be matches.

3.9.5 Using Position Information

Consider the strings $s = $ `acdefghijk` and $t = $ `bcdefghijk`, and assume $J = 0.9$. Since both strings are of length 10, they are indexed under their first two symbols. Thus, s is indexed under `a` and `c`, while t is indexed under `b` and `c`. Whichever is added last will find the other in the bucket for `c`, and they will be compared. However, since `c` is the second symbol of both, we know there will be two symbols, `a` and `b` in this case, that are in the union of the two sets but not in the intersection. Indeed, even though s and t are identical from `c` to the end, their intersection is 9 symbols and their union is 11; thus $\text{SIM}(s,t) = 9/11$, which is less than 0.9.

If we build our index based not only on the symbol, but on the position of the symbol within the string, we could avoid comparing s and t above. That is, let our index have a bucket for each pair (x, i), containing the strings that have symbol x in position i of their prefix. Given a string s, and assuming J is the minimum desired Jaccard similarity, we look at the prefix of s, that is, the positions 1 through $\lfloor (1 - J)L_s \rfloor + 1$. If the symbol in position i of the prefix is x, add s to the index bucket for (x, i).

Now consider s as a probe string. With what buckets must it be compared? We shall visit the symbols of the prefix of s from the left, and we shall take advantage of the fact that we only need to find a possible matching string t if none of the previous buckets we have examined for matches held t. That is, we only need to find a candidate match once. Thus, if we find that the ith symbol of s is x, then we need look in the bucket (x, j) for certain small values of j.

Figure 3.15 Strings s and t begin with $i - 1$ and $j - 1$ unique symbols, respectively, and then agree beyond that

To compute the upper bound on j, suppose t is a string none of whose first $j - 1$ symbols matched anything in s, but the ith symbol of s is the same as the jth symbol of t. The highest value of $\text{SIM}(s,t)$ occurs if s and t are identical beyond their ith and jth symbols, respectively, as suggested by Fig. 3.15. If that is the case, the size of their intersection is $L_s - i + 1$, since that is the number of symbols of s that could possibly be in t. The size of their union is at least $L_s + j - 1$. That is, s surely contributes L_s symbols to the union, and there are also at least $j - 1$ symbols of t that are not in s. The ratio of the sizes of the intersection and union must be at least J, so we must have:

$$\frac{L_s - i + 1}{L_s + j - 1} \geq J$$

If we isolate j in this inequality, we have $j \leq \big(L_s(1 - J) - i + 1 + J\big)/J$.

EXAMPLE 3.28   Consider the string $s = \texttt{acdefghijk}$ with $J = 0.9$ discussed at the beginning of this section. Suppose s is now a probe string. We already established that we need to consider the first two positions; that is, i can be 1 or 2. Suppose $i = 1$. Then $j \leq (10 \times 0.1 - 1 + 1 + 0.9)/0.9$. That is, we only have to compare the symbol a with strings in the bucket for $(\texttt{a}, j)$ if $j \leq 2.11$. Thus, j can be 1 or 2, but nothing higher.

Now suppose $i = 2$. Then we require $j \leq (10 \times 0.1 - 2 + 1 + 0.9)/0.9$, Or $j \leq 1$. We conclude that we must look in the buckets for $(\texttt{a}, 1)$, $(\texttt{a}, 2)$, and $(\texttt{c}, 1)$, but in no other bucket. In comparison, using the buckets of Section 3.9.4, we would look into the buckets for a and c, which is equivalent to looking to all buckets $(\texttt{a}, j)$ and $(\texttt{c}, j)$ for any j.   □

3.9.6   Using Position and Length in Indexes

When we considered the upper limit on j in the previous section, we assumed that what follows positions i and j were as in Fig. 3.15, where what followed these positions in strings s and t matched exactly. We do not want to build an index that involves every symbol in the strings, because that makes the total work excessive. However, we can add to our index a summary of what follows the positions being indexed. Doing so expands the number of buckets, but not beyond reasonable bounds, and yet enables us to eliminate many candidate matches without comparing entire strings. The idea is to use index buckets corresponding to a symbol, a position, and the *suffix length*, that is, the number of symbols following the position in question.

EXAMPLE 3.29   The string $s = \texttt{acdefghijk}$, with $J = 0.9$, would be indexed in the buckets for $(\texttt{a}, 1, 9)$ and $(\texttt{c}, 2, 8)$. That is, the first position of s has symbol a, and its suffix is of length 9. The second position has symbol c and its suffix is of length 8.   □

Figure 3.15 assumes that the suffixes for position i of s and position j of t have the same length. If not, then we can either get a smaller upper bound on the size of the intersection of s and t (if t is shorter) or a larger lower bound on the size of the union (if t is longer). Suppose s has suffix length p and t has suffix length q.

Case 1: $p \geq q$. Here, the maximum size of the intersection is

$$L_s - i + 1 - (p - q)$$

Since $L_s = i + p$, we can write the above expression for the intersection size as $q + 1$. The minimum size of the union is $L_s + j - 1$, as it was when we did not take suffix length into account. Thus, we require

$$\frac{q + 1}{L_s + j - 1} \geq J$$

whenever $p \geq q$.

Case 2: $p < q$. Here, the maximum size of the intersection is $L_s - i + 1$, as when suffix length was not considered. However, the minimum size of the union is now $L_s + j - 1 + q - p$. If we again use the relationship $L_s = i + p$, we can replace $L_s - p$ by i and get the formula $i + j - 1 + q$ for the size of the union. If the Jaccard similarity is at least J, then

$$\frac{L_s - i + 1}{i + j - 1 + q} \geq J$$

whenever $p < q$.

EXAMPLE 3.30   Let us again consider the string $s = $ acdefghijk, but to make the example show some details, let us choose $J = 0.8$ instead of 0.9. We know that $L_s = 10$. Since $\lfloor (1 - J)L_s \rfloor + 1 = 3$, we must consider prefix positions $i = 1$, 2, and 3 in what follows. As before, let p be the suffix length of s and q the suffix length of t.

First, consider the case $p \geq q$. The additional constraint we have on q and j is $(q + 1)/(9 + j) \geq 0.8$. We can enumerate the pairs of values of j and q for each i between 1 and 3, as follows.

$i = 1$: Here, $p = 9$, so $q \leq 9$. Let us consider the possible values of q:

   $q = 9$: We must have $10/(9 + j) \geq 0.8$. Thus, we can have $j = 1$, $j = 2$, or $j = 3$. Note that for $j = 4$, $10/13 > 0.8$.

   $q = 8$: We must have $9/(9 + j) \geq 0.8$. Thus, we can have $j = 1$ or $j = 2$. For $j = 3$, $9/12 > 0.8$.

   $q = 7$: We must have $8/(9 + j) \geq 0.8$. Only $j = 1$ satisfies this inequality.

   $q = 6$: There are no possible values of j, since $7/(9 + j) > 0.8$ for every positive integer j. The same holds for every smaller value of q.

$i = 2$: Here, $p = 8$, so we require $q \leq 8$. Since the constraint $(q+1)/(9+j) \geq 0.8$ does not depend on i,[8] we can use the analysis from the above case, but exclude the case $q = 9$. Thus, the only possible values of j and q when $i = 2$ are

    (1) $q = 8$; $j = 1$.
    (2) $q = 8$; $j = 2$.
    (3) $q = 7$; $j = 1$.

$i = 3$: Now, $p = 7$ and the constraints are $q \leq 7$ and $(q + 1)/(9 + j) \geq 0.8$. The only option is $q = 7$ and $j = 1$.

Next, we must consider the case $p < q$. The additional constraint is

$$\frac{11 - i}{i + j + q - 1} \geq 0.8$$

Again, consider each possible value of i.

$i = 1$: Then $p = 9$, so we require $q \geq 10$ and $10/(q + j) \geq 0.8$. The possible values of q and j are

    (1) $q = 10$; $j = 1$.
    (2) $q = 10$; $j = 2$.
    (3) $q = 11$; $j = 1$.

$i = 2$: Now, $p = 8$, so we require $q \geq 9$ and $9/(q + j + 1) \geq 0.8$. Since j must be a positive integer, the only solution is $q = 9$ and $j = 1$, a possibility that we already knew about.

$i = 3$: Here, $p = 7$, so we require $q \geq 8$ and $8/(q + j + 2) \geq 0.8$. There are no solutions.

	q	$j = 1$	$j = 2$	$j = 3$
	7	x		
	8	x	x	
$i = 1$	9	x	x	x
	10	x	x	
	11	x		
	7	x		
$i = 2$	8	x	x	
	9	x		
$i = 3$	7	x		

Figure 3.16 The buckets that must be examined to find possible matches for the string $s =$ `acdefghijk` with $J = 0.8$ are marked with an x

When we accumulate the possible combinations of i, j, and q, we see that the set of index buckets in which we must look forms a pyramid. Figure 3.16 shows

---

[8] Note that i does influence the value of p, and through p, puts a limit on q.

the buckets in which we must search. That is, we must look in those buckets (x, j, q) such that the ith symbol of the string s is x, j is the position associated with the bucket and q the suffix length. □

3.9.7 Exercises for Section 3.9

EXERCISE 3.9.1   Suppose our universal set is the lower-case letters, and the order of elements is taken to be the vowels, in alphabetic order, followed by the consonants in reverse alphabetic order. Represent the following sets as strings.

(a) $\{q, w, e, r, t, y\}$.
(b) $\{a, s, d, f, g, h, j, u, i\}$.

EXERCISE 3.9.2   Suppose we filter candidate pairs based only on length, as in Section 3.9.3. If s is a string of length 20, with what strings is s compared when J, the lower bound on Jaccard similarity has the following values: (a) $J = 0.85$; (b) $J = 0.95$; (c) $J = 0.98$?

EXERCISE 3.9.3   Suppose we have a string s of length 15, and we wish to index its prefix as in Section 3.9.4.

(a) How many positions are in the prefix if $J = 0.85$?
(b) How many positions are in the prefix if $J = 0.95$?
! (c) For what range of values of J will s be indexed under its first four symbols, but no more?

EXERCISE 3.9.4   Suppose s is a string of length 12. With what symbol-position pairs will s be compared with if we use the indexing approach of Section 3.9.5, and (a) $J = 0.75$; (b) $J = 0.95$?

! EXERCISE 3.9.5   Suppose we use position information in our index, as in Section 3.9.5. Strings s and t are both chosen at random from a universal set of 100 elements. Assume $J = 0.9$. What is the probability that s and t will be compared if

(a) s and t are both of length 9.
(b) s and t are both of length 10.

EXERCISE 3.9.6   Suppose we use indexes based on both position and suffix length, as in Section 3.9.6. If s is a string of length 20, with what symbol-position-length triples will s be compared with, if (a) $J = 0.8$; (b) $J = 0.9$?

3.10   Summary of Chapter 3

✦ *Jaccard Similarity*: The Jaccard similarity of sets is the ratio of the size of the intersection of the sets to the size of the union. This measure of similarity is suitable for many applications, including textual similarity of documents and similarity of buying habits of customers.

♦ *Shingling*: A k-shingle is any k characters that appear consecutively in a document. If we represent a document by its set of k-shingles, then the Jaccard similarity of the shingle sets measures the textual similarity of documents. Sometimes, it is useful to hash shingles to bit strings of shorter length, and use sets of hash values to represent documents.

♦ *Minhashing*: A minhash function on sets is based on a permutation of the universal set. Given any such permutation, the minhash value for a set is that element of the set that appears first in the permuted order.

♦ *Minhash Signatures*: We may represent sets by picking some list of permutations and computing for each set its minhash signature, which is the sequence of minhash values obtained by applying each permutation on the list to that set. Given two sets, the expected fraction of the permutations that will yield the same minhash value is exactly the Jaccard similarity of the sets.

♦ *Efficient Minhashing*: Since it is not really possible to generate random permutations, it is normal to simulate a permutation by picking a random hash function and taking the minhash value for a set to be the least hash value of any of the set's members. An additional efficiency can be had by restricting the search for the smallest minhash value to only a small subset of the universal set.

♦ *Locality-Sensitive Hashing for Signatures*: This technique allows us to avoid computing the similarity of every pair of sets or their minhash signatures. If we are given signatures for the sets, we may divide them into bands, and only measure the similarity of a pair of sets if they are identical in at least one band. By choosing the size of bands appropriately, we can eliminate from consideration most of the pairs that do not meet our threshold of similarity.

♦ *Distance Measures*: A distance measure is a function on pairs of points in a space that satisfy certain axioms. The distance between two points is 0 if the points are the same, but greater than 0 if the points are different. The distance is symmetric; it does not matter in which order we consider the two points. A distance measure must satisfy the triangle inequality: the distance between two points is never more than the sum of the distances between those points and some third point.

♦ *Euclidean Distance*: The most common notion of distance is the Euclidean distance in an n-dimensional space. This distance, sometimes called the L_2-norm, is the square root of the sum of the squares of the differences between the points in each dimension. Another distance suitable for Euclidean spaces, called Manhattan distance or the L_1-norm is the sum of the magnitudes of the differences between the points in each dimension.

♦ *Jaccard Distance*: One minus the Jaccard similarity is a distance measure, called the Jaccard distance.

♦ *Cosine Distance*: The angle between vectors in a vector space is the cosine distance measure. We can compute the cosine of that angle by taking the dot product of the vectors and dividing by the lengths of the vectors.

◆ *Edit Distance*: This distance measure applies to a space of strings, and is the number of insertions and/or deletions needed to convert one string into the other. The edit distance can also be computed as the sum of the lengths of the strings minus twice the length of the longest common subsequence of the strings.

◆ *Hamming Distance*: This distance measure applies to a space of vectors. The Hamming distance between two vectors is the number of positions in which the vectors differ.

◆ *Generalized Locality-Sensitive Hashing*: We may start with any collection of functions, such as the minhash functions, that can render a decision as to whether or not a pair of items should be candidates for similarity checking. The only constraint on these functions is that they provide a lower bound on the probability of saying "yes" if the distance (according to some distance measure) is below a given limit, and an upper bound on the probability of saying "yes" if the distance is above another given limit. We can then increase the probability of saying "yes" for nearby items and at the same time decrease the probability of saying "yes" for distant items to as great an extent as we wish, by applying an AND construction and an OR construction.

◆ *Random Hyperplanes and LSH for Cosine Distance*: We can get a set of basis functions to start a generalized LSH for the cosine distance measure by identifying each function with a list of randomly chosen vectors. We apply a function to a given vector v by taking the dot product of v with each vector on the list. The result is a sketch consisting of the signs ($+1$ or -1) of the dot products. The fraction of positions in which the sketches of two vectors agree, multiplied by 180, is an estimate of the angle between the two vectors.

◆ *LSH For Euclidean Distance*: A set of basis functions to start LSH for Euclidean distance can be obtained by choosing random lines and projecting points onto those lines. Each line is broken into fixed-length intervals, and the function answers "yes" to a pair of points that fall into the same interval.

◆ *High-Similarity Detection by String Comparison*: An alternative approach to finding similar items, when the threshold of Jaccard similarity is close to 1, avoids using minhashing and LSH. Rather, the universal set is ordered, and sets are represented by strings, consisting their elements in order. The simplest way to avoid comparing all pairs of sets or their strings is to note that highly similar sets will have strings of approximately the same length. If we sort the strings, we can compare each string with only a small number of the immediately following strings.

◆ *Character Indexes*: If we represent sets by strings, and the similarity threshold is close to 1, we can index all strings by their first few characters. The prefix whose characters must be indexed is approximately the length of the string times the maximum Jaccard distance (1 minus the minimum Jaccard similarity).

◆ *Position Indexes*: We can index strings not only on the characters in their prefixes, but on the position of that character within the prefix. We reduce the number of pairs of strings that must be compared, because if two strings share a character that is not in the first position in both strings, then we know that either there are some preceding characters that are in the union but not the intersection, or there is an earlier symbol that appears in both strings.

◆ *Suffix Indexes*: We can also index strings based not only on the characters in their prefixes and the positions of those characters, but on the length of the character's suffix – the number of positions that follow it in the string. This structure further reduces the number of pairs that must be compared, because a common symbol with different suffix lengths implies additional characters that must be in the union but not in the intersection.

3.11   References for Chapter 3

The technique we called shingling is attributed to [11]. The use in the manner we discussed here is from [2].

Minhashing comes from [3]. The improvement that avoids looking at all elements is from [10].

The original works on locality-sensitive hashing were [9] and [7]. [1] is a useful summary of ideas in this field.

[4] introduces the idea of using random-hyperplanes to summarize items in a way that respects the cosine distance. [8] suggests that random hyperplanes plus LSH can be more accurate at detecting similar documents than minhashing plus LSH.

Techniques for summarizing points in a Euclidean space are covered in [6]. [12] presented the shingling technique based on stop words.

The length and prefix-based indexing schemes for high-similarity matching comes from [5]. The technique involving suffix length is from [13].

[1] A. Andoni and P. Indyk, "Near-optimal hashing algorithms for approximate nearest neighbor in high dimensions," *Comm. ACM* **51**:1, pp. 117–122, 2008.

[2] A.Z. Broder, "On the resemblance and containment of documents," *Proc. Compression and Complexity of Sequences*, pp. 21–29, Positano Italy, 1997.

[3] A.Z. Broder, M. Charikar, A.M. Frieze, and M. Mitzenmacher, "Min-wise independent permutations," *ACM Symposium on Theory of Computing*, pp. 327–336, 1998.

[4] M. Charikar, "Similarity estimation techniques from rounding algorithms," *ACM Symposium on Theory of Computing*, pp. 380–388, 2002.

[5] S. Chaudhuri, V. Ganti, and R. Kaushik, "A primitive operator for similarity joins in data cleaning," *Proc. Intl. Conf. on Data Engineering*, 2006.

[6] M. Datar, N. Immorlica, P. Indyk, and V.S. Mirrokni, "Locality-sensitive

hashing scheme based on p-stable distributions," *Symposium on Computational Geometry* pp. 253–262, 2004.

[7] A. Gionis, P. Indyk, and R. Motwani, "Similarity search in high dimensions via hashing," *Proc. Intl. Conf. on Very Large Databases*, pp. 518–529, 1999.

[8] M. Henzinger, "Finding near-duplicate web pages: a large-scale evaluation of algorithms," *Proc. 29th SIGIR Conf.*, pp. 284–291, 2006.

[9] P. Indyk and R. Motwani. "Approximate nearest neighbor: towards removing the curse of dimensionality," *ACM Symposium on Theory of Computing*, pp. 604–613, 1998.

[10] P. Li, A.B. Owen, and C.H. Zhang. "One permutation hashing," *Conf. on Neural Information Processing Systems* 2012, pp. 3122–3130.

[11] U. Manber, "Finding similar files in a large file system," *Proc. USENIX Conference*, pp. 1–10, 1994.

[12] M. Theobald, J. Siddharth, and A. Paepcke, "SpotSigs: robust and efficient near duplicate detection in large web collections," *31st Annual ACM SIGIR Conference*, July, 2008, Singapore.

[13] C. Xiao, W. Wang, X. Lin, and J.X. Yu, "Efficient similarity joins for near duplicate detection," *Proc. WWW Conference*, pp. 131–140, 2008.

4   Mining Data Streams

Most of the algorithms described in this book assume that we are mining a database. That is, all our data is available when and if we want it. In this chapter, we shall make another assumption: data arrives in a stream or streams, and if it is not processed immediately or stored, then it is lost forever. Moreover, we shall assume that the data arrives so rapidly that it is not feasible to store it all in active storage (i.e., in a conventional database), and then interact with it at the time of our choosing.

The algorithms for processing streams each involve summarization of the stream in some way. We shall start by considering how to make a useful sample of a stream and how to filter a stream to eliminate most of the "undesirable" elements. We then show how to estimate the number of different elements in a stream using much less storage than would be required if we listed all the elements we have seen.

Another approach to summarizing a stream is to look at only a fixed-length "window" consisting of the last n elements for some (typically large) n. We then query the window as if it were a relation in a database. If there are many streams and/or n is large, we may not be able to store the entire window for every stream, so we need to summarize even the windows. We address the fundamental problem of maintaining an approximate count on the number of 1s in the window of a bit stream, while using much less space than would be needed to store the entire window itself. This technique generalizes to approximating various kinds of sums.

4.1   The Stream Data Model

Let us begin by discussing the elements of streams and stream processing. We explain the difference between streams and databases and the special problems that arise when dealing with streams. Some typical applications where the stream model applies will be examined.

4.1.1   A Data-Stream-Management System

In analogy to a database-management system, we can view a stream processor as a kind of data-management system, the high-level organization of which is suggested in Fig. 4.1. Any number of streams can enter the system. Each stream

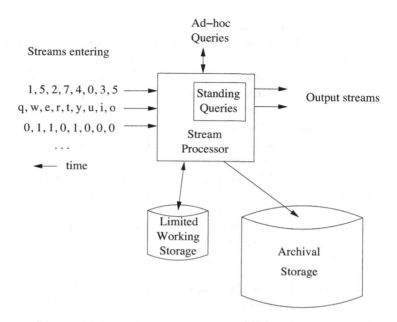

Figure 4.1 A data-stream-management system

can provide elements at its own schedule; they need not have the same data rates or data types, and the time between elements of one stream need not be uniform. The fact that the rate of arrival of stream elements is not under the control of the system distinguishes stream processing from the processing of data that goes on within a database-management system. The latter system controls the rate at which data is read from the disk, and therefore never has to worry about data getting lost as it attempts to execute queries.

Streams may be archived in a large *archival store*, but we assume it is not possible to answer queries from the archival store. It could be examined only under special circumstances using time-consuming retrieval processes. There is also a *working store*, into which summaries or parts of streams may be placed, and which can be used for answering queries. The working store might be disk, or it might be main memory, depending on how fast we need to process queries. But either way, it is of sufficiently limited capacity that it cannot store all the data from all the streams.

4.1.2   Examples of Stream Sources

Before proceeding, let us consider some of the ways in which stream data arises naturally.

Sensor Data

Imagine a temperature sensor bobbing about in the ocean, sending back to a base station a reading of the surface temperature each hour. The data produced by this sensor is a stream of real numbers. It is not a very interesting stream, since the data rate is so low. It would not stress modern technology, and the entire stream could be kept in main memory, essentially forever.

Now, give the sensor a GPS unit, and let it report surface height instead of temperature. The surface height varies quite rapidly compared with temperature, so we might have the sensor send back a reading every tenth of a second. If it sends a 4-byte real number each time, then it produces 3.5 megabytes per day. It will still take some time to fill up main memory, let alone a single disk.

But one sensor might not be that interesting. To learn something about ocean behavior, we might want to deploy a million sensors, each sending back a stream, at the rate of ten per second. A million sensors isn't very many; there would be one for every 150 square miles of ocean. Now we have 3.5 terabytes arriving every day, and we definitely need to think about what can be kept in working storage and what can only be archived.

Image Data

Satellites often send down to earth streams consisting of many terabytes of images per day. Surveillance cameras produce images with lower resolution than satellites, but there can be many of them, each producing a stream of images at intervals like one second. London is said to have six million such cameras, each producing a stream.

Internet and Web Traffic

A switching node in the middle of the Internet receives streams of IP packets from many inputs and routes them to its outputs. Normally, the job of the switch is to transmit data and not to retain it or query it. But there is a tendency to put more capability into the switch, e.g., the ability to detect denial-of-service attacks or the ability to reroute packets based on information about congestion in the network.

Web sites receive streams of various types. For example, Google receives several hundred million search queries per day. Yahoo! accepts billions of "clicks" per day on its various sites. Many interesting things can be learned from these streams. For example, an increase in queries like "sore throat" enables us to track the spread of viruses. A sudden increase in the click rate for a link could indicate some news connected to that page, or it could mean that the link is broken and needs to be repaired.

4.1.3   Stream Queries

There are two ways that queries get asked about streams. We show in Fig. 4.1 a place within the processor where *standing queries* are stored. These queries are, in a sense, permanently executing, and produce outputs at appropriate times.

EXAMPLE 4.1   The stream produced by the ocean-surface-temperature sensor mentioned at the beginning of Section 4.1.2 might have a standing query to output an alert whenever the temperature exceeds 25 degrees centigrade. This query is easily answered, since it depends only on the most recent stream element.

Alternatively, we might have a standing query that, each time a new reading arrives, produces the average of the 24 most recent readings. That query also can be answered easily, if we store the 24 most recent stream elements. When a new stream element arrives, we can drop from the working store the 25th most recent element, since it will never again be needed (unless there is some other standing query that requires it).

Another query we might ask is the maximum temperature ever recorded by that sensor. We can answer this query by retaining a simple summary: the maximum of all stream elements ever seen. It is not necessary to record the entire stream. When a new stream element arrives, we compare it with the stored maximum, and set the maximum to whichever is larger. We can then answer the query by producing the current value of the maximum. Similarly, if we want the average temperature over all time, we have only to record two values: the number of readings ever sent in the stream and the sum of those readings. We can adjust these values easily each time a new reading arrives, and we can produce their quotient as the answer to the query.   □

The other form of query is *ad-hoc*, a question asked once about the current state of a stream or streams. If we do not store all streams in their entirety, as normally we can not, then we cannot expect to answer arbitrary queries about streams. If we have some idea what kind of queries will be asked through the ad-hoc query interface, then we can prepare for them by storing appropriate parts or summaries of streams as in Example 4.1.

If we want the facility to ask a wide variety of ad-hoc queries, a common approach is to store a *sliding window* of each stream in the working store. A sliding window can be the most recent n elements of a stream, for some n, or it can be all the elements that arrived within the last t time units, e.g., one day. If we regard each stream element as a tuple, we can treat the window as a relation and query it with any SQL query. Of course the stream-management system must keep the window fresh, deleting the oldest elements as new ones come in.

EXAMPLE 4.2   Web sites often like to report the number of unique users over the past month. If we think of each login as a stream element, we can maintain a window that is all logins in the most recent month. We must associate the arrival time with each login, so we know when it no longer belongs to the window. If we think of the window as a relation Logins(name, time), then it is simple to get the number of unique users over the past month. The SQL query is:

```
SELECT COUNT(DISTINCT(name))
FROM Logins
WHERE time >= t;
```

Here, t is a constant that represents the time one month before the current time.

Note that we must be able to maintain the entire stream of logins for the past month in working storage. However, for even the largest sites, that data is not more than a few terabytes, and so surely can be stored on disk. □

4.1.4   Issues in Stream Processing

Before proceeding to discuss algorithms, let us consider the constraints under which we work when dealing with streams. First, streams often deliver elements very rapidly. We must process elements in real time, or we lose the opportunity to process them at all, without accessing the archival storage. Thus, it often is important that the stream-processing algorithm is executed in main memory, without access to secondary storage or with only rare accesses to secondary storage. Moreover, even when streams are "slow," as in the sensor-data example of Section 4.1.2, there may be many such streams. Even if each stream by itself can be processed using a small amount of main memory, the requirements of all the streams together can easily exceed the amount of available main memory.

Thus, many problems about streaming data would be easy to solve if we had enough memory, but become rather hard and require the invention of new techniques in order to execute them at a realistic rate on a machine of realistic size. Here are two generalizations about stream algorithms worth bearing in mind as you read through this chapter:

- Often, it is much more efficient to get an approximate answer to our problem than an exact solution.
- As in Chapter 3, a variety of techniques related to hashing turn out to be useful. Generally, these techniques introduce useful randomness into the algorithm's behavior, in order to produce an approximate answer that is very close to the true result.

4.2   Sampling Data in a Stream

As our first example of managing streaming data, we shall look at extracting reliable samples from a stream. As with many stream algorithms, the "trick" involves using hashing in a somewhat unusual way.

4.2.1   A Motivating Example

The general problem we shall address is selecting a subset of a stream so that we can ask queries about the selected subset and have the answers be statistically representative of the stream as a whole. If we know what queries are to be asked, then there are a number of methods that might work, but we are looking for a technique that will allow ad-hoc queries on the sample. We shall look at a particular problem, from which the general idea will emerge.

Our running example is the following. A search engine receives a stream of queries, and it would like to study the behavior of typical users.[1] We assume the stream consists of tuples (user, query, time). Suppose that we want to answer queries such as "What fraction of the typical user's queries were repeated over the past month?" Assume also that we wish to store only 1/10th of the stream elements.

The obvious approach would be to generate a random number, say an integer from 0 to 9, in response to each search query. Store the tuple if and only if the random number is 0. If we do so, each user has, on average, 1/10th of their queries stored. Statistical fluctuations will introduce some noise into the data, but if users issue many queries, the law of large numbers will assure us that most users will have a fraction quite close to 1/10th of their queries stored.

However, this scheme gives us the wrong answer to the query asking for the average number of duplicate queries for a user. Suppose a user has issued s search queries one time in the past month, d search queries twice, and no search queries more than twice. If we have a 1/10th sample, of queries, we shall see in the sample for that user an expected $s/10$ of the search queries issued once. Of the d search queries issued twice, only $d/100$ will appear twice in the sample; that fraction is d times the probability that both occurrences of the query will be in the 1/10th sample. Of the queries that appear twice in the full stream, $18d/100$ will appear exactly once. To see why, note that $18/100$ is the probability that one of the two occurrences will be in the 1/10th of the stream that is selected, while the other is in the 9/10th that is not selected.

The correct answer to the query about the fraction of repeated searches is $d/(s+d)$. However, the answer we shall obtain from the sample is $d/(10s+19d)$. To derive the latter formula, note that $d/100$ appear twice, while $s/10+18d/100$ appear once. Thus, the fraction appearing twice in the sample is $d/100$ divided by $d/100 + s/10 + 18d/100$. This ratio is $d/(10s + 19d)$. For no positive values of s and d is $d/(s + d) = d/(10s + 19d)$.

4.2.2 Obtaining a Representative Sample

The query of Section 4.2.1, like many queries about the statistics of typical users, cannot be answered by taking a sample of each user's search queries. Thus, we must strive to pick 1/10th of the users, and take all their searches for the sample, while taking none of the searches from other users. If we can store a list of all users, and whether or not they are in the sample, then we could do the following. Each time a search query arrives in the stream, we look up the user to see whether or not they are in the sample. If so, we add this search query to the sample, and if not, then not. However, if we have no record of ever having seen this user before, then we generate a random integer between 0 and 9. If the number is 0,

---

[1] While we shall refer to "users," the search engine really receives IP addresses from which the search query was issued. We shall assume that these IP addresses identify unique users, which is approximately true, but not exactly true.

we add this user to our list with value "in," and if the number is other than 0, we add the user with the value "out."

That method works as long as we can afford to keep the list of all users and their in/out decision in main memory, because there isn't time to go to disk for every search that arrives. By using a hash function, one can avoid keeping the list of users. That is, we hash each user name to one of ten buckets, 0 through 9. If the user hashes to bucket 0, then accept this search query for the sample, and if not, then not.

Note we do not actually store the user in the bucket; in fact, there is no data in the buckets at all. Effectively, we use the hash function as a random-number generator, with the important property that, when applied to the same user several times, we always get the same "random" number. That is, without storing the in/out decision for any user, we can reconstruct that decision any time a search query by that user arrives.

More generally, we can obtain a sample consisting of any rational fraction a/b of the users by hashing user names to b buckets, 0 through $b-1$. Add the search query to the sample if the hash value is less than a.

4.2.3   The General Sampling Problem

The running example is typical of the following general problem. Our stream consists of tuples with n components. A subset of the components are the *key* components, on which the selection of the sample will be based. In our running example, there are three components – user, query, and time – of which only *user* is in the key. However, we could also take a sample of queries by making *query* be the key, or even take a sample of user-query pairs by making both those components form the key.

To take a sample of size a/b, we hash the key value for each tuple to b buckets, and accept the tuple for the sample if the hash value is less than a. If the key consists of more than one component, the hash function needs to combine the values for those components to make a single hash-value. The result will be a sample consisting of all tuples with certain key values. The selected key values will be approximately a/b of all the key values appearing in the stream.

4.2.4   Varying the Sample Size

Often, the sample will grow as more of the stream enters the system. In our running example, we retain all the search queries of the selected 1/10th of the users, forever. As time goes on, more searches for the same users will be accumulated, and new users that are selected for the sample will appear in the stream.

If we have a budget for how many tuples from the stream can be stored as the sample, then the fraction of key values must vary, lowering as time goes on. In order to assure that at all times, the sample consists of all tuples from a subset of the key values, we choose a hash function h from key values to a very large number of values $0, 1, \ldots, B - 1$. We maintain a *threshold* t, which initially can be the largest bucket number, $B - 1$. At all times, the sample consists of those tuples whose key K satisfies $h(K) \le t$. New tuples from the stream are added to the sample if and only if they satisfy the same condition.

If the number of stored tuples of the sample exceeds the allotted space, we lower t to $t - 1$ and remove from the sample all those tuples whose key K hashes to t. For efficiency, we can lower t by more than 1, and remove the tuples with several of the highest hash values, whenever we need to throw some key values out of the sample. Further efficiency is obtained by maintaining an index on the hash value, so we can find all those tuples whose keys hash to a particular value quickly.

4.2.5 Exercises for Section 4.2

EXERCISE 4.2.1 Suppose we have a stream of tuples with the schema

Grades(university, courseID, studentID, grade)

Assume universities are unique, but a courseID is unique only within a university (i.e., different universities may have different courses with the same ID, e.g., "CS101") and likewise, studentID's are unique only within a university (different universities may assign the same ID to different students). Suppose we want to answer certain queries approximately from a 1/20th sample of the data. For each of the queries below, indicate how you would construct the sample. That is, tell what the key attributes should be.

(a) For each university, estimate the average number of students in a course.
(b) Estimate the fraction of students who have a GPA of 3.5 or more.
(c) Estimate the fraction of courses where at least half the students got "A."

4.3 Filtering Streams

Another common process on streams is selection, or filtering. We want to accept those tuples in the stream that meet a criterion. Accepted tuples are passed to another process as a stream, while other tuples are dropped. If the selection criterion is a property of the tuple that can be calculated (e.g., the first component is less than 10), then the selection is easy to do. The problem becomes harder when the criterion involves lookup for membership in a set. It is especially hard, when that set is too large to store in main memory. In this section, we shall discuss the technique known as "Bloom filtering" as a way to eliminate most of the tuples that do not meet the criterion.

4.3.1 A Motivating Example

Again let us start with a running example that illustrates the problem and what we can do about it. Suppose we have a set S of one billion allowed email addresses – those that we will allow through because we believe them not to be spam. The stream consists of pairs: an email address and the email itself. Since the typical email address is 20 bytes or more, it is not reasonable to store S in main memory. Thus, we can either use disk accesses to determine whether or not to let through any given stream element, or we can devise a method that requires no more main memory than we have available, and yet will filter most of the undesired stream elements.

Suppose for argument's sake that we have one gigabyte of available main memory. In the technique known as *Bloom filtering*, we use that main memory as a bit array. In this case, we have room for eight billion bits, since one byte equals eight bits. Devise a hash function h from email addresses to eight billion buckets. Hash each member of S to a bit, and set that bit to 1. All other bits of the array remain 0.

Since there are one billion members of S, approximately 1/8th of the bits will be 1. The exact fraction of bits set to 1 will be slightly less than 1/8th, because it is possible that two members of S hash to the same bit. We shall discuss the exact fraction of 1s in Section 4.3.3. When a stream element arrives, we hash its email address. If the bit to which that email address hashes is 1, then we let the email through. But if the email address hashes to a 0, we are certain that the address is not in S, so we can drop this stream element.

Unfortunately, some spam email will get through. Approximately 1/8th of the stream elements whose email address is not in S will happen to hash to a bit whose value is 1 and will be let through. Nevertheless, since the majority of emails are spam (about 80% according to some reports), eliminating 7/8th of the spam is a significant benefit. Moreover, if we want to eliminate every spam, we need only check for membership in S those good and bad emails that get through the filter. Those checks will require the use of secondary memory to access S itself. There are also other options, as we shall see when we study the general Bloom-filtering technique. As a simple example, we could use a cascade of filters, each of which would eliminate 7/8th of the remaining spam.

4.3.2   The Bloom Filter

A *Bloom filter* consists of:

(1) An array of n bits, initially all 0s.
(2) A collection of hash functions $h_1, h_2, \ldots, h_k$. Each hash function maps "key" values to n buckets, corresponding to the n bits of the bit-array.
(3) A set S of m key values.

The purpose of the Bloom filter is to allow through all stream elements whose keys are in S, while rejecting most of the stream elements whose keys are not in S.

To initialize the bit array, begin with all bits 0. Take each key value in S and hash it using each of the k hash functions. Set to 1 each bit that is $h_i(K)$ for some hash function h_i and some key value K in S.

To test a key K that arrives in the stream, check that all of

$$h_1(K), h_2(K), \ldots, h_k(K)$$

are 1s in the bit-array. If all are 1s, then let the stream element through. If one or more of these bits are 0, then K could not be in S, so reject the stream element.

4.3.3 Analysis of Bloom Filtering

If a key value is in S, then the element will surely pass through the Bloom filter. However, if the key value is not in S, it might still pass. We need to understand how to calculate the probability of a *false positive*, as a function of n, the bit-array length, m the number of members of S, and k, the number of hash functions.

The model to use is throwing darts at targets. Suppose we have x targets and y darts. Any dart is equally likely to hit any target. After throwing the darts, how many targets can we expect to be hit at least once? The analysis is similar to the analysis in Section 3.4.2, and goes as follows:

- The probability that a given dart will not hit a given target is $(x-1)/x$.
- The probability that none of the y darts will hit a given target is $\left(\frac{x-1}{x}\right)^y$. We can write this expression as $(1 - \frac{1}{x})^{x(\frac{y}{x})}$.
- Using the approximation $(1 - \epsilon)^{1/\epsilon} = 1/e$ for small ϵ (recall Section 1.3.5), we conclude that the probability that none of the y darts hit a given target is $e^{-y/x}$.

EXAMPLE 4.3 Consider the running example of Section 4.3.1. We can use the above calculation to get the true expected number of 1s in the bit array. Think of each bit as a target, and each member of S as a dart. Then the probability that a given bit will be 1 is the probability that the corresponding target will be hit by one or more darts. Since there are one billion members of S, we have $y = 10^9$ darts. As there are eight billion bits, there are $x = 8 \times 10^9$ targets. Thus, the probability that a given target is not hit is $e^{-y/x} = e^{-1/8}$ and the probability that it *is* hit is $1 - e^{-1/8}$. That quantity is about 0.1175. In Section 4.3.1 we suggested that $1/8 = 0.125$ is a good approximation, which it is, but now we have the exact calculation. □

We can apply the rule to the more general situation, where set S has m members, the array has n bits, and there are k hash functions. The number of targets is $x = n$, and the number of darts is $y = km$. Thus, the probability that a bit remains 0 is $e^{-km/n}$. We want the fraction of 0 bits to be fairly large, or else the probability that a nonmember of S will hash at least once to a 0 becomes too small, and there are too many false positives. For example, we might choose k, the number of hash functions to be n/m or less. Then the probability of a 0 is at least e^{-1} or 37%. In general, the probability of a false positive is the probability of a 1 bit, which is $1 - e^{-km/n}$, raised to the kth power, i.e., $(1 - e^{-km/n})^k$.

EXAMPLE 4.4   In Example 4.3 we found that the fraction of 1s in the array of our running example is 0.1175, and this fraction is also the probability of a false positive. That is, a nonmember of S will pass through the filter if it hashes to a 1, and the probability of it doing so is 0.1175.

Suppose we used the same S and the same array, but used two different hash functions. This situation corresponds to throwing two billion darts at eight billion targets, and the probability that a bit remains 0 is $e^{-1/4}$. In order to be a false positive, a nonmember of S must hash twice to bits that are 1, and this probability is $(1 - e^{-1/4})^2$, or approximately 0.0493. Thus, adding a second hash function for our running example is an improvement, reducing the false-positive rate from 0.1175 to 0.0493.   □

4.3.4   Exercises for Section 4.3

EXERCISE 4.3.1   For the situation of our running example (8 billion bits, 1 billion members of the set S), calculate the false-positive rate if we use three hash functions? What if we use four hash functions?

! EXERCISE 4.3.2   Suppose we have n bits of memory available, and our set S has m members. Instead of using k hash functions, we could divide the n bits into k arrays, and hash once to each array. As a function of n, m, and k, what is the probability of a false positive? How does it compare with using k hash functions into a single array?

!! EXERCISE 4.3.3   As a function of n, the number of bits and m the number of members in the set S, what number of hash functions minimizes the false-positive rate?

4.4   Counting Distinct Elements in a Stream

In this section we look at a third simple kind of processing we might want to do on a stream. As with the previous examples – sampling and filtering – it is somewhat tricky to do what we want in a reasonable amount of main memory, so we use a variety of hashing and a randomized algorithm to get approximately what we want with little space needed per stream.

4.4.1   The Count-Distinct Problem

Suppose stream elements are chosen from some universal set. We would like to know how many different elements have appeared in the stream, counting either from the beginning of the stream or from some known time in the past.

EXAMPLE 4.5   As a useful example of this problem, consider a Web site gathering statistics on how many unique users it has seen in each given month. The universal set is the set of logins for that site, and a stream element is generated each time someone logs in. This measure is appropriate for a site like Amazon, where the typical user logs in with their unique login name.

A similar problem is a Web site like Google that does not require login to issue a search query, and may be able to identify users only by the IP address from which they send the query. There are about 4 billion IP addresses,[2] sequences of four 8-bit bytes will serve as the universal set in this case.   □

The obvious way to solve the problem is to keep in main memory a list of all the elements seen so far in the stream. Keep them in an efficient search structure such as a hash table or search tree, so one can quickly add new elements and check whether or not the element that just arrived on the stream was already seen. As long as the number of distinct elements is not too great, this structure can fit in main memory and there is little problem obtaining an exact answer to the question how many distinct elements appear in the stream.

However, if the number of distinct elements is too great, or if there are too many streams that need to be processed at once (e.g., Yahoo! wants to count the number of unique users viewing each of its pages in a month), then we cannot store the needed data in main memory. There are several options. We could use more machines, each machine handling only one or several of the streams. We could store most of the data structure in secondary memory and batch stream elements so whenever we brought a disk block to main memory there would be many tests and updates to be performed on the data in that block. Or we could use the strategy to be discussed in this section, where we only estimate the number of distinct elements but use much less memory than the number of distinct elements.

4.4.2   The Flajolet–Martin Algorithm

It is possible to estimate the number of distinct elements by hashing the elements of the universal set to a bit-string that is sufficiently long. The length of the bit-string must be sufficient that there are more possible results of the hash function than there are elements of the universal set. For example, 64 bits is sufficient to hash URL's. We shall pick many different hash functions and hash each element of the stream using these hash functions. The important property of a hash function is that when applied to the same element, it always produces the same result. Notice that this property was also essential for the sampling technique of Section 4.2.

The idea behind the Flajolet-Martin Algorithm is that the more different elements we see in the stream, the more different hash-values we shall see. As we see more different hash-values, it becomes more likely that one of these values will be "unusual." The particular unusual property we shall exploit is that the value ends in many 0's, although many other options exist.

Whenever we apply a hash function h to a stream element a, the bit string

---

[2] At least that will be the case until IPv6 becomes the norm.

$h(a)$ will end in some number of 0s, possibly none. Call this number the *tail length* for a and h. Let R be the maximum tail length of any a seen so far in the stream. Then we shall use estimate 2^R for the number of distinct elements seen in the stream.

This estimate makes intuitive sense. The probability that a given stream element a has $h(a)$ ending in at least r 0s is 2^{-r}. Suppose there are m distinct elements in the stream. Then the probability that none of them has tail length at least r is $(1 - 2^{-r})^m$. This sort of expression should be familiar by now. We can rewrite it as $\left((1 - 2^{-r})^{2^r}\right)^{m2^{-r}}$. Assuming r is reasonably large, the inner expression is of the form $(1 - \epsilon)^{1/\epsilon}$, which is approximately $1/e$. Thus, the probability of not finding a stream element with as many as r 0s at the end of its hash value is $e^{-m2^{-r}}$. We can conclude:

(1) If m is much larger than 2^r, then the probability that we shall find a tail of length at least r approaches 1.
(2) If m is much less than 2^r, then the probability of finding a tail length at least r approaches 0.

We conclude from these two points that the proposed estimate of m, which is 2^R (recall R is the largest tail length for any stream element) is unlikely to be either much too high or much too low.

4.4.3 Combining Estimates

Unfortunately, there is a trap regarding the strategy for combining the estimates of m, the number of distinct elements, that we obtain by using many different hash functions. Our first assumption would be that if we take the average of the values 2^R that we get from each hash function, we shall get a value that approaches the true m, the more hash functions we use. However, that is not the case, and the reason has to do with the influence an overestimate has on the average.

Consider a value of r such that 2^r is much larger than m. There is some probability p that we shall discover r to be the largest number of 0s at the end of the hash value for any of the m stream elements. Then the probability of finding $r + 1$ to be the largest number of 0s instead is at least $p/2$. However, if we do increase by 1 the number of 0s at the end of a hash value, the value of 2^R doubles. Consequently, the contribution from each possible large R to the expected value of 2^R grows as R grows, and the expected value of 2^R is actually infinite.[3]

Another way to combine estimates is to take the median of all estimates. The median is not affected by the occasional outsized value of 2^R, so the worry described above for the average should not carry over to the median. Unfortunately,

---

[3] Technically, since the hash value is a bit-string of finite length, there is no contribution to 2^R for Rs that are larger than the length of the hash value. However, this effect is not enough to avoid the conclusion that the expected value of 2^R is much too large.

the median suffers from another defect: it is always a power of 2. Thus, no matter how many hash functions we use, should the correct value of m be between two powers of 2, say 400, then it will be impossible to obtain a close estimate.

There is a solution to the problem, however. We can combine the two methods. First, group the hash functions into small groups, and take their average. Then, take the median of the averages. It is true that an occasional outsized 2^R will bias some of the groups and make them too large. However, taking the median of group averages will reduce the influence of this effect almost to nothing. Moreover, if the groups themselves are large enough, then the averages can be essentially any number, which enables us to approach the true value m as long as we use enough hash functions. In order to guarantee that any possible average can be obtained, groups should be of size at least a small multiple of $\log_2 m$.

4.4.4 Space Requirements

Observe that as we read the stream it is not necessary to store the elements seen. The only thing we need to keep in main memory is one integer per hash function; this integer records the largest tail length seen so far for that hash function and any stream element. If we are processing only one stream, we could use millions of hash functions, which is far more than we need to get a close estimate. Only if we are trying to process many streams at the same time would main memory constrain the number of hash functions we could associate with any one stream. In practice, the time it takes to compute hash values for each stream element would be the more significant limitation on the number of hash functions we use.

4.4.5 Exercises for Section 4.4

EXERCISE 4.4.1 Suppose our stream consists of the integers 3, 1, 4, 1, 5, 9, 2, 6, 5. Our hash functions will all be of the form $h(x) = ax + b \mod 32$ for some a and b. You should treat the result as a 5-bit binary integer. Determine the tail length for each stream element and the resulting estimate of the number of distinct elements if the hash function is:

(a) $h(x) = 2x + 1 \mod 32$.
(b) $h(x) = 3x + 7 \mod 32$.
(c) $h(x) = 4x \mod 32$.

! EXERCISE 4.4.2 Do you see any problems with the choice of hash functions in Exercise 4.4.1? What advice could you give someone who was going to use a hash function of the form $h(x) = ax + b \mod 2^k$?

4.5 Estimating Moments

In this section we consider a generalization of the problem of counting distinct elements in a stream. The problem, called computing "moments," involves the distribution of frequencies of different elements in the stream. We shall define moments of all orders and concentrate on computing second moments, from which the general algorithm for all moments is a simple extension.

4.5.1   Definition of Moments

Suppose a stream consists of elements chosen from a universal set. Assume the universal set is ordered so we can speak of the ith element for any i. Let m_i be the number of occurrences of the ith element for any i. Then the *kth-order moment* (or just kth moment) of the stream is the sum over all i of $(m_i)^k$.

EXAMPLE 4.6   The 0th moment is the sum of 1 for each m_i that is greater than 0.[4] That is, the 0th moment is a count of the number of distinct elements in the stream. We can use the method of Section 4.4 to estimate the 0th moment of a stream.

The 1st moment is the sum of the m_i, which must be the length of the stream. Thus, first moments are especially easy to compute; just count the length of the stream seen so far.

The second moment is the sum of the squares of the m_i. It is sometimes called the *surprise number*, since it measures how uneven the distribution of elements in the stream is. To see the distinction, suppose we have a stream of length 100, in which eleven different elements appear. The most even distribution of these eleven elements would have one appearing 10 times and the other ten appearing 9 times each. In this case, the surprise number is $10^2 + 10 \times 9^2 = 910$. At the other extreme, one of the eleven elements could appear 90 times and the other ten appear 1 time each. Then, the surprise number would be $90^2 + 10 \times 1^2 = 8110$. □

As in Section 4.4, there is no problem computing moments of any order if we can afford to keep in main memory a count for each element that appears in the stream. However, also as in that section, if we cannot afford to use that much memory, then we need to estimate the kth moment by keeping a limited number of values in main memory and computing an estimate from these values. For the case of distinct elements, each of these values were counts of the longest tail produced by a single hash function. We shall see another form of value that is useful for second and higher moments.

4.5.2   The Alon–Matias–Szegedy Algorithm for Second Moments

For now, let us assume that a stream has a particular length n. We shall show how to deal with growing streams in the next section. Suppose we do not have

---

[4] Technically, since m_i could be 0 for some elements in the universal set, we need to make explicit in the definition of "moment" that 0^0 is taken to be 0. For moments 1 and above, the contribution of the m_i that are 0 is surely 0.

enough space to count all the m_i for all the elements of the stream. We can still estimate the second moment of the stream using a limited amount of space; the more space we use, the more accurate the estimate will be. We compute some number of *variables*. For each variable X, we store:

(1) A particular element of the universal set, which we refer to as $X.element$, and

(2) An integer $X.value$, which is the *value* of the variable. To determine the value of a variable X, we choose a position in the stream between 1 and n, uniformly and at random. Set $X.element$ to be the element found there, and initialize $X.value$ to 1. As we read the stream, add 1 to $X.value$ each time we encounter another occurrence of $X.element$.

EXAMPLE 4.7 Suppose the stream is $a, b, c, b, d, a, c, d, a, b, d, c, a, a, b$. Its length is $n = 15$. Since a appears five times, b appears four times, and c and d appear three times each, the second moment for the stream is $5^2 + 4^2 + 3^2 + 3^2 = 59$. Suppose we keep three variables, X_1, X_2, and X_3. Also, assume that at "random" we pick the 3rd, 8th, and 13th positions to define these three variables.

When we reach position 3, we find element c, so we set $X_1.element = c$ and $X_1.value = 1$. Position 4 holds b, so we do not change X_1. Likewise, nothing happens at positions 5 or 6. At position 7, we see c again, so we set $X_1.value = 2$.

At position 8 we find d, and so set $X_2.element = d$ and $X_2.value = 1$. Positions 9 and 10 hold a and b, so they do not affect X_1 or X_2. Position 11 holds d so we set $X_2.value = 2$, and position 12 holds c so we set $X_1.value = 3$. At position 13, we find element a, and so set $X_3.element = a$ and $X_3.value = 1$. Then, at position 14 we see another a and so set $X_3.value = 2$. Position 15, with element b does not affect any of the variables, so we are done, with final values $X_1.value = 3$ and $X_2.value = X_3.value = 2$. □

We can derive an estimate of the second moment from any variable X. This estimate is $n(2X.value - 1)$.

EXAMPLE 4.8 Consider the three variables from Example 4.7. From X_1 we derive the estimate $n(2X_1.value - 1) = 15 \times (2 \times 3 - 1) = 75$. The other two variables, X_2 and X_3, each have value 2 at the end, so their estimates are $15 \times (2 \times 2 - 1) = 45$. Recall that the true value of the second moment for this stream is 59. On the other hand, the average of the three estimates is 55, a fairly close approximation. □

4.5.3 Why the Alon–Matias–Szegedy Algorithm Works

We can prove that the expected value of any variable constructed as in Section 4.5.2 is the second moment of the stream from which it is constructed. Some notation will make the argument easier to follow. Let $e(i)$ be the stream element that appears at position i in the stream, and let $c(i)$ be the number of times element $e(i)$ appears in the stream among positions $i, i + 1, \ldots, n$.

EXAMPLE 4.9   Consider the stream of Example 4.7. $e(6) = a$, since the 6th position holds a. Also, $c(6) = 4$, since a appears at positions 9, 13, and 14, as well as at position 6. Note that a also appears at position 1, but that fact does not contribute to $c(6)$. □

The expected value of $n(2X.value-1)$ is the average over all positions i between 1 and n of $n(2c(i) - 1)$; that is,

$$E\big(n(2X.value - 1)\big) = \frac{1}{n}\sum_{i=1}^{n} n(2c(i) - 1)$$

We can simplify the above by canceling factors $1/n$ and n, to get

$$E\big(n(2X.value - 1)\big) = \sum_{i=1}^{n} \big(2c(i) - 1\big)$$

However, to make sense of the formula, we need to change the order of summation by grouping all those positions that have the same element. For instance, concentrate on some element a that appears m_a times in the stream. The term for the last position in which a appears must be $2 \times 1 - 1 = 1$. The term for the next-to-last position in which a appears is $2 \times 2 - 1 = 3$. The positions with a before that yield terms 5, 7, and so on, up to $2m_a - 1$, which is the term for the first position in which a appears. That is, the formula for the expected value of $2X.value - 1$ can be written:

$$E\big(n(2X.value - 1)\big) = \sum_{a} 1 + 3 + 5 + \cdots + (2m_a - 1)$$

Note that $1+3+5+\cdots+(2m_a-1) = (m_a)^2$. The proof is an easy induction on the number of terms in the sum. Thus, $E\big(n(2X.value - 1)\big) = \sum_{a}(m_a)^2$, which is the definition of the second moment.

4.5.4   Higher-Order Moments

We estimate kth moments, for $k > 2$, in essentially the same way as we estimate second moments. The only thing that changes is the way we derive an estimate from a variable. In Section 4.5.2 we used the formula $n(2v - 1)$ to turn a value v, the count of the number of occurrences of some particular stream element a, into an estimate of the second moment. Then, in Section 4.5.3 we saw why this formula works: the terms $2v - 1$, for $v = 1, 2, \ldots, m$ sum to m^2, where m is the number of times a appears in the stream.

Notice that $2v-1$ is the difference between v^2 and $(v-1)^2$. Suppose we wanted the third moment rather than the second. Then all we have to do is replace $2v-1$ by $v^3 - (v - 1)^3 = 3v^2 - 3v + 1$. Then $\sum_{v=1}^{m} 3v^2 - 3v + 1 = m^3$, so we can use as our estimate of the third moment the formula $n(3v^2 - 3v + 1)$, where $v = X.value$ is the value associated with some variable X. More generally, we can estimate kth moments for any $k \geq 2$ by turning value $v = X.value$ into $n\big(v^k - (v - 1)^k\big)$.

4.5.5 Dealing With Infinite Streams

Technically, the estimate we used for second and higher moments assumes that n, the stream length, is a constant. In practice, n grows with time. That fact, by itself, doesn't cause problems, since we store only the values of variables and multiply some function of that value by n when it is time to estimate the moment. If we count the number of stream elements seen and store this value, which only requires $\log n$ bits, then we have n available whenever we need it.

A more serious problem is that we must be careful how we select the positions for the variables. If we do this selection once and for all, then as the stream gets longer, we are biased in favor of early positions, and the estimate of the moment will be too large. On the other hand, if we wait too long to pick positions, then early in the stream we do not have many variables and so will get an unreliable estimate.

The proper technique is to maintain as many variables as we can store at all times, and to throw some out as the stream grows. The discarded variables are replaced by new ones, in such a way that at all times, the probability of picking any one position for a variable is the same as that of picking any other position. Suppose we have space to store s variables. Then the first s positions of the stream are each picked as the position of one of the s variables.

Inductively, suppose we have seen n stream elements, and the probability of any particular position being the position of a variable is uniform, that is s/n. When the $(n+1)$st element arrives, pick that position with probability $s/(n+1)$. If not picked, then the s variables keep their same positions. However, if the $(n+1)$st position is picked, then throw out one of the current s variables, with equal probability. Replace the one discarded by a new variable whose element is the one at position $n+1$ and whose value is 1.

Surely, the probability that position $n+1$ is selected for a variable is what it should be: $s/(n+1)$. However, the probability of every other position also is $s/(n+1)$, as we can prove by induction on n. By the inductive hypothesis, before the arrival of the $(n+1)$st stream element, this probability was s/n. With probability $1 - s/(n+1)$ the $(n+1)$st position will not be selected, and the probability of each of the first n positions remains s/n. However, with probability $s/(n+1)$, the $(n+1)$st position is picked, and the probability for each of the first n positions is reduced by factor $(s-1)/s$. Considering the two cases, the probability of selecting each of the first n positions is

$$\left(1 - \frac{s}{n+1}\right)\left(\frac{s}{n}\right) + \left(\frac{s}{n+1}\right)\left(\frac{s-1}{s}\right)\left(\frac{s}{n}\right)$$

This expression simplifies to

$$\left(1 - \frac{s}{n+1}\right)\left(\frac{s}{n}\right) + \left(\frac{s-1}{n+1}\right)\left(\frac{s}{n}\right)$$

and then to

$$\left(\left(1 - \frac{s}{n+1}\right) + \left(\frac{s-1}{n+1}\right)\right)\left(\frac{s}{n}\right)$$

> ### A General Stream-Sampling Problem
>
> Notice that the technique described in Section 4.5.5 actually solves a more general problem. It gives us a way to maintain a sample of s stream elements so that at all times, all stream elements are equally likely to be selected for the sample.
>
> As an example of where this technique can be useful, recall that in Section 4.2 we arranged to select all the tuples of a stream having key value in a randomly selected subset. Suppose that, as time goes on, there are too many tuples associated with any one key. We can arrange to limit the number of tuples for any key K to a fixed constant s by using the technique of Section 4.5.5 whenever a new tuple for key K arrives.

which in turn simplifies to

$$\left(\frac{n}{n+1}\right)\left(\frac{s}{n}\right) = \frac{s}{n+1}$$

Thus, we have shown by induction on the stream length n that all positions have equal probability s/n of being chosen as the position of a variable.

4.5.6   Exercises for Section 4.5

EXERCISE 4.5.1   Compute the surprise number (second moment) for the stream 3, 1, 4, 1, 3, 4, 2, 1, 2. What is the third moment of this stream?

! EXERCISE 4.5.2   If a stream has n elements, of which m are distinct, what are the minimum and maximum possible surprise number, as a function of m and n?

EXERCISE 4.5.3   Suppose we are given the stream of Exercise 4.5.1, to which we apply the Alon–Matias–Szegedy Algorithm to estimate the surprise number. For each possible value of i, if X_i is a variable starting position i, what is the value of $X_i.value$?

EXERCISE 4.5.4   Repeat Exercise 4.5.3 if the intent of the variables is to compute third moments. What is the value of each variable at the end? What estimate of the third moment do you get from each variable? How does the average of these estimates compare with the true value of the third moment?

EXERCISE 4.5.5   Prove by induction on m that $1 + 3 + 5 + \cdots + (2m - 1) = m^2$.

EXERCISE 4.5.6   If we wanted to compute fourth moments, how would we convert $X.value$ to an estimate of the fourth moment?

4.6 Counting Ones in a Window

We now turn our attention to counting problems for streams. Suppose we have a window of length N on a binary stream. We want at all times to be able to answer queries of the form "how many 1s are there in the last k bits?" for any $k \le N$. As in previous sections, we focus on the situation where we cannot afford to store the entire window. After showing an approximate algorithm for the binary case, we discuss how this idea can be extended to summing numbers.

4.6.1 The Cost of Exact Counts

To begin, suppose we want to be able to count exactly the number of 1s in the last k bits for any $k \le N$. Then we claim it is necessary to store all N bits of the window, as any representation that used fewer than N bits could not work. In proof, suppose we have a representation that uses fewer than N bits to represent the N bits in the window. Since there are 2^N sequences of N bits, but fewer than 2^N representations, there must be two different bit strings w and x that have the same representation. Since $w \ne x$, they must differ in at least one bit. Let the last $k - 1$ bits of w and x agree, but let them differ on the kth bit from the right end.

EXAMPLE 4.10 If $w = 0101$ and $x = 1010$, then $k = 1$, since scanning from the right, they first disagree at position 1. If $w = 1001$ and $x = 0101$, then $k = 3$, because they first disagree at the third position from the right. □

Suppose the data representing the contents of the window is whatever sequence of bits represents both w and x. Ask the query "how many 1s are in the last k bits?" The query-answering algorithm will produce the same answer, whether the window contains w or x, because the algorithm can only see their representation. But the correct answers are surely different for these two bit-strings. Thus, we have proved that we must use at least N bits to answer queries about the last k bits for any k.

In fact, we need N bits, even if the only query we can ask is "how many 1s are in the entire window of length N?" The argument is similar to that used above. Suppose we use fewer than N bits to represent the window, and therefore we can find w, x, and k as above. It might be that w and x have the same number of 1s, as they did in both cases of Example 4.10. However, if we follow the current window by any $N - k$ bits, we will have a situation where the true window contents resulting from w and x are identical except for the leftmost bit, and therefore, their counts of 1s are unequal. However, since the representations of w and x are the same, the representation of the window must still be the same if we feed the same bit sequence to these representations. Thus, we can force the answer to the query "how many 1s in the window?" to be incorrect for one of the two possible window contents.

4.6.2   The Datar–Gionis–Indyk–Motwani Algorithm

We shall present the simplest case of an algorithm called DGIM. This version of the algorithm uses $O(\log^2 N)$ bits to represent a window of N bits, and allows us to estimate the number of 1s in the window with an error of no more than 50%. Later, we shall discuss an improvement of the method that limits the error to any fraction $\epsilon > 0$, and still uses only $O(\log^2 N)$ bits (although with a constant factor that grows as ϵ shrinks).

To begin, each bit of the stream has a *timestamp*, the position in which it arrives. The first bit has timestamp 1, the second has timestamp 2, and so on. Since we only need to distinguish positions within the window of length N, we shall represent timestamps modulo N, so they can be represented by $\log_2 N$ bits. If we also store the total number of bits ever seen in the stream (i.e., the most recent timestamp) modulo N, then we can determine from a timestamp modulo N where in the current window the bit with that timestamp is.

We divide the window into *buckets*,[5] consisting of:

(1) The timestamp of its right (most recent) end.
(2) The number of 1s in the bucket. This number must be a power of 2, and we refer to the number of 1s as the *size* of the bucket.

To represent a bucket, we need $\log_2 N$ bits to represent the timestamp (modulo N) of its right end. To represent the number of 1s we only need $\log_2 \log_2 N$ bits. The reason is that we know this number i is a power of 2, say 2^j, so we can represent i by coding j in binary. Since j is at most $\log_2 N$, it requires $\log_2 \log_2 N$ bits. Thus, $O(\log N)$ bits suffice to represent a bucket.

There are six rules that must be followed when representing a stream by buckets.

- The right end of a bucket is always a position with a 1.
- Every position with a 1 is in some bucket.
- No position is in more than one bucket.
- There are one or two buckets of any given size, up to some maximum size.
- All sizes must be a power of 2.
- Buckets cannot decrease in size as we move to the left (back in time).

EXAMPLE 4.11   Figure 4.2 shows a bit stream divided into buckets in a way that satisfies the DGIM rules. At the right (most recent) end we see two buckets of size 1. To its left we see one bucket of size 2. Note that this bucket covers four positions, but only two of them are 1. Proceeding left, we see two buckets of size 4, and we suggest that a bucket of size 8 exists further left.

Notice that it is OK for some 0s to lie between buckets. Also, observe from Fig. 4.2 that the buckets do not overlap; there are one or two of each size up to the largest size, and sizes only increase moving left.   □

---

[5] Do not confuse these "buckets" with the "buckets" discussed in connection with hashing.

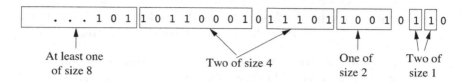

. . 1 0 1 1 0 1 1 0 0 0 1 0 1 1 1 0 1 1 0 0 1 0 1 1 0

At least one
of size 8   Two of size 4   One of
size 2   Two of
size 1

Figure 4.2 A bit-stream divided into buckets following the DGIM rules

In the next sections, we shall explain the following about the DGIM algorithm:

(1) Why the number of buckets representing a window must be small.

(2) How to estimate the number of 1s in the last k bits for any k, with an error no greater than 50%.

(3) How to maintain the DGIM conditions as new bits enter the stream.

4.6.3 Storage Requirements for the DGIM Algorithm

We observed that each bucket can be represented by $O(\log N)$ bits. If the window has length N, then there are no more than N 1s, surely. Suppose the largest bucket is of size 2^j. Then j cannot exceed $\log_2 N$, or else there are more 1s in this bucket than there are 1s in the entire window. Thus, there are at most two buckets of all sizes from $\log_2 N$ down to 1, and no buckets of larger sizes.

We conclude that there are $O(\log N)$ buckets. Since each bucket can be represented in $O(\log N)$ bits, the total space required for all the buckets representing a window of size N is $O(\log^2 N)$.

4.6.4 Query Answering in the DGIM Algorithm

Suppose we are asked how many 1s there are in the last k bits of the window, for some $1 \leq k \leq N$. Find the bucket b with the earliest timestamp that includes at least some of the k most recent bits. Estimate the number of 1s to be the sum of the sizes of all the buckets to the right (more recent) than bucket b, plus half the size of b itself.

EXAMPLE 4.12   Suppose the stream is that of Fig. 4.2, and $k = 10$. Then the query asks for the number of 1s in the ten rightmost bits, which happen to be 0110010110. Let the current timestamp (time of the rightmost bit) be t. Then the two buckets with one 1, having timestamps $t - 1$ and $t - 2$ are completely included in the answer. The bucket of size 2, with timestamp $t - 4$, is also completely included. However, the rightmost bucket of size 4, with timestamp $t - 8$ is only partly included. We know it is the last bucket to contribute to the answer, because the next bucket to its left has timestamp less than $t - 9$ and thus is completely out of the window. On the other hand, we know the buckets to its right are completely inside the range of the query because of the existence of a bucket to their left with timestamp $t - 9$ or greater.

Our estimate of the number of 1s in the last ten positions is thus 6. This number is the two buckets of size 1, the bucket of size 2, and half the bucket of size 4 that is partially within range. Of course the correct answer is 5. □

Suppose the above estimate of the answer to a query involves a bucket b of size 2^j that is partially within the range of the query. Let us consider how far from the correct answer c our estimate could be. There are two cases: the estimate could be larger or smaller than c.

Case 1: The estimate is less than c. In the worst case, all the 1s of b are actually within the range of the query, so the estimate misses half bucket b, or 2^{j-1} 1s. But in this case, c is at least 2^j; in fact it is at least $2^{j+1} - 1$, since there is at least one bucket of each of the sizes $2^{j-1}, 2^{j-2}, \ldots, 1$. We conclude that our estimate is at least 50% of c.

Case 2: The estimate is greater than c. In the worst case, only the rightmost bit of bucket b is within range, and there is only one bucket of each of the sizes smaller than b. Then $c = 1 + 2^{j-1} + 2^{j-2} + \cdots + 1 = 2^j$ and the estimate we give is $2^{j-1} + 2^{j-1} + 2^{j-2} + \cdots + 1 = 2^j + 2^{j-1} - 1$. We see that the estimate is no more than 50% greater than c.

4.6.5 Maintaining the DGIM Conditions

Suppose we have a window of length N properly represented by buckets that satisfy the DGIM conditions. When a new bit comes in, we may need to modify the buckets, so they continue to represent the window and continue to satisfy the DGIM conditions. First, whenever a new bit enters:

- Check the leftmost (earliest) bucket. If its timestamp has now reached the current timestamp minus N, then this bucket no longer has any of its 1s in the window. Therefore, drop it from the list of buckets.

Now, we must consider whether the new bit is 0 or 1. If it is 0, then no further change to the buckets is needed. If the new bit is a 1, however, we may need to make several changes. First:

- Create a new bucket with the current timestamp and size 1.

If there was only one bucket of size 1, then nothing more needs to be done. However, if there are now three buckets of size 1, that is one too many. We fix this problem by combining the leftmost (earliest) two buckets of size 1.

- To combine any two adjacent buckets of the same size, replace them by one bucket of twice the size. The timestamp of the new bucket is the timestamp of the rightmost (later in time) of the two buckets.

Combining two buckets of size 1 may create a third bucket of size 2. If so, we combine the leftmost two buckets of size 2 into a bucket of size 4. That, in turn, may create a third bucket of size 4, and if so we combine the leftmost two into a bucket of size 8. This process may ripple through the bucket sizes, but there are at most $\log_2 N$ different sizes, and the combination of two adjacent buckets of the same size only requires constant time. As a result, any new bit can be processed in $O(\log N)$ time.

EXAMPLE 4.13 Suppose we start with the buckets of Fig. 4.2 and a 1 enters. First, the leftmost bucket evidently has not fallen out of the window, so we do not drop any buckets. We create a new bucket of size 1 with the current timestamp, say t. There are now three buckets of size 1, so we combine the leftmost two. They are replaced with a single bucket of size 2. Its timestamp is $t - 2$, the timestamp of the bucket on the right (i.e., the rightmost bucket that actually appears in Fig. 4.2.

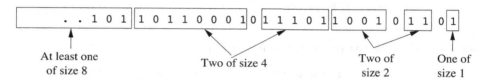

Figure 4.3 Modified buckets after a new 1 arrives in the stream

There are now two buckets of size 2, but that is allowed by the DGIM rules. Thus, the final sequence of buckets after the addition of the 1 is as shown in Fig. 4.3. □

4.6.6 Reducing the Error

Instead of allowing either one or two of each size bucket, suppose we allow either $r - 1$ or r of each of the exponentially growing sizes $1, 2, 4, \ldots$, for some integer $r > 2$. In order to represent any possible number of 1s, we must relax this condition for the buckets of size 1 and buckets of the largest size present; there may be any number, from 1 to r, of buckets of these sizes.

The rule for combining buckets is essentially the same as in Section 4.6.5. If we get $r + 1$ buckets of size 2^j, combine the leftmost two into a bucket of size 2^{j+1}. That may, in turn, cause there to be $r + 1$ buckets of size 2^{j+1}, and if so we continue combining buckets of larger sizes.

The argument used in Section 4.6.4 can also be used here. However, because there are more buckets of smaller sizes, we can get a stronger bound on the error. We saw there that the largest relative error occurs when only one 1 from the leftmost bucket b is within the query range, and we therefore overestimate the true count. Suppose bucket b is of size 2^j. Then the true count is at least $1 + (r - 1)(2^{j-1} + 2^{j-2} + \cdots + 1) = 1 + (r - 1)(2^j - 1)$. The overestimate is

---

Bucket Sizes and Ripple-Carry Adders

There is a pattern to the distribution of bucket sizes as we execute the basic algorithm of Section 4.6.5. Think of two buckets of size 2^j as a "1" in position j and one bucket of size 2^j as a "0" in that position. Then as 1s arrive in the stream, the bucket sizes after each 1 form consecutive binary integers. The occasional long sequences of bucket combinations are analogous to the occasional long rippling of carries as we go from an integer like 101111 to 110000.

$2^{j-1} - 1$. Thus, the fractional error is

$$\frac{2^{j-1} - 1}{1 + (r - 1)(2^j - 1)}$$

No matter what j is, this fraction is upper bounded by $1/(r-1)$. Thus, by picking r sufficiently large, we can limit the error to any desired $\epsilon > 0$.

4.6.7 Extensions to the Counting of Ones

It is natural to ask whether we can extend the technique of this section to handle aggregations more general than counting 1s in a binary stream. An obvious direction to look is to consider streams of integers and ask if we can estimate the sum of the last k integers for any $1 \leq k \leq N$, where N, as usual, is the window size.

It is unlikely that we can use the DGIM approach to streams containing both positive and negative integers. We could have a stream containing both very large positive integers and very large negative integers, but with a sum in the window that is very close to 0. Any imprecision in estimating the values of these large integers would have a huge effect on the estimate of the sum, and so the fractional error could be unbounded.

For example, suppose we broke the stream into buckets as we have done, but represented the bucket by the sum of the integers therein, rather than the count of 1s. If b is the bucket that is partially within the query range, it could be that b has, in its first half, very large negative integers and in its second half, equally large positive integers, with a sum of 0. If we estimate the contribution of b by half its sum, that contribution is essentially 0. But the actual contribution of that part of bucket b that is in the query range could be anything from 0 to the sum of all the positive integers. This difference could be far greater than the actual query answer, and so the estimate would be meaningless.

On the other hand, some other extensions involving integers do work. Suppose that the stream consists of only positive integers in the range 1 to 2^m for some m. We can treat each of the m bits of each integer as if it were a separate stream. We then use the DGIM method to count the 1s in each bit. Suppose the count of the ith bit (assuming bits count from the low-order end, starting at 0) is c_i.

Then the sum of the integers is

$$\sum_{i=0}^{m-1} c_i 2^i$$

If we use the technique of Section 4.6.6 to estimate each c_i with fractional error at most ϵ, then the estimate of the true sum has error at most ϵ. The worst case occurs when all the c_i are overestimated or all are underestimated by the same fraction.

4.6.8 Exercises for Section 4.6

EXERCISE 4.6.1 Suppose the window is as shown in Fig. 4.2. Estimate the number of 1s the the last k positions, for (a) $k = 5$; (b)$k = 15$. In each case, how far off the correct value is your estimate?

! EXERCISE 4.6.2 There are several ways that the bit-stream 1001011011101 could be partitioned into buckets. Find all of them.

EXERCISE 4.6.3 Describe what happens to the buckets if three more 1s enter the window represented by Fig. 4.3. You may assume none of the 1s shown leave the window.

4.7 Decaying Windows

We have assumed that a sliding window held a certain tail of the stream, either the most recent N elements for fixed N, or all the elements that arrived after some time in the past. Sometimes we do not want to make a sharp distinction between recent elements and those in the distant past, but want to weight the recent elements more heavily. In this section, we consider "exponentially decaying windows," and an application where they are quite useful: finding the most common "recent" elements.

4.7.1 The Problem of Most-Common Elements

Suppose we have a stream whose elements are the movie tickets purchased all over the world, with the name of the movie as part of the element. We want to keep a summary of the stream that is the most popular movies "currently." While the notion of "currently" is imprecise, intuitively, we want to discount the popularity of a movie like *Star Wars–Episode 4*, which sold many tickets, but most of these were sold decades ago. On the other hand, a movie that sold n tickets in each of the last 10 weeks is probably more popular than a movie that sold $2n$ tickets last week but nothing in previous weeks.

One solution would be to imagine a bit stream for each movie. The ith bit has value 1 if the ith ticket is for that movie, and 0 otherwise. Pick a window size N, which is the number of most recent tickets that would be considered in evaluating popularity. Then, use the method of Section 4.6 to estimate the number of tickets for each movie, and rank movies by their estimated counts. This technique might work for movies, because there are only thousands of movies, but it would fail if we were instead recording the popularity of items sold at Amazon, or the rate at which different Twitter-users tweet, because there are too many Amazon products and too many tweeters. Further, it only offers approximate answers.

4.7.2   Definition of the Decaying Window

An alternative approach is to redefine the question so that we are not asking for a count of 1s in a window. Rather, let us compute a smooth aggregation of all the 1s ever seen in the stream, with decaying weights, so the further back in the stream, the less weight is given. Formally, let a stream currently consist of the elements $a_1, a_2, \ldots, a_t$, where a_1 is the first element to arrive and a_t is the current element. Let c be a small constant, such as 10^{-6} or 10^{-9}. Define the *exponentially decaying window* for this stream to be the sum

$$\sum_{i=0}^{t-1} a_{t-i}(1-c)^i$$

The effect of this definition is to spread out the weights of the stream elements as far back in time as the stream goes. In contrast, a fixed window with the same sum of the weights, $1/c$, would put equal weight 1 on each of the most recent $1/c$ elements to arrive and weight 0 on all previous elements. The distinction is suggested by Fig. 4.4.

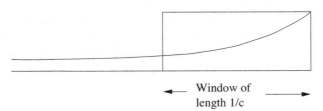

Window of
length 1/c

Figure 4.4 A decaying window and a fixed-length window of equal weight

It is much easier to adjust the sum in an exponentially decaying window than in a sliding window of fixed length. In the sliding window, we have to worry about the element that falls out of the window each time a new element arrives. That forces us to keep the exact elements along with the sum, or to use an approximation scheme such as DGIM. However, when a new element a_{t+1} arrives at the stream input, all we need to do is:

(1) Multiply the current sum by $1 - c$.
(2) Add a_{t+1}.

The reason this method works is that each of the previous elements has now moved one position further from the current element, so its weight is multiplied by $1 - c$. Further, the weight on the current element is $(1 - c)^0 = 1$, so adding a_{t+1} is the correct way to include the new element's contribution.

4.7.3 Finding the Most Popular Elements

Let us return to the problem of finding the most popular movies in a stream of ticket sales.[6] We shall use an exponentially decaying window with a constant c, which you might think of as 10^{-9}. That is, we approximate a sliding window holding the last one billion ticket sales. For each movie, we imagine a separate stream with a 1 each time a ticket for that movie appears in the stream, and a 0 each time a ticket for some other movie arrives. The decaying sum of the 1s measures the current popularity of the movie.

We imagine that the number of possible movies in the stream is huge, so we do not want to record values for the unpopular movies. Therefore, we establish a threshold, say $1/2$, so that if the popularity score for a movie goes below this number, its score is dropped from the counting. For reasons that will become obvious, the threshold must be less than 1, although it can be any number less than 1. When a new ticket arrives on the stream, do the following:

(1) For each movie whose score we are currently maintaining, multiply its score by $(1 - c)$.
(2) Suppose the new ticket is for movie M. If there is currently a score for M, add 1 to that score. If there is no score for M, create one and initialize it to 1.
(3) If any score is below the threshold $1/2$, drop that score.

It may not be obvious that the number of movies whose scores are maintained at any time is limited. However, note that the sum of all scores is $1/c$. There cannot be more than $2/c$ movies with score of $1/2$ or more, or else the sum of the scores would exceed $1/c$. Thus, $2/c$ is a limit on the number of movies being counted at any time. Of course in practice, the ticket sales would be concentrated on only a small number of movies at any time, so the number of actively counted movies would be much less than $2/c$.

4.8 Summary of Chapter 4

◆ *The Stream Data Model*: This model assumes data arrives at a processing engine at a rate that makes it infeasible to store everything in active storage. One strategy to dealing with streams is to maintain summaries of the

---

[6] This example should be taken with a grain of salt, because, as we pointed out, there aren't enough different movies for this technique to be essential. Imagine, if you will, that the number of movies is extremely large, so counting ticket sales of each one separately is not feasible.

streams, sufficient to answer the expected queries about the data. A second approach is to maintain a sliding window of the most recently arrived data.

✦ *Sampling of Streams*: To create a sample of a stream that is usable for a class of queries, we identify a set of key attributes for the stream. By hashing the key of any arriving stream element, we can use the hash value to decide consistently whether all or none of the elements with that key will become part of the sample.

✦ *Bloom Filters*: This technique allows us to filter streams so elements that belong to a particular set are allowed through, while most nonmembers are deleted. We use a large bit array, and several hash functions. Members of the selected set are hashed to buckets, which are bits in the array, and those bits are set to 1. To test a stream element for membership, we hash the element to a set of bits using each of the hash functions, and only accept the element if all these bits are 1.

✦ *Counting Distinct Elements*: To estimate the number of different elements appearing in a stream, we can hash elements to integers, interpreted as binary numbers. 2 raised to the power that is the longest sequence of 0s seen in the hash value of any stream element is an estimate of the number of different elements. By using many hash functions and combining these estimates, first by taking averages within groups, and then taking the median of the averages, we get a reliable estimate.

✦ *Moments of Streams*: The kth moment of a stream is the sum of the kth powers of the counts of each element that appears at least once in the stream. The 0th moment is the number of distinct elements, and the 1st moment is the length of the stream.

✦ *Estimating Second Moments*: A good estimate for the second moment, or surprise number, is obtained by choosing a random position in the stream, taking twice the number of times this element appears in the stream from that position onward, subtracting 1, and multiplying by the length of the stream. Many random variables of this type can be combined like the estimates for counting the number of distinct elements, to produce a reliable estimate of the second moment.

✦ *Estimating Higher Moments*: The technique for second moments works for kth moments as well, as long as we replace the formula $2x - 1$ (where x is the number of times the element appears at or after the selected position) by $x^k - (x - 1)^k$.

✦ *Estimating the Number of 1s in a Window*: We can estimate the number of 1s in a window of 0s and 1s by grouping the 1s into buckets. Each bucket has a number of 1s that is a power of 2; there are one or two buckets of each size, and sizes never decrease as we go back in time. If we record only the position and size of the buckets, we can represent the contents of a window of size N with $O(\log^2 N)$ space.

✦ *Answering Queries About Numbers of 1s*: If we want to know the approximate numbers of 1s in the most recent k elements of a binary stream, we find the earliest bucket B that is at least partially within the last k positions of the window and estimate the number of 1s to be the sum of the sizes of each of the more recent buckets plus half the size of B. This estimate can never be off by more that 50% of the true count of 1s.

✦ *Closer Approximations to the Number of 1s*: By changing the rule for how many buckets of a given size can exist in the representation of a binary window, so that either r or $r - 1$ of a given size may exist, we can assure that the approximation to the true number of 1s is never off by more than $1/r$.

✦ *Exponentially Decaying Windows*: Rather than fixing a window size, we can imagine that the window consists of all the elements that ever arrived in the stream, but with the element that arrived t time units ago weighted by e^{-ct} for some time-constant c. Doing so allows us to maintain certain summaries of an exponentially decaying window easily. For instance, the weighted sum of elements can be recomputed, when a new element arrives, by multiplying the old sum by $1 - c$ and then adding the new element.

✦ *Maintaining Frequent Elements in an Exponentially Decaying Window*: We can imagine that each item is represented by a binary stream, where 0 means the item was not the element arriving at a given time, and 1 means that it was. We can find the elements whose sum of their binary stream is at least $1/2$. When a new element arrives, multiply all recorded sums by 1 minus the time constant, add 1 to the count of the item that just arrived, and delete from the record any item whose sum has fallen below $1/2$.

4.9   References for Chapter 4

Many ideas associated with stream management appear in the "chronicle data model" of [8]. An early survey of research in stream-management systems is [2]. Also, [6] is a recent book on the subject of stream management.

The sampling technique of Section 4.2 is from [7]. The Bloom Filter is generally attributed to [3], although essentially the same technique appeared as "superimposed codes" in [9].

The algorithm for counting distinct elements is essentially that of [5], although the particular method we described appears in [1]. The latter is also the source for the algorithm for calculating the surprise number and higher moments. However, the technique for maintaining a uniformly chosen sample of positions in the stream is called "reservoir sampling" and comes from [10].

The technique for approximately counting 1s in a window is from [4].

[1] N. Alon, Y. Matias, and M. Szegedy, "The space complexity of approximating frequency moments," *28th ACM Symposium on Theory of Computing*, pp. 20–29, 1996.

[2] B. Babcock, S. Babu, M. Datar, R. Motwani, and J. Widom, "Models and

issues in data stream systems," *Symposium on Principles of Database Systems*, pp. 1–16, 2002.

[3] B.H. Bloom, "Space/time trade-offs in hash coding with allowable errors," *Comm. ACM* **13**:7, pp. 422–426, 1970.

[4] M. Datar, A. Gionis, P. Indyk, and R. Motwani, "Maintaining stream statistics over sliding windows," *SIAM J. Computing* **31**, pp. 1794–1813, 2002.

[5] P. Flajolet and G.N. Martin, "Probabilistic counting for database applications," *24th Symposium on Foundations of Computer Science*, pp. 76–82, 1983.

[6] M. Garofalakis, J. Gehrke, and R. Rastogi (editors), *Data Stream Management*, Springer, 2009.

[7] P.B. Gibbons, "Distinct sampling for highly-accurate answers to distinct values queries and event reports," *Intl. Conf. on Very Large Databases*, pp. 541–550, 2001.

[8] H.V. Jagadish, I.S. Mumick, and A. Silberschatz, "View maintenance issues for the chronicle data model," *Proc. ACM Symp. on Principles of Database Systems*, pp. 113–124, 1995.

[9] W.H. Kautz and R.C. Singleton, "Nonadaptive binary superimposed codes," *IEEE Transactions on Information Theory* **10**, pp. 363–377, 1964.

[10] J. Vitter, "Random sampling with a reservoir," *ACM Transactions on Mathematical Software* **11**:1, pp. 37–57, 1985.

5 Link Analysis

One of the biggest changes in our lives in the decade following the turn of the century was the availability of efficient and accurate Web search, through search engines such as Google. While Google was not the first search engine, it was the first able to defeat the spammers who had made search almost useless. Moreover, the innovation provided by Google was a nontrivial technological advance, called "PageRank." We shall begin the chapter by explaining what PageRank is and how it is computed efficiently.

Yet the war between those who want to make the Web useful and those who would exploit it for their own purposes is never over. When PageRank was established as an essential technique for a search engine, spammers invented ways to manipulate the PageRank of a Web page, often called link spam.[1] That development led to the response of TrustRank and other techniques for preventing spammers from attacking PageRank. We shall discuss TrustRank and other approaches to detecting link spam.

Finally, this chapter also covers some variations on PageRank. These techniques include topic-sensitive PageRank (which can also be adapted for combating link spam) and the HITS, or "hubs and authorities" approach to evaluating pages on the Web.

5.1 PageRank

We begin with a portion of the history of search engines, in order to motivate the definition of PageRank,[2] a tool for evaluating the importance of Web pages in a way that it is not easy to fool. We introduce the idea of "random surfers," to explain why PageRank is effective. We then introduce the technique of "taxation" or recycling of random surfers, in order to avoid certain Web structures that present problems for the simple version of PageRank.

---

[1] Link spammers sometimes try to make their unethicality less apparent by referring to what they do as "search-engine optimization."

[2] The term PageRank comes from Larry Page, the inventor of the idea and a founder of Google.

5.1.1   Early Search Engines and Term Spam

There were many search engines before Google. Largely, they worked by crawling the Web and listing the *terms* (words or other strings of characters other than white space) found in each page, in an inverted index. An *inverted index* is a data structure that makes it easy, given a term, to find (pointers to) all the places where that term occurs.

When a *search query* (list of terms) was issued, the pages with those terms were extracted from the inverted index and ranked in a way that reflected the use of the terms within the page. Thus, presence of a term in a header of the page made the page more relevant than would the presence of the term in ordinary text, and large numbers of occurrences of the term would add to the assumed relevance of the page for the search query.

As people began to use search engines to find their way around the Web, unethical people saw the opportunity to fool search engines into leading people to their page. Thus, if you were selling shirts on the Web, all you cared about was that people would see your page, regardless of what they were looking for. Thus, you could add a term like "movie" to your page, and do it thousands of times, so a search engine would think you were a terribly important page about movies. When a user issued a search query with the term "movie," the search engine would list your page first. To prevent the thousands of occurrences of "movie" from appearing on your page, you could give it the same color as the background. And if simply adding "movie" to your page didn't do the trick, then you could go to the search engine, give it the query "movie," and see what page *did* come back as the first choice. Then, copy that page into your own, again using the background color to make it invisible.

Techniques for fooling search engines into believing your page is about something it is not, are called *term spam*. The ability of term spammers to operate so easily rendered early search engines almost useless. To combat term spam, Google introduced two innovations:

(1) PageRank was used to simulate where Web surfers, starting at a random page, would tend to congregate if they followed randomly chosen outlinks from the page at which they were currently located, and this process were allowed to iterate many times. Pages that would have a large number of surfers were considered more "important" than pages that would rarely be visited. Google prefers important pages to unimportant pages when deciding which pages to show first in response to a search query.

(2) The content of a page was judged not only by the terms appearing on that page, but by the terms used in or near the links to that page. Note that while it is easy for a spammer to add false terms to a page they control, they cannot as easily get false terms added to the pages that link to their own page, if they do not control those pages.

These two techniques together make it very hard for the hypothetical shirt

---

> ## Simplified PageRank Doesn't Work
>
> As we shall see, computing PageRank by simulating random surfers is a time-consuming process. One might think that simply counting the number of in-links for each page would be a good approximation to where random surfers would wind up. However, if that is all we did, then the hypothetical shirt-seller could simply create a "spam farm" of a million pages, each of which linked to his shirt page. Then, the shirt page looks very important indeed, and a search engine would be fooled.

vendor to fool Google. While the shirt-seller can still add "movie" to his page, the fact that Google believed what other pages say about him, over what he says about himself would negate the use of false terms. The obvious countermeasure is for the shirt seller to create many pages of his own, and link to his shirt-selling page with a link that says "movie." But those pages would not be given much importance by PageRank, since other pages would not link to them. The shirt-seller could create many links among his own pages, but none of these pages would get much importance according to the PageRank algorithm, and therefore, he still would not be able to fool Google into thinking his page was about movies.

It is reasonable to ask why simulation of random surfers should allow us to approximate the intuitive notion of the "importance" of pages. There are two related motivations that inspired this approach.

- Users of the Web "vote with their feet." They tend to place links to pages they think are good or useful pages to look at, rather than bad or useless pages.
- The behavior of a random surfer indicates which pages users of the Web are likely to visit. Users are more likely to visit useful pages than useless pages.

But regardless of the reason, the PageRank measure has been proved empirically to work, and so we shall study in detail how it is computed.

5.1.2   Definition of PageRank

PageRank is a function that assigns a real number to each page in the Web (or at least to that portion of the Web that has been crawled and its links discovered). The intent is that the higher the PageRank of a page, the more "important" it is. There is not one fixed algorithm for assignment of PageRank, and in fact variations on the basic idea can alter the relative PageRank of any two pages. We begin by defining the basic, idealized PageRank, and follow it by modifications that are necessary for dealing with some real-world problems concerning the structure of the Web.

Think of the Web as a directed graph, where pages are the nodes, and there is an arc from page p_1 to page p_2 if there are one or more links from p_1 to p_2. Figure 5.1 is an example of a tiny version of the Web, where there are only four pages. Page A has links to each of the other three pages; page B has links to A and D only; page C has a link only to A, and page D has links to B and C only.

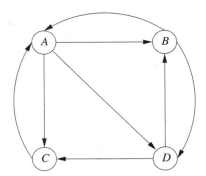

Figure 5.1 A hypothetical example of the Web

Suppose a random surfer starts at page A in Fig. 5.1. There are links to B, C, and D, so this surfer will next be at each of those pages with probability $1/3$, and has zero probability of being at A. A random surfer at B has, at the next step, probability $1/2$ of being at A, $1/2$ of being at D, and 0 of being at B or C.

In general, we can define the *transition matrix of the Web* to describe what happens to random surfers after one step. This matrix M has n rows and columns, if there are n pages. The element m_{ij} in row i and column j has value $1/k$ if page j has k arcs out, and one of them is to page i. Otherwise, $m_{ij} = 0$.

EXAMPLE 5.1   The transition matrix for the Web of Fig. 5.1 is

$$
M = \begin{bmatrix}
0 & 1/2 & 1 & 0 \\
1/3 & 0 & 0 & 1/2 \\
1/3 & 0 & 0 & 1/2 \\
1/3 & 1/2 & 0 & 0
\end{bmatrix}
$$

In this matrix, the order of the pages is the natural one, A, B, C, and D. Thus, the first column expresses the fact, already discussed, that a surfer at A has a $1/3$ probability of next being at each of the other pages. The second column expresses the fact that a surfer at B has a $1/2$ probability of being next at A and the same of being at D. The third column says a surfer at C is certain to be at A next. The last column says a surfer at D has a $1/2$ probability of being next at B and the same at C.   □

The probability distribution for the location of a random surfer can be de-scribed by a column vector whose jth component is the probability that the surfer is at page j. This probability is the (idealized) *PageRank* function.

Suppose we start a random surfer at any of the n pages of the Web with equal probability. Then the initial vector $\mathbf{v}_0$ will have $1/n$ for each component. If M is the transition matrix of the Web, then after one step, the distribution of the surfer will be $M\mathbf{v}_0$, after two steps it will be $M(M\mathbf{v}_0) = M^2\mathbf{v}_0$, and so on. In general, multiplying the initial vector $\mathbf{v}_0$ by M a total of i times will give us the distribution of the surfer after i steps.

To see why multiplying a distribution vector $\mathbf{v}$ by M gives the distribution $\mathbf{x} = M\mathbf{v}$ at the next step, we reason as follows. The probability $\mathbf{x}_i$ that a random surfer will be at node i at the next step, is $\sum_j m_{ij}\mathbf{v}_j$. Here, m_{ij} is the probability that a surfer at node j will move to node i at the next step (often 0 because there is no link from j to i), and $\mathbf{v}_j$ is the probability that the surfer was at node j at the previous step.

This sort of behavior is an example of the ancient theory of *Markov processes*. It is known that the distribution of the surfer approaches a limiting distribution $\mathbf{v}$ that satisfies $\mathbf{v} = M\mathbf{v}$, provided two conditions are met:

(1) The graph is *strongly connected*; that is, it is possible to get from any node to any other node.
(2) There are no *dead ends*: nodes that have no arcs out.

Note that Fig. 5.1 satisfies both these conditions.

The limit is reached when multiplying the distribution by M another time does not change the distribution. In other terms, the limiting $\mathbf{v}$ is an eigenvector of M (an *eigenvector* of a matrix M is a vector $\mathbf{v}$ that satisfies $\mathbf{v} = \lambda M\mathbf{v}$ for some constant *eigenvalue* λ). In fact, because M is *stochastic*, meaning that its columns each add up to 1, $\mathbf{v}$ is the *principal* eigenvector (its associated eigenvalue is the largest of all eigenvalues). Note also that, because M is stochastic, the eigenvalue associated with the principal eigenvector is 1.

The principal eigenvector of M tells us where the surfer is most likely to be after a long time. Recall that the intuition behind PageRank is that the more likely a surfer is to be at a page, the more important the page is. We can compute the principal eigenvector of M by starting with the initial vector $\mathbf{v}_0$ and multiplying by M some number of times, until the vector we get shows little change at each round. In practice, for the Web itself, 50–75 iterations are sufficient to converge to within the error limits of double-precision arithmetic.

EXAMPLE 5.2   Suppose we apply the process described above to the matrix M from Example 5.1. Since there are four nodes, the initial vector $\mathbf{v}_0$ has four components, each $1/4$. The sequence of approximations to the limit that we get by multiplying at each step by M is:

$$
\begin{bmatrix} 1/4 \\ 1/4 \\ 1/4 \\ 1/4 \end{bmatrix},
\begin{bmatrix} 9/24 \\ 5/24 \\ 5/24 \\ 5/24 \end{bmatrix},
\begin{bmatrix} 15/48 \\ 11/48 \\ 11/48 \\ 11/48 \end{bmatrix},
\begin{bmatrix} 11/32 \\ 7/32 \\ 7/32 \\ 7/32 \end{bmatrix}, \ldots,
\begin{bmatrix} 3/9 \\ 2/9 \\ 2/9 \\ 2/9 \end{bmatrix}
$$

Notice that in this example, the probabilities for B, C, and D remain the same. It is easy to see that B and C must always have the same values at any iteration, because their rows in M are identical. To show that their values are

---

Solving Linear Equations

If you look at the 4-node "Web" of Example 5.2, you might think that the way to solve the equation $\mathbf{v} = M\mathbf{v}$ is by Gaussian elimination. Indeed, in that example, we argued what the limit would be essentially by doing so. However, in realistic examples, where there are tens or hundreds of billions of nodes, Gaussian elimination is not feasible. The reason is that Gaussian elimination takes time that is cubic in the number of equations. Thus, the only way to solve equations on this scale is to iterate as we have suggested. Even that iteration is quadratic at each round, but we can speed it up by taking advantage of the fact that the matrix M is very sparse; there are on average about ten links per page, i.e., ten nonzero entries per column.

Moreover, there is another difference between PageRank calculation and solving linear equations. The equation $\mathbf{v} = M\mathbf{v}$ has an infinite number of solutions, since we can take any solution $\mathbf{v}$, multiply its components by any fixed constant c, and get another solution to the same equation. When we include the constraint that the sum of the components is 1, as we have done, then we get a unique solution.

---

also the same as the value for D, an inductive proof works, and we leave it as an exercise. Given that the last three values of the limiting vector must be the same, it is easy to discover the limit of the above sequence. The first row of M tells us that the probability of A must be $3/2$ the other probabilities, so the limit has the probability of A equal to $3/9$, or $1/3$, while the probability for the other three nodes is $2/9$.

This difference in probability is not great. But in the real Web, with billions of nodes of greatly varying importance, the true probability of being at a node like `www.amazon.com` is orders of magnitude greater than the probability of typical nodes. □

5.1.3   Structure of the Web

It would be nice if the Web were strongly connected like Fig. 5.1. However, it is not, in practice. An early study of the Web found it to have the structure shown in Fig. 5.2. There was a large strongly connected component (SCC), but there were several other portions that were almost as large.

(1) The *in-component*, consisting of pages that could reach the SCC by following links, but were not reachable from the SCC.
(2) The *out-component*, consisting of pages reachable from the SCC but unable to reach the SCC.
(3) *Tendrils*, which are of two types. Some tendrils consist of pages reachable from the in-component but not able to reach the in-component. The other tendrils can reach the out-component, but are not reachable from the out-component.

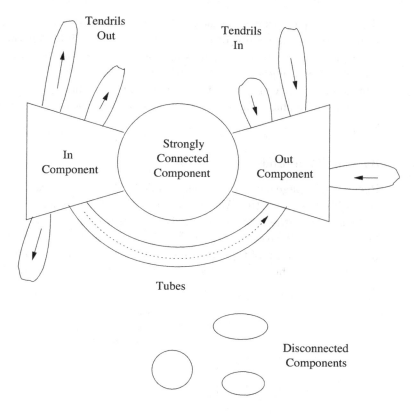

Figure 5.2 The "bowtie" picture of the Web

In addition, there were small numbers of pages found either in

(a) *Tubes*, which are pages reachable from the in-component and able to reach the out-component, but unable to reach the SCC or be reached from the SCC.

(b) Isolated components that are unreachable from the large components (the SCC, in- and out-components) and unable to reach those components.

Several of these structures violate the assumptions needed for the Markov-process iteration to converge to a limit. For example, when a random surfer enters the out-component, they can never leave. As a result, surfers starting in either the SCC or in-component are going to wind up in either the out-component or a tendril off the in-component. Thus, no page in the SCC or in-component winds up with any probability of a surfer being there. If we interpret this probability as measuring the importance of a page, then we conclude falsely that nothing in the SCC or in-component is of any importance.

As a result, PageRank is usually modified to prevent such anomalies. There are really two problems we need to avoid. First is the dead end, a page that has no links out. Surfers reaching such a page disappear, and the result is that in the limit no page that can reach a dead end can have any PageRank at all. The second problem is groups of pages that all have outlinks but they never link to any other pages. These structures are called *spider traps*.[3] Both these problems are solved by a method called "taxation," where we assume a random surfer has a finite probability of leaving the Web at any step, and new surfers are started at each page. We shall illustrate this process as we study each of the two problem cases.

5.1.4   Avoiding Dead Ends

Recall that a page with no link out is called a dead end. If we allow dead ends, the transition matrix of the Web is no longer stochastic, since some of the columns will sum to 0 rather than 1. A matrix whose column sums are at most 1 is called *substochastic*. If we compute $M^i\mathbf{v}$ for increasing powers of a substochastic matrix M, then some or all of the components of the vector go to 0. That is, importance "drains out" of the Web, and we get no information about the relative importance of pages.

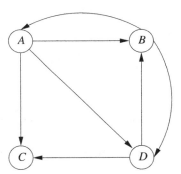

Figure 5.3 C is now a dead end

EXAMPLE 5.3   In Fig. 5.3 we have modified Fig. 5.1 by removing the arc from C to A. Thus, C becomes a dead end. In terms of random surfers, when a surfer reaches C they disappear at the next round. The matrix M that describes Fig. 5.3 is

$$M = \begin{bmatrix} 0 & 1/2 & 0 & 0 \\ 1/3 & 0 & 0 & 1/2 \\ 1/3 & 0 & 0 & 1/2 \\ 1/3 & 1/2 & 0 & 0 \end{bmatrix}$$

Note that it is substochastic, but not stochastic, because the sum of the third column, for C, is 0, not 1. Here is the sequence of vectors that result by starting

---

[3] They are so called because the programs that crawl the Web, recording pages and links, are often referred to as "spiders." Once a spider enters a spider trap, it can never leave.

with the vector with each component $1/4$, and repeatedly multiplying the vector by M:

$$\begin{bmatrix} 1/4 \\ 1/4 \\ 1/4 \\ 1/4 \end{bmatrix},\ \begin{bmatrix} 3/24 \\ 5/24 \\ 5/24 \\ 5/24 \end{bmatrix},\ \begin{bmatrix} 5/48 \\ 7/48 \\ 7/48 \\ 7/48 \end{bmatrix},\ \begin{bmatrix} 21/288 \\ 31/288 \\ 31/288 \\ 31/288 \end{bmatrix},\ \dots,\ \begin{bmatrix} 0 \\ 0 \\ 0 \\ 0 \end{bmatrix}$$

As we see, the probability of a surfer being anywhere goes to 0, as the number of steps increase. □

There are two approaches to dealing with dead ends.

(1) We can drop the dead ends from the graph, and also drop their incoming arcs. Doing so may create more dead ends, which also have to be dropped, recursively. However, eventually we wind up with a strongly-connected component, none of whose nodes are dead ends. In terms of Fig. 5.2, recursive deletion of dead ends will remove parts of the out-component, tendrils, and tubes, but leave the SCC and the in-component, as well as parts of any small isolated components.[4]

(2) We can modify the process by which random surfers are assumed to move about the Web. This method, which we refer to as "taxation," also solves the problem of spider traps, so we shall defer it to Section 5.1.5.

If we use the first approach, recursive deletion of dead ends, then we solve the remaining graph G by whatever means are appropriate, including the taxation method if there might be spider traps in G. Then, we restore the graph, but keep the PageRank values for the nodes of G. Nodes not in G, but with predecessors all in G can have their PageRank computed by summing, over all predecessors p, the PageRank of p divided by the number of successors of p in the full graph. Now there may be other nodes, not in G, that have the PageRank of all their predecessors computed. These may have their own PageRank computed by the same process. Eventually, all nodes outside G will have their PageRank computed; they can surely be computed in the order opposite to that in which they were deleted.

EXAMPLE 5.4   Figure 5.4 is a variation on Fig. 5.3, where we have introduced a successor E for C. But E is a dead end, and when we remove it, and the arc entering from C, we find that C is now a dead end. After removing C, no more nodes can be removed, since each of A, B, and D have arcs leaving. The resulting graph is shown in Fig. 5.5.

---

[4] You might suppose that the entire out-component and all the tendrils will be removed, but remember that they can have within them smaller strongly connected components, including spider traps, which cannot be deleted.

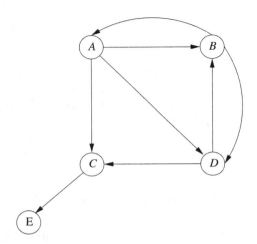

Figure 5.4 A graph with two levels of dead ends

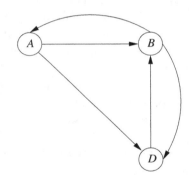

Figure 5.5 The reduced graph with no dead ends

The matrix for the graph of Fig. 5.5 is

$$
M = \begin{bmatrix} 0 & 1/2 & 0 \\ 1/2 & 0 & 1 \\ 1/2 & 1/2 & 0 \end{bmatrix}
$$

The rows and columns correspond to A, B, and D in that order. To get the PageRanks for this matrix, we start with a vector with all components equal to $1/3$, and repeatedly multiply by M. The sequence of vectors we get is

$$
\begin{bmatrix} 1/3 \\ 1/3 \\ 1/3 \end{bmatrix}, \begin{bmatrix} 1/6 \\ 3/6 \\ 2/6 \end{bmatrix}, \begin{bmatrix} 3/12 \\ 5/12 \\ 4/12 \end{bmatrix}, \begin{bmatrix} 5/24 \\ 11/24 \\ 8/24 \end{bmatrix}, \ldots, \begin{bmatrix} 2/9 \\ 4/9 \\ 3/9 \end{bmatrix}
$$

We now know that the PageRank of A is $2/9$, the PageRank of B is $4/9$, and the PageRank of D is $3/9$. We still need to compute PageRanks for C and E, and we do so in the order opposite to that in which they were deleted. Since C was last to be deleted, we know all its predecessors have PageRanks computed. These predecessors are A and D. In Fig. 5.4, A has three successors, so it contributes $1/3$ of its PageRank to C. Page D has two successors in Fig. 5.4, so it contributes half its PageRank to C. Thus, the PageRank of C is $\frac{1}{3} \times \frac{2}{9} + \frac{1}{2} \times \frac{3}{9} = 13/54$.

Now we can compute the PageRank for E. That node has only one predecessor, C, and C has only one successor. Thus, the PageRank of E is the same as that of C. Note that the sums of the PageRanks exceed 1, and they no longer represent the distribution of a random surfer. Yet they do represent decent estimates of the relative importance of the pages. □

5.1.5 Spider Traps and Taxation

As we mentioned, a spider trap is a set of nodes with no dead ends but no arcs out. These structures can appear intentionally or unintentionally on the Web, and they cause the PageRank calculation to place all the PageRank within the spider traps.

EXAMPLE 5.5 Consider Fig. 5.6, which is Fig. 5.1 with the arc out of C changed to point to C itself. That change makes C a simple spider trap of one node. Note that in general spider traps can have many nodes, and as we shall see in Section 5.4, there are spider traps with millions of nodes that spammers construct intentionally.

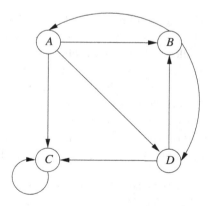

Figure 5.6 A graph with a one-node spider trap

The transition matrix for Fig. 5.6 is

$$
M = \begin{bmatrix}
0 & 1/2 & 0 & 0 \\
1/3 & 0 & 0 & 1/2 \\
1/3 & 0 & 1 & 1/2 \\
1/3 & 1/2 & 0 & 0
\end{bmatrix}
$$

If we perform the usual iteration to compute the PageRank of the nodes, we get

$$
\begin{bmatrix} 1/4 \\ 1/4 \\ 1/4 \\ 1/4 \end{bmatrix}, \begin{bmatrix} 3/24 \\ 5/24 \\ 11/24 \\ 5/24 \end{bmatrix}, \begin{bmatrix} 5/48 \\ 7/48 \\ 29/48 \\ 7/48 \end{bmatrix}, \begin{bmatrix} 21/288 \\ 31/288 \\ 205/288 \\ 31/288 \end{bmatrix}, \ldots, \begin{bmatrix} 0 \\ 0 \\ 1 \\ 0 \end{bmatrix}
$$

As predicted, all the PageRank is at C, since once there a random surfer can never leave. □

To avoid the problem illustrated by Example 5.5, we modify the calculation of PageRank by allowing each random surfer a small probability of *teleporting* to a random page, rather than following an out-link from their current page. The iterative step, where we compute a new vector estimate of PageRanks $\mathbf{v}'$ from the current PageRank estimate $\mathbf{v}$ and the transition matrix M is

$$
\mathbf{v}' = \beta M \mathbf{v} + (1 - \beta)\mathbf{e}/n
$$

where β is a chosen constant, usually in the range 0.8 to 0.9, $\mathbf{e}$ is a vector of all 1s with the appropriate number of components, and n is the number of nodes in the Web graph. The term $\beta M \mathbf{v}$ represents the case where, with probability β, the random surfer decides to follow an out-link from their present page. The term $(1 - \beta)\mathbf{e}/n$ is a vector each of whose components has value $(1 - \beta)/n$ and represents the introduction, with probability $1 - \beta$, of a new random surfer at a random page.

Note that if the graph has no dead ends, then the probability of introducing a new random surfer is exactly equal to the probability that the random surfer will decide *not* to follow a link from their current page. In this case, it is reasonable to visualize the surfer as deciding either to follow a link or teleport to a random page. However, if there are dead ends, then there is a third possibility, which is that the surfer goes nowhere. Since the term $(1 - \beta)\mathbf{e}/n$ does not depend on the sum of the components of the vector $\mathbf{v}$, there will always be some fraction of a surfer operating on the Web. That is, when there are dead ends, the sum of the components of $\mathbf{v}$ may be less than 1, but it will never reach 0.

EXAMPLE 5.6   Let us see how the new approach to computing PageRank fares on the graph of Fig. 5.6. We shall use $\beta = 0.8$ in this example. Thus, the equation for the iteration becomes

$$
\mathbf{v}' = \begin{bmatrix} 0 & 2/5 & 0 & 0 \\ 4/15 & 0 & 0 & 2/5 \\ 4/15 & 0 & 4/5 & 2/5 \\ 4/15 & 2/5 & 0 & 0 \end{bmatrix} \mathbf{v} + \begin{bmatrix} 1/20 \\ 1/20 \\ 1/20 \\ 1/20 \end{bmatrix}
$$

Notice that we have incorporated the factor β into M by multiplying each of its elements by 4/5. The components of the vector $(1 - \beta)\mathbf{e}/n$ are each 1/20, since

$1 - \beta = 1/5$ and $n = 4$. Here are the first few iterations:

$$\begin{bmatrix} 1/4 \\ 1/4 \\ 1/4 \\ 1/4 \end{bmatrix}, \begin{bmatrix} 9/60 \\ 13/60 \\ 25/60 \\ 13/60 \end{bmatrix}, \begin{bmatrix} 41/300 \\ 53/300 \\ 153/300 \\ 53/300 \end{bmatrix}, \begin{bmatrix} 543/4500 \\ 707/4500 \\ 2543/4500 \\ 707/4500 \end{bmatrix}, \cdots, \begin{bmatrix} 15/148 \\ 19/148 \\ 95/148 \\ 19/148 \end{bmatrix}$$

By being a spider trap, C has managed to get more than half of the PageRank for itself. However, the effect has been limited, and each of the nodes gets some of the PageRank. □

5.1.6 Using PageRank in a Search Engine

Having seen how to calculate the PageRank vector for the portion of the Web that a search engine has crawled, we should examine how this information is used. Each search engine has a secret formula that decides the order in which to show pages to the user in response to a search query consisting of one or more search terms (words). Google is said to use over 250 different properties of pages, from which a linear order of pages is decided.

First, in order to be considered for the ranking at all, a page has to have at least one of the search terms in the query. Normally, the weighting of properties is such that unless all the search terms are present, a page has very little chance of being in the top ten that are normally shown first to the user. Among the qualified pages, a score is computed for each, and an important component of this score is the PageRank of the page. Other components include the presence or absence of search terms in prominent places, such as headers or the links to the page itself.

5.1.7 Exercises for Section 5.1

EXERCISE 5.1.1 Compute the PageRank of each page in Fig. 5.7, assuming no taxation.

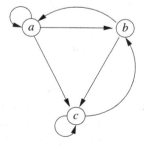

Figure 5.7 An example graph for exercises

EXERCISE 5.1.2   Compute the PageRank of each page in Fig. 5.7, assuming $\beta = 0.8$.

! EXERCISE 5.1.3   Suppose the Web consists of a *clique* (set of nodes with all possible arcs from one to another) of n nodes and a single additional node that is the successor of each of the n nodes in the clique. Figure 5.8 shows this graph for the case $n = 4$. Determine the PageRank of each page, as a function of n and β.

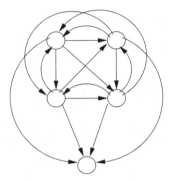

Figure 5.8 Example of graphs discussed in Exercise 5.1.3

!! EXERCISE 5.1.4   Construct, for any integer n, a Web such that, depending on β, any of the n nodes can have the highest PageRank among those n. It is allowed for there to be other nodes in the Web besides these n.

! EXERCISE 5.1.5   Show by induction on n that if the second, third, and fourth components of a vector $\mathbf{v}$ are equal, and M is the transition matrix of Example 5.1, then the second, third, and fourth components are also equal in $M^n\mathbf{v}$ for any $n \geq 0$.

Figure 5.9 A chain of dead ends

EXERCISE 5.1.6   Suppose we recursively eliminate dead ends from the graph, solve the remaining graph, and estimate the PageRank for the dead-end pages as described in Section 5.1.4. Suppose the graph is a chain of dead ends, headed by a node with a self-loop, as suggested in Fig. 5.9. What would be the PageRank assigned to each of the nodes?

EXERCISE 5.1.7   Repeat Exercise 5.1.6 for the tree of dead ends suggested by

Fig. 5.10. That is, there is a single node with a self-loop, which is also the root of a complete binary tree of n levels.

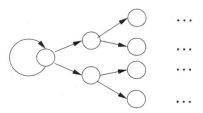

Figure 5.10 A tree of dead ends

5.2   Efficient Computation of PageRank

To compute the PageRank for a large graph representing the Web, we have to perform a matrix–vector multiplication on the order of 50 times, until the vector is close to unchanged at one iteration. To a first approximation, the MapReduce method given in Section 2.3.1 is suitable. However, we must deal with two issues:

(1) The transition matrix of the Web M is very sparse. Thus, representing it by all its elements is highly inefficient. Rather, we want to represent the matrix by its nonzero elements.
(2) We may not be using MapReduce, or for efficiency reasons we may wish to use a combiner (see Section 2.2.4) with the Map tasks to reduce the amount of data that must be passed from Map tasks to Reduce tasks. In this case, the striping approach discussed in Section 2.3.1 is not sufficient to avoid heavy use of disk (thrashing).

We discuss the solution to these two problems in this section.

5.2.1   Representing Transition Matrices

The transition matrix is very sparse, since the average Web page has about 10 out-links. If, say, we are analyzing a graph of ten billion pages, then only one in a billion entries is not 0. The proper way to represent any sparse matrix is to list the locations of the nonzero entries and their values. If we use 4-byte integers for coordinates of an element and an 8-byte double-precision number for the value, then we need 16 bytes per nonzero entry. That is, the space needed is linear in the number of nonzero entries, rather than quadratic in the side of the matrix.

However, for a transition matrix of the Web, there is one further compression that we can do. If we list the nonzero entries by column, then we know what each nonzero entry is; it is 1 divided by the out-degree of the page. We can thus represent a column by one integer for the out-degree, and one integer per nonzero entry in that column, giving the row number where that entry is located. Thus, we need slightly more than 4 bytes per nonzero entry to represent a transition matrix.

EXAMPLE 5.7   Let us reprise the example Web graph from Fig. 5.1, whose transition matrix is

$$M = \begin{bmatrix} 0 & 1/2 & 1 & 0 \\ 1/3 & 0 & 0 & 1/2 \\ 1/3 & 0 & 0 & 1/2 \\ 1/3 & 1/2 & 0 & 0 \end{bmatrix}$$

Recall that the rows and columns represent nodes A, B, C, and D, in that order. In Fig. 5.11 is a compact representation of this matrix.[5]

Source	Degree	Destinations
A	3	B, C, D
B	2	A, D
C	1	A
D	2	B, C

Figure 5.11 Represent a transition matrix by the out-degree of each node and the list of its successors

For instance, the entry for A has degree 3 and a list of three successors. From that row of Fig. 5.11 we can deduce that the column for A in matrix M has 0 in the row for A (since it is not on the list of destinations) and 1/3 in the rows for B, C, and D. We know that the value is 1/3 because the degree column in Fig. 5.11 tells us there are three links out of A.   □

5.2.2   PageRank Iteration Using MapReduce

One iteration of the PageRank algorithm involves taking an estimated PageRank vector $\mathbf{v}$ and computing the next estimate $\mathbf{v}'$ by

$$\mathbf{v}' = \beta M \mathbf{v} + (1 - \beta)\mathbf{e}/n$$

Recall β is a constant slightly less than 1, $\mathbf{e}$ is a vector of all 1s, and n is the number of nodes in the graph that transition matrix M represents.

If n is small enough that each Map task can store the full vector $\mathbf{v}$ in main memory and also have room in main memory for the result vector $\mathbf{v}'$, then there is little more here than a matrix–vector multiplication. The additional steps are

---

[5] Because M is not sparse, this representation is not very useful for M. However, the example illustrates the process of representing matrices in general, and the sparser the matrix is, the more this representation will save.

to multiply each component of $M\mathbf{v}$ by constant β and to add $(1-\beta)/n$ to each component.

However, it is likely, given the size of the Web today, that $\mathbf{v}$ is much too large to fit in main memory. As we discussed in Section 2.3.1, the method of striping, where we break M into vertical stripes (see Fig. 2.4) and break $\mathbf{v}$ into corresponding horizontal stripes, will allow us to execute the MapReduce process efficiently, with no more of $\mathbf{v}$ at any one Map task than can conveniently fit in main memory.

5.2.3 Use of Combiners to Consolidate the Result Vector

There are two reasons the method of Section 5.2.2 might not be adequate.

(1) We might wish to add terms for $\mathbf{v}'_i$, the ith component of the result vector $\mathbf{v}$, at the Map tasks. This improvement is the same as using a combiner, since the Reduce function simply adds terms with a common key. Recall that for a MapReduce implementation of matrix–vector multiplication, the key is the value of i for which a term $m_{ij}\mathbf{v}_j$ is intended.
(2) We might not be using MapReduce at all, but rather executing the iteration step at a single machine or a collection of machines.

We shall assume that we are trying to implement a combiner in conjunction with a Map task; the second case uses essentially the same idea.

Suppose that we are using the stripe method to partition a matrix and vector that do not fit in main memory. Then a vertical stripe from the matrix M and a horizontal stripe from the vector $\mathbf{v}$ will contribute to all components of the result vector $\mathbf{v}'$. Since that vector is the same length as $\mathbf{v}$, it will not fit in main memory either. Moreover, as M is stored column-by-column for efficiency reasons, a column can affect any of the components of $\mathbf{v}'$. As a result, it is unlikely that when we need to add a term to some component $\mathbf{v}'_i$, that component will already be in main memory. Thus, most terms will require that a page be brought into main memory to add it to the proper component. That situation, called *thrashing*, takes orders of magnitude too much time to be feasible.

An alternative strategy is based on partitioning the matrix into k^2 blocks, while the vectors are still partitioned into k stripes. A picture, showing the division for $k=4$, is in Fig. 5.12. Note that we have not shown the multiplication of the matrix by β or the addition of $(1-\beta)\mathbf{e}/n$, because these steps are straightforward, regardless of the strategy we use.

In this method, we use k^2 Map tasks. Each task gets one square of the matrix M, say M_{ij}, and one stripe of the vector $\mathbf{v}$, which must be $\mathbf{v}_j$. Notice that each stripe of the vector is sent to k different Map tasks; $\mathbf{v}_j$ is sent to the task handling M_{ij} for each of the k possible values of i. Thus, $\mathbf{v}$ is transmitted over the network k times. However, each piece of the matrix is sent only once. Since the size of the matrix, properly encoded as described in Section 5.2.1, can be expected to be several times the size of the vector, the transmission cost is not too much greater

Figure 5.12 Partitioning a matrix into square blocks

than the minimum possible. And because we are doing considerable combining at the Map tasks, we save as data is passed from the Map tasks to the Reduce tasks.

The advantage of this approach is that we can keep both the jth stripe of $\mathbf{v}$ and the ith stripe of $\mathbf{v}'$ in main memory as we process M_{ij}. Note that all terms generated from M_{ij} and $\mathbf{v}_j$ contribute to $\mathbf{v}'_i$ and no other stripe of $\mathbf{v}'$.

5.2.4 Representing Blocks of the Transition Matrix

Since we are representing transition matrices in the special way described in Section 5.2.1, we need to consider how the blocks of Fig. 5.12 are represented. Unfortunately, the space required for a column of blocks (a "stripe" as we called it earlier) is greater than the space needed for the stripe as a whole, but not too much greater.

For each block, we need data about all those columns that have at least one nonzero entry within the block. If k, the number of stripes in each dimension, is large, then most columns will have nothing in most blocks of its stripe. For a given block, we not only have to list those rows that have a nonzero entry for that column, but we must repeat the out-degree for the node represented by the column. Consequently, it is possible that the out-degree will be repeated as many times as the out-degree itself. That observation bounds from above the space needed to store the blocks of a stripe at twice the space needed to store the stripe as a whole.

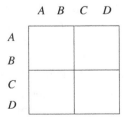

Figure 5.13 A four-node graph is divided into four 2×2 blocks

EXAMPLE 5.8   Let us suppose the matrix from Example 5.7 is partitioned into blocks, with $k = 2$. That is, the upper-left quadrant represents links from A or B to A or B, the upper-right quadrant represents links from C or D to A or B, and so on. It turns out that in this small example, the only entry that we can avoid is the entry for C in M_{22}, because C has no arcs to either C or D. The tables representing each of the four blocks are shown in Fig. 5.14.

Source	Degree	Destinations
A	3	B
B	2	A

(a) Representation of M_{11} connecting A and B to A and B

Source	Degree	Destinations
C	1	A
D	2	B

(b) Representation of M_{12} connecting C and D to A and B

Source	Degree	Destinations
A	3	C, D
B	2	D

(c) Representation of M_{21} connecting A and B to C and D

Source	Degree	Destinations
D	2	C

(d) Representation of M_{22} connecting C and D to C and D

Figure 5.14 Sparse representation of the blocks of a matrix

If we examine Fig. 5.14(a), we see the representation of the upper-left quadrant. Notice that the degrees for A and B are the same as in Fig. 5.11, because we need to know the entire number of successors, not the number of successors within the relevant block. However, each successor of A or B is represented in Fig. 5.14(a) or Fig. 5.14(c), but not both. Notice also that in Fig. 5.14(d), there is no entry for C, because there are no successors of C within the lower half of the matrix (rows C and D).   □

5.2.5   Other Efficient Approaches to PageRank Iteration

The algorithm discussed in Section 5.2.3 is not the only option. We shall discuss several other approaches that use fewer processors. These algorithms share with the algorithm of Section 5.2.3 the good property that the matrix M is read only once, although the vector $\mathbf{v}$ is read k times, where the parameter k is chosen so that $1/k$th of the vectors $\mathbf{v}$ and $\mathbf{v}'$ can be held in main memory. Recall that the algorithm of Section 5.2.3 uses k^2 processors, assuming all Map tasks are executed in parallel at different processors.

We can assign all the blocks in one row of blocks to a single Map task, and thus reduce the number of Map tasks to k. For instance, in Fig. 5.12, M_{11}, M_{12}, M_{13}, and M_{14} would be assigned to a single Map task. If we represent the blocks as in Fig. 5.14, we can read the blocks in a row of blocks one-at-a-time, so the matrix does not consume a significant amount of main-memory. At the same time that we read M_{ij}, we must read the vector stripe $\mathbf{v}_j$. As a result, each of the k Map tasks reads the entire vector $\mathbf{v}$, along with $1/k$th of the matrix.

The work reading M and $\mathbf{v}$ is thus the same as for the algorithm of Section 5.2.3, but the advantage of this approach is that each Map task can combine all the terms for the portion $\mathbf{v}'_i$ for which it is exclusively responsible. In other words, the Reduce tasks have nothing to do but to concatenate the pieces of $\mathbf{v}'$ received from the k Map tasks.

We can extend this idea to an environment in which MapReduce is not used. Suppose we have a single processor, with M and $\mathbf{v}$ stored on its disk, using the same sparse representation for M that we have discussed. We can first simulate the first Map task, the one that uses blocks M_{11} through M_{1k} and all of $\mathbf{v}$ to compute $\mathbf{v}'_1$. Then we simulate the second Map task, reading M_{21} through M_{2k} and all of $\mathbf{v}$ to compute $\mathbf{v}'_2$, and so on. As for the previous algorithms, we thus read M once and $\mathbf{v}$ k times. We can make k as small as possible, subject to the constraint that there is enough main memory to store $1/k$th of $\mathbf{v}$ and $1/k$th of $\mathbf{v}'$, along with as small a portion of M as we can read from disk (typically, one disk block).

5.2.6   Exercises for Section 5.2

EXERCISE 5.2.1   Suppose we wish to store an $n \times n$ Boolean matrix (0 and 1 elements only). We could represent it by the bits themselves, or we could represent the matrix by listing the positions of the 1s as pairs of integers, each integer requiring $\lceil \log_2 n \rceil$ bits. The former is suitable for dense matrices; the latter is suitable for sparse matrices. How sparse must the matrix be (i.e., what fraction of the elements should be 1s) for the sparse representation to save space?

EXERCISE 5.2.2   Using the method of Section 5.2.1, represent the transition matrices of the following graphs:

(a) Figure 5.4.
(b) Figure 5.7.

EXERCISE 5.2.3   Using the method of Section 5.2.4, represent the transition matrices of the graph of Fig. 5.3, assuming blocks have side 2.

EXERCISE 5.2.4   Consider a Web graph that is a chain, like Fig. 5.9, with n nodes. As a function of k, which you may assume divides n, describe the representation of the transition matrix for this graph, using the method of Section 5.2.4

5.3   Topic-Sensitive PageRank

There are several improvements we can make to PageRank. One, to be studied in this section, is that we can weight certain pages more heavily because of their topic. The mechanism for enforcing this weighting is to alter the way random surfers behave, having them prefer to land on a page that is known to cover the chosen topic. In the next section, we shall see how the topic-sensitive idea can also be applied to negate the effects of a new kind of spam, called "link spam," that has developed to try to fool the PageRank algorithm.

5.3.1   Motivation for Topic-Sensitive Page Rank

Different people have different interests, and sometimes distinct interests are expressed using the same term in a query. The canonical example is the search query `jaguar`, which might refer to the animal, the automobile, a version of the MAC operating system, or even an ancient game console. If a search engine can deduce that the user is interested in automobiles, for example, then it can do a better job of returning relevant pages to the user.

Ideally, each user would have a private PageRank vector that gives the importance of each page to that user. It is not feasible to store a vector of length many billions for each of a billion users, so we need to do something simpler. The *topic-sensitive PageRank* approach creates one vector for each of some small number of topics, biasing the PageRank to favor pages of that topic. We then endeavour to classify users according to the degree of their interest in each of the selected topics. While we surely lose some accuracy, the benefit is that we store only a short vector for each user, rather than an enormous vector for each user.

EXAMPLE 5.9   One useful topic set is the 16 top-level categories (sports, medicine, etc.) of the Open Directory (DMOZ).[6] We could create 16 PageRank vectors, one for each topic. If we could determine that the user is interested in one of these topics, perhaps by the content of the pages they have recently viewed, then we could use the PageRank vector for that topic when deciding on the ranking of pages.   □

---

[6] This directory, found at `www.dmoz.org`, is a collection of human-classified Web pages.

5.3.2   Biased Random Walks

Suppose we have identified some pages that represent a topic such as "sports." To create a topic-sensitive PageRank for sports, we can arrange that the random surfers are introduced only to a random sports page, rather than to a random page of any kind. The consequence of this choice is that random surfers are likely to be at an identified sports page, or a page reachable along a short path from one of these known sports pages. Our intuition is that pages linked to by sports pages are themselves likely to be about sports. The pages they link to are also likely to be about sports, although the probability of being about sports surely decreases as the distance from an identified sports page increases.

The mathematical formulation for the iteration that yields topic-sensitive PageRank is similar to the equation we used for general PageRank. The only difference is how we add the new surfers. Suppose S is a set of integers consisting of the row/column numbers for the pages we have identified as belonging to a certain topic (called the *teleport set*). Let $\mathbf{e}_S$ be a vector that has 1 in the components in S and 0 in other components. Then the *topic-sensitive PageRank for S* is the limit of the iteration

$$\mathbf{v}' = \beta M \mathbf{v} + (1 - \beta)\mathbf{e}_S/|S|$$

Here, as usual, M is the transition matrix of the Web, and $|S|$ is the size of set S.

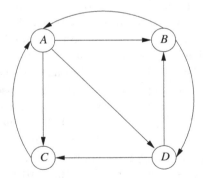

Figure 5.15 Repeat of example Web graph

EXAMPLE 5.10   Let us reconsider the original Web graph we used in Fig. 5.1, which we reproduce as Fig. 5.15. Suppose we use $\beta = 0.8$. Then the transition matrix for this graph, multiplied by β, is

$$\beta M = \begin{bmatrix} 0 & 2/5 & 4/5 & 0 \\ 4/15 & 0 & 0 & 2/5 \\ 4/15 & 0 & 0 & 2/5 \\ 4/15 & 2/5 & 0 & 0 \end{bmatrix}$$

Suppose that our topic is represented by the teleport set $S = \{B, D\}$. Then the vector $(1 - \beta)\mathbf{e}_S/|S|$ has $1/10$ for its second and fourth components and 0 for the other two components. The reason is that $1 - \beta = 1/5$, the size of S is 2, and $\mathbf{e}_S$ has 1 in the components for B and D and 0 in the components for A and C. Thus, the equation that must be iterated is

$$
\mathbf{v}' =
\begin{bmatrix}
0 & 2/5 & 4/5 & 0 \\
4/15 & 0 & 0 & 2/5 \\
4/15 & 0 & 0 & 2/5 \\
4/15 & 2/5 & 0 & 0
\end{bmatrix}
\mathbf{v} +
\begin{bmatrix}
0 \\
1/10 \\
0 \\
1/10
\end{bmatrix}
$$

Here are the first few iterations of this equation. We have also started with the surfers only at the pages in the teleport set. Although the initial distribution has no effect on the limit, it may help the computation to converge faster.

$$
\begin{bmatrix}
0/2 \\
1/2 \\
0/2 \\
1/2
\end{bmatrix},
\begin{bmatrix}
2/10 \\
3/10 \\
2/10 \\
3/10
\end{bmatrix},
\begin{bmatrix}
42/150 \\
41/150 \\
26/150 \\
41/150
\end{bmatrix},
\begin{bmatrix}
62/250 \\
71/250 \\
46/250 \\
71/250
\end{bmatrix}, \ldots,
\begin{bmatrix}
54/210 \\
59/210 \\
38/210 \\
59/210
\end{bmatrix}
$$

Notice that because of the concentration of surfers at B and D, these nodes get a higher PageRank than they did in Example 5.2. In that example, A was the node of highest PageRank. □

5.3.3 Using Topic-Sensitive PageRank

In order to integrate topic-sensitive PageRank into a search engine, we must:

(1) Decide on the topics for which we shall create specialized PageRank vectors.
(2) Pick a teleport set for each of these topics, and use that set to compute the topic-sensitive PageRank vector for that topic.
(3) Find a way of determining the topic or set of topics that are most relevant for a particular search query.
(4) Use the PageRank vectors for that topic or topics in the ordering of the responses to the search query.

We have mentioned one way of selecting the topic set: use the top-level topics of the Open Directory. Other approaches are possible, but there is probably a need for human classification of at least some pages.

The third step is probably the trickiest, and several methods have been proposed. Some possibilities:

(a) Allow the user to select a topic from a menu.
(b) Infer the topic(s) by the words that appear in the Web pages recently searched by the user, or recent queries issued by the user. We need to discuss how one goes from a collection of words to a topic, and we shall do so in Section 5.3.4
(c) Infer the topic(s) by information about the user, e.g., their bookmarks or their stated interests on Facebook.

5.3.4   Inferring Topics from Words

The question of classifying documents by topic is a subject that has been studied for decades, and we shall not go into great detail here. Suffice it to say that topics are characterized by words that appear surprisingly often in documents on that topic. For example, neither `fullback` nor `measles` appear very often in documents on the Web. But `fullback` will appear far more often than average in pages about sports, and `measles` will appear far more often than average in pages about medicine.

If we examine the entire Web, or a large, random sample of the Web, we can get the background frequency of each word. Suppose we then go to a large sample of pages known to be about a certain topic, say the pages classified under sports by the Open Directory. Examine the frequencies of words in the sports sample, and identify the words that appear significantly more frequently in the sports sample than in the background. In making this judgment, we must be careful to avoid some extremely rare word that appears in the sports sample with relatively higher frequency. This word is probably a misspelling that happened to appear only in one or a few of the sports pages. Thus, we probably want to put a floor on the number of times a word appears, before it can be considered characteristic of a topic.

Once we have identified a large collection of words that appear much more frequently in the sports sample than in the background, and we do the same for all the topics on our list, we can examine other pages and classify them by topic. Here is a simple approach. Suppose that $S_1, S_2, \ldots, S_k$ are the sets of words that have been determined to be characteristic of each of the topics on our list. Let P be the set of words that appear in a given page P. Compute the Jaccard similarity (recall Section 3.1.1) between P and each of the S_i. Classify the page as that topic with the highest Jaccard similarity. Note that all Jaccard similarities may be very low, especially if the sizes of the sets S_i are small. Thus, it is important to pick reasonably large sets S_i to make sure that we cover all aspects of the topic represented by the set.

We can use this method, or a number of variants, to classify the pages the user has most recently retrieved. We could say the user is interested in the topic into which the largest number of these pages fall. Or we could blend the topic-sensitive PageRank vectors in proportion to the fraction of these pages that fall into each topic, thus constructing a single PageRank vector that reflects the user's current blend of interests. We could also use the same procedure on the pages that the user currently has bookmarked, or combine the bookmarked pages with the recently viewed pages.

5.3.5   Exercises for Section 5.3

EXERCISE 5.3.1   Compute the topic-sensitive PageRank for the graph of Fig. 5.15, assuming the teleport set is:

(a) *A* only.

(b) *A* and *C*.

5.4   Link Spam

When it became apparent that PageRank and other techniques used by Google made term spam ineffective, spammers turned to methods designed to fool the PageRank algorithm into overvaluing certain pages. The techniques for artificially increasing the PageRank of a page are collectively called *link spam*. In this section we shall first examine how spammers create link spam, and then see several methods for decreasing the effectiveness of these spamming techniques, including TrustRank and measurement of spam mass.

5.4.1   Architecture of a Spam Farm

A collection of pages whose purpose is to increase the PageRank of a certain page or pages is called a *spam farm*. Figure 5.16 shows the simplest form of spam farm. From the point of view of the spammer, the Web is divided into three parts:

(1) *Inaccessible pages*: the pages that the spammer cannot affect. Most of the Web is in this part.

(2) *Accessible pages*: those pages that, while they are not controlled by the spammer, can be affected by the spammer.

(3) *Own pages*: the pages that the spammer owns and controls.

The spam farm consists of the spammer's own pages, organized in a special way as seen on the right, and some links from the accessible pages to the spammer's pages. Without some links from the outside, the spam farm would be useless, since it would not even be crawled by a typical search engine.

Concerning the accessible pages, it might seem surprising that one can affect a page without owning it. However, today there are many sites, such as blogs or newspapers that invite others to post their comments on the site. In order to get as much PageRank flowing to his own pages from outside, the spammer posts many comments such as "I agree. Please see my article at www.mySpamFarm.com."

In the spam farm, there is one page t, the *target page*, at which the spammer attempts to place as much PageRank as possible. There are a large number m of *supporting* pages, that accumulate the portion of the PageRank that is distributed equally to all pages (the fraction $1-\beta$ of the PageRank that represents surfers going to a random page). The supporting pages also prevent the Page-Rank of t from being lost, to the extent possible, since some will be taxed away at each round. Notice that t has a link to every supporting page, and every supporting page links only to t.

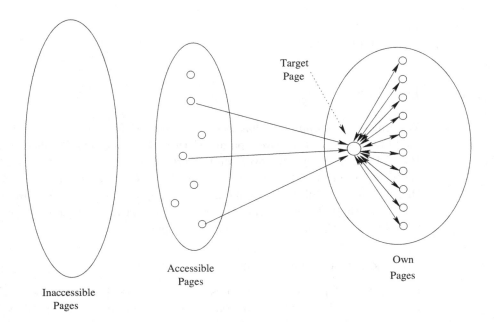

Figure 5.16 The Web from the point of view of the link spammer

5.4.2   Analysis of a Spam Farm

Suppose that PageRank is computed using a taxation parameter β, typically around 0.85. That is, β is the fraction of a page's PageRank that gets distributed to its successors at the next round. Let there be n pages on the Web in total, and let some of them be a spam farm of the form suggested in Fig. 5.16, with a target page t and m supporting pages. Let x be the amount of PageRank contributed by the accessible pages. That is, x is the sum, over all accessible pages p with a link to t, of the PageRank of p times β, divided by the number of successors of p. Finally, let y be the unknown PageRank of t. We shall solve for y.

First, the PageRank of each supporting page is

$$\beta y/m + (1 - \beta)/n$$

The first term represents the contribution from t. The PageRank y of t is taxed, so only βy is distributed to ts successors. That PageRank is divided equally among the m supporting pages. The second term is the supporting page's share of the fraction $1 - \beta$ of the PageRank that is divided equally among all pages on the Web.

Now, let us compute the PageRank y of target page t. Its PageRank comes from three sources:

(1) Contribution x from outside, as we have assumed.

(2) β times the PageRank of every supporting page; that is,

$$\beta(\beta y/m + (1 - \beta)/n)$$

(3) $(1 - \beta)/n$, the share of the fraction $1 - \beta$ of the PageRank that belongs to t. This amount is negligible and will be dropped to simplify the analysis.

Thus, from (1) and (2) above, we can write

$$y = x + \beta m \left(\frac{\beta y}{m} + \frac{1 - \beta}{n}\right) = x + \beta^2 y + \beta(1 - \beta)\frac{m}{n}$$

We may solve the above equation for y, yielding

$$y = \frac{x}{1 - \beta^2} + c\frac{m}{n}$$

where $c = \beta(1 - \beta)/(1 - \beta^2) = \beta/(1 + \beta)$.

EXAMPLE 5.11 If we choose $\beta = 0.85$, then $1/(1 - \beta^2) = 3.6$, and $c = \beta/(1 + \beta) = 0.46$. That is, the structure has amplified the external PageRank contribution by 360%, and also obtained an amount of PageRank that is 46% of the fraction of the Web, m/n, that is in the spam farm. □

5.4.3 Combating Link Spam

It has become essential for search engines to detect and eliminate link spam, just as it was necessary in the previous decade to eliminate term spam. There are two approaches to link spam. One is to look for structures such as the spam farm in Fig. 5.16, where one page links to a very large number of pages, each of which links back to it. Search engines surely search for such structures and eliminate those pages from their index. That causes spammers to develop different structures that have essentially the same effect of capturing PageRank for a target page or pages. There is essentially no end to variations of Fig. 5.16, so this war between the spammers and the search engines will likely go on for a long time.

However, there is another approach to eliminating link spam that doesn't rely on locating the spam farms. Rather, a search engine can modify its definition of PageRank to lower the rank of link-spam pages automatically. We shall consider two different formulas:

(1) *TrustRank*, a variation of topic-sensitive PageRank designed to lower the score of spam pages.

(2) *Spam mass*, a calculation that identifies the pages that are likely to be spam and allows the search engine to eliminate those pages or to lower their PageRank strongly.

5.4.4   TrustRank

TrustRank is topic-sensitive PageRank, where the "topic" is a set of pages believed to be trustworthy (not spam). The theory is that while a spam page might
easily be made to link to a trustworthy page, it is unlikely that a trustworthy page
would link to a spam page. The borderline area is a site with blogs or other opportunities for spammers to create links, as was discussed in Section 5.4.1. These
pages cannot be considered trustworthy, even if their own content is highly reliable, as would be the case for a reputable newspaper that allowed readers to
post comments.

    To implement TrustRank, we need to develop a suitable teleport set of trust-
worthy pages. Two approaches that have been tried are:

(1) Let humans examine a set of pages and decide which of them are trustworthy.
    For example, we might pick the pages of highest PageRank to examine, on
    the theory that, while link spam can raise a page's rank from the bottom
    to the middle of the pack, it is essentially impossible to give a spam page a
    PageRank near the top of the list.
(2) Pick a domain whose membership is controlled, on the assumption that it is
    hard for a spammer to get their pages into these domains. For example, we
    could pick the .edu domain, since university pages are unlikely to be spam
    farms. We could likewise pick .mil, or .gov. However, the problem with these
    specific choices is that they are almost exclusively US sites. To get a good
    distribution of trustworthy Web pages, we should include the analogous sites
    from foreign countries, e.g., ac.il, or edu.sg.

It is likely that search engines today implement a strategy of the second type
routinely, so that what we think of as PageRank really is a form of TrustRank.

5.4.5   Spam Mass

The idea behind spam mass is that we measure for each page the fraction of
its PageRank that comes from spam. We do so by computing both the ordinary
PageRank and the TrustRank based on some teleport set of trustworthy pages.
Suppose page p has PageRank r and TrustRank t. Then the *spam mass* of p is
$(r - t)/r$. A negative or small positive spam mass means that p is probably not
a spam page, while a spam mass close to 1 suggests that the page probably is
spam. It is possible to eliminate pages with a high spam mass from the index
of Web pages used by a search engine, thus eliminating a great deal of the link
spam without having to identify particular structures that spam farmers use.

EXAMPLE 5.12   Let us consider both the PageRank and topic-sensitive Page-
Rank that were computed for the graph of Fig. 5.1 in Examples 5.2 and 5.10, respectively. In the latter case, the teleport set was nodes B and D, so let us assume
those are the trusted pages. Figure 5.17 tabulates the PageRank, TrustRank, and
spam mass for each of the four nodes.

Node	PageRank	TrustRank	Spam Mass
A	3/9	54/210	0.229
B	2/9	59/210	-0.264
C	2/9	38/210	0.186
D	2/9	59/210	-0.264

Figure 5.17 Calculation of spam mass

In this simple example, the only conclusion is that the nodes B and D, which were a priori determined not to be spam, have negative spam mass and are therefore not spam. The other two nodes, A and C, each have a positive spam mass, since their PageRanks are higher than their TrustRanks. For instance, the spam mass of A is computed by taking the difference $3/9 - 54/210 = 8/105$ and dividing $8/105$ by the PageRank $3/9$ to get $8/35$ or about 0.229. However, their spam mass is still closer to 0 than to 1, so it is probable that they are not spam. □

5.4.6 Exercises for Section 5.4

EXERCISE 5.4.1   In Section 5.4.2 we analyzed the spam farm of Fig. 5.16, where every supporting page links back to the target page. Repeat the analysis for a spam farm in which:

(a) Each supporting page links to itself instead of to the target page.
(b) Each supporting page links nowhere.
(c) Each supporting page links both to itself and to the target page.

EXERCISE 5.4.2   For the original Web graph of Fig. 5.1, assuming only B is a trusted page:

(a) Compute the TrustRank of each page.
(b) Compute the spam mass of each page.

! EXERCISE 5.4.3   Suppose two spam farmers agree to link their spam farms. How would you link the pages in order to increase as much as possible the Page-Rank of each spam farm's target page? Is there an advantage to linking spam farms?

5.5   Hubs and Authorities

An idea called "hubs and authorities' was proposed shortly after PageRank was first implemented. The algorithm for computing hubs and authorities bears some resemblance to the computation of PageRank, since it also deals with the iterative computation of a fixedpoint involving repeated matrix–vector multiplication.

However, there are also significant differences between the two ideas, and neither can substitute for the other.

This hubs-and-authorities algorithm, sometimes known as *HITS* (*hyperlink-induced topic search*), was originally intended not as a preprocessing step before handling search queries, as PageRank is, but as a step to be done along with the processing of a search query, to rank only the responses to that query. We shall, however, describe it as a technique for analyzing the entire Web, or the portion crawled by a search engine. There is reason to believe that something like this approach is, in fact, used by the Ask search engine.

5.5.1   The Intuition Behind HITS

While PageRank assumes a one-dimensional notion of importance for pages, HITS views important pages as having two flavors of importance.

(1) Certain pages are valuable because they provide information about a topic. These pages are called *authorities*.
(2) Other pages are valuable not because they provide information about any topic, but because they tell you where to go to find out about that topic. These pages are called *hubs*.

EXAMPLE 5.13   A typical department at a university maintains a Web page listing all the courses offered by the department, with links to a page for each course, telling about the course – the instructor, the text, an outline of the course content, and so on. If you want to know about a certain course, you need the page for that course; the departmental course list will not do. The course page is an authority for that course. However, if you want to find out what courses the department is offering, it is not helpful to search for each courses' page; you need the page with the course list first. This page is a hub for information about courses.   □

Just as PageRank uses the recursive definition of importance that "a page is important if important pages link to it," HITS uses a mutually recursive definition of two concepts: "a page is a good hub if it links to good authorities, and a page is a good authority if it is linked to by good hubs."

5.5.2   Formalizing Hubbiness and Authority

To formalize the above intuition, we shall assign two scores to each Web page. One score represents the *hubbiness* of a page – that is, the degree to which it is a good hub, and the second score represents the degree to which the page is a good authority. Assuming that pages are enumerated, we represent these scores by vectors $\mathbf{h}$ and $\mathbf{a}$. The ith component of $\mathbf{h}$ gives the hubbiness of the ith page, and the ith component of $\mathbf{a}$ gives the authority of the same page.

While importance is divided among the successors of a page, as expressed by the transition matrix of the Web, the normal way to describe the computation of hubbiness and authority is to add the authority of successors to estimate hubbiness and to add hubbiness of predecessors to estimate authority. If that is all we did, then the hubbiness and authority values would typically grow beyond bounds. Thus, we normally scale the values of the vectors **h** and **a** so that the largest component is 1. An alternative is to scale so that the sum of components is 1.

To describe the iterative computation of **h** and **a** formally, we use the *link matrix of the Web, L*. If we have n pages, then L is an $n \times n$ matrix, and $L_{ij} = 1$ if there is a link from page i to page j, and $L_{ij} = 0$ if not. We shall also have need for L^T, the *transpose* of L. That is, $L_{ij}^T = 1$ if there is a link from page j to page i, and $L_{ij}^T = 0$ otherwise. Notice that L^T is similar to the matrix M that we used for PageRank, but where L^T has 1, M has a fraction – 1 divided by the number of out-links from the page represented by that column.

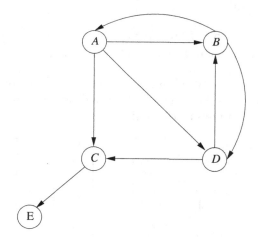

Figure 5.18 Sample data used for HITS examples

EXAMPLE 5.14   For a running example, we shall use the Web of Fig. 5.4, which we reproduce here as Fig. 5.18. An important observation is that dead ends or spider traps do not prevent the HITS iteration from converging to a meaningful pair of vectors. Thus, we can work with Fig. 5.18 directly, with no "taxation" or alteration of the graph needed. The link matrix L and its transpose are shown in Fig. 5.19.   □

The fact that the hubbiness of a page is proportional to the sum of the authority of its successors is expressed by the equation $\mathbf{h} = \lambda L \mathbf{a}$, where λ is an unknown constant representing the scaling factor needed. Likewise, the fact that the authority of a page is proportional to the sum of the hubbinesses of its predecessors is expressed by $\mathbf{a} = \mu L^T \mathbf{h}$, where μ is another scaling constant. These equations allow us to compute the hubbiness and authority independently, by substituting one equation in the other, as:

$$
L = \begin{bmatrix} 0 & 1 & 1 & 1 & 0 \\ 1 & 0 & 0 & 1 & 0 \\ 0 & 0 & 0 & 0 & 1 \\ 0 & 1 & 1 & 0 & 0 \\ 0 & 0 & 0 & 0 & 0 \end{bmatrix} \qquad L^T = \begin{bmatrix} 0 & 1 & 0 & 0 & 0 \\ 1 & 0 & 0 & 1 & 0 \\ 1 & 0 & 0 & 1 & 0 \\ 1 & 1 & 0 & 0 & 0 \\ 0 & 0 & 1 & 0 & 0 \end{bmatrix}
$$

Figure 5.19 The link matrix for the Web of Fig. 5.18 and its transpose

- $\mathbf{h} = \lambda\mu L L^T \mathbf{h}$.
- $\mathbf{a} = \lambda\mu L^T L \mathbf{a}$.

However, since LL^T and $L^T L$ are not as sparse as L and L^T, we are usually better off computing $\mathbf{h}$ and $\mathbf{a}$ in a true mutual recursion. That is, start with $\mathbf{h}$ a vector of all 1s.

(1) Compute $\mathbf{a} = L^T\mathbf{h}$ and then scale so the largest component is 1.
(2) Next, compute $\mathbf{h} = L\mathbf{a}$ and scale again.

Now, we have a new $\mathbf{h}$ and can repeat steps (1) and (2) until at some iteration the changes to the two vectors are sufficiently small that we can stop and accept the current values as the limit.

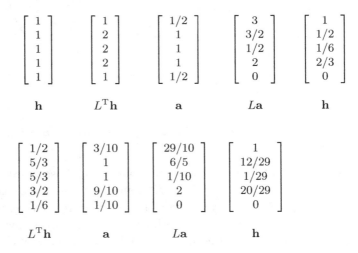

Figure 5.20 First two iterations of the HITS algorithm

EXAMPLE 5.15   Let us perform the first two iterations of the HITS algorithm on the Web of Fig. 5.18. In Fig. 5.20 we see the succession of vectors computed. The first column is the initial $\mathbf{h}$, all 1s. In the second column, we have estimated the relative authority of pages by computing $L^T\mathbf{h}$, thus giving each page the sum of the hubbinesses of its predecessors. The third column gives us the first estimate of **a**. It is computed by scaling the second column; in this case we have divided each component by 2, since that is the largest value in the second column.

The fourth column is $L\mathbf{a}$. That is, we have estimated the hubbiness of each page by summing the estimate of the authorities of each of its successors. Then, the fifth column scales the fourth column. In this case, we divide by 3, since that is the largest value in the fourth column. Columns six through nine repeat the process outlined in our explanations for columns two through five, but with the better estimate of hubbiness given by the fifth column.

The limit of this process may not be obvious, but it can be computed by a simple program. The limits are:

$$\mathbf{h} = \begin{bmatrix} 1 \\ 0.3583 \\ 0 \\ 0.7165 \\ 0 \end{bmatrix} \qquad \mathbf{a} = \begin{bmatrix} 0.2087 \\ 1 \\ 1 \\ 0.7913 \\ 0 \end{bmatrix}$$

This result makes sense. First, we notice that the hubbiness of E is surely 0, since it leads nowhere. The hubbiness of C depends only on the authority of E and vice versa, so it should not surprise us that both are 0. A is the greatest hub, since it links to the three biggest authorities, B, C, and D. Also, B and C are the greatest authorities, since they are linked to by the two biggest hubs, A and D.

For Web-sized graphs, the only way of computing the solution to the hubs-and-authorities equations is iteratively. However, for this tiny example, we can compute the solution by solving equations. We shall use the equations $\mathbf{h} = \lambda\mu LL^{\mathrm{T}}\mathbf{h}$. First, LL^{T} is

$$LL^{\mathrm{T}} = \begin{bmatrix} 3 & 1 & 0 & 2 & 0 \\ 1 & 2 & 0 & 0 & 0 \\ 0 & 0 & 1 & 0 & 0 \\ 2 & 0 & 0 & 2 & 0 \\ 0 & 0 & 0 & 0 & 0 \end{bmatrix}$$

Let $\nu = 1/(\lambda\mu)$ and let the components of $\mathbf{h}$ for nodes A through E be a through e, respectively. Then the equations for $\mathbf{h}$ can be written

$$\begin{aligned} \nu a &= 3a + b + 2d & \nu b &= a + 2b \\ \nu c &= c & \nu d &= 2a + 2d \\ \nu e &= 0 \end{aligned}$$

The equation for b tells us $b = a/(\nu - 2)$ and the equation for d tells us $d = 2a/(\nu-2)$. If we substitute these expressions for b and d in the equation for a, we get $\nu a = a\big(3 + 5/(\nu - 2)\big)$. From this equation, since a is a factor of both sides, we are left with a quadratic equation for ν which simplifies to $\nu^2 - 5\nu + 1 = 0$. The positive root is $\nu = (5 + \sqrt{21})/2 = 4.791$. Now that we know ν is neither 0 or 1, the equations for c and e tell us immediately that $c = e = 0$.

Finally, if we recognize that a is the largest component of $\mathbf{h}$ and set $a = 1$, we get $b = 0.3583$ and $d = 0.7165$. Along with $c = e = 0$, these values give us the limiting value of h. The value of $\mathbf{a}$ can be computed from $\mathbf{h}$ by multiplying by L^{T} and scaling.   □

5.5.3   Exercises for Section 5.5

EXERCISE 5.5.1   Compute the hubbiness and authority of each of the nodes in our original Web graph of Fig. 5.1.

! EXERCISE 5.5.2   Suppose our graph is a chain of n nodes, as was suggested by Fig. 5.9. Compute the hubs and authorities vectors, as a function of n.

5.6   Summary of Chapter 5

✦   *Term Spam*: Early search engines were unable to deliver relevant results because they were vulnerable to term spam – the introduction into Web pages of words that misrepresented what the page was about.

✦   *The Google Solution to Term Spam*: Google was able to counteract term spam by two techniques. First was the PageRank algorithm for determining the relative importance of pages on the Web. The second was a strategy of believing what other pages said about a given page, in or near their links to that page, rather than believing only what the page said about itself.

✦   *PageRank*: PageRank is an algorithm that assigns a real number, called its PageRank, to each page on the Web. The PageRank of a page is a measure of how important the page is, or how likely it is to be a good response to a search query. In its simplest form, PageRank is a solution to the recursive equation "a page is important if important pages link to it."

✦   *Transition Matrix of the Web*: We represent links in the Web by a matrix whose ith row and ith column represent the ith page of the Web. If there are one or more links from page j to page i, then the entry in row i and column j is $1/k$, where k is the number of pages to which page j links. Other entries of the transition matrix are 0.

✦   *Computing PageRank on Strongly Connected Web Graphs*: For strongly connected Web graphs (those where any node can reach any other node), Page-Rank is the principal eigenvector of the transition matrix. We can compute PageRank by starting with any nonzero vector and repeatedly multiplying the current vector by the transition matrix, to get a better estimate.[7] After about 50 iterations, the estimate will be very close to the limit, which is the true PageRank.

---

[7] Technically, the condition for this method to work is more restricted than simply "strongly connected." However, the other necessary conditions will surely be met by any large strongly connected component of the Web that was not artificially constructed.

✦ *The Random Surfer Model*: Calculation of PageRank can be thought of as simulating the behavior of many random surfers, who each start at a random page and at any step move, at random, to one of the pages to which their current page links. The limiting probability of a surfer being at a given page is the PageRank of that page. The intuition is that people tend to create links to the pages they think are useful, so random surfers will tend to be at a useful page.

✦ *Dead Ends*: A dead end is a Web page with no links out. The presence of dead ends will cause the PageRank of some or all of the pages to go to 0 in the iterative computation, including pages that are not dead ends. We can eliminate all dead ends before undertaking a PageRank calculation by recursively dropping nodes with no arcs out. Note that dropping one node can cause another, which linked only to it, to become a dead end, so the process must be recursive.

✦ *Spider Traps*: A spider trap is a set of nodes that, while they may link to each other, have no links out to other nodes. In an iterative calculation of Page-Rank, the presence of spider traps cause all the PageRank to be captured within that set of nodes.

✦ *Taxation Schemes*: To counter the effect of spider traps (and of dead ends, if we do not eliminate them), PageRank is normally computed in a way that modifies the simple iterative multiplication by the transition matrix. A parameter β is chosen, typically around 0.85. Given an estimate of the PageRank, the next estimate is computed by multiplying the estimate by β times the transition matrix, and then adding $(1 - \beta)/n$ to the estimate for each page, where n is the total number of pages.

✦ *Taxation and Random Surfers*: The calculation of PageRank using taxation parameter β can be thought of as giving each random surfer a probability $1 - \beta$ of leaving the Web, and introducing an equivalent number of surfers randomly throughout the Web.

✦ *Efficient Representation of Transition Matrices*: Since a transition matrix is very sparse (almost all entries are 0), it saves both time and space to represent it by listing its nonzero entries. However, in addition to being sparse, the nonzero entries have a special property: they are all the same in any given column; the value of each nonzero entry is the inverse of the number of nonzero entries in that column. Thus, the preferred representation is column-by-column, where the representation of a column is the number of nonzero entries, followed by a list of the rows where those entries occur.

✦ *Very Large-Scale Matrix–Vector Multiplication*: For Web-sized graphs, it may not be feasible to store the entire PageRank estimate vector in the main memory of one machine. Thus, we can break the vector into k segments and break the transition matrix into k^2 squares, called blocks, assigning each square to one machine. The vector segments are each sent to k machines, so there is a small additional cost in replicating the vector.

✦ *Representing Blocks of a Transition Matrix*: When we divide a transition matrix into square blocks, the columns are divided into k segments. To represent a segment of a column, nothing is needed if there are no nonzero entries in that segment. However, if there are one or more nonzero entries, then we need to represent the segment of the column by the total number of nonzero entries in the column (so we can tell what value the nonzero entries have) followed by a list of the rows with nonzero entries.

◆ *Topic-Sensitive PageRank*: If we know the queryer is interested in a certain topic, then it makes sense to bias the PageRank in favor of pages on that topic. To compute this form of PageRank, we identify a set of pages known to be on that topic, and we use it as a "teleport set." The PageRank calculation is modified so that only the pages in the teleport set are given a share of the tax, rather than distributing the tax among all pages on the Web.

◆ *Creating Teleport Sets*: For topic-sensitive PageRank to work, we need to identify pages that are very likely to be about a given topic. One approach is to start with the pages that the open directory (DMOZ) identifies with that topic. Another is to identify words known to be associated with the topic, and select for the teleport set those pages that have an unusually high number of occurrences of such words.

◆ *Link Spam*: To fool the PageRank algorithm, unscrupulous actors have created spam farms. These are collections of pages whose purpose is to concentrate high PageRank on a particular target page.

◆ *Structure of a Spam Farm*: Typically, a spam farm consists of a target page and very many supporting pages. The target page links to all the supporting pages, and the supporting pages link only to the target page. In addition, it is essential that some links from outside the spam farm be created. For example, the spammer might introduce links to their target page by writing comments in other people's blogs or discussion groups.

◆ *TrustRank*: One way to ameliorate the effect of link spam is to compute a topic-sensitive PageRank called TrustRank, where the teleport set is a collection of trusted pages. For example, the home pages of universities could serve as the trusted set. This technique avoids sharing the tax in the PageRank calculation with the large numbers of supporting pages in spam farms and thus preferentially reduces their PageRank.

◆ *Spam Mass*: To identify spam farms, we can compute both the conventional PageRank and the TrustRank for all pages. Those pages that have much lower TrustRank than PageRank are likely to be part of a spam farm.

◆ *Hubs and Authorities*: While PageRank gives a one-dimensional view of the importance of pages, an algorithm called HITS tries to measure two different aspects of importance. Authorities are those pages that contain valuable information. Hubs are pages that, while they do not themselves contain the information, link to places where the information can be found.

◆ *Recursive Formulation of the HITS Algorithm*: Calculation of the hubs and authorities scores for pages depends on solving the recursive equations: "a hub links to many authorities, and an authority is linked to by many hubs."

The solution to these equations is essentially an iterated matrix–vector multiplication, just like PageRank's. However, the existence of dead ends or spider traps does not affect the solution to the HITS equations in the way they do for PageRank, so no taxation scheme is necessary.

5.7 References for Chapter 5

The PageRank algorithm was first expressed in [1]. The experiments on the structure of the Web, which we used to justify the existence of dead ends and spider traps, were described in [2]. The block-stripe method for performing the PageRank iteration is taken from [5].

Topic-sensitive PageRank is taken from [6]. TrustRank is described in [4], and the idea of spam mass is taken from [3].

The HITS (hubs and authorities) idea was described in [7].

[1] S. Brin and L. Page, "Anatomy of a large-scale hypertextual web search engine," *Proc. 7th Intl. World-Wide-Web Conference*, pp. 107–117, 1998.

[2] A. Broder, R. Kumar, F. Maghoul, P. Raghavan, S. Rajagopalan, R. Stata, A. Tomkins, and J. Weiner, "Graph structure in the web," *Computer Networks* **33**:1–6, pp. 309–320, 2000.

[3] Z. Gyöngi, P. Berkhin, H. Garcia-Molina, and J. Pedersen, "Link spam detection based on mass estimation," *Proc. 32nd Intl. Conf. on Very Large Databases*, pp. 439–450, 2006.

[4] Z. Gyöngi, H. Garcia-Molina, and J. Pedersen, "Combating link spam with trustrank," *Proc. 30th Intl. Conf. on Very Large Databases*, pp. 576–587, 2004.

[5] T.H. Haveliwala, "Efficient computation of PageRank," Stanford Univ. Dept. of Computer Science technical report, Sept., 1999. Available as

    `http://infolab.stanford.edu/~taherh/papers/efficient-pr.pdf`

[6] T.H. Haveliwala, "Topic-sensitive PageRank," *Proc. 11th Intl. World-Wide-Web Conference*, pp. 517–526, 2002

[7] J.M. Kleinberg, "Authoritative sources in a hyperlinked environment," *J. ACM* **46**:5, pp. 604–632, 1999.

6 Frequent Itemsets

We turn in this chapter to one of the major families of techniques for characterizing data: the discovery of frequent itemsets. This problem is often viewed as the discovery of "association rules," although the latter is a more complex characterization of data, whose discovery depends fundamentally on the discovery of frequent itemsets.

To begin, we introduce the "market-basket" model of data, which is essentially a many-many relationship between two kinds of elements, called "items" and "baskets," but with some assumptions about the shape of the data. The frequent-itemsets problem is that of finding sets of items that appear in (are related to) many of the same baskets.

The problem of finding frequent itemsets differs from the similarity search discussed in Chapter 3. Here we are interested in the absolute number of baskets that contain a particular set of items. In Chapter 3 we wanted items that have a large fraction of their baskets in common, even if the absolute number of baskets is small.

The difference leads to a new class of algorithms for finding frequent itemsets. We begin with the A-Priori Algorithm, which works by eliminating most large sets as candidates by looking first at smaller sets and recognizing that a large set cannot be frequent unless all its subsets are. We then consider various improvements to the basic A-Priori idea, concentrating on very large data sets that stress the available main memory.

Next, we consider approximate algorithms that work faster but are not guaranteed to find all frequent itemsets. Also in this class of algorithms are those that exploit parallelism, including the parallelism we can obtain through a MapReduce formulation. Finally, we discuss briefly how to find frequent itemsets in a data stream.

6.1 The Market-Basket Model

The *market-basket* model of data is used to describe a common form of many-many relationship between two kinds of objects. On the one hand, we have *items*, and on the other we have *baskets*, sometimes called "transactions." Each basket consists of a set of items (an *itemset*), and usually we assume that the number of items in a basket is small – much smaller than the total number of items. The number of baskets is usually assumed to be very large, bigger than what can fit in main memory. The data is assumed to be represented in a file consisting of a sequence of baskets. In terms of the distributed file system described in Section 2.1, the baskets are the objects of the file, and each basket is of type "set of items."

6.1.1 Definition of Frequent Itemsets

Intuitively, a set of items that appears in many baskets is said to be "frequent." To be formal, we assume there is a number s, called the *support threshold*. If I is a set of items, the *support* for I is the number of baskets for which I is a subset. We say I is *frequent* if its support is s or more.

EXAMPLE 6.1   In Fig. 6.1 are sets of words. Each set is a basket, and the words are items. We took these sets by Googling `cat dog` and taking snippets from the highest-ranked pages. Do not be concerned if a word appears twice in a basket, as baskets are sets, and in principle items can appear only once. Also, ignore capitalization.

(1) {Cat, and, dog, bites}
(2) {Yahoo, news, claims, a, cat, mated, with, a, dog, and, produced, viable, offspring}
(3) {Cat, killer, likely, is, a, big, dog}
(4) {Professional, free, advice, on, dog, training, puppy, training}
(5) {Cat, and, kitten, training, and, behavior}
(6) {Dog, &, Cat, provides, dog, training, in, Eugene, Oregon}
(7) { "Dog, and, cat", is, a, slang, term, used, by, police, officers, for, a, male–female, relationship}
(8) {Shop, for, your, show, dog, grooming, and, pet, supplies}

Figure 6.1 Here are eight baskets, each consisting of items that are words

Since the empty set is a subset of any set, the support for $\emptyset$ is 8. However, we shall not generally concern ourselves with the empty set, since it tells us nothing.

Among the singleton sets, obviously {cat} and {dog} are quite frequent. "Dog" appears in all but basket (5), so its support is 7, while "cat" appears in all but (4) and (8), so its support is 6. The word "and" is also quite frequent; it appears in (1), (2), (5), (7), and (8), so its support is 5. The words "a" and "training" appear in three sets, while "for" and "is" appear in two each. No other word appears more than once.

Suppose that we set our threshold at $s = 3$. Then there are five frequent singleton itemsets: {dog}, {cat}, {and}, {a}, and {training}.

Now, let us look at the doubletons. A doubleton cannot be frequent unless both items in the set are frequent by themselves. Thus, there are only ten possible frequent doubletons. Fig. 6.2 is a table indicating which baskets contain which doubletons.

	training	a	and	cat
dog	4, 6	2, 3, 7	1, 2, 7, 8	1, 2, 3, 6, 7
cat	5, 6	2, 3, 7	1, 2, 5, 7	
and	5	2, 7		
a	none			

Figure 6.2 Occurrences of doubletons

For example, we see from the table of Fig. 6.2 that doubleton {dog, training} appears only in baskets (4) and (6). Therefore, its support is 2, and it is not frequent. There are five frequent doubletons if $s = 3$; they are

$$\{dog, a\} \quad \{dog, and\} \quad \{dog, cat\}$$
$$\{cat, a\} \quad \{cat, and\}$$

Each appears at least three times; for instance, {dog, cat} appears five times.

Next, let us see if there are frequent triples. In order to be a frequent triple, each pair of elements in the set must be a frequent doubleton. For example, {dog, a, and} cannot be a frequent itemset, because if it were, then surely {a, and} would be frequent, but it is not. The triple {dog, cat, and} might be frequent, because each of its doubleton subsets is frequent. Unfortunately, the three words appear together only in baskets (1) and (2), so it is not a frequent triple. The triple {dog, cat, a} might be frequent, since its doubletons are all frequent. In fact, all three words do appear in baskets (2), (3), and (7), so it is a frequent triple. No other triple of words is even a candidate for being a frequent triple, since for no other triple of words are its three doubleton subsets frequent. As there is only one frequent triple, there can be no frequent quadruples or larger sets. □

6.1.2 Applications of Frequent Itemsets

The original application of the market-basket model was in the analysis of true market baskets. That is, supermarkets and chain stores record the contents of every market basket (physical shopping cart) brought to the register for checkout. Here the "items" are the different products that the store sells, and the "baskets" are the sets of items in a single market basket. A major chain might sell 100,000 different items and collect data about millions of market baskets.

By finding frequent itemsets, a retailer can learn what is commonly bought together. Especially important are pairs or larger sets of items that occur much more frequently than would be expected were the items bought independently.

> ## On-Line versus Brick-and-Mortar Retailing
>
> We suggested in Section 3.1.3 that an on-line retailer would use similarity measures for items to find pairs of items that, while they might not be bought by many customers, had a significant fraction of their customers in common. An on-line retailer could then advertise one item of the pair to the few customers who had bought the other item of the pair. This methodology makes no sense for a bricks-and-mortar retailer, because unless lots of people buy an item, it cannot be cost effective to advertise a sale on the item. Thus, the techniques of Chapter 3 are not often useful for brick-and-mortar retailers.
>
> Conversely, the on-line retailer has little need for the analysis we discuss in this chapter, since it is designed to search for itemsets that appear frequently. If the on-line retailer was limited to frequent itemsets, they would miss all the opportunities that are present in the "long tail" to select advertisements for each customer individually.

We shall discuss this aspect of the problem in Section 6.1.3, but for the moment let us simply consider the search for frequent itemsets. We will discover by this analysis that many people buy bread and milk together, but that is of little interest, since we already knew that these were popular items individually. We might discover that many people buy hot dogs and mustard together. That, again, should be no surprise to people who like hot dogs, but it offers the supermarket an opportunity to do some clever marketing. They can advertise a sale on hot dogs and raise the price of mustard. When people come to the store for the cheap hot dogs, they often will remember that they need mustard, and buy that too. Either they will not notice the price is high, or they reason that it is not worth the trouble to go somewhere else for cheaper mustard.

The famous example of this type is "diapers and beer." One would hardly expect these two items to be related, but through data analysis one chain store discovered that people who buy diapers are unusually likely to buy beer. The theory is that if you buy diapers, you probably have a baby at home, and if you have a baby, then you are unlikely to be drinking at a bar; hence you are more likely to bring beer home. The same sort of marketing ploy that we suggested for hot dogs and mustard could be used for diapers and beer.

However, applications of frequent-itemset analysis is not limited to market baskets. The same model can be used to mine many other kinds of data. Some examples are:

(1) *Related concepts*: Let items be words, and let baskets be documents (e.g., Web pages, blogs, tweets). A basket/document contains those items/words that are present in the document. If we look for sets of words that appear together in many documents, the sets will be dominated by the most common words (stop words), as we saw in Example 6.1. There, even though the intent was to find snippets that talked about cats and dogs, the stop words

"and" and "a" were prominent among the frequent itemsets. However, if we ignore all the most common words, then we would hope to find among the frequent pairs some pairs of words that represent a joint concept. For example, we would expect a pair like {Brad, Angelina} to appear with surprising frequency.

(2) *Plagiarism*: Let the items be documents and the baskets be sentences. An item/document is "in" a basket/sentence if the sentence is in the document. This arrangement appears backwards, but it is exactly what we need, and we should remember that the relationship between items and baskets is an arbitrary many-many relationship. That is, "in" need not have its conventional meaning: "part of." In this application, we look for pairs of items that appear together in several baskets. If we find such a pair, then we have two documents that share several sentences in common. In practice, even one or two sentences in common is a good indicator of plagiarism.

(3) *Biomarkers*: Let the items be of two types – biomarkers such as genes or blood proteins, and diseases. Each basket is the set of data about a patient: their genome and blood-chemistry analysis, as well as their medical history of disease. A frequent itemset that consists of one disease and one or more biomarkers suggests a test for the disease.

6.1.3   Association Rules

While the subject of this chapter is extracting frequent sets of items from data, this information is often presented as a collection of if–then rules, called *association rules*. The form of an association rule is $I \rightarrow j$, where I is a set of items and j is an item. The implication of this association rule is that if all of the items in I appear in some basket, then j is "likely" to appear in that basket as well.

We formalize the notion of "likely" by defining the *confidence* of the rule $I \rightarrow j$ to be the ratio of the support for $I \cup \{j\}$ to the support for I. That is, the confidence of the rule is the fraction of the baskets with all of I that also contain j.

EXAMPLE 6.2   Consider the baskets of Fig. 6.1. The confidence of the rule $\{cat,\ dog\} \rightarrow and$ is 3/5. The words "cat" and "dog" appear in five baskets: (1), (2), (3), (6), and (7). Of these, "and" appears in (1), (2), and (7), or 3/5 of the baskets.

For another illustration, the confidence of $\{cat\} \rightarrow kitten$ is 1/6. The word "cat" appears in six baskets, (1), (2), (3), (5), (6), and (7). Of these, only (5) has the word "kitten."   □

Confidence alone can be useful, provided the support for the left side of the rule is fairly large. For example, we don't need to know that people are unusually likely to buy mustard when they buy hot dogs, as long as we know that many people buy hot dogs, and many people buy both hot dogs and mustard. We can still use the sale-on-hot-dogs trick discussed in Section 6.1.2. However, there is often more value to an association rule if it reflects a true relationship, where the item or items on the left somehow affect the item on the right.

Thus, we define the *interest* of an association rule $I \rightarrow j$ to be the difference between its confidence and the fraction of baskets that contain j. That is, if I has no influence on j, then we would expect that the fraction of baskets including I that contain j would be exactly the same as the fraction of all baskets that contain j. Such a rule has interest 0. However, it is interesting, in both the informal and technical sense, if a rule has either high interest, meaning that the presence of I in a basket somehow causes the presence of j, or highly negative interest, meaning that the presence of I discourages the presence of j.

EXAMPLE 6.3   The story about beer and diapers is really a claim that the association rule $\{diapers\} \rightarrow beer$ has high interest. That is, the fraction of diaper-buyers who buy beer is significantly greater than the fraction of all customers that buy beer. An example of a rule with negative interest is $\{coke\} \rightarrow pepsi$. That is, people who buy Coke are unlikely to buy Pepsi as well, even though a good fraction of all people buy Pepsi – people typically prefer one or the other, but not both. Similarly, the rule $\{pepsi\} \rightarrow coke$ can be expected to have negative interest.

For some numerical calculations, let us return to the data of Fig. 6.1. The rule $\{dog\} \rightarrow cat$ has confidence 5/7, since "dog" appears in seven baskets, of which five have "cat." However, "cat" appears in six out of the eight baskets, so we would expect that 75% of the seven baskets with "dog" would have "cat" as well. Thus, the interest of the rule is $5/7 - 3/4 = -0.036$, which is essentially 0. The rule $\{cat\} \rightarrow kitten$ has interest $1/6 - 1/8 = 0.042$. The justification is that one out of the six baskets with "cat" have "kitten" as well, while "kitten" appears in only one of the eight baskets. This interest, while positive, is close to 0 and therefore indicates the association rule is not very "interesting."   □

6.1.4   Finding Association Rules with High Confidence

Identifying useful association rules is not much harder than finding frequent itemsets. We shall take up the problem of finding frequent itemsets in the balance of this chapter, but for the moment, assume it is possible to find those frequent itemsets whose support is at or above a support threshold s.

If we are looking for association rules $I \rightarrow j$ that apply to a reasonable fraction of the baskets, then the support of I must be reasonably high. In practice, such as for marketing in brick-and-mortar stores, "reasonably high" is often around 1% of the baskets. We also want the confidence of the rule to be reasonably high, perhaps 50%, or else the rule has little practical effect. As a result, the set $I \cup \{j\}$ will also have fairly high support.

Suppose we have found all itemsets that meet a threshold of support, and that we have the exact support calculated for each of these itemsets. We can find within them all the association rules that have both high support and high confidence. That is, if J is a set of n items that is found to be frequent, there are only n possible association rules involving this set of items, namely $J - \{j\} \to j$ for each j in J. If J is frequent, $J - \{j\}$ must be at least as frequent. Thus, it too is a frequent itemset, and we have already computed the support of both J and $J - \{j\}$. Their ratio is the confidence of the rule $J - \{j\} \to j$.

It must be assumed that there are not too many frequent itemsets and thus not too many candidates for high-support, high-confidence association rules. The reason is that each one found must be acted upon. If we give the store manager a million association rules that meet our thresholds for support and confidence, they cannot even read them, let alone act on them. Likewise, if we produce a million candidates for biomarkers, we cannot afford to run the experiments needed to check them out. Thus, it is normal to adjust the support threshold so that we do not get too many frequent itemsets. This assumption leads, in later sections, to important consequences about the efficiency of algorithms for finding frequent itemsets.

6.1.5 Exercises for Section 6.1

EXERCISE 6.1.1 Suppose there are 100 items, numbered 1 to 100, and also 100 baskets, also numbered 1 to 100. Item i is in basket b if and only if i divides b with no remainder. Thus, item 1 is in all the baskets, item 2 is in all fifty of the even-numbered baskets, and so on. Basket 12 consists of items $\{1, 2, 3, 4, 6, 12\}$, since these are all the integers that divide 12. Answer the following questions:

(a) If the support threshold is 5, which items are frequent?
! (b) If the support threshold is 5, which pairs of items are frequent?
! (c) What is the sum of the sizes of all the baskets?

! EXERCISE 6.1.2 For the item-basket data of Exercise 6.1.1, which basket is the largest?

EXERCISE 6.1.3 Suppose there are 100 items, numbered 1 to 100, and also 100 baskets, also numbered 1 to 100. Item i is in basket b if and only if b divides i with no remainder. For example, basket 12 consists of items

$$\{12, 24, 36, 48, 60, 72, 84, 96\}$$

Repeat Exercise 6.1.1 for this data.

! EXERCISE 6.1.4 This question involves data from which nothing interesting can be learned about frequent itemsets, because there are no sets of items that are correlated. Suppose the items are numbered 1 to 10, and each basket is constructed by including item i with probability $1/i$, each decision being made independently of all other decisions. That is, all the baskets contain item 1, half contain item 2, a third contain item 3, and so on. Assume the number of baskets is sufficiently large that the baskets collectively behave as one would expect statistically. Let the support threshold be 1% of the baskets. Find the frequent itemsets.

EXERCISE 6.1.5 For the data of Exercise 6.1.1, what is the confidence of the following association rules?

(a) $\{5, 7\} \to 2$.
(b) $\{2, 3, 4\} \to 5$.

EXERCISE 6.1.6 For the data of Exercise 6.1.3, what is the confidence of the following association rules?

(a) $\{24, 60\} \to 8$.
(b) $\{2, 3, 4\} \to 5$.

!! EXERCISE 6.1.7 Describe all the association rules that have 100% confidence for the market-basket data of:

(a) Exercise 6.1.1.
(b) Exercise 6.1.3.

! EXERCISE 6.1.8 Prove that in the data of Exercise 6.1.4 there are no interesting association rules; i.e., the interest of every association rule is 0.

6.2 Market Baskets and the A-Priori Algorithm

We shall now begin a discussion of how to find frequent itemsets or information derived from them, such as association rules with high support and confidence. The original improvement on the obvious algorithms, known as "A-Priori," from which many variants have been developed, will be covered here. The next two sections will discuss certain further improvements. Before discussing the A-priori Algorithm itself, we begin the section with an outline of the assumptions about how data is stored and manipulated when searching for frequent itemsets.

6.2.1 Representation of Market-Basket Data

As we mentioned, we assume that market-basket data is stored in a file basket-by-basket. Possibly, the data is in a distributed file system as in Section 2.1, and the baskets are the objects the file contains. Or the data may be stored in a conventional file, with a character code to represent the baskets and their items.

EXAMPLE 6.4 We could imagine that such a file begins:

        {23,456,1001}{3,18,92,145}{...

Here, the character { begins a basket and the character } ends it. The items in a basket are represented by integers and are separated by commas. Thus, the first basket contains items 23, 456, and 1001; the second basket contains items 3, 18, 92, and 145. □

It may be that one machine receives the entire file. Or we could be using MapReduce or a similar tool to divide the work among many processors, in which case each processor receives only a part of the file. It turns out that combining the work of parallel processors to get the exact collection of itemsets that meet a global support threshold is hard, and we shall address this question only in Section 6.4.4.

We also assume that the size of the file of baskets is sufficiently large that it does not fit in main memory. Thus, a major cost of any algorithm is the time it takes to read the baskets from disk. Once a disk block full of baskets is in main memory, we can expand it, generating all the subsets of size k. Since one of the assumptions of our model is that the average size of a basket is small, generating all the pairs in main memory should take time that is much less than the time it took to read the basket from disk. For example, if there are 20 items in a basket, then there are $\binom{20}{2} = 190$ pairs of items in the basket, and these can be generated easily in a pair of nested for-loops.

As the size of the subsets we want to generate gets larger, the time required grows larger; in fact takes approximately time $n^k/k!$ to generate all the subsets of size k for a basket with n items. Eventually, this time dominates the time needed to transfer the data from disk. However:

(1) Often, we need only small frequent itemsets, so k never grows beyond 2 or 3.

(2) And when we do need the itemsets for a large size k, it is usually possible to eliminate many of the items in each basket as not able to participate in a frequent itemset, so the value of n drops as k increases.

The conclusion we would like to draw is that the work of examining each of the baskets can usually be assumed proportional to the size of the file. We can thus measure the running time of a frequent-itemset algorithm by the number of times that each disk block of the data file is read.

Moreover, all the algorithms we discuss have the property that they read the basket file sequentially. Thus, algorithms can be characterized by the number of passes through the basket file that they make, and their running time is proportional to the product of the number of passes they make through the basket file times the size of that file. Since we cannot control the amount of data, only the number of passes taken by the algorithm matters, and it is that aspect of the algorithm that we shall focus upon when measuring the running time of a frequent-itemset algorithm.

6.2.2 Use of Main Memory for Itemset Counting

There is a second data-related issue that we must examine, however. All frequent-itemset algorithms require us to maintain many different counts as we make a pass through the data. For example, we might need to count the number of times that each pair of items occurs in baskets. If we do not have enough main memory to store each of the counts, then adding 1 to a random count will most likely require us to load a page from disk. In that case, the algorithm will thrash and run many orders of magnitude slower than if we were certain to find each count in main memory. The conclusion is that we cannot count anything that doesn't fit in main memory. Thus, each algorithm has a limit on how many items it can deal with.

EXAMPLE 6.5 Suppose a certain algorithm has to count all pairs of items, and there are n items. We thus need space to store $\binom{n}{2}$ integers, or about $n^2/2$ integers. If integers take 4 bytes, we require $2n^2$ bytes. If our machine has 2 gigabytes, or 2^{31} bytes of main memory, then we require $n \leq 2^{15}$, or approximately $n < 33,000$. □

It is not trivial to store the $\binom{n}{2}$ counts in a way that makes it easy to find the count for a pair $\{i, j\}$. First, we have not assumed anything about how items are represented. They might, for instance, be strings like "bread." It is more space-efficient to represent items by consecutive integers from 1 to n, where n is the number of distinct items. Unless items are already represented this way, we need a hash table that translates items as they appear in the file to integers. That is, each time we see an item in the file, we hash it. If it is already in the hash table, we can obtain its integer code from its entry in the table. If the item is not there, we assign it the next available number (from a count of the number of distinct items seen so far) and enter the item and its code into the table.

The Triangular-Matrix Method

Even after coding items as integers, we still have the problem that we must count a pair $\{i, j\}$ in only one place. For example, we could order the pair so that $i < j$, and only use the entry $a[i, j]$ in a two-dimensional array a. That strategy would make half the array useless. A more space-efficient way is to use a one-dimensional *triangular array*. We store in $a[k]$ the count for the pair $\{i, j\}$, with $1 \leq i < j \leq n$, where

$$k = (i - 1)\left(n - \frac{i}{2}\right) + j - i$$

The result of this layout is that the pairs are stored in lexicographic order, that is first $\{1, 2\}$, $\{1, 3\}, \ldots, \{1, n\}$, then $\{2, 3\}$, $\{2, 4\}, \ldots, \{2, n\}$, and so on, down to $\{n - 2, n - 1\}$, $\{n - 2, n\}$, and finally $\{n - 1, n\}$.

The Triples Method

There is another approach to storing counts that may be more appropriate, depending on the fraction of the possible pairs of items that actually appear in some basket. We can store counts as triples $[i, j, c]$, meaning that the count of pair $\{i, j\}$, with $i < j$, is c. A data structure, such as a hash table with i and j as the search key, is used so we can tell if there is a triple for a given i and j and, if so, to find it quickly. We call this approach the *triples method* of storing counts.

Unlike the triangular matrix, the triples method does not require us to store anything if the count for a pair is 0. On the other hand, the triples method requires us to store three integers, rather than one, for every pair that does appear in some basket. In addition, there is the space needed for the hash table or other data structure used to support efficient retrieval. The conclusion is that the triangular matrix will be better if at least $1/3$ of the $\binom{n}{2}$ possible pairs actually appear in some basket, while if significantly fewer than $1/3$ of the possible pairs occur, we should consider using the triples method.

EXAMPLE 6.6   Suppose there are 100,000 items, and 10,000,000 baskets of 10 items each. Then the triangular-matrix method requires $\binom{100000}{2} = 5 \times 10^9$ (approximately) integer counts.[1] On the other hand, the total number of pairs among all the baskets is $10^7\binom{10}{2} = 4.5 \times 10^8$. Even in the extreme case that every pair of items appeared only once, there could be only 4.5×10^8 pairs with nonzero counts. If we used the triples method to store counts, we would need only three times that number of integers, or 1.35×10^9 integers. Thus, in this case the triples method will surely take much less space than the triangular matrix.

However, even if there were ten or a hundred times as many baskets, it would be normal for there to be a sufficiently uneven distribution of items that we might still be better off using the triples method. That is, some pairs would have very high counts, and the number of different pairs that occurred in one or more baskets would be much less than the theoretical maximum number of such pairs. □

6.2.3   Monotonicity of Itemsets

Much of the effectiveness of the algorithms we shall discuss is driven by a single observation, called *monotonicity* for itemsets:

- If a set I of items is frequent, then so is every subset of I.

The reason is simple. Let $J \subseteq I$. Then every basket that contains all the items in I surely contains all the items in J. Thus, the count for J must be at least as great as the count for I, and if the count for I is at least s, then the count for J is at least s. Since J may be contained in some baskets that are missing one or more elements of $I - J$, it is entirely possible that the count for J is strictly greater than the count for I.

In addition to making the A-Priori Algorithm work, monotonicity offers us a way to compact the information about frequent itemsets. If we are given a support threshold s, then we say an itemset is *maximal* if no superset is frequent. If we list only the maximal itemsets, then we know that all subsets of a maximal itemset are frequent, and no set that is not a subset of some maximal itemset can be frequent.

---

[1] Here, and throughout the chapter, we shall use the approximation that $\binom{n}{2} = n^2/2$ for large n.

EXAMPLE 6.7 Let us reconsider the data of Example 6.1 with support threshold $s = 3$. We found that there were five frequent singletons, those with words "cat," "dog," "a," "and," and "training." Each of these is contained in a frequent doubleton, except for "training," so one maximal frequent itemset is {training}. There are also five frequent doubletons with $s = 3$, namely

$$\{dog, a\} \quad \{dog, and\} \quad \{dog, cat\}$$
$$\{cat, a\} \quad \{cat, and\}$$

We also found one frequent triple, {dog, cat, a}, and there are no larger frequent itemsets. Thus, this triple is maximal, but the three frequent doubletons it contains are *not* maximal. The other frequent doubletons, {dog, and} and {cat, and}, are maximal. Notice that we can deduce from the frequent doubletons that singletons like {dog} are frequent. □

6.2.4 Tyranny of Counting Pairs

As you may have noticed, we have focused on the matter of counting pairs in the discussion so far. There is a good reason to do so: in practice the most main memory is required for determining the frequent pairs. The number of items, while possibly very large, is rarely so large we cannot count all the singleton sets in main memory at the same time.

What about larger sets – triples, quadruples, and so on? Recall that in order for frequent-itemset analysis to make sense, the result has to be a small number of sets, or we cannot even *read* them all, let alone consider their significance. Thus, in practice the support threshold is set high enough that it is only a rare set that is frequent. Monotonicity tells us that if there is a frequent triple, then there are three frequent pairs contained within it. And of course there may be frequent pairs contained in no frequent triple as well. Thus, we expect to find more frequent pairs than frequent triples, more frequent triples than frequent quadruples, and so on.

That argument would not be enough were it impossible to avoid counting all the triples, since there are many more triples than pairs. It is the job of the A-Priori Algorithm and related algorithms to avoid counting many triples or larger sets, and they are, as we shall see, effective in doing so. Thus, in what follows, we concentrate on algorithms for computing frequent pairs.

6.2.5 The A-Priori Algorithm

For the moment, let us concentrate on finding the frequent pairs only. If we have enough main memory to count all pairs, using either of the methods discussed in Section 6.2.2 (triangular matrix or triples), then it is a simple matter to read the file of baskets in a single pass. For each basket, we use a double loop to generate all the pairs. Each time we generate a pair, we add 1 to its count. At the end, we examine all pairs to see which have counts that are equal to or greater than the support threshold s; these are the frequent pairs.

However, this simple approach fails if there are too many pairs of items to count them all in main memory. The *A-Priori* Algorithm is designed to reduce the number of pairs that must be counted, at the expense of performing two passes over data, rather than one pass.

The First Pass of A-Priori

In the first pass, we create two tables. The first table, if necessary, translates item names into integers from 1 to n, as described in Section 6.2.2. The other table is an array of counts; the ith array element counts the occurrences of the item numbered i. Initially, the counts for all the items are 0.

As we read baskets, we look at each item in the basket and translate its name into an integer. Next, we use that integer to index into the array of counts, and we add 1 to the integer found there.

Between the Passes of A-Priori

After the first pass, we examine the counts of the items to determine which of them are frequent as singletons. It might appear surprising that many singletons are not frequent. But remember that we set the threshold s sufficiently high that we do not get too many frequent sets; a typical s would be 1% of the baskets. If we think about our own visits to a supermarket, we surely buy certain things more than 1% of the time: perhaps milk, bread, Coke or Pepsi, and so on. We can even believe that 1% of the customers buy diapers, even though we may not do so. However, many of the items on the shelves are surely not bought by 1% of the customers: Creamy Caesar Salad Dressing for example.

For the second pass of A-Priori, we create a new numbering from 1 to m for just the frequent items. This table is an array indexed 1 to n, and the entry for i is either 0, if item i is not frequent, or a unique integer in the range 1 to m if item i is frequent. We shall refer to this table as the *frequent-items table*.

The Second Pass of A-Priori

During the second pass, we count all the pairs that consist of two frequent items. Recall from Section 6.2.3 that a pair cannot be frequent unless both its members are frequent. Thus, we miss no frequent pairs. The space required on the second pass is $2m^2$ bytes, rather than $2n^2$ bytes, if we use the triangular-matrix method for counting. Notice that the renumbering of just the frequent items is necessary if we are to use a triangular matrix of the right size. The complete set of main-memory structures used in the first and second passes is shown in Fig. 6.3.

Also notice that the benefit of eliminating infrequent items is amplified; if only half the items are frequent we need one quarter of the space to count. Likewise, if we use the triples method, we need to count only those pairs of two frequent items that occur in at least one basket.

The mechanics of the second pass are as follows.

(1) For each basket, look in the frequent-items table to see which of its items are frequent.
(2) In a double loop, generate all pairs of frequent items in that basket.

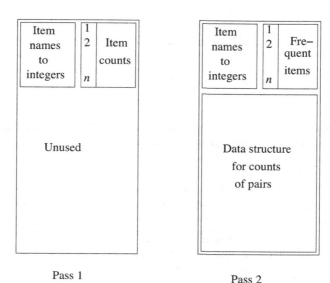

Figure 6.3 Schematic of main-memory use during the two passes of the A-Priori Algorithm

(3) For each such pair, add one to its count in the data structure used to store counts.

Finally, at the end of the second pass, examine the structure of counts to determine which pairs are frequent.

6.2.6   A-Priori for All Frequent Itemsets

The same technique used for finding frequent pairs without counting all pairs lets us find larger frequent itemsets without an exhaustive count of all sets. In the A-Priori Algorithm, one pass is taken for each set-size k. If no frequent itemsets of a certain size are found, then monotonicity tells us there can be no larger frequent itemsets, so we can stop.

The pattern of moving from one size k to the next size $k+1$ can be summarized as follows. For each size k, there are two sets of itemsets:

(1) C_k is the set of *candidate* itemsets of size k – the itemsets that we must count in order to determine whether they are in fact frequent.

(2) L_k is the set of truly frequent itemsets of size k.

The pattern of moving from one set to the next and one size to the next is suggested by Fig. 6.4.

We start with C_1, which is all singleton itemsets, i.e., the items themselves. That is, before we examine the data, any item could be frequent as far as we know. The first filter step is to count all items, and those whose counts are at least the support threshold s form the set L_1 of frequent items.

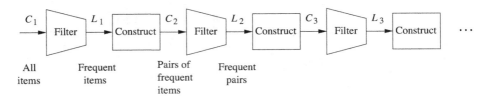

Figure 6.4 The A-Priori Algorithm alternates between constructing candidate sets and filtering to find those that are truly frequent

The set C_2 of candidate pairs is the set of pairs both of whose items are in L_1; that is, they are frequent items. Note that we do not construct C_2 explicitly. Rather we use the definition of C_2, and we test membership in C_2 by testing whether both of its members are in L_1. The second pass of the A-Priori Algorithm counts all the candidate pairs and determines which appear at least s times. These pairs form L_2, the frequent pairs.

We can follow this pattern as far as we wish. The set C_3 of candidate triples is constructed (implicitly) as the set of triples, any two of which is a pair in L_2. Our assumption about the sparsity of frequent itemsets, outlined in Section 6.2.4 implies that there will not be too many frequent pairs, so they can be listed in a main-memory table. Likewise, there will not be too many candidate triples, so these can all be counted by a generalization of the triples method. That is, while triples are used to count pairs, we would use quadruples, consisting of the three item codes and the associated count, when we want to count triples. Similarly, we can count sets of size k using tuples with $k+1$ components, the last of which is the count, and the first k of which are the item codes, in sorted order.

To find L_3 we make a third pass through the basket file. For each basket, we need only look at those items that are in L_1. From these items, we can examine each pair and determine whether or not that pair is in L_2. Any item of the basket that does not appear in at least two frequent pairs, both of which consist of items in the basket, cannot be part of a frequent triple that the basket contains. Thus, we have a fairly limited search for triples that are both contained in the basket and are candidates in C_3. Any such triples found have 1 added to their count.

EXAMPLE 6.8   Suppose our basket consists of items 1 through 10. Of these, 1 through 5 have been found to be frequent items, and the following pairs have been found frequent: $\{1,2\}$, $\{2,3\}$, $\{3,4\}$, and $\{4,5\}$. At first, we eliminate the nonfrequent items, leaving only 1 through 5. However, 1 and 5 appear in only one frequent pair in the itemset, and therefore cannot contribute to a frequent triple contained in the basket. Thus, we must consider adding to the count of triples that are contained in $\{2,3,4\}$. There is only one such triple, of course. However, we shall not find it in C_3, because $\{2,4\}$ evidently is not frequent.   □

The construction of the collections of larger frequent itemsets and candidates proceeds in essentially the same manner, until at some pass we find no new frequent itemsets and stop. That is:

(1) Define C_k to be all those itemsets of size k, every $k-1$ of which is an itemset in L_{k-1}.
(2) Find L_k by making a pass through the baskets and counting all and only the itemsets of size k that are in C_k. Those itemsets that have count at least s are in L_k.

6.2.7 Exercises for Section 6.2

EXERCISE 6.2.1 If we use a triangular matrix to count pairs, and n, the number of items, is 20, what pair's count is in $a[100]$?

! EXERCISE 6.2.2 In our description of the triangular-matrix method in Section 6.2.2, the formula for k involves dividing an arbitrary integer i by 2. Yet we need to have k always be an integer. Prove that k will, in fact, be an integer.

! EXERCISE 6.2.3 Let there be I items in a market-basket data set of B baskets. Suppose that every basket contains exactly K items. As a function of I, B, and K:

(a) How much space does the triangular-matrix method take to store the counts of all pairs of items, assuming four bytes per array element?
(b) What is the largest possible number of pairs with a nonzero count?
(c) Under what circumstances can we be certain that the triples method will use less space than the triangular array?

!! EXERCISE 6.2.4 How would you count all itemsets of size 3 by a generalization of the triangular-matrix method? That is, arrange that in a one-dimensional array there is exactly one element for each set of three items.

! EXERCISE 6.2.5 Suppose the support threshold is 5. Find the maximal frequent itemsets for the data of:

(a) Exercise 6.1.1.
(b) Exercise 6.1.3.

EXERCISE 6.2.6 Apply the A-Priori Algorithm with support threshold 5 to the data of:

(a) Exercise 6.1.1.
(b) Exercise 6.1.3.

! EXERCISE 6.2.7 Suppose we have market baskets that satisfy the following assumptions:

(1) The support threshold is 10,000.
(2) There are one million items, represented by the integers $0, 1, \ldots, 999999$.

(3) There are N frequent items, that is, items that occur 10,000 times or more.

(4) There are one million pairs that occur 10,000 times or more.

(5) There are $2M$ pairs that occur exactly once. Of these pairs, M consist of two frequent items; the other M each have at least one nonfrequent item.

(6) No other pairs occur at all.

(7) Integers are always represented by 4 bytes.

Suppose we run the A-Priori Algorithm and can choose on the second pass between the triangular-matrix method for counting candidate pairs and a hash table of item-item-count triples. Neglect in the first case the space needed to translate between original item numbers and numbers for the frequent items, and in the second case neglect the space needed for the hash table. As a function of N and M, what is the minimum number of bytes of main memory needed to execute the A-Priori Algorithm on this data?

6.3   Handling Larger Datasets in Main Memory

The A-Priori Algorithm is fine as long as the step with the greatest requirement for main memory – typically the counting of the candidate pairs C_2 – has enough memory that it can be accomplished without thrashing (repeated moving of data between disk and main memory). Several algorithms have been proposed to cut down on the size of candidate set C_2. Here, we consider the PCY Algorithm, which takes advantage of the fact that in the first pass of A-Priori there is typically lots of main memory not needed for the counting of single items. Then we look at the Multistage Algorithm, which uses the PCY trick and also inserts extra passes to further reduce the size of C_2.

6.3.1   The Algorithm of Park, Chen, and Yu

This algorithm, which we call *PCY* after its authors, exploits the observation that there may be much unused space in main memory on the first pass. If there are a million items and gigabytes of main memory, we do not need more than 10% of the main memory for the two tables suggested in Fig. 6.3 – a translation table from item names to small integers and an array to count those integers. The PCY Algorithm uses that space for an array of integers that generalizes the idea of a Bloom filter (see Section 4.3). The idea is shown schematically in Fig. 6.5.

Think of this array as a hash table, whose buckets hold integers rather than sets of keys (as in an ordinary hash table) or bits (as in a Bloom filter). Pairs of items are hashed to buckets of this hash table. As we examine a basket during the first pass, we not only add 1 to the count for each item in the basket, but we generate all the pairs, using a double loop. We hash each pair, and we add 1 to the bucket into which that pair hashes. Note that the pair itself doesn't go into the bucket; the pair only affects the single integer in the bucket.

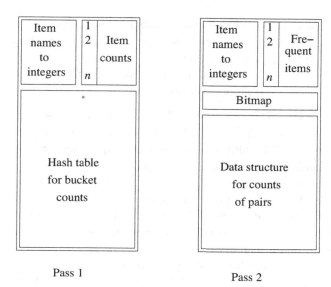

Figure 6.5 Organization of main memory for the first two passes of the PCY Algorithm

At the end of the first pass, each bucket has a count, which is the sum of the counts of all the pairs that hash to that bucket. If the count of a bucket is at least as great as the support threshold s, it is called a *frequent bucket*. We can say nothing about the pairs that hash to a frequent bucket; they could all be frequent pairs from the information available to us. But if the count of the bucket is less than s (an *infrequent bucket*), we know no pair that hashes to this bucket can be frequent, even if the pair consists of two frequent items. That fact gives us an advantage on the second pass. We can define the set of candidate pairs C_2 to be those pairs $\{i, j\}$ such that:

(1) i and j are frequent items.
(2) $\{i, j\}$ hashes to a frequent bucket.

It is the second condition that distinguishes PCY from A-Priori.

EXAMPLE 6.9 Depending on the data and the amount of available main memory, there may or may not be a benefit to using the hash table on pass 1. In the worst case, all buckets are frequent, and the PCY Algorithm counts exactly the same pairs as A-Priori does on the second pass. However, sometimes, we can expect most of the buckets to be infrequent. In that case, PCY reduces the memory requirements of the second pass.

Suppose we have a gigabyte of main memory available for the hash table on the first pass. Suppose also that the data file has a billion baskets, each with ten items. A bucket is an integer, typically 4 bytes, so we can maintain a quarter of a billion buckets. The number of pairs in all the baskets is $10^9 \times \binom{10}{2}$ or 4.5×10^{10} pairs; this number is also the sum of the counts in the buckets. Thus, the average count is $4.5 \times 10^{10}/2.5 \times 10^8$, or 180. If the support threshold s is around 180 or less, we might expect few buckets to be infrequent. However, if s is much larger, say 1000, then it must be that the great majority of the buckets are infrequent. The greatest possible number of frequent buckets is $4.5 \times 10^{10}/1000$, or 45 million out of the 250 million buckets. □

Between the passes of PCY, the hash table is summarized as a *bitmap*, with one bit for each bucket. The bit is 1 if the bucket is frequent and 0 if not. Thus integers of 32 bits are replaced by single bits, and the bitmap shown in the second pass in Fig. 6.5 takes up only 1/32 of the space that would otherwise be available to store counts. However, if most buckets are infrequent, we expect that the number of pairs being counted on the second pass will be much smaller than the total number of pairs of frequent items. Thus, PCY can handle some data sets without thrashing during the second pass, while A-Priori would run out of main memory and thrash.

There is another subtlety regarding the second pass of PCY that affects the amount of space needed. While we were able to use the triangular-matrix method on the second pass of A-Priori if we wished, because the frequent items could be renumbered from 1 to some m, we cannot do so for PCY. The reason is that the pairs of frequent items that PCY lets us avoid counting are placed randomly within the triangular matrix; they are the pairs that happen to hash to an infrequent bucket on the first pass. There is no known way of compacting the matrix to avoid leaving space for the uncounted pairs.

Consequently, we are forced to use the triples method in PCY. That restriction may not matter if the fraction of pairs of frequent items that actually appear in buckets were small; we would then want to use triples for A-Priori anyway. However, if most pairs of frequent items appear together in at least one bucket, then we are forced in PCY to use triples, while A-Priori can use a triangular matrix. Thus, unless PCY lets us avoid counting at least 2/3 of the pairs of frequent items, we cannot gain by using PCY instead of A-Priori.

While the discovery of frequent pairs by PCY differs significantly from A-Priori, the later stages, where we find frequent triples and larger sets if desired, are essentially the same as A-Priori. This statement holds as well for each of the improvements to A-Priori that we cover in this section. As a result, we shall cover only the construction of the frequent pairs from here on.

6.3.2   The Multistage Algorithm

The *Multistage Algorithm* improves upon PCY by using several successive hash tables to reduce further the number of candidate pairs. The tradeoff is that Multistage takes more than two passes to find the frequent pairs. An outline of the Multistage Algorithm is shown in Fig. 6.6.

The first pass of Multistage is the same as the first pass of PCY. After that pass, the frequent buckets are identified and summarized by a bitmap, again the same as in PCY. But the second pass of Multistage does not count the candidate

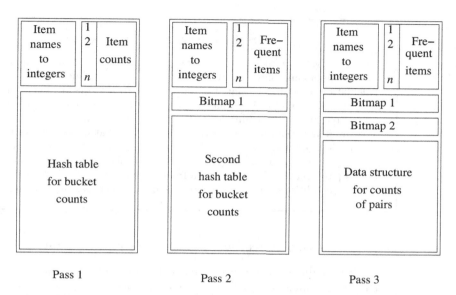

Figure 6.6 The Multistage Algorithm uses additional hash tables to reduce the number of candidate pairs

pairs. Rather, it uses the available main memory for another hash table, using another hash function. Since the bitmap from the first hash table takes up 1/32 of the available main memory, the second hash table has almost as many buckets as the first.

On the second pass of Multistage, we again go through the file of baskets. There is no need to count the items again, since we have those counts from the first pass. However, we must retain the information about which items are frequent, since we need it on both the second and third passes. During the second pass, we hash certain pairs of items to buckets of the second hash table. A pair is hashed only if it meets the two criteria for being counted in the second pass of PCY; that is, we hash $\{i, j\}$ if and only if i and j are both frequent, and the pair hashed to a frequent bucket on the first pass. As a result, the sum of the counts in the second hash table should be significantly less than the sum for the first pass. The result is that, even though the second hash table has only 31/32 of the number of buckets that the first table has, we expect there to be many fewer frequent buckets in the second hash table than in the first.

After the second pass, the second hash table is also summarized as a bitmap, and that bitmap is stored in main memory. The two bitmaps together take up slightly less than 1/16th of the available main memory, so there is still plenty of space to count the candidate pairs on the third pass. A pair $\{i, j\}$ is in C_2 if and only if:

(1) i and j are both frequent items.

(2) $\{i, j\}$ hashed to a frequent bucket in the first hash table.

A Subtle Error in Multistage

Occasionally, an implementation tries to eliminate the second requirement for $\{i, j\}$ to be a candidate – that it hashes to a frequent bucket on the first pass. The (false) reasoning is that if it didn't hash to a frequent bucket on the first pass, it wouldn't have been hashed at all on the second pass, and thus would not contribute to the count of its bucket on the second pass. While it is true that the pair is not counted on the second pass, that doesn't mean it wouldn't have hashed to a frequent bucket had it been hashed. Thus, it is entirely possible that $\{i, j\}$ consists of two frequent items and hashes to a frequent bucket on the second pass, yet it did not hash to a frequent bucket on the first pass. Therefore, all three conditions must be checked on the counting pass of Multistage.

---

(3) $\{i, j\}$ hashed to a frequent bucket in the second hash table.

The third condition is the distinction between Multistage and PCY.

It might be obvious that it is possible to insert any number of passes between the first and last in the multistage Algorithm. There is a limiting factor that each pass must store the bitmaps from each of the previous passes. Eventually, there is not enough space left in main memory to do the counts. No matter how many passes we use, the truly frequent pairs will always hash to a frequent bucket, so there is no way to avoid counting them.

6.3.3   The Multihash Algorithm

Sometimes, we can get most of the benefit of the extra passes of the Multistage Algorithm in a single pass. This variation of PCY is called the *Multihash Algorithm*. Instead of using two different hash tables on two successive passes, use two hash functions and two separate hash tables that share main memory on the first pass, as suggested by Fig. 6.7.

The danger of using two hash tables on one pass is that each hash table has half as many buckets as the one large hash table of PCY. As long as the average count of a bucket for PCY is much lower than the support threshold, we can operate two half-sized hash tables and still expect most of the buckets of both hash tables to be infrequent. Thus, in this situation we might well choose the multihash approach.

EXAMPLE 6.10   Suppose that if we run PCY, the average bucket will have a count $s/10$, where s is the support threshold. Then if we used the Multihash approach with two half-sized hash tables, the average count would be $s/5$. As a result, at most 1/5th of the buckets in either hash table could be frequent, and a random infrequent pair has at most probability $(1/5)^2 = 0.04$ of being in a frequent bucket in both hash tables.

By the same reasoning, the upper bound on the infrequent pair being in a frequent bucket in the one PCY hash table is at most 1/10. That is, we might

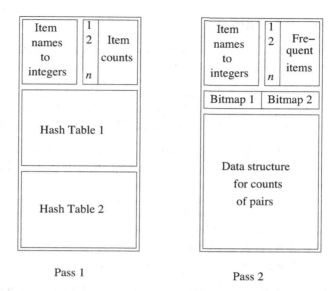

Figure 6.7 The Multihash Algorithm uses several hash tables in one pass

expect to have to count 2.5 times as many infrequent pairs in PCY as in the version of Multihash suggested above. We would therefore expect Multihash to have a smaller memory requirement for the second pass than would PCY.

But these upper bounds do not tell the complete story. There may be many fewer frequent buckets than the maximum for either algorithm, since the presence of some very frequent pairs will skew the distribution of bucket counts. However, this analysis is suggestive of the possibility that for some data and support thresholds, we can do better by running several hash functions in main memory at once.   □

For the second pass of Multihash, each hash table is converted to a bitmap, as usual. Note that the two bitmaps for the two hash functions in Fig. 6.7 occupy exactly as much space as a single bitmap would for the second pass of the PCY Algorithm. The conditions for a pair $\{i, j\}$ to be in C_2, and thus to require a count on the second pass, are the same as for the third pass of Multistage: i and j must both be frequent, and the pair must have hashed to a frequent bucket according to both hash tables.

Just as Multistage is not limited to two hash tables, we can divide the available main memory into as many hash tables as we like on the first pass of Multihash. The risk is that should we use too many hash tables, the average count for a bucket will exceed the support threshold. At that point, there may be very few infrequent buckets in any of the hash tables. Even though a pair must hash to a frequent bucket in every hash table to be counted, we may find that the probability an infrequent pair will be a candidate rises, rather than falls, if we add another hash table.

6.3.4   Exercises for Section 6.3

EXERCISE 6.3.1   Here is a collection of twelve baskets. Each contains three of the six items 1 through 6.

$$\{1,2,3\} \quad \{2,3,4\} \quad \{3,4,5\} \quad \{4,5,6\}$$
$$\{1,3,5\} \quad \{2,4,6\} \quad \{1,3,4\} \quad \{2,4,5\}$$
$$\{3,5,6\} \quad \{1,2,4\} \quad \{2,3,5\} \quad \{3,4,6\}$$

Suppose the support threshold is 4. On the first pass of the PCY Algorithm we use a hash table with 11 buckets, and the set $\{i,j\}$ is hashed to bucket $i \times j$ mod 11.

(a) By any method, compute the support for each item and each pair of items.
(b) Which pairs hash to which buckets?
(c) Which buckets are frequent?
(d) Which pairs are counted on the second pass of the PCY Algorithm?

EXERCISE 6.3.2   Suppose we run the Multistage Algorithm on the data of Exercise 6.3.1, with the same support threshold of 4. The first pass is the same as in that exercise, and for the second pass, we hash pairs to nine buckets, using the hash function that hashes $\{i,j\}$ to bucket $i+j$ mod 9. Determine the counts of the buckets on the second pass. Does the second pass reduce the set of candidate pairs? Note that all items are frequent, so the only reason a pair would not be hashed on the second pass is if it hashed to an infrequent bucket on the first pass.

EXERCISE 6.3.3   Suppose we run the Multihash Algorithm on the data of Exercise 6.3.1. We shall use two hash tables with five buckets each. For one, the set $\{i,j\}$, is hashed to bucket $2i + 3j + 4$ mod 5, and for the other, the set is hashed to $i+4j$ mod 5. Since these hash functions are not symmetric in i and j, order the items so that $i < j$ when evaluating each hash function. Determine the counts of each of the 10 buckets. How large does the support threshold have to be for the Multistage Algorithm to eliminate more pairs than the PCY Algorithm would, using the hash table and function described in Exercise 6.3.1?

! EXERCISE 6.3.4   Suppose we perform the PCY Algorithm to find frequent pairs, with market-basket data meeting the following specifications:

(1) The support threshold is 10,000.
(2) There are one million items, represented by the integers $0, 1, \ldots, 999999$.
(3) There are 250,000 frequent items, that is, items that occur 10,000 times or more.
(4) There are one million pairs that occur 10,000 times or more.
(5) There are P pairs that occur exactly once and consist of two frequent items.
(6) No other pairs occur at all.
(7) Integers are always represented by 4 bytes.

(8) When we hash pairs, they distribute among buckets randomly, but as evenly as possible; i.e., you may assume that each bucket gets exactly its fair share of the P pairs that occur once.

Suppose there are S bytes of main memory. In order to run the PCY Algorithm successfully, the number of buckets must be sufficiently large that most buckets are not frequent. In addition, on the second pass, there must be enough room to count all the candidate pairs. As a function of S, what is the largest value of P for which we can successfully run the PCY Algorithm on this data?

! EXERCISE 6.3.5   Under the assumptions given in Exercise 6.3.4, will the Multihash Algorithm reduce the main-memory requirements for the second pass? As a function of S and P, what is the optimum number of hash tables to use on the first pass?

! EXERCISE 6.3.6   Suppose we perform the 3-pass Multistage Algorithm to find frequent pairs, with market-basket data meeting the following specifications:

(1) The support threshold is 10,000.
(2) There are one million items, represented by the integers $0, 1, \ldots, 999999$. All items are frequent; that is, they occur at least 10,000 times.
(3) There are one million pairs that occur 10,000 times or more.
(4) There are P pairs that occur exactly once.
(5) No other pairs occur at all.
(6) Integers are always represented by 4 bytes.
(7) When we hash pairs, they distribute among buckets randomly, but as evenly as possible; i.e., you may assume that each bucket gets exactly its fair share of the P pairs that occur once.
(8) The hash functions used on the first two passes are completely independent.

Suppose there are S bytes of main memory. As a function of S and P, what is the expected number of candidate pairs on the third pass of the Multistage Algorithm?

6.4   Limited-Pass Algorithms

The algorithms for frequent itemsets discussed so far use one pass for each size of itemset we investigate. If main memory is too small to hold the data and the space needed to count frequent itemsets of one size, there does not seem to be any way to avoid k passes to compute the exact collection of frequent itemsets. However, there are many applications where it is not essential to discover every frequent itemset. For instance, if we are looking for items purchased together at a supermarket, we are not going to run a sale based on every frequent itemset we find, so it is quite sufficient to find most but not all of the frequent itemsets.

    In this section we explore some algorithms that have been proposed to find

---

> ### Why Not Just Pick the First Part of the File?
>
> The risk in selecting a sample from one portion of a large file is that the data is
> not uniformly distributed in the file. For example, suppose the file were a list of
> true market-basket contents at a department store, organized by date of sale. If
> you took only the first baskets in the file, you would have old data. For example,
> there would be no iPods in these baskets, even though iPods might have become
> a popular item later.
>
> As another example, consider a file of medical tests performed at different
> hospitals. If each chunk comes from a different hospital, then picking chunks at
> random will give us a sample drawn from only a small subset of the hospitals.
> If hospitals perform different tests or perform them in different ways, the data
> may be highly biased.

all or most frequent itemsets using at most two passes. We begin with the obvious approach of using a sample of the data rather than the entire dataset. An algorithm called SON uses two passes, gets the exact answer, and lends itself to implementation by MapReduce or another parallel computing regime. Finally, Toivonen's Algorithm uses two passes on average, gets an exact answer, but may, rarely, not terminate in any given amount of time.

6.4.1   The Simple, Randomized Algorithm

Instead of using the entire file of baskets, we could pick a random subset of the baskets and pretend it is the entire dataset. We must adjust the support threshold to reflect the smaller number of baskets. For instance, if the support threshold for the full dataset is s, and we choose a sample of 1% of the baskets, then we should examine the sample for itemsets that appear in at least $s/100$ of the baskets.

The safest way to pick the sample is to read the entire dataset, and for each basket, select that basket for the sample with some fixed probability p. Suppose there are m baskets in the entire file. At the end, we shall have a sample whose size is very close to pm baskets. However, if we have reason to believe that the baskets appear in random order in the file already, then we do not even have to read the entire file. We can select the first pm baskets for our sample. Or, if the file is part of a distributed file system, we can pick some chunks at random to serve as the sample.

Having selected our sample of the baskets, we use part of main memory to store these baskets. The balance of the main memory is used to execute one of the algorithms we have discussed, such as A-Priori, PCY, Multistage, or Multihash. However, the algorithm must run passes over the main-memory sample for each itemset size, until we find a size with no frequent items. There are no disk accesses needed to read the sample, since it resides in main memory. As frequent itemsets of each size are discovered, they can be written out to disk; this operation and the initial reading of the sample from disk are the only disk I/O's the algorithm does.

Of course the algorithm will fail if whichever method from Section 6.2 or 6.3 we choose cannot be run in the amount of main memory left after storing the sample. If we need more main memory, then an option is to read the sample from disk for each pass. Since the sample is much smaller than the full dataset, we still avoid most of the disk I/O's that the algorithms discussed previously would use.

6.4.2 Avoiding Errors in Sampling Algorithms

We should be mindful of the problem with the simple algorithm of Section 6.4.1: it cannot be relied upon either to produce all the itemsets that are frequent in the whole dataset, nor will it produce only itemsets that are frequent in the whole. An itemset that is frequent in the whole but not in the sample is a *false negative*, while an itemset that is frequent in the sample but not the whole is a *false positive*.

If the sample is large enough, there are unlikely to be serious errors. That is, an itemset whose support is much larger than the threshold will almost surely be identified from a random sample, and an itemset whose support is much less than the threshold is unlikely to appear frequent in the sample. However, an itemset whose support in the whole is very close to the threshold is as likely to be frequent in the sample as not.

We can eliminate false positives by making a pass through the full dataset and counting all the itemsets that were identified as frequent in the sample. Retain as frequent only those itemsets that were frequent in the sample and also frequent in the whole. Note that this improvement will eliminate all false positives, but a false negative is not counted and therefore remains undiscovered.

To accomplish this task in a single pass, we need to be able to count all frequent itemsets of all sizes at once, within main memory. If we were able to run the simple algorithm successfully with the main memory available, then there is a good chance we shall be able to count all the frequent itemsets at once, because:

(a) The frequent singletons and pairs are likely to dominate the collection of all frequent itemsets, and we had to count them all in one pass already.
(b) We now have all of main memory available, since we do not have to store the sample in main memory.

We cannot eliminate false negatives completely, but we can reduce their number if the amount of main memory allows it. We have assumed that if s is the support threshold, and the sample is fraction p of the entire dataset, then we use ps as the support threshold for the sample. However, we can use something smaller than that as the threshold for the sample, such a $0.9ps$. Having a lower threshold means that more itemsets of each size will have to be counted, so the main-memory requirement rises. On the other hand, if there is enough main memory, then we shall identify as having support at least $0.9ps$ in the sample almost all those itemsets that have support at least s is the whole. If we then make a complete pass to eliminate those itemsets that were identified as frequent in the sample but are not frequent in the whole, we have no false positives and hopefully have none or very few false negatives.

6.4.3   The Algorithm of Savasere, Omiecinski, and Navathe

Our next improvement avoids both false negatives and false positives, at the cost of making two full passes. It is called the *SON* Algorithm after the authors. The idea is to divide the input file into chunks (which may be "chunks" in the sense of a distributed file system, or simply a piece of the file). Treat each chunk as a sample, and run the algorithm of Section 6.4.1 on that chunk. We use ps as the threshold, if each chunk is fraction p of the whole file, and s is the support threshold. Store on disk all the frequent itemsets found for each chunk.

Once all the chunks have been processed in that way, take the union of all the itemsets that have been found frequent for one or more chunks. These are the *candidate* itemsets. Notice that if an itemset is not frequent in any chunk, then its support is less than ps in each chunk. Since the number of chunks is $1/p$, we conclude that the total support for that itemset is less than $(1/p)ps = s$. Thus, every itemset that is frequent in the whole is frequent in at least one chunk, and we can be sure that all the truly frequent itemsets are among the candidates; i.e., there are no false negatives.

We have made a total of one pass through the data as we read each chunk and processed it. In a second pass, we count all the candidate itemsets and select those that have support at least s as the frequent itemsets.

6.4.4   The SON Algorithm and MapReduce

The SON algorithm lends itself well to a parallel-computing environment. Each of the chunks can be processed in parallel, and the frequent itemsets from each chunk combined to form the candidates. We can distribute the candidates to many processors, have each processor count the support for each candidate in a subset of the baskets, and finally sum those supports to get the support for each candidate itemset in the whole dataset. This process does not have to be implemented in MapReduce, but there is a natural way of expressing each of the two passes as a MapReduce operation. We shall summarize this MapReduce-MapReduce sequence below.

First Map Function: Take the assigned subset of the baskets and find the itemsets frequent in the subset using the algorithm of Section 6.4.1. As described there, lower the support threshold from s to ps if each Map task gets fraction p of the total input file. The output is a set of key-value pairs $(F, 1)$, where F is a frequent itemset from the sample. The value is always 1 and is irrelevant.

First Reduce Function: Each Reduce task is assigned a set of keys, which are itemsets. The value is ignored, and the Reduce task simply produces those keys (itemsets) that appear one or more times. Thus, the output of the first Reduce function is the candidate itemsets.

Second Map Function: The Map tasks for the second Map function take all the output from the first Reduce Function (the candidate itemsets) and a portion of the input data file. Each Map task counts the number of occurrences of each of the candidate itemsets among the baskets in the portion of the dataset that it was assigned. The output is a set of key-value pairs (C, v), where C is one of the candidate sets and v is the support for that itemset among the baskets that were input to this Map task.

Second Reduce Function: The Reduce tasks take the itemsets they are given as keys and sum the associated values. The result is the total support for each of the itemsets that the Reduce task was assigned to handle. Those itemsets whose sum of values is at least s are frequent in the whole dataset, so the Reduce task outputs these itemsets with their counts. Itemsets that do not have total support at least s are not transmitted to the output of the Reduce task.[2]

6.4.5   Toivonen's Algorithm

This algorithm uses randomness in a different way from the simple sampling algorithm of Section 6.4.1. Toivonen's Algorithm, given sufficient main memory, will use one pass over a small sample and one full pass over the data. It will give neither false negatives nor positives, but there is a small yet nonzero probability that it will fail to produce any answer at all. In that case it needs to be repeated until it gives an answer. However, the average number of passes needed before it produces all and only the frequent itemsets is a small constant.

Toivonen's algorithm begins by selecting a small sample of the input dataset, and finding from it the candidate frequent itemsets. The process is exactly that of Section 6.4.1, except that it is essential the threshold be set to something less than its proportional value. That is, if the support threshold for the whole dataset is s, and the sample size is fraction p, then when looking for frequent itemsets in the sample, use a threshold such as $0.9ps$ or $0.8ps$. The smaller we make the threshold, the more main memory we need for computing all itemsets that are frequent in the sample, but the more likely we are to avoid the situation where the algorithm fails to provide an answer.

Having constructed the collection of frequent itemsets for the sample, we next construct the *negative border*. This is the collection of itemsets that are not frequent in the sample, but all of their *immediate subsets* (subsets constructed by deleting exactly one item) are frequent in the sample.

---

[2] Strictly speaking, the Reduce function has to produce a value for each key. It can produce 1 as the value for itemsets found frequent and 0 for those not frequent.

EXAMPLE 6.11   Suppose the items are $\{A, B, C, D, E\}$ and we have found the following itemsets to be frequent in the sample: $\{A\}$, $\{B\}$, $\{C\}$, $\{D\}$, $\{B, C\}$, $\{C, D\}$. Note that $\emptyset$ is also frequent, as long as there are at least as many baskets as the support threshold, although technically the algorithms we have described omit this obvious fact. First, $\{E\}$ is in the negative border, because it is not frequent in the sample, but its only immediate subset, $\emptyset$, is frequent.

The sets $\{A, B\}$, $\{A, C\}$, $\{A, D\}$ and $\{B, D\}$ are in the negative border. None of these sets are frequent, and each has two immediate subsets, both of which are frequent. For instance, $\{A, B\}$ has immediate subsets $\{A\}$ and $\{B\}$. Of the other six doubletons, none are in the negative border. The sets $\{B, C\}$ and $\{C, D\}$ are not in the negative border, because they are frequent. The remaining four pairs are each E together with another item, and those are not in the negative border because they have an immediate subset $\{E\}$ that is not frequent.

None of the triples or larger sets are in the negative border. For instance, $\{B, C, D\}$ is not in the negative border because it has an immediate subset $\{B, D\}$ that is not frequent. Thus, the negative border consists of five sets: $\{E\}$, $\{A, B\}$, $\{A, C\}$, $\{A, D\}$ and $\{B, D\}$.   □

To complete Toivonen's algorithm, we make a pass through the entire dataset, counting all the itemsets that are frequent in the sample or are in the negative border. There are two possible outcomes.

(1) No member of the negative border is frequent in the whole dataset. In this case, the correct set of frequent itemsets is exactly those itemsets from the sample that were found to be frequent in the whole.
(2) Some member of the negative border is frequent in the whole. Then we cannot be sure that there are not some even larger sets, in neither the negative border nor the collection of frequent itemsets for the sample, that are also frequent in the whole. Thus, we can give no answer at this time and must repeat the algorithm with a new random sample.

6.4.6   Why Toivonen's Algorithm Works

Clearly Toivonen's algorithm never produces a false positive, since it only reports as frequent those itemsets that have been counted and found to be frequent in the whole. To argue that it never produces a false negative, we must show that when no member of the negative border is frequent in the whole, then there can be no itemset whatsoever that is:

(1) Frequent in the whole, but
(2) In neither the negative border nor the collection of frequent itemsets for the sample.

Suppose the contrary. That is, there is a set S that is frequent in the whole, but not in the negative border and not frequent in the sample. Also, this round of Toivonen's Algorithm produced an answer, which would certainly not include S

among the frequent itemsets. By monotonicity, all subsets of S are also frequent in the whole. Let T be a subset of S that is of the smallest possible size among all subsets of S that are not frequent in the sample.

We claim that T must be in the negative border. Surely T meets one of the conditions for being in the negative border: it is not frequent in the sample. It also meets the other condition for being in the negative border: each of its immediate subsets is frequent in the sample. For if some immediate subset of T were not frequent in the sample, then there would be a subset of S that is smaller than T and not frequent in the sample, contradicting our selection of T as a subset of S that was not frequent in the sample, yet as small as any such set.

Now we see that T is both in the negative border and frequent in the whole dataset. Consequently, this round of Toivonen's algorithm did not produce an answer.

6.4.7 Exercises for Section 6.4

EXERCISE 6.4.1 Suppose there are eight items, $A, B, \ldots, H$, and the following are the maximal frequent itemsets: $\{A, B\}$, $\{B, C\}$, $\{A, C\}$, $\{A, D\}$, $\{E\}$, and $\{F\}$. Find the negative border.

EXERCISE 6.4.2 Apply Toivonen's Algorithm to the data of Exercise 6.3.1, with a support threshold of 4. Take as the sample the first row of baskets: $\{1, 2, 3\}$, $\{2, 3, 4\}$, $\{3, 4, 5\}$, and $\{4, 5, 6\}$, i.e., one-third of the file. Our scaled-down support theshold will be 1.

(a) What are the itemsets frequent in the sample?
(b) What is the negative border?
(c) What is the outcome of the pass through the full dataset? Are any of the itemsets in the negative border frequent in the whole?

!! EXERCISE 6.4.3 Suppose item i appears exactly s times in a file of n baskets, where s is the support threshold. If we take a sample of $n/100$ baskets, and lower the support threshold for the sample to $s/100$, what is the probability that i will be found to be frequent? You may assume that both s and n are divisible by 100.

6.5 Counting Frequent Items in a Stream

Suppose that instead of a file of baskets we have a stream of baskets, from which we want to mine the frequent itemsets. Recall from Chapter 4 that the difference between a stream and a data file is that stream elements are only available when they arrive, and typically the arrival rate is so great that we cannot store the entire stream in a way that allows easy querying. Further, it is common that streams evolve over time, so the itemsets that are frequent in today's stream may not be frequent tomorrow.

A clear distinction between streams and files, when frequent itemsets are considered, is that there is no end to a stream, so eventually an itemset is going to exceed the support threshold, as long as it appears repeatedly in the stream. As a result, for streams, we must think of the support threshold s as a fraction of the baskets in which an itemset must appear in order to be considered frequent. Even with this adjustment, we still have several options regarding the portion of the stream over which that fraction is measured.

In this section, we shall discuss several ways that we might extract frequent itemsets from a stream. First, we consider ways to use the sampling techniques of the previous section. Then, we consider the decaying-window model from Section 4.7, and extend the method described in Section 4.7.3 for finding "popular" items.

6.5.1 Sampling Methods for Streams

In what follows, we shall assume that stream elements are baskets of items. Perhaps the simplest approach to maintaining a current estimate of the frequent itemsets in a stream is to collect some number of baskets and store it as a file. Run one of the frequent-itemset algorithms discussed in this chapter, meanwhile ignoring the stream elements that arrive, or storing them as another file to be analyzed later. When the frequent-itemsets algorithm finishes, we have an estimate of the frequent itemsets in the stream. We then have several options.

(1) We can use this collection of frequent itemsets for whatever application is at hand, but start running another iteration of the chosen frequent-itemset algorithm immediately. This algorithm can either:

  (a) Use the file that was collected while the first iteration of the algorithm was running. At the same time, collect yet another file to be used at another iteration of the algorithm, when this current iteration finishes.

  (b) Start collecting another file of baskets now, and run the algorithm when an adequate number of baskets has been collected.

(2) We can continue to count the numbers of occurrences of each of these frequent itemsets, along with the total number of baskets seen in the stream, since the counting started. If any itemset is discovered to occur in a fraction of the baskets that is significantly below the threshold fraction s, then this set can be dropped from the collection of frequent itemsets. When computing the fraction, it is important to include the occurrences from the original file of baskets, from which the frequent itemsets were derived. If not, we run the risk that we shall encounter a short period in which a truly frequent itemset does not appear sufficiently frequently and throw it out. We should also allow some way for new frequent itemsets to be added to the current collection. Possibilities include:

(a) Periodically gather a new segment of the baskets in the stream and use it as the data file for another iteration of the chosen frequent-itemsets algorithm. The new collection of frequent items is formed from the result of this iteration and the frequent itemsets from the previous collection that have survived the possibility of having been deleted for becoming infrequent.

(b) Add some random itemsets to the current collection, and count their fraction of occurrences for a while, until one has a good idea of whether or not they are currently frequent. Rather than choosing new itemsets completely at random, one might focus on sets with items that appear in many itemsets already known to be frequent. For example, a good choice is to pick new itemsets from the negative border (Section 6.4.5) of the current set of frequent itemsets.

6.5.2 Frequent Itemsets in Decaying Windows

Recall from Section 4.7 that a decaying window on a stream is formed by picking a small constant c and giving the ith element prior to the most recent element the weight $(1-c)^i$, or approximately e^{-ci}. Section 4.7.3 actually presented a method for computing the frequent items, provided the support threshold is defined in a somewhat different way. That is, we considered, for each item, a stream that had 1 if the item appeared at a certain stream element and 0 if not. We defined the "score" for that item to be the sum of the weights where its stream element was 1. We were constrained to record all items whose score was at least $1/2$. We can not use a score threshold above 1, because we do not initiate a count for an item until the item appears in the stream, and the first time it appears, its score is only 1 (since 1, or $(1-c)^0$, is the weight of the current item).

If we wish to adapt this method to streams of baskets, there are two modifications we must make. The first is simple. Stream elements are baskets rather than individual items, so many items may appear at a given stream element. Treat each of those items as if they were the "current" item and add 1 to their score after multiplying all current scores by $1-c$, as described in Section 4.7.3. If some items in a basket have no current score, initialize the scores of those items to 1.

The second modification is trickier. We want to find all frequent itemsets, not just singleton itemsets. If we were to initialize a count for an itemset whenever we saw it, we would have too many counts. For example, one basket of 20 items has over a million subsets, and all of these would have to be initiated for one basket. On the other hand, as we mentioned, if we use a requirement above 1 for initiating the scoring of an itemset, then we would never get any itemsets started, and the method would not work.

A way of dealing with this problem is to start scoring certain itemsets as soon as we see one instance, but be conservative about which itemsets we start. We may borrow from the A-Priori trick, and only start an itemset I if all its immediate proper subsets are already being scored. The consequence of this restriction is that if I is truly frequent, eventually we shall begin to count it, but we never start an itemset unless it would at least be a candidate in the sense used in the A-Priori Algorithm.

EXAMPLE 6.12   Suppose I is a large itemset, but it appears in the stream periodically, once every $1/2c$ baskets. Then its score, and that of its subsets, never falls below $e^{-1/2}$, which is greater than $1/2$. Thus, once a score is created for some subset of I, that subset will continue to be scored forever. The first time I appears, only its singleton subsets will have scores created for them. However, the next time I appears, each of its doubleton subsets will commence scoring, since each of the immediate subsets of those doubletons is already being scored. Likewise, the kth time I appears, its subsets of size $k-1$ are all being scored, so we initiate scores for each of its subsets of size k. Eventually, we reach the size $|I|$, at which time we start scoring I itself.   □

6.5.3   Hybrid Methods

The approach of Section 6.5.2 offers certain advantages. It requires a limited amount of work each time a stream element arrives, and it always provides an up-to-date picture of what is frequent in the decaying window. Its big disadvantage is that it requires us to maintain scores for each itemset with a score of at least $1/2$. We can limit the number of itemsets being scored by increasing the value of the parameter c. But the larger c is, the smaller the decaying window is. Thus, we could be forced to accept information that tracks the local fluctuations in frequency too closely, rather than integrating over a long period.

We can combine the ideas from Sections 6.5.1 and 6.5.2. For example, we could run a standard algorithm for frequent itemsets on a sample of the stream, with a conventional threshold for support. The itemsets that are found frequent by this algorithm will be treated as if they all arrived at the current time. That is, they each get a score equal to a fixed fraction of their count.

More precisely, suppose the initial sample has b baskets, c is the decay constant for the decaying window, and the minimum score we wish to accept for a frequent itemset in the decaying window is s. Then the support threshold for the initial run of the frequent-itemset algorithm is bcs. If an itemset I is found to have support t in the sample, then it is initially given a score of $t/(bc)$.

EXAMPLE 6.13   Suppose $c = 10^{-6}$ and the minimum score we wish to accept in the decaying window is 10. Suppose also we take a sample of 10^8 baskets from the stream. Then when analyzing that sample, we use a support threshold of $10^8 \times 10^{-6} \times 10 = 1000$.

Consider an itemset I that has support 2000 in the sample. Then the initial score we use for I is $2000/(10^8 \times 10^{-6}) = 20$. After this initiation step, each time a basket arrives in the stream, the current score will be multiplied by $1 - c = 0.999999$. If I is a subset of the current basket, then add 1 to the score.

If the score for I goes below 10, then it is considered to be no longer frequent, so it is dropped from the collection of frequent itemsets. □

We do not, sadly, have a reasonable way of initiating the scoring of new itemsets. If we have no score for itemset I, and 10 is the minimum score we want to maintain, there is no way that a single basket can jump its score from 0 to anything more than 1. The best strategy for adding new sets is to run a new frequent-itemsets calculation on a sample from the stream, and add to the collection of itemsets being scored any that meet the threshold for that sample but were not previously being scored.

6.5.4   Exercises for Section 6.5

!! EXERCISE 6.5.1   Suppose we are counting frequent itemsets in a decaying window with a decay constant c. Suppose also that with probability p, a given stream element (basket) contains both items i and j. Additionally, with probability p the basket contains i but not j, and with probability p it contains j but not i. As a function of c and p, what is the fraction of time we shall be scoring the pair $\{i, j\}$?

6.6   Summary of Chapter 6

✦ *Market-Basket Data*: This model of data assumes there are two kinds of entities: items and baskets. There is a many–many relationship between items and baskets. Typically, baskets are related to small sets of items, while items may be related to many baskets.

✦ *Frequent Itemsets*: The support for a set of items is the number of baskets containing all those items. Itemsets with support that is at least some threshold are called frequent itemsets.

✦ *Association Rules*: These are implications that if a basket contains a certain set of items I, then it is likely to contain another particular item j as well. The probability that j is also in a basket containing I is called the confidence of the rule. The interest of the rule is the amount by which the confidence deviates from the fraction of all baskets that contain j.

✦ *The Pair-Counting Bottleneck*: To find frequent itemsets, we need to examine all baskets and count the number of occurrences of sets of a certain size. For typical data, with a goal of producing a small number of itemsets that are the most frequent of all, the part that often takes the most main memory is the counting of pairs of items. Thus, methods for finding frequent itemsets typically concentrate on how to minimize the main memory needed to count pairs.

✦ *Triangular Matrices*: While one could use a two-dimensional array to count pairs, doing so wastes half the space, because there is no need to count pair $\{i, j\}$ in both the i-j and j-i array elements. By arranging the pairs (i, j) for which $i < j$ in lexicographic order, we can store only the needed counts in a one-dimensional array with no wasted space, and yet be able to access the count for any pair efficiently.

◆ *Storage of Pair Counts as Triples*: If fewer than 1/3 of the possible pairs actually occur in baskets, then it is more space-efficient to store counts of pairs as triples (i, j, c), where c is the count of the pair $\{i, j\}$, and $i < j$. An index structure such as a hash table allows us to find the triple for (i, j) efficiently.

◆ *Monotonicity of Frequent Itemsets*: An important property of itemsets is that if a set of items is frequent, then so are all its subsets. We exploit this property to eliminate the need to count certain itemsets by using its contrapositive: if an itemset is not frequent, then neither are its supersets.

◆ *The A-Priori Algorithm for Pairs*: We can find all frequent pairs by making two passes over the baskets. On the first pass, we count the items themselves, and then determine which items are frequent. On the second pass, we count only the pairs of items both of which are found frequent on the first pass. Monotonicity justifies our ignoring other pairs.

◆ *Finding Larger Frequent Itemsets*: A-Priori and many other algorithms allow us to find frequent itemsets larger than pairs, if we make one pass over the baskets for each size itemset, up to some limit. To find the frequent itemsets of size k, monotonicity lets us restrict our attention to only those itemsets such that all their subsets of size $k - 1$ have already been found frequent.

◆ *The PCY Algorithm*: This algorithm improves on A-Priori by creating a hash table on the first pass, using all main-memory space that is not needed to count the items. Pairs of items are hashed, and the hash-table buckets are used as integer counts of the number of times a pair has hashed to that bucket. Then, on the second pass, we only have to count pairs of frequent items that hashed to a frequent bucket (one whose count is at least the support threshold) on the first pass.

◆ *The Multistage Algorithm*: We can insert additional passes between the first and second pass of the PCY Algorithm to hash pairs to other, independent hash tables. At each intermediate pass, we only have to hash pairs of frequent items that have hashed to frequent buckets on all previous passes.

◆ *The Multihash Algorithm*: We can modify the first pass of the PCY Algorithm to divide available main memory into several hash tables. On the second pass, we only have to count a pair of frequent items if they hashed to frequent buckets in all hash tables.

◆ *Randomized Algorithms*: Instead of making passes through all the data, we may choose a random sample of the baskets, small enough that it is possible to store both the sample and the needed counts of itemsets in main memory. The support threshold must be scaled down in proportion. We can then find the frequent itemsets for the sample, and hope that it is a good representation of the data as whole. While this method uses at most one pass through the whole dataset, it is subject to false positives (itemsets that are frequent in the sample but not the whole) and false negatives (itemsets that are frequent in the whole but not the sample).

✦ *The SON Algorithm*: An improvement on the simple randomized algorithm is to divide the entire file of baskets into segments small enough that all frequent itemsets for the segment can be found in main memory. Candidate itemsets are those found frequent for at least one segment. A second pass allows us to count all the candidates and find the exact collection of frequent itemsets. This algorithm is especially appropriate in a MapReduce setting.

✦ *Toivonen's Algorithm*: This algorithm starts by finding frequent itemsets in a sample, but with the threshold lowered so there is little chance of missing an itemset that is frequent in the whole. Next, we examine the entire file of baskets, counting not only the itemsets that are frequent in the sample, but also, the negative border – itemsets that have not been found frequent, but all their immediate subsets are. If no member of the negative border is found frequent in the whole, then the answer is exact. But if a member of the negative border is found frequent, then the whole process has to repeat with another sample.

✦ *Frequent Itemsets in Streams*: If we use a decaying window with constant c, then we can start counting an item whenever we see it in a basket. We start counting an itemset if we see it contained within the current basket, and all its immediate proper subsets already are being counted. As the window is decaying, we multiply all counts by $1 - c$ and eliminate those that are less than $1/2$.

6.7   References for Chapter 6

The market-basket data model, including association rules and the A-Priori Algorithm, are from [1] and [2].

The PCY Algorithm is from [4]. The Multistage and Multihash Algorithms are found in [3].

The SON Algorithm is from [5]. Toivonen's Algorithm appears in [6].

[1] R. Agrawal, T. Imielinski, and A. Swami, "Mining associations between sets of items in massive databases," *Proc. ACM SIGMOD Intl. Conf. on Management of Data*, pp. 207–216, 1993.

[2] R. Agrawal and R. Srikant, "Fast algorithms for mining association rules," *Intl. Conf. on Very Large Databases*, pp. 487–499, 1994.

[3] M. Fang, N. Shivakumar, H. Garcia-Molina, R. Motwani, and J.D. Ullman, "Computing iceberg queries efficiently," *Intl. Conf. on Very Large Databases*, pp. 299-310, 1998.

[4] J.S. Park, M.-S. Chen, and P.S. Yu, "An effective hash-based algorithm for mining association rules," *Proc. ACM SIGMOD Intl. Conf. on Management of Data*, pp. 175–186, 1995.

[5] A. Savasere, E. Omiecinski, and S.B. Navathe, "An efficient algorithm for mining association rules in large databases," *Intl. Conf. on Very Large Databases*, pp. 432–444, 1995.

[6] H. Toivonen, "Sampling large databases for association rules," *Intl. Conf. on Very Large Databases*, pp. 134–145, 1996.

7 Clustering

Clustering is the process of examining a collection of "points," and grouping the points into "clusters" according to some distance measure. The goal is that points in the same cluster have a small distance from one another, while points in different clusters are at a large distance from one another. A suggestion of what clusters might look like was seen in Fig. 1.1. However, there the intent was that there were three clusters around three different road intersections, but two of the clusters blended into one another because they were not sufficiently separated.

Our goal in this chapter is to offer methods for discovering clusters in data. We are particularly interested in situations where the data is very large, and/or where the space either is high-dimensional, or the space is not Euclidean at all. We shall therefore discuss several algorithms that assume the data does not fit in main memory. However, we begin with the basics: the two general approaches to clustering and the methods for dealing with clusters in a non-Euclidean space.

7.1 Introduction to Clustering Techniques

We begin by reviewing the notions of distance measures and spaces. The two major approaches to clustering – hierarchical and point-assignment – are defined. We then turn to a discussion of the "curse of dimensionality," which makes clustering in high-dimensional spaces difficult, but also, as we shall see, enables some simplifications if used correctly in a clustering algorithm.

7.1.1 Points, Spaces, and Distances

A dataset suitable for clustering is a collection of *points*, which are objects belonging to some *space*. In its most general sense, a space is just a universal set of points, from which the points in the dataset are drawn. However, we should be mindful of the common case of a Euclidean space (see Section 3.5.2), which has a number of important properties useful for clustering. In particular, a Euclidean space's points are vectors of real numbers. The length of the vector is the number of dimensions of the space. The components of the vector are commonly called *coordinates* of the represented points.

All spaces for which we can perform a clustering have a distance measure, giving a distance between any two points in the space. We introduced distances in Section 3.5. The common Euclidean distance (square root of the sums of the squares of the differences between the coordinates of the points in each dimension) serves for all Euclidean spaces, although we also mentioned some other options for distance measures in Euclidean spaces, including the Manhattan distance (sum of the magnitudes of the differences in each dimension) and the L_∞-distance (maximum magnitude of the difference in any dimension).

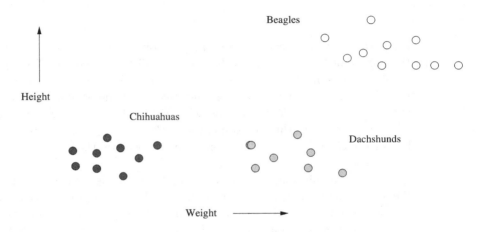

Figure 7.1 Heights and weights of dogs taken from three varieties

EXAMPLE 7.1   Classical applications of clustering often involve low-dimensional Euclidean spaces. For example, Fig. 7.1 shows height and weight measurements of dogs of several varieties. Without knowing which dog is of which variety, we can see just by looking at the diagram that the dogs fall into three clusters, and those clusters happen to correspond to three varieties. With small amounts of data, any clustering algorithm will establish the correct clusters, and simply plotting the points and "eyeballing" the plot will suffice as well.   □

However, modern clustering problems are not so simple. They may involve Euclidean spaces of very high dimension or spaces that are not Euclidean at all. For example, it is challenging to cluster documents by their topic, based on the occurrence of common, unusual words in the documents. It is challenging to cluster moviegoers by the type or types of movies they like.

We also considered in Section 3.5 distance measures for non-Euclidean spaces. These include the Jaccard distance, cosine distance, Hamming distance, and edit distance. Recall that the requirements for a function on pairs of points to be a distance measure are that

(1) Distances are always nonnegative, and only the distance between a point and itself is 0.

(2) Distance is symmetric; it doesn't matter in which order you consider the points when computing their distance.

(3) Distance measures obey the triangle inequality; the distance from x to y to z is never less than the distance going from x to z directly.

7.1.2 Clustering Strategies

We can divide (cluster!) clustering algorithms into two groups that follow two fundamentally different strategies.

(1) *Hierarchical* or *agglomerative* algorithms start with each point in its own cluster. Clusters are combined based on their "closeness," using one of many possible definitions of "close." Combination stops when further combination leads to clusters that are undesirable for one of several reasons. For example, we may stop when we have a predetermined number of clusters, or we may use a measure of compactness for clusters, and refuse to construct a cluster by combining two smaller clusters if the resulting cluster has points that are spread out over too large a region.

(2) The other class of algorithms involve *point assignment*. Points are considered in some order, and each one is assigned to the cluster into which it best fits. This process is normally preceded by a short phase in which initial clusters are estimated. Variations allow occasional combining or splitting of clusters, or may allow points to be unassigned if they are *outliers* (points too far from any of the current clusters).

Algorithms for clustering can also be distinguished by:

(a) Whether the algorithm assumes a Euclidean space, or whether the algorithm works for an arbitrary distance measure. We shall see that a key distinction is that in a Euclidean space it is possible to summarize a collection of points by their *centroid* – the average of the points. In a non-Euclidean space, there is no notion of a centroid, and we are forced to develop another way to summarize clusters.

(b) Whether the algorithm assumes that the data is small enough to fit in main memory, or whether data must reside in secondary memory, primarily. Algorithms for large amounts of data often must take shortcuts, since it is infeasible to look at all pairs of points, for example. It is also necessary to summarize clusters in main memory, since we cannot hold all the points of all the clusters in main memory at the same time.

7.1.3 The Curse of Dimensionality

High-dimensional Euclidean spaces have a number of unintuitive properties that are sometimes referred to as the "curse of dimensionality." Non-Euclidean spaces usually share these anomalies as well. One manifestation of the "curse" is that in high dimensions, almost all pairs of points are equally far away from one another.

Another manifestation is that almost any two vectors are almost orthogonal. We shall explore each of these in turn.

The Distribution of Distances in a High-Dimensional Space

Let us consider a d-dimensional Euclidean space. Suppose we choose n random points in the unit cube, i.e., points $[x_1, x_2, \ldots, x_d]$, where each x_i is in the range 0 to 1. If $d = 1$, we are placing random points on a line of length 1. We expect that some pairs of points will be very close, e.g., consecutive points on the line. We also expect that some points will be very far away – those at or near opposite ends of the line. The average distance between a pair of points is $1/3$.[1]

Suppose that d is very large. The Euclidean distance between two random points $[x_1, x_2, \ldots, x_d]$ and $[y_1, y_2, \ldots, y_d]$ is

$$\sqrt{\sum_{i=1}^{d}(x_i - y_i)^2}$$

Here, each x_i and y_i is a random variable chosen uniformly in the range 0 to 1. Since d is large, we can expect that for some i, $|x_i - y_i|$ will be close to 1. That puts a lower bound of 1 on the distance between almost any two random points. In fact, a more careful argument can put a stronger lower bound on the distance between all but a vanishingly small fraction of the pairs of points. However, the maximum distance between two points is $\sqrt{d}$, and one can argue that all but a vanishingly small fraction of the pairs do not have a distance close to this upper limit. In fact, almost all points will have a distance close to the average distance.

If there are essentially no pairs of points that are close, it is hard to build clusters at all. There is little justification for grouping one pair of points and not another. Of course, the data may not be random, and there may be useful clusters, even in very high-dimensional spaces. However, the argument about random data suggests that it will be hard to find these clusters among so many pairs that are all at approximately the same distance.

Angles Between Vectors

Suppose again that we have three random points A, B, and C in a d-dimensional space, where d is large. Here, we do not assume points are in the unit cube; they can be anywhere in the space. What is angle ABC? We may assume that A is the point $[x_1, x_2, \ldots, x_d]$ and C is the point $[y_1, y_2, \ldots, y_d]$, while B is the origin. Recall from Section 3.5.4 that the cosine of the angle ABC is the dot product of A and C divided by the product of the lengths of the vectors A and C. That is, the cosine is

$$\frac{\sum_{i=1}^{d} x_i y_i}{\sqrt{\sum_{i=1}^{d} x_i^2}\sqrt{\sum_{i=1}^{d} y_i^2}}$$

---

[1] You can prove this fact by evaluating a double integral, but we shall not do the math here, as it is not central to the discussion.

As d grows, the denominator grows linearly in d, but the numerator is a sum of random values, which are as likely to be positive as negative. Thus, the expected value of the numerator is 0, and as d grows, its standard deviation grows only as $\sqrt{d}$. Thus, for large d, the cosine of the angle between any two vectors is almost certain to be close to 0, which means the angle is close to 90 degrees.

An important consequence of random vectors being orthogonal is that if we have three random points A, B, and C, and we know the distance from A to B is d_1, while the distance from B to C is d_2, we can assume the distance from A to C is approximately $\sqrt{d_1^2 + d_2^2}$. That rule does not hold, even approximately, if the number of dimensions is small. As an extreme case, if $d = 1$, then the distance from A to C would necessarily be $d_1 + d_2$ if A and C were on opposite sides of B, or $|d_1 - d_2|$ if they were on the same side.

7.1.4 Exercises for Section 7.1

! EXERCISE 7.1.1 Prove that if you choose two points uniformly and independently on a line of length 1, then the expected distance between the points is $1/3$.

!! EXERCISE 7.1.2 If you choose two points uniformly in the unit square, what is their expected Euclidean distance?

! EXERCISE 7.1.3 Suppose we have a d-dimensional Euclidean space. Consider vectors whose components are only $+1$ or -1 in each dimension. Note that each vector has length $\sqrt{d}$, so the product of their lengths (denominator in the formula for the cosine of the angle between them) is d. If we chose each component independently, and a component is as likely to be $+1$ as -1, what is the distribution of the value of the numerator of the formula (i.e., the sum of the products of the corresponding components from each vector)? What can you say about the expected value of the cosine of the angle between the vectors, as d grows large?

7.2 Hierarchical Clustering

We begin by considering hierarchical clustering in a Euclidean space. This algorithm can only be used for relatively small datasets, but even so, there are some efficiencies we can make by careful implementation. When the space is non-Euclidean, there are additional problems associated with hierarchical clustering. We therefore consider "clustroids" and the way we can represent a cluster when there is no centroid or average point in a cluster.

7.2.1   Hierarchical Clustering in a Euclidean Space

Any hierarchical clustering algorithm works as follows. We begin with every point in its own cluster. As time goes on, larger clusters will be constructed by combining two smaller clusters, and we have to decide in advance:

(1) How will clusters be represented?
(2) How will we choose which two clusters to merge?
(3) When will we stop combining clusters?

Once we have answers to these questions, the algorithm can be described succinctly as:

```
WHILE it is not time to stop DO
        pick the best two clusters to merge;
        combine those two clusters into one cluster;
END;
```

To begin, we shall assume the space is Euclidean. That allows us to represent a cluster by its centroid or average of the points in the cluster. Note that in a cluster of one point, that point is the centroid, so we can initialize the clusters straightforwardly. We can then use the merging rule that the distance between any two clusters is the Euclidean distance between their centroids, and we should pick the two clusters at the shortest distance. Other ways to define intercluster distance are possible, and we can also pick the best pair of clusters on a basis other than their distance. We shall discuss some options in Section 7.2.3.

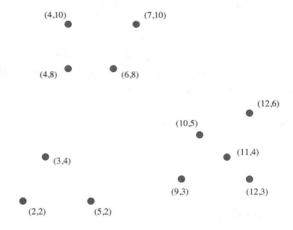

Figure 7.2 Twelve points to be clustered hierarchically

EXAMPLE 7.2   Let us see how the basic hierarchical clustering would work on the data of Fig. 7.2. These points live in a 2-dimensional Euclidean space, and each point is named by its (x, y) coordinates. Initially, each point is in a cluster by itself and is the centroid of that cluster. Among all the pairs of points, there are two pairs that are closest: (10,5) and (11,4) or (11,4) and (12,3). Each is at distance $\sqrt{2}$. Let us break ties arbitrarily and decide to combine (11,4) with (12,3). The result is shown in Fig. 7.3, including the centroid of the new cluster, which is at (11.5, 3.5).

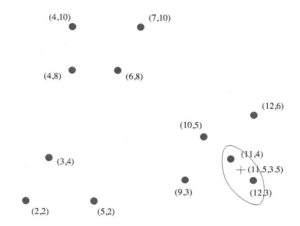

Figure 7.3 Combining the first two points into a cluster

You might think that (10,5) gets combined with the new cluster next, since it is so close to (11,4). But our distance rule requires us to compare only cluster centroids, and the distance from (10,5) to the centroid of the new cluster is $1.5\sqrt{2}$, which is slightly greater than 2. Thus, now the two closest clusters are those of the points (4,8) and (4,10). We combine them into one cluster with centroid (4,9).

At this point, the two closest centroids are (10,5) and (11.5, 3.5), so we combine these two clusters. The result is a cluster of three points (10,5), (11,4), and (12,3). The centroid of this cluster is (11,4), which happens to be one of the points of the cluster, but that situation is coincidental. The state of the clusters is shown in Fig. 7.4.

Now, there are several pairs of centroids that are at distance $\sqrt{5}$, and these are the closest centroids. We show in Fig. 7.5 the result of picking three of these:

(1) (6,8) is combined with the cluster of two elements having centroid (4,9).
(2) (2,2) is combined with (3,4).
(3) (9,3) is combined with the cluster of three elements having centroid (11,4).

We can proceed to combine clusters further. We shall discuss alternative stopping rules next. ☐

There are several approaches we might use to stopping the clustering process.

(1) We could be told, or have a belief, about how many clusters there are in the data. For example, if we are told that the data about dogs is taken from

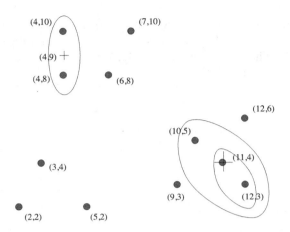

Figure 7.4 Clustering after two additional steps

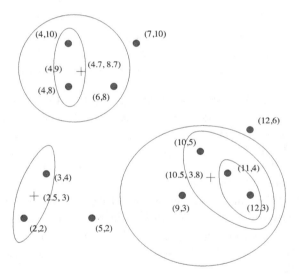

Figure 7.5 Three more steps of the hierarchical clustering

Chihuahuas, Dachshunds, and Beagles, then we know to stop when there are three clusters left.

(2) We could stop combining when at some point the best combination of existing clusters produces a cluster that is inadequate. We shall discuss various tests for the adequacy of a cluster in Section 7.2.3, but for an example, we could insist that any cluster have an average distance between the centroid and its points no greater than some limit. This approach is only sensible if we have a reason to believe that no cluster extends over too much of the space.

(3) We could continue clustering until there is only one cluster. However, it is

meaningless to return a single cluster consisting of all the points. Rather, we return the tree representing the way in which all the points were combined. This form of answer makes good sense in some applications, such as one in which the points are genomes of different species, and the distance measure reflects the difference in the genome.[2] Then, the tree represents the evolution of these species, that is, the likely order in which two species branched from a common ancestor.

EXAMPLE 7.3   If we complete the clustering of the data of Fig. 7.2, the tree describing how clusters were grouped is the tree shown in Fig. 7.6.   □

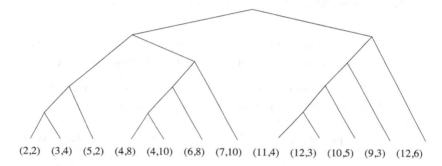

(2,2)   (3,4)   (5,2)   (4,8)   (4,10)   (6,8)   (7,10)   (11,4)   (12,3)   (10,5)   (9,3)   (12,6)

Figure 7.6 Tree showing the complete grouping of the points of Fig. 7.2

7.2.2   Efficiency of Hierarchical Clustering

The basic algorithm for hierarchical clustering is not very efficient. At each step, we must compute the distances between each pair of clusters, in order to find the best merger. The initial step takes $O(n^2)$ time, but subsequent steps take time proportional to $(n-1)^2, (n-2)^2, \ldots$. The sum of squares up to n is $O(n^3)$, so this algorithm is cubic. Thus, it cannot be run except for fairly small numbers of points.

However, there is a somewhat more efficient implementation of which we should be aware.

(1) We start, as we must, by computing the distances between all pairs of points, and this step is $O(n^2)$.

(2) Form the pairs and their distances into a priority queue, so we can always find the smallest distance in one step. This operation is also $O(n^2)$.

(3) When we decide to merge two clusters C and D, we remove all entries in the priority queue involving one of these two clusters; that requires work $O(n \log n)$ since there are at most $2n$ deletions to be performed, and priority-queue deletion can be performed in $O(\log n)$ time.

---

[2] This space would not be Euclidean, of course, but the principles regarding hierarchical clustering carry over, with some modifications, to non-Euclidean clustering.

(4) We then compute all the distances between the new cluster and the remaining clusters. This work is also $O(n \log n)$, as there are at most n entries to be inserted into the priority queue, and insertion into a priority queue can also be done in $O(\log n)$ time.

Since the last two steps are executed at most n times, and the first two steps are executed only once, the overall running time of this algorithm is $O(n^2 \log n)$. That is better than $O(n^3)$, but it still puts a strong limit on how large n can be before it becomes infeasible to use this clustering approach.

7.2.3   ### Alternative Rules for Controlling Hierarchical Clustering

We have seen one rule for picking the best clusters to merge: find the pair with the smallest distance between their centroids. Some other options are:

(1) Take the distance between two clusters to be the minimum of the distances between any two points, one chosen from each cluster. For example, in Fig. 7.3 we would next chose to cluster the point (10,5) with the cluster of two points, since (10,5) has distance $\sqrt{2}$, and no other pair of unclustered points is that close. Note that in Example 7.2, we did make this combination eventually, but not until we had combined another pair of points. In general, it is possible that this rule will result in an entirely different clustering from that obtained using the distance-of-centroids rule.

(2) Take the distance between two clusters to be the average distance of all pairs of points, one from each cluster.

(3) The *radius* of a cluster is the maximum distance between all the points and the centroid. Combine the two clusters whose resulting cluster has the lowest radius. A slight modification is to combine the clusters whose result has the lowest average distance between a point and the centroid. Another modification is to use the sum of the squares of the distances between the points and the centroid. In some algorithms, we shall find these variant definitions of "radius" referred to as "the radius."

(4) The *diameter* of a cluster is the maximum distance between any two points of the cluster. Note that the radius and diameter of a cluster are not related directly, as they are in a circle, but there is a tendency for them to be proportional. We may choose to merge those clusters whose resulting cluster has the smallest diameter. Variants of this rule, analogous to the rule for radius, are possible.

EXAMPLE 7.4   Let us consider the cluster consisting of the five points at the right of Fig. 7.2. The centroid of these five points is (10.8, 4.2). There is a tie for the two furthest points from the centroid: (9,3) and (12,6), both at distance $\sqrt{4.68} = 2.16$. Thus, the radius is 2.16. For the diameter, we find the two points in the cluster having the greatest distance. These are again (9,3) and (12,6).

Their distance is $\sqrt{18} = 4.24$, so that is the diameter. Notice that the diameter is not exactly twice the radius, although it is close in this case. The reason is that the centroid is not on the line between (9,3) and (12,6). □

We also have options in determining when to stop the merging process. We already mentioned "stop when we have k clusters" for some predetermined k. Here are some other options.

(1) Stop if the diameter of the cluster that results from the best merger exceeds a threshold. We can also base this rule on the radius, or on any of the variants of the radius mentioned above.

(2) Stop if the *density* of the cluster that results from the best merger is below some threshold. The density can be defined in many different ways. Roughly, it should be the number of cluster points per unit volume of the cluster. That ratio can be estimated by the number of points divided by some power of the diameter or radius of the cluster. The correct power could be the number of dimensions of the space. Sometimes, 1 or 2 is chosen as the power, regardless of the number of dimensions.

(3) Stop when there is evidence that the next pair of clusters to be combined yields a bad cluster. For example, we could track the average diameter of all the current clusters. As long as we are combining points that truly belong in a cluster, this average will rise gradually. However, if we combine two clusters that really don't deserve to be combined, then the average diameter will take a sudden jump.

EXAMPLE 7.5   Let us reconsider Fig. 7.2. It has three natural clusters. We computed the diameter of the largest – the five points at the right – in Example 7.4; it is 4.24. The diameter of the 3-node cluster at the lower left is 3, the distance between (2,2) and (5,2). The diameter of the 4-node cluster at the upper left is $\sqrt{13} = 3.61$. The average diameter, 3.62, was reached starting from 0 after nine mergers, so the rise is evidently slow: about 0.4 per merger.

If we are forced to merge two of these natural clusters, the best we can do is merge the two at the left. The diameter of this cluster is $\sqrt{89} = 9.43$; that is the distance between the two points (2,2) and (7,10). Now, the average of the diameters is $(9.43 + 4.24)/2 = 6.84$. This average has jumped almost as much in one step as in all nine previous steps. That comparison indicates that the last merger was inadvisable, and we should roll it back and stop. □

7.2.4   Hierarchical Clustering in Non-Euclidean Spaces

When the space is non-Euclidean, we need to use some distance measure that is computed from points, such as Jaccard, cosine, or edit distance. That is, we cannot base distances on "location" of points. The algorithm of Section 7.2.1 requires distances between points to be computed, but presumably we have a way to compute those distances. A problem arises when we need to represent a cluster, because we cannot replace a collection of points by their centroid.

EXAMPLE 7.6   The problem arises for any of the non-Euclidean distances we have discussed, but to be concrete, suppose we are using edit distance, and we decide to merge the strings abcd and aecdb. These have edit distance 3 and might well be merged. However, there is no string that represents their average, or that could be thought of as lying naturally between them. We could take one of the strings that we might pass through when transforming one string to the other by single insertions or deletions, such as aebcd, but there are many such options. Moreover, when clusters are formed from more than two strings, the notion of "on the path between" stops making sense. □

Given that we cannot combine points in a cluster when the space is non-Euclidean, our only choice is to pick one of the points of the cluster itself to represent the cluster. Ideally, this point is close to all the points of the cluster, so it in some sense lies in the "center." We call the representative point the *clustroid*. We can select the clustroid in various ways, each designed to, in some sense, minimize the distances between the clustroid and the other points in the cluster. Common choices include selecting as the clustroid the point that minimizes:

(1) The sum of the distances to the other points in the cluster.
(2) The maximum distance to another point in the cluster.
(3) The sum of the squares of the distances to the other points in the cluster.

EXAMPLE 7.7   Suppose we are using edit distance, and a cluster consists of the four points abcd, aecdb, abecb, and ecdab. Their distances are found in the following table:

	ecdab	abecb	aecdb
abcd	5	3	3
aecdb	2	2	
abecb	4		

If we apply the three criteria for being the centroid to each of the four points of the cluster, we find:

Point	Sum	Max	Sum-Sq
abcd	11	5	43
aecdb	7	3	17
abecb	9	4	29
ecdab	11	5	45

We can see from these measurements that whichever of the three criteria we choose, aecdb will be selected as the clustroid. In general, different criteria could yield different clustroids. □

The options for measuring the distance between clusters that were outlined in Section 7.2.3 can be applied in a non-Euclidean setting, provided we use the clustroid in place of the centroid. For example, we can merge the two clusters whose clustroids are closest. We could also use the average or minimum distance between all pairs of points from the clusters.

Other suggested criteria involved measuring the density of a cluster, based on the radius or diameter. Both these notions make sense in the non-Euclidean environment. The diameter is still the maximum distance between any two points in the cluster. The radius can be defined using the clustroid in place of the centroid. Moreover, it makes sense to use the same sort of evaluation for the radius as we used to select the clustroid in the first place. For example, if we take the clustroid to be the point with the smallest sum of squares of distances to the other nodes, then define the radius to be that sum of squares (or its square root).

Finally, Section 7.2.3 also discussed criteria for stopping the merging of clusters. None of these criteria made direct use of the centroid, except through the notion of radius, and we have already observed that "radius" makes good sense in non-Euclidean spaces. Thus, there is no substantial change in the options for stopping criteria when we move from Euclidean to non-Euclidean spaces.

7.2.5   Exercises for Section 7.2

EXERCISE 7.2.1   Perform a hierarchical clustering of the one-dimensional set of points 1, 4, 9, 16, 25, 36, 49, 64, 81, assuming clusters are represented by their centroid (average), and at each step the clusters with the closest centroids are merged.

EXERCISE 7.2.2   How would the clustering of Example 7.2 change if we used for the distance between two clusters:

(a) The minimum of the distances between any two points, one from each cluster.
(b) The average of the distances between pairs of points, one from each of the two clusters.

EXERCISE 7.2.3   Repeat the clustering of Example 7.2 if we choose to merge the two clusters whose resulting cluster has:

(a) The smallest radius.
(b) The smallest diameter.

EXERCISE 7.2.4   Compute the density of each of the three clusters in Fig. 7.2, if "density" is defined to be the number of points divided by

(a) The square of the radius.
(b) The diameter (not squared).

What are the densities, according to (a) and (b), of the clusters that result from the merger of any two of these three clusters. Does the difference in densities suggest the clusters should or should not be merged?

EXERCISE 7.2.5   We can select clustroids for clusters, even if the space is Euclidean. Consider the three natural clusters in Fig. 7.2, and compute the clustroids of each, assuming the criterion for selecting the clustroid is the point with the minimum sum of distances to the other point in the cluster.

! EXERCISE 7.2.6   Consider the space of strings with edit distance as the distance measure. Give an example of a set of strings such that if we choose the clustroid by minimizing the sum of the distances to the other points we get one point as the clustroid, but if we choose the clustroid by minimizing the maximum distance to the other points, another point becomes the clustroid.

7.3   K-means Algorithms

In this section we begin the study of point-assignment algorithms. The best known family of clustering algorithms of this type is called k-means. They assume a Euclidean space, and they also assume the number of clusters, k, is known in advance. It is, however, possible to deduce k by trial and error. After an introduction to the family of k-means algorithms, we shall focus on a particular algorithm, called BFR after its authors, that enables us to execute k-means on data that is too large to fit in main memory.

7.3.1   K-Means Basics

A k-means algorithm is outlined in Fig. 7.7. There are several ways to select the initial k points that represent the clusters, and we shall discuss them in Section 7.3.2. The heart of the algorithm is the for-loop, in which we consider each point other than the k selected points and assign it to the closest cluster, where "closest" means closest to the centroid of the cluster. Note that the centroid of a cluster can migrate as points are assigned to it. However, since only points near the cluster are likely to be assigned, the centroid tends not to move too much.

```
Initially choose k points that are likely to be in
    different clusters;
Make these points the centroids of their clusters;
FOR each remaining point p DO
    find the centroid to which p is closest;
    Add p to the cluster of that centroid;
    Adjust the centroid of that cluster to account for p;
END;
```

Figure 7.7 Outline of k-means algorithms

An optional step at the end is to fix the centroids of the clusters and to reassign each point, including the k initial points, to the k clusters. Usually, a point p will be assigned to the same cluster in which it was placed on the first pass. However, there are cases where the centroid of p's original cluster moved quite far from p after p was placed there, and p is assigned to a different cluster on the second pass. In fact, even some of the original k points could wind up being reassigned. As these examples are unusual, we shall not dwell on the subject.

7.3.2   Initializing Clusters for K-Means

We want to pick points that have a good chance of lying in different clusters. There are two approaches.

(1) Pick points that are as far away from one another as possible.
(2) Cluster a sample of the data, perhaps hierarchically, so there are k clusters. Pick a point from each cluster, perhaps that point closest to the centroid of the cluster.

The second approach requires little elaboration. For the first approach, there are variations. One good choice is:

```
Pick the first point at random;
WHILE there are fewer than k points DO
    Add the point whose minimum distance from the selected
        points is as large as possible;
END;
```

EXAMPLE 7.8   Let us consider the twelve points of Fig. 7.2, which we reproduce here as Fig. 7.8. In the worst case, our initial choice of a point is near the center, say (6,8). The furthest point from (6,8) is (12,3), so that point is chosen next.

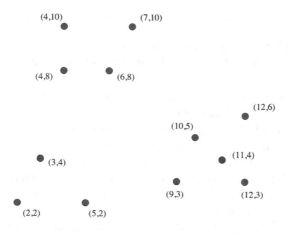

Figure 7.8 Repeat of Fig. 7.2

Among the remaining ten points, the one whose minimum distance to either (6,8) or (12,3) is a maximum is (2,2). That point has distance $\sqrt{52} = 7.21$ from (6,8) and distance $\sqrt{101} = 10.05$ to (12,3); thus its "score" is 7.21. You can check easily that any other point is less than distance 7.21 from at least one of (6,8) and (12,3). Our selection of three starting points is thus (6,8), (12,3), and (2,2). Notice that these three belong to different clusters.

Had we started with a different point, say (10,5), we would get a different set of three initial points. In this case, the starting points would be (10,5), (2,2), and (4,10). Again, these points belong to the three different clusters.   □

7.3.3   Picking the Right Value of k

We may not know the correct value of k to use in a k-means clustering. However, if we can measure the quality of the clustering for various values of k, we can usually guess what the right value of k is. Recall the discussion in Section 7.2.3, especially Example 7.5, where we observed that if we take a measure of appropriateness for clusters, such as average radius or diameter, that value will grow slowly, as long as the number of clusters we assume remains at or above the true number of clusters. However, as soon as we try to form fewer clusters than there really are, the measure will rise precipitously. The idea is expressed by the diagram of Fig. 7.9.

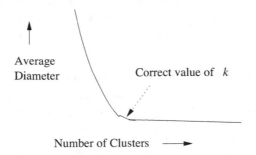

Figure 7.9 Average diameter or another measure of diffuseness rises quickly as soon as the number of clusters falls below the true number present in the data

If we have no idea what the correct value of k is, we can find a good value in a number of clustering operations that grows only logarithmically with the true number. Begin by running the k-means algorithm for $k = 1, 2, 4, 8, \ldots$. Eventually, you will find two values v and $2v$ between which there is very little decrease in the average diameter, or whatever measure of cluster cohesion you are using. We may conclude that the value of k that is justified by the data lies between $v/2$ and v. If you use a binary search (discussed below) in that range, you can find the best value for k in another $\log_2 v$ clustering operations, for a total of $2 \log_2 v$ clusterings. Since the true value of k is at least $v/2$, we have used a number of clusterings that is logarithmic in k.

Since the notion of "not much change" is imprecise, we cannot say exactly how much change is too much. However, the binary search can be conducted as follows, assuming the notion of "not much change" is made precise by some formula. We know that there is too much change between $v/2$ and v, or else we would not have gone on to run a clustering for $2v$ clusters. Suppose at some point we have narrowed the range of k to between x and y. Let $z = (x + y)/2$. Run a clustering with z as the target number of clusters. If there is not too much change between z and y, then the true value of k lies between x and z. So recursively narrow that range to find the correct value of k. On the other hand, if there is too much change between z and y, then use binary search in the range between z and y instead.

7.3.4 The Algorithm of Bradley, Fayyad, and Reina

This algorithm, which we shall refer to as *BFR* after its authors, is a variant of k-means that is designed to cluster data in a high-dimensional Euclidean space. It makes a very strong assumption about the shape of clusters: they must be normally distributed about a centroid. The mean and standard deviation for a cluster may differ for different dimensions, but the dimensions must be independent. For instance, in two dimensions a cluster may be cigar-shaped, but the cigar must not be rotated off of the axes. Figure 7.10 makes the point.

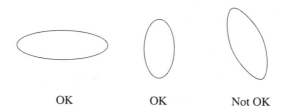

OK   OK   Not OK

Figure 7.10 The clusters in data for which the BFR algorithm may be used can have standard deviations that differ along different axes, but the axes of the cluster must align with the axes of the space

The BFR Algorithm begins by selecting k points, using one of the methods discussed in Section 7.3.2. Then, the points of the data file are read in chunks. These might be chunks from a distributed file system or a conventional file might be partitioned into chunks of the appropriate size. Each chunk must consist of few enough points that they can be processed in main memory. Also stored in main memory are summaries of the k clusters and some other data, so the entire memory is not available to store a chunk. The main-memory data other than the chunk from the input consists of three types of objects:

(1) *The Discard Set*: These are simple summaries of the clusters themselves. We shall address the form of cluster summarization shortly. Note that the cluster summaries are not "discarded"; they are in fact essential. However, the points

that the summary represents *are* discarded and have no representation in main memory other than through this summary.

(2) *The Compressed Set*: These are summaries, similar to the cluster summaries, but for sets of points that have been found close to one another, but not close to any cluster. The points represented by the compressed set are also discarded, in the sense that they do not appear explicitly in main memory. We call the represented sets of points *miniclusters*.

(3) *The Retained Set*: Certain points can neither be assigned to a cluster nor are they sufficiently close to any other points that we can represent them by a compressed set. These points are held in main memory exactly as they appear in the input file.

The picture in Fig. 7.11 suggests how the points processed so far are represented.

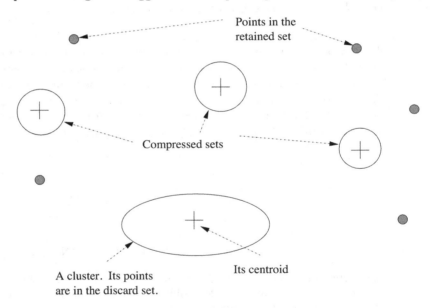

Figure 7.11 Points in the discard, compressed, and retained sets

The discard and compressed sets are represented by $2d + 1$ values, if the data is d-dimensional. These numbers are:

(a) The number of points represented, N.
(b) The sum of the components of all the points in each dimension. This data is a vector SUM of length d, and the component in the ith dimension is SUM_i.
(c) The sum of the squares of the components of all the points in each dimension. This data is a vector SUMSQ of length d, and its component in the ith dimension is SUMSQ_i.

Our real goal is to represent a set of points by their count, their centroid and the standard deviation in each dimension. However, these $2d + 1$ values give us

---

Benefits of the N, SUM, SUMSQ Representation

There is a significant advantage to representing sets of points as it is done in the BFR Algorithm, rather than by storing N, the centroid, and the standard deviation in each dimension. Consider what we need to do when we add a new point to a cluster. N is increased by 1, of course. But we can also add the vector representing the location of the point to SUM to get the new SUM, and we can add the squares of the components of the vector to SUMSQ to get the new SUMSQ. Had we used the centroid in place of SUM, then we could not adjust the centroid to account for the new point without doing some calculation involving N, and the recomputation of the standard deviations would be far more complex as well. Similarly, if we want to combine two sets, we just add corresponding values of N, SUM, and SUMSQ, while if we used the centroid and standard deviations as a representation, the calculation would be far more complex.

---

those statistics. N is the count. The centroid's coordinate in the ith dimension is the SUM_i/N, that is the sum in that dimension divided by the number of points. The variance in the ith dimension is $\text{SUMSQ}_i/N - (\text{SUM}_i/N)^2$. We can compute the standard deviation in each dimension, since it is the square root of the variance.

EXAMPLE 7.9   Suppose a cluster consists of the points $(5, 1)$, $(6, -2)$, and $(7, 0)$. Then $N = 3$, SUM $= [18, -1]$, and SUMSQ $= [110, 5]$. The centroid is SUM$/N$, or $[6, -1/3]$. The variance in the first dimension is $110/3 - (18/3)^2 = 0.667$, so the standard deviation is $\sqrt{0.667} = 0.816$. In the second dimension, the variance is $5/3 - (-1/3)^2 = 1.56$, so the standard deviation is 1.25.   □

7.3.5   Processing Data in the BFR Algorithm

We shall now outline what happens when we process a chunk of points.

(1) First, all points that are sufficiently close to the centroid of a cluster are added to that cluster. As described in the box on benefits, it is simple to add the information about the point to the N, SUM, and SUMSQ that represent the cluster. We then discard the point. The question of what "sufficiently close" means will be addressed shortly.

(2) For the points that are not sufficiently close to any centroid, we cluster them, along with the points in the retained set. Any main-memory clustering algorithm can be used, such as the hierarchical methods discussed in Section 7.2. We must use some criterion for deciding when it is reasonable to combine two points into a cluster or two clusters into one. Section 7.2.3 covered the ways we might make this decision. Clusters of more than one point are summarized and added to the compressed set. Singleton clusters become the retained set of points.

(3) We now have miniclusters derived from our attempt to cluster new points and the old retained set, and we have the miniclusters from the old compressed set. Although none of these miniclusters can be merged with one of the k clusters, they might merge with one another. The criterion for merger may again be chosen according to the discussion in Section 7.2.3. Note that the form of representation for compressed sets (N, SUM, and SUMSQ) makes it easy to compute statistics such as the variance for the combination of two miniclusters that we consider merging.

(4) Points that are assigned to a cluster or a minicluster, i.e., those that are not in the retained set, are written out, with their assignment, to secondary memory.

Finally, if this is the last chunk of input data, we need to do something with the compressed and retained sets. We can treat them as outliers, and never cluster them at all. Or, we can assign each point in the retained set to the cluster of the nearest centroid. We can combine each minicluster with the cluster whose centroid is closest to the centroid of the minicluster.

An important decision that must be examined is how we decide whether a new point p is close enough to one of the k clusters that it makes sense to add p to the cluster. Two approaches have been suggested.

(a) Add p to a cluster if it not only has the centroid closest to p, but it is very unlikely that, after all the points have been processed, some other cluster centroid will be found to be nearer to p. This decision is a complex statistical calculation. It must assume that points are ordered randomly, and that we know how many points will be processed in the future. Its advantage is that if we find one centroid to be significantly closer to p than any other, we can add p to that cluster and be done with it, even if p is very far from all centroids.

(b) We can measure the probability that, if p belongs to a cluster, it would be found as far as it is from the centroid of that cluster. This calculation makes use of the fact that we believe each cluster to consist of normally distributed points with the axes of the distribution aligned with the axes of the space. It allows us to make the calculation through the *Mahalanobis distance* of the point, which we shall describe next.

The Mahalanobis distance is essentially the distance between a point and the centroid of a cluster, normalized by the standard deviation of the cluster in each dimension. Since the BFR Algorithm assumes the axes of the cluster align with the axes of the space, the computation of Mahalanobis distance is especially simple. Let $p = [p_1, p_2, \ldots, p_d]$ be a point and $c = [c_1, c_2, \ldots, c_d]$ the centroid of a cluster. Let σ_i be the standard deviation of points in the cluster in the ith dimension. Then the Mahalanobis distance between p and c is

$$\sqrt{\sum_{i=1}^{d}(\frac{p_i - c_i}{\sigma_i})^2}$$

That is, we normalize the difference between p and c in the ith dimension by dividing by the standard deviation of the cluster in that dimension. The rest of the formula combines the normalized distances in each dimension in the normal way for a Euclidean space.

To assign point p to a cluster, we compute the Mahalanobis distance between p and each of the cluster centroids. We choose that cluster whose centroid has the least Mahalanobis distance, and we add p to that cluster provided the Mahalanobis distance is less than a threshold. For instance, suppose we pick four as the threshold. If data is normally distributed, then the probability of a value as far as four standard deviations from the mean is less than one in a million. Thus, if the points in the cluster are really normally distributed, then the probability that we will fail to include a point that truly belongs is less than 10^{-6}. And such a point is likely to be assigned to that cluster eventually anyway, as long as it does not wind up closer to some other centroid as centroids migrate in response to points added to their cluster.

7.3.6   Exercises for Section 7.3

EXERCISE 7.3.1   For the points of Fig. 7.8, if we select three starting points using the method of Section 7.3.2, and the first point we choose is (3,4), which other points are selected.

!! EXERCISE 7.3.2   Prove that no matter what point we start with in Fig. 7.8, if we select three starting points by the method of Section 7.3.2 we obtain points in each of the three clusters. *Hint*: You could solve this exhaustively by begining with each of the twelve points in turn. However, a more generally applicable solution is to consider the diameters of the three clusters and also consider the *minimum intercluster distance*, that is, the minimum distance between two points chosen from two different clusters. Can you prove a general theorem based on these two parameters of a set of points?

! EXERCISE 7.3.3   Give an example of a dataset and a selection of k initial centroids such that when the points are reassigned to their nearest centroid at the end, at least one of the initial k points is reassigned to a different cluster.

EXERCISE 7.3.4   For the three clusters of Fig. 7.8:

(a) Compute the representation of the cluster as in the BFR Algorithm. That is, compute N, SUM, and SUMSQ.
(b) Compute the variance and standard deviation of each cluster in each of the two dimensions.

EXERCISE 7.3.5   Suppose a cluster of three-dimensional points has standard deviations of 2, 3, and 5, in the three dimensions, in that order. Compute the Mahalanobis distance between the origin $(0, 0, 0)$ and the point $(1, -3, 4)$.

7.4   The CURE Algorithm

We now turn to another large-scale-clustering algorithm in the point-assignment class. This algorithm, called *CURE* (Clustering Using REpresentatives), assumes a Euclidean space. However, it does not assume anything about the shape of clusters; they need not be normally distributed, and can even have strange bends, S-shapes, or even rings. Instead of representing clusters by their centroid, it uses a collection of representative points, as the name implies.

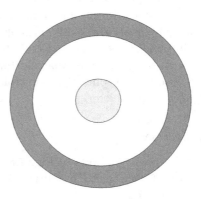

Figure 7.12 Two clusters, one surrounding the other

EXAMPLE 7.10   Figure 7.12 is an illustration of two clusters. The inner cluster is an ordinary circle, while the second is a ring around the circle. This arrangement is not completely pathological. A creature from another galaxy might look at our solar system and observe that the objects cluster into an inner circle (the planets) and an outer ring (the Kuyper belt), with little in between.   □

7.4.1   Initialization in CURE

We begin the CURE algorithm by:

(1) Take a small sample of the data and cluster it in main memory. In principle, any clustering method could be used, but as CURE is designed to handle oddly shaped clusters, it is often advisable to use a hierarchical method in which clusters are merged when they have a close pair of points. This issue is discussed in more detail in Example 7.11 below.

(2) Select a small set of points from each cluster to be *representative points*.

These points should be chosen to be as far from one another as possible, using the method described in Section 7.3.2.

(3) Move each of the representative points a fixed fraction of the distance between its location and the centroid of its cluster. Perhaps 20% is a good fraction to choose. Note that this step requires a Euclidean space, since otherwise, there might not be any notion of a line between two points.

EXAMPLE 7.11 We could use a hierarchical clustering algorithm on a sample of the data from Fig. 7.12. If we took as the distance between clusters the shortest distance between any pair of points, one from each cluster, then we would correctly find the two clusters. That is, pieces of the ring would stick together, and pieces of the inner circle would stick together, but pieces of ring would always be far away from the pieces of the circle. Note that if we used the rule that the distance between clusters was the distance between their centroids, then we might not get the intuitively correct result. The reason is that the centroids of both clusters are in the center of the diagram.

Figure 7.13 Select representative points from each cluster, as far from one another as possible

For the second step, we pick the representative points. If the sample from which the clusters are constructed is large enough, we can count on a cluster's sample points at greatest distance from one another lying on the boundary of the cluster. Figure 7.13 suggests what our initial selection of sample points might look like.

Finally, we move the representative points a fixed fraction of the distance from their true location toward the centroid of the cluster. Note that in Fig. 7.13 both clusters have their centroid in the same place: the center of the inner circle. Thus, the representative points from the circle move inside the cluster, as was intended. Points on the outer edge of the ring also move into their cluster, but points on the ring's inner edge move outside the cluster. The final locations of the representative points from Fig. 7.13 are suggested by Fig. 7.14. □

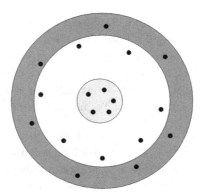

Figure 7.14 Moving the representative points 20% of the distance to the cluster's centroid

7.4.2   Completion of the CURE Algorithm

The next phase of CURE is to merge two clusters if they have a pair of representative points, one from each cluster, that are sufficiently close. The user may pick the distance that defines "close." This merging step can repeat, until there are no more sufficiently close clusters.

EXAMPLE 7.12   The situation of Fig. 7.14 serves as a useful illustration. There is some argument that the ring and circle should really be merged, because their centroids are the same. For instance, if the gap between the ring and circle were much smaller, it might well be argued that combining the points of the ring and circle into a single cluster reflected the true state of affairs. For instance, the rings of Saturn have narrow gaps between them, but it is reasonable to visualize the rings as a single object, rather than several concentric objects. In the case of Fig. 7.14 the choice of

(1) The fraction of the distance to the centroid that we move the representative points and
(2) The choice of how far apart representative points of two clusters need to be to avoid merger

together determine whether we regard Fig. 7.12 as one cluster or two.   □

The last step of CURE is point assignment. Each point p is brought from secondary storage and compared with the representative points. We assign p to the cluster of the representative point that is closest to p.

EXAMPLE 7.13   In our running example, points within the ring will surely be closer to one of the ring's representative points than to any representative point of the circle. Likewise, points within the circle will surely be closest to a representative point of the circle. An outlier – a point not within the ring or the circle – will be assigned to the ring if it is outside the ring. If the outlier is between the ring and the circle, it will be assigned to one or the other, somewhat favoring the ring because its representative points have been moved toward the circle.   □

7.4.3   Exercises for Section 7.4

EXERCISE 7.4.1   Consider two clusters that are a circle and a surrounding ring, as in the running example of this section. Suppose:

i.   The radius of the circle is c.

ii.   The inner and outer circles forming the ring have radii i and o, respectively.

iii. All representative points for the two clusters are on the boundaries of the clusters.

iv.   Representative points are moved 20% of the distance from their initial position toward the centroid of their cluster.

v.   Clusters are merged if, after repositioning, there are representative points from the two clusters at distance d or less.

In terms of d, c, i, and o, under what circumstances will the ring and circle be merged into a single cluster?

7.5   Clustering in Non-Euclidean Spaces

We shall next consider an algorithm that handles non-main-memory data, but does not require a Euclidean space. The algorithm, which we shall refer to as GRGPF for its authors (V. Ganti, R. Ramakrishnan, J. Gehrke, A. Powell, and J. French), takes ideas from both hierarchical and point-assignment approaches. Like CURE, it represents clusters by sample points in main memory. However, it also tries to organize the clusters hierarchically, in a tree, so a new point can be assigned to the appropriate cluster by passing it down the tree. Leaves of the tree hold summaries of some clusters, and interior nodes hold subsets of the information describing the clusters reachable through that node. An attempt is made to group clusters by their distance from one another, so the clusters at a leaf are close, and the clusters reachable from one interior node are relatively close as well.

7.5.1   Representing Clusters in the GRGPF Algorithm

As we assign points to clusters, the clusters can grow large. Most of the points in a cluster are stored on disk, and are not used in guiding the assignment of points, although they can be retrieved. The representation of a cluster in main memory consists of several *features*. Before listing these features, if p is any point in a cluster, let ROWSUM(p) be the sum of the squares of the distances from p to each of the other points in the cluster. Note that, although we are not in a Euclidean space, there is some distance measure d that applies to points, or else it is not possible to cluster points at all. The following features form the *representation* of a cluster.

(1) N, the number of points in the cluster.
(2) The clustroid of the cluster, which is defined specifically to be the point in the cluster that minimizes the sum of the squares of the distances to the other points; that is, the clustroid is the point in the cluster with the smallest ROWSUM.
(3) The rowsum of the clustroid of the cluster.
(4) For some chosen constant k, the k points of the cluster that are closest to the clustroid, and their rowsums. These points are part of the representation in case the addition of points to the cluster causes the clustroid to change. The assumption is made that the new clustroid would be one of these k points near the old clustroid.
(5) The k points of the cluster that are furthest from the clustroid and their rowsums. These points are part of the representation so that we can consider whether two clusters are close enough to merge. The assumption is made that if two clusters are close, then a pair of points distant from their respective clustroids would be close.

7.5.2   Initializing the Cluster Tree

The clusters are organized into a tree, and the nodes of the tree may be very large, perhaps disk blocks or pages, as would be the case for a B-tree or R-tree, which the cluster-representing tree resembles. Each leaf of the tree holds as many cluster representations as can fit. Note that a cluster representation has a size that does not depend on the number of points in the cluster.

An interior node of the cluster tree holds a sample of the clustroids of the clusters represented by each of its subtrees, along with pointers to the roots of those subtrees. The samples are of fixed size, so the number of children that an interior node may have is independent of its level. Notice that as we go up the tree, the probability that a given cluster's clustroid is part of the sample diminishes.

We initialize the cluster tree by taking a main-memory sample of the dataset and clustering it hierarchically. The result of this clustering is a tree T, but T is not exactly the tree used by the GRGPF Algorithm. Rather, we select from T certain of its nodes that represent clusters of approximately some desired size n. These are the initial clusters for the GRGPF Algorithm, and we place their representations at the leaf of the cluster-representing tree. We then group clusters with a common ancestor in T into interior nodes of the cluster-representing tree, so in some sense, clusters descended from one interior node are as close as possible. In some cases, rebalancing of the cluster-representing tree will be necessary. This process is similar to the reorganization of a B-tree, and we shall not examine this issue in detail.

7.5.3   Adding Points in the GRGPF Algorithm

We now read points from secondary storage and insert each one into the nearest cluster. We start at the root, and look at the samples of clustroids for each of the children of the root. Whichever child has the clustroid closest to the new point p is the node we examine next. When we reach any node in the tree, we look at the sample clustroids for its children and go next to the child with the clustroid closest to p. Note that some of the sample clustroids at a node may have been seen at a higher level, but each level provides more detail about the clusters lying below, so we see many new sample clustroids each time we go a level down the tree.

Finally, we reach a leaf. This leaf has the cluster features for each cluster represented by that leaf, and we pick the cluster whose clustroid is closest to p. We adjust the representation of this cluster to account for the new node p. In particular, we:

(1) Add 1 to N.
(2) Add the square of the distance between p and each of the nodes q mentioned in the representation to ROWSUM(q). These points q include the clustroid, the k nearest points, and the k furthest points.

We also estimate the rowsum of p, in case p needs to be part of the representation (e.g., it turns out to be one of the k points closest to the clustroid). Note we cannot compute ROWSUM(p) exactly, without going to disk and retrieving all the points of the cluster. The estimate we use is

$$\text{ROWSUM}(p) = \text{ROWSUM}(c) + Nd^2(p, c)$$

where $d(p, c)$ is the distance between p and the clustroid c. Note that N and ROWSUM(c) in this formula are the values of these features before they were adjusted to account for the addition of p.

We might well wonder why this estimate works. In Section 7.1.3 we discussed the "curse of dimensionality," in particular the observation that in a high-dimensional Euclidean space, almost all angles are right angles. Of course the assumption of the GRGPF Algorithm is that the space might not be Euclidean, but typically a non-Euclidean space also suffers from the curse of dimensionality, in that it behaves in many ways like a high-dimensional Euclidean space. If we assume that the angle between p, c, and another point q in the cluster is a right angle, then the Pythagorean theorem tell us that

$$d^2(p, q) = d^2(p, c) + d^2(c, q)$$

If we sum over all q other than c, and then add $d^2(p, c)$ to ROWSUM(p) to account for the fact that the clustroid is one of the points in the cluster, we derive ROWSUM(p) = ROWSUM(c) + $Nd^2(p, c)$.

Now, we must see if the new point p is one of the k closest or furthest points from the clustroid, and if so, p and its rowsum become a cluster feature, replacing one of the other features – whichever is no longer one of the k closest or furthest. We also need to consider whether the rowsum for one of the k closest points q is now less than ROWSUM(c). That situation could happen if p were closer to one of these points than to the current clustroid. If so, we swap the roles of c and q. Eventually, it is possible that the true clustroid will no longer be one of the original k closest points. We have no way of knowing, since we do not see the other points of the cluster in main memory. However, they are all stored on disk, and can be brought into main memory periodically for a recomputation of the cluster features.

7.5.4   Splitting and Merging Clusters

The GRGPF Algorithm assumes that there is a limit on the radius that a cluster may have. The particular definition used for the radius is $\sqrt{\text{ROWSUM}(c)/N}$, where c is the clustroid of the cluster and N the number of points in the cluster. That is, the radius is the square root of the average square of the distance from the clustroid of the points in the cluster. If a cluster's radius grows too large, it is split into two. The points of that cluster are brought into main memory, and divided into two clusters to minimize the rowsums. The cluster features for both clusters are computed.

As a result, the leaf of the split cluster now has one more cluster to represent. We should manage the cluster tree like a B-tree, so usually, there will be room in a leaf to add one more cluster. However, if not, then the leaf must be split into two leaves. To implement the split, we must add another pointer and more sample clustroids at the parent node. Again, there may be extra space, but if not, then this node too must be split, and we do so to minimize the squares of the distances between the sample clustroids assigned to different nodes. As in a B-tree, this splitting can ripple all the way up to the root, which can then be split if needed.

The worst thing that can happen is that the cluster-representing tree is now too large to fit in main memory. There is only one thing to do: we make it smaller by raising the limit on how large the radius of a cluster can be, and we consider merging pairs of clusters. It is normally sufficient to consider clusters that are "nearby," in the sense that their representatives are at the same leaf or at leaves with a common parent. However, in principle, we can consider merging any two clusters C_1 and C_2 into one cluster C.

To merge clusters, we assume that the clustroid of C will be one of the points that are as far as possible from the clustroid of C_1 or the clustroid of C_2. Suppose we want to compute the rowsum in C for the point p, which is one of the k points in C_1 that are as far as possible from the centroid of C_1. We use the curse-of-dimensionality argument that says all angles are approximately right angles, to justify the following formula.

$$\text{ROWSUM}_C(p) = \text{ROWSUM}_{C_1}(p) + N_{C_2}\left(d^2(p, c_1) + d^2(c_1, c_2)\right) + \text{ROWSUM}_{C_2}(c_2)$$

In the above, we subscript N and ROWSUM by the cluster to which that feature refers. We use c_1 and c_2 for the clustroids of C_1 and C_2, respectively.

In detail, we compute the sum of the squares of the distances from p to all the nodes in the combined cluster C by beginning with $\text{ROWSUM}_{C_1}(p)$ to get the terms for the points in the same cluster as p. For the N_{C_2} points q in C_2, we consider the path from p to the clustroid of C_1, then to the clustroid of C_2, and finally to q. We assume there is a right angle between the legs from p to c_1 and c_1 to c_2, and another right angle between the shortest path from p to c_2 and the leg from c_2 to q. We then use the Pythagorean theorem to justify computing the square of the length of the path to each q as the sum of the squares of the three legs.

We must then finish computing the features for the merged cluster. We need to consider all the points in the merged cluster for which we know the rowsum. These are, the centroids of the two clusters, the k points closest to the clustroids for each cluster, and the k points furthest from the clustroids for each cluster, with the exception of the point that was chosen as the new clustroid. We can compute the distances from the new clustroid for each of these $4k + 1$ points. We select the k with the smallest distances as the "close" points and the k with the largest distances as the "far" points. We can then compute the rowsums for the chosen points, using the same formulas above that we used to compute the rowsums for the candidate clustroids.

7.5.5 Exercises for Section 7.5

EXERCISE 7.5.1 Using the cluster representation of Section 7.5.1, represent the twelve points of Fig. 7.8 as a single cluster. Use parameter $k = 2$ as the number of close and distant points to be included in the representation. *Hint*: Since the distance is Euclidean, we can get the square of the distance between two points by taking the sum of the squares of the differences along the x- and y-axes.

EXERCISE 7.5.2 Compute the radius, in the sense used by the GRGPF Algorithm (square root of the average square of the distance from the clustroid) for the cluster that is the five points in the lower right of Fig. 7.8. Note that (11,4) is the clustroid.

7.6 Clustering for Streams and Parallelism

In this section, we shall consider briefly how one might cluster a stream. The model we have in mind is one where there is a sliding window (recall Section 4.1.3) of N points, and we can ask for the centroids or clustroids of the best clusters formed from the last m of these points, for any $m \leq N$. We also study a similar approach to clustering a large, fixed set of points using MapReduce on a computing cluster (no pun intended). This section provides only a rough outline to suggest the possibilities, which depend on our assumptions about how clusters evolve in a stream.

7.6.1   The Stream-Computing Model

We assume that each stream element is a point in some space. The sliding window consists of the most recent N points. Our goal is to precluster subsets of the points in the stream, so that we may quickly answer queries of the form "what are the clusters of the last m points?" for any $m \le N$. There are many variants of this query, depending on what we assume about what constitutes a cluster. For instance, we may use a k-means approach, where we are really asking that the last m points be partitioned into exactly k clusters. Or, we may allow the number of clusters to vary, but use one of the criteria in Section 7.2.3 or 7.2.4 to determine when to stop merging clusters into larger clusters.

We make no restriction regarding the space in which the points of the stream live. It may be a Euclidean space, in which case the answer to the query is the centroids of the selected clusters. The space may be non-Euclidean, in which case the answer is the clustroids of the selected clusters, where any of the definitions for "clustroid" may be used (see Section 7.2.4).

The problem is considerably easier if we assume that all stream elements are chosen with statistics that do not vary along the stream. Then, a sample of the stream is good enough to estimate the clusters, and we can in effect ignore the stream after a while. However, the stream model normally assumes that the statistics of the stream elements varies with time. For example, the centroids of the clusters may migrate slowly as time goes on, or clusters may expand, contract, divide, or merge.

7.6.2   A Stream-Clustering Algorithm

In this section, we shall present a greatly simplified version of an algorithm referred to as BDMO (for the authors, B. Babcock, M. Datar, R. Motwani, and L. O'Callaghan). The true version of the algorithm involves much more complex structures, which are designed to provide performance guarantees in the worst case.

The BDMO Algorithm builds on the methodology for counting ones in a stream that was described in Section 4.6. Here are the key similarities and differences:

- Like that algorithm, the points of the stream are partitioned into, and summarized by, buckets whose sizes are a power of two. Here, the *size* of a bucket is the number of points it represents, rather than the number of stream elements that are 1.

- As before, the sizes of buckets obey the restriction that there are one or two of each size, up to some limit. However, we do not assume that the sequence of allowable bucket sizes starts with 1. Rather, they are required only to form a sequence where each size is twice the previous size, e.g., $3, 6, 12, 24, \ldots$.

- Bucket sizes are again restrained to be nondecreasing as we go back in time. As in Section 4.6, we can conclude that there will be $O(\log N)$ buckets.
- The *contents* of a bucket consists of:
  (1) The size of the bucket.
  (2) The timestamp of the bucket, that is, the most recent point that contributes to the bucket. As in Section 4.6, timestamps can be recorded modulo N.
  (3) A collection of records that represent the clusters into which the points of that bucket have been partitioned. These records contain:
     (a) The number of points in the cluster.
     (b) The centroid or clustroid of the cluster.
     (c) Any other parameters necessary to enable us to merge clusters and maintain approximations to the full set of parameters for the merged cluster. We shall give some examples when we discuss the merger process in Section 7.6.4.

7.6.3 Initializing Buckets

Our smallest bucket size will be p, a power of 2. Thus, every p stream elements, we create a new bucket, with the most recent p points. The timestamp for this bucket is the timestamp of the most recent point in the bucket. We may leave each point in a cluster by itself, or we may perform a clustering of these points according to whatever clustering strategy we have chosen. For instance, if we choose a k-means algorithm, then (assuming $k < p$) we cluster the points into k clusters by some algorithm.

Whatever method we use to cluster initially, we assume it is possible to compute the centroids or clustroids for the clusters and count the points in each cluster. This information becomes part of the record for each cluster. We also compute whatever other parameters for the clusters will be needed in the merging process.

7.6.4 Merging Buckets

Following the strategy from Section 4.6, whenever we create a new bucket, we need to review the sequence of buckets. First, if some bucket has a timestamp that is more than N time units prior to the current time, then nothing of that bucket is in the window, and we may drop it from the list. Second, we may have created three buckets of size p, in which case we must merge the oldest two of the three. The merger may create two buckets of size $2p$, in which case we may have to merge buckets of increasing sizes, recursively, just as in Section 4.6.

To merge two consecutive buckets, we need to do several things:

(1) The size of the bucket is twice the sizes of the two buckets being merged.

(2) The timestamp for the merged bucket is the timestamp of the more recent of the two consecutive buckets.

(3) We must consider whether to merge clusters, and if so, we need to compute the parameters of the merged clusters. We shall elaborate on this part of the algorithm by considering several examples of criteria for merging and ways to estimate the needed parameters.

EXAMPLE 7.14   Perhaps the simplest case is where we are using a k-means approach in a Euclidean space. We represent clusters by the count of their points and their centroids. Each bucket has exactly k clusters, so we can pick $p = k$, or we can pick p larger than k and cluster the p points into k clusters when we create a bucket initially as in Section 7.6.3. We must find the best matching between the k clusters of the first bucket and the k clusters of the second. Here, "best" means the matching that minimizes the sum of the distances between the centroids of the matched clusters.

Note that we do not consider merging two clusters from the same bucket, because our assumption is that clusters do not evolve too much between consecutive buckets. Thus, we would expect to find in each of two adjacent buckets a representation of each of the k "true" clusters that exist in the stream.

When we decide to merge two clusters, one from each bucket, the number of points in the merged cluster is surely the sum of the numbers of points in the two clusters. The centroid of the merged cluster is the weighted average of the centroids of the two clusters, where the weighting is by the numbers of points in the clusters. That is, if the two clusters have n_1 and n_2 points, respectively, and have centroids c_1 and c_2 (the latter are d-dimensional vectors for some d), then the combined cluster has $n = n_1 + n_2$ points and has centroid

$$c = \frac{n_1 c_1 + n_2 c_2}{n_1 + n_2} \qquad \square$$

EXAMPLE 7.15   The method of Example 7.14 suffices when the clusters are changing very slowly. Suppose we might expect the cluster centroids to migrate sufficiently quickly that when matching the centroids from two consecutive buckets, we might be faced with an ambiguous situation, where it is not clear which of two clusters best matches a given cluster from the other bucket. One way to protect against such a situation is to create more than k clusters in each bucket, even if we know that, when we query (see Section 7.6.5), we shall have to merge into exactly k clusters. For example, we might choose p to be much larger than k, and, when we merge, only merge clusters when the result is sufficiently coherent according to one of the criteria outlined in Section 7.2.3. Or, we could use a hierarchical strategy, and make the best merges, so as to maintain $p > k$ clusters in each bucket.

Suppose, to be specific, that we want to put a limit on the sum of the distances between all the points of a cluster and its centroid. Then in addition to the count of points and the centroid of a cluster, we can include an estimate of this sum in the record for a cluster. When we initialize a bucket, we can compute the sum exactly. But as we merge clusters, this parameter becomes an estimate only. Suppose we merge two clusters, and want to compute the sum of distances for the merged cluster. Use the notation for centroids and counts in Example 7.14, and in addition, let s_1 and s_2 be the sums for the two clusters. Then we may estimate the radius of the merged cluster to be

$$n_1|\mathbf{c}_1 - \mathbf{c}| + n_2|\mathbf{c}_2 - \mathbf{c}| + s_1 + s_2$$

That is, we estimate the distance between any point x and the new centroid $\mathbf{c}$ to be the distance of that point to its old centroid (these distances sum to $s_1 + s_2$, the last two terms in the above expression) plus the distance from the old centroid to the new (these distances sum to the first two terms of the above expression). Note that this estimate is an upper bound, by the triangle inequality.

An alternative is to replace the sum of distances by the sum of the squares of the distances from the points to the centroid. If these sums for the two clusters are t_1 and t_2, respectively, then we can produce an estimate for the same sum in the new cluster as

$$n_1|\mathbf{c}_1 - \mathbf{c}|^2 + n_2|\mathbf{c}_2 - \mathbf{c}|^2 + t_1 + t_2$$

This estimate is close to correct if the space is high-dimensional, by the "curse of dimensionality." □

EXAMPLE 7.16 Our third example will assume a non-Euclidean space and no constraint on the number of clusters. We shall borrow several of the techniques from the GRGPF Algorithm of Section 7.5. Specifically, we represent clusters by their clustroid and rowsum (sum of the squares of the distances from each node of the cluster to its clustroid). We include in the record for a cluster information about a set of points at maximum distance from the clustroid, including their distances from the clustroid and their rowsums. Recall that their purpose is to suggest a clustroid when this cluster is merged with another.

When we merge buckets, we may choose one of many ways to decide which clusters to merge. For example, we may consider pairs of clusters in order of the distance between their clustroids. We may also choose to merge clusters when we consider them, provided the sum of their rowsums is below a certain limit. Alternatively, we may perform the merge if the sum of rowsums divided by the number of points in the clusters is below a limit. Any of the other strategies discussed for deciding when to merge clusters may be used as well, provided we arrange to maintain the data (e.g., cluster diameter) necessary to make decisions.

We then must pick a new clustroid, from among the points most distant from the clustroids of the two merged clusters. We can compute rowsums for each of these candidate clustroids using the formulas given in Section 7.5.4. We also follow the strategy given in that section to pick a subset of the distant points from each cluster to be the set of distant points for the merged cluster, and to compute the new rowsum and distance-to-clustroid for each. □

7.6.5   Answering Queries

Recall that we assume a query is a request for the clusters of the most recent m points in the stream, where $m \leq N$. Because of the strategy we have adopted of combining buckets as we go back in time, we may not be able to find a set of buckets that covers exactly the last m points. However, if we choose the smallest set of buckets that cover the last m points, we shall include in these buckets no more than the last $2m$ points. We shall produce, as answer to the query, the centroids or clustroids of all the points in the selected buckets. In order for the result to be a good approximation to the clusters for exactly the last m points, we must assume that the points between $2m$ and $m + 1$ will not have radically different statistics from the most recent m points. However, if the statistics vary too rapidly, recall from Section 4.6.6 that a more complex bucketing scheme can guarantee that we can find buckets to cover at most the last $m(1 + \epsilon)$ points, for any $\epsilon > 0$.

Having selected the desired buckets, we pool all their clusters. We then use some methodology for deciding which clusters to merge. Examples 7.14 and 7.16 are illustrations of two approaches to this merger. For instance, if we are required to produce exactly k clusters, then we can merge the clusters with the closest centroids until we are left with only k clusters, as in Example 7.14. Or we can make a decision whether or not to merge clusters in various ways, as we sampled in Example 7.16.

7.6.6   Clustering in a Parallel Environment

Now, let us briefly consider the use of parallelism available in a computing cluster.[3] We assume we are given a very large collection of points, and we wish to exploit parallelism to compute the centroids of their clusters. The simplest approach is to use a MapReduce strategy, but in most cases we are constrained to use a single Reduce task.

Begin by creating many Map tasks. Each task is assigned a subset of the points. The Map function's job is to cluster the points it is given. Its output is a set of key-value pairs with a fixed key 1, and a value that is the description of one cluster. This description can be any of the possibilities suggested in Section 7.6.2, such as the centroid, count, and diameter of the cluster.

Since all key-value pairs have the same key, there can be only one Reduce task. This task gets descriptions of the clusters produced by each of the Map tasks, and must merge them appropriately. We may use the discussion in Section 7.6.4 as representative of the various strategies we might use to produce the final clustering, which is the output of the Reduce task.

---

[3] Do not forget that the term "cluster" has two completely different meanings in this section.

7.6.7   Exercises for Section 7.6

EXERCISE 7.6.1   Execute the BDMO Algorithm with $p = 3$ on the following 1-dimensional, Euclidean data:

$$1, 45, 80, 24, 56, 71, 17, 40, 66, 32, 48, 96, 9, 41, 75, 11, 58, 93, 28, 39, 77$$

The clustering algorithms is k-means with $k = 3$. Only the centroid of a cluster, along with its count, is needed to represent a cluster.

EXERCISE 7.6.2   Using your clusters from Exercise 7.6.1, produce the best centroids in response to a query asking for a clustering of the last 10 points.

7.7   Summary of Chapter 7

✦ *Clustering*: Clusters are often a useful summary of data that is in the form of points in some space. To cluster points, we need a distance measure on that space. Ideally, points in the same cluster have small distances between them, while points in different clusters have large distances between them.

✦ *Clustering Algorithms*: Clustering algorithms generally have one of two forms. Hierarchical clustering algorithms begin with all points in a cluster of their own, and nearby clusters are merged iteratively. Point-assignment clustering algorithms consider points in turn and assign them to the cluster in which they best fit.

✦ *The Curse of Dimensionality*: Points in high-dimensional Euclidean spaces, as well as points in non-Euclidean spaces often behave unintuitively. Two unexpected properties of these spaces are that random points are almost always at about the same distance, and random vectors are almost always orthogonal.

✦ *Centroids and Clustroids*: In a Euclidean space, the members of a cluster can be averaged, and this average is called the centroid. In non-Euclidean spaces, there is no guarantee that points have an "average," so we are forced to use one of the members of the cluster as a representative or typical element of the cluster. That representative is called the clustroid.

✦ *Choosing the Clustroid*: There are many ways we can define a typical point of a cluster in a non-Euclidean space. For example, we could choose the point with the smallest sum of distances to the other points, the smallest sum of the squares of those distances, or the smallest maximum distance to any other point in the cluster.

✦ *Radius and Diameter*: Whether or not the space is Euclidean, we can define the radius of a cluster to be the maximum distance from the centroid or clustroid to any point in that cluster. We can define the diameter of the cluster to be the maximum distance between any two points in the cluster. Alternative definitions, especially of the radius, are also known, for example, average distance from the centroid to the other points.

◆ *Hierarchical Clustering*: This family of algorithms has many variations, which differ primarily in two areas. First, we may chose in various ways which two clusters to merge next. Second, we may decide when to stop the merge process in various ways.

◆ *Picking Clusters to Merge*: One strategy for deciding on the best pair of clusters to merge in a hierarchical clustering is to pick the clusters with the closest centroids or clustroids. Another approach is to pick the pair of clusters with the closest points, one from each cluster. A third approach is to use the average distance between points from the two clusters.

◆ *Stopping the Merger Process*: A hierarchical clustering can proceed until there are a fixed number of clusters left. Alternatively, we could merge until it is impossible to find a pair of clusters whose merger is sufficiently compact, e.g., the merged cluster has a radius or diameter below some threshold. Another approach involves merging as long as the resulting cluster has a sufficiently high "density," which can be defined in various ways, but is the number of points divided by some measure of the size of the cluster, e.g., the radius.

◆ *K-Means Algorithms*: This family of algorithms is of the point-assignment type and assumes a Euclidean space. It is assumed that there are exactly k clusters for some known k. After picking k initial cluster centroids, the points are considered one at a time and assigned to the closest centroid. The centroid of a cluster can migrate during point assignment, and an optional last step is to reassign all the points, while holding the centroids fixed at their final values obtained during the first pass.

◆ *Initializing K-Means Algorithms*: One way to find k initial centroids is to pick a random point, and then choose $k - 1$ additional points, each as far away as possible from the previously chosen points. An alternative is to start with a small sample of points and use a hierarchical clustering to merge them into k clusters.

◆ *Picking K in a K-Means Algorithm*: If the number of clusters is unknown, we can use a binary-search technique, trying a k-means clustering with different values of k. We search for the largest value of k for which a decrease below k clusters results in a radically higher average diameter of the clusters. This search can be carried out in a number of clustering operations that is logarithmic in the true value of k.

◆ *The BFR Algorithm*: This algorithm is a version of k-means designed to handle data that is too large to fit in main memory. It assumes clusters are normally distributed about the axes.

◆ *Representing Clusters in BFR*: Points are read from disk one chunk at a time. Clusters are represented in main memory by the count of the number of points, the vector sum of all the points, and the vector formed by summing the squares of the components of the points in each dimension. Other collection of points, too far from a cluster centroid to be included in a cluster, are represented as "miniclusters" in the same way as the k clusters, while still other points, which are not near any other point will be represented as themselves and called "retained" points.

✦ *Processing Points in BFR*: Most of the points in a main-memory load will be assigned to a nearby cluster and the parameters for that cluster will be adjusted to account for the new points. Unassigned points can be formed into new miniclusters, and these miniclusters can be merged with previously discovered miniclusters or retained points. After the last memory load, the miniclusters and retained points can be merged to their nearest cluster or kept as outliers.

✦ *The CURE Algorithm*: This algorithm is of the point-assignment type. It is designed for a Euclidean space, but clusters can have any shape. It handles data that is too large to fit in main memory.

✦ *Representing Clusters in CURE*: The algorithm begins by clustering a small sample of points. It then selects representative points for each cluster, by picking points in the cluster that are as far away from each other as possible. The goal is to find representative points on the fringes of the cluster. However, the representative points are then moved a fraction of the way toward the centroid of the cluster, so they lie somewhat in the interior of the cluster.

✦ *Processing Points in CURE*: After creating representative points for each cluster, the entire set of points can be read from disk and assigned to a cluster. We assign a given point to the cluster of the representative point that is closest to the given point.

✦ *The GRGPF Algorithm*: This algorithm is of the point-assignment type. It handles data that is too big to fit in main memory, and it does not assume a Euclidean space.

✦ *Representing Clusters in GRGPF*: A cluster is represented by the count of points in the cluster, the clustroid, a set of points nearest the clustroid and a set of points furthest from the clustroid. The nearby points allow us to change the clustroid if the cluster evolves, and the distant points allow for merging clusters efficiently in appropriate circumstances. For each of these points, we also record the rowsum, that is the square root of the sum of the squares of the distances from that point to all the other points of the cluster.

✦ *Tree Organization of Clusters in GRGPF*: Cluster representations are organized into a tree structure like a B-tree, where nodes of the tree are typically disk blocks and contain information about many clusters. The leaves hold the representation of as many clusters as possible, while interior nodes hold a sample of the clustroids of the clusters at their descendant leaves. We organize the tree so that the clusters whose representatives are in any subtree are as close as possible.

✦ *Processing Points in GRGPF*: After initializing clusters from a sample of points, we insert each point into the cluster with the nearest clustroid. Because of the tree structure, we can start at the root and choose to visit the child with the sample clustroid nearest to the given point. Following this rule down one path in the tree leads us to a leaf, where we insert the point into the cluster with the nearest clustroid on that leaf.

✦ *Clustering Streams*: A generalization of the DGIM Algorithm (for counting 1s in the sliding window of a stream) can be used to cluster points that are part of a slowly evolving stream. The BDMO Algorithm uses buckets similar to those of DGIM, with allowable bucket sizes forming a sequence where each size is twice the previous size.

✦ *Representation of Buckets in BDMO*: The size of a bucket is the number of points it represents. The bucket itself holds only a representation of the clusters of these points, not the points themselves. A cluster representation includes a count of the number of points, the centroid or clustroid, and other information that is needed for merging clusters according to some selected strategy.

✦ *Merging Buckets in BDMO*: When buckets must be merged, we find the best matching of clusters, one from each of the buckets, and merge them in pairs. If the stream evolves slowly, then we expect consecutive buckets to have almost the same cluster centroids, so this matching makes sense.

✦ *Answering Queries in BDMO*: A query is a length of a suffix of the sliding window. We take all the clusters in all the buckets that are at least partially within that suffix and merge them using some strategy. The resulting clusters are the answer to the query.

✦ *Clustering Using MapReduce*: We can divide the data into chunks and cluster each chunk in parallel, using a Map task. The clusters from each Map task can be further clustered in a single Reduce task.

7.8   References for Chapter 7

The ancestral study of clustering for large-scale data is the BIRCH Algorithm of [6]. The BFR Algorithm is from [2]. The CURE Algorithm is found in [5].

The paper on the GRGPF Algorithm is [3]. The necessary background regarding B-trees and R-trees can be found in [4]. The study of clustering on streams is taken from [1].

[1] B. Babcock, M. Datar, R. Motwani, and L. O'Callaghan, "Maintaining variance and k-medians over data stream windows," *Proc. ACM Symp. on Principles of Database Systems*, pp. 234–243, 2003.

[2] P.S. Bradley, U.M. Fayyad, and C. Reina, "Scaling clustering algorithms to large databases," *Proc. Knowledge Discovery and Data Mining*, pp. 9–15, 1998.

[3] V. Ganti, R. Ramakrishnan, J. Gehrke, A.L. Powell, and J.C. French:, "Clustering large datasets in arbitrary metric spaces," *Proc. Intl. Conf. on Data Engineering*, pp. 502–511, 1999.

[4] H. Garcia-Molina, J.D. Ullman, and J. Widom, *Database Systems: The Complete Book* Second Edition, Prentice-Hall, Upper Saddle River, NJ, 2009.

[5] S. Guha, R. Rastogi, and K. Shim, "CURE: An efficient clustering algorithm for large databases," *Proc. ACM SIGMOD Intl. Conf. on Management of Data*, pp. 73–84, 1998.

[6] T. Zhang, R. Ramakrishnan, and M. Livny, "BIRCH: an efficient data clustering method for very large databases," *Proc. ACM SIGMOD Intl. Conf. on Management of Data*, pp. 103–114, 1996.

8 Advertising on the Web

One of the big surprises of the 21st century has been the ability of all sorts of interesting Web applications to support themselves through advertising, rather than subscription. While radio and television have managed to use advertising as their primary revenue source, most media – newspapers and magazines, for example – have had to use a hybrid approach, combining revenue from advertising and subscriptions.

By far the most lucrative venue for on-line advertising has been search, and much of the effectiveness of search advertising comes from the "adwords" model of matching search queries to advertisements. We shall therefore devote much of this chapter to algorithms for optimizing the way this assignment is done. The algorithms used are of an unusual type; they are greedy and they are "on-line" in a particular technical sense to be discussed. We shall therefore digress to discuss these two algorithmic issues – greediness and on-line algorithms – in general, before tackling the adwords problem.

A second interesting on-line advertising problem involves selecting items to advertise at an on-line store. This problem involves "collaborative filtering," where we try to find customers with similar behavior in order to suggest they buy things that similar customers have bought. This subject will be treated in Section 9.3.

8.1 Issues in On-Line Advertising

In this section, we summarize the technical problems that are presented by the opportunities for on-line advertising. We begin by surveying the types of ads found on the Web.

8.1.1 Advertising Opportunities

The Web offers many ways for an advertiser to show their ads to potential customers. Here are the principal venues.

(1) Some sites, such as eBay, Craig's List or auto trading sites allow advertisers to post their ads directly, either for free, for a fee, or a commission.
(2) Display ads are placed on many Web sites. Advertisers pay for the display

at a fixed rate per *impression* (one display of the ad with the download of the page by some user). Normally, a second download of the page, even by the same user, will result in the display of a different ad and is a second impression.

(3) On-line stores such as Amazon show ads in many contexts. The ads are not paid for by the manufacturers of the product advertised, but are selected by the store to maximize the probability that the customer will be interested in the product. We consider this kind of advertising in Chapter 9.

(4) Search ads are placed among the results of a search query. Advertisers bid for the right to have their ad shown in response to certain queries, but they pay only if the ad is clicked on. The particular ads to be shown are selected by a complex process, to be discussed in this chapter, involving the search terms that the advertiser has bid for, the amount of their bid, the observed probability that the ad will be clicked on, and the total budget that the advertiser has offered for the service.

8.1.2 Direct Placement of Ads

When advertisers can place ads directly, such as a free ad on Craig's List or the "buy it now" feature at eBay, there are several problems that the site must deal with. Ads are displayed in response to query terms, e.g., "apartment Palo Alto." The Web site can use an inverted index of words, just as a search engine does (see Section 5.1.1) and return those ads that contain all the words in the query. Alternatively, one can ask the advertiser to specify parameters of the ad, which are stored in a database. For instance, an ad for a used car could specify the manufacturer, model, color, and year from pull-down menus, so only clearly understood terms can be used. Queryers can use the same menus of terms in their queries.

Ranking ads is a bit more problematic, since there is nothing like the links on the Web to tell us which ads are more "important." One strategy used is "most-recent first." That strategy, while equitable, is subject to abuse, where advertisers post small variations of their ads at frequent intervals. The technology for discovering ads that are too similar has already been covered, in Section 3.4.

An alternative approach is to try to measure the attractiveness of an ad. Each time it is displayed, record whether or not the queryer clicked on it. Presumably, attractive ads will be clicked on more frequently than those that are not. However, there are several factors that must be considered in evaluating ads:

(1) The position of the ad in a list has great influence on whether or not it is clicked. The first on the list has by far the highest probability, and the probability drops off exponentially as the position increases.

(2) The ad may have attractiveness that depends on the query terms. For example, an ad for a used convertible would be more attractive if the search query includes the term "convertible," even though it might be a valid response to

queries that look for that make of car, without specifying whether or not a convertible is wanted.

(3) All ads deserve the opportunity to be shown until their click probability can be approximated closely. If we start all ads out with a click probability of 0, we shall never show them and thus never learn whether or not they are attractive ads.

8.1.3 Issues for Display Ads

This form of advertising on the Web most resembles advertising in traditional media. An ad for a Chevrolet run in the pages of the *New York Times* is a display ad, and its effectiveness is limited. It may be seen by many people, but most of them are not interested in buying a car, just bought a car, don't drive, or have another good reason to ignore the ad. Yet the cost of printing the ad was still borne by the newspaper and hence by the advertiser. An impression of a similar ad on the Yahoo! home page is going to be relatively ineffective for essentially the same reason. The fee for placing such an ad is typically a fraction of a cent per impression.

The response of traditional media to this lack of focus was to create newspapers or magazines for special interests. If you are a manufacturer of golf clubs, running your ad in *Golf Digest* would give you an order-of-magnitude increase in the probability that the person seeing your ad would be interested in it. This phenomenon explains the existence of many specialized, low-circulation magazines. They are able to charge much more per impression for an ad than is a general-purpose outlet such as a daily newspaper. The same phenomenon appears on the Web. An ad for golf clubs on `sports.yahoo.com/golf` has much more value per impression than does the same ad on the Yahoo! home page or an ad for Chevrolets on the Yahoo! golf page.

However, the Web offers an opportunity to tailor display ads in a way that hardcopy media cannot: it is possible to use information about the user to determine which ad they should be shown, regardless of what page they are looking at. If it is known that Sally likes golf, then it makes sense to show her an ad for golf clubs, regardless of what page she is looking at. We could determine Sally's love for golf in various ways:

(1) She may belong to a golf-related group on Facebook.
(2) She may mention "golf" frequently in emails posted on her gmail account.
(3) She may spend a lot of time on the Yahoo! golf page.
(4) She may issue search queries with golf-related terms frequently.
(5) She may bookmark the Web sites of one or more golf courses.

Each of these methods, and many others like these, raise enormous privacy issues. It is not the purpose of this book to try to resolve those issues, which in practice probably have no solution that will satisfy all concerns. On the one hand, people like the free services that have recently become advertising-supported, and these services depend on advertising being much more effective than conventional ads. There is a general agreement that, if there must be ads, it is better to see things you might actually use than to have what pages you view cluttered with irrelevancies. On the other hand, there is great potential for misuse if the information leaves the realm of the machines that execute advertising algorithms and get into the hands of real people.

8.2   On-Line Algorithms

Before addressing the question of matching advertisements to search queries, we shall digress slightly by examining the general class to which such algorithms belong. This class is referred to as "on-line," and they generally involve an approach called "greedy." We also give, in the next section, a preliminary example of an on-line greedy algorithm for a simpler problem: maximal matching.

8.2.1   On-Line and Off-Line Algorithms

Typical algorithms work as follows. All the data needed by the algorithm is presented initially. The algorithm can access the data in any order. At the end, the algorithm produces its answer. Such an algorithm is called *off-line*.

However, there are times when we cannot see all the data before our algorithm must make some decisions. Chapter 4 covered stream mining, where we could store only a limited amount of the stream, and had to answer queries about the entire stream when called upon to do so. There is an extreme form of stream processing, where we must respond with an output after each stream element arrives. We thus must decide about each stream element knowing nothing at all of the future. Algorithms of this class are called *on-line* algorithms.[1]

As the case in point, selecting ads to show with search queries would be relatively simple if we could do it off-line. We would see a month's worth of search queries, and look at the bids advertisers made on search terms, as well as their advertising budgets for the month, and we could then assign ads to the queries in a way that maximized both the revenue to the search engine and the number of impressions that each advertiser got. The problem with off-line algorithms is that most queryers don't want to wait a month to get their search results.

Thus, we must use an on-line algorithm to assign ads to search queries. That is, when a search query arrives, we must select the ads to show with that query immediately. We can use information about the past, e.g., we do not have to show an ad if the advertiser's budget has already been spent, and we can examine the

---

[1] Unfortunately, we are faced with another case of dual meanings, like the coincidence involving the term "cluster" that we noted in Section 7.6.6, where we needed to interpret properly phrases such as "algorithms for computing clusters on computer clusters." Here, the term "on-line" refers to the nature of the algorithm, and should not be confused with "on-line" meaning "on the Internet" in phrases such as "on-line algorithms for on-line advertising."

click-through rate (fraction of the time the ad is clicked on when it is displayed) that an ad has obtained so far. However, we cannot use anything about future search queries. For instance, we cannot know whether there will be lots of queries arriving later and using search terms on which this advertiser has made higher bids.

EXAMPLE 8.1   Let us take a very simple example of why knowing the future could help. A manufacturer A of replica antique furniture has bid 10 cents on the search term "chesterfield".[2] A more conventional manufacturer B has bid 20 cents on both the terms "chesterfield" and "sofa." Both have monthly budgets of $100, and there are no other bidders on either of these terms. It is the beginning of the month, and a search query "chesterfield" has just arrived. We are allowed to display only one ad with the query.

The obvious thing to do is to display B's ad, because they bid more. However, suppose there will be lots of search queries this month for "sofa," but very few for "chesterfield." Then A will never spend its $100 budget, while B will spend its full budget even if we give the query to A. Specifically, if there will be at least 500 more queries for either "sofa" or "chesterfield," then there is no harm, and potentially a benefit, in giving the query to A. It will still be possible for B to spend its entire budget, while we are increasing the amount of A's budget that will be spent. Note that this argument makes sense both from the point of view of the search engine, which wants to maximize total revenue, and from the point of view of both A and B, who presumably want to get all the impressions that their budgets allow.

If we could know the future, then we would know how many more "sofa" queries and how many more "chesterfield" queries were going to arrive this month. If that number is below 500, then we want to give the query to B to maximize revenue, but if it is 500 or more, then we want to give it to A. Since we don't know the future, an on-line algorithm cannot always do as well as an off-line algorithm.   □

8.2.2   Greedy Algorithms

Many on-line algorithms are of the *greedy algorithm* type. These algorithms make their decision in response to each input element by maximizing some function of the input element and the past.

EXAMPLE 8.2   The obvious greedy algorithm for the situation described in Example 8.1 is to assign a query to the highest bidder who still has budget left. For the data of that example, what will happen is that the first 500 "sofa" or "chesterfield" queries will be assigned to B. At that time, B runs out of budget and is assigned no more queries. After that, the next 1000 "chesterfield" queries are assigned to A, and "sofa" queries get no ad and therefore earn the search engine no money.

---

[2] A chesterfield is a type of sofa. See, for example, `www.chesterfields.info`.

The worst thing that can happen is that 500 "chesterfield" queries arrive, followed by 500 "sofa" queries. An off-line algorithm could optimally assign the first 500 to A, earning \$50, and the next 500 to B, earning \$100, or a total of \$150. However, the greedy algorithm will assign the first 500 to B, earning \$100, and then has no ad for the next 500, earning nothing. □

8.2.3   The Competitive Ratio

As we see from Example 8.2, an on-line algorithm need not give as good a result as the best off-line algorithm for the same problem. The most we can expect is that there will be some constant c less than 1, such that on any input, the result of a particular on-line algorithm is at least c times the result of the optimum off-line algorithm. The constant c, if it exists, is called the *competitive ratio* for the on-line algorithm.

EXAMPLE 8.3   The greedy algorithm, on the particular data of Example 8.2, gives a result that is 2/3 as good as that of the optimum algorithm: \$100 versus \$150. That proves that the competitive ratio is no greater than 2/3. But it could be less. The competitive ratio for an algorithm may depend on what kind of data is allowed to be input to the algorithm. Even if we restrict inputs to the situation described in Example 8.2, but with the bids allowed to vary, then we can show the greedy algorithm has a competitive ratio no greater than 1/2. Just raise the bid by A to ϵ less than 20 cents. As ϵ approaches 0, the greedy algorithm still produces only \$100, but the return from the optimum algorithm approaches \$200. We can show that it is impossible to do worse than half the optimum in this simple case, so the competitive ratio is indeed 1/2. However, we'll leave this sort of proof for later sections. □

8.2.4   Exercises for Section 8.2

! EXERCISE 8.2.1   A popular example of the design of an on-line algorithm to minimize the competitive ratio is the *ski-buying problem*.[3] Suppose you can buy skis for \$100, or you can rent skis for \$10 per day. You decide to take up skiing, but you don't know if you will like it. You may try skiing for any number of days and then give it up. The merit of an algorithm is the cost per day of skis, and we must try to minimize this cost.

One on-line algorithm for making the rent/buy decision is "buy skis immediately." If you try skiing once, fall down and give it up, then this on-line algorithm costs you \$100 per day, while the optimum off-line algorithm would have you rent skis for \$10 for the one day you used them. Thus, the competitive ratio of the algorithm "buy skis immediately" is at most 1/10th, and that is in fact the exact competitive ratio, since using the skis one day is the worst possible outcome for this algorithm. On the other hand, the on-line algorithm "always rent skis" has

---

[3] Thanks to Anna Karlin for this example.

an arbitrarily small competitive ratio. If you turn out to really like skiing and go regularly, then after n days, you will have paid $10n$ or $10/day, while the optimum off-line algorithm would have bought skis at once, and paid only $100, or $100/n$ per day.

Your question: design an on-line algorithm for the ski-buying problem that has the best possible competitive ratio. What is that competitive ratio? *Hint*: Since you could, at any time, have a fall and decide to give up skiing, the only thing the on-line algorithm can use in making its decision is how many times previously you have gone skiing.

8.3   The Matching Problem

We shall now take up a problem that is a simplified version of the problem of matching ads to search queries. This problem, called "maximal matching," is an abstract problem involving *bipartite graphs* (graphs with two sets of nodes – left and right – with all edges connecting a node in the left set to a node in the right set. Figure 8.1 is an example of a bipartite graph. Nodes 1, 2, 3, and 4 form the left set, while nodes a, b, c, and d form the right set.

8.3.1   Matches and Perfect Matches

Suppose we are given a bipartite graph. A *matching* is a subset of the edges such that no node is an end of two or more edges. A matching is said to be *perfect* if every node appears in the matching. Note that a matching can only be perfect if the left and right sets are of the same size. A matching that is as large as any other matching for the graph in question is said to be *maximal*.

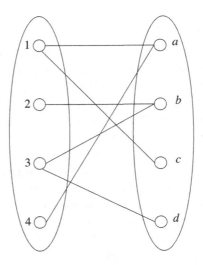

Figure 8.1 A bipartite graph

EXAMPLE 8.4   The set of edges $\{(1, a),\ (2, b),\ (3, d)\}$ is a matching for the bipartite graph of Fig. 8.1. Each member of the set is an edge of the bipartite graph, and no node appears more than once. The set of edges

$$\{(1, c),\ (2, b),\ (3, d),\ (4, a)\}$$

is a perfect matching, represented by heavy lines in Fig. 8.2. Every node appears exactly once. It is, in fact, the sole perfect matching for this graph, although some bipartite graphs have more than one perfect matching. The matching of Fig. 8.2 is also maximal, since every perfect matching is maximal.   □

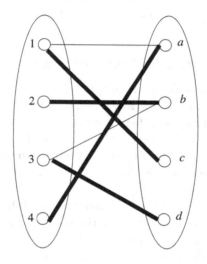

Figure 8.2 The only perfect matching for the graph of Fig. 8.1

8.3.2   The Greedy Algorithm for Maximal Matching

Off-line algorithms for finding a maximal matching have been studied for decades, and one can get very close to $O(n^2)$ for an n-node graph. On-line algorithms for the problem have also been studied, and it is this class of algorithms we shall consider here. In particular, the greedy algorithm for maximal matching works as follows. We consider the edges in whatever order they are given. When we consider (x, y), add this edge to the matching if neither x nor y are ends of any edge selected for the matching so far. Otherwise, skip (x, y).

EXAMPLE 8.5   Let us consider a greedy match for the graph of Fig. 8.1. Suppose we order the nodes lexicographically, that is, by order of their left node, breaking ties by the right node. Then we consider the edges in the order $(1, a)$, $(1, c)$, $(2, b)$, $(3, b)$, $(3, d)$, $(4, a)$. The first edge, $(1, a)$, surely becomes part of the matching. The second edge, $(1, c)$, cannot be chosen, because node 1 already appears in the matching. The third edge, $(2, b)$, is selected, because neither node 2 nor node b

appears in the matching so far. Edge $(3, b)$ is rejected for the match because b is already matched, but then $(3, d)$ is added to the match because neither 3 nor d has been matched so far. Finally, $(4, a)$ is rejected because a appears in the match. Thus, the matching produced by the greedy algorithm for this ordering of the edges is $\{(1, a), (2, b), (3, d)\}$. As we saw, this matching is not maximal. □

EXAMPLE 8.6   A greedy match can be even worse than that of Example 8.5. On the graph of Fig. 8.1, any ordering that begins with the two edges $(1, a)$ and $(3, b)$, in either order, will match those two pairs but then will be unable to match nodes 2 or 4. Thus, the size of the resulting match is only 2.   □

8.3.3   Competitive Ratio for Greedy Matching

We can show a competitive ratio of $1/2$ for the greedy matching algorithm of Section 8.3.2. First, the ratio cannot be more than $1/2$. We already saw that for the graph of Fig. 8.1, there is a perfect matching of size 4. However, if the edges are presented in any of the orders discussed in Example 8.6, the size of the match is only 2, or half the optimum. Since the competitive ratio for an algorithm is the minimum over all possible inputs of the ratio of what that algorithm achieves to the optimum result, we see that $1/2$ is an upper bound on the competitive ratio.

Suppose M_o is a maximal matching, and M_g is the matching that the greedy algorithm produces. Let L be the set of left nodes that are matched in M_o but not in M_g. Let R be the set of right nodes that are connected by edges to any node in L. We claim that every node in R is matched in M_g. Suppose not; in particular, suppose node r in R is not matched in M_g. Then the greedy algorithm will eventually consider some edge (ℓ, r), where ℓ is in L. At that time, neither end of this edge is matched, because we have supposed that neither ℓ nor r is ever matched by the greedy algorithm. That observation contradicts the definition of how the greedy algorithm works; that is, the greedy algorithm would indeed match (ℓ, r). We conclude that every node in R is matched in M_g.

Now, we know several things about the sizes of sets and matchings.

(1) $|M_o| \leq |M_g| + |L|$, since among the nodes on the left, only nodes in L can be matched in M_o but not M_g.

(2) $|L| \leq |R|$, because in M_o, all the nodes in L were matched.

(3) $|R| \leq |M_g|$, because every node in R is matched in M_g.

Now, (2) and (3) give us $|L| \leq |M_g|$. That, together with (1), gives us $|M_o| \leq 2|M_g|$, or $|M_g| \geq \frac{1}{2}|M_o|$. The latter inequality says that the competitive ratio is at least $1/2$. Since we already observed that the competitive ratio is no more than $1/2$, we now conclude the ratio is exactly $1/2$.

8.3.4 Exercises for Section 8.3

EXERCISE 8.3.1 Define the graph G_n to have the $2n$ nodes

$$a_0, a_1, \ldots, a_{n-1}, b_0, b_1, \ldots, b_{n-1}$$

and the following edges. Each node a_i, for $i = 0, 1, \ldots, n-1$, is connected to the nodes b_j and b_k, where

$$j = 2i \mod n \text{ and } k = (2i+1) \mod n$$

For instance, the graph G_4 has the following edges: (a_0, b_0), (a_0, b_1), (a_1, b_2), (a_1, b_3), (a_2, b_0), (a_2, b_1), (a_3, b_2), and (a_3, b_3).

(a) Find a perfect matching for G_4.

(b) Find a perfect matching for G_5.

!! (c) Prove that for every n, G_n has a perfect matching.

! EXERCISE 8.3.2 How many perfect matchings do the graphs G_4 and G_5 of Exercise 8.3.1 have?

! EXERCISE 8.3.3 Whether or not the greedy algorithm gives us a perfect matching for the graph of Fig. 8.1 depends on the order in which we consider the edges. Of the 6! possible orders of the six edges, how many give us a perfect matching? Give a simple test for distinguishing those orders that do give the perfect matching from those that do not.

8.4 The Adwords Problem

We now consider the fundamental problem of search advertising, which we term the "adwords problem," because it was first encountered in the Google Adwords system. We then discuss a greedy algorithm called "Balance" that offers a good competitive ratio. We analyze this algorithm for a simplified case of the adwords problem.

8.4.1 History of Search Advertising

Around the year 2000, a company called Overture (later bought by Yahoo!) introduced a new kind of search. Advertisers bid on *keywords* (words in a search query), and when a user searched for that keyword, the links to all the advertisers who bid on that keyword are displayed in the order highest-bid-first. If the advertiser's link was clicked on, they paid what they had bid.

That sort of search was very useful for the case where the search queryer really was looking for advertisements, but it was rather useless for the queryer who was just looking for information. Recall our discussion in Section 5.1.1 about the point that unless a search engine can provide reliable responses to queries that are for general information, no one will want to use the search engine when they are looking to buy something.

Several years later, Google adapted the idea in a system called *Adwords*. By that time, the reliability of Google was well established, so people were willing to trust the ads they were shown. Google kept the list of responses based on PageRank and other objective criteria separate from the list of ads, so the same system was useful for the queryer who just wanted information as well as the queryer looking to buy something.

The Adwords system went beyond the earlier system in several ways that made the selection of ads more complex.

(1) Google would show only a limited number of ads with each query. Thus, while Overture simply ordered all ads for a given keyword, Google had to decide which ads to show, as well as the order in which to show them.

(2) Users of the Adwords system specified a budget: the amount they were willing to pay for all clicks on their ads in a month. These constraints make the problem of assigning ads to search queries more complex, as we hinted at in Example 8.1.

(3) Google did not simply order ads by the amount of the bid, but by the amount they expected to receive for display of each ad. That is, the click-through rate was observed for each ad, based on the history of displays of that ad. The value of an ad was taken to be the product of the bid and the click-through rate.

8.4.2   Definition of the Adwords Problem

Of course, the decision regarding which ads to show must be made on-line. Thus, we are only going to consider on-line algorithms for solving the *adwords problem*, which is as follows.

- Given:
    (1) A set of bids by advertisers for search queries.
    (2) A click-through rate for each advertiser-query pair.
    (3) A budget for each advertiser. We shall assume budgets are for a month, although any unit of time could be used.
    (4) A limit on the number of ads to be displayed with each search query.
- Respond to each search query with a set of advertisers such that:
    (1) The size of the set is no larger than the limit on the number of ads per query.
    (2) Each advertiser has bid on the search query.
    (3) Each advertiser has enough budget left to pay for the ad if it is clicked upon.

The *revenue* of a selection of ads is the total value of the ads selected, where the *value* of an ad is the product of the bid and the click-through rate for the ad and query. The merit of an on-line algorithm is the total revenue obtained over a month (the time unit over which budgets are assumed to apply). We shall try to measure the competitive ratio for algorithms, that is, the minimum total revenue for that algorithm, on any sequence of search queries, divided by the revenue of the optimum off-line algorithm for the same sequence of search queries.

8.4.3 The Greedy Approach to the Adwords Problem

Since only an on-line algorithm is suitable for the adwords problem, we should first examine the performance of the obvious greedy algorithm. We shall make a number of simplifications to the environment; our purpose is to show eventually that there is a better algorithm than the obvious greedy algorithm. The simplifications:

(a) There is one ad shown for each query.
(b) All advertisers have the same budget.
(c) All click-through rates are the same.
(d) All bids are either 0 or 1. Alternatively, we may assume that the value of each ad (product of bid and click-through rate) is the same.

The greedy algorithm picks, for each search query, any advertiser who has bid 1 for that query. The competitive ratio for this algorithm is 1/2, as the following example shows.

EXAMPLE 8.7   Suppose there are two advertisers A and B, and only two possible queries, x and y. Advertiser A bids only on x, while B bids on both x and y. The budget for each advertiser is 2. Notice the similarity to the situation in Example 8.1; the only differences are the fact that the bids by each advertiser are the same and the budgets are smaller here.

Let the sequence of queries be $xxyy$. The greedy algorithm is able to allocate the first two xs to B, whereupon there is no one with an unexpended budget to pay for the two ys. The revenue for the greedy algorithm in this case is thus 2. However, the optimum off-line algorithm will allocate the xs to A and the ys to B, achieving a revenue of 4. The competitive ratio for the greedy algorithm is thus no more than 1/2. We can argue that on any sequence of queries the ratio of the revenues for the greedy and optimal algorithms is at least 1/2, using essentially the same idea as in Section 8.3.3. □

8.4.4 The Balance Algorithm

There is a simple improvement to the greedy algorithm that gives a competitive ratio of 3/4 for the simple case of Section 8.4.3. This algorithm, called the *Balance Algorithm*, assigns a query to the advertiser who bids on the query and has the largest remaining budget. Ties may be broken arbitrarily.

EXAMPLE 8.8   Consider the same situation as in Example 8.7. The Balance

---

Adwords Aspects not in Our Model

There are several ways in which the real AdWords system differs from the simplified model of this section.

Matching Bids and Search Queries: In our simplified model, advertisers bid on sets of words, and an advertiser's bid is eligible to be shown for search queries that have exactly the same set of words as the advertiser's bid. In reality, Google, Yahoo!, and Microsoft all offer advertisers a feature known as *broad matching*, where an ad is eligible to be shown for search queries that are inexact matches of the bid keywords. Examples include queries that include a subset or superset of keywords, and also queries that use words with very similar meanings to the words the advertiser bid on. For such broad matches, search engines charge the advertiser based on complicated formulas taking into account how closely related the search query is to the advertiser's bid. These formulas vary across search engines and are not made public.

Charging Advertisers for Clicks: In our simplified model, when a user clicks on an advertiser's ad, the advertiser is charged the amount they bid. This policy is known as a *first-price auction*. In reality, search engines use a more complicated system known as a *second-price auction*, where each advertiser pays approximately the bid of the advertiser who placed immediately behind them in the auction. For example, the first-place advertiser for a search might pay the bid of the advertiser in second place, plus one cent. It has been shown that second-price auctions are less susceptible to being gamed by advertisers than first-price auctions and lead to higher revenues for the search engine.

Algorithm can assign the first query x to either A or B, because they both bid on x and their remaining budgets are the same. However, the second x must be assigned to the other of A and B, because they then have the larger remaining budget. The first y is assigned to B, since it has budget remaining and is the only bidder on y. The last y cannot be assigned, since B is out of budget, and A did not bid. Thus, the total revenue for the Balance Algorithm on this data is 3. In comparison, the total revenue for the optimum off-line algorithm is 4, since it can assign the xs to A and the ys to B. Our conclusion is that, for the simplified adwords problem of Section 8.4.3, the competitive ratio of the Balance Algorithm is no more than $3/4$. We shall see next that with only two advertisers, $3/4$ is exactly the competitive ratio, although as the number of advertisers grows, the competitive ratio lowers to 0.63 (actually $1 - 1/e$) but no lower. □

8.4.5　A Lower Bound on Competitive Ratio for Balance

In this section we shall prove that in the simple case of the Balance Algorithm that we are considering, the competitive ratio is $3/4$. Given Example 8.8, we have only to prove that the total revenue obtained by the Balance Algorithm is at least $3/4$ of the revenue for the optimum off-line algorithm. Thus, consider a situation in which there are two advertisers, A_1 and A_2, each with a budget of B. We shall assume that each query is assigned to an advertiser by the optimum algorithm. If not, we can delete those queries without affecting the revenue of the optimum algorithm and possibly reducing the revenue of Balance. Thus, the lowest possible competitive ratio is achieved when the query sequence consists only of ads assigned by the optimum algorithm.

We shall also assume that both advertisers' budgets are consumed by the optimum algorithm. If not, we can reduce the budgets, and again argue that the revenue of the optimum algorithm is not reduced while that of Balance can only shrink. That change may force us to use different budgets for the two advertisers, but we shall continue to assume the budgets are both B. We leave as an exercise the extension of the proof to the case where the budgets of the two advertisers are different.

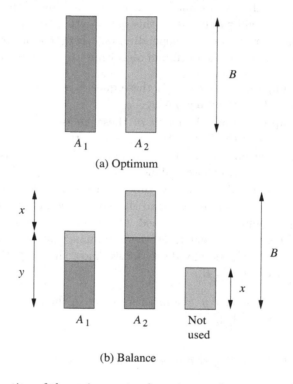

Figure 8.3 Illustration of the assignments of queries to advertisers in the optimum and Balance algorithms

Figure 8.3 suggests how the $2B$ queries are assigned to advertisers by the two algorithms. In (a) we see that B queries are assigned to each of A_1 and A_2 by the optimum algorithm. Now, consider how these same queries are assigned by Balance. First, observe that Balance must exhaust the budget of at least one of the advertisers, say A_2. If not, then there would be some query assigned to neither advertiser, even though both had budget. We know at least one of the advertisers bids on each query, because that query is assigned in the optimum algorithm. That situation contradicts how Balance is defined to operate; it always assigns a query if it can.

Thus, we see in Fig. 8.3(b) that A_2 is assigned B queries. These queries could have been assigned to either A_1 or A_2 by the optimum algorithm. We also see in Fig. 8.3(b) that we use y as the number of queries assigned to A_1 and x as $B - y$. It is our goal to show $y \geq x$. That inequality will show the revenue of Balance is at least $3B/2$, or 3/4th the revenue of the optimum algorithm.

We note that x is also the number of unassigned queries for the Balance Algorithm, and that all the unassigned queries must have been assigned to A_2 by the optimum algorithm. The reason is that A_1 never runs out of budget, so any query assigned by the optimum algorithm to A_1 is surely bid on by A_1. Since A_1 always has budget during the running of the Balance Algorithm, that algorithm will surely assign this query, either to A_1 or to A_2.

There are two cases, depending on whether more of the queries that are assigned to A_1 by the optimum algorithm are assigned to A_1 or A_2 by Balance.

(1) Suppose at least half of these queries are assigned by Balance to A_1. Then $y \geq B/2$, so surely $y \geq x$.
(2) Suppose more than half of these queries are assigned by Balance to A_2. Consider the last of these queries q that is assigned to A_2 by the Balance Algorithm. At that time, A_2 must have had at least as great a budget available as A_1, or else Balance would have assigned query q to A_1, just as the optimum algorithm did. Since more than half of the B queries that the optimum algorithm assigns to A_1 are assigned to A_2 by Balance, we know that just before q was assigned, the remaining budget of A_2 was at most $B/2$. Therefore, at that time, the remaining budget of A_1 was also at most $B/2$. Since budgets only decrease, we know that $x \leq B/2$. It follows that $y \geq x$, since $x + y = B$.

We conclude that $y \geq x$ in either case, so the competitive ratio of the Balance Algorithm is 3/4.

8.4.6   The Balance Algorithm with Many Bidders

When there are many advertisers, the competitive ratio for the Balance Algorithm can be under 3/4, but not too far below that fraction. The worst case for Balance is as follows.

(1) There are N advertisers, $A_1, A_2, \ldots, A_N$.
(2) Each advertiser has a budget $B = N!$.
(3) There are N queries $q_1, q_2, \ldots, q_N$.
(4) Advertiser A_i bids on queries $q_1, q_2, \ldots, q_i$ and no other queries.
(5) The query sequence consists of N rounds. The ith round consists of B occurrences of query q_i and nothing else.

The optimum off-line algorithm assigns the B queries q_i in the ith round to A_i for all i. Thus, all queries are assigned to a bidder, and the total revenue of the optimum algorithm is NB.

However, the Balance Algorithm assigns each of the queries in round 1 to the N advertisers equally, because all bid on q_1, and the Balance Algorithm prefers the bidder with the greatest remaining budget. Thus, each advertiser gets B/N of the queries q_1. Now consider the queries q_2 in round 2. All but A_1 bid on these queries, so they are divided equally among A_2 through A_N, with each of these $N-1$ bidders getting $B/(N-1)$ queries. The pattern, suggested by Fig. 8.4, repeats for each round $i = 3, 4, \ldots$, with A_i through A_N getting $B/(N-i+1)$ queries.

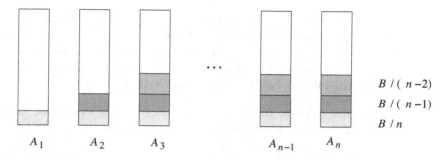

Figure 8.4 Apportioning queries to N advertisers in the worst case

However, eventually, the budgets of the higher-numbered advertisers will be exhausted. That will happen at the lowest round j such that

$$B\left(\frac{1}{N} + \frac{1}{N-1} + \cdots + \frac{1}{N-j+1}\right) \geq B$$

that is,

$$\frac{1}{N} + \frac{1}{N-1} + \cdots + \frac{1}{N-j+1} \geq 1$$

Euler showed that as k gets large, $\sum_{i=1}^{k} 1/i$ approaches $\log_e k$. Using this observation, we can approximate the above sum as $\log_e N - \log_e(N-j)$.

We are thus looking for the j such that $\log_e N - \log_e(N-j) = 1$, approximately. If we replace $\log_e N - \log_e(N-j)$ by the equivalent $\log_e(N/(N-j))$ and exponentiate both sides of the equation $\log_e(N/(N-j)) = 1$, we get $N/(N-j) = e$. Solving this equation for j, we get

$$j = N\left(1 - \frac{1}{e}\right)$$

as the approximate value of j for which all advertisers are either out of budget or do not bid on any of the remaining queries. Thus, the approximate revenue obtained by the Balance Algorithm is $BN(1 - \frac{1}{e})$, that is, the queries of the first j rounds. Therefore, the competitive ratio is $1 - \frac{1}{e}$, or approximately 0.63.

8.4.7   The Generalized Balance Algorithm

The Balance Algorithm works well when all bids are 0 or 1. However, in practice, bids can be arbitrary, and with arbitrary bids and budgets Balance fails to weight the sizes of the bids properly. The following example illustrates the point.

EXAMPLE 8.9   Suppose there are two advertisers A_1 and A_2, and one query q. The bids on q and budgets are:

Bidder	Bid	Budget
A_1	1	110
A_2	10	100

If there are 10 occurrences of q, the optimum off-line algorithm will assign them all to A_2 and gain revenue 100. However, because A_1's budget is larger, Balance will assign all ten queries to A_1 for a revenue of 10. In fact, one can extend this idea easily to show that for situations like this one, there is no competitive ratio higher than 0 that holds for the Balance Algorithm.   □

In order to make Balance work in more general situations, we need to make two modifications. First, we need to bias the choice of ad in favor of higher bids. Second, we need to be less absolute about the remaining budget. Rather, we consider the fraction of the budgets remaining, so we are biased toward using some of each advertiser's budget. The latter change will make the Balance Algorithm more "risk averse"; it will not leave too much of any advertiser's budget unused. It can be shown (see the chapter references) that the following generalization of the Balance Algorithm has a competitive ratio of $1 - 1/e = 0.63$.

- Suppose that a query q arrives, advertiser A_i has bid x_i for this query (note that x_i could be 0). Also, suppose that fraction f_i of the budget of A_i is currently unspent. Let $\Psi_i = x_i(1 - e^{-f_i})$. Then assign q to the advertiser A_i such that Ψ_i is a maximum. Break ties arbitrarily.

EXAMPLE 8.10   Consider how the generalized Balance Algorithm would work on the data of Example 8.9. For the first occurrence of query q,

$$\Psi_1 = 1 \times (1 - e^{-1})$$

since A_1 has bid 1, and fraction 1 of A_1's budget remains. That is,

$$\Psi_1 = 1 - 1/e = 0.63$$

On the other hand, $\Psi_2 = 10 \times (1 - e^{-1}) = 6.3$. Thus, the first q is awarded to A_2.

The same thing happens for each of the qs. That is, Ψ_1 stays at 0.63, while Ψ_2 decreases. However, it never goes below 0.63. Even for the 10th q, when 90% of A_2's budget has already been used, $\Psi_2 = 10 \times (1 - e^{-1/10})$. Recall (Section 1.3.5) the Taylor expansion for $e^x = 1 + x + x^2/2! + x^3/3! + \cdots$. Thus,

$$e^{-1/10} = 1 - \frac{1}{10} + \frac{1}{200} - \frac{1}{6000} + \cdots$$

or approximately, $e^{-1/10} = 0.905$. Thus, $\Psi_2 = 10 \times 0.095 = 0.95$. □

We leave unproved the assertion that the competitive ratio for this algorithm is $1-1/e$. We also leave unproved an additional surprising fact: no on-line algorithm for the adwords problem as described in this section can have a competitive ratio above $1 - 1/e$.

8.4.8 Final Observations About the Adwords Problem

The Balance Algorithm, as described, does not take into account the possibility that the click-through rate differs for different ads. It is simple to multiply the bid by the click-through rate when computing the Ψ_i, and doing so will maximize the expected revenue. We can even incorporate information about the click-through rate for each ad on each query for which a nonzero amount has been bid. When faced with the problem of allocating a particular query q, we incorporate a factor that is the click-through rate for that ad on query q, when computing each of the Ψs.

Another issue we must consider in practice is the historical frequency of queries. If, for example, we know that advertiser A_i has a budget sufficiently small that there are sure to be enough queries coming later in the month to satisfy A_i's demand, then there is no point in boosting Ψ_i if some of A_i's budget has already been expended. That is, maintain $\Psi_i = x_i(1 - e^{-1})$ as long as we can expect that there will be enough queries remaining in the month to give A_i its full budget of ads. This change can cause Balance to perform worse if the sequence of queries is governed by an adversary who can control the sequence of queries. Such an adversary can cause the queries A_i bid on suddenly to disappear. However, search engines get so many queries, and their generation is so random, that it is not necessary in practice to imagine significant deviation from the norm.

8.4.9 Exercises for Section 8.4

EXERCISE 8.4.1 Using the simplifying assumptions of Example 8.7, suppose that there are three advertisers, A, B, and C. There are three queries, x, y, and z. Each advertiser has a budget of 2. Advertiser A bids only on x; B bids on x and y, while C bids on x, y, and z. Note that on the query sequence $xxyyzz$, the optimum off-line algorithm would yield a revenue of 6, since all queries can be assigned.

! (a) Show that the greedy algorithm will assign at least 4 of these 6 queries.

!! (b) Find another sequence of queries such that the greedy algorithm can assign as few as half the queries that the optimum off-line algorithm assigns on that sequence.

!! EXERCISE 8.4.2   Extend the proof of Section 8.4.5 to the case where the two advertisers have unequal budgets.

! EXERCISE 8.4.3   Show how to modify Example 8.9 by changing the bids and/or budgets to make the competitive ratio come out as close to 0 as you like.

8.5   Adwords Implementation

While we should now have an idea of how ads are selected to go with the answer to a search query, we have not addressed the problem of finding the bids that have been made on a given query. As long as bids are for the exact set of words in a query, the solution is relatively easy. However, there are a number of extensions to the query/bid matching process that are not as simple. We shall explain the details in this section.

8.5.1   Matching Bids and Search Queries

As we have described the adwords problem, and as it normally appears in practice, advertisers bid on sets of words. If a search query occurs having exactly that set of words in some order, then the bid is said to match the query, and it becomes a candidate for selection. We can avoid having to deal with word order by storing all sets of words representing a bid in lexicographic (alphabetic) order. The list of words in sorted order forms the hash-key for the bid, and these bids may be stored in a hash table used as an index, as discussed in Section 1.3.2.

Search queries also have their words sorted prior to lookup. When we hash the sorted list, we find in the hash table all the bids for exactly that set of words. They can be retrieved quickly, since we have only to look at the contents of that bucket.

Moreover, there is a good chance that we can keep the entire hash table in main memory. If there are a million advertisers, each bidding on 100 queries, and the record of the bid requires 100 bytes, then we require ten gigabytes of main memory, which is well within the limits of what is feasible for a single machine. If more space is required, we can split the buckets of the hash table among as many machines as we need. Search queries can be hashed and sent to the appropriate machine.

In practice, search queries may be arriving far too rapidly for a single machine, or group of machines that collaborate on a single query at a time, to handle them all. In that case, the stream of queries is split into as many pieces as necessary, and each piece is handled by one group of machines. In fact, answering the search query, independent of ads, will require a group of machines working in parallel anyway, in order that the entire processing of a query can be done in main memory.

8.5.2 More Complex Matching Problems

However, the potential for matching bids to objects is not limited to the case where the objects are search queries and the match criterion is same-set-of-words. For example, Google also matches adwords bids to emails. There, the match criterion is not based on the equality of sets. Rather, a bid on a set of words S matches an email if all the words in S appear anywhere in the email.

This matching problem is much harder. We can still maintain a hash-table index for the bids, but the number of subsets of words in a hundred-word email is much too large to look up all the sets, or even all the small sets of (say) three or fewer words. There are a number of other potential applications of this sort of matching that, at the time of this writing, are not implemented but could be. They all involve *standing queries* – queries that users post to a site, expecting the site to notify them whenever something matching the query becomes available at the site. For example:

(1) Twitter allows one to follow all the "tweets" of a given person. However, it is feasible to allow users to specify a set of words, such as

> `ipod free music`

and see all the tweets where all these words appear, not necessarily in order, and not necessarily adjacent.

(2) On-line news sites often allow users to select from among certain keywords or phrases, e.g., "healthcare" or "Barack Obama," and receive alerts whenever a new news article contains that word or consecutive sequence of words. This problem is simpler than the email/adwords problem for several reasons. Matching single words or consecutive sequences of words, even in a long article, is not as time-consuming as matching small sets of words. Further, the sets of terms that one can search for is limited, so there aren't too many "bids." Even if many people want alerts about the same term, only one index entry, with the list of all those people associated, is required. However, a more advanced system could allow users to specify alerts for sets of words in a news article, just as the Adwords system allows anyone to bid on a set of words in an email.

8.5.3 A Matching Algorithm for Documents and Bids

We shall offer an algorithm that will match many "bids" against many "documents." As before, a *bid* is a (typically small) set of words. A document is a larger set of words, such as an email, tweet, or news article. We assume there may be hundreds of documents per second arriving, although if there are that many, the document stream may be split among many machines or groups of machines. We assume there are many bids, perhaps on the order of a hundred million or a billion. As always, we want to do as much in main memory as we can.

We shall, as before, represent a bid by its words listed in some order. There are two new elements in the representation. First, we shall include a *status* with each list of words. The status is an integer indicating how many of the first words on the list have been matched by the current document. When a bid is stored in the index, its status is always 0.

Second, while the order of words could be lexicographic, we can lower the amount of work by ordering words rarest-first. However, since the number of different words that can appear in emails is essentially unlimited, it is not feasible to order all words in this manner. As a compromise, we might identify the n most common words on the Web or in a sample of the stream of documents we are processing. Here, n might be a hundred thousand or a million. These n words are sorted by frequency, and they occupy the *end* of the list, with the most frequent words at the very end. All words not among the n most frequent can be assumed equally infrequent and ordered lexicographically. Then, the words of any document can be ordered. If a word does not appear on the list of n frequent words, place it at the front of the order, lexicographically. Those words in the document that do appear on the list of most frequent words appear after the infrequent words, in the reverse order of frequency (i.e., with the most frequent words of the documents ordered last).

EXAMPLE 8.11   Suppose our document is

        'Twas brillig, and the slithy toves

"The" is the most frequent word in English, and "and" is only slightly less frequent. Let us suppose that "twas" makes the list of frequent words, although its frequency is surely lower than that of "the" or "and." The other words do not make the list of frequent words.

Then the end of the list consists of "twas," "and," and "the," in that order, since that is the inverse order of frequency. The other three words are placed at the front of the list in lexicographic order. Thus,

        brillig slithy toves twas and the

is the sequence of words in the document, properly ordered.   □

The bids are stored in a hash-table, whose hash key is the first word of the bid, in the order explained above. The record for the bid will also include information about what to do when the bid is matched. The status is 0 and need not be stored explicitly. There is another hash table, whose job is to contain copies of those bids that have been partially matched. These bids have a status that is at least 1, but less than the number of words in the set. If the status is i, then the hash-key for this hash table is the $(i+1)$st word. The arrangement of hash tables is suggested by Fig. 8.5. To process a document, do the following.

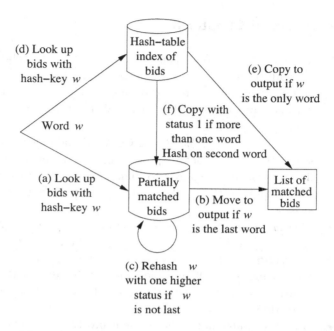

Figure 8.5 Managing large numbers of bids and large numbers of documents

(1) Sort the words of the document in the order discussed above. Eliminate duplicate words.
(2) For each word w, in the sorted order:
    (i) Using w as the hash-key for the table of partially matched bids, find those bids having w as key.
    (ii) For each such bid b, if w is the last word of b, move b to the table of matched bids.
    (iii) If w is not the last word of b, add 1 to b's status, and rehash b using the word whose position is one more than the new status, as the hash-key.
    (iv) Using w as the hash key for the table of all bids, find those bids for which w is their first word in the sorted order.
    (v) For each such bid b, if there is only one word on its list, copy it to the table of matched bids.
    (vi) If b consists of more than one word, add it, with status 1, to the table of partially matched bids, using the second word of b as the hash-key.
(3) Produce the list of matched bids as the output.

The benefit of the rarest-first order should now be visible. A bid is only copied to the second hash table if its rarest word appears in the document. In comparison, if lexicographic order was used, more bids would be copied to the second hash table. By minimizing the size of that table, we not only reduce the amount of work in steps 2(i)–2(iii), but we make it more likely that this entire table can be kept in main memory.

8.6   Summary of Chapter 8

✦ *Targeted Advertising*: The big advantage that Web-based advertising has over advertising in conventional media such as newspapers is that Web advertising can be selected according to the interests of each individual user. This advantage has enabled many Web services to be supported entirely by advertising revenue.

✦ *On- and Off-Line Algorithms*: Conventional algorithms that are allowed to see all their data before producing an answer are called off-line. An on-line algorithm is required to make a response to each element in a stream immediately, with knowledge of only the past, not the future elements in the stream.

✦ *Greedy Algorithms*: Many on-line algorithms are greedy, in the sense that they select their action at every step by minimizing some objective function.

✦ *Competitive Ratio*: We can measure the quality of an on-line algorithm by minimizing, over all possible inputs, the value of the result of the on-line algorithm compared with the value of the result of the best possible off-line algorithm.

✦ *Bipartite Matching*: This problem involves two sets of nodes and a set of edges between members of the two sets. The goal is to find a maximal matching – as large a set of edges as possible that includes no node more than once.

✦ *On-Line Solution to the Matching Problem*: One greedy algorithm for finding a match in a bipartite graph (or any graph, for that matter) is to order the edges in some way, and for each edge in turn, add it to the match if neither of its ends are yet part of an edge previously selected for the match. This algorithm can be proved to have a competitive ratio of 1/2; that is, it never fails to match at least half as many nodes as the best off-line algorithm matches.

✦ *Search Ad Management*: A search engine receives bids from advertisers on certain search queries. Some ads are displayed with each search query, and the search engine is paid the amount of the bid only if the queryer clicks on the ad. Each advertiser can give a budget, the total amount they are willing to pay for clicks in a month.

✦ *The Adwords Problem*: The data for the adwords problem is a set of bids by advertisers on certain search queries, together with a total budget for each advertiser and information about the historical click-through rate for each ad for each query. Another part of the data is the stream of search queries received by the search engine. The objective is to select on-line a fixed-size set of ads in response to each query that will maximize the revenue to the search engine.

✦ *Simplified Adwords Problem*: To see some of the nuances of ad selection, we considered a simplified version in which all bids are either 0 or 1, only one ad is shown with each query, and all advertisers have the same budget. Under this model the obvious greedy algorithm of giving the ad placement to anyone who has bid on the query and has budget remaining can be shown to have a competitive ratio of 1/2.

✦ *The Balance Algorithm*: This algorithm improves on the simple greedy algorithm. A query's ad is given to the advertiser who has bid on the query and has the largest remaining budget. Ties can be broken arbitrarily.

✦ *Competitive Ratio of the Balance Algorithm*: For the simplified adwords model, the competitive ratio of the Balance Algorithm is 3/4 for the case of two advertisers and $1 - 1/e$, or about 63% for any number of advertisers.

✦ *The Balance Algorithm for the Generalized Adwords Problem*: When bidders can make differing bids, have different budgets, and have different click-through rates for different queries, the Balance Algorithm awards an ad to the advertiser with the highest value of the function $\Psi = x(1 - e^{-f})$. Here, x is the product of the bid and the click-through rate for that advertiser and query, and f is the fraction of the advertiser's budget that remains unspent.

✦ *Implementing an Adwords Algorithm*: The simplest version of the implementation serves in situations where the bids are on exactly the set of words in the search query. We can represent a query by the list of its words, in sorted order. Bids are stored in a hash table or similar structure, with a hash key equal to the sorted list of words. A search query can then be matched against bids by a straightforward lookup in the table.

✦ *Matching Word Sets Against Documents*: A harder version of the adwords-implementation problem allows bids, which are still small sets of words as in a search query, to be matched against larger documents, such as emails or tweets. A bid set matches the document if all the words appear in the document, in any order and not necessarily adjacent.

✦ *Hash Storage of Word Sets*: A useful data structure stores the words of each bid set in the order rarest-first. Documents have their words sorted in the same order. Word sets are stored in a hash table with the first word, in the rarest-first order, as the key.

✦ *Processing Documents for Bid Matches*: We process the words of the document rarest-first. Word sets whose first word is the current word are copied to a temporary hash table, with the second word as the key. Sets already in the temporary hash table are examined to see if the word that is their key matches the current word, and, if so, they are rehashed using their next word. Sets whose last word is matched are copied to the output.

8.7   References for Chapter 8

[1] is an investigation of the way ad position influences the click-through rate.

The Balance Algorithm was developed in [2] and its application to the adwords problem is from [3].

[1] N. Craswell, O. Zoeter, M. Taylor, and W. Ramsey, "An experimental comparison of click-position bias models," *Proc. Intl. Conf. on Web Search and Web Data Mining* pp. 87–94, 2008.

[2] B. Kalyanasundaram and K.R. Pruhs, "An optimal deterministic algorithm for b-matching," *Theoretical Computer Science* **233**:1–2, pp. 319–325, 2000.

[3] A Mehta, A. Saberi, U. Vazirani, and V. Vazirani, "Adwords and generalized on-line matching," *IEEE Symp. on Foundations of Computer Science*, pp. 264–273, 2005.

9 Recommendation Systems

There is an extensive class of Web applications that involve predicting user responses to options. Such a facility is called a *recommendation system*. We shall begin this chapter with a survey of the most important examples of these systems. However, to bring the problem into focus, two good examples of recommendation systems are:

(1) Offering news articles to on-line newspaper readers, based on a prediction of reader interests.

(2) Offering customers of an on-line retailer suggestions about what they might like to buy, based on their past history of purchases and/or product searches.

Recommendation systems use a number of different technologies. We can classify these systems into two broad groups.

- *Content-based systems* examine properties of the items recommended. For instance, if a Netflix user has watched many cowboy movies, then recommend a movie classified in the database as having the "cowboy" genre.

- *Collaborative filtering* systems recommend items based on similarity measures between users and/or items. The items recommended to a user are those preferred by similar users. This sort of recommendation system can use the groundwork laid in Chapter 3 on similarity search and Chapter 7 on clustering. However, these technologies by themselves are not sufficient, and there are some new algorithms that have proven effective for recommendation systems.

9.1 A Model for Recommendation Systems

In this section we introduce a model for recommendation systems, based on a utility matrix of preferences. We introduce the concept of a "long-tail," which explains the   advantage of on-line vendors over conventional, brick-and-mortar vendors. We then briefly survey the sorts of applications in which recommendation systems have proved useful.

9.1.1   The Utility Matrix

In a recommendation-system application there are two classes of entities, which we shall refer to as *users* and *items*. Users have preferences for certain items, and these preferences must be teased out of the data. The data itself is represented as a *utility matrix*, giving for each user-item pair, a value that represents what is known about the degree of preference of that user for that item. Values come from an ordered set, e.g., integers 1–5 representing the number of stars that the user gave as a rating for that item. We assume that the matrix is sparse, meaning that most entries are "unknown." An unknown rating implies that we have no explicit information about the user's preference for the item.

EXAMPLE 9.1   In Fig. 9.1 we see an example utility matrix, representing users' ratings of movies on a 1–5 scale, with 5 the highest rating. Blanks represent the situation where the user has not rated the movie. The movie names are HP1, HP2, and HP3 for *Harry Potter* I, II, and III, TW for *Twilight*, and SW1, SW2, and SW3 for *Star Wars* episodes 1, 2, and 3. The users are represented by capital letters A through D.

	HP1	HP2	HP3	TW	SW1	SW2	SW3
A	4			5	1		
B	5	5	4				
C				2	4	5	
D		3					3

Figure 9.1 A utility matrix representing ratings of movies on a 1–5 scale

Notice that most user-movie pairs have blanks, meaning the user has not rated the movie. In practice, the matrix would be even sparser, with the typical user rating only a tiny fraction of all available movies.   □

The goal of a recommendation system is to predict the blanks in the utility matrix. For example, would user A like SW2? There is little evidence from the tiny matrix in Fig. 9.1. We might design our recommendation system to take into account properties of movies, such as their producer, director, stars, or even the similarity of their names. If so, we might then note the similarity between SW1 and SW2, and then conclude that since A did not like SW1, they were unlikely to enjoy SW2 either. Alternatively, with much more data, we might observe that the people who rated both SW1 and SW2 tended to give them similar ratings. Thus, we could conclude that A would also give SW2 a low rating, similar to A's rating of SW1.

We should also be aware of a slightly different goal that makes sense in many applications. It is not necessary to predict every blank entry in a utility matrix. Rather, it is only necessary to discover some entries in each row that are likely to be high. In most applications, the recommendation system does not offer users a ranking of all items, but rather suggests a few that the user should value highly.

It may not even be necessary to find all items with the highest expected ratings, but only to find a large subset of those with the highest ratings.

9.1.2 The Long Tail

Before discussing the principal applications of recommendation systems, let us ponder the *long tail* phenomenon that makes recommendation systems necessary. Physical delivery systems are characterized by a scarcity of resources. Brick-and-mortar stores have limited shelf space, and can show the customer only a small fraction of all the choices that exist. On the other hand, on-line stores can make anything that exists available to the customer. Thus, a physical bookstore may have several thousand books on its shelves, but Amazon offers millions of books. A physical newspaper can print several dozen articles per day, while on-line news services offer thousands per day.

Recommendation in the physical world is fairly simple. First, it is not possible to tailor the store to each individual customer. Thus, the choice of what is made available is governed only by the aggregate numbers. Typically, a bookstore will display only the books that are most popular, and a newspaper will print only the articles it believes the most people will be interested in. In the first case, sales figures govern the choices, in the second case, editorial judgement serves.

The Long Tail

Figure 9.2 The long tail: physical institutions can only provide what is popular, while on-line institutions can make everything available

The distinction between the physical and on-line worlds has been called the *long tail* phenomenon, and it is suggested in Fig. 9.2. The vertical axis represents *popularity* (the number of times an item is chosen). The items are ordered on the horizontal axis according to their popularity. Physical institutions provide only

> ### *Into Thin Air* and *Touching the Void*
>
> An extreme example of how the long tail, together with a well designed recommendation system can influence events is the story told by Chris Anderson about a book called *Touching the Void*. This mountain-climbing book was not a big seller in its day, but many years after it was published, another book on the same topic, called *Into Thin Air* was published. Amazon's recommendation system noticed a few people who bought both books, and started recommending *Touching the Void* to people who bought, or were considering, *Into Thin Air*. Had there been no on-line bookseller, *Touching the Void* might never have been seen by potential buyers, but in the on-line world, *Touching the Void* eventually became very popular in its own right, in fact, more so than *Into Thin Air*.

the most popular items to the left of the vertical line, while the corresponding on-line institutions provide the entire range of items: the tail as well as the popular items.

The long-tail phenomenon forces on-line institutions to recommend items to individual users. It is not possible to present all available items to the user, the way physical institutions can. Neither can we expect users to have heard of each of the items they might like.

9.1.3 Applications of Recommendation Systems

We have mentioned several important applications of recommendation systems, but here we shall consolidate the list in a single place.

(1) *Product Recommendations*: Perhaps the most important use of recommendation systems is at on-line retailers. We have noted how Amazon or similar on-line vendors strive to present each returning user with some suggestions of products that they might like to buy. These suggestions are not random, but are based on the purchasing decisions made by similar customers or on other techniques we shall discuss in this chapter.

(2) *Movie Recommendations*: Netflix offers its customers recommendations of movies they might like. These recommendations are based on ratings provided by users, much like the ratings suggested in the example utility matrix of Fig. 9.1. The importance of predicting ratings accurately is so high, that Netflix offered a prize of one million dollars for the first algorithm that could beat its own recommendation system by 10%.[1] The prize was finally won in 2009, by a team of researchers called "Bellkor's Pragmatic Chaos," after over three years of competition.

---

[1] To be exact, the algorithm had to have a root-mean-square error (RMSE) that was 10% less than the RMSE of the Netflix algorithm on a test set taken from actual ratings of Netflix users. To develop an algorithm, contestants were given a training set of data, also taken from actual Netflix data.

(3) *News Articles*: News services have attempted to identify articles of interest to readers, based on the articles that they have read in the past. The similarity might be based on the similarity of important words in the documents, or on the articles that are read by people with similar reading tastes. The same principles apply to recommending blogs from among the millions of blogs available, videos on YouTube, or other sites where content is provided regularly.

9.1.4 Populating the Utility Matrix

Without a utility matrix, it is almost impossible to recommend items. However, acquiring data from which to build a utility matrix is often difficult. There are two general approaches to discovering the value users place on items.

(1) We can ask users to rate items. Movie ratings are generally obtained this way, and some on-line stores try to obtain ratings from their purchasers. Sites providing content, such as some news sites or YouTube also ask users to rate items. This approach is limited in its effectiveness, since generally users are unwilling to provide responses, and the information from those who do may be biased by the very fact that it comes from people willing to provide ratings.

(2) We can make inferences from users' behavior. Most obviously, if a user buys a product at Amazon, watches a movie on YouTube, or reads a news article, then the user can be said to "like" this item. Note that this sort of rating system really has only one value: 1 means that the user likes the item. Often, we find a utility matrix with this kind of data shown with 0s rather than blanks where the user has not purchased or viewed the item. However, in this case 0 is not a lower rating than 1; it is no rating at all. More generally, one can infer interest from behavior other than purchasing. For example, if an Amazon customer views information about an item, we can infer that they are interested in the item, even if they don't buy it.

9.2   Content-Based Recommendations

As we mentioned at the beginning of the chapter, there are two basic architectures for a recommendation system:

(1) *Content-Based* systems focus on properties of items. Similarity of items is determined by measuring the similarity in their properties.
(2) *Collaborative-Filtering* systems focus on the relationship between users and items. Similarity of items is determined by the similarity of the ratings of those items by the users who have rated both items.

In this section, we focus on content-based recommendation systems. The next section will cover collaborative filtering.

9.2.1   Item Profiles

In a content-based system, we must construct for each item a *profile*, which is a record or collection of records representing important characteristics of that item. In simple cases, the profile consists of some characteristics of the item that are easily discovered. For example, consider the features of a movie that might be relevant to a recommendation system.

(1) The set of actors of the movie. Some viewers prefer movies with their favorite actors.
(2) The director. Some viewers have a preference for the work of certain directors.
(3) The year in which the movie was made. Some viewers prefer old movies; others watch only the latest releases.
(4) The *genre* or general type of movie. Some viewers like only comedies, others dramas or romances.

There are many other features of movies that could be used as well. Except for the last, genre, the information is readily available from descriptions of movies. Genre is a vaguer concept. However, movie reviews generally assign a genre from a set of commonly used terms. For example the *Internet Movie Database* (IMDB) assigns a genre or genres to every movie. We shall discuss mechanical construction of genres in Section 9.3.3.

Many other classes of items also allow us to obtain features from available data, even if that data must at some point be entered by hand. For instance, products often have descriptions written by the manufacturer, giving features relevant to that class of product (e.g., the screen size and cabinet color for a TV). Books have descriptions similar to those for movies, so we can obtain features such as author, year of publication, and genre. Music products such as CD's and MP3 downloads have available features such as artist, composer, and genre.

9.2.2   Discovering Features of Documents

There are other classes of items where it is not immediately apparent what the values of features should be. We shall consider two of them: document collections and images. Documents present special problems, and we shall discuss the technology for extracting features from documents in this section. Images will be discussed in Section 9.2.3 as an important example where user-supplied features have some hope of success.

There are many kinds of documents for which a recommendation system can be useful. For example, there are many news articles published each day, and we cannot read all of them. A recommendation system can suggest articles on topics a user is interested in, but how can we distinguish among topics? Web pages are also a collection of documents. Can we suggest pages a user might want to see? Likewise, blogs could be recommended to interested users, if we could classify blogs by topics.

Unfortunately, these classes of documents do not tend to have readily available information giving features. A substitute that has been useful in practice is the identification of words that characterize the topic of a document. How we do the identification was outlined in Section 1.3.1. First, eliminate stop words – the several hundred most common words, which tend to say little about the topic of a document. For the remaining words, compute the TF.IDF score for each word in the document. The ones with the highest scores are the words that characterize the document.

We may then take as the features of a document the n words with the highest TF.IDF scores. It is possible to pick n to be the same for all documents, or to let n be a fixed percentage of the words in the document. We could also choose to make all words whose TF.IDF scores are above a given threshold to be a part of the feature set.

Now, documents are represented by sets of words. Intuitively, we expect these words to express the subjects or main ideas of the document. For example, in a news article, we would expect the words with the highest TF.IDF score to include the names of people discussed in the article, unusual properties of the event described, and the location of the event. To measure the similarity of two documents, there are several natural distance measures we can use:

(1) We could use the Jaccard distance between the sets of words (recall Section 3.5.3).
(2) We could use the cosine distance (recall Section 3.5.4) between the sets, treated as vectors.

To compute the cosine distance in option (2), think of the sets of high-TF.IDF words as a vector, with one component for each possible word. The vector has 1 if the word is in the set and 0 if not. Since between two documents there are only a finite number of words among their two sets, the infinite dimensionality of the vectors is unimportant. Almost all components are 0 in both, and 0s do not impact the value of the dot product. To be precise, the dot product is the size of the intersection of the two sets of words, and the lengths of the vectors are the square roots of the numbers of words in each set. That calculation lets us compute the cosine of the angle between the vectors as the dot product divided by the product of the vector lengths.

9.2.3 Obtaining Item Features From Tags

Let us consider a database of images as an example of a way that features have been obtained for items. The problem with images is that their data, typically an array of pixels, does not tell us anything useful about their features. We can calculate simple properties of pixels, such as the average amount of red in the picture, but few users are looking for red pictures or especially like red pictures. There have been a number of attempts to obtain information about features of items by inviting users to *tag* the items by entering words or phrases that describe

---

Two Kinds of Document Similarity

Recall that in Section 3.4 we gave a method for finding documents that were "similar," using shingling, minhashing, and LSH. There, the notion of similarity was lexical – documents are similar if they contain large, identical sequences of characters. For recommendation systems, the notion of similarity is different. We are interested only in the occurrences of many important words in both documents, even if there is little lexical similarity between the documents. However, the methodology for finding similar documents remains almost the same. Once we have a distance measure, either Jaccard or cosine, we can use minhashing (for Jaccard) or random hyperplanes (for cosine distance; see Section 3.7.2) feeding data to an LSH algorithm to find the pairs of documents that are similar in the sense of sharing many common keywords.

Tags from Computer Games

An interesting direction for encouraging tagging is the "games" approach pioneered by Luis von Ahn. He enabled two players to collaborate on the tag for an image. In rounds, they would suggest a tag, and the tags would be exchanged. If they agreed, then they "won," and if not, they would play another round with the same image, trying to agree simultaneously on a tag. While an innovative direction to try, it is questionable whether sufficient public interest can be generated to produce enough free work to satisfy the needs for tagged data.

---

the item. Thus, one picture with a lot of red might be tagged "Tiananmen Square," while another is tagged "sunset at Malibu." The distinction is not something that could be discovered by existing image-analysis programs.

Almost any kind of data can have its features described by tags. One of the earliest attempts to tag massive amounts of data was the site del.icio.us, later bought by Yahoo!, which invited users to tag Web pages. The goal of this tagging was to make a new method of search available, where users entered a set of tags as their search query, and the system retrieved the Web pages that had been tagged that way. However, it is also possible to use the tags as a recommendation system. If it is observed that a user retrieves or bookmarks many pages with a certain set of tags, then we can recommend other pages with the same tags.

The problem with tagging as an approach to feature discovery is that the process only works if users are willing to take the trouble to create the tags, and there are enough tags that occasional erroneous ones will not bias the system too much.

9.2.4   Representing Item Profiles

Our ultimate goal for content-based recommendation is to create both an item profile consisting of feature-value pairs and a user profile summarizing the preferences of the user, based of their row of the utility matrix. In Section 9.2.2 we suggested how an item profile could be constructed. We imagined a vector of 0s and 1s, where a 1 represented the occurrence of a high-TF.IDF word in the document. Since features for documents were all words, it was easy to represent profiles this way.

We shall try to generalize this vector approach to all sorts of features. It is easy to do so for features that are sets of discrete values. For example, if one feature of movies is the set of actors, then imagine that there is a component for each actor, with 1 if the actor is in the movie, and 0 if not. Likewise, we can have a component for each possible director, and each possible genre. All these features can be represented using only 0s and 1s.

There is another class of features that is not readily represented by Boolean vectors: those features that are numerical. For instance, we might take the average rating for movies to be a feature,[2] and this average is a real number. It does not make sense to have one component for each of the possible average ratings, and doing so would cause us to lose the structure implicit in numbers. That is, two ratings that are close but not identical should be considered more similar than widely differing ratings. Likewise, numerical features of products, such as screen size or disk capacity for PC's, should be considered similar if their values do not differ greatly.

Numerical features should be represented by single components of vectors representing items. These components hold the exact value of that feature. There is no harm if some components of the vectors are Boolean and others are real-valued or integer-valued. We can still compute the cosine distance between vectors, although if we do so, we should give some thought to the appropriate scaling of the non-Boolean components, so that they neither dominate the calculation nor are they irrelevant.

EXAMPLE 9.2 Suppose the only features of movies are the set of actors and the average rating. Consider two movies with five actors each. Two of the actors are in both movies. Also, one movie has an average rating of 3 and the other an average of 4. The vectors look something like

$$0 \quad 1 \quad 1 \quad 0 \quad 1 \quad 1 \quad 0 \quad 1 \quad 3\alpha$$
$$1 \quad 1 \quad 0 \quad 1 \quad 0 \quad 1 \quad 1 \quad 0 \quad 4\alpha$$

However, there are in principle an infinite number of additional components, each with 0s for both vectors, representing all the possible actors that neither movie has. Since cosine distance of vectors is not affected by components in which both vectors have 0, we need not worry about the effect of actors that are in neither movie.

The last component shown represents the average rating. We have shown it as having an unknown scaling factor α. In terms of α, we can compute the cosine of the angle between the vectors. The dot product is $2 + 12\alpha^2$, and the lengths of

---

[2] The rating is not a very reliable feature, but it will serve as an example.

the vectors are $\sqrt{5 + 9\alpha^2}$ and $\sqrt{5 + 16\alpha^2}$. Thus, the cosine of the angle between the vectors is

$$\frac{2 + 12\alpha^2}{\sqrt{25 + 125\alpha^2 + 144\alpha^4}}$$

If we choose $\alpha = 1$, that is, we take the average ratings as they are, then the value of the above expression is 0.816. If we use $\alpha = 2$, that is, we double the ratings, then the cosine is 0.940. That is, the vectors appear much closer in direction than if we use $\alpha = 1$. Likewise, if we use $\alpha = 1/2$, then the cosine is 0.619, making the vectors look quite different. We cannot tell which value of α is "right," but we see that the choice of scaling factor for numerical features affects our decision about how similar items are. $\square$

9.2.5   User Profiles

We not only need to create vectors describing items; we need to create vectors with the same components that describe the user's preferences. We have the utility matrix representing the connection between users and items. Recall the nonblank matrix entries could be just 1s representing user purchases or a similar connection, or they could be arbitrary numbers representing a rating or degree of affection that the user has for the item.

With this information, the best estimate we can make regarding which items the user likes is some aggregation of the profiles of those items. If the utility matrix has only 1s, then the natural aggregate is the average of the components of the vectors representing the item profiles for the items in which the utility matrix has 1 for that user.

EXAMPLE 9.3   Suppose items are movies, represented by Boolean profiles with components corresponding to actors. Also, the utility matrix has a 1 if the user has seen the movie and is blank otherwise. If 20% of the movies that user U likes have Julia Roberts as one of the actors, then the user profile for U will have 0.2 in the component for Julia Roberts. $\square$

If the utility matrix is not Boolean, e.g., ratings 1–5, then we can weight the vectors representing the profiles of items by the utility value. It makes sense to normalize the utilities by subtracting the average value for a user. That way, we get negative weights for items with a below-average rating, and positive weights for items with above-average ratings. That effect will prove useful when we discuss in Section 9.2.6 how to find items that a user should like.

EXAMPLE 9.4   Consider the same movie information as in Example 9.3, but now suppose the utility matrix has nonblank entries that are ratings in the 1–5 range. Suppose user U gives an average rating of 3. There are three movies with Julia Roberts as an actor, and those movies got ratings of 3, 4, and 5. Then in the user profile of U, the component for Julia Roberts will have value that is the average of $3 - 3$, $4 - 3$, and $5 - 3$, that is, a value of 1.

On the other hand, user V gives an average rating of 4, and has also rated three movies with Julia Roberts (it doesn't matter whether or not they are the same three movies U rated). User V gives these three movies ratings of 2, 3, and 5. The user profile for V has, in the component for Julia Roberts, the average of $2 - 4$, $3 - 4$, and $5 - 4$, that is, the value $-2/3$. □

9.2.6 Recommending Items to Users Based on Content

With profile vectors for both users and items, we can estimate the degree to which a user would prefer an item by computing the cosine distance between the user's and item's vectors. As in Example 9.2, we may wish to scale various components whose values are not Boolean. The random-hyperplane and locality-sensitive-hashing techniques can be used to place (just) item profiles in buckets. In that way, given a user to whom we want to recommend some items, we can apply the same two techniques – random hyperplanes and LSH – to determine in which buckets we must look for items that might have a small cosine distance from the user.

EXAMPLE 9.5 Consider first the data of Example 9.3. The user's profile will have components for actors proportional to the likelihood that the actor will appear in a movie the user likes. Thus, the highest recommendations (lowest cosine distance) belong to the movies with lots of actors that appear in many of the movies the user likes. As long as actors are the only information we have about features of movies, that is probably the best we can do.[3]

Now, consider Example 9.4. There, we observed that the vector for a user will have positive numbers for actors that tend to appear in movies the user likes and negative numbers for actors that tend to appear in movies the user doesn't like. Consider a movie with many actors the user likes, and only a few or none that the user doesn't like. The cosine of the angle between the user's and movie's vectors will be a large positive fraction. That implies an angle close to 0, and therefore a small cosine distance between the vectors.

Next, consider a movie with about as many actors that the user likes as those the user doesn't like. In this situation, the cosine of the angle between the user and movie is around 0, and therefore the angle between the two vectors is around 90 degrees. Finally, consider a movie with mostly actors the user doesn't like. In that case, the cosine will be a large negative fraction, and the angle between the two vectors will be close to 180 degrees – the maximum possible cosine distance. □

---

[3] Note that the fact all user-vector components will be small fractions does not affect the recommendation, since the cosine calculation involves dividing by the length of each vector. That is, user vectors will tend to be much shorter than movie vectors, but only the direction of vectors matters.

9.2.7   Classification Algorithms

A completely different approach to a recommendation system using item profiles and utility matrices is to treat the problem as one of machine learning. Regard the given data as a training set, and for each user, build a classifier that predicts the rating of all items. There are a great number of different classifiers, and it is not our purpose to teach this subject here. However, you should be aware of the option of developing a classifier for recommendation, so we shall discuss one common classifier – decision trees – briefly.

A *decision tree* is a collection of nodes, arranged as a binary tree. The leaves render decisions; in our case, the decision would be "likes" or "doesn't like." Each interior node is a condition on the objects being classified; in our case the condition would be a predicate involving one or more features of an item.

To classify an item, we start at the root, and apply the predicate at the root to the item. If the predicate is true, go to the left child, and if it is false, go to the right child. Then repeat the same process at the node visited, until a leaf is reached. That leaf classifies the item as liked or not.

Construction of a decision tree requires selection of a predicate for each interior node. There are many ways of picking the best predicate, but they all try to arrange that one of the children gets all or most of the positive examples in the training set (i.e, the items that the given user likes, in our case) and the other child gets all or most of the negative examples (the items this user does not like).

Once we have selected a predicate for a node N, we divide the items into the two groups: those that satisfy the predicate and those that do not. For each group, we again find the predicate that best separates the positive and negative examples in that group. These predicates are assigned to the children of N. This process of dividing the examples and building children can proceed to any number of levels. We can stop, and create a leaf, if the group of items for a node is homogeneous; i.e., they are all positive or all negative examples.

However, we may wish to stop and create a leaf with the majority decision for a group, even if the group contains both positive and negative examples. The reason is that the statistical significance of a small group may not be high enough to rely on. For that reason a variant strategy is to create an *ensemble* of decision trees, each using different predicates, but allow the trees to be deeper than what the available data justifies. Such trees are called *overfitted*. To classify an item, apply all the trees in the ensemble, and let them vote on the outcome. We shall not consider this option here, but give a simple hypothetical example of a decision tree.

EXAMPLE 9.6   Suppose our items are news articles, and features are the high-TF.IDF words (*keywords*) in those documents. Further suppose there is a user U who likes articles about baseball, except articles about the New York Yankees. The row of the utility matrix for U has 1 if U has read the article and is blank if not. We shall take the 1s as "like" and the blanks as "doesn't like." Predicates will be Boolean expressions of keywords.

Since U generally likes baseball, we might find that the best predicate for the root is "homerun" OR ("batter" AND "pitcher"). Items that satisfy the predicate will tend to be positive examples (articles with 1 in the row for U in the utility matrix), and items that fail to satisfy the predicate will tend to be negative examples (blanks in the utility-matrix row for U). Figure 9.3 shows the root as well as the rest of the decision tree.

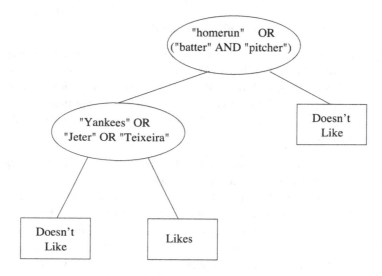

Figure 9.3 A decision tree

Suppose that the group of articles that do not satisfy the predicate includes sufficiently few positive examples that we can conclude all of these items are in the "don't-like" class. We may then put a leaf with decision "don't like" as the right child of the root. However, the articles that satisfy the predicate includes a number of articles that user U doesn't like; these are the articles that mention the Yankees. Thus, at the left child of the root, we build another predicate. We might find that the predicate "Yankees" OR "Jeter" OR "Teixeira" is the best possible indicator of an article about baseball and about the Yankees. Thus, we see in Fig. 9.3 the left child of the root, which applies this predicate. Both children of this node are leaves, since we may suppose that the items satisfying this predicate are predominantly negative and those not satisfying it are predominantly positive. □

Unfortunately, classifiers of all types tend to take a long time to construct. For instance, if we wish to use decision trees, we need one tree per user. Constructing a tree not only requires that we look at all the item profiles, but we have to consider many different predicates, which could involve complex combinations of features. Thus, this approach tends to be used only for relatively small problem sizes.

9.2.8   Exercises for Section 9.2

EXERCISE 9.2.1   Three computers, A, B, and C, have the numerical features listed below:

Feature	A	B	C
Processor Speed	3.06	2.68	2.92
Disk Size	500	320	640
Main-Memory Size	6	4	6

We may imagine these values as defining a vector for each computer; for instance, A's vector is $[3.06, 500, 6]$. We can compute the cosine distance between any two of the vectors, but if we do not scale the components, then the disk size will dominate and make differences in the other components essentially invisible. Let us use 1 as the scale factor for processor speed, α for the disk size, and β for the main memory size.

(a) In terms of α and β, compute the cosines of the angles between the vectors for each pair of the three computers.

(b) What are the angles between the vectors if $\alpha = \beta = 1$?

(c) What are the angles between the vectors if $\alpha = 0.01$ and $\beta = 0.5$?

! (d) One fair way of selecting scale factors is to make each inversely proportional to the average value in its component. What would be the values of α and β, and what would be the angles between the vectors?

EXERCISE 9.2.2   An alternative way of scaling components of a vector is to begin by normalizing the vectors. That is, compute the average for each component and subtract it from that component's value in each of the vectors.

(a) Normalize the vectors for the three computers described in Exercise 9.2.1.

!! (b) This question does not require difficult calculation, but it requires some serious thought about what angles between vectors mean. When all components are nonnegative, as they are in the data of Exercise 9.2.1, no vectors can have an angle greater than 90 degrees. However, when we normalize vectors, we can (and must) get some negative components, so the angles can now be anything, that is, 0 to 180 degrees. Moreover, averages are now 0 in every component, so the suggestion in part (d) of Exercise 9.2.1 that we should scale in inverse proportion to the average makes no sense. Suggest a way of finding an appropriate scale for each component of normalized vectors. How would you interpret a large or small angle between normalized vectors? What would the angles be for the normalized vectors derived from the data in Exercise 9.2.1?

EXERCISE 9.2.3   A certain user has rated the three computers of Exercise 9.2.1 as follows: A: 4 stars, B: 2 stars, C: 5 stars.

(a) Normalize the ratings for this user.

(b) Compute a user profile for the user, with components for processor speed, disk size, and main memory size, based on the data of Exercise 9.2.1.

9.3   Collaborative Filtering

We shall now take up a significantly different approach to recommendation. Instead of using features of items to determine their similarity, we focus on the similarity of the user ratings for two items. That is, in place of the item-profile vector for an item, we use its column in the utility matrix. Further, instead of contriving a profile vector for users, we represent them by their rows in the utility matrix. Users are similar if their vectors are close according to some distance measure such as Jaccard or cosine distance. Recommendation for a user U is then made by looking at the users that are most similar to U in this sense, and recommending items that these users like. The process of identifying similar users and recommending what similar users like is called *collaborative filtering*.

9.3.1   Measuring Similarity

The first question we must deal with is how to measure similarity of users or items from their rows or columns in the utility matrix. We have reproduced Fig. 9.1 here as Fig. 9.4. This data is too small to draw any reliable conclusions, but its small size will make clear some of the pitfalls in picking a distance measure. Observe specifically the users A and C. They rated two movies in common, but they appear to have almost diametrically opposite opinions of these movies. We would expect that a good distance measure would make them rather far apart. Here are some alternative measures to consider.

	HP1	HP2	HP3	TW	SW1	SW2	SW3
A	4			5	1		
B	5	5	4				
C				2	4	5	
D		3					3

Figure 9.4 The utility matrix introduced in Fig. 9.1

Jaccard Distance

We could ignore values in the matrix and focus only on the sets of items rated. If the utility matrix only reflected purchases, this measure would be a good one to choose. However, when utilities are more detailed ratings, the Jaccard distance loses important information.

EXAMPLE 9.7 A and B have an intersection of size 1 and a union of size 5. Thus, their Jaccard similarity is 1/5, and their Jaccard distance is 4/5; i.e., they are very far apart. In comparison, A and C have a Jaccard similarity of $2/4$, so their Jaccard distance is the same, $1/2$. Thus, A appears closer to C than to B. Yet that conclusion seems intuitively wrong. A and C disagree on the two movies they both watched, while A and B seem both to have liked the one movie they watched in common. □

Cosine Distance

We can treat blanks as a 0 value. This choice is questionable, since it has the effect of treating the lack of a rating as more similar to disliking the movie than liking it.

EXAMPLE 9.8   The cosine of the angle between A and B is

$$\frac{4 \times 5}{\sqrt{4^2 + 5^2 + 1^2}\sqrt{5^2 + 5^2 + 4^2}} = 0.380$$

The cosine of the angle between A and C is

$$\frac{5 \times 2 + 1 \times 4}{\sqrt{4^2 + 5^2 + 1^2}\sqrt{2^2 + 4^2 + 5^2}} = 0.322$$

Since a larger (positive) cosine implies a smaller angle and therefore a smaller distance, this measure tells us that A is slightly closer to B than to C. □

Rounding the Data

We could try to eliminate the apparent similarity between movies a user rates highly and those with low scores by rounding the ratings. For instance, we could consider ratings of 3, 4, and 5 as a "1" and consider ratings 1 and 2 as unrated. The utility matrix would then look as in Fig. 9.5. Now, the Jaccard distance between A and B is $3/4$, while between A and C it is 1; i.e., C appears further from A than B does, which is intuitively correct. Applying cosine distance to Fig. 9.5 allows us to draw the same conclusion.

	HP1	HP2	HP3	TW	SW1	SW2	SW3
A	1			1			
B	1	1	1				
C					1	1	
D		1					1

Figure 9.5 Utilities of 3, 4, and 5 have been replaced by 1, while ratings of 1 and 2 are omitted

Normalizing Ratings

If we normalize ratings, by subtracting from each rating the average rating of that user, we turn low ratings into negative numbers and high ratings into positive numbers. If we then take the cosine distance, we find that users with opposite views of the movies they viewed in common will have vectors in almost opposite directions, and can be considered as far apart as possible. However, users with similar opinions about the movies rated in common will have a relatively small angle between them.

EXAMPLE 9.9   Figure 9.6 shows the matrix of Fig. 9.4 with all ratings normalized. An interesting effect is that D's ratings have effectively disappeared, because a 0 is the same as a blank when cosine distance is computed. Note that D gave only 3s and did not differentiate among movies, so it is quite possible that D's opinions are not worth taking seriously.

	HP1	HP2	HP3	TW	SW1	SW2	SW3
A	2/3			5/3	−7/3		
B	1/3	1/3	−2/3				
C				−5/3	1/3	4/3	
D		0					0

Figure 9.6 The utility matrix introduced in Fig. 9.1

Let us compute the cosine of the angle between A and B:

$$\frac{(2/3) \times (1/3)}{\sqrt{(2/3)^2 + (5/3)^2 + (-7/3)^2}\sqrt{(1/3)^2 + (1/3)^2 + (-2/3)^2}} = 0.092$$

The cosine of the angle between between A and C is

$$\frac{(5/3) \times (-5/3) + (-7/3) \times (1/3)}{\sqrt{(2/3)^2 + (5/3)^2 + (-7/3)^2}\sqrt{(-5/3)^2 + (1/3)^2 + (4/3)^2}} = -0.559$$

Notice that under this measure, A and C are much further apart than A and B, and neither pair is very close. Both these observations make intuitive sense, given that A and C disagree on the two movies they rated in common, while A and B give similar scores to the one movie they rated in common.   □

9.3.2   The Duality of Similarity

The utility matrix can be viewed as telling us about users or about items, or both. It is important to realize that any of the techniques we suggested in Section 9.3.1 for finding similar users can be used on columns of the utility matrix to find similar items. There are two ways in which the symmetry is broken in practice.

(1) We can use information about users to recommend items. That is, given a user, we can find some number of the most similar users, perhaps using the techniques of Chapter 3. We can base our recommendation on the decisions made by these similar users, e.g., recommend the items that the greatest number of them have purchased or rated highly. However, there is no symmetry. Even if we find pairs of similar items, we need to take an additional step in order to recommend items to users. This point is explored further at the end of this subsection.

(2) There is a difference in the typical behavior of users and items, as it pertains to similarity. Intuitively, items tend to be classifiable in simple terms. For example, music tends to belong to a single genre. It is impossible, e.g., for a piece of music to be both 60's rock and 1700's baroque. On the other hand, there are individuals who like both 60's rock and 1700's baroque, and who buy examples of both types of music. The consequence is that it is easier to discover items that are similar because they belong to the same genre, than it is to detect that two users are similar because they prefer one genre in common, while each also likes some genres that the other doesn't care for.

As we suggested in (1) above, one way of predicting the value of the utility-matrix entry for user U and item I is to find the n users (for some predetermined n) most similar to U and average their ratings for item I, counting only those among the n similar users who have rated I. It is generally better to normalize the matrix first. That is, for each of the n users subtract their average rating for items from their rating for i. Average the difference for those users who have rated I, and then add this average to the average rating that U gives for all items. This normalization adjusts the estimate in the case that U tends to give very high or very low ratings, or a large fraction of the similar users who rated I (of which there may be only a few) are users who tend to rate very high or very low.

Dually, we can use item similarity to estimate the entry for user U and item I. Find the m items most similar to I, for some m, and take the average rating, among the m items, of the ratings that U has given. As for user-user similarity, we consider only those items among the m that U has rated, and it is probably wise to normalize item ratings first.

Note that whichever approach to estimating entries in the utility matrix we use, it is not sufficient to find only one entry. In order to recommend items to a user U, we need to estimate every entry in the row of the utility matrix for U, or at least find all or most of the entries in that row that are blank but have a high estimated value. There is a tradeoff regarding whether we should work from similar users or similar items.

- If we find similar users, then we only have to do the process once for user U. From the set of similar users we can estimate all the blanks in the utility matrix for U. If we work from similar items, we have to compute similar items for almost all items, before we can estimate the row for U.

- On the other hand, item-item similarity often provides more reliable information, because of the phenomenon observed above, namely that it is easier to find items of the same genre than it is to find users that like only items of a single genre.

Whichever method we choose, we should precompute preferred items for each user, rather than waiting until we need to make a decision. Since the utility matrix evolves slowly, it is generally sufficient to compute it infrequently and assume that it remains fixed between recomputations.

9.3.3 Clustering Users and Items

It is hard to detect similarity among either items or users, because we have little information about user-item pairs in the sparse utility matrix. In the perspective of Section 9.3.2, even if two items belong to the same genre, there are likely to be very few users who bought or rated both. Likewise, even if two users both like a genre or genres, they may not have bought any items in common.

One way of dealing with this pitfall is to cluster items and/or users. Select any of the distance measures suggested in Section 9.3.1, or any other distance measure, and use it to perform a clustering of, say, items. Any of the methods suggested in Chapter 7 can be used. However, we shall see that there may be little reason to try to cluster into a small number of clusters immediately. Rather, a hierarchical approach, where we leave many clusters unmerged may suffice as a first step. For example, we might leave half as many clusters as there are items.

	HP	TW	SW
A	4	5	1
B	4.67		
C		2	4.5
D	3		3

Figure 9.7 Utility matrix for users and clusters of items

EXAMPLE 9.10   Figure 9.7 shows what happens to the utility matrix of Fig. 9.4 if we manage to cluster the three Harry-Potter movies into one cluster, denoted HP, and also cluster the three Star-Wars movies into one cluster SW.   □

Having clustered items to an extent, we can revise the utility matrix so the columns represent clusters of items, and the entry for user U and cluster C is the average rating that U gave to those members of cluster C that U did rate. Note that U may have rated none of the cluster members, in which case the entry for U and C is still blank.

We can use this revised utility matrix to cluster users, again using the distance measure we consider most appropriate. Use a clustering algorithm that again leaves many clusters, e.g., half as many clusters as there are users. Revise the utility matrix, so the rows correspond to clusters of users, just as the columns correspond to clusters of items. As for item-clusters, compute the entry for a user cluster by averaging the ratings of the users in the cluster.

Now, this process can be repeated several times if we like. That is, we can cluster the item clusters and again merge the columns of the utility matrix that belong to one cluster. We can then turn to the users again, and cluster the user clusters. The process can repeat until we have an intuitively reasonable number of clusters of each kind.

Once we have clustered the users and/or items to the desired extent and computed the cluster-cluster utility matrix, we can estimate entries in the original utility matrix as follows. Suppose we want to predict the entry for user U and item I:

(a) Find the clusters to which U and I belong, say clusters C and D, respectively.
(b) If the entry in the cluster-cluster utility matrix for C and D is something other than blank, use this value as the estimated value for the U–I entry in the original utility matrix.
(c) If the entry for C–D is blank, then use the method outlined in Section 9.3.2 to estimate that entry by considering clusters similar to C or D. Use the resulting estimate as the estimate for the U-I entry.

9.3.4   Exercises for Section 9.3

	a	b	c	d	e	f	g	h
A	4	5		5	1		3	2
B		3	4	3	1	2	1	
C	2		1	3		4	5	3

Figure 9.8 A utility matrix for exercises

EXERCISE 9.3.1   Figure 9.8 is a utility matrix, representing the ratings, on a 1–5 star scale, of eight items, a through h, by three users A, B, and C. Compute the following from the data of this matrix.

(a) Treating the utility matrix as boolean, compute the Jaccard distance between each pair of users.
(b) Repeat Part (a), but use the cosine distance.
(c) Treat ratings of 3, 4, and 5 as 1 and 1, 2, and blank as 0. Compute the Jaccard distance between each pair of users.
(d) Repeat Part (c), but use the cosine distance.
(e) Normalize the matrix by subtracting from each nonblank entry the average value for its user.
(f) Using the normalized matrix from Part (e), compute the cosine distance between each pair of users.

EXERCISE 9.3.2   In this exercise, we cluster items in the matrix of Fig. 9.8. Do the following steps.

(a) Cluster the eight items hierarchically into four clusters. The following method should be used to cluster. Replace all 3s, 4s, and 5s by 1 and replace 1s, 2s, and blanks by 0. use the Jaccard distance to measure the distance between the resulting column vectors. For clusters of more than one element, take the distance between clusters to be the minimum distance between pairs of elements, one from each cluster.

(b) Then, construct from the original matrix of Fig. 9.8 a new matrix whose rows correspond to users, as before, and whose columns correspond to clusters. Compute the entry for a user and cluster of items by averaging the nonblank entries for that user and all the items in the cluster.

(c) Compute the cosine distance between each pair of users, according to your matrix from Part (b).

9.4 Dimensionality Reduction

An entirely different approach to estimating the blank entries in the utility matrix is to conjecture that the utility matrix is actually the product of two long, thin matrices. This view makes sense if there are a relatively small set of features of items and users that determine the reaction of most users to most items. In this section, we sketch one approach to discovering two such matrices; the approach is called "UV-decomposition," and it is an instance of a more general theory called SVD (*singular-value decomposition*).

9.4.1 UV-Decomposition

Consider movies as a case in point. Most users respond to a small number of features; they like certain genres, they may have certain famous actors or actresses that they like, and perhaps there are a few directors with a significant following. If we start with the utility matrix M, with n rows and m columns (i.e., there are n users and m items), then we might be able to find a matrix U with n rows and d columns and a matrix V with d rows and m columns, such that UV closely approximates M in those entries where M is nonblank. If so, then we have established that there are d dimensions that allow us to characterize both users and items closely. We can then use the entry in the product UV to estimate the corresponding blank entry in utility matrix M. This process is called *UV-decomposition* of M.

$$
\begin{bmatrix}
5 & 2 & 4 & 4 & 3 \\
3 & 1 & 2 & 4 & 1 \\
2 &   & 3 & 1 & 4 \\
2 & 5 & 4 & 3 & 5 \\
4 & 4 & 5 & 4 &
\end{bmatrix}
=
\begin{bmatrix}
u_{11} & u_{12} \\
u_{21} & u_{22} \\
u_{31} & u_{32} \\
u_{41} & u_{42} \\
u_{51} & u_{52}
\end{bmatrix}
\times
\begin{bmatrix}
v_{11} & v_{12} & v_{13} & v_{14} & v_{15} \\
v_{21} & v_{22} & v_{23} & v_{24} & v_{25}
\end{bmatrix}
$$

Figure 9.9 UV-decomposition of matrix M

EXAMPLE 9.11 We shall use as a running example a 5×5 matrix M with all but two of its entries known. We wish to decompose M into a 5×2 and 2×5 matrix, U and V, respectively. The matrices M, U, and V are shown in Fig. 9.9 with the known entries of M indicated and the matrices U and V shown with their entries as variables to be determined. This example is essentially the smallest nontrivial case where there are more known entries than there are entries in U and V combined, and we therefore can expect that the best decomposition will not yield a product that agrees exactly in the nonblank entries of M.   □

9.4.2   Root-Mean-Square Error

While we can pick among several measures of how close the product UV is to M, the typical choice is the root-mean-square error (RMSE), where we

(1) Sum, over all nonblank entries in M the square of the difference between that entry and the corresponding entry in the product UV.
(2) Take the mean (average) of these squares by dividing by the number of terms in the sum (i.e., the number of nonblank entries in M).
(3) Take the square root of the mean.

Minimizing the sum of the squares is the same as minimizing the square root of the average square, so we generally omit the last two steps in our running example.

$$
\begin{bmatrix} 1 & 1 \\ 1 & 1 \\ 1 & 1 \\ 1 & 1 \\ 1 & 1 \end{bmatrix} \times \begin{bmatrix} 1 & 1 & 1 & 1 & 1 \\ 1 & 1 & 1 & 1 & 1 \end{bmatrix} = \begin{bmatrix} 2 & 2 & 2 & 2 & 2 \\ 2 & 2 & 2 & 2 & 2 \\ 2 & 2 & 2 & 2 & 2 \\ 2 & 2 & 2 & 2 & 2 \\ 2 & 2 & 2 & 2 & 2 \end{bmatrix}
$$

Figure 9.10 Matrices U and V with all entries 1

EXAMPLE 9.12   Suppose we guess that U and V should each have entries that are all 1s, as shown in Fig. 9.10. This is a poor guess, since the product, consisting of all 2s, has entries that are much below the average of the entries in M. Nonetheless, we can compute the RMSE for this U and V; in fact the regularity in the entries makes the calculation especially easy to follow. Consider the first rows of M and UV. We subtract 2 (each entry in UV) from the entries in the first row of M, to get $3, 0, 2, 2, 1$. We square and sum these to get 18. In the second row, we do the same to get $1, -1, 0, 2, -1$, square and sum to get 7. In the third row, the second column is blank, so that entry is ignored when computing the RMSE. The differences are $0, 1, -1, 2$ and the sum of squares is 6. For the fourth row, the differences are $0, 3, 2, 1, 3$ and the sum of squares is 23. The fifth row has a blank entry in the last column, so the differences are $2, 2, 3, 2$ and the sum of squares is 21. When we sum the sums from each of the five rows, we get $18 + 7 + 6 + 23 + 21 = 75$. Generally, we shall stop at this point, but if we want to compute the true RMSE, we divide by 23 (the number of nonblank entries in M) and take the square root. In this case $\sqrt{75/23} = 1.806$ is the RMSE. □

9.4.3 Incremental Computation of a UV-Decomposition

Finding the UV-decomposition with the least RMSE involves starting with some arbitrarily chosen U and V, and repeatedly adjusting U and V to make the RMSE smaller. We shall consider only adjustments to a single element of U or V, although in principle, one could make more complex adjustments. Whatever adjustments we allow, in a typical example there will be many *local minima* – matrices U and V such that no allowable adjustment reduces the RMSE. Unfortunately, only one of these local minima will be the *global minimum* – the matrices U and V that produce the least possible RMSE. To increase our chances of finding the global minimum, we need to pick many different starting points, that is, different choices of the initial matrices U and V. However, there is never a guarantee that our best local minimum will be the global minimum.

We shall start with the U and V of Fig. 9.10, where all entries are 1, and do a few adjustments to some of the entries, finding the values of those entries that give the largest possible improvement to the RMSE. From these examples, the general calculation should become obvious, but we shall follow the examples by the formula for minimizing the RMSE by changing a single entry. In what follows, we shall refer to entries of U and V by their variable names u_{11}, and so on, as given in Fig. 9.9.

EXAMPLE 9.13   Suppose we start with U and V as in Fig. 9.10, and we decide to alter u_{11} to reduce the RMSE as much as possible. Let the value of u_{11} be x. Then the new U and V can be expressed as in Fig. 9.11.

$$
\begin{bmatrix} x & 1 \\ 1 & 1 \\ 1 & 1 \\ 1 & 1 \\ 1 & 1 \end{bmatrix} \times \begin{bmatrix} 1 & 1 & 1 & 1 & 1 \\ 1 & 1 & 1 & 1 & 1 \end{bmatrix} = \begin{bmatrix} x+1 & x+1 & x+1 & x+1 & x+1 \\ 2 & 2 & 2 & 2 & 2 \\ 2 & 2 & 2 & 2 & 2 \\ 2 & 2 & 2 & 2 & 2 \\ 2 & 2 & 2 & 2 & 2 \end{bmatrix}
$$

Figure 9.11 Making u_{11} a variable

Notice that the only entries of the product that have changed are those in the first row. Thus, when we compare UV with M, the only change to the RMSE comes from the first row. The contribution to the sum of squares from the first row is

$$
\left(5 - (x+1)\right)^2 + \left(2 - (x+1)\right)^2 + \left(4 - (x+1)\right)^2 + \left(4 - (x+1)\right)^2 + \left(3 - (x+1)\right)^2
$$

This sum simplifies to

$$
(4 - x)^2 + (1 - x)^2 + (3 - x)^2 + (3 - x)^2 + (2 - x)^2
$$

We want the value of x that minimizes the sum, so we take the derivative and set that equal to 0, as:

$$-2 \times \left((4-x) + (1-x) + (3-x) + (3-x) + (2-x)\right) = 0$$

or $-2 \times (13 - 5x) = 0$, from which it follows that $x = 2.6$.

$$
\begin{bmatrix}
2.6 & 1 \\
1 & 1 \\
1 & 1 \\
1 & 1 \\
1 & 1
\end{bmatrix}
\times
\begin{bmatrix}
1 & 1 & 1 & 1 & 1 \\
1 & 1 & 1 & 1 & 1
\end{bmatrix}
=
\begin{bmatrix}
3.6 & 3.6 & 3.6 & 3.6 & 3.6 \\
2 & 2 & 2 & 2 & 2 \\
2 & 2 & 2 & 2 & 2 \\
2 & 2 & 2 & 2 & 2 \\
2 & 2 & 2 & 2 & 2
\end{bmatrix}
$$

Figure 9.12 The best value for u_{11} is found to be 2.6

Figure 9.12 shows U and V after u_{11} has been set to 2.6. Note that the sum of the squares of the errors in the first row has been reduced from 18 to 5.2, so the total RMSE (ignoring average and square root) has been reduced from 75 to 62.2.

$$
\begin{bmatrix}
2.6 & 1 \\
1 & 1 \\
1 & 1 \\
1 & 1 \\
1 & 1
\end{bmatrix}
\times
\begin{bmatrix}
y & 1 & 1 & 1 & 1 \\
1 & 1 & 1 & 1 & 1
\end{bmatrix}
=
\begin{bmatrix}
2.6y + 1 & 3.6 & 3.6 & 3.6 & 3.6 \\
y + 1 & 2 & 2 & 2 & 2 \\
y + 1 & 2 & 2 & 2 & 2 \\
y + 1 & 2 & 2 & 2 & 2 \\
y + 1 & 2 & 2 & 2 & 2
\end{bmatrix}
$$

Figure 9.13 v_{11} becomes a variable y

Suppose our next entry to vary is v_{11}. Let the value of this entry be y, as suggested in Fig. 9.13. Only the first column of the product is affected by y, so we need only to compute the sum of the squares of the differences between the entries in the first columns of M and UV. This sum is

$$\left(5 - (2.6y + 1)\right)^2 + \left(3 - (y+1)\right)^2 + \left(2 - (y+1)\right)^2 + \left(2 - (y+1)\right)^2 + \left(4 - (y+1)\right)^2$$

This expression simplifies to

$$(4 - 2.6y)^2 + (2 - y)^2 + (1 - y)^2 + (1 - y)^2 + (3 - y)^2$$

As before, we find the minimum value of this expression by differentiating and equating to 0, as:

$$-2 \times \left(2.6(4 - 2.6y) + (2 - y) + (1 - y) + (1 - y) + (3 - y)\right) = 0$$

The solution for y is $y = 17.4/10.76 = 1.617$. The improved estimates of U and V are shown in Fig. 9.14.

We shall do one more change, to illustrate what happens when entries of M are blank. We shall vary u_{31}, calling it z temporarily. The new U and V are shown in Fig. 9.15. The value of z affects only the entries in the third row.

$$
\begin{bmatrix} 2.6 & 1 \\ 1 & 1 \\ 1 & 1 \\ 1 & 1 \\ 1 & 1 \end{bmatrix} \times \begin{bmatrix} 1.617 & 1 & 1 & 1 & 1 \\ 1 & & 1 & 1 & 1 & 1 \end{bmatrix} = \begin{bmatrix} 5.204 & 3.6 & 3.6 & 3.6 & 3.6 \\ 2.617 & 2 & 2 & 2 & 2 \\ 2.617 & 2 & 2 & 2 & 2 \\ 2.617 & 2 & 2 & 2 & 2 \\ 2.617 & 2 & 2 & 2 & 2 \end{bmatrix}
$$

Figure 9.14 Replace y by 1.617

$$
\begin{bmatrix} 2.6 & 1 \\ 1 & 1 \\ z & 1 \\ 1 & 1 \\ 1 & 1 \end{bmatrix} \times \begin{bmatrix} 1.617 & 1 & 1 & 1 & 1 \\ 1 & & 1 & 1 & 1 & 1 \end{bmatrix} = \begin{bmatrix} 5.204 & 3.6 & 3.6 & 3.6 & 3.6 \\ 2.617 & 2 & 2 & 2 & 2 \\ 1.617z+1 & z+1 & z+1 & z+1 & z+1 \\ 2.617 & 2 & 2 & 2 & 2 \\ 2.617 & 2 & 2 & 2 & 2 \end{bmatrix}
$$

Figure 9.15 u_{31} becomes a variable z

We can express the sum of the squares of the errors as

$$
\bigl(2 - (1.617z + 1)\bigr)^2 + \bigl(3 - (z + 1)\bigr)^2 + \bigl(1 - (z + 1)\bigr)^2 + \bigl(4 - (z + 1)\bigr)^2
$$

Note that there is no contribution from the element in the second column of the third row, since this element is blank in M. The expression simplifies to

$$
(1 - 1.617z)^2 + (2 - z)^2 + (-z)^2 + (3 - z)^2
$$

The usual process of setting the derivative to 0 gives us

$$
-2 \times \bigl(1.617(1 - 1.617z) + (2 - z) + (-z) + (3 - z)\bigr) = 0
$$

whose solution is $z = 6.617/5.615 = 1.178$. The next estimate of the decomposition UV is shown in Fig. 9.16. □

$$
\begin{bmatrix} 2.6 & 1 \\ 1 & 1 \\ 1.178 & 1 \\ 1 & 1 \\ 1 & 1 \end{bmatrix} \times \begin{bmatrix} 1.617 & 1 & 1 & 1 & 1 \\ 1 & & 1 & 1 & 1 & 1 \end{bmatrix} = \begin{bmatrix} 5.204 & 3.6 & 3.6 & 3.6 & 3.6 \\ 2.617 & 2 & 2 & 2 & 2 \\ 2.905 & 2.178 & 2.178 & 2.178 & 2.178 \\ 2.617 & 2 & 2 & 2 & 2 \\ 2.617 & 2 & 2 & 2 & 2 \end{bmatrix}
$$

Figure 9.16 Replace z by 1.178

9.4.4 Optimizing an Arbitrary Element

Having seen some examples of picking the optimum value for a single element in the matrix U or V, let us now develop the general formula. As before, assume that M is an $n \times m$ utility matrix with some entries blank, while U and V are matrices of dimensions $n \times d$ and $d \times m$, for some d. We shall use m_{ij}, u_{ij}, and

v_{ij} for the entries in row i and column j of M, U, and V, respectively. Also, let $P = UV$, and use p_{ij} for the element in row i and column j of the product matrix P.

Suppose we want to vary u_{rs} and find the value of this element that minimizes the RMSE between M and UV. Note that u_{rs} affects only the elements in row r of the product $P = UV$. Thus, we need only concern ourselves with the elements

$$p_{rj} = \sum_{k=1}^{d} u_{rk} v_{kj} = \sum_{k \neq s} u_{rk} v_{kj} + x v_{sj}$$

for all values of j such that m_{rj} is nonblank. In the expression above, we have replaced u_{rs}, the element we wish to vary, by a variable x, and we use the convention

- $\sum_{k \neq s}$ is shorthand for the sum for $k = 1, 2, \ldots, d$, except for $k = s$.

If m_{rj} is a nonblank entry of the matrix M, then the contribution of this element to the sum of the squares of the errors is

$$(m_{rj} - p_{rj})^2 = \left(m_{rj} - \sum_{k \neq s} u_{rk} v_{kj} - x v_{sj}\right)^2$$

We shall use another convention:

- $\sum_j$ is shorthand for the sum over all j such that m_{rj} is nonblank.

Then we can write the sum of the squares of the errors that are affected by the value of $x = u_{rs}$ as

$$\sum_j \left(m_{rj} - \sum_{k \neq s} u_{rk} v_{kj} - x v_{sj}\right)^2$$

Take the derivative of the above with respect to x, and set it equal to 0, in order to find the value of x that minimizes the RMSE. That is,

$$\sum_j -2 v_{sj} \left(m_{rj} - \sum_{k \neq s} u_{rk} v_{kj} - x v_{sj}\right) = 0$$

As in the previous examples, the common factor -2 can be dropped. We solve the above equation for x, and get

$$x = \frac{\sum_j v_{sj} \left(m_{rj} - \sum_{k \neq s} u_{rk} v_{kj}\right)}{\sum_j v_{sj}^2}$$

There is an analogous formula for the optimum value of an element of V. If we want to vary $v_{rs} = y$, then the value of y that minimizes the RMSE is

$$y = \frac{\sum_i u_{ir} \left(m_{is} - \sum_{k \neq r} u_{ik} v_{ks}\right)}{\sum_i u_{ir}^2}$$

Here, $\sum_i$ is shorthand for the sum over all i such that m_{is} is nonblank, and $\sum_{k \neq r}$ is the sum over all values of k between 1 and d, except for $k = r$.

9.4.5 Building a Complete UV-Decomposition Algorithm

Now, we have the tools to search for the global optimum decomposition of a utility matrix M. There are four areas where we shall discuss the options.

(1) Preprocessing of the matrix M.
(2) Initializing U and V.
(3) Ordering the optimization of the elements of U and V.
(4) Ending the attempt at optimization.

Preprocessing

Because the differences in the quality of items and the rating scales of users are such important factors in determining the missing elements of the matrix M, it is often useful to remove these influences before doing anything else. The idea was introduced in Section 9.3.1. We can subtract from each nonblank element m_{ij} the average rating of user i. Then, the resulting matrix can be modified by subtracting the average rating (in the modified matrix) of item j. It is also possible to first subtract the average rating of item j and then subtract the average rating of user i in the modified matrix. The results one obtains from doing things in these two different orders need not be the same, but will tend to be close. A third option is to normalize by subtracting from m_{ij} the average of the average rating of user i and item j, that is, subtracting one half the sum of the user average and the item average.

If we choose to normalize M, then when we make predictions, we need to undo the normalization. That is, if whatever prediction method we use results in estimate e for an element m_{ij} of the normalized matrix, then the value we predict for m_{ij} in the true utility matrix is e plus whatever amount was subtracted from row i and from column j during the normalization process.

Initialization

As we mentioned, it is essential that there be some randomness in the way we seek an optimum solution, because the existence of many local minima justifies our running many different optimizations in the hope of reaching the global minimum on at least one run. We can vary the initial values of U and V, or we can vary the way we seek the optimum (to be discussed next), or both.

A simple starting point for U and V is to give each element the same value, and a good choice for this value is that which gives the elements of the product UV the average of the nonblank elements of M. Note that if we have normalized M, then this value will necessarily be 0. If we have chosen d as the lengths of the short sides of U and V, and a is the average nonblank element of M, then the elements of U and V should be $\sqrt{a/d}$.

If we want many starting points for U and V, then we can perturb the value $\sqrt{a/d}$ randomly and independently for each of the elements. There are many options for how we do the perturbation. We have a choice regarding the distribution of the difference. For example we could add to each element a normally distributed value with mean 0 and some chosen standard deviation. Or we could add a value uniformly chosen from the range $-c$ to $+c$ for some c.

Performing the Optimization

In order to reach a local minimum from a given starting value of U and V, we need to pick an order in which we visit the elements of U and V. The simplest thing to do is pick an order, e.g., row-by-row, for the elements of U and V, and visit them in round-robin fashion. Note that just because we optimized an element once does not mean we cannot find a better value for that element after other elements have been adjusted. Thus, we need to visit elements repeatedly, until we have reason to believe that no further improvements are possible.

Alternatively, we can follow many different optimization paths from a single starting value by randomly picking the element to optimize. To make sure that every element is considered in each round, we could instead choose a permutation of the elements and follow that order for every round.

Converging to a Minimum

Ideally, at some point the RMSE becomes 0, and we know we cannot do better. In practice, since there are normally many more nonblank elements in M than there are elements in U and V together, we have no right to expect that we can reduce the RMSE to 0. Thus, we have to detect when there is little benefit to be had in revisiting elements of U and/or V. We can track the amount of improvement in the RMSE obtained in one round of the optimization, and stop when that improvement falls below a threshold. A small variation is to observe the improvements resulting from the optimization of individual elements, and stop when the maximum improvement during a round is below a threshold.

Avoiding Overfitting

One problem that often arises when performing a UV-decomposition is that we arrive at one of the many local minima that conform well to the given data, but picks up values in the data that don't reflect well the underlying process that gives rise to the data. That is, although the RMSE may be small on the given data, it doesn't do well predicting future data. There are several things that can be done to cope with this problem, which is called *overfitting* by statisticians.

(1) Avoid favoring the first components to be optimized by only moving the value of a component a fraction of the way, say half way, from its current value toward its optimized value.

(2) Stop revisiting elements of U and V well before the process has converged.

(3) Take several different UV decompositions, and when predicting a new entry in the matrix M, take the average of the results of using each decomposition.

Gradient Descent

The technique for finding a UV-decomposition discussed in Section 9.4 is an example of *gradient descent*. We are given some data points – the nonblank elements of the matrix M – and for each data point we find the direction of change that most decreases the error function: the RMSE between the current UV product and M. We shall have much more to say about gradient descent in Section 12.3.4. It is also worth noting that while we have described the method as visiting each nonblank point of M several times until we approach a minimum-error decomposition, that may well be too much work on a large matrix M. Thus, an alternative approach has us look at only a randomly chosen fraction of the data when seeking to minimize the error. This approach, called *stochastic gradient descent* is discussed in Section 12.3.5.

9.4.6 Exercises for Section 9.4

EXERCISE 9.4.1 Starting with the decomposition of Fig. 9.10, we may choose any of the 20 entries in U or V to optimize first. Perform this first optimization step assuming we choose: (a) u_{32} (b) v_{41}.

EXERCISE 9.4.2 If we wish to start out, as in Fig. 9.10, with all U and V entries set to the same value, what value minimizes the RMSE for the matrix M of our running example?

EXERCISE 9.4.3 Starting with the U and V matrices in Fig. 9.16, do the following in order:

(a) Reconsider the value of u_{11}. Find its new best value, given the changes that have been made so far.

(b) Then choose the best value for u_{52}.

(c) Then choose the best value for v_{22}.

EXERCISE 9.4.4 Derive the formula for y (the optimum value of element v_{rs} given at the end of Section 9.4.4.

EXERCISE 9.4.5 Normalize the matrix M of our running example by:

(a) First subtracting from each element the average of its row, and then subtracting from each element the average of its (modified) column.

(b) First subtracting from each element the average of its column, and then subtracting from each element the average of its (modified) row.

Are there any differences in the results of (a) and (b)?

9.5   The Netflix Challenge

A significant boost to research into recommendation systems was given when NetFlix offered a prize of $1,000,000 to the first person or team to beat their own recommendation algorithm, called CineMatch, by 10%. After over three years of work, the prize was awarded in September, 2009.

The Netflix challenge consisted of a published dataset, giving the ratings by approximately half a million users on (typically small subsets of) approximately 17,000 movies. This data was selected from a larger dataset, and proposed algorithms were tested on their ability to predict the ratings in a secret remainder of the larger dataset. The information for each (user, movie) pair in the published dataset included a rating (1–5 stars) and the date on which the rating was made.

The RMSE was used to measure the performance of algorithms. CineMatch has an RMSE of approximately 0.95; i.e., the typical rating would be off by almost one full star. To win the prize, it was necessary that your algorithm have an RMSE that was at most 90% of the RMSE of CineMatch.

The bibliographic notes for this chapter include references to descriptions of the winning algorithms. Here, we mention some interesting and perhaps unintuitive facts about the challenge.

- CineMatch was not a very good algorithm. In fact, it was discovered early that the obvious algorithm of predicting, for the rating by user u on movie m, the average of:

  (1)The average rating given by u on all rated movies and

  (2)The average of the ratings for movie m by all users who rated that movie.

  was only 3% worse than CineMatch.

- The UV-decomposition algorithm described in Section 9.4 was found by three students (Michael Harris, Jeffrey Wang, and David Kamm) to give a 7% improvement over CineMatch, when coupled with normalization and a few other tricks.

- The winning entry was actually a combination of several different algorithms that had been developed independently. A second team, which submitted an entry that would have won, had it been submitted a few minutes earlier, also was a blend of independent algorithms. This strategy – combining different algorithms – has been used before in a number of hard problems and is something worth remembering.

- Several attempts have been made to use the data contained in IMDB, the Internet movie database, to match the names of movies from the Netflix challenge with their names in IMDB, and thus extract useful information not contained in the Netflix data itself. IMDB has information about actors and directors, and classifies movies into one or more of 28 genres. It was found that genre and other information was not useful. One possible reason is the machine-learning algorithms were able to discover the relevant information anyway, and a second is that the entity resolution problem of matching movie names as given in Netflix and IMDB data is not that easy to solve exactly.

- Time of rating turned out to be useful. It appears there are movies that are more likely to be appreciated by people who rate it immediately after viewing than by those who wait a while and then rate it. "Patch Adams" was given as an example of such a movie. Conversely, there are other movies that were not liked by those who rated it immediately, but were better appreciated after a while; "Memento" was cited as an example. While one cannot tease out of the data information about how long was the delay between viewing and rating, it is generally safe to assume that most people see a movie shortly after it comes out. Thus, one can examine the ratings of any movie to see if its ratings have an upward or downward slope with time.

9.6   Summary of Chapter 9

- *Utility Matrices*: Recommendation systems deal with users and items. A utility matrix offers known information about the degree to which a user likes an item. Normally, most entries are unknown, and the essential problem of recommending items to users is predicting the values of the unknown entries based on the values of the known entries.

- *Two Classes of Recommendation Systems*: These systems attempt to predict a user's response to an item by discovering similar items and the response of the user to those. One class of recommendation system is content-based; it measures similarity by looking for common features of the items. A second class of recommendation system uses collaborative filtering; these measure similarity of users by their item preferences and/or measure similarity of items by the users who like them.

- *Item Profiles*: These consist of features of items. Different kinds of items have different features on which content-based similarity can be based. Features of documents are typically important or unusual words. Products have attributes such as screen size for a television. Media such as movies have a genre and details such as actor or performer. Tags can also be used as features if they can be acquired from interested users.

- *User Profiles*: A content-based collaborative filtering system can construct profiles for users by measuring the frequency with which features appear in the items the user likes. We can then estimate the degree to which a user will like an item by the closeness of the item's profile to the user's profile.

- *Classification of Items*: An alternative to constructing a user profile is to build a classifier for each user, e.g., a decision tree. The row of the utility matrix for that user becomes the training data, and the classifier must predict the response of the user to all items, whether or not the row had an entry for that item.

◆ *Similarity of Rows and Columns of the Utility Matrix*: Collaborative filtering algorithms must measure the similarity of rows and/or columns of the utility matrix. Jaccard distance is appropriate when the matrix consists only of 1s and blanks (for "not rated"). Cosine distance works for more general values in the utility matrix. It is often useful to normalize the utility matrix by subtracting the average value (either by row, by column, or both) before measuring the cosine distance.

◆ *Clustering Users and Items*: Since the utility matrix tends to be mostly blanks, distance measures such as Jaccard or cosine often have too little data with which to compare two rows or two columns. A preliminary step or steps, in which similarity is used to cluster users and/or items into small groups with strong similarity, can help provide more common components with which to compare rows or columns.

◆ *UV-Decomposition*: One way of predicting the blank values in a utility matrix is to find two long, thin matrices U and V, whose product is an approximation to the given utility matrix. Since the matrix product UV gives values for all user-item pairs, that value can be used to predict the value of a blank in the utility matrix. The intuitive reason this method makes sense is that often there are a relatively small number of issues (that number is the "thin" dimension of U and V) that determine whether or not a user likes an item.

◆ *Root-Mean-Square Error*: A good measure of how close the product UV is to the given utility matrix is the RMSE (root-mean-square error). The RMSE is computed by averaging the square of the differences between UV and the utility matrix, in those elements where the utility matrix is nonblank. The square root of this average is the RMSE.

◆ *Computing U and V*: One way of finding a good choice for U and V in a UV-decomposition is to start with arbitrary matrices U and V. Repeatedly adjust one of the elements of U or V to minimize the RMSE between the product UV and the given utility matrix. The process converges to a local optimum, although to have a good chance of obtaining a global optimum we must either repeat the process from many starting matrices, or search from the starting point in many different ways.

◆ *The Netflix Challenge*: An important driver of research into recommendation systems was the Netflix challenge. A prize of $1,000,000 was offered for a contestant who could produce an algorithm that was 10% better than Netflix's own algorithm at predicting movie ratings by users. The prize was awarded in Sept., 2009.

9.7   References for Chapter 9

[1] is a survey of recommendation systems as of 2005. The argument regarding the importance of the long tail in on-line systems is from [2], which was expanded into a book [3].

[8] discusses the use of computer games to extract tags for items.

See [5] for a discussion of item–item similarity and how Amazon designed its collaborative-filtering algorithm for product recommendations.

There are three papers describing the three algorithms that, in combination, won the NetFlix challenge. They are [4], [6], and [7].

[1] G. Adomavicius and A. Tuzhilin, "Towards the next generation of recommender systems: a survey of the state-of-the-art and possible extensions," *IEEE Trans. on Data and Knowledge Engineering* **17**:6, pp. 734–749, 2005.

[2] C. Anderson,

http://www.wired.com/wired/archive/12.10/tail.html

2004.

[3] C. Anderson, *The Long Tail: Why the Future of Business is Selling Less of More*, Hyperion Books, New York, 2006.

[4] Y. Koren, "The BellKor solution to the Netflix grand prize,"

www.netflixprize.com/assets/GrandPrize2009_BPC_BellKor.pdf

2009.

[5] G. Linden, B. Smith, and J. York, "Amazon.com recommendations: item-to-item collaborative filtering," *Internet Computing* **7**:1, pp. 76–80, 2003.

[6] M. Piotte and M. Chabbert, "The Pragmatic Theory solution to the Netflix grand prize,"

www.netflixprize.com/assets/
GrandPrize2009_BPC_PragmaticTheory.pdf

2009.

[7] A. Toscher, M. Jahrer, and R. Bell, "The BigChaos solution to the Netflix grand prize,"

www.netflixprize.com/assets/GrandPrize2009_BPC_BigChaos.pdf

2009.

[8] L. von Ahn, "Games with a purpose," *IEEE Computer Magazine*, pp. 96–98, June 2006.

10 Mining Social-Network Graphs

There is much information to be gained by analyzing the large-scale data that is derived from social networks. The best-known example of a social network is the "friends" relation found on sites like Facebook. However, as we shall see there are many other sources of data that connect people or other entities.

In this chapter, we shall study techniques for analyzing such networks. An important question about a social network is how to identify "communities," that is, subsets of the nodes (people or other entities that form the network) with unusually strong connections. Some of the techniques used to identify communities are similar to the clustering algorithms we discussed in Chapter 7. However, communities almost never partition the set of nodes in a network. Rather, communities usually overlap. For example, you may belong to several communities of friends or classmates. The people from one community tend to know each other, but people from two different communities rarely know each other. You would not want to be assigned to only one of the communities, nor would it make sense to cluster all the people from all your communities into one cluster.

Also in this chapter we explore efficient algorithms for discovering other properties of graphs. We look at "simrank," a way to discover similarities among nodes of a graph. One of the interesting applications of simrank is that it gives us a way to identify communities as sets of "similar" nodes. We then explore triangle counting as a way to measure the connectedness of a community. In addition, we give efficient algorithms for exact and approximate measurement of the neighborhood sizes of nodes in a graph, and we look at efficient algorithms for computing the transitive closure.

10.1 Social Networks as Graphs

We begin our discussion of social networks by introducing a graph model. Not every graph is a suitable representation of what we intuitively regard as a social network. We therefore discuss the idea of "locality," the property of social networks that says nodes and edges of the graph tend to cluster in communities. This section also looks at some of the kinds of social networks that occur in practice.

10.1.1 What is a Social Network?

When we think of a social network, we think of Facebook, Twitter, Google+, or another website that is called a "social network," and indeed this kind of network is representative of the broader class of networks called "social." The essential characteristics of a social network are:

(1) There is a collection of entities that participate in the network. Typically, these entities are people, but they could be something else entirely. We shall discuss some other examples in Section 10.1.3.

(2) There is at least one relationship between entities of the network. On Facebook or its ilk, this relationship is called *friends*. Sometimes the relationship is all-or-nothing; two people are either friends or they are not. However, in other examples of social networks, the relationship has a degree. This degree could be discrete; e.g., friends, family, acquaintances, or none as in Google+. It could be a real number; an example would be the fraction of the average day that two people spend talking to each other.

(3) There is an assumption of nonrandomness or locality. This condition is the hardest to formalize, but the intuition is that relationships tend to cluster. That is, if entity A is related to both B and C, then there is a higher probability than average that B and C are related.

10.1.2 Social Networks as Graphs

Social networks are naturally modeled as graphs, which we sometimes refer to as a *social graph*. The entities are the nodes, and an edge connects two nodes if the nodes are related by the relationship that characterizes the network. If there is a degree associated with the relationship, this degree is represented by labeling the edges. Often, social graphs are undirected, as for the Facebook friends graph. But they can be directed graphs, as for example the graphs of followers on Twitter or Google+.

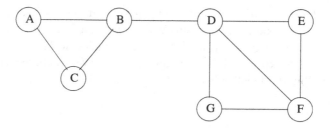

Figure 10.1 Example of a small social network

EXAMPLE 10.1 Figure 10.1 is an example of a tiny social network. The entities are the nodes A through G. The relationship, which we might think of as "friends," is represented by the edges. For instance, B is friends with A, C, and D.

Is this graph really typical of a social network, in the sense that it exhibits locality of relationships? First, note that the graph has nine edges out of the $\binom{7}{2} = 21$ pairs of nodes that could have had an edge between them. Suppose X, Y, and Z are nodes of Fig. 10.1, with edges between X and Y and also between X and Z. What would we expect the probability of an edge between Y and Z to be? If the graph were large, that probability would be very close to the fraction of the pairs of nodes that have edges between them, i.e., $9/21 = .429$ in this case. However, because the graph is small, there is a noticeable difference between the true probability and the ratio of the number of edges to the number of pairs of nodes. Since we already know there are edges (X, Y) and (X, Z), there are only seven edges remaining. Those seven edges could run between any of the 19 remaining pairs of nodes. Thus, the probability of an edge (Y, Z) is $7/19 = .368$.

Now, we must compute the probability that the edge (Y, Z) exists in Fig. 10.1, given that edges (X, Y) and (X, Z) exist. What we shall actually count is pairs of nodes that could be Y and Z, without worrying about which node is Y and which is Z. If X is A, then Y and Z must be B and C, in some order. Since the edge (B, C) exists, A contributes one positive example (where the edge does exist) and no negative examples (where the edge is absent). The cases where X is C, E, or G are essentially the same. In each case, X has only two neighbors, and the edge between the neighbors exists. Thus, we have seen four positive examples and zero negative examples so far.

Now, consider $X = F$. F has three neighbors, D, E, and G. There are edges between two of the three pairs of neighbors, but no edge between G and E. Thus, we see two more positive examples and we see our first negative example. If $X = B$, there are again three neighbors, but only one pair of neighbors, A and C, has an edge. Thus, we have two more negative examples, and one positive example, for a total of seven positive and three negative. Finally, when $X = D$, there are four neighbors. Of the six pairs of neighbors, only two have edges between them.

Thus, the total number of positive examples is nine and the total number of negative examples is seven. We see that in Fig. 10.1, the fraction of times the third edge exists is thus $9/16 = .563$. This fraction is considerably greater than the .368 expected value for that fraction. We conclude that Fig. 10.1 does indeed exhibit the locality expected in a social network. □

10.1.3 Varieties of Social Networks

There are many examples of social networks other than "friends" networks. Here, let us enumerate some of the other examples of networks that also exhibit locality of relationships.

Telephone Networks

Here the nodes represent phone numbers, which are really individuals. There is an edge between two nodes if a call has been placed between those phones in some fixed period of time, such as last month, or "ever." The edges could be weighted by the number of calls made between these phones during the period. Communities in a telephone network will form from groups of people that communicate frequently: groups of friends, members of a club, or people working at the same company, for example.

Email Networks

The nodes represent email addresses, which are again individuals. An edge represents the fact that there was at least one email in at least one direction between the two addresses. Alternatively, we may only place an edge if there were emails in both directions. In that way, we avoid viewing spammers as "friends" with all their victims. Another approach is to label edges as *weak* or *strong*. Strong edges represent communication in both directions, while weak edges indicate that the communication was in one direction only. The communities seen in email networks come from the same sorts of groupings we mentioned in connection with telephone networks. A similar sort of network involves people who text other people through their cell phones.

Collaboration Networks

Nodes represent individuals who have published research papers. There is an edge between two individuals who published one or more papers jointly. Optionally, we can label edges by the number of joint publications. The communities in this network are authors working on a particular topic.

An alternative view of the same data is as a graph in which the nodes are papers. Two papers are connected by an edge if they have at least one author in common. Now, we form communities that are collections of papers on the same topic.

There are several other kinds of data that form two networks in a similar way. For example, we can look at the people who edit Wikipedia articles and the articles that they edit. Two editors are connected if they have edited an article in common. The communities are groups of editors that are interested in the same subject. Dually, we can build a network of articles, and connect articles if they have been edited by the same person. Here, we get communities of articles on similar or related subjects.

In fact, the data involved in collaborative filtering, as was discussed in Chapter 9, often can be viewed as forming a pair of networks, one for the customers and one for the products. Customers who buy the same sorts of products, e.g., science-fiction books, will form communities, and dually, products that are bought by the same customers will form communities, e.g., all science-fiction books.

Other Examples of Social Graphs

Many other phenomena give rise to graphs that look something like social graphs, especially exhibiting locality. Examples include: information networks (documents, web graphs, patents), infrastructure networks (roads, planes, water pipes, powergrids), biological networks (genes, proteins, food-webs of animals eating each other), as well as other types, like product co-purchasing networks (e.g., Groupon).

10.1.4   Graphs With Several Node Types

There are other social phenomena that involve entities of different types. We just discussed, under the heading of "collaboration networks," several kinds of graphs that are really formed from two types of nodes. Authorship networks can be seen to have author nodes and paper nodes. In the discussion above, we built two social networks by eliminating the nodes of one of the two types, but we do not have to do that. We can rather think of the structure as a whole.

For a more complex example, users at a site like del.icio.us place tags on Web pages. There are thus three different kinds of entities: users, tags, and pages. We might think that users were somehow connected if they tended to use the same tags frequently, or if they tended to tag the same pages. Similarly, tags could be considered related if they appeared on the same pages or were used by the same users, and pages could be considered similar if they had many of the same tags or were tagged by many of the same users.

The natural way to represent such information is as a k-partite graph for some $k > 1$. We met bipartite graphs, the case $k = 2$, in Section 8.3. In general, a *k-partite graph* consists of k disjoint sets of nodes, with no edges between nodes of the same set.

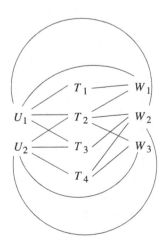

Figure 10.2 A tripartite graph representing users, tags, and Web pages

EXAMPLE 10.2   Figure 10.2 is an example of a tripartite graph (the case $k = 3$ of a k-partite graph). There are three sets of nodes, which we may think of as users $\{U_1, U_2\}$, tags $\{T_1, T_2, T_3, T_4\}$, and Web pages $\{W_1, W_2, W_3\}$. Notice that all edges connect nodes from two different sets. We may assume this graph represents information about the three kinds of entities. For example, the edge (U_1, T_2) means that user U_1 has placed the tag T_2 on at least one page. Note that the graph does not tell us a detail that could be important: who placed which tag on which page? To represent such ternary information would require a more complex representation, such as a database relation with three columns corresponding to users, tags, and pages.   □

10.1.5   Exercises for Section 10.1

EXERCISE 10.1.1   It is possible to think of the edges of one graph G as the nodes of another graph G'. We construct G' from G by the *dual construction*:

(1) If (X, Y) is an edge of G, then XY, representing the unordered set of X and Y is a node of G'. Note that XY and YX represent the same node of G', not two different nodes.

(2) If (X, Y) and (X, Z) are edges of G, then in G' there is an edge between XY and XZ. That is, nodes of G' have an edge between them if the edges of G that these nodes represent have a node (of G) in common.

(a) If we apply the dual construction to a network of friends, what is the interpretation of the edges of the resulting graph?

(b) Apply the dual construction to the graph of Fig. 10.1.

! (c) How is the degree of a node XY in G' related to the degrees of X and Y in G?

!! (d) The number of edges of G' is related to the degrees of the nodes of G by a certain formula. Discover that formula.

! (e) What we called the dual is not a true dual, because applying the construction to G' does not necessarily yield a graph isomorphic to G. Give an example graph G where the dual of G' *is* isomorphic to G and another example where the dual of G' is *not* isomorphic to G.

10.2   Clustering of Social-Network Graphs

An important aspect of social networks is that they contain communities of entities that are connected by many edges. These typically correspond to groups of friends at school or groups of researchers interested in the same topic, for example. In this section, we shall consider clustering of the graph as a way to identify communities. It turns out that the techniques we learned in Chapter 7 are generally unsuitable for the problem of clustering social-network graphs.

10.2.1   Distance Measures for Social-Network Graphs

If we were to apply standard clustering techniques to a social-network graph, our first step would be to define a distance measure. When the edges of the graph have labels, these labels might be usable as a distance measure, depending on what they represented. But when the edges are unlabeled, as in a "friends" graph, there is not much we can do to define a suitable distance.

Our first instinct is to assume that nodes are close if they have an edge between them and distant if not. Thus, we could say that the distance $d(x, y)$ is 0 if there is an edge (x, y) and 1 if there is no such edge. We could use any other two values, such as 1 and ∞, as long as the distance is closer when there is an edge.

Neither of these two-valued "distance measures" – 0 and 1 or 1 and ∞ – is a true distance measure. The reason is that they violate the triangle inequality when there are three nodes, with two edges between them. That is, if there are edges (A, B) and (B, C), but no edge (A, C), then the distance from A to C exceeds the sum of the distances from A to B to C. We could fix this problem by using, say, distance 1 for an edge and distance 1.5 for a missing edge. But the problem with two-valued distance functions is not limited to the triangle inequality, as we shall see in the next section.

10.2.2   Applying Standard Clustering Methods

Recall from Section 7.1.2 that there are two general approaches to clustering: hierarchical (agglomerative) and point-assignment. Let us consider how each of these would work on a social-network graph. First, consider the hierarchical methods covered in Section 7.2. In particular, suppose we use as the intercluster distance the minimum distance between nodes of the two clusters.

Hierarchical clustering of a social-network graph starts by combining some two nodes that are connected by an edge. Successively, edges that are not between two nodes of the same cluster would be chosen randomly to combine the clusters to which their two nodes belong. The choices would be random, because all distances represented by an edge are the same.

EXAMPLE 10.3   Consider again the graph of Fig. 10.1, repeated here as Fig. 10.3. First, let us agree on what the communities are. At the highest level, it appears that there are two communities $\{A, B, C\}$ and $\{D, E, F, G\}$. However, we could also view $\{D, E, F\}$ and $\{D, F, G\}$ as two subcommunities of $\{D, E, F, G\}$; these two subcommunities overlap in two of their members, and thus could never be identified by a pure clustering algorithm. Finally, we could consider each pair of individuals that are connected by an edge as a community of size 2, although such communities are uninteresting.

The problem with hierarchical clustering of a graph like that of Fig. 10.3 is that at some point we are likely to chose to combine B and D, even though they surely belong in different clusters. The reason we are likely to combine B and D is that D, and any cluster containing it, is as close to B and any cluster

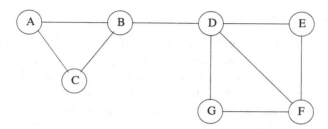

Figure 10.3 Repeat of Fig. 10.1

containing it, as A and C are to B. There is even a 1/9 probability that the first thing we do is to combine B and D into one cluster.

There are things we can do to reduce the probability of error. We can run hierarchical clustering several times and pick the run that gives the most coherent clusters. We can use a more sophisticated method for measuring the distance between clusters of more than one node, as discussed in Section 7.2.3. But no matter what we do, in a large graph with many communities there is a significant chance that in the initial phases we shall use some edges that connect two nodes that do not belong together in any large community. □

Now consider a point-assignment approach to clustering social networks. Again, the fact that all edges are at the same distance will introduce a number of random factors that will lead to some nodes being assigned to the wrong cluster. An example should illustrate the point.

EXAMPLE 10.4 Suppose we try a k-means approach to clustering Fig. 10.3. As we want two clusters, we pick $k = 2$. If we pick two starting nodes at random, they might both be in the same cluster. If, as suggested in Section 7.3.2, we start with one randomly chosen node and then pick another as far away as possible, we don't do much better; we could thereby pick any pair of nodes not connected by an edge, e.g., E and G in Fig. 10.3.

However, suppose we do get two suitable starting nodes, such as B and F. We shall then assign A and C to the cluster of B and assign E and G to the cluster of F. But D is as close to B as it is to F, so it could go either way, even though it is "obvious" that D belongs with F.

If the decision about where to place D is deferred until we have assigned some other nodes to the clusters, then we shall probably make the right decision. For instance, if we assign a node to the cluster with the shortest average distance to all the nodes of the cluster, then D should be assigned to the cluster of F, as long as we do not try to place D before any other nodes are assigned. However, in large graphs, we shall surely make mistakes on some of the first nodes we place. □

10.2.3   Betweenness

Since there are problems with standard clustering methods, several specialized clustering techniques have been developed to find communities in social networks. In this section we shall consider one of the simplest, based on finding the edges that are least likely to be inside a community.

Define the *betweenness* of an edge (a, b) to be the number of pairs of nodes x and y such that the edge (a, b) lies on the shortest path between x and y. To be more precise, since there can be several shortest paths between x and y, edge (a, b) is credited with the fraction of those shortest paths that include the edge (a, b). As in golf, a high score is bad. It suggests that the edge (a, b) runs between two different communities; that is, a and b do not belong to the same community.

EXAMPLE 10.5   In Fig. 10.3 the edge (B, D) has the highest betweenness, as should surprise no one. In fact, this edge is on every shortest path between any of A, B, and C to any of D, E, F, and G. Its betweenness is therefore $3 \times 4 = 12$. In contrast, the edge (D, F) is on only four shortest paths: those from A, B, C, and D to F.   □

10.2.4   The Girvan–Newman Algorithm

In order to exploit the betweenness of edges, we need to calculate the number of shortest paths going through each edge. We shall describe a method called the *Girvan-Newman* (GN) Algorithm, which visits each node X once and computes the number of shortest paths from X to each of the other nodes that go through each of the edges. The algorithm begins by performing a breadth-first search (BFS) of the graph, starting at the node X. Note that the level of each node in the BFS presentation is the length of the shortest path from X to that node. Thus, the edges that go between nodes at the same level can never be part of a shortest path from X.

Edges between levels are called *DAG* edges ("DAG" stands for directed, acyclic graph). Each DAG edge will be part of at least one shortest path from root X. If there is a DAG edge (Y, Z), where Y is at the level above Z (i.e., closer to the root), then we shall call Y a *parent* of Z and Z a *child* of Y, although parents are not necessarily unique in a DAG as they would be in a tree.

EXAMPLE 10.6   Figure 10.4 is a breadth-first presentation of the graph of Fig. 10.3, starting at node E. Solid edges are DAG edges and dashed edges connect nodes at the same level.   □

The second step of the GN algorithm is to label each node by the number of shortest paths that reach it from the root. Start by labeling the root 1. Then, from the top down, label each node Y by the sum of the labels of its parents.

EXAMPLE 10.7   In Fig. 10.4 are the labels for each of the nodes. First, label the root E with 1. At level 1 are the nodes D and F. Each has only E as a parent, so

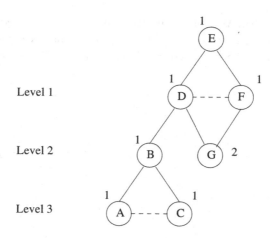

Figure 10.4 Step 1 of the Girvan-Newman Algorithm

they too are labeled 1. Nodes B and G are at level 2. B has only D as a parent, so B's label is the same as the label of D, which is 1. However, G has parents D and F, so its label is the sum of their labels, or 2. Finally, at level 3, A and C each have only parent B, so their labels are the label of B, which is 1. □

The third and final step is to calculate for each edge e the sum over all nodes Y of the fraction of shortest paths from the root X to Y that go through e. This calculation involves computing this sum for both nodes and edges, from the bottom. Each node other than the root is given a *credit* of 1, representing the shortest path to that node. This credit may be divided among nodes and edges above, since there could be several different shortest paths to the node. The rules for the calculation are as follows:

(1) Each leaf in the DAG (a *leaf* is a node with no DAG edges to nodes at levels below) gets a credit of 1.
(2) Each node that is not a leaf gets a credit equal to 1 plus the sum of the credits of the DAG edges from that node to the level below.
(3) A DAG edge e entering node Z from the level above is given a share of the credit of Z proportional to the fraction of shortest paths from the root to Z that go through e. Formally, let the parents of Z be $Y_1, Y_2, \ldots, Y_k$. Let p_i be the number of shortest paths from the root to Y_i; this number was computed in Step 2 and is illustrated by the labels in Fig. 10.4. Then the credit for the edge (Y_i, Z) is the credit of Z times p_i divided by $\sum_{j=1}^{k} p_j$.

After performing the credit calculation with each node as the root, we sum the credits for each edge. Then, since each shortest path will have been discovered twice – once when each of its endpoints is the root – we must divide the credit for each edge by 2.

EXAMPLE 10.8   Let us perform the credit calculation for the BFS presentation of Fig. 10.4. We shall start from level 3 and proceed upwards. First, A and C, being leaves, get credit 1. Each of these nodes have only one parent, so their credit is given to the edges (B, A) and (B, C), respectively.

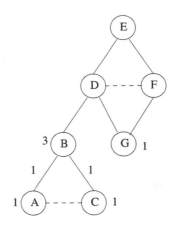

Figure 10.5 Final step of the Girvan-Newman Algorithm – levels 3 and 2

At level 2, G is a leaf, so it gets credit 1. B is not a leaf, so it gets credit equal to 1 plus the credits on the DAG edges entering it from below. Since both these edges have credit 1, the credit of B is 3. Intuitively 3 represents the fact that all shortest paths from E to A, B, and C go through B. Figure 10.5 shows the credits assigned so far.

Now, let us proceed to level 1. B has only one parent, D, so the edge (D, B) gets the entire credit of B, which is 3. However, G has two parents, D and F. We therefore need to divide the credit of 1 that G has between the edges (D, G) and (F, G). In what proportion do we divide? If you examine the labels of Fig. 10.4, you see that both D and F have label 1, representing the fact that there is one shortest path from E to each of these nodes. Thus, we give half the credit of G to each of these edges; i.e., their credit is each $1/(1 + 1) = 0.5$. Had the labels of D and F in Fig. 10.4 been 5 and 3, meaning there were five shortest paths to D and only three to F, then the credit of edge (D, G) would have been 5/8 and the credit of edge (F, G) would have been 3/8.

Now, we can assign credits to the nodes at level 1. D gets 1 plus the credits of the edges entering it from below, which are 3 and 0.5. That is, the credit of D is 4.5. The credit of F is 1 plus the credit of the edge (F, G), or 1.5. Finally, the edges (E, D) and (E, F) receive the credit of D and F, respectively, since each of these nodes has only one parent. These credits are all shown in Fig. 10.6.

The credit on each of the edges in Fig. 10.6 is the contribution to the betweenness of that edge due to shortest paths from E. For example, this contribution for the edge (E, D) is 4.5. □

To complete the betweenness calculation, we have to repeat this calculation

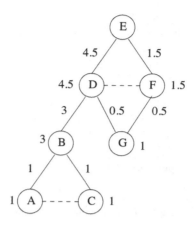

Figure 10.6 Final step of the Girvan–Newman Algorithm – completing the credit calculation

for every node as the root and sum the contributions. Finally, we must divide by 2 to get the true betweenness, since every shortest path will be discovered twice, once for each of its endpoints.

10.2.5 Using Betweenness to Find Communities

The betweenness scores for the edges of a graph behave something like a distance measure on the nodes of the graph. It is not exactly a distance measure, because it is not defined for pairs of nodes that are unconnected by an edge, and might not satisfy the triangle inequality even when defined. However, we can cluster by taking the edges in order of increasing betweenness and add them to the graph one at a time. At each step, the connected components of the graph form some clusters. The higher the betweenness we allow, the more edges we get, and the larger the clusters become.

More commonly, this idea is expressed as a process of edge removal. Start with the graph and all its edges; then remove edges with the highest betweenness, until the graph has broken into a suitable number of connected components.

EXAMPLE 10.9 Let us start with our running example, the graph of Fig. 10.1. We see it with the betweenness for each edge in Fig. 10.7. The calculation of the betweenness will be left to the reader. The only tricky part of the count is to observe that between E and G there are two shortest paths, one going through D and the other through F. Thus, each of the edges (D, E), (E, F), (D, G), and (G, F) are credited with half a shortest path.

Clearly, edge (B, D) has the highest betweenness, so it is removed first. That leaves us with exactly the communities we observed make the most sense, namely: $\{A, B, C\}$ and $\{D, E, F, G\}$. However, we can continue to remove edges. Next to leave are (A, B) and (B, C) with a score of 5, followed by (D, E) and (D, G) with

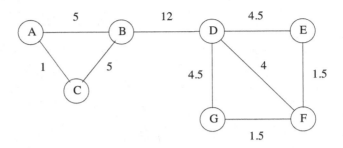

Figure 10.7 Betweenness scores for the graph of Fig. 10.1

a score of 4.5. Then (D, F), whose score is 4, would leave the graph. We see in Fig. 10.8 the graph that remains.

Figure 10.8 All the edges with betweenness 4 or more have been removed

The "communities" of Fig. 10.8 look strange. One implication is that A and C are more closely knit to each other than to B. That is, in some sense B is a "traitor" to the community $\{A, B, C\}$ because he has a friend D outside that community. Likewise, D can be seen as a "traitor" to the group $\{D, E, F, G\}$, which is why in Fig. 10.8, only E, F, and G remain connected. □

10.2.6   Exercises for Section 10.2

EXERCISE 10.2.1   Figure 10.9 is an example of a social-network graph. Use the Girvan–Newman approach to find the number of shortest paths from each of the following nodes that pass through each of the edges. (a) A (b) B.

EXERCISE 10.2.2   Using symmetry, the calculations of Exercise 10.2.1 are all you need to compute the betweenness of each edge. Do the calculation.

EXERCISE 10.2.3   Using the betweenness values from Exercise 10.2.2, determine reasonable candidates for the communities in Fig. 10.9 by removing all edges with a betweenness above some threshold.

Speeding Up the Betweenness Calculation

If we apply the method of Section 10.2.4 to a graph of n nodes and e edges, it takes $O(ne)$ running time to compute the betweenness of each edge. That is, BFS from a single node takes $O(e)$ time, as do the two labeling steps. We must start from each node, so there are n of the computations described in Section 10.2.4.

If the graph is large – and even a million nodes is large when the algorithm takes $O(ne)$ time – we cannot afford to execute it as suggested. However, if we pick a subset of the nodes at random and use these as the roots of breadth-first searches, we can get an approximation to the betweenness of each edge that will serve in most applications.

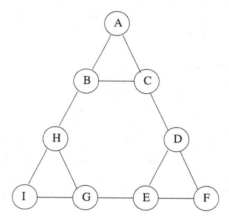

Figure 10.9 Graph for exercises

10.3 Direct Discovery of Communities

In the previous section we searched for communities by partitioning all the individuals in a social network. While this approach is relatively efficient, it does have several limitations. It is not possible to place an individual in two different communities, and everyone is assigned to a community. In this section, we shall see a technique for discovering communities directly by looking for subsets of the nodes that have a relatively large number of edges among them. Interestingly, the technique for doing this search on a large graph involves finding large frequent itemsets, as was discussed in Chapter 6.

10.3.1 Finding Cliques

Our first thought about how we could find sets of nodes with many edges between them is to start by finding a large *clique* (a set of nodes with edges between any two of them). However, that task is not easy. Not only is finding maximal cliques NP-complete, but it is among the hardest of the NP-complete problems in the sense that even approximating the maximal clique is hard. Further, it is possible to have a set of nodes with almost all edges between them, and yet have only relatively small cliques.

EXAMPLE 10.10 Suppose our graph has nodes numbered $1, 2, \ldots, n$ and there is an edge between two nodes i and j unless i and j have the same remainder when divided by k. Then the fraction of possible edges that are actually present is approximately $(k-1)/k$. There are many cliques of size k, of which $\{1, 2, \ldots, k\}$ is but one example.

Yet there are no cliques larger than k. To see why, observe that any set of $k+1$ nodes has two that leave the same remainder when divided by k. This point is an application of the "pigeonhole principle." Since there are only k different remainders possible, we cannot have distinct remainders for each of $k + 1$ nodes. Thus, no set of $k + 1$ nodes can be a clique in this graph. □

10.3.2 Complete Bipartite Graphs

Recall our discussion of bipartite graphs from Section 8.3. A *complete bipartite graph* consists of s nodes on one side and t nodes on the other side, with all st possible edges between the nodes of one side and the other present. We denote this graph by $K_{s,t}$. You should draw an analogy between complete bipartite graphs as subgraphs of general bipartite graphs and cliques as subgraphs of general graphs. In fact, a clique of s nodes is often referred to as a *complete graph* and denoted K_s, while a complete bipartite subgraph is sometimes called a *bi-clique*.

While as we saw in Example 10.10, it is not possible to guarantee that a graph with many edges necessarily has a large clique, it *is* possible to guarantee that a bipartite graph with many edges has a large complete bipartite subgraph.[1] We can regard a complete bipartite subgraph (or a clique if we discovered a large one) as the nucleus of a community and add to it nodes with many edges to existing members of the community. If the graph itself is k-partite as discussed in Section 10.1.4, then we can take nodes of two types and the edges between them to form a bipartite graph. In this bipartite graph, we can search for complete bipartite subgraphs as the nuclei of communities. For instance, in Example 10.2, we could focus on the tag and page nodes of a graph like Fig. 10.2 and try to find communities of tags and Web pages. Such a community would consist of related tags and related pages that deserved many or all of those tags.

However, we can also use complete bipartite subgraphs for community finding in ordinary graphs where nodes all have the same type. Divide the nodes into two equal groups at random. If a community exists, then we would expect about half its nodes to fall into each group, and we would expect that about half its edges

---

[1] It is important to understand that we do not mean a *generated* subgraph – one formed by selecting some nodes and including all edges. In this context, we only require that there be edges between any pair of nodes on different sides. It is also possible that some nodes on the same side are connected by edges as well.

would go between groups. Thus, we still have a reasonable chance of identifying a large complete bipartite subgraph in the community. To this nucleus we can add nodes from either of the two groups, if they have edges to many of the nodes already identified as belonging to the community.

10.3.3 Finding Complete Bipartite Subgraphs

Suppose we are given a large bipartite graph G, and we want to find instances of $K_{s,t}$ within it. It is possible to view the problem of finding instances of $K_{s,t}$ within G as one of finding frequent itemsets. For this purpose, let the "items" be the nodes on one side of G, which we shall call the *left* side. We assume that the instance of $K_{s,t}$ we are looking for has t nodes on the left side, and we shall also assume for efficiency that $t \leq s$. The "baskets" correspond to the nodes on the other side of G (the *right* side). The members of the basket for node v are the nodes of the left side to which v is connected. Finally, let the support threshold be s, the number of nodes that the instance of $K_{s,t}$ has on the right side.

We can now state the problem of finding instances of $K_{s,t}$ as that of finding frequent itemsets F of size t. That is, if a set of t nodes on the left side is frequent, then they all occur together in at least s baskets. But the baskets are the nodes on the right side. Each basket corresponds to a node that is connected to all t of the nodes in F. Thus, the frequent itemset of size t and s of the baskets in which all those items appear form an instance of $K_{s,t}$.

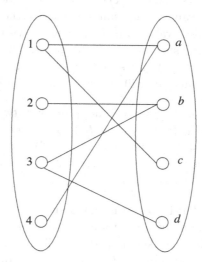

Figure 10.10 The bipartite graph from Fig. 8.1

EXAMPLE 10.11   Recall the bipartite graph of Fig. 8.1, which we repeat here as Fig. 10.10. The left side is the nodes $\{1, 2, 3, 4\}$ and the right side is $\{a, b, c, d\}$. The latter are the baskets, so basket a consists of "items" 1 and 4; that is, $a = \{1, 4\}$. Similarly, $b = \{2, 3\}$, $c = \{1\}$ and $d = \{3\}$.

If $s = 2$ and $t = 1$, we must find itemsets of size 1 that appear in at least two baskets. $\{1\}$ is one such itemset, and $\{3\}$ is another. However, in this tiny example there are no itemsets for larger, more interesting, values of s and t, such as $s = t = 2$. □

10.3.4 Why Complete Bipartite Graphs Must Exist

We must now turn to the matter of demonstrating that any bipartite graph with a sufficiently high fraction of the edges present will have an instance of $K_{s,t}$. In what follows, assume that the graph G has n nodes on the left and another n nodes on the right. Assuming the two sides have the same number of nodes simplifies the calculation, but the argument generalizes to sides of any size. Finally, let d be the average degree of all nodes.

The argument involves counting the number of frequent itemsets of size t that a basket with d items contributes to. When we sum this number over all nodes on the right side, we get the total frequency of all the subsets of size t on the left. When we divide by $\binom{n}{t}$, we get the average frequency of all itemsets of size t. At least one must have a frequency that is at least average, so if this average is at least s, we know an instance of $K_{s,t}$ exists.

Now we provide the detailed calculation. Suppose the degree of the ith node on the right is d_i; that is, d_i is the size of the ith basket. Then this basket contributes to $\binom{d_i}{t}$ itemsets of size t. The total contribution of the n nodes on the right is $\sum_i \binom{d_i}{t}$. The value of this sum depends on the d_i, of course. However, we know that the average value of d_i is d. It is known that this sum is minimized when each d_i is d. We shall not prove this point, but a simple example will suggest the reasoning: since $\binom{d_i}{t}$ grows roughly as the tth power of d_i, moving 1 from a large d_i to some smaller d_j will reduce the sum of $\binom{d_i}{t} + \binom{d_j}{t}$.

EXAMPLE 10.12   Suppose there are only two nodes, $t = 2$, and the average degree of the nodes is 4. Then $d_1 + d_2 = 8$, and the sum of interest is $\binom{d_1}{2} + \binom{d_2}{2}$. If $d_1 = d_2 = 4$, then the sum is $\binom{4}{2} + \binom{4}{2} = 6 + 6 = 12$. However, if $d_1 = 5$ and $d_2 = 3$, the sum is $\binom{5}{2} + \binom{3}{2} = 10 + 3 = 13$. If $d_1 = 6$ and $d_2 = 2$, then the sum is $\binom{6}{2} + \binom{2}{2} = 15 + 1 = 16$. □

Thus, in what follows, we shall assume that all nodes have the average degree d. So doing minimizes the total contribution to the counts for the itemsets, and thus makes it least likely that there will be a frequent itemset (itemset with with support s or more) of size t. Observe the following:

- The total contribution of the n nodes on the right to the counts of the itemsets of size t is $n\binom{d}{t}$.

- The number of itemsets of size t is $\binom{n}{t}$.

- Thus, the average count of an itemset of size t is $n\binom{d}{t} / \binom{n}{t}$; this expression must be at least s if we are to argue that an instance of $K_{s,t}$ exists.

If we expand the binomial coefficients in terms of factorials, we find

$$n\binom{d}{t}\bigg/\binom{n}{t} = nd!(n-t)!t!/((d-t)!t!n!) =$$

$$n(d)(d-1)\cdots(d-t+1)/(n(n-1)\cdots(n-t+1))$$

To simplify the formula above, let us assume that n is much larger than d, and d is much larger than t. Then $d(d-1)\cdots(d-t+1)$ is approximately d^t, and $n(n-1)\cdots(n-t+1)$ is approximately n^t. We thus require that

$$n(d/n)^t \geq s$$

That is, if there is a community with n nodes on each side, the average degree of the nodes is d, and $n(d/n)^t \geq s$, then this community is guaranteed to have a complete bipartite subgraph $K_{s,t}$. Moreover, we can find the instance of $K_{s,t}$ efficiently, using the methods of Chapter 6, even if this small community is embedded in a much larger graph. That is, we can treat all nodes in the entire graph as baskets and as items, and run A-priori or one of its improvements on the entire graph, looking for sets of t items with support s.

EXAMPLE 10.13 Suppose there is a community with 100 nodes on each side, and the average degree of nodes is 50; i.e., half the possible edges exist. This community will have an instance of $K_{s,t}$, provided $100(1/2)^t \geq s$. For example, if $t = 2$, then s can be as large as 25. If $t = 3$, s can be 11, and if $t = 4$, s can be 6.

Unfortunately, the approximation we made gives us a bound on s that is a little too high. If we revert to the original formula $n\binom{d}{t}/\binom{n}{t} \geq s$, we see that for the case $t = 4$ we need $100\binom{50}{4}/\binom{100}{4} \geq s$. That is,

$$\frac{100 \times 50 \times 49 \times 48 \times 47}{100 \times 99 \times 98 \times 97} \geq s$$

The expression on the left is not 6, but only 5.87. However, if the average support for an itemset of size 4 is 5.87, then it is impossible that all those itemsets have support 5 or less. Thus, we can be sure that at least one itemset of size 4 has support 6 or more, and an instance of $K_{6,4}$ exists in this community. □

10.3.5 Exercises for Section 10.3

EXERCISE 10.3.1 For the running example of a social network from Fig. 10.1, how many instances of $K_{s,t}$ are there for:

(a) $s = 1$ and $t = 3$.
(b) $s = 2$ and $t = 2$.
(c) $s = 2$ and $t = 3$.

EXERCISE 10.3.2 Suppose there is a community of $2n$ nodes. Divide the community into two groups of n members, at random, and form the bipartite graph between the two groups. Suppose that the average degree of the nodes of the bipartite graph is d. Find the set of maximal pairs (t, s), with $t \leq s$, such that an instance of $K_{s,t}$ is guaranteed to exist, for the following combinations of n and d:

(a) $n = 20$ and $d = 5$.
(b) $n = 200$ and $d = 150$.
(c) $n = 1000$ and $d = 400$.

By "maximal," we mean there is no different pair (s', t') such that both $s' \geq s$ and $t' \geq t$ hold.

10.4   Partitioning of Graphs

In this section, we examine another approach to organizing social-network graphs. We use some important tools from matrix theory ("spectral methods") to formulate the problem of partitioning a graph to minimize the number of edges that connect different components. The goal of minimizing the "cut" size needs to be understood carefully before proceeding. For instance, if you just joined Facebook, you are not yet connected to any friends. We do not want to partition the friends graph with you in one group and the rest of the world in the other group, even though that would partition the graph without there being any edges that connect members of the two groups. This cut is not desirable because the two components are too unequal in size.

10.4.1   What Makes a Good Partition?

Given a graph, we would like to divide the nodes into two sets so that the *cut*, or set of edges that connect nodes in different sets is minimized. However, we also want to constrain the selection of the cut so that the two sets are approximately equal in size. The next example illustrates the point.

EXAMPLE 10.14   Recall our running example of the graph in Fig. 10.1. There, it is evident that the best partition puts $\{A, B, C\}$ in one set and $\{D, E, F, G\}$ in the other. The cut consists only of the edge (B, D) and is of size 1. No nontrivial cut can be smaller.

In Fig. 10.11 is a variant of our example, where we have added the node H and two extra edges, (H, C) and (C, G). If all we wanted was to minimize the size of the cut, then the best choice would be to put H in one set and all the other nodes in the other set. But it should be apparent that if we reject partitions where one set is too small, then the best we can do is to use the cut consisting of edges (B, D) and (C, G), which partitions the graph into two equal-sized sets $\{A, B, C, H\}$ and $\{D, E, F, G\}$.   □

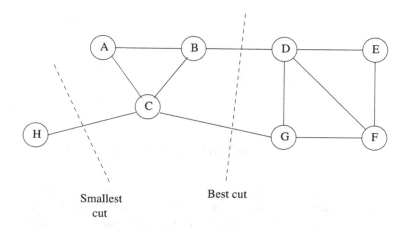

Figure 10.11 The smallest cut might not be the best cut

10.4.2 Normalized Cuts

A proper definition of a "good" cut must balance the size of the cut itself against the difference in the sizes of the sets that the cut creates. One choice that serves well is the "normalized cut." First, define the *volume* of a set S of nodes, denoted $Vol(S)$, to be the number of edges with at least one end in S.

Suppose we partition the nodes of a graph into two disjoint sets S and T. Let $Cut(S, T)$ be the number of edges that connect a node in S to a node in T. Then the *normalized cut* value for S and T is

$$\frac{Cut(S,T)}{Vol(S)} + \frac{Cut(S,T)}{Vol(T)}$$

EXAMPLE 10.15 Again consider the graph of Fig. 10.11. If we choose $S = \{H\}$ and $T = \{A, B, C, D, E, F, G\}$, then $Cut(S, T) = 1$. $Vol(S) = 1$, because there is only one edge connected to H. On the other hand, $Vol(T) = 11$, because all the edges have at least one end at a node of T. Thus, the normalized cut for this partition is $1/1 + 1/11 = 1.09$.

Now, consider the preferred cut for this graph consisting of the edges (B, D) and (C, G). Then $S = \{A, B, C, H\}$ and $T = \{D, E, F, G\}$. $Cut(S, T) = 2$, $Vol(S) = 6$, and $Vol(T) = 7$. The normalized cut for this partition is thus only $2/6 + 2/7 = 0.62$. □

10.4.3 Some Matrices That Describe Graphs

To develop the theory of how matrix algebra can help us find good graph partitions, we first need to learn about three different matrices that describe aspects of a graph. The first should be familiar: the *adjacency matrix* that has a 1 in row i and column j if there is an edge between nodes i and j, and 0 otherwise.

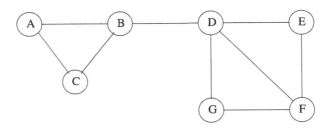

Figure 10.12 Repeat of the graph of Fig. 10.1

EXAMPLE 10.16   We repeat our running example graph in Fig. 10.12. Its adjacency matrix appears in Fig. 10.13. Note that the rows and columns correspond to the nodes $A, B, \ldots, G$ in that order. For example, the edge (B, D) is reflected by the fact that the entry in row 2 and column 4 is 1 and so is the entry in row 4 and column 2.   □

$$
\begin{bmatrix}
0 & 1 & 1 & 0 & 0 & 0 & 0 \\
1 & 0 & 1 & 1 & 0 & 0 & 0 \\
1 & 1 & 0 & 0 & 0 & 0 & 0 \\
0 & 1 & 0 & 0 & 1 & 1 & 1 \\
0 & 0 & 0 & 1 & 0 & 1 & 0 \\
0 & 0 & 0 & 1 & 1 & 0 & 1 \\
0 & 0 & 0 & 1 & 0 & 1 & 0
\end{bmatrix}
$$

Figure 10.13 The adjacency matrix for Fig. 10.12

The second matrix we need is the *degree matrix* for a graph. This graph has nonzero entries only on the diagonal. The entry for row and column i is the degree of the ith node.

EXAMPLE 10.17   The degree matrix for the graph of Fig. 10.12 is shown in Fig. 10.14. We use the same order of the nodes as in Example 10.16. For instance, the entry in row 4 and column 4 is 4 because node D has edges to four other nodes. The entry in row 4 and column 5 is 0, because that entry is not on the diagonal.   □

Suppose our graph has adjacency matrix A and degree matrix D. Our third matrix, called the *Laplacian matrix*, is $L = D - A$, the difference between the degree matrix and the adjacency matrix. That is, the Laplacian matrix L has the same entries as D on the diagonal. Off the diagonal, at row i and column j, L has -1 if there is an edge between nodes i and j and 0 if not.

EXAMPLE 10.18   The Laplacian matrix for the graph of Fig. 10.12 is shown in Fig. 10.15. Notice that each row and each column sums to zero, as must be the case for any Laplacian matrix.   □

$$\begin{bmatrix} 2 & 0 & 0 & 0 & 0 & 0 & 0 \\ 0 & 3 & 0 & 0 & 0 & 0 & 0 \\ 0 & 0 & 2 & 0 & 0 & 0 & 0 \\ 0 & 0 & 0 & 4 & 0 & 0 & 0 \\ 0 & 0 & 0 & 0 & 2 & 0 & 0 \\ 0 & 0 & 0 & 0 & 0 & 3 & 0 \\ 0 & 0 & 0 & 0 & 0 & 0 & 2 \end{bmatrix}$$

Figure 10.14 The degree matrix for Fig. 10.12

$$\begin{bmatrix} 2 & -1 & -1 & 0 & 0 & 0 & 0 \\ -1 & 3 & -1 & -1 & 0 & 0 & 0 \\ -1 & -1 & 2 & 0 & 0 & 0 & 0 \\ 0 & -1 & 0 & 4 & -1 & -1 & -1 \\ 0 & 0 & 0 & -1 & 2 & -1 & 0 \\ 0 & 0 & 0 & -1 & -1 & 3 & -1 \\ 0 & 0 & 0 & -1 & 0 & -1 & 2 \end{bmatrix}$$

Figure 10.15 The Laplacian matrix for Fig. 10.12

10.4.4 Eigenvalues of the Laplacian Matrix

We can get a good idea of the best way to partition a graph from the eigenvalues and eigenvectors of its Laplacian matrix. In Section 5.1.2 we observed how the principal eigenvector (eigenvector associated with the largest eigenvalue) of the transition matrix of the Web told us something useful about the importance of Web pages. In fact, in simple cases (no taxation) the principal eigenvector is the PageRank vector. When dealing with the Laplacian matrix, however, it turns out that the smallest eigenvalues and their eigenvectors reveal the information we desire.

The smallest eigenvalue for every Laplacian matrix is 0, and its corresponding eigenvector is $[1, 1, \ldots, 1]$. To see why, let L be the Laplacian matrix for a graph of n nodes, and let $\mathbf{1}$ be the column vector of all 1s with length n. We claim $L\mathbf{1}$ is a column vector of all 0s. To see why, consider row i of L. Its diagonal element has the degree d of node i. Row i also will have d occurrences of -1, and all other elements of row i are 0. Multiplying row i by column vector $\mathbf{1}$ has the effect of summing the row, and this sum is clearly $d + (-1)d = 0$. Thus, we can conclude $L\mathbf{1} = 0\mathbf{1}$, which demonstrates that 0 is an eigenvalue and $\mathbf{1}$ its corresponding eigenvector.

There is a simple way to find the second-smallest eigenvalue for any matrix, such as the Laplacian matrix, that is *symmetric* (the entry in row i and column j equals the entry in row j and column i). While we shall not prove this fact, the second-smallest eigenvalue of L is the minimum of $\mathbf{x}^T L \mathbf{x}$, where $\mathbf{x} = [x_1, x_2, \ldots, x_n]$ is a column vector with n components, and the minimum is taken under the constraints:

(1) The length of $\mathbf{x}$ is 1; that is, $\sum_{i=1}^{n} x_i^2 = 1$.

(2) $\mathbf{x}$ is orthogonal to the eigenvector associated with the smallest eigenvalue.

Moreover, the value of $\mathbf{x}$ that achieves this minimum is the second eigenvector.

When L is a Laplacian matrix for an n-node graph, we know something more. The eigenvector associated with the smallest eigenvalue is $\mathbf{1}$. Thus, if $\mathbf{x}$ is orthogonal to $\mathbf{1}$, we must have

$$\mathbf{x}^T \mathbf{1} = \sum_{i=1}^{n} x_i = 0$$

In addition for the Laplacian matrix, the expression $\mathbf{x}^T L \mathbf{x}$ has a useful equivalent expression. Recall that $L = D - A$, where D and A are the degree and adjacency matrices of the same graph. Thus, $\mathbf{x}^T L \mathbf{x} = \mathbf{x}^T D \mathbf{x} - \mathbf{x}^T A \mathbf{x}$. Let us evaluate the term with D and then the term for A. Here $D\mathbf{x}$ is the column vector $[d_1 x_1, d_2 x_2, \ldots, d_n x_n]$, where d_i is the degree of the ith node of the graph. Thus, $\mathbf{x}^T D \mathbf{x}$ is $\sum_{i=1}^{n} d_i x_i^2$.

Now, turn to $\mathbf{x}^T A \mathbf{x}$. The ith component of the column vector $A\mathbf{x}$ is the sum of x_j over all j such that there is an edge (i, j) in the graph. Thus, $-\mathbf{x}^T A \mathbf{x}$ is the sum of $-2x_i x_j$ over all pairs of nodes $\{i, j\}$ such that there is an edge between them. Note that the factor 2 appears because each set $\{i, j\}$ corresponds to two terms, $-x_i x_j$ and $-x_j x_i$.

We can group the terms of $\mathbf{x}^T L \mathbf{x}$ in a way that distributes the terms to each pair $\{i, j\}$. From $-\mathbf{x}^T A \mathbf{x}$, we already have the term $-2x_i x_j$. From $\mathbf{x}^T D \mathbf{x}$, we distribute the term $d_i x_i^2$ to the d_i pairs that include node i. As a result, we can associate with each pair $\{i, j\}$ that has an edge between nodes i and j the terms $x_i^2 - 2x_i x_j + x_j^2$. This expression is equivalent to $(x_i - x_j)^2$. Therefore, we have proved that $\mathbf{x}^T L \mathbf{x}$ equals the sum over all graph edges (i, j) of $(x_i - x_j)^2$.

Recall that the second-smallest eigenvalue is the minimum of this expression under the constraint that $\sum_{i=1}^{n} x_i^2 = 1$. Intuitively, we minimize it by making x_i and x_j close whenever there is an edge between nodes i and j in the graph. We might imagine that we could choose $x_i = 1/\sqrt{n}$ for all i and thus make this sum 0. However, recall that we are constrained to choose $\mathbf{x}$ to be orthogonal to $\mathbf{1}$, which means the sum of the x_i is 0. We are also forced to make $\sum_{i=1}^{n} x_i^2$ be 1, so all components cannot be 0. As a consequence, $\mathbf{x}$ must have some positive and some negative components.

We can obtain a partition of the graph by taking one set to be the nodes i whose corresponding vector component x_i is positive and the other set to be those whose components are negative. This choice does not guarantee a partition into sets of equal size, but the sizes are likely to be close. We believe that the cut between the two sets will have a small number of edges because $(x_i - x_j)^2$ is likely to be smaller if both x_i and x_j have the same sign than if they have different signs. Thus, minimizing $\mathbf{x}^T L \mathbf{x}$ under the required constraints will tend to give x_i and x_j the same sign if there is an edge (i, j).

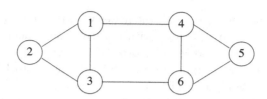

Figure 10.16 Graph for illustrating partitioning by spectral analysis

EXAMPLE 10.19   Let us apply the above technique to the graph of Fig. 10.16.
The Laplacian matrix for this graph is shown in Fig. 10.17. By standard methods
or math packages we can find all the eigenvalues and eigenvectors of this matrix.
We shall simply tabulate them in Fig. 10.18, from lowest eigenvalue to highest.
Note that we have not scaled the eigenvectors to have length 1, but could do so
easily if we wished.

$$\begin{bmatrix} 3 & -1 & -1 & -1 & 0 & 0 \\ -1 & 2 & -1 & 0 & 0 & 0 \\ -1 & -1 & 3 & 0 & 0 & -1 \\ -1 & 0 & 0 & 3 & -1 & -1 \\ 0 & 0 & 0 & -1 & 2 & -1 \\ 0 & 0 & -1 & -1 & -1 & 3 \end{bmatrix}$$

Figure 10.17 The Laplacian matrix for Fig. 10.16

The second eigenvector has three positive and three negative components. It
makes the unsurprising suggestion that one group should be $\{1, 2, 3\}$, the nodes
with positive components, and the other group should be $\{4, 5, 6\}$.   □

Eigenvalue	0	1	3	3	4	5
Eigenvector	1	1	−5	−1	−1	−1
	1	2	4	−2	1	0
	1	1	1	3	−1	1
	1	−1	−5	−1	1	1
	1	−2	4	−2	−1	0
	1	−1	1	3	1	−1

Figure 10.18 Eigenvalues and eigenvectors for the matrix of Fig. 10.17

10.4.5   Alternative Partitioning Methods

The method of Section 10.4.4 gives us a good partition of the graph into two
pieces that have a small cut between them. There are several ways we can use
the same eigenvectors to suggest other good choices of partition. First, we are

not constrained to put all the nodes with positive components in the eigenvector into one group and those with negative components in the other. We could set the threshold at some point other than zero.

For instance, suppose we modified Example 10.19 so that the threshold was not zero, but -1.5. Then the two nodes 4 and 6, with components -1 in the second eigenvector of Fig. 10.18, would join 1, 2, and 3, leaving five nodes in one component and only node 5 in the other. That partition would have a cut of size two, as did the choice based on the threshold of zero, but the two components have radically different sizes, so we would tend to prefer our original choice. However, there are other cases where the threshold zero gives unequally sized components, as would be the case if we used the third eigenvector in Fig. 10.18.

We may also want a partition into more than two components. One approach is to use the method described above to split the graph into two, and then use it repeatedly on the components to split them as far as desired. A second approach is to use several of the eigenvectors, not just the second, to partition the graph. If we use m eigenvectors, and set a threshold for each, we can get a partition into 2^m groups, each group consisting of the nodes that are above or below threshold for each of the eigenvectors, in a particular pattern.

It is worth noting that each eigenvector except the first is the vector $\mathbf{x}$ that minimizes $\mathbf{x}^T L\mathbf{x}$, subject to the constraint that it is orthogonal to all previous eigenvectors. This constraint generalizes the constraints we described for the second eigenvector in a natural way. As a result, while each eigenvector tries to produce a minimum-sized cut, the fact that successive eigenvectors have to satisfy more and more constraints generally causes the cuts they describe to be progressively worse.

EXAMPLE 10.20   Let us reconsider the graph of Fig. 10.16, for which the eigenvectors of its Laplacian matrix were tabulated in Fig. 10.18. The third eigenvector, with a threshold of 0, puts nodes 1 and 4 in one group and the other four nodes in the other. That is not a bad partition, but its cut size is four, compared with the cut of size two that we get from the second eigenvector.

If we use both the second and third eigenvectors, we put nodes 2 and 3 in one group, because their components are positive in both eigenvectors. Nodes 5 and 6 are in another group, because their components are negative in the second eigenvector and positive in the third. Node 1 is in a group by itself because it is positive in the second eigenvector and negative in the third, while node 4 is also in a group by itself because its component is negative in both eigenvectors. This partition of a six-node graph into four groups is too fine a partition to be meaningful. But at least the groups of size two each have an edge between the nodes, so it is as good as we could ever get for a partition into groups of these sizes.   □

10.4.6   Exercises for Section 10.4

EXERCISE 10.4.1   For the graph of Fig. 10.9, construct:

(a) The adjacency matrix.

(b) The degree matrix.

(c) The Laplacian matrix.

! EXERCISE 10.4.2   For the Laplacian matrix constructed in Exercise 10.4.1(c), find the second-smallest eigenvalue and its eigenvector. What partition of the nodes does it suggest?

!! EXERCISE 10.4.3   For the Laplacian matrix constructed in Exercise 10.4.1(c), construct the third and subsequent smallest eigenvalues and their eigenvectors.

10.5   Finding Overlapping Communities

So far, we have concentrated on clustering a social graph to find communities. But communities are in practice rarely disjoint. In this section, we explain a method for taking a social graph and fitting a model to it that best explains how it could have been generated by a mechanism that assumes the probability that two individuals are connected by an edge (are "friends") increases as they become members of more communities in common. An important tool in this analysis is "maximum-likelihood estimation," which we shall explain before getting to the matter of finding overlapping communities.

10.5.1   The Nature of Communities

To begin, let us consider what we would expect two overlapping communities to look like. Our data is a social graph, where nodes are people and there is an edge between two nodes if the people are "friends." Let us imagine that this graph represents students at a school, and there are two clubs in this school: the Chess Club and the Spanish Club. It is reasonable to suppose that each of these clubs forms a community. It is also reasonable to suppose that two people in the Chess Club are more likely to be friends in the graph because they know each other from the club. Likewise, if two people are in the Spanish Club, then there is a good chance they know each other, and are likely to be friends.

What if two people are in both clubs? They now have two reasons why they might know each other, and so we would expect an even greater probability that they will be friends in the social graph. Our conclusion is that we expect edges to be dense within any community, but we expect edges to be even denser in the intersection of two communities, denser than that in the intersection of three communities, and so on. The idea is suggested by Fig. 10.19.

10.5.2   Maximum-Likelihood Estimation

Before we see the algorithm for finding communities that have overlap of the kind suggested in Section 10.5.1, let us digress and learn a useful modeling tool called

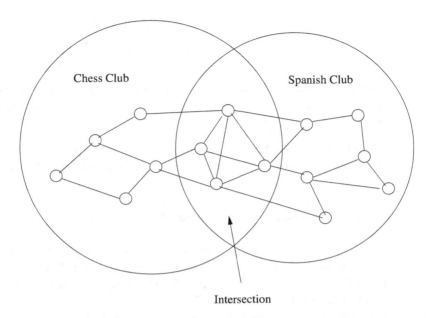

Figure 10.19 The overlap of two communities is denser than the nonoverlapping parts of these communities

maximum-likelihood estimation, or MLE. The idea behind MLE is that we make an assumption about the generative process (the *model*) that creates instances of some artifact, for example, "friends graphs." The model has parameters that determine the probability of generating any particular instance of the artifact; this probability is called the *likelihood* of those parameter values. We assume that the value of the parameters that gives the largest value of the likelihood is the correct model for the observed artifact.

An example should make the MLE principle clear. For instance, we might wish to generate random graphs. We suppose that each edge is present with probability p and not present with probability $1 - p$, with the presence or absence of each edge chosen independently. The only parameter we can adjust is p. For each value of p there is a small but nonzero probability that the graph generated will be exactly the one we see. Following the MLE principle, we shall declare that the true value of p is the one for which the probability of generating the observed graph is the highest.

EXAMPLE 10.21 Consider the graph of Fig. 10.19. There are 15 nodes and 23 edges. As there are $\binom{15}{2} = 105$ pairs of 15 nodes, we see that if each edge is chosen with probability p, then the probability (likelihood) of generating exactly the graph of Fig. 10.19 is given by the function $p^{23}(1 - p)^{82}$. No matter what value p has between 0 and 1, that is an incredibly tiny number. But the function does have a maximum, which we can determine by taking its derivative and

---

Prior Probabilities

When we do an MLE analysis, we generally assume that the parameters can take any value in their range, and there is no bias in favor of particular values. However, if that is not the case, then we can multiply the formula we get for the probability of the observed artifact being generated, as a function of the parameter values, by the function that represents the relative likelihood of those values of the parameter being the true values. The exercises offer examples of MLE with assumptions about the prior distribution of the parameters.

---

setting that to 0. That is:

$$23p^{22}(1-p)^{82} - 82p^{23}(1-p)^{81} = 0$$

We can group terms to rewrite the above as

$$p^{22}(1-p)^{81}\big(23(1-p) - 82p\big) = 0$$

The only way the right side can be 0 is if p is 0 or 1, or the last factor,

$$\big(23(1-p) - 82p\big)$$

is 0. When p is 0 or 1, the value of the likelihood function $p^{23}(1-p)^{82}$ is minimized, not maximized, so it must be the last factor that is 0. That is, the likelihood of generating the graph of Fig. 10.19 is maximized when

$$23 - 23p - 82p = 0$$

or $p = 23/105$.

That outcome is hardly a surprise. It says the most likely value for p is the observed fraction of possible edges that are present in the graph. However, when we use a more complicated mechanism to generate graphs or other artifacts, the value of the parameters that produce the observed artifact with maximum likelihood is far from obvious. ☐

10.5.3 The Affiliation-Graph Model

We shall now introduce a reasonable mechanism, called the *affiliation-graph model*, to generate social graphs from communities. Once we see how the parameters of the model influence the likelihood of seeing a given graph, we can address how one would solve for the values of the parameters that give the maximum likelihood. The elements of the graph-generation mechanism are:

(1) There is a given number of communities, and there is a given number of individuals (nodes of the graph).
(2) Each community can have any set of individuals as members. That is, the memberships in the communities are parameters of the model.

(3) Each community C has a probability p_C associated with it, the probability that two members of community C are connected by an edge because they are both members of C. These probabilities are also parameters of the model.

(4) If a pair of nodes is in two or more communities, then there is an edge between them if any of the communities of which both are members induces that edge according to Rule (3).

(5) The decision whether a community induces an edge between two of its members is independent of that decision for any other community of which these two individuals are also members.

We must compute the likelihood that a given graph with the proper number of nodes is generated by this mechanism. The key observation is how the edge probabilities are computed, given an assignment of individuals to communities and values of the p_C. Consider an edge (u, v) between nodes u and v. Suppose u and v are members of communities C and D, but not any other communities. Then because of the indepenence assumption, Rule (5) above, the probability that there is *no* edge between u and v is the product of the probabilities that there is no edge due to community C and no edge due to community D. That is, with probability $(1 - p_C)(1 - p_D)$ there is no edge (u, v) in the graph, and of course the probability that there *is* such an edge is 1 minus that.

More generally, if u and v are members of a nonempty set of communities M and not any others, then p_{uv}, the probability of an edge between u and v is given by:

$$p_{uv} = 1 - \prod_{C \text{ in } M} (1 - p_C) \tag{10.1}$$

As an important special case, if u and v are not in any communities together, then we take p_{uv} to be ϵ, some very tiny number. We have to choose this probability to be nonzero, or else we can never assign a nonzero likelihood to any set of communities that do not have every pair of individuals sharing a community. But by taking the probability to be very small, we bias our computation to favor solutions such that every observed edge is explained by joint membership in some community.

If we know which nodes are in which communities, then we can compute the likelihood of the given graph for these edge probabilities using a simple generalization of Example 10.21. Let p_{uv} be the probability of an edge between nodes u and v, as defined by Equation (10.1), or ϵ if u and v do not share a community. Then the likelihood of E being exactly the set of edges in the observed graph is

$$\prod_{(u,v) \text{ in } E} p_{uv} \prod_{(u,v) \text{ not in } E} (1 - p_{uv})$$

EXAMPLE 10.22   Consider the tiny social graph in Fig. 10.20. Suppose there are two communities C and D, with associated probabilities p_C and p_D. Also, suppose that we have determined (or are using as a temporary hypothesis) that

$C = \{w, x, y\}$ and $D = \{w, y, z\}$. To begin, consider the pair of nodes w and x. $M_{wx} = \{C\}$; that is, this pair is in community C but not in community D. Therefore, $p_{wx} = 1 - (1 - p_C) = p_C$.

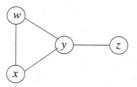

Figure 10.20 A social graph

Similarly, x and y are only together in C, y and z are only together in D, and likewise w and z are only together in D. Thus, we find $p_{xy} = p_C$ and $p_{yz} = p_{wz} = p_D$. Now the pair w and y are together in both communities, so $p_{wy} = 1 - (1 - p_C)(1 - p_D) = p_C + p_D - p_C p_D$. Finally, x and z are not together in either community, so $p_{xz} = \epsilon$.

Now, we can compute the likelihood of the graph in Fig. 10.20, given our assumptions about membership in the two communities. This likelihood is the product of the probabilities associated with each of the four pairs of nodes whose edges appear in the graph, times one minus the probability for each of the two pairs whose edges are not there. That is, we want

$$p_{wx} p_{wy} p_{xy} p_{yz} (1 - p_{wz})(1 - p_{xz})$$

Substituting the expressions we developed above for each of these probabilities, we get

$$(p_C)^2 p_D (p_C + p_D - p_C p_D)(1 - p_D)(1 - \epsilon) \tag{10.2}$$

Note that ϵ is very small, so the last factor is essentially 1 and can be dropped.

We must find the values of p_C and p_D that maximize Expression (10.2). First, notice that all factors are either independent of p_C or grow with p_C. The only hard step in this argument is to remember that $p_D \leq 1$, so

$$p_C + p_D - p_C p_D$$

must grow positively with p_C. It follows that the likelihood is maximized when p_C is as large as possible; that is, $p_C = 1$.

Next, we must find the value of p_D that maximizes the expression, given that $p_C = 1$. The expression becomes $p_D(1 - p_D)$, and it is easy to see that this expression has its maximum at $p_D = 0.5$. That is, given $C = \{w, x, y\}$ and $D = \{w, y, z\}$, the maximum likelihood for the graph in Fig. 10.20 occurs when members of C are certain to have an edge between them and there is a 50% chance that joint membership in D will cause an edge between the members. □

10.5.4   Discrete Optimization of Community Assignments

Example 10.22 reflects only part of the process whereby we develop an affiliation-graph model for a given network. We also need to find an assignment of members to communities such that the maximum-likelihood solution for that assignment has the largest likelihood for any assignment. Once we fix on an assignment, we can find the probabilities p_C associated with each community C. The most popular method for doing so is "gradient descent," a technique that we introduced in Section 9.4.5 and that will be discussed further starting in Section 12.3.4.

Unfortunately, it is not obvious how one incorporates the set of members of each community into the gradient-descent solution, since changes to the membership of communities is by discrete steps, not according to some continuous function as is required for gradient descent. The only feasible way to search the space of possible assignments of members to communities is by starting with an assignment, perhaps chosen at random. As we search for better assignments, we always have one assignment that is "current."

We consider small changes to the assignment, say by insertion or deletion of one member for one community. For each such assignment, we can solve for the best community probabilities (the p_C) by gradient descent. If a change to the current assignment leads to a higher likelihood, then make the resulting assignment be the current assignment. If the change does not improve the likelihood, then try another change from the current assignment. Eventually, you will reach a current assignment for which no small change to the assignment leads to a higher likelihood. The resulting assignment, along with the probabilities for the communities that maximizes the likelihood for this assignment, forms the affiliation-graph model for this graph.

Note that because we allow only a particular set of simple changes, such as insertion or deletion of one member, the resulting assignment of nodes to communities may not be globally optimum. It is possible that the model with the highest likelihood is radically different from the best assignment we can reach. It is possible, and often appropriate, to repeat this process with many different random starting solutions, and to take the best of the resulting models.

Finally, in the above discussion we assumed the number of communities was fixed. We can also permit "small" changes that adjust the number of communities, e.g., by merging two communities or by adding a new community with a random set of initial members. Another approach is to fix the number of communities, but after finding the best model for that number of communities, add one more community and solve again, to see if the likelihood of the best model improves. If not, subtract one from the number of communities to see if the likelihood improves. If either of those changes improves things, then repeat the process of moving in the direction or more or fewer communities, whichever led to an improvement.

Log Likelihood

Usually, we compute the logarithm of the likelihood function (the *log likelihood*), rather than the function itself. Doing so offers several advantages. Products become sums, which often simplifies the expression. Also, summing many numbers is less prone to numerical rounding errors than is taking the product of many tiny numbers.

10.5.5 Avoiding the Use of Discrete Membership Changes

There is a solution to the problem caused by the affiliation-graph model, where membership of individuals in communities is discrete: either you are a member of the community or not. Instead of "all-or-nothing" membership of nodes in communities, we can suppose that for each node and each community, there is a "strength of membership" for that node and community. Intuitively, the stronger the membership of two individuals in the same community is, the more likely it is that this community will cause there to be an edge between them. In this model, we can adjust the strength of membership for an individual in a community continuously, just as we can adjust the probability associated with a community in the affiliation-graph model. That improvement allows us to use methods for optimizing continuous functions, such as gradient descent, to maximize the expression for likelihood. In the new model, we have

(1) Fixed sets of communities and individuals, as before.
(2) For each community C and individual x, there is a *strength of membership* parameter F_{xC}. These parameters can take any nonnegative value, and a value of 0 means the individual is definitely not in the community.
(3) The probability that community C causes there to be an edge between nodes u and v is

$$p_C(u, v) = 1 - e^{-F_{uC}F_{vC}}$$

As before, the probability of there being an edge between u and v is 1 minus the probability that none of the communities causes there to be an edge between them. That is, each community independently causes edges, and an edge exists between two nodes if any community causes it to exist. More formally, p_{uv}, the probability of an edge between nodes u and v, is

$$p_{uv} = 1 - \prod_C (1 - p_C(u, v))$$

If we substitute the formula for $p_C(u, v)$ that is assumed in the model, we get

$$p_{uv} = 1 - e^{-\sum_C F_{uC}F_{vC}}$$

Finally, let E be the set of edges in the observed graph. As before, we can write the formula for the likelihood of the observed graph as the product of the

---

Continuous Versus Discrete Optimization

The trick used in Section 10.5.5 is surprisingly common. Whenever you are trying to find an optimum solution to a problem where some of the elements are continuous (e.g., the probabilities of communities inducing edges) and some elements are discrete (e.g., the memberships of the communities), it might make sense to replace each discrete element by a continuous variable. That change, while it doesn't strictly speaking represent reality, enables us to perform only one optimization, which will use a continuous-optimization method such as gradient descent. Note, however, that whether we perform a discrete optimization, as in Section 10.5.4 or a continuous optimization as in Section 10.5.5, we run the risk of winding up in a local optimum that is not the globally best solution.

expression for p_{uv} for each edge (u, v) that is in E, times the product of $1 - p_{uv}$ for each edge (u, v) that is not in E. Thus, in the new model, the formula for the likelihood of the graph with edges E is

$$\prod_{(u,v) \text{ in } E} (1 - e^{-\sum_C F_{uC} F_{vC}}) \prod_{(u,v) \text{ not in } E} e^{-\sum_C F_{uC} F_{vC}} \tag{10.3}$$

We can simplify Expression (10.3) somewhat by taking its logarithm. Remember that maximizing a function also maximizes the logarithm of that function, and vice versa. So we can take the natural logarithm of the Expression (10.3) to replace the products by sums. We also get simplification from the fact that $\log(e^x) = x$.

$$\sum_{(u,v) \text{ in } E} \log(1 - e^{-\sum_C F_{uC} F_{vC}}) - \sum_{(u,v) \text{ not in } E} \sum_C F_{uC} F_{vC} \tag{10.4}$$

We can now find the values for the F_{xC} that maximizes the expression (10.4). One way is to use gradient descent in a manner similar to what was done in Section 9.4.5. That is, we pick one node x, and adjust all the values of the F_{xC} in the direction that most improves the value of (10.4). Notice that the only factors whose values change in response to changes to the F_{xC} are those where one of u and v is x and the other of u and v is a node adjacent to x. Since the degree of a node is typically much less than the number of edges in the graph, we can avoid looking at most of the terms in (10.4) at each step.

10.5.6 Exercises for Section 10.5

EXERCISE 10.5.1 Suppose graphs are generated by picking a probability p and choosing each edge independently with probability p, as in Example 10.21. For the graph of Fig. 10.20, what value of p gives the maximum likelihood of seeing that graph? What is the probability this graph is generated?

EXERCISE 10.5.2 Compute the MLE for the graph in Example 10.22 for the following guesses of the memberships of the two communities.

(a) $C = \{w, x\}$; $C = \{y, z\}$.

(b) $C = \{w, x, y, z\}$; $C = \{x, y, z\}$.

EXERCISE 10.5.3   Example 10.22 considered the initial assignment of nodes to two communities $C = \{w, x, y\}$ and $D = \{w, y, z\}$. Suppose we keep the number of communities fixed at 2, but allow incremental changes to the communities that add or delete a single node. What would be the final assignment of nodes to the communities C and D that maximizes the likelihood of seeing the graph of Fig. 10.20? What is that likelihood?

! EXERCISE 10.5.4   Are there any other assignments of nodes to (any number of) communities for Fig. 10.20 that would lead to the same likelihood as the solution you obtained for Exercise 10.5.3?

EXERCISE 10.5.5   Suppose we have a coin, which may not be a fair coin, and we flip it some number of times, seeing h heads and t tails.

(a) If the probability p of getting a head on any flip is p, what is the MLE for p, in terms of h and t?

! (b) Suppose we are told that there is a 90% probability that the coin is fair (i.e., $p = 0.5$), and a 10% chance that $p = 0.1$. For what values of h and t is it more likely that the coin is fair?

!! (c) Suppose the a-priori likelihood that p has a particular value is proportional to $|p - 0.5|$. That is, p is more likely to be near 0 or 1, than around $1/2$. If we see h heads and t tails, what is the maximum likelihood estimate of p?

10.6   Simrank

In this section, we shall take up another approach to analyzing social-network graphs. This technique, called "simrank," applies best to graphs with several types of nodes, although it can in principle be applied to any graph. The purpose of simrank is to measure the similarity between nodes of the same type, and it does so by seeing where random walkers on the graph wind up when starting at a particular node, the *source* node. Because calculation must be carried out once for each source node, there is a limit to the size of graphs that can be analyzed completely in this manner. However, we shall also offer an algorithm that approximates simrank, but is far more efficient than iterated matrix-vector multiplication. Finally, we show how simrank can be used to find communities.

10.6.1   Random Walkers on a Social Graph

Recall our view of PageRank in Section 5.1 as reflecting what a "random surfer" would do if they walked on the Web graph. We can similarly think of a person "walking" on a social network. The graph of a social network is generally undirected, while the Web graph is directed. However, the difference is unimportant.

A walker at a node N of an undirected graph will move with equal probability to any of the *neighbors* of N (those nodes with which N shares an edge).

Suppose, for example, that such a *walker* starts out at node T_1 of Fig. 10.2, which we reproduce here as Fig. 10.21. At the first step, it would go either to U_1 or W_1. If to W_1, then it would next either come back to T_1 or go to T_2. If the walker first moved to U_1, it would wind up at either T_1, T_2, or T_3 next.

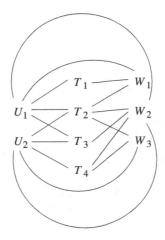

Figure 10.21 Repeat of Fig. 10.2

We conclude that, starting at T_1, there is a good chance the walker would visit T_2, at least initially, and that chance is better than the chance it would visit T_3 or T_4. It would be interesting if we could infer that tags T_1 and T_2 are therefore related or similar in some way. The evidence is that they have both been placed on a common Web page, W_1, and they have also been used by a common tagger, U_1.

However, if we allow the walker to continue traversing the graph at random, then the probability that the walker will be at any particular node does not depend on where it starts out. This conclusion comes from the theory of Markov processes that we mentioned in Section 5.1.2, although the independence from the starting point requires additional conditions besides connectedness that the graph of Fig. 10.21 does satisfy.

10.6.2   Random Walks with Restart

We see from the observations above that it is not possible to measure similarity to a particular node by looking at the limiting distribution of the walker. However, we have already seen, in Section 5.1.5, the introduction of a small probability that the walker will stop walking at random. Later, we saw in Section 5.3.2 that there were reasons to select only a subset of Web pages as the teleport set, the pages that the walker would go to when they stopped surfing the Web at random.

Here, we take this idea to the extreme. We are focused on one particular source node S of a social network, and we want to see where the random walker winds up on short walks from S. To learn where the walker would tend to be, we modify the matrix of transition probabilities to have a small probability of transitioning back to S from any node. That is, we shall compute the topic-sensitive PageRank calculation with a teleport set consisting of only the node S. Formally, let M be the *transition matrix* of the graph G. That is, the entry in row i and column j of M is $1/k$ if node j of G has degree k, and one of the adjacent nodes is i. Otherwise, this entry is 0. We shall discuss teleporting in a moment, but first, let us look at a simple example of a transition matrix.

EXAMPLE 10.23   Figure 10.22 is an example of a very simple network involving three pictures, and two tags, "Sky" and "Tree" that have been placed on some of them. Pictures 1 and 3 have both tags, while Picture 2 has only the tag "Sky." Intuitively, we expect that Picture 3 is more similar to Picture 1 than Picture 2 is, and an analysis using a random walker with restart at Picture 1 will support that intuition.

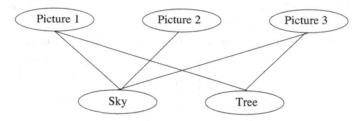

Figure 10.22 A simple bipartite social graph

Let us order the nodes as Picture 1, Picture 2, Picture 3, Sky, Tree. Then the transition matrix for the graph of Fig. 10.22 is

$$
\begin{bmatrix}
0 & 0 & 0 & 1/3 & 1/2 \\
0 & 0 & 0 & 1/3 & 0 \\
0 & 0 & 0 & 1/3 & 1/2 \\
1/2 & 1 & 1/2 & 0 & 0 \\
1/2 & 0 & 1/2 & 0 & 0
\end{bmatrix}
$$

For example, the fourth column corresponds to the node "Sky," and this node connects to each of the tree picture nodes. It therefore has degree three, so the nonzero entries in its column must be $1/3$. The picture nodes correspond to the first three rows and columns, so the entry $1/3$ appears in the first three rows of column 4. Since the "Sky" node does not have an edge to either itself or the "Tree" node, the entries in the last two rows of column 4 are 0.   □

As before, let us use β as the probability that the walker continues at random, so $1 - \beta$ is the probability the walker will teleport to the source node S. Let e_S be the column vector that has 1 in the row for node S and 0s elsewhere. Then if

$\mathbf{v}$ is the column vector that reflects the probability the walker is at each of the nodes at a particular round, and $\mathbf{v}'$ is the probability the walker is at each of the nodes at the next round, then $\mathbf{v}'$ is related to $\mathbf{v}$ by:

$$\mathbf{v}' = \beta M \mathbf{v} + (1 - \beta)\mathbf{e}_S$$

EXAMPLE 10.24 Assume M is the matrix of Example 10.23 and $\beta = 0.8$. Also, assume that node S is Picture 1; that is, we want to compute the similarity of other pictures to Picture 1. Then the equation for the new value $\mathbf{v}'$ of the distribution that we must iterate is

$$\mathbf{v}' = \begin{bmatrix} 0 & 0 & 0 & 4/15 & 2/5 \\ 0 & 0 & 0 & 4/15 & 0 \\ 0 & 0 & 0 & 4/15 & 2/5 \\ 2/5 & 4/5 & 2/5 & 0 & 0 \\ 2/5 & 0 & 2/5 & 0 & 0 \end{bmatrix} \mathbf{v} + \begin{bmatrix} 1/5 \\ 0 \\ 0 \\ 0 \\ 0 \end{bmatrix}$$

Since the graph of Fig. 10.22 is connected, the original matrix M is stochastic, and we can deduce that if the initial vector $\mathbf{v}$ has components that sum to 1, then $\mathbf{v}'$ will also have components that sum to 1. As a result, we can simplify the above equation by adding 1/5 to each of the entries in the first row of the matrix. That is, we can iterate the matrix-vector multiplication

$$\mathbf{v}' = \begin{bmatrix} 1/5 & 1/5 & 1/5 & 7/15 & 3/5 \\ 0 & 0 & 0 & 4/15 & 0 \\ 0 & 0 & 0 & 4/15 & 2/5 \\ 2/5 & 4/5 & 2/5 & 0 & 0 \\ 2/5 & 0 & 2/5 & 0 & 0 \end{bmatrix} \mathbf{v}$$

If we start with $\mathbf{v} = \mathbf{e}_S$, then the sequence of estimates of the distribution of the walker that we get is

$$\begin{bmatrix} 1 \\ 0 \\ 0 \\ 0 \\ 0 \end{bmatrix}, \begin{bmatrix} 1/5 \\ 0 \\ 0 \\ 2/5 \\ 2/5 \end{bmatrix}, \begin{bmatrix} 35/75 \\ 8/75 \\ 20/75 \\ 6/75 \\ 6/75 \end{bmatrix}, \begin{bmatrix} 95/375 \\ 8/375 \\ 20/375 \\ 142/375 \\ 110/375 \end{bmatrix}, \begin{bmatrix} 2353/5625 \\ 568/5625 \\ 1228/5625 \\ 786/5625 \\ 690/5625 \end{bmatrix}, \ldots, \begin{bmatrix} .345 \\ .066 \\ .145 \\ .249 \\ .196 \end{bmatrix}$$

We observe from the above that in the limit, the walker is more than twice as likely to be at Picture 3 than at Picture 2. This analysis confirms the intuition that Picture 3 is more like Picture 1 than Picture 2 is. □

There are several additional observations that we may take away from Example 10.24. First, remember that this analysis applies only to Picture 1. If we wanted to know what pictures were most similar to another picture, we would have to start the analysis over for that picture. Likewise, if we wanted to know about which tags were most closely associated with the tag "Sky" (an uninteresting question in this small example, since there is only one other tag), then we would have to arrange to have the walker teleport only to the "Sky" node.

Second, notice that convergence takes time, since there is an initial oscillation. That is, initially, all the weight is at the pictures, and at the second step most of the weight is at the tags. At the third step, most weight is back at the pictures, but at the fourth step much of the weight moves to the tags again. However, in the limit there is convergence, with 5/9 of the weight at the pictures and 4/9 of the weight at the tags. In general, the process converges for any connected k-partite graph.

10.6.3   Approximate Simrank

The straightforward calculation of simrank involves repeated matrix-vector multiplications, just as for any PageRank-type calculation. However, when there is a single node S in the teleport set, nodes that are far from S are certain to get a very small simrank. If we are willing to accept an approximation to the true simrank, we can use another approach, where we never even look at the nodes that are far away from S.

We shall simulate a different kind of walk on the graph. Instead of the walker moving to a random neighbor (if it does not teleport to the source node), it will either move or stay where it is, with equal probability. If it decides to move, then it will move to any neighbor with equal probability. However, there is another aspect to the decision whether to move or not. We can regard a walker as either part of the limiting PageRank for its node, or part of the *residual* PageRank, that is, PageRank that has not yet been assigned to any node. Only in the latter case do we consider moving that walker.

We shall therefore use two vectors, $\mathbf{r}$ and $\mathbf{q}$, each with one component for each node. In what follows, $\mathbf{r}$ will be our current estimates for the PageRank of each node, and $\mathbf{q}$ will be the current residual PageRank for each node. However, note that as the computation proceeds, we may never compute many of the components of these vectors. We shall also use the notation q_U for the component of $\mathbf{q}$ for node U, and use r_U analogously. Initailly, we assume $\mathbf{r}$ is the all-0s vector, while $\mathbf{q}$ is all 0s except for $q_S = 1$. That is, $\mathbf{q}$ says that we assume all walkers start at S, while $\mathbf{r}$ says that we have not yet resolved where any of them will wind up asymptotically.

The approximate simrank calculation uses two parameters. We continue to use β as the nontaxed fraction; i.e., $1 - \beta$ is the probability that a walker will teleport to the source node S. The second parameter we need is ϵ, a small fraction that gives the maximum amount of residual PageRank that we shall be willing *not* to pass from one node to a neighbor. Thus, the smaller ϵ is, the closer we get to the true PageRank, but also the longer the computation takes. We should choose ϵ to be very small, say 0.01 divided by the number of edges in the graph. That way we do not terminate until the total amount of residual PageRank is at most 0.01. The approximate-simrank algorithm is to repeat the following steps until we can no longer find any node U whose residual PageRank divided by its degree (i.e., the amount of PageRank it could pass to any one of its neighbors) is greater than ϵ.

(1) Let U be any node such that q_U, the component of $\mathbf{q}$ for node U, exceeds ϵ times the degree of U.
(2) Add $(1 - \beta)q_U$ to the current value of r_U. That is, we credit node U with an amount of true PageRank equal to the tax on its current residual.
(3) Set q_U to $\beta q_U / 2$. That is, of the portion of U's residual that is not taxed, half that residual remains at U.
(4) Suppose U has degree d. Then for each node V adjacent to U, add to q_V an amount equal to $\beta q_U / (2d)$. That is, the other half of the untaxed residual for U is divided equally among its neighbors.

EXAMPLE 10.25   Let us reconsider Example 10.23 from the point of view of appreoximate PageRank, again using Picture1 as the source node S. We shall again use $\beta = 0.8$, but we shall leave ϵ unspecified, since we are not going to carry out the computation to completion for any reasonably small ϵ. Figure 10.23 summarizes what could be the first five steps of the algorithm.

U	r_{P1}	r_{P2}	r_{P3}	r_{Sk}	r_{Tr}	q_{P1}	q_{P2}	q_{P3}	q_{Sk}	q_{Tr}
Initial	0	0	0	0	0	1	0	0	0	0
Picture1	.2	0	0	0	0	.4	0	0	.2	.2
Tree	.2	0	0	0	.04	.44	0	.04	.2	.08
Picture1	.288	0	0	0	.04	.176	0	.04	.288	.168
Sky	.288	0	0	.058	.04	.214	.038	.078	.115	.168
Picture3	.288	0	.016	.058	.04	.214	.038	.031	.131	.184

Figure 10.23 The first five steps in an approximate PageRank calculation

The first row, labeled "Initial," shows the initial values of $\mathbf{r}$ and $\mathbf{q}$. We show each component for each vector, in the same order as in Example 10.23: Pictures 1, 2, and 3, then Sky and Tree. Our first choice of U has to be Picture1, the source node, since it is the only node with any residual PageRank. In step (1) we convert $(1 - \beta)q_{P1}$ of the residual for Picture1 to approximate PageRank. Thus, r_{P1} is set to 0.2. Of the remaining value 0.8 for q_{P1}, 0.4 remains, and the other 0.4 is divided equally among the neighbors Sky and Tree of Picture1. These observations explain the second row of the table.

Suppose we then choose Tree as the next value of node U. The value of q_{Tr} is now 0.2, so we move one fifth of this value to r_{Tr}, which makes that value be 0.04. Of the remaining 0.16, half remains as q_{Tr}, and the remainder is divided between q_{P1}, which becomes 0.44, and q_{P3}, which becomes 0.04. These steps explain the third row. We show a sequence of three additional steps, each with a possible choice of U, assuming ϵ is large enough to justify continuing the algorithm. You are invited to work the next three steps by yourself and continue the simulation, which is shown only to three decimal places.   □

10.6.4   Why Approximate Simrank Works

There are several questions you may naturally ask about the algorithm described in the previous section.

(1) Why is this algorithm more efficient than the straightforward implementation of PageRank with a single source node as the teleport set?

(2) Why does this algorithm converge to an approximation of the true simrank?

(3) Why do we distribute only half the residual value for node U, rather than the entire residual?

The answer to the last question is simplest. It is there to help distribute the residual values as quickly as possible. For some graphs, it is fine to skip step (3) and in step (4) to give each node V an additional residual of $\beta q_U/d$. However, in other cases, such as a bipartite graph, distributing the entire residual of node U will cause the residuals to bounce back and forth between the two sides of the graph, thus causing there to be at least one large residual for a longer time, than if we distributed only half the residual.

For the first question, we note that every node that qualifies as a possible choice of U has $q_U > \epsilon$; usually it will be comsiderably larger than ϵ because the actual lower bound on q_U is ϵ times the degree of U. Observe that if $q_U > \epsilon$, then a quantity of at least $\epsilon(1 - \beta)$ is moved from the residual vector $\mathbf{q}$ to the approximate PageRank vector $\mathbf{r}$. However, the sum of all the components of both vectors is 1, so we cannot have a number of rounds of this algorithm that exceeds $\frac{1}{\epsilon(1-\beta)}$. That is a constant number of rounds, while the customary PageRank algorithm takes time that is at least proportional to the number of nodes in the graph times the number of iterations of matrix-vector multiplication. Further, if we are careful, we can organize the components of $\mathbf{q}$ into a priority queue, so we can select a candidate for U in $O(\log n)$ time if there are n nodes in the graph.

Finally, we need to address the second question: why does the result approximate the true simrank? Here is an intuitive argument. First, moving residual values around the graph is a simulation of random walkers on the graph. The fact that the walkers are moving asynchronously (since they move with 50% probability rather than certainly move at each step) is not important. the walkers will still distribute themselves eventually as they would if they took a synchronous random walk. But the distribution of residuals is not the answer that the algorithm gives. Rather, the answer is the vector $\mathbf{r}$ when the algorithm terminates. In fact, the values that get moved from $\mathbf{q}$ to $\mathbf{r}$ are fraction $1 - \beta$ of the values of the residuals at random times, depending on the order in which we select nodes to be U. However, the true PageRank for any node V is the probability that a walker is at node V at a random time, given that it started out at the source S. By picking U at random (among nodes with sufficiently large residual), we are simulating the selection of a random time at which to view each walker, and therefore, getting approximately the correct distribution of the walkers.

10.6.5   Application of Simrank to Finding Communities

An interesting application of simrank is finding the communities to which a given node (the source node) belongs. We could then find all the reasonable communities in a network by selecting as source nodes those nodes that have not yet been assigned to any community, or that have been assigned to only a small number of communities.

Suppose we start with source node S and find the simrank for all the nodes for this source. We could use either the exact or approximate simrank algorithm to do so. Then, order the nodes other than S by their simrank, and consider adding each, highest simrank first, to a community containing S. We need to know when to stop adding nodes, so we need a stopping criterion. A simple approach is to add nodes until the *density* of edges – the fraction of edges that connect nodes in the community divided by the number of possible edges connecting nodes in the community (i.e., $\binom{n}{2}$ for an n-node community) – goes below a threshold.

EXAMPLE 10.26   Let us consider the very simple network from Fig. 10.22. We shall use Picture1 as the source node, so we are trying to find good communities containing that node. The network is too small to give a reasonable set of communities, but it will serve for an example of the algorithm.

We learned from Example 10.23 that with Picture1 as the source node, the simrank values for the five nodes are in the order Picture1, Sky, Tree, Picture3, Picture2. The community consisting of the first two nodes on this list has a density of 1, since the one possible edge between Picture1 and Sky is indeed present. When we add the third node, Tree, the density falls to $2/3$, since only two of the possible three edges are present. Adding the fourth node, Picture3, keeps the density at $2/3$; now four of the six possible edges are present. If we add the last node, the density is down to $1/2$ – five of the ten possible edges are present in the entire network. If our threshold in density is greater than $2/3$, then we would pick only the first two nodes as the community, while if we have a threshhold t, with $2/3 \geq t > 1/2$, then we would pick the first four nodes as the community. □

Another measure of the goodness of a community C is the *conductance*. To define conductance, we need first to define the *volume* of a community C, which is the smaller of the sum of the degress of the nodes in C and the sum of the degrees of the nodes not in C. Then the conductance of C is the ratio of the number of edges with *exactly* one end in C divided by the volume of C. The intuitive idea behind conductance is that it looks for sets C that are neither too small nor too large, and yet can be disconnected from the network by cutting a relatively small number of edges. Small conductance suggests a closely knit community.

When we consider the sequence of communities formed by adding one node at a time, in order of their simrank, we often find that there are several points in the sequence where the conductance is a local minimum. These are the best choices for a community containing the source node. If there is more than one local minimum, then there are several communities, one nested within another, to which the source node can be said to belong.

EXAMPLE 10.27 Let us repeat Example 10.26, but use conductance as the criterion for goodness of a community. Recall the order in which we add nodes is Picture1, Sky, Tree, Picture3, Picture2. Let C_i be the community containing the first i of these nodes, and let c_i be the conductance of that community.

The first possibility is C_1 consisting of only the node Picture1. There are two edges with exactly one end in C_1. The volume of C_1 is the smaller of 2 (the degree of its one node) and 8 (the sum of the degrees of the other four nodes. Thus, $c_1 = 2/\min(2, 8) = 1$.

Now consider $C_2 = \{$Picture1, Sky$\}$. There are three edges that have exactly one end in C_2. The volume of C_2 is the smaller of the sum of the degrees of the two nodes in C_2 (i,e., $2 + 3 = 5$) and the sum of the degrees of the other three nodes, which is also 5. Thus, $c_2 = 3/\min(5, 5) = 3/5$.

Now, consider adding Tree to form $C_3 = \{Picture1, Sky, Tree\}$. The number of edges with exactly one end in C_3 is three. The sum of the degrees of the three nodes is $2 + 3 + 2 = 7$, while the sum of the degrees of the other two nodes is three. Thus, $c_3 = 3/\min(7, 3) = 1$. You may continue this sequence and find that $c_4 = 1/\min(9, 1) = 1$. In this case, there is only one minimum, and that is $c_2 = 3/5$. We thus conclude that the "best" community containing Picture1 is $C_2 = \{$Picture1, Sky$\}$. □

10.6.6 Exercises for Section 10.6

EXERCISE 10.6.1 If, in Fig. 10.22 you start the walk from Picture 2, what will be the similarity to Picture 2 of the other two pictures? Which do you expect to be more similar to Picture 2?

EXERCISE 10.6.2 If, in Fig. 10.22 you start the walk from Picture 3, what do you expect the similarity to the other two pictures to be?

! EXERCISE 10.6.3 Repeat the analysis of Example 10.24, and compute the similarities of Picture 1 to the other pictures, if the following modifications are made to Fig. 10.22:

(a) The tag "Tree" is added to Picture 2.
(b) A third tag "Water" is added to Picture 3.
(c) A third tag "Water" is added to both Picture 1 and Picture 2.

Note: the changes are independently done for each part; they are not cumulative.

EXERCISE 10.6.4 Continue the simulation started in Fig. 10.23, assuming the next three values for U are Picture1, Sky, and Tree.

EXERCISE 10.6.5 What is the smallest value of ϵ for which we can say that Fig. 10.23 is a complete execution of the approximate PageRank algorithm?

!! EXERCISE 10.6.6   Suppose our network consists of only two nodes with an edge between them. Let the nodes be S (the source, to which teleports occur) and T, the other node.

(a) Suppose that we run a modified version of the approximate-PageRank algorithm of Section 10.6.3, where all (rather than only half) of the untaxed residual of the selected node is distributed to its neighbors (in this case, to the one neighbor). What is the sequence of values for the vectors $\mathbf{r}$ and $\mathbf{q}$ that results? Note that in this case, the choice of U is deterministic, since at any step only one of the two nodes has residual PageRank. For very small ϵ, what is the limit of the approximate PageRank vector?

(b) Suppose that for the same network, we instead run the original algorithm, where only half the residual is distributed to the neighbor. What is the limiting PageRank in this case, assuming ϵ is tiny?

EXERCISE 10.6.7   For the network of Fig. 10.22, compute the simrank when the source node is Tree. Then find the best choice of communities containing Tree if your requirement on a community is

(a) Density at least 2/3.

(b) Local minimum in conductance.

! EXERCISE 10.6.8   Suppose our network consists of nodes in a single chain, that is, nodes $U_1, U_2, \ldots, U_n$, with an edge between U_i and U_{i+1}, for $1 \le i < n$.

(a) As a function of k, compute the density of the "community" consisting of the first k nodes: $\{U_1, U_2, \ldots, U_k\}$.

(b) As a function of k, compute the conductance of the community consisting of the first k nodes.

(c) Using density as the measure of goodness for a community, what is the best value of k?

(d) Using conductance as the measure of goodness for a community, what is the best value of k?

10.7   Counting Triangles

One of the most useful properties of social-network graphs is the count of triangles and other simple subgraphs. In this section we shall give methods for estimating or getting an exact count of triangles in a very large graph. We begin with a motivation for such counts and then give some methods for counting efficiently.

10.7.1 Why Count Triangles?

If we start with n nodes and add m edges to a graph at random, there will be an expected number of triangles in the graph. We can calculate this number without too much difficulty. There are $\binom{n}{3}$ sets of three nodes, or approximately $n^3/6$ sets of three nodes that might be a triangle. The probability of an edge between any two given nodes being added is $m/\binom{n}{2}$, or approximately $2m/n^2$. The probability that any set of three nodes has edges between each pair, if those edges are independently chosen to be present or absent is approximately $(2m/n^2)^3 = 8m^3/n^6$. Thus, the expected number of triangles in a graph of n nodes and m randomly selected edges is approximately $(8m^3/n^6)(n^3/6) = \frac{4}{3}(m/n)^3$.

If a graph is a social network with n participants and m pairs of "friends," we would expect the number of triangles to be much greater than the value for a random graph. The reason is that if A and B are friends, and A is also a friend of C, there should be a much greater chance than average that B and C are also friends. Thus, counting the number of triangles helps us to measure the extent to which a graph looks like a social network.

We can also look at communities within a social network. It has been demonstrated that the age of a community is related to the density of triangles. That is, when a group has just formed, people pull in their like-minded friends, but the number of triangles is relatively small. If A brings in friends B and C, it may well be that B and C do not know each other. As the community matures, B and C may interact because of their membership in the community. Thus, there is a good chance that at sometime the triangle $\{A, B, C\}$ will be completed.

10.7.2 An Algorithm for Finding Triangles

We shall begin our study with an algorithm that has the fastest possible running time on a single processor. Suppose we have a graph of n nodes and $m \geq n$ edges. For convenience, assume the nodes are integers $1, 2, \ldots, n$.

Call a node a *heavy hitter* if its degree is at least $\sqrt{m}$. A *heavy-hitter triangle* is a triangle all three of whose nodes are heavy hitters. We use separate algorithms to count the heavy-hitter triangles and all other triangles. Note that the number of heavy-hitter nodes is no more than $2\sqrt{m}$, since otherwise the sum of the degrees of the heavy hitter nodes would be more than $2m$. Since each edge contributes to the degree of only two nodes, there would then have to be more than m edges.

Assuming the graph is represented by its edges, we preprocess the graph as follows:

(1) Compute the degree of each node. This part requires only that we examine each edge and add 1 to the count of each of its two nodes. The total time required is $O(m)$.

(2) Create an index on edges, with the pair of nodes at its ends as the key. That is, the index allows us to determine, given two nodes, whether the edge

between them exists. A hash table suffices. It can be constructed in $O(m)$ time, and the expected time to answer a query about the existence of an edge is a constant, at least in the expected sense.[2]

(3) Create another index of edges, this one with key equal to a single node. Given a node v, we can retrieve the nodes adjacent to v in time proportional to the number of those nodes. Again, a hash table, this time with single nodes as the key, suffices in the expected sense.

We shall order the nodes as follows. First, order nodes by degree. Then, if v and u have the same degree, recall that both v and u are integers, so order them numerically. That is, we say $v \prec u$ if and only if either

(i) The degree of v is less than the degree of u, or
(ii) The degrees of u and v are the same, and $v < u$.

Heavy-Hitter Triangles: There are only $O(\sqrt{m})$ heavy-hitter nodes, so we can consider all sets of three of these nodes. There are $O(m^{3/2})$ possible heavy-hitter triangles, and using the index on edges we can check if all three edges exist in $O(1)$ time. Therefore, $O(m^{3/2})$ time is needed to find all the heavy-hitter triangles.

Other Triangles: We find the other triangles a different way. Consider each edge (v_1, v_2). If both v_1 and v_2 are heavy hitters, ignore this edge. Suppose, however, that v_1 is not a heavy hitter and moreover $v_1 \prec v_2$. Let $u_1, u_2, \ldots, u_k$ be the nodes adjacent to v_1. Note that $k < \sqrt{m}$. We can find these nodes, using the index on nodes, in $O(k)$ time, which is surely $O(\sqrt{m})$ time. For each u_i we can use the first index to check whether edge (u_i, v_2) exists in $O(1)$ time. We can also determine the degree of u_i in $O(1)$ time, because we have counted all the nodes' degrees. We count the triangle $\{v_1, v_2, u_i\}$ if and only if the edge (u_i, v_2) exists, and $v_1 \prec u_i$. In that way, a triangle is counted only once – when v_1 is the node of the triangle that precedes both other nodes of the triangle according to the $\prec$ ordering. Thus, the time to process all the nodes adjacent to v_1 is $O(\sqrt{m})$. Since there are m edges, the total time spent counting other triangles is $O(m^{3/2})$.

We now see that preprocessing takes $O(m)$ time. The time to find heavy-hitter triangles is $O(m^{3/2})$, and so is the time to find the other triangles. Thus, the total time of the algorithm is $O(m^{3/2})$.

10.7.3 Optimality of the Triangle-Finding Algorithm

It turns out that the algorithm described in Section 10.7.2 is, to within an order of magnitude, the best possible. To see why, consider a complete graph on n nodes. This graph has $m = \binom{n}{2}$ edges and the number of triangles is $\binom{n}{3}$. Since

---

[2] Thus, technically, our algorithm is only optimal in the sense of expected running time, not worst-case running time. However, hashing of large numbers of items has an extremely high probability of behaving according to expectation, and if we happened to choose a hash function that made some buckets too big, we could rehash until we found a good hash function.

we cannot enumerate triangles in less time than the number of those triangles, we know any algorithm will take $\Omega(n^3)$ time on this graph. However, $m = O(n^2)$, so any algorithm takes $\Omega(m^{3/2})$ time on this graph.

One might wonder if there were a better algorithm that worked on sparser graphs than the complete graph. However, we can add to the complete graph a chain of nodes with any length up to n^2. This chain adds no more triangles. It no more than doubles the number of edges, but makes the number of nodes as large as we like, in effect lowering the ratio of edges to nodes to be as close to 1 as we like. Since there are still $\Omega(m^{3/2})$ triangles, we see that this lower bound holds for the full range of possible ratios of m/n.

10.7.4 Finding Triangles Using MapReduce

For a very large graph, we want to use parallelism to speed the computation. We can express triangle-finding as a multiway join and use the technique of Section 2.5.3 to optimize the use of a single MapReduce job to count triangles. It turns out that this use is one where the multiway-join technique of that section is generally much more efficient than taking two two-way joins. Moreover, the total execution time of the parallel algorithm is essentially the same as the execution time on a single processor using the algorithm of Section 10.7.2.

To begin, assume that the nodes of a graph are numbered $1, 2, \ldots, n$. We use a relation E to represent edges. To avoid representing each edge twice, we assume that if $E(A, B)$ is a tuple of this relation, then not only is there an edge between nodes A and B, but also, as integers, we have $A < B$.[3] This requirement also eliminates loops (edges from a node to itself), which we generally assume do not exist in social-network graphs anyway, but which could lead to "triangles" that really do not involve three different nodes.

Using this relation, we can express the set of triangles of the graph whose edges are E by the natural join

$$E(X, Y) \bowtie E(X, Z) \bowtie E(Y, Z) \tag{10.5}$$

To understand this join, we have to recognize that the attributes of the relation E are given different names in each of the three uses of E. That is, we imagine there are three copies of E, each with the same tuples, but with a different schemas. In SQL, this join would be written using a single relation $E(A, B)$ as follows:

```
SELECT e1.A, e1.B, e2.B
FROM E e1, E e2, E e3
WHERE e1.A = e2.A AND e1.B = e3.A AND e2.B = e3.B
```

In this query, the equated attributes $e1.A$ and $e2.A$ are represented in our join

---

[3] Do not confuse this simple numerical ordering of the nodes with the order $\prec$ that we discussed in Section 10.7.2 and which involved the degrees of the nodes. Here, node degrees are not computed and are not relevant.

by the attribute X. Also, $e1.B$ and $e3.A$ are each represented by Y; $e2.B$ and $e3.B$ are represented by Z.

Notice that each triangle appears once in this join. The triangle consisting of nodes v_1, v_2, and v_3 is generated when X, Y, and Z are these three nodes in numerical order, i.e., $X < Y < Z$. For instance, if the numerical order of the nodes is $v_1 < v_2 < v_3$, then X can only be v_1, Y is v_2, and Z is v_3.

The technique of Section 2.5.3 can be used to optimize the join of Equation 10.5. Recall the ideas in Example 2.15, where we considered the number of ways in which the values of each attribute should be hashed. In the present example, the matter is quite simple. The three occurrences of relation E surely have the same size, so by symmetry, attributes X, Y, and Z will each be hashed to the same number of buckets. In particular, if we hash nodes to b buckets, then there will be b^3 reducers. Each Reduce task is associated with a sequence of three bucket numbers (x, y, z), where each of x, y, and z is in the range 1 to b.

The Map tasks divide the relation E into as many parts as there are Map tasks. Suppose one Map task is given the tuple $E(u, v)$ to send to certain Reduce tasks. First, think of (u, v) as a tuple of the join term $E(X, Y)$. We can hash u and v to get the bucket numbers for X and Y, but we don't know the bucket to which Z hashes. Thus, we must send $E(u, v)$ to all Reducer tasks that correspond to a sequence of three bucket numbers $(h(u), h(v), z)$ for any of the b possible buckets z.

But the same tuple $E(u, v)$ must also be treated as a tuple for the term $E(X, Z)$. We therefore also send the tuple $E(u, v)$ to all Reduce tasks that correspond to a triple $(h(u), y, h(v))$ for any y. Finally, we treat $E(u, v)$ as a tuple of the term $E(Y, Z)$ and send that tuple to all Reduce tasks corresponding to a triple $(x, h(u), h(v))$ for any x. The total communication required is thus $3b$ key-value pairs for each of the m tuples of the edge relation E. That is, the minimum communication cost is $O(mb)$ if we use b^3 Reduce tasks.

Next, let us compute the total execution cost at all the Reduce tasks. Assume that the hash function distributes edges sufficiently randomly that the Reduce tasks each get approximately the same number of edges. Since the total number of edges distributed to the b^3 Reduce tasks is $O(mb)$, it follows that each task receives $O(m/b^2)$ edges. If we use the algorithm of Section 10.7.2 at each Reduce task, the total computation at a task is $O\big((m/b^2)^{3/2}\big)$, or $O(m^{3/2}/b^3)$. Since there are b^3 Reduce tasks, the total computation cost is $O(m^{3/2})$, exactly as for the one-processor algorithm of Section 10.7.2.

10.7.5 Using Fewer Reduce Tasks

By a judicious ordering of the nodes, we can lower the number of reduce tasks by approximately a factor of 6. Think of the "name" of the node i as the pair $(h(i), i)$, where h is the hash function that we used in Section 10.7.4 to hash nodes to b buckets. Order nodes by their name, considering only the first component (i.e., the bucket to which the node hashes), and only using the second component to break ties among nodes that are in the same bucket.

If we use this ordering of nodes, then the Reduce task corresponding to list of buckets (i, j, k) will be needed only if $i \leq j \leq k$. If b is large, then approximately $1/6$ of all b^3 sequences of integers, each in the range 1 to b, will satisfy these inequalities. For any b, the number of such sequences is $\binom{b+2}{3}$ (see Exercise 10.7.4). Thus, the exact ratio is $(b+2)(b+1)/(6b^2)$.

As there are fewer reducers, we get a substantial decrease in the number of key-value pairs that must be communicated. Instead of having to send each of the m edges to $3b$ Reduce tasks, we need to send each edge to only b tasks. Specifically, consider an edge e whose two nodes hash to i and j; these buckets could be the same or different. For each of the b values of k between 1 and b, consider the list formed from i, j, and k in sorted order. Then the Reduce task that corresponds to this list requires the edge e. But no other Reduce tasks require e.

To compare the communication cost of the method of this section with that of Section 10.7.4, let us fix the number of Reduce tasks, say k. Then the method of Section 10.7.4 hashes nodes to $\sqrt[3]{k}$ buckets, and therefore communicates $3m\sqrt[3]{k}$ key-value pairs. On the other hand, the method of this section hashes nodes to approximately $\sqrt[3]{6k}$ buckets, thus requiring $m\sqrt[3]{6}\sqrt[3]{k}$ communication. Thus, the ratio of the communication needed by the method of Section 10.7.4 to what is needed here is $3/\sqrt[3]{6} = 1.65$.

EXAMPLE 10.28   Consider the straightforward algorithm of Section 10.7.4 with $b = 6$. That is, there are $b^3 = 216$ Reduce tasks and the communication cost is $3mb = 18m$. We cannot use exactly 216 Reduce tasks with the method of this section, but we can come very close if we choose $b = 10$. Then, the number of Reduce tasks is $\binom{12}{3} = 220$, and the communication cost is $mb = 10m$. That is, the communication cost is 5/9th of the cost of the straightforward method. □

10.7.6   Exercises for Section 10.7

EXERCISE 10.7.1   How many triangles are there in the graphs of:

(a) Figure 10.1.
(b) Figure 10.9.
! (c) Figure 10.2.

EXERCISE 10.7.2   For each of the graphs of Exercise 10.7.1 determine:

(i) What is the minimum degree for a node to be considered a "heavy hitter"?
(ii) Which nodes are heavy hitters?
(iii) Which triangles are heavy-hitter triangles?

! EXERCISE 10.7.3   In this exercise we consider the problem of finding squares in a graph. That is, we want to find quadruples of nodes a, b, c, d such that the four edges (a,b), (b,c), (c,d), and (a,d) exist in the graph. Assume the graph is represented by a relation E as in Section 10.7.4. It is not possible to write a single join of four copies of E that expresses all possible squares in the graph, but we can write three such joins. Moreover, in some cases, we need to follow the join by a selection that eliminates "squares" where one pair of opposite corners are really the same node. We can assume that node a is numerically lower than its neighbors b and d, but there are three cases, depending on whether c is

(i)   also lower than b and d,
(ii) between b and d, or
(iii) higher than both b and d.

(a) Write the natural joins that produce squares satisfying each of the three conditions above. You can use four different attributes W, X, Y, and Z, and assume that there are four copies of relation E with different schemas, so the joins can each be expressed as natural joins.

(b) For which of these joins do we need a selection to assure that opposite corners are really different nodes?

!! (c) Assume we plan to use k Reduce tasks. For each of your joins from (a), into how many buckets should you hash each of W, X, Y, and Z in order to minimize the communication cost?

(d) Unlike the case of triangles, it is not guaranteed that each square is produced only once, although we can be sure that each square is produced by only one of the three joins. For example, a square in which the two nodes at opposite corners are each lower numerically than each of the other two nodes will only be produced by the join (i). For each of the three joins, how many times does it produce any square that it produces at all?

! EXERCISE 10.7.4   Show that the number of sequences of integers $1 \leq i \leq j \leq k \leq b$ is $\binom{b+2}{3}$. *Hint*: show that these sequences can be placed in a 1-to-1 correspondence with the binary strings of length $b+2$ having exactly three 1s.

10.8   Neighborhood Properties of Graphs

There are several important properties of graphs that relate to the number of nodes one can reach from a given node along a short path. In this section we look at algorithms for solving problems about paths and neighborhoods for very large graphs. In some cases, exact solutions are not feasible for graphs with millions of nodes. We therefore look at approximation algorithms as well as exact algorithms.

10.8.1   Directed Graphs and Neighborhoods

In this section we shall use a directed graph as a model of a network. A *directed graph* has a set of nodes and a set of *arcs*; the latter is a pair of nodes written

$u \to v$. We call u the *source* and v the *target* of the arc. The arc is said to be *from u to v*.

Many kinds of graphs can be modeled by directed graphs. The Web is a major example, where the arc $u \to v$ is a link from page u to page v. Or, the arc $u \to v$ could mean that telephone subscriber u has called subscriber v in the past month. For another example, the arc could mean that individual u is following individual v on Twitter. In yet another graph, the arc could mean that research paper u references paper v.

Moreover, all undirected graphs can be represented by directed graphs. Instead of the undirected edge (u, v), use two arcs $u \to v$ and $v \to u$. Thus, the material of this section also applies to graphs that are inherently undirected, such as a friends graph in a social network.

A *path* in a directed graph is a sequence of nodes $v_0, v_1, \ldots, v_k$ such that there are arcs $v_i \to v_{i+1}$ for all $i = 0, 1, \ldots, k - 1$. The *length* of this path is k, the number of arcs along the path. Note that there are $k + 1$ nodes in a path of length k, and a node by itself is considered a path of length 0.

The *neighborhood of radius d* for a node v is the set of nodes u for which there is a path of length at most d from v to u. We denote this neighborhood by $N(v, d)$. For example, $N(v, 0)$ is always $\{v\}$, and $N(v, 1)$ is v plus the set of nodes to which there is an arc from v. More generally, if V is a set of nodes, then $N(V, d)$ is the set of nodes u for which there is a path of length d or less from at least one node in the set V.

The *neighborhood profile* of a node v is the sequence of sizes of its neighborhoods $|N(v, 1)|, |N(v, 2)|, \ldots$. We do not include the neighborhood of distance 0, since its size is always 1.

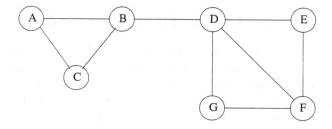

Figure 10.24 Our small social network; think of it as a directed graph

EXAMPLE 10.29 Consider the undirected graph of Fig. 10.1, which we reproduce here as Fig. 10.24. To turn it into a directed graph, think of each edge as a pair of arcs, one in each direction. For instance, the edge (A, B) becomes the arcs $A \to B$ and $B \to A$. First, consider the neighborhoods of node A. We know $N(A, 0) = \{A\}$. Moreover, $N(A, 1) = \{A, B, C\}$, since there are arcs from A only to B and C. Furthermore, $N(A, 2) = \{A, B, C, D\}$ and $N(A, 3) = \{A, B, C, D, E, F, G\}$. Neighborhoods for larger radius are all the same as $N(A, 3)$.

On the other hand, consider node B. We find $N(B,0) = \{B\}$, $N(B,1) = \{A,B,C,D\}$, and $N(B,2) = \{A,B,C,D,E,F,G\}$. We know that B is more central to the network than A, and this fact is reflected by the neighborhood profiles of the two nodes. Node A has profile $3, 4, 7, 7, \ldots$, while B has profile $4, 7, 7, \ldots$. Evidently, B is more central than A, because at every distance, its neighborhood is at least as large as that of A. In fact, D is even more central than B, because its neighborhood profile $5, 7, 7, \ldots$ dominates the profile of each of the nodes. $\square$

10.8.2   The Diameter of a Graph

The *diameter* of a directed graph is the smallest integer d such that for every two nodes u and v there is a path of length d or less from u to v. In a directed graph, this definition only makes sense if the graph is *strongly connected*; that is, there is a path from any node to any other node. Recall our discussion of the Web in Section 5.1.3, where we observed that there is a large strongly connected subset of the Web in the "center," but that the Web as a whole is not strongly connected. Rather, there are some pages that reach nowhere by links, and some pages that cannot be reached by links.

If the graph is undirected, the definition of diameter is the same as for directed graphs, but the path may traverse the undirected edges in either direction. That is, we treat an undirected edge as a pair of arcs, one in each direction. The notion of diameter makes sense in an undirected graph as long as that graph is connected.

EXAMPLE 10.30   For the graph of Fig. 10.24, the diameter is 3. There are some pairs of nodes, such as A and E, that have no path of length less than 3. But every pair of nodes has a path from one to the other with length at most 3. $\square$

We can compute the diameter of a graph by computing the sizes of its neighborhoods of increasing radius, until at some radius we fail to add any more nodes. That is, for each node v, find the smallest d such that $|N(v,d)| = |N(v,d+1)|$. This d is the tight upper bound on the length of the shortest path from v to any node it can reach. Call it $d(v)$. For instance, we saw from Example 10.29 that $d(A) = 3$ and $d(B) = 2$. If there is any node v such that $|N(v,d(v))|$ is not the number of nodes in the entire graph, then the graph is not strongly connected, and we cannot offer any finite integer as its diameter. However, if the graph is strongly connected, then the diameter of the graph is $\max_v\big(d(v)\big)$.

The reason this computation works is that one way to express $N(v,d+1)$ is the union of $N(v,d)$ and the set of all nodes w such that for some u in $N(v,d)$ there is an arc $u \to w$. That is, we start with $N(v,d)$ and add to it the targets of all arcs that have a source in $N(v,d)$. If all the arcs with source in $N(v,d)$ are already in $N(v,d)$, then not only is $N(v,d+1)$ equal to $N(v,d)$, but all of $N(v,d+2), N(v,d+3), \ldots$ will equal $N(v,d)$. Finally, we observe that since $N(v,d) \subseteq N(v,d+1)$ the only way $|N(v,d)|$ can equal $|N(v,d+1)|$ is for $N(v,d)$

Six Degrees of Separation

There is a famous game called "six degrees of Kevin Bacon," the object of which is to find paths of length at most six in the graph whose nodes are movie stars and whose edges connect stars that played in the same movie. The conjecture is that in this graph, no movie star is of distance more than six from Kevin Bacon. More generally, any two movie stars can be connected by a path of length at most six; i.e., the diameter of the graph is six. A small diameter makes computation of neighborhoods more efficient, so it would be nice if all social-network graphs exhibited a similar small diameter. In fact, the phrase "six degrees of separation," refers to the conjecture that in the network of all people in the world, where an edge means that the two people know each other, the diameter is six. Unfortunately, as we shall discuss in Section 10.8.3, not all important graphs exhibit such tight connections.

---

and $N(v, d + 1)$ to be the same set. Thus, if d is the smallest integer such that $|N(v, d)| = |N(v, d + 1)|$, it follows that every node v can reach is reached by a path of length at most d.

10.8.3   Transitive Closure and Reachability

The *transitive closure* of a graph is the set of pairs of nodes (u, v) such that there is a path from u to v of length one or more. We shall sometimes write this assertion as $Path(u, v)$. A related concept is *reachability*. We say node u *reaches* node v if $u = v$ or $Path(u, v)$ is true.[4] The problem of computing the transitive closure is to find all pairs of nodes u and v in a graph for which $Path(u, v)$ is true. The reachability problem is, given a node u in the graph, find all $v \neq u$ such that $Path(u, v)$ is true.

These two concepts relate to the notions of neighborhoods that we have seen earlier. Define $N(u, \infty)$ to be $\bigcup_{i \geq 0} N(u, i)$. Then v is in $N(u, \infty)$ if and only if $v = u$ or $Path(u, v)$ is true. Thus, the reachability problem is to compute the union of all the neighborhoods of any radius for a given node u. The discussion in Section 10.8.2 reminds us that we can compute the reachable set for u by computing its neighborhoods up to that smallest radius d for which $N(u, d) = N(u, d + 1)$.

The two problems – transitive closure and reachability – are related, but there are many examples of graphs where reachability is feasible and transitive closure is not. For instance, suppose we have a Web graph of a billion nodes. If we want to find the pages (nodes) reachable from a given page, we can do so, even on a single machine with a large main memory. However, just to produce the transitive closure of the graph could involve 10^{18} pairs of nodes, which is not practical, even using a large computer cluster.[5]

---

[4] Note that both may be true, if there is a cycle involving node u.
[5] While we cannot compute the transitive closure completely, we can still learn a great deal

10.8.4   Reachability Via MapReduce

When it comes to parallel implementation, transitive closure is actually more readily parallelizable than is reachability. If we want to compute $N(v, \infty)$, the set of nodes reachable from node v, without computing the entire transitive closure, we have no option but to compute the sequence of neighborhoods, which is essentially a breadth-first search of the graph from v. In relational terms, suppose we have a relation $Arc(X, Y)$ containing those pairs (x, y) such that there is an arc $x \to y$. We want to compute iteratively a relation $Reach(X)$ that is the set of nodes reachable from node v. After i rounds, $Reach(X)$ will contain all those nodes in $N(v, i)$.

Initially, $Reach(X)$ contains only the node v. Suppose it contains all the nodes in $N(v, i)$ after some round of MapReduce. To construct $N(v, i + 1)$ we need to join $Reach$ with the Arc relation, then project onto the second component and perform a union of the result with the old value of $Reach$. In SQL terms, we perform

```
SELECT DISTINCT Arc.Y
FROM Reach, Arc
WHERE Arc.X = Reach.X;
```

This query asks us to compute the natural join of $Reach(X)$ and $Arc(X, Y)$, which we can do by MapReduce as explained in Section 2.3.7. Then, we have to group the result by Y and eliminate duplicates, a process that can be done by another MapReduce job as in Section 2.3.8.

We then take the union of the result of this query with the current value of $Reach$. At some round, we will find that there are no new $Reach$ facts added, and at that point we can stop. The current value of $Reach$ will be $N(v, \infty)$.

How many rounds this process requires depends on how far from v is the furthest node that v can reach. In many social-network graphs, the diameter is small, as discussed in the box on "Six Degrees of Separation." If so, computing reachability in parallel, using MapReduce or another approach, is feasible. Few rounds of computation will be needed, and the space requirements are not greater than the space it takes to represent the graph.

However, there are some graphs where the number of rounds is a serious impediment. For instance, in a typical portion of the Web, it has been found that most pages reachable from a given page are reachable by paths of length 10–15. Yet there are some pairs of pages such that the first reaches the second, but only through paths whose length is measured in the hundreds. For instance, blogs are sometimes structured so each response is reachable only through the comment to which it responds. Running arguments lead to long paths with no way to

about the structure of a graph, provided there are large strongly connected components. For example, the Web graph experiments discussed in Section 5.1.3 were done on a graph of about 200 million nodes. Although they never listed all the pairs of nodes in the transitive closure, they were able to describe the structure of the Web. We discuss the needed algorithm in Section 10.8.10.

"shortcut" around that path. Or a tutorial on the Web, with 50 chapters, may be structured so you can only get to Chapter i through the page for Chapter $i-1$.

10.8.5 Semi-naive Evaluation

There is a common trick that can make iterative evaluations such as that of Section 10.8.4 more efficient. There, at each round we joined the entire set of known reachable nodes with the arcs. However, if we knew at a previous round that node u was reachable, and there is an arc from u to some node w, then we have already discovered that w is reachable. Therefore, it is not necessary to consider node u again in the current round. By considering each member of *Reach* only at the round after its reachability was discovered, we save a lot of work.

The improved algorithm, which is an instance of what is called *seminaive evaluation*,[6] uses not only a set $Reach(X)$ but also a set $NewReach(X)$, consisting of all and only those nodes that were first discovered reachable at the previous round. Initially, we set *NewReach* to be $\{v\}$, the source node, while *Reach* is empty. We repeat the following steps until at some round, *NewReach* is a subset of *Reach*; i.e., no new *Reach* facts can be discovered.

(1) Insert each node in *NewReach* into *Reach*. If no change to *Reach* occurs, then we have discovered all reachable nodes, and the iteration ends.

(2) Otherwise, compute a new value for relation $NewReach(X)$ by setting it to be the result of the following query:

```
SELECT DISTINCT Arc.Y
FROM NewReach, Arc
WHERE Arc.X = NewReach.X;
```

10.8.6 Linear Transitive Closure

The method of Section 10.8.4 can be applied to compute the entire transitive closure in parallel, if we compute the reachable set from each node. However, there are more straightforward ways to compute the relation $Path(X, Y)$ from the relation $Arc(X, Y)$, and also ways that are more efficient. The simplest way to compute transitive closure is to start with $Path(x, Y)$ equal to $Arc(x, Y)$, and in each parallel round extend the lengths of paths that we know about by extending paths by a single arc. This approach is called *linear transitive closure*. In SQL terms, each round computes the new paths by

---

[6] This rather strange term has a history behind it. In the 1980s when it was first observed that "naive" algorithms for computing relations recursively by using the entire recursive relation at each round could be improved by only considering the new tuples at each round, it was assumed that shortly an even better approach, which could justify the name "not naive," would be discovered. Alas, no such improvement has ever been found, so we are left with the term "seminaive."

```
SELECT DISTINCT Path.X, Arc.Y
FROM Path, Arc
WHERE Arc.X = Path.Y;
```

As for reachability, we use the MapReduce algorithms for join and grouping-and-aggregation to execute this query, and then take the union of the query result with the old value of *Path*. The result will be the value of *Path* for the next round. The number of rounds we must execute is the same as for reachability. After d rounds, where d is the diameter of the graph, we will have followed all paths of length up to $d + 1$, and will therefore discover no new *Path* facts on the last round. At that point, we know we can stop.

As for rechability, we can use seminaive evaluation to speed up the join at each round. A fact $Path(v, u)$ that was discovered more than one round ago will already have been joined with every useful $Arc(u, w)$ fact, and therefore will not add any new *Path* facts at the current round. Therefore, we can implement linear TC by the following seminaive algorithm.

The improved algorithm uses the relation $Path(X, Y)$ as well as a relation $NewPath(X, Y)$, which contains all and only the *Path* facts that have been discovered at the previous round. Initially, we set $NewPath$ to be Arc, while $Path$ is empty. We repeat the following steps until at some round, $NewPath$ is a subset of $Path$.

(1) Insert each node in $NewPath$ into $Path$. If no change to $Path$ occurs, then we have discovered all $Path$ facts, and the iteration ends.

(2) Otherwise, compute a new value for relation $NewPath(X, Y)$ by setting it to be the result of the following query:

```
SELECT DISTINCT NewPath.X, Arc.Y
FROM NewPath, Arc
WHERE Arc.X = NewPath.Y;
```

10.8.7   Transitive Closure by Recursive Doubling

Interestingly, the transitive closure can be computed much faster in parallel than can strict reachability or linear transitive closure. By a recursive-doubling technique, we can double the length of paths we know about in a single round. Thus, on a graph of diameter d, we need only $\log_2 d$ rounds, rather than d rounds. If $d = 6$, the difference is not important, but if $d = 1000$, $\log_2 d$ is about 10, so there is a hundredfold reduction in the number of rounds.

The simplest recursive-doubling approach is to start with relation $Path(X, Y)$ equal to the arc relation $Arc(X, Y)$. Suppose that after i rounds, $Path(X, Y)$ contains all pairs (x, y) such that there is a path from x to y of length at most 2^i. Then if we join $Path$ with itself at the next round, we shall discover all those pairs (x, y) such that there is a path from x to y of length at most $2 \times 2^i = 2^{i+1}$. The recursive-doubling query in SQL is

---

Reachability From Recursive Doubling

We have claimed that computing reachability inherently requires a number of rounds equal to the diameter of the graph. That is not strictly true, but there is a downside to deviating from the method given in Section 10.8.4 for reachability. If we want the set $Reach(v)$, we can compute the transitive closure of the entire graph by recursive doubling, and then throw away all pairs that do not have v as their first component. But we cannot throw away all those pairs until we are done. During the computation of the transitive closure, we could wind up computing many facts $Path(x, y)$, where neither x nor y is reachable from v, and even if they are reachable from v, we may not need to know x can reach y. If the graph is large, it may be infeasible to store all the $Path$ facts, even though we could store the $Reach$ facts.

```
SELECT DISTINCT p1.X, p2.Y
FROM Path p1, Path p2
WHERE p1.Y = p2.X;
```

After computing this query, we get all pairs connected by a path of length between 2 and 2^{i+1}, assuming $Path$ contains pairs connected by paths of length between 1 and 2^i. If we take the union of the result of this query with the Arc relation itself, then we get all paths of length between 1 and 2^{i+1} and can use the union as the $Path$ relation in the next round of recursive doubling. The query itself can be implemented by two MapReduce jobs, one to do the join and the other to do the union and eliminate duplicates. As we observed for the parallel reachability computation, the methods of Sections 2.3.7 and 2.3.8 suffice. The union, discussed in Section 2.3.6 doesn't really require a MapReduce job of its own; it can be combined with the duplicate-elimination.

If a graph has diameter d, then after $\log_2 d$ rounds of the above algorithm $Path$ contains all pairs (x, y) connected by a path of length at most d; that is, it contains all pairs in the transitive closure. Unless we already know d, one more round will be necessary to verify that no more pairs can be found, but for large d, this process takes many fewer rounds than the breadth-first search that we used for reachability.

However, the above recursive-doubling method does a lot of redundant work. An example should make the point clear.

EXAMPLE 10.31   Suppose the shortest path from x_0 to x_{17} is of length 17; in particular, let there be a path $x_0 \to x_1 \to \cdots \to x_{17}$. We shall discover the fact $Path(x_0, x_{17})$ on the fifth round, when $Path$ contains all pairs connected by paths of length up to 16. The same path from x_0 to x_{17} will be discovered 16 times when we join $Path$ with itself. That is, we can take the fact $Path(x_0, x_{16})$ and combine it with $Path(x_{16}, x_{17})$ to obtain $Path(x_0, x_{17})$. Or we can combine $Path(x_0, x_{15})$ with $Path(x_{15}, x_{17})$ to discover the same fact, and so on. On the other hand, linear TC would discover this path only once: when $Path(x_0, x_{16})$ was in *NewPath*. □

As for the previous algorithms, the recursive-doubling algorithm has a more efficient version that uses seminaive evaluation. Again, we use two relations, $Path(X, Y)$ and $NewPath(X, Y)$. Instead of joining two copies of *Path*, we replace the second *Path* relation by *NewPath*. Note that if the shortest path from u to v has length k, then we can break this path into a head of length $\lfloor k/2 \rfloor$ at the beginning and a tail of length $\lceil k/2 \rceil$ at the end. The tail will not be discovered until the round $\lceil k/2 \rceil$, whereupon it appears in *NewPath*, while the head will surely be discovered at that round (if k is even) or before (if k is odd), and will thus be in *Path* for the next join with *NewPath*. Thus, the following seminaive version of recursive doubling will work.

Initially, we set *NewPath* to be *Arc*, while *Path* is empty. We repeat the following steps until at some round, *NewPath* is a subset of *Path*.

(1) Insert each node in *NewPath* into *Path*. If no change to *Path* occurs, then we have discovered all *Path* facts, and the iteration ends.
(2) Otherwise, compute a new value for relation $NewPath(X, Y)$ by setting it to be the result of the following query:

```
SELECT DISTINCT Path.X, NewPath.Y
FROM Path, NewPath
WHERE NewPath.X = Path.Y;
```

10.8.8   Smart Transitive Closure

There is a variant of recursive doubling, called *smart* transitive closure, that avoids discovering the same path more than once. Every path of length greater than 1 can be broken into a *head* whose length is a power of 2, followed by a *tail* whose length is no greater than the length of the head.

EXAMPLE 10.32   A path of length 13 has a head consisting of the first 8 arcs, followed by a tail consisting of the last 5 arcs. A path of length 2 is a head of length 1 followed by a tail of length 1. Note that 1 is a power of 2 (the 0th power), and the tail will be as long as the head whenever the path itself has a length that is a power of 2. □

To implement smart transitive closure in SQL, we introduce a relation $Q(X, Y)$ whose function after the ith round is to hold all pairs of nodes (x, y) such that the shortest path from x to y has length exactly 2^i. Also, after the ith round, $Path(x, y)$ will be true if the shortest path from x to y is of length at most $2^{i+1} - 1$. Note that this interpretation of *Path* is slightly different from the interpretation of *Path* in the simple recursive-doubling method given in Section 10.8.7.

Initially, set both Q and *Path* to be copies of the relation *Arc*. After the ith round, assume that Q and *Path* have the contents described in the previous paragraph. Note that for the round $i = 1$, the initial values of Q and *Path* initially satisfy the conditions as described for $i = 0$. On the $(i+1)$st round, we do the following:

(1) Compute a new value for Q by joining it with itself and thus discovering paths of twice the length as those in Q, using the SQL query

```
SELECT DISTINCT q1.X, q2.Y
FROM Q q1, Q q2
WHERE q1.Y = q2.X;
```

(2) Subtract *Path* from the relation Q computed in Step (1) Note that Step (1) discovers all paths of length 2^{i+1}. But some pairs connected by these paths may also have shorter paths. The result of Step (2) is to leave in Q all and only those pairs (u, v) such that the shortest path from u to v has length exactly 2^{i+1}.

(3) Join *Path* with the new value of Q computed in Step (2), using the SQL query

```
SELECT DISTINCT Q.X, Path.Y
FROM Q, Path
WHERE Q.Y = Path.X;
```

At the beginning of the round, *Path* contains all (y, z) such that the shortest path from y to z has a length up to $2^{i+1} - 1$, and the new value of Q contains all pairs (x, y) for which the shortest path from x to y is of length 2^{i+1}. Thus, the result of this query is the set of pairs (x, y) such that the shortest path from x to y has a length between $2^{i+1} + 1$ and $2^{i+2} - 1$, inclusive.

(4) Set the new value of *Path* to be the union of the relation computed in Step (3), the new value of Q computed in step (1), and the old value of *Path*. These three terms give us all pairs (x, y) whose shortest path is of length $2^{i+1} + 1$ through $2^{i+2} - 1$, exactly 2^{i+1}, and 1 through $2^{i+1} - 1$, respectively. Thus, the union gives us all shortest paths up to length $2^{i+2} - 1$, as required by the inductive hypothesis about what is true after each round.

Each round of the smart transitive-closure algorithm uses steps that are joins, aggregations (duplicate eliminations), or unions. A round can thus be implemented as a short sequence of MapReduce jobs. Further, a good deal of work can be saved if these operations can be combined, say by using the more general patterns of communication permitted by a workflow system (see Section 2.4.1).

Interestingly, smart TC already incorporates the seminaive trick. At each round, the relation Q contains only facts $Q(u, v)$ that have never been in Q before, since the shortest path from U to v is longer than the shortest paths that were represented in Q at any previous round. Further, when we join Q with *Path*, we are using only facts in Q that were not in Q in previous rounds, so Q is a subset of what would be *NewPath* in the algorithm of Section 10.8.7.

Path Facts Versus Paths

We should be careful to distinguish between a path, which is a sequence of arcs, and a path fact, which is a statement that there exists a path from some node x to some node y. The path fact has been shown typically as $Path(x, y)$. Smart transitive closure discovers each path only once, but it may discover a path fact more than once. The reason is that often a graph will have many paths from x to y, and may even have many different paths from x to y that are of the same length.

Not all paths are discovered independently by smart transitive closure. For instance, if there are arcs $w \rightarrow x \rightarrow y \rightarrow z$ and also arcs $x \rightarrow u \rightarrow z$, then the path fact $Path(w, z)$ will be discovered twice, once by combining $Path(w, y)$ with $Path(y, z)$ and again when combining $Path(w, u)$ with $Path(u, z)$. On the other hand, if the arcs were $w \rightarrow x \rightarrow y \rightarrow z$ and $w \rightarrow v \rightarrow y$, then $Path(w, z)$ would be discovered only once, when combining $Path(w, y)$ with $Path(y, z)$.

10.8.9   Comparison of Methods

The methods discussed in Sections 10.8.4 through 10.8.8 have their advantages and disadvantages. The principal issues are the number of rounds required and the time it takes to execute each round. We shall consider these costs on a directed graph with n nodes, e arcs, and diameter d.

For all the algorithms discussed, the cost of the joins dominates the cost of the other operations at a round – grouping, aggregation, and union. Thus, we shall think only about the cost of the joins. Further, we shall assume that the join is implemented efficiently, as in the algorithm of Section 2.3.7. In that algorithm, each tuple from each of the two relations is sent to one reducer, and the work at each reducer is the product of the numbers of tuples from each of the two relations at that reducer. Finally, we shall assume all the algorithms are implemented by their seminaive versions, since that is more efficient than the "naive" version. Figure 10.25 summarizes the analysis.

Algorithm	Computation	Rounds
Reachability	$O(e)$	d
Linear TC	$O(ne)$	d
Recursive Doubling	$O(n^3)$	$\log_2 d$
Smart TC	$O(n^3)$	$\log_2 d$

Figure 10.25 Costs of transitive-closure algorithms

The numbers of rounds for these algorithms have already been discussed. Reachability and linear transitive closure will find new *Reach* or *Path* facts until the search implied by their iterations allow any node to be reached from any other. That number of rounds is bounded by the diameter of the graph. When computing the full transitive closure, there will always be some nodes u and v such that the shortest path from u to v has distance d. Thus, linear transitive closure always requires d rounds. However, when we search from one particular node u, it is possible that it can reach all of the nodes it ever reaches using paths much shorter than the diameter of the graph. That is, the value of d could be determined by a pair of nodes that does not include u. For the two recursive-doubling methods, the last two lines of Fig. 10.25, we noted that in $\log_2 d$ rounds, we discover all paths of length up to d, and therefore discover all *Path* facts.

Now, consider the cost of the join in the seminaive version of the reachability algorithm of Section 10.8.4. Each node u can be in *NewReach* at only one round. In that round, it will meet all the arcs with head u at a reducer. Thus, over all the rounds and all the reducers at each round, the cost of joining node u with arcs is equal to the out-degree of u. Notice that each arc contributes to the out-degree of exactly one node – the node at its tail. Thus, the sum of the out-degrees of the nodes of a directed graph equals the number of arcs in the graph. That observation justifies the $O(e)$ bound for the cost of a round for reachability.

For seminaive linear transitive closure, consider a node u and the reducers corresponding to u over all the rounds. For each node v, only one of these reducers can receive the fact *NewPath*(v, u). At that round, this reducer will join this fact with all the *Arc*(u, w) facts and thereby incur cost equal to the out-degree of u. If we fix v and let u vary, then the total work of all reducers handling facts of the form *NewPath*(v, u) for any u is the sum of the out-degrees of all nodes u, which is the total number of edges, e. Then, when we sum this cost over all n of the nodes v, we find that the total number of facts joined among all the reducers at all the rounds is $O(ne)$.

Next, look at the join associated with the seminaive recursive-doubling algorithm of Section 10.8.7. Each fact *NewPath*(u, w) appears in *NewPath* at only one round. At that round, it may meet any *Path*(v, u) fact. Thus, the total work of all the reducers at all the rounds is n^2 (for the number of different facts that may ever appear in *NewPath*) times n (for the number of *Path* facts with which it may be joined when it appears. This argument justifies the $O(n^3)$ bound for seminaive recursive doubling.

Finally, look at smart transitive closure. Now, we are doing two joins at each round: Q with itself, and Q with *Path*. A fact $Q(u, w)$ can only appear at one round, and at worst it will be joined with n other facts $Q(v, u)$ at that round. Thus, the total work is at most $O(n^3)$, which is the product of n^2 facts times a join with n facts. The argument for the second join, Q with *Path*, is similar. Note that the upper bound on computation for smart TC is the same as for recursive doubling. However, as we discussed in Section 10.8.8, there is a strong likelihood that fewer pairs of *Path* facts will be connected using the smart-TC approach than if we use brute-force recursive doubling, even if the theoretical worst cases are the same.

10.8.10 Transitive Closure by Graph Reduction

A *strongly connected component* (SCC) of a graph is a set of nodes S such that:

(1) Every node in S reaches every other node in S.
(2) S is maximal, in the sense that there is no node outside S that both reaches every node in S and is reached by every node in S.

A typical directed graph such as the Web contains many strongly connected components (SCCs). We can collapse an SCC to a single node as far as computing the transitive closure is concerned, since all the nodes in an SCC reach exactly the same nodes. There is an elegant algorithm for finding the SCCs of a graph in time linear in the size of the graph, due to J.E. Hopcroft and R.E. Tarjan. However, this algorithm is inherently sequential, based on depth-first search, and so not well suited to parallel impelementation on large graphs.

We can find most of the SCCs in a graph by some random node selections, with two reachability calculations for each selected node. Moreover, the larger an SCC is, the more likely it is to be collapsed early, thus reducing the size of the graph quickly. The algorithm for reducing SCCs to single nodes is as follows. Let G be the graph to be reduced, and let G' be G with all the arcs reversed.

(1) Pick a node v from G at random.
(2) Find $N_G(v, \infty)$, the set of nodes reachable from v in G.
(3) Find $N_{G'}(v, \infty)$, the set of nodes that v reaches in the graph G' that has the arcs of G reversed. Equivalently, this set is those nodes that reach v in G.
(4) Construct the SCC S containing v, which is $N_G(v, \infty) \cap N_{G'}(v, \infty)$. That is, v and u are in the same SCC of G if and only if v can reach u and u can reach v.
(5) Replace SCC S by a single node s in G. To do so, delete all nodes in S from G and add s to the node set of G. Delete from G all arcs one or both ends of which are in S. Then, add to the arc set of G an arc $s \rightarrow x$ whenever there was an arc in G from any member of S to x. Finally, add an arc $x \rightarrow s$ if there was an arc from x to any member of S.

We can iterate the above steps a fixed number of times. Alternatively, we can iterate until the graph becomes sufficiently small. We even could examine all nodes until each is assigned to some SCC. Note that in the extreme case, a node v is in an SCC consisting of itself only, if

$$N_G(v, \infty) \cap N_{G'}(v, \infty) = \{v\}$$

If we make the latter choice, the resulting graph is called the *transitive reduction* of the original graph G. The transitive reduction is always acyclic, since if it had a cycle there would remain an SCC of more than one node. However, it is not necessary to reduce to an acyclic graph, as long as the resulting graph has sufficiently few nodes that it is feasible to compute the full transitive closure of this graph; that is, the number of nodes is small enough that we can deal with a result whose size is proportional to the square of that number of nodes.

While the transitive closure of the reduced graph is not exactly the same as the transitive closure of the original graph, the former, plus the information about what SCC each original node belongs to is enough to tell us anything that the transitive closure of the original graph tells us. If we want to know whether $Path(u, v)$ is true in the original graph, find the SCCs containing u and v. If u and v belong to the same SCC, then surely u can reach v. If they belong to different SCCs s and t, respectively, determine whether s reaches t in the reduced graph. If so, then u reaches v in the original graph, and if not, then not.

EXAMPLE 10.33   Let us reconsider the "bowtie" picture of the Web from Section 5.1.3. The number of nodes in the part of the graph examined was over 200 million; surely too large to deal with data of size proportional to the square of that number. There was one large set of nodes called "the SCC" that was regarded as the center of the graph. Since about one node in four was in this SCC, it would be collapsed to a single node as soon as any one of its members was chosen at random. But there are many other SCCs in the Web, even though they were not shown explicitly in the "bowtie." For instance, the in-component would have within it many large SCCs. The nodes in one of these SCCs can reach each other, and can reach some of the other nodes in the in-component, and of course they can reach all the nodes in the central SCC. The SCCs in the in- and out-components, the tubes, and other structures can all be collapsed, leading to a far smaller graph.   □

10.8.11   Approximating the Sizes of Neighborhoods

In this section we shall take up the problem of computing the neighborhood profile for each node of a large graph. A variant of the problem, which yields to the same technique, is to find the size of the reachable set for each node v, i.e., the set we have called $N(v, \infty)$. Recall that for a graph of a billion nodes, it is totally infeasible to compute the neighborhoods for each node, even using a very large cluster of machines. Even if we want only a count of the nodes in each neighborhood, rather than the nodes themselves, we need to remember the nodes found so far as we explore the graph, or else we shall not know whether a found node is new or one we have seen already.

On the other hand, it is not so hard to find an approximation to the size of each neighborhood, using the Flajolet–Martin technique discussed in Section 4.4.2. Recall that this technique uses some large number of hash functions; in this case, the hash functions are applied to the nodes of the graph. The important property of the bit string we get when we apply hash function h to node v is the "tail length" – the number of 0s at the end of the string. For any set of nodes, an estimate of the size of the set is 2^R, where R is the length of the longest tail for any member of the set. Thus, instead of storing all the members of the set, we can instead record only the value of R for that set. Of course, the Flajolet–Martin technique uses many different hash functions and combines the value of R obtained from each, so we need to record the value of R for each hash function. Nevertheless, the total space needed for (say) several hundred values of R is much less than the spece needed to list all the members of a large neighborhood.

EXAMPLE 10.34   If we use a hash function that produces a 64-bit string, then six bits are all that we need to store each value of R. For instance, if there are a billion nodes, and we want to estimate the size of the neighborhood for each, we can store the value of R for 20 hash functions for each node in 15 gigabytes.   □

If we store tail lengths for each neighborhood, we can use this information to compute estimates for the larger neighborhoods from our estimates for the smaller neighborhoods. That is, suppose we have computed our estimates for $|N(v, d)|$ for all nodes v, and we want to compute estimates for the neighborhoods of radius $d + 1$. For each hash function h, the value of R for $N(v, d + 1)$ is the largest of:

(1) The tail of v itself and
(2) The values of R associated with h and $N(u, d)$, where $v \to u$ is an arc of the graph.

Notice that it doesn't matter whether a node is reachable through only one successor of v in the graph, or through many different successors. We get the same estimate in either case. This useful property was the same one we exploited in Section 4.4.2 to avoid having to know whether a stream element appeared once or many times in the stream.

We shall now describe the complete algorithm, called *ANF* (Approximate Neighborhood Function). We choose K hash functions $h_1, h_2, \ldots, h_k$. For each node v and radius d, let $R_i(v, d)$ denote the maximum tail length of any node in $N(v, d)$ using hash function h_i.

BASIS: To initialize, let $R_i(v, 0)$ be the length of the tail of $h_i(v)$, for all i and v.

INDUCTION: Suppose we have computed $R_i(v, d)$ for all i and v. Initialize $R_i(v, d + 1)$ to be $R_i(v, d)$, for all i and v. Then, consider all arcs $x \to y$ in the graph, in any order. For each $x \to y$, set $R_i(x, d + 1)$ to the larger of its current value and $R_i(y, d)$.

Observe that the fact we can consider the arcs in any order may provide a big speedup in the case that we can store the R_i in main memory, while the set of arcs is so large it must be stored on disk. We can stream all the disk blocks containing arcs one at a time, thus using only one disk access per iteration per disk block used for arc storage. This advantage is similar to the one we observed in Section 6.2.1, where we pointed out how frequent-itemset algorithms like A-priori could take advantage of reading market-basket data in a stream, where each disk block was read only once for each round.

To estimate the size of $N(v, d)$, combine the values of the $R_i(v, d)$ for $i = 1, 2, \ldots, k$, as discussed in Section 4.4.3. That is, group the Rs into small groups, take the average, and take the median of the averages.

Another improvement to the ANF Algorithm can be had if we are only interested in estimating the sizes of the reachable sets, $N(v, \infty)$. It is not then necessary to save $R_i(v, d)$ for different radii d. We can maintain one value $R_i(v)$ for each hash function h_i and each node v. When on any round, we consider arc $x \rightarrow y$, we simply assign

$$R_i(x) := \max\big(R_i(x), R_i(y)\big)$$

We can stop the iteration when at some round no value of any $R_i(v)$ changes. Or if we know d is the diameter of the graph, we can just iterate d times.

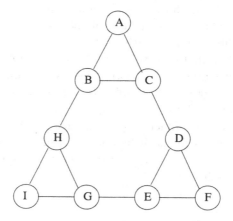

Figure 10.26 A graph for exercises on neighborhoods and transitive closure

10.8.12   Exercises for Section 10.8

EXERCISE 10.8.1   For the graph of Fig. 10.9, which we repeat here as Fig. 10.26:

(a) If the graph is represented as a directed graph, how many arcs are there?
(b) What are the neighborhood profiles for nodes A and B?
(c) What is the diameter of the graph?
(d) How many pairs are in the transitive closure? *Hint*: Do not forget that there are paths of length greater than zero from a node to itself in this graph.
(e) If we compute the transitive closure by recursive doubling, how many rounds are needed?

EXERCISE 10.8.2   The smart transitive-closure algorithm breaks paths of any length into head and tail of specific lengths. What are the head and tail lengths for paths of length 7, 8, and 9?

! EXERCISE 10.8.3   Fill in the values of the table in Fig. 10.25 for the versions of the algorithms for reachability, linear TC and recursive doubling if the seminaive trick is not used.

! EXERCISE 10.8.4   In Section 10.8.9 we observed that the sum of the out-degrees of the nodes in a directed graph equals the number of arcs in the graph. There is a similar relationship for an undirected graph, between the degrees of its nodes and its number of edges. Find and prove this relationship.

EXERCISE 10.8.5   Consider the running example of a social network, last shown in Fig. 10.24. Suppose we use one hash function h which maps each node (capital letter) to its ASCII code. Note that the ASCII code for A is 01000001, and the codes for $B, C, \ldots$ are sequential, $01000010, 01000011, \ldots$.

(a) Using this hash function, compute the values of R for each node and radius 1. What are the estimates of the sizes of each neighborhood? How do the estimates compare with reality?

(b) Next, compute the values of R for each node and radius 2. Again compute the estimates of neighborhood sizes and compare with reality.

(c) The diameter of the graph is 3. Compute the value of R and the size estimate for the set of reachable nodes for each of the nodes of the graph.

(d) Another hash function g is one plus the ASCII code for a letter. Repeat (a) through (c) for hash function g. Take the estimate of the size of a neighborhood to be the average of the estimates given by h and g. How close are these estimates?

10.9   Summary of Chapter 10

◆ *Social-Network Graphs*: Graphs that represent the connections in a social network are not only large, but they exhibit a form of locality, where small subsets of nodes (communities) have a much higher density of edges than the average density.

◆ *Communities and Clusters*: While communities resemble clusters in some ways, there are also significant differences. Individuals (nodes) normally belong to several communities, and the usual distance measures fail to represent closeness among nodes of a community. As a result, standard algorithms for finding clusters in data do not work well for community finding.

◆ *Betweenness*: One way to separate nodes into communities is to measure the betweenness of edges, which is the sum over all pairs of nodes of the fraction of shortest paths between those nodes that go through the given edge. Communities are formed by deleting the edges whose betweenness is above a given threshold.

◆ *The Girvan–Newman Algorithm*: The Girvan–Newman Algorithm is an efficient technique for computing the betweenness of edges. A breadth-first search from each node is performed, and a sequence of labeling steps computes the share of paths from the root to each other node that go through each of the edges. The shares for an edge that are computed for each root are summed to get the betweenness.

✦ *Communities and Complete Bipartite Graphs*: A complete bipartite graph has two groups of nodes, all possible edges between pairs of nodes chosen one from each group, and no edges between nodes of the same group. Any sufficiently dense community (a set of nodes with many edges among them) will have a large complete bipartite graph.

✦ *Finding Complete Bipartite Graphs*: We can find complete bipartite graphs by the same techniques we used for finding frequent itemsets. Nodes of the graph can be thought of both as the items and as the baskets. The basket corresponding to a node is the set of adjacent nodes, thought of as items. A complete bipartite graph with node groups of size t and s can be thought of as finding frequent itemsets of size t with support s.

✦ *Graph Partitioning*: One way to find communities is to partition a graph repeatedly into pieces of roughly similar sizes. A cut is a partition of the nodes of the graph into two sets, and its size is the number of edges that have one end in each set. The volume of a set of nodes is the number of edges with at least one end in that set.

✦ *Normalized Cuts*: We can normalize the size of a cut by taking the ratio of the size of the cut and the volume of each of the two sets formed by the cut. Then add these two ratios to get the normalized cut value. Normalized cuts with a low sum are good, in the sense that they tend to divide the nodes into two roughly equal parts, and have a relatively small size.

✦ *Adjacency Matrices*: These matrices describe a graph. The entry in row i and column j is 1 if there is an edge between nodes i and j, and 0 otherwise.

✦ *Degree Matrices*: The degree matrix for a graph has d in the ith diagonal entry if d is the degree of the ith node. Off the diagonal, all entries are 0.

✦ *Laplacian Matrices*: The Laplacian matrix for a graph is its degree matrix minus its adjacency matrix. That is, the entry in row i and column i of the Laplacian matrix is the degree of the ith node of the graph, and the entry in row i and column j, for $i \neq j$, is -1 if there is an edge between nodes i and j, and 0 otherwise.

✦ *Spectral Method for Partitioning Graphs*: The lowest eigenvalue for any Laplacian matrix is 0, and its corresponding eigenvector consists of all 1s. The eigenvectors corresponding to small eigenvalues can be used to guide a partition of the graph into two parts of similar size with a small cut value. For one example, putting the nodes with a positive component in the eigenvector with the second-smallest eigenvalue into one set and those with a negative component into the other is usually good.

✦ *Overlapping Communities*: Typically, individuals are members of several communities. In graphs describing social networks, it is normal for the probability that two individuals are friends to rise as the number of communities of which both are members grows.

◆ *The Affiliation-Graph Model*: An appropriate model for membership in communities is to assume that for each community there is a probability that because of this community two members become friends (have an edge in the social network graph). Thus, the probability that two nodes have an edge is 1 minus the product of the probabilities that none of the communities of which both are members cause there to be an edge between them. We then find the assignment of nodes to communities and the values of those probabilities that best describes the observed social graph.

◆ *Maximum-Likelihood Estimation*: An important modeling technique, useful for modeling communities as well as many other things, is to compute, as a function of all choices of parameter values that the model allows, the probability that the observed data would be generated. The values that yield the highest probability are assumed to be correct, and called the maximum-likelihood estimate (MLE).

◆ *Use of Gradient Descent*: If we know membership in communities, we can find the MLE by gradient descent or other methods. However, we cannot find the best membership in communities by gradient descent, because membership is discrete, not continuous.

◆ *Improved Community Modeling by Strength of Membership*: We can formulate the problem of finding the MLE of communities in a social graph by assuming individuals have a strength of membership in each community, possibly 0 if they are not a member. If we define the probability of an edge between two nodes to be a function of their membership strengths in their common communities, we can turn the problem of finding the MLE into a continuous problem and solve it using gradient descent.

◆ *Simrank*: One way to measure the similarity of nodes in a graph with several types of nodes is to start a random walker at one node and allow it to wander, with a fixed probability of restarting at the same node. The distribution of where the walker can be expected to be is a good measure of the similarity of nodes to the starting node. This process must be repeated with each node as the starting node if we are to get all-pairs similarity.

◆ *Triangles in Social Networks*: The number of triangles per node is an important measure of the closeness of a community and often reflects its maturity. We can enumerate or count the triangles in a graph with m edges in $O(m^{3/2})$ time, but no more efficient algorithm exists in general.

◆ *Triangle Finding by MapReduce*: We can find triangles in a single round of MapReduce by treating it as a three-way join. Each edge must be sent to a number of reducers proportional to the cube root of the total number of reducers, and the total computation time spent at all the reducers is proportional to the time of the serial algorithm for triangle finding.

◆ *Neighborhoods*: The neighborhood of radius d for a node v in a directed or undirected graph is the set of nodes reachable from v along paths of length at most d. The neighborhood profile of a node is the sequence of neighborhood sizes for all distances from 1 upwards. The diameter of a connected graph is the smallest d for which the neighborhood of radius d for any starting node includes the entire graph.

✦ *Transitive Closure*: A node v can reach node u if u is in the neighborhood of v for some radius. The transitive closure of a graph is the set of pairs of nodes (v, u) such that v can reach u.

✦ *Computing Transitive Closure*: Since the transitive closure can have a number of facts equal to the square of the number of nodes of a graph, it is infeasible to compute transitive closure directly for large graphs. One approach is to find strongly connected components of the graph and collapse them each to a single node before computing the transitive closure.

✦ *Transitive Closure and MapReduce*: We can view transitive closure computation as the iterative join of a path relation (pairs of nodes v and u such that u is known to be reachable from v) and the arc relation of the graph. Such an approach requires a number of MapReduce rounds equal to the diameter of the graph.

✦ *Semi-naive Evaluation*: When computing the transitive closure for a graph, we can speed up the iterative evaluation of the *Path* relation by recognizing that a *Path* fact is only useful on the round after that round when it was first discovered. A similar idea speeds up the reachability calculation and many similar iterative algorithms.

✦ *Transitive Closure by Recursive Doubling*: An approach that uses fewer MapReduce rounds is to join the path relation with itself at each round. At each round, we double the length of paths that are able to contribute to the transitive closure. Thus, the number of needed rounds is only the base-2 logarithm of the diameter of the graph.

✦ *Smart Transitive Closure*: While recursive doubling can cause the same path to be considered many times, and thus increases the total computation time (compared with iteratively joining paths with single arcs), a variant called smart transitive closure avoids discovering the same path more than once. The trick is to require that when joining two paths, the first has a length that is a power of 2.

✦ *Approximating Neighborhood Sizes*: By using the Flajolet–Martin technique for approximating the number of distinct elements in a stream, we can find the neighborhood sizes at different radii approximately. We maintain a set of tail lengths for each node. To increase the radius by 1, we examine each edge (u, v) and for each tail length for u we set it equal to the corresponding tail length for v if the latter is larger than the former.

10.10   References for Chapter 10

Simrank comes from [8]. An alternative approach in [11] views similarity of two nodes as the propability that random walks from the two nodes will be at the same node. [3] combines random walks with node classification to predict links in a social-network graph. [16] looks at the efficiency of computing simrank as a personalized PageRank.

The Girvan–Newman Algorithm is from [6]. Finding communities by searching for complete bipartite graphs appears in [9].

Normalized cuts for spectral analysis were introduced in [13]. [19] is a survey of spectral methods for finding clusters, and [5] is a more general survey of community finding in graphs. [10] is an analysis of communities in many networks encountered in practice.

Detection of overlapping communities is explored in [20], [21], and [22].

Counting triangles using MapReduce was discussed in [15]. The method descirbed here is from [1], which also gives a technique that works for any subgraph. [17] discusses randomized algorithms for triangle finding.

The ANF Algorithm was first investigated in [12]. [4] gives an additional speedup to ANF.

The Smart Transitive-Closure Algorithm was discovered by [7] and [18] independently. Implementation of transitive closure using MapReduce or similar systems is discussed in [2].

An open-source C++ implementation of many of the algorithms described in this chapter can be found in the SNAP library [[14]].

[1] F. N. Afrati, D. Fotakis, and J. D. Ullman, "Enumerating subgraph instances by map-reduce,"

http://ilpubs.stanford.edu:8090/1020

[2] F.N. Afrati and J.D. Ullman, "Transitive closure and recursive Datalog implemented on clusters," in *Proc. EDBT* (2012).

[3] L. Backstrom and J. Leskovec, "Supervised random walks: predicting and recommending links in social networks," *Proc. Fourth ACM Intl. Conf. on Web Search and Data Mining* (2011), pp. 635–644.

[4] P. Boldi, M. Rosa, and S. Vigna, "HyperANF: approximating the neighbourhood function of very large graphs on a budget," *Proc. WWW Conference* (2011), pp. 625–634.

[5] S. Fortunato, "Community detection in graphs," *Physics Reports* **486**:3–5 (2010), pp. 75–174.

[6] M. Girvan and M.E.J. Newman, "Community structure in social and biological networks," *Proc. Natl. Acad. Sci.* **99** (2002), pp. 7821–7826.

[7] Y.E. Ioannidis, "On the computation of the transitive closure of relational operators," *Proc. 12th Intl. Conf. on Very Large Data Bases*, pp. 403–411.

[8] G. Jeh and J. Widom, "Simrank: a measure of structural-context similarity," *Proceedings of the eighth ACM SIGKDD International Conference on Knowledge Discovery and Data Mining* (2002), pp. 538–543.

[9] R. Kumar, P. Raghavan, S. Rajagopalan, and A. Tomkins, "Trawling the Web for emerging cyber-communities, *Computer Networks* **31**:11–16 (May, 1999), pp. 1481–1493.

[10] J. Leskovec, K.J. Lang, A. Dasgupta, and M.W. Mahoney, "Community structure in large networks: natural cluster sizes and the absence of large well-defined clusters," `http://arxiv.org/abs/0810.1355`.

[11] S. Melnik, H. Garcia-Molina, and E. Rahm, "Similarity flooding: a versatile graph matching algorithm and its application to schema matching, *Proc. Intl. Conf. on Data Engineering* (2002), pp. 117–128.

[12] C.R. Palmer, P.B. Gibbons, and C. Faloutsos, "ANF: a fast and scalable tool for data mining in massive graphs," *Proc. Eighth ACM SIGKDD Intl. Conf. on Knowledge Discovery and Data Mining* (2002), pp. 81–90.

[13] J. Shi and J. Malik, "Normalized cuts and image segmentation," *IEEE Trans. on Pattern Analysis and Machine Intelligence*," **22**:8 (2000), pp. 888–905.

[14] Stanford Network Analysis Platform, `http://snap.stanford.edu`.

[15] S. Suri and S. Vassilivitskii, "Counting triangles and the curse of the last reducer," *Proc. WWW Conference* (2011).

[16] H. Tong, C. Faloutsos, and J.-Y. Pan, "Fast random walk with restart and its applications," *ICDM* 2006, pp. 613–622.

[17] C.E. Tsourakakis, U. Kang, G.L. Miller, and C. Faloutsos, "DOULION: counting triangles in massive graphs with a coin," *Proc. Fifteenth ACM SIGKDD Intl. Conf. on Knowledge Discovery and Data Mining* (2009).

[18] P. Valduriez and H. Boral, "Evaluation of recursive queries using join indices," *Expert Database Conf.* (1986), pp. 271–293.

[19] U. von Luxburg, "A tutorial on spectral clustering," *Statistics and Computing* bf17:4 (2007), 2007, pp. 395–416.

[20] J. Yang and J. Leskovec, "Overlapping community detection at scale: a non-negative matrix factorization approach," *ACM International Conference on Web Search and Data Mining*, 2013.

[21] J. Yang, J. McAuley, J. Leskovec, "Detecting cohesive and 2-mode communities in directed and undirected networks," *ACM International Conference on Web Search and Data Mining*, 2014.

[22] J. Yang, J. McAuley, J. Leskovec, "Community detection in networks with node attributes," *IEEE International Conference On Data Mining*, 2013.

11 Dimensionality Reduction

There are many sources of data that can be viewed as a large matrix. We saw in Chapter 5 how the Web can be represented as a transition matrix. In Chapter 9, the utility matrix was a point of focus. And in Chapter 10 we examined matrices that represent social networks. In many of these matrix applications, the matrix can be summarized by finding "narrower" matrices that in some sense are close to the original. These narrow matrices have only a small number of rows or a small number of columns, and therefore can be used much more efficiently than can the original large matrix. The process of finding these narrow matrices is called *dimensionality reduction*.

We saw a preliminary example of dimensionality reduction in Section 9.4. There, we discussed UV-decomposition of a matrix and gave a simple algorithm for finding this decomposition. Recall that a large matrix M was decomposed into two matrices U and V whose product UV was approximately M. The matrix U had a small number of columns whereas V had a small number of rows, so each was significantly smaller than M, and yet together they represented most of the information in M that was useful in predicting ratings of items by individuals.

In this chapter we shall explore the idea of dimensionality reduction in more detail. We begin with a discussion of eigenvalues and their use in "principal component analysis" (PCA). We cover singular-value decomposition, a more powerful version of UV-decomposition. Finally, because we are always interested in the largest data sizes we can handle, we look at another form of decomposition, called CUR-decomposition, which is a variant of singular-value decomposition that keeps the matrices of the decomposition sparse if the original matrix is sparse.

11.1 Eigenvalues and Eigenvectors of Symmetric Matrices

We shall assume that you are familiar with the basics of matrix algebra: multiplication, transpose, determinants, and solving linear equations for example. In this section, we shall define eigenvalues and eigenvectors of a symmetric matrix and show how to find them. Recall a matrix is symmetric if the element in row i and column j equals the element in row j and column i.

11.1.1   Definitions

Let M be a square matrix. Let λ be a constant and $\mathbf{e}$ a nonzero column vector with the same number of rows as M. Then λ is an *eigenvalue* of M and $\mathbf{e}$ is the corresponding *eigenvector* of M if $M\mathbf{e} = \lambda\mathbf{e}$.

If $\mathbf{e}$ is an eigenvector of M and c is any constant, then it is also true that $c\mathbf{e}$ is an eigenvector of M with the same eigenvalue. Multiplying a vector by a constant changes the length of a vector, but not its direction. Thus, to avoid ambiguity regarding the length, we shall require that every eigenvector be a *unit vector*, meaning that the sum of the squares of the components of the vector is 1. Even that is not quite enough to make the eigenvector unique, since we may still multiply by -1 without changing the sum of squares of the components. Thus, we shall normally require that the first nonzero component of an eigenvector be positive.

EXAMPLE 11.1   Let M be the matrix

$$\begin{bmatrix} 3 & 2 \\ 2 & 6 \end{bmatrix}$$

One of the eigenvectors of M is

$$\begin{bmatrix} 1/\sqrt{5} \\ 2/\sqrt{5} \end{bmatrix}$$

and its corresponding eigenvalue is 7. The equation

$$\begin{bmatrix} 3 & 2 \\ 2 & 6 \end{bmatrix} \begin{bmatrix} 1/\sqrt{5} \\ 2/\sqrt{5} \end{bmatrix} = 7 \begin{bmatrix} 1/\sqrt{5} \\ 2/\sqrt{5} \end{bmatrix}$$

demonstrates the truth of this claim. Note that both sides are equal to

$$\begin{bmatrix} 7/\sqrt{5} \\ 14/\sqrt{5} \end{bmatrix}$$

Also observe that the eigenvector is a unit vector, because $(1/\sqrt{5})^2 + (2/\sqrt{5})^2 = 1/5 + 4/5 = 1$.   □

11.1.2   Computing Eigenvalues and Eigenvectors

We have already seen one approach to finding an *eigenpair* (an eigenvalue and its corresponding eigenvector) for a suitable matrix M in Section 5.1: start with any unit vector $\mathbf{v}$ of the appropriate length and compute $M^i\mathbf{v}$ iteratively until it converges.[1] When M is a stochastic matrix, the limiting vector is the *principal eigenvector* (the eigenvector with the largest eigenvalue), and its corresponding eigenvalue is 1.[2] This method for finding the principal eigenvector, called *power*

---

[1] Recall M^i denotes multiplying by the matrix M i times, as discussed in Section 5.1.2.
[2] Note that a stochastic matrix is not generally symmetric. Symmetric matrices and stochastic matrices are two classes of matrices for which eigenpairs exist and can be exploited. In this chapter, we focus on techniques for symmetric matrices.

iteration, works quite generally, although if the principal eigenvalue (eigenvalue associated with the principal eigenvector) is not 1, then as i grows, the ratio of $M^{i+1}\mathbf{v}$ to $M^i\mathbf{v}$ approaches the principal eigenvalue while $M^i\mathbf{v}$ approaches a vector (probably not a unit vector) with the same direction as the principal eigenvector.

We shall take up the generalization of the power-iteration method to find all eigenpairs in Section 11.1.3. However, there is an $O(n^3)$-running-time method for computing all the eigenpairs of a symmetric $n \times n$ matrix exactly, and this method will be presented first. There will always be n eigenpairs, although in some cases, some of the eigenvalues will be identical. The method starts by restating the equation that defines eigenpairs, $M\mathbf{e} = \lambda\mathbf{e}$ as $(M - \lambda I)\mathbf{e} = \mathbf{z}$, where

(1) I is the $n \times n$ *identity matrix* with 1s along the main diagonal and 0s elsewhere.

(2) $\mathbf{z}$ is a vector of all 0s.

A fact of linear algebra is that in order for $(M - \lambda I)\mathbf{e} = \mathbf{z}$ to hold for a vector $\mathbf{e} \neq \mathbf{z}$, the determinant of $M - \lambda I$ must be 0. Notice that $(M - \lambda I)$ looks almost like the matrix M, but if M has c in one of its diagonal elements, then $(M - \lambda I)$ has $c - \lambda$ there. While the determinant of an $n \times n$ matrix has $n!$ terms, it can be computed in various ways in $O(n^3)$ time; an example is the method of "pivotal condensation."

The determinant of $(M - \lambda I)$ is an nth-degree polynomial in λ, from which we can get the n values of λ that are the eigenvalues of M. For any such value, say c, we can then solve the equation $M\mathbf{e} = c\mathbf{e}$. There are n equations in n unknowns (the n components of $\mathbf{e}$), but since there is no constant term in any equation, we can only solve for $\mathbf{e}$ to within a constant factor. However, using any solution, we can normalize it so the sum of the squares of the components is 1, thus obtaining the eigenvector that corresponds to eigenvalue c.

EXAMPLE 11.2 Let us find the eigenpairs for the 2×2 matrix M from Example 11.1. Recall $M =$

$$\begin{bmatrix} 3 & 2 \\ 2 & 6 \end{bmatrix}$$

Then $M - \lambda I$ is

$$\begin{bmatrix} 3 - \lambda & 2 \\ 2 & 6 - \lambda \end{bmatrix}$$

The determinant of this matrix is $(3 - \lambda)(6 - \lambda) - 4$, which we must set to 0. The equation in λ to solve is thus $\lambda^2 - 9\lambda + 14 = 0$. The roots of this equation are $\lambda = 7$ and $\lambda = 2$; the first is the principal eigenvalue, since it is the larger. Let $\mathbf{e}$ be the vector of unknowns

$$\begin{bmatrix} x \\ y \end{bmatrix}$$

We must solve

$$\begin{bmatrix} 3 & 2 \\ 2 & 6 \end{bmatrix} \begin{bmatrix} x \\ y \end{bmatrix} = 7 \begin{bmatrix} x \\ y \end{bmatrix}$$

When we multiply the matrix and vector we get two equations

$$\begin{aligned} 3x + 2y &= 7x \\ 2x + 6y &= 7y \end{aligned}$$

Notice that both of these equations really say the same thing: $y = 2x$. Thus, a possible eigenvector is

$$\begin{bmatrix} 1 \\ 2 \end{bmatrix}$$

But that vector is not a unit vector, since the sum of the squares of its components is 5, not 1. Thus to get the unit vector in the same direction, we divide each component by $\sqrt{5}$. That is, the principal eigenvector is

$$\begin{bmatrix} 1/\sqrt{5} \\ 2/\sqrt{5} \end{bmatrix}$$

and its eigenvalue is 7. Note that this was the eigenpair we explored in Example 11.1.

For the second eigenpair, we repeat the above with eigenvalue 2 in place of 7. The equation involving the components of e is $x = -2y$, and the second eigenvector is

$$\begin{bmatrix} 2/\sqrt{5} \\ -1/\sqrt{5} \end{bmatrix}$$

Its corresponding eigenvalue is 2, of course. □

11.1.3 Finding Eigenpairs by Power Iteration

We now examine the generalization of the process we used in Section 5.1 to find the principal eigenvector, which in that section was the PageRank vector – all we needed from among the various eigenvectors of the stochastic matrix of the Web. We start by computing the principal eigenvector by a slight generalization of the approach used in Section 5.1. We then modify the matrix to, in effect, remove the principal eigenvector. The result is a new matrix whose principal eigenvector is the second eigenvector (eigenvector with the second-largest eigenvalue) of the original matrix. The process proceeds in that manner, removing each eigenvector as we find it, and then using power iteration to find the principal eigenvector of the matrix that remains.

Let M be the matrix whose eigenpairs we would like to find. Start with any nonzero vector $\mathbf{x}_0$ and then iterate:

$$\mathbf{x}_{k+1} := \frac{M\mathbf{x}_k}{\|M\mathbf{x}_k\|}$$

where $\|N\|$ for a matrix or vector N denotes the *Frobenius norm*; that is, the square root of the sum of the squares of the elements of N. We multiply the current vector $\mathbf{x}_k$ by the matrix M until convergence (i.e., $\|x_k - x_{k+1}\|$ is less than some small, chosen constant). Let $\mathbf{x}$ be $\mathbf{x}_k$ for that value of k at which convergence is obtained. Then $\mathbf{x}$ is (approximately) the principal eigenvector of M. To obtain the corresponding eigenvalue we simply compute $\lambda_1 = \mathbf{x}^T M \mathbf{x}$, which is the equation $M\mathbf{x} = \lambda \mathbf{x}$ solved for λ, since $\mathbf{x}$ is a unit vector.

EXAMPLE 11.3   Take the matrix from Example 11.2:

$$M = \begin{bmatrix} 3 & 2 \\ 2 & 6 \end{bmatrix}$$

and let us start with $\mathbf{x}_0$ a vector with 1 for both components. To compute $\mathbf{x}_1$, we multiply $M\mathbf{x}_0$ to get

$$\begin{bmatrix} 3 & 2 \\ 2 & 6 \end{bmatrix} \begin{bmatrix} 1 \\ 1 \end{bmatrix} = \begin{bmatrix} 5 \\ 8 \end{bmatrix}$$

The Frobenius norm of the result is $\sqrt{5^2 + 8^2} = \sqrt{89} = 9.434$. We obtain $\mathbf{x}_1$ by dividing 5 and 8 by 9.434; that is:

$$\mathbf{x}_1 = \begin{bmatrix} 0.530 \\ 0.848 \end{bmatrix}$$

For the next iteration, we compute

$$\begin{bmatrix} 3 & 2 \\ 2 & 6 \end{bmatrix} \begin{bmatrix} 0.530 \\ 0.848 \end{bmatrix} = \begin{bmatrix} 3.286 \\ 6.148 \end{bmatrix}$$

The Frobenius norm of the result is 6.971, so we divide to obtain

$$\mathbf{x}_2 = \begin{bmatrix} 0.471 \\ 0.882 \end{bmatrix}$$

We are converging toward a normal vector whose second component is twice the first. That is, the limiting value of the vector that we obtain by power iteration is the principal eigenvector:

$$\mathbf{x} = \begin{bmatrix} 0.447 \\ 0.894 \end{bmatrix}$$

Finally, we compute the principal eigenvalue by

$$\lambda = \mathbf{x}^T M \mathbf{x} = \begin{bmatrix} 0.447 & 0.894 \end{bmatrix} \begin{bmatrix} 3 & 2 \\ 2 & 6 \end{bmatrix} \begin{bmatrix} 0.447 \\ 0.894 \end{bmatrix} = 6.993$$

Recall from Example 11.2 that the true principal eigenvalue is 7. Power iteration will introduce small errors due either to limited precision, as was the case here, or due to the fact that we stop the iteration before reaching the exact value of the eigenvector. When we computed PageRank, the small inaccuracies did not matter, but when we try to compute all eigenpairs, inaccuracies accumulate if we are not careful. □

To find the second eigenpair we create a new matrix $M^* = M - \lambda_1 \mathbf{x}\mathbf{x}^\mathrm{T}$. Then, use power iteration on M^* to compute its largest eigenvalue. The obtained $\mathbf{x}*$ and $\lambda*$ correspond to the second largest eigenvalue and the corresponding eigenvector of matrix M.

Intuitively, what we have done is eliminate the influence of a given eigenvector by setting its associated eigenvalue to zero. The formal justification is the following two observations. If $M^* = M - \lambda \mathbf{x}\mathbf{x}^\mathrm{T}$, where $\mathbf{x}$ and λ are the eigenpair with the largest eigenvalue, then:

(1) $\mathbf{x}$ is also an eigenvector of M^*, and its corresponding eigenvalue is 0. In proof, observe that

$$M^*\mathbf{x} = (M - \lambda \mathbf{x}\mathbf{x}^\mathrm{T})\mathbf{x} = M\mathbf{x} - \lambda \mathbf{x}\mathbf{x}^\mathrm{T}\mathbf{x} = M\mathbf{x} - \lambda\mathbf{x} = 0$$

At the next-to-last step we use the fact that $\mathbf{x}^\mathrm{T}\mathbf{x} = 1$ because $\mathbf{x}$ is a unit vector.

(2) Conversely, if $\mathbf{v}$ and λ_v are an eigenpair of a symmetric matrix M other than the first eigenpair $(\mathbf{x}, \lambda)$, then they are also an eigenpair of M^*. *Proof*:

$$M^*\mathbf{v} = (M^*)^\mathrm{T}\mathbf{v} = (M - \lambda \mathbf{x}\mathbf{x}^\mathrm{T})^\mathrm{T}\mathbf{v} = M^\mathrm{T}\mathbf{v} - \lambda\mathbf{x}(\mathbf{x}^\mathrm{T}\mathbf{v}) = M^\mathrm{T}\mathbf{v} = \lambda_v\mathbf{v}$$

This sequence of equalities needs the following justifications:
(a) If M is symmetric, then $M = M^\mathrm{T}$.
(b) The eigenvectors of a symmetric matrix are *orthogonal*. That is, the dot product of any two distinct eigenvectors of a matrix is 0. We do not prove this statement here.

EXAMPLE 11.4 Continuing Example 11.3, we compute

$$M^* = \begin{bmatrix} 3 & 2 \\ 2 & 6 \end{bmatrix} - 6.993 \begin{bmatrix} 0.447 \\ 0.894 \end{bmatrix} \begin{bmatrix} 0.447 & 0.894 \end{bmatrix} =$$

$$\begin{bmatrix} 3 & 2 \\ 2 & 6 \end{bmatrix} - \begin{bmatrix} 1.397 & 2.795 \\ 2.795 & 5.589 \end{bmatrix} = \begin{bmatrix} 1.603 & -0.795 \\ -0.795 & 0.411 \end{bmatrix}$$

We may find the second eigenpair by processing the matrix above as we did the original matrix M. □

11.1.4 The Matrix of Eigenvectors

Suppose we have an $n \times n$ symmetric matrix M whose eigenvectors, viewed as column vectors, are $\mathbf{e}_1, \mathbf{e}_2, \ldots, \mathbf{e}_n$. Let E be the matrix whose ith column is $\mathbf{e}_i$. Then $EE^\mathrm{T} = E^\mathrm{T}E = I$. The explanation is that the eigenvectors of a symmetric matrix are *orthonormal*. That is, they are orthogonal unit vectors.

EXAMPLE 11.5 For the matrix M of Example 11.2, the matrix E is

$$\begin{bmatrix} 2/\sqrt{5} & 1/\sqrt{5} \\ -1/\sqrt{5} & 2/\sqrt{5} \end{bmatrix}$$

E^{T} is therefore

$$\begin{bmatrix} 2/\sqrt{5} & -1/\sqrt{5} \\ 1/\sqrt{5} & 2/\sqrt{5} \end{bmatrix}$$

When we compute EE^{T} we get

$$\begin{bmatrix} 4/5+1/5 & -2/5+2/5 \\ -2/5+2/5 & 1/5+4/5 \end{bmatrix} = \begin{bmatrix} 1 & 0 \\ 0 & 1 \end{bmatrix}$$

The calculation is similar when we compute $E^{\mathrm{T}}E$. Notice that the 1s along the main diagonal are the sums of the squares of the components of each of the eigenvectors, which makes sense because they are unit vectors. The 0s off the diagonal reflect the fact that the entry in the ith row and jth column is the dot product of the ith and jth eigenvectors. Since eigenvectors are orthogonal, these dot products are 0. □

11.1.5 Exercises for Section 11.1

EXERCISE 11.1.1 Find the unit vector in the same direction as the vector $[1, 2, 3]$.

EXERCISE 11.1.2 Complete Example 11.4 by computing the principal eigenvector of the matrix that was constructed in this example. How close to the correct solution (from Example 11.2) are you?

EXERCISE 11.1.3 For any symmetric 3×3 matrix

$$\begin{bmatrix} a-\lambda & b & c \\ b & d-\lambda & e \\ c & e & f-\lambda \end{bmatrix}$$

there is a cubic equation in λ that says the determinant of this matrix is 0. In terms of a through f, find this equation.

EXERCISE 11.1.4 Find the eigenpairs for the following matrix:

$$\begin{bmatrix} 1 & 1 & 1 \\ 1 & 2 & 3 \\ 1 & 3 & 5 \end{bmatrix}$$

using the method of Section 11.1.2.

! EXERCISE 11.1.5 Find the eigenpairs for the following matrix:

$$\begin{bmatrix} 1 & 1 & 1 \\ 1 & 2 & 3 \\ 1 & 3 & 6 \end{bmatrix}$$

using the method of Section 11.1.2.

EXERCISE 11.1.6 For the matrix of Exercise 11.1.4:

(a) Starting with a vector of three 1s, use power iteration to find an approximate value of the principal eigenvector.

(b) Compute an estimate the principal eigenvalue for the matrix.

(c) Construct a new matrix by subtracting out the effect of the principal eigenpair, as in Section 11.1.3.

(d) From your matrix of (c), find the second eigenpair for the original matrix of Exercise 11.1.4.

(e) Repeat (c) and (d) to find the third eigenpair for the original matrix.

EXERCISE 11.1.7   Repeat Exercise 11.1.6 for the matrix of Exercise 11.1.5.

11.2   Principal-Component Analysis

Principal-component analysis, or PCA, is a technique for taking a dataset consisting of a set of tuples representing points in a high-dimensional space and finding the directions along which the tuples line up best. The idea is to treat the set of tuples as a matrix M and find the eigenvectors for MM^T or M^TM. The matrix of these eigenvectors can be thought of as a rigid rotation in a high-dimensional space. When you apply this transformation to the original data, the axis corresponding to the principal eigenvector is the one along which the points are most "spread out," More precisely, this axis is the one along which the variance of the data is maximized. Put another way, the points can best be viewed as lying along this axis, with small deviations from this axis. Likewise, the axis corresponding to the second eigenvector (the eigenvector corresponding to the second-largest eigenvalue) is the axis along which the variance of distances from the first axis is greatest, and so on.

We can view PCA as a data-mining technique. The high-dimensional data can be replaced by its projection onto the most important axes. These axes are the ones corresponding to the largest eigenvalues. Thus, the original data is approximated by data that has many fewer dimensions and that summarizes well the original data.

11.2.1   An Illustrative Example

We shall start the exposition with a contrived and simple example. In this example, the data is two-dimensional, a number of dimensions that is too small to make PCA really useful. Moreover, the data, shown in Fig. 11.1 has only four points, and they are arranged in a simple pattern along the 45-degree line to make our calculations easy to follow. That is, to anticipate the result, the points can best be viewed as lying along the axis that is at a 45-degree angle, with small deviations in the perpendicular direction.

To begin, let us represent the points by a matrix M with four rows – one for each point – and two columns, corresponding to the x-axis and y-axis. This

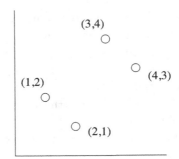

Figure 11.1 Four points in a two-dimensional space

matrix is

$$M = \begin{bmatrix} 1 & 2 \\ 2 & 1 \\ 3 & 4 \\ 4 & 3 \end{bmatrix}$$

Compute $M^T M$, which is

$$M^T M = \begin{bmatrix} 1 & 2 & 3 & 4 \\ 2 & 1 & 4 & 3 \end{bmatrix} \begin{bmatrix} 1 & 2 \\ 2 & 1 \\ 3 & 4 \\ 4 & 3 \end{bmatrix} = \begin{bmatrix} 30 & 28 \\ 28 & 30 \end{bmatrix}$$

We may find the eigenvalues of the matrix above by solving the equation

$$(30 - \lambda)(30 - \lambda) - 28 \times 28 = 0$$

as we did in Example 11.2. The solution is $\lambda = 58$ and $\lambda = 2$.

Following the same procedure as in Example 11.2, we must solve

$$\begin{bmatrix} 30 & 28 \\ 28 & 30 \end{bmatrix} \begin{bmatrix} x \\ y \end{bmatrix} = 58 \begin{bmatrix} x \\ y \end{bmatrix}$$

When we multiply out the matrix and vector we get two equations

$$30x + 28y = 58x$$
$$28x + 30y = 58y$$

Both equations tell us the same thing: $x = y$. Thus, the unit eigenvector corresponding to the principal eigenvalue 58 is

$$\begin{bmatrix} 1/\sqrt{2} \\ 1/\sqrt{2} \end{bmatrix}$$

For the second eigenvalue, 2, we perform the same process. Multiply out

$$\begin{bmatrix} 30 & 28 \\ 28 & 30 \end{bmatrix} \begin{bmatrix} x \\ y \end{bmatrix} = 2 \begin{bmatrix} x \\ y \end{bmatrix}$$

to get the two equations

$$30x + 28y = 2x$$
$$28x + 30y = 2y$$

Both equations tell us the same thing: $x = -y$. Thus, the unit eigenvector corresponding to the principal eigenvalue 2 is

$$\begin{bmatrix} -1/\sqrt{2} \\ 1/\sqrt{2} \end{bmatrix}$$

While we promised to write eigenvectors with their first component positive, we choose the opposite here because it makes the transformation of coordinates easier to follow in this case.

Now, let us construct E, the matrix of eigenvectors for the matrix $M^{\mathrm{T}}M$. Placing the principal eigenvector first, the matrix of eigenvectors is

$$E = \begin{bmatrix} 1/\sqrt{2} & -1/\sqrt{2} \\ 1/\sqrt{2} & 1/\sqrt{2} \end{bmatrix}$$

Any matrix of *orthonormal vectors* (unit vectors that are orthogonal to one another) represents a rotation and/or reflection of the axes of a Euclidean space. The matrix above can be viewed as a rotation 45 degrees counterclockwise. For example, let us multiply the matrix M that represents each of the points of Fig. 11.1 by E. The product is

$$ME = \begin{bmatrix} 1 & 2 \\ 2 & 1 \\ 3 & 4 \\ 4 & 3 \end{bmatrix} \begin{bmatrix} 1/\sqrt{2} & -1/\sqrt{2} \\ 1/\sqrt{2} & 1/\sqrt{2} \end{bmatrix} = \begin{bmatrix} 3/\sqrt{2} & 1/\sqrt{2} \\ 3/\sqrt{2} & -1/\sqrt{2} \\ 7/\sqrt{2} & 1/\sqrt{2} \\ 7/\sqrt{2} & -1/\sqrt{2} \end{bmatrix}$$

Figure 11.2 Figure 11.1 with the axes rotated 45 degrees counterclockwise

We see the first point, $[1, 2]$, has been transformed into the point

$$[3/\sqrt{2}, 1/\sqrt{2}]$$

If we examine Fig. 11.2, with the dashed line representing the new x-axis, we see that the projection of the first point onto that axis places it at distance $3/\sqrt{2}$

from the origin. To check this fact, notice that the point of projection for both the first and second points is $[1.5, 1.5]$ in the original coordinate system, and the distance from the origin to this point is

$$\sqrt{(1.5)^2 + (1.5)^2} = \sqrt{9/2} = 3/\sqrt{2}$$

Moreover, the new y-axis is, of course, perpendicular to the dashed line. The first point is at distance $1/\sqrt{2}$ above the new x-axis in the direction of the y-axis. That is, the distance between the points $[1, 2]$ and $[1.5, 1.5]$ is

$$\sqrt{(1 - 1.5)^2 + (2 - 1.5)^2} = \sqrt{(-1/2)^2 + (1/2)^2} = \sqrt{1/2} = 1/\sqrt{2}$$

Figure 11.3 shows the four points in the rotated coordinate system.

$(3/\sqrt{2}, 1/\sqrt{2})$ $(7/\sqrt{2}, 1/\sqrt{2})$

$(3/\sqrt{2}, -1/\sqrt{2})$ $(7/\sqrt{2}, -1/\sqrt{2})$

Figure 11.3 The points of Fig. 11.1 in the new coordinate system

The second point, $[2, 1]$ happens by coincidence to project onto the same point of the new x-axis. It is $1/\sqrt{2}$ below that axis along the new y-axis, as is confirmed by the fact that the second row in the matrix of transformed points is $[3/\sqrt{2}, -1/\sqrt{2}]$. The third point, $[3, 4]$, is transformed into $[7/\sqrt{2}, 1/\sqrt{2}]$; and the fourth point, $[4, 3]$, is transformed to $[7/\sqrt{2}, -1/\sqrt{2}]$. That is, they both project onto the same point of the new x-axis, and that point is at distance $7/\sqrt{2}$ from the origin, while they are $1/\sqrt{2}$ above and below the new x-axis in the direction of the new y-axis.

11.2.2   Using Eigenvectors for Dimensionality Reduction

From the example we have just worked out, we can see a general principle. If M is a matrix whose rows each represent a point in a Euclidean space with any number of dimensions, we can compute $M^{\mathrm{T}}M$ and compute its eigenpairs. Let E be the matrix whose columns are the eigenvectors, ordered as largest eigenvalue first. Define the matrix L to have the eigenvalues of $M^{\mathrm{T}}M$ along the diagonal, largest first, and 0s in all other entries. Then, since $M^{\mathrm{T}}M\mathbf{e} = \lambda\mathbf{e} = \mathbf{e}\lambda$ for each eigenvector $\mathbf{e}$ and its corresponding eigenvalue λ, it follows that $M^{\mathrm{T}}ME = EL$.

We observed that ME is the points of M transformed into a new coordinate space. In this space, the first axis (the one corresponding to the largest eigenvalue) is the most significant; formally, the variance of points along that axis is the greatest. The second axis, corresponding to the second eigenpair, is next most significant in the same sense, and the pattern continues for each of the eigenpairs. If we want to transform M to a space with fewer dimensions, then the choice that preserves the most significance is the one that uses the eigenvectors associated with the largest eigenvalues and ignores the other eigenvalues.

That is, let E_k be the first k columns of E. Then ME_k is a k-dimensional representation of M.

EXAMPLE 11.6 Let M be the matrix from Section 11.2.1. This data has only two dimensions, so the only dimensionality reduction we can do is to use $k = 1$; i.e., project the data onto a one dimensional space. That is, we compute ME_1 by

$$
\begin{bmatrix} 1 & 2 \\ 2 & 1 \\ 3 & 4 \\ 4 & 3 \end{bmatrix} \begin{bmatrix} 1/\sqrt{2} \\ 1/\sqrt{2} \end{bmatrix} = \begin{bmatrix} 3/\sqrt{2} \\ 3/\sqrt{2} \\ 7/\sqrt{2} \\ 7/\sqrt{2} \end{bmatrix}
$$

The effect of this transformation is to replace the points of M by their projections onto the x-axis of Fig. 11.3. While the first two points project to the same point, as do the third and fourth points, this representation makes the best possible one-dimensional distinctions among the points. $\square$

11.2.3 The Matrix of Distances

Let us return to the example of Section 11.2.1, but instead of starting with $M^T M$, let us examine the eigenvalues of MM^T. Since our example M has more rows than columns, the latter is a bigger matrix than the former, but if M had more columns than rows, we would actually get a smaller matrix. In the running example, we have

$$
MM^T = \begin{bmatrix} 1 & 2 \\ 2 & 1 \\ 3 & 4 \\ 4 & 3 \end{bmatrix} \begin{bmatrix} 1 & 2 & 3 & 4 \\ 2 & 1 & 4 & 3 \end{bmatrix} = \begin{bmatrix} 5 & 4 & 11 & 10 \\ 4 & 5 & 10 & 11 \\ 11 & 10 & 25 & 24 \\ 10 & 11 & 24 & 25 \end{bmatrix}
$$

Like $M^T M$, we see that MM^T is symmetric. The entry in the ith row and jth column has a simple interpretation; it is the dot product of the vectors represented by the ith and jth points (rows of M).

There is a strong relationship between the eigenvalues of $M^T M$ and MM^T. Suppose $\mathbf{e}$ is an eigenvector of $M^T M$; that is,

$$
M^T M \mathbf{e} = \lambda \mathbf{e}
$$

Multiply both sides of this equation by M on the left. Then

$$
MM^T(M\mathbf{e}) = M\lambda \mathbf{e} = \lambda(M\mathbf{e})
$$

Thus, as long as $M\mathbf{e}$ is not the zero vector $\mathbf{z}$, it will be an eigenvector of MM^{T} and λ will be an eigenvalue of MM^{T} as well as of $M^{\mathrm{T}}M$.

The converse holds as well. That is, if $\mathbf{e}$ is an eigenvector of MM^{T} with corresponding eigenvalue λ, then start with $MM^{\mathrm{T}}\mathbf{e} = \lambda\mathbf{e}$ and multiply on the left by M^{T} to conclude that $M^{\mathrm{T}}M(M^{\mathrm{T}}\mathbf{e}) = \lambda(M^{\mathrm{T}}\mathbf{e})$. Thus, if $M^{\mathrm{T}}\mathbf{e}$ is not $\mathbf{z}$, then λ is also an eigenvalue of $M^{\mathrm{T}}M$.

We might wonder what happens when $M^{\mathrm{T}}\mathbf{e} = \mathbf{z}$. In that case, $MM^{\mathrm{T}}\mathbf{e}$ is also $\mathbf{z}$, but $\mathbf{e}$ is not $\mathbf{z}$ because $\mathbf{z}$ cannot be an eigenvector. However, since $\mathbf{z} = \lambda\mathbf{e}$, we conclude that $\lambda = 0$.

We conclude that the eigenvalues of MM^{T} are the eigenvalues of $M^{\mathrm{T}}M$ plus additional 0s. If the dimension of MM^{T} were less than the dimension of $M^{\mathrm{T}}M$, then the opposite would be true; the eigenvalues of $M^{\mathrm{T}}M$ would be those of MM^{T} plus additional 0s.

$$
\begin{bmatrix}
3/\sqrt{116} & 1/2 & 7/\sqrt{116} & 1/2 \\
3/\sqrt{116} & -1/2 & 7/\sqrt{116} & -1/2 \\
7/\sqrt{116} & 1/2 & -3/\sqrt{116} & -1/2 \\
7/\sqrt{116} & -1/2 & -3/\sqrt{116} & 1/2
\end{bmatrix}
$$

Figure 11.4 Eigenvector matrix for MM^{T}

EXAMPLE 11.7   The eigenvalues of MM^{T} for our running example must include 58 and 2, because those are the eigenvalues of $M^{\mathrm{T}}M$ as we observed in Section 11.2.1. Since MM^{T} is a 4×4 matrix, it has two other eigenvalues, which must both be 0. The matrix of eigenvectors corresponding to 58, 2, 0, and 0 is shown in Fig. 11.4.   □

11.2.4   Exercises for Section 11.2

EXERCISE 11.2.1   Let M be the matrix of data points

$$
\begin{bmatrix}
1 & 1 \\
2 & 4 \\
3 & 9 \\
4 & 16
\end{bmatrix}
$$

(a) What are $M^{\mathrm{T}}M$ and MM^{T}?

(b) Compute the eigenpairs for $M^{\mathrm{T}}M$.

! (c) What do you expect to be the eigenvalues of MM^{T}?

! (d) Find the eigenvectors of MM^{T}, using your eigenvalues from part (c).

! EXERCISE 11.2.2   Prove that if M is any matrix, then $M^{\mathrm{T}}M$ and MM^{T} are symmetric.

11.3   Singular-Value Decomposition

We now take up a second form of matrix analysis that leads to a low-dimensional representation of a high-dimensional matrix. This approach, called *singular-value decomposition* (SVD), allows an exact representation of any matrix, and also makes it easy to eliminate the less important parts of that representation to produce an approximate representation with any desired number of dimensions. Of course the fewer the dimensions we choose, the less accurate will be the approximation.

We begin with the necessary definitions. Then, we explore the idea that the SVD defines a small number of "concepts" that connect the rows and columns of the matrix. We show how eliminating the least important concepts gives us a smaller representation that closely approximates the original matrix. Next, we see how these concepts can be used to query the original matrix more efficiently, and finally we offer an algorithm for performing the SVD itself.

11.3.1   Definition of SVD

Let M be an $m \times n$ matrix, and let the rank of M be r. Recall that the *rank* of a matrix is the largest number of rows (or equivalently columns) we can choose for which no nonzero linear combination of the rows is the all-zero vector $\mathbf{z}$ (we say a set of such rows or columns is *independent*). Then we can find matrices U, Σ, and V as shown in Fig. 11.5 with the following properties:

(1) U is an $m \times r$ *column-orthonormal matrix*; that is, each of its columns is a unit vector and the dot product of any two columns is 0.

(2) V is an $n \times r$ column-orthonormal matrix. Note that we always use V in its transposed form, so it is the rows of V^{T} that are orthonormal.

(3) Σ is a diagonal matrix; that is, all elements not on the main diagonal are 0. The elements of Σ are called the *singular values* of M.

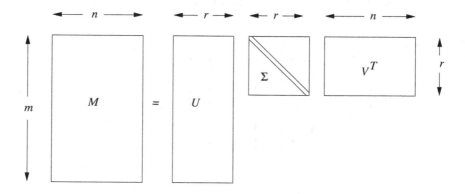

Figure 11.5 The form of a singular-value decomposition

EXAMPLE 11.8   Figure 11.6 gives a rank-2 matrix representing ratings of movies by users. In this contrived example there are two "concepts" underlying the movies: science-fiction and romance. All the boys rate only science-fiction, and all the girls rate only romance. It is this existence of two strictly adhered to concepts that gives the matrix a rank of 2. That is, we may pick one of the first four rows and one of the last three rows and observe that there is no nonzero linear sum of these rows that is 0. But we cannot pick three independent rows. For example, if we pick rows 1, 2, and 7, then three times the first minus the second, plus zero times the seventh is $\mathbf{z}$.

	Matrix	Alien	Star Wars	Casablanca	Titanic
Joe	1	1	1	0	0
Jim	3	3	3	0	0
John	4	4	4	0	0
Jack	5	5	5	0	0
Jill	0	0	0	4	4
Jenny	0	0	0	5	5
Jane	0	0	0	2	2

Figure 11.6 Ratings of movies by users

We can make a similar observation about the columns. We may pick one of the first three columns and one of the last two coluns, and they will be independent, but no set of three columns is independent.

The decomposition of the matrix M from Fig. 11.6 into U, Σ, and V, with all elements correct to two significant digits, is shown in Fig. 11.7. Since the rank of M is 2, we can use $r = 2$ in the decomposition. We shall see how to compute this decomposition in Section 11.3.6.   □

$$
\underbrace{\begin{bmatrix} 1 & 1 & 1 & 0 & 0 \\ 3 & 3 & 3 & 0 & 0 \\ 4 & 4 & 4 & 0 & 0 \\ 5 & 5 & 5 & 0 & 0 \\ 0 & 0 & 0 & 4 & 4 \\ 0 & 0 & 0 & 5 & 5 \\ 0 & 0 & 0 & 2 & 2 \end{bmatrix}}_{M}
=
\underbrace{\begin{bmatrix} .14 & 0 \\ .42 & 0 \\ .56 & 0 \\ .70 & 0 \\ 0 & .60 \\ 0 & .75 \\ 0 & .30 \end{bmatrix}}_{U}
\underbrace{\begin{bmatrix} 12.4 & 0 \\ 0 & 9.5 \end{bmatrix}}_{\Sigma}
\underbrace{\begin{bmatrix} .58 & .58 & .58 & 0 & 0 \\ 0 & 0 & 0 & .71 & .71 \end{bmatrix}}_{V^{\mathrm{T}}}
$$

Figure 11.7 SVD for the matrix M of Fig. 11.6

11.3.2   Interpretation of SVD

The key to understanding what SVD offers is in viewing the r columns of U, Σ, and V as representing *concepts* that are hidden in the original matrix M. In Example 11.8, these concepts are clear; one is "science fiction" and the other is "romance." Let us think of the rows of M as people and the columns of M as movies. Then matrix U connects people to concepts. For example, the person Joe, who corresponds to row 1 of M in Fig. 11.6, likes only the concept science fiction. The value 0.14 in the first row and first column of U is smaller than some of the other entries in that column, because while Joe watches only science fiction, he doesn't rate those movies highly. The second column of the first row of U is 0, because Joe doesn't rate romance movies at all.

The matrix V relates movies to concepts. The 0.58 in each of the first three columns of the first row of V^{T} indicates that the first three movies – *The Matrix*, *Alien*, and *Star Wars* – each are of the science-fiction genre, while the 0s in the last two columns of the first row say that these movies do not partake of the concept romance at all. Likewise, the second row of V^{T} tells us that the movies *Casablanca* and *Titanic* are exclusively romances.

Finally, the matrix Σ gives the strength of each of the concepts. In our example, the strength of the science-fiction concept is 12.4, while the strength of the romance concept is 9.5. Intuitively, the science-fiction concept is stronger because the data provides more information about the movies of that genre and the people who like them.

In general, the concepts will not be so clearly delineated. There will be fewer 0s in U and V, although Σ is always a diagonal matrix and will always have 0s off the diagonal. The entities represented by the rows and columns of M (analogous to people and movies in our example) will partake of several different concepts to varying degrees. In fact, the decomposition of Example 11.8 was especially simple, since the rank of the matrix M was equal to the desired number of columns of U, Σ, and V. We were therefore able to get an exact decomposition of M with only two columns for each of the three matrices U, Σ, and V; the product $U\Sigma V^{\mathrm{T}}$, if carried out to infinite precision, would be exactly M. In practice, life is not so simple. When the rank of M is greater than the number of columns we want for the matrices U, Σ, and V, the decomposition is not exact. We need to eliminate from the exact decomposition those columns of U and V that correspond to the smallest singular values, in order to get the best approximation. The following example is a slight modification of Example 11.8 that will illustrate the point.

EXAMPLE 11.9   Figure 11.8 is almost the same as Fig. 11.6, but Jill and Jane rated *Alien*, although neither liked it very much. The rank of the matrix in Fig. 11.8 is 3; for example the first, sixth, and seventh rows are independent, but you can check that no four rows are independent. Figure 11.9 shows the decomposition of the matrix from Fig. 11.8.

We have used three columns for U, Σ, and V because they decompose a matrix

$$\begin{array}{r|ccccc} & \text{Matrix} & \text{Alien} & \text{Star Wars} & \text{Casablanca} & \text{Titanic} \\ \hline \text{Joe} & 1 & 1 & 1 & 0 & 0 \\ \text{Jim} & 3 & 3 & 3 & 0 & 0 \\ \text{John} & 4 & 4 & 4 & 0 & 0 \\ \text{Jack} & 5 & 5 & 5 & 0 & 0 \\ \text{Jill} & 0 & 2 & 0 & 4 & 4 \\ \text{Jenny} & 0 & 0 & 0 & 5 & 5 \\ \text{Jane} & 0 & 1 & 0 & 2 & 2 \end{array}$$

Figure 11.8 The new matrix M', with ratings for *Alien* by two additional raters

$$\begin{bmatrix} 1 & 1 & 1 & 0 & 0 \\ 3 & 3 & 3 & 0 & 0 \\ 4 & 4 & 4 & 0 & 0 \\ 5 & 5 & 5 & 0 & 0 \\ 0 & 2 & 0 & 4 & 4 \\ 0 & 0 & 0 & 5 & 5 \\ 0 & 1 & 0 & 2 & 2 \end{bmatrix} =$$

$$M'$$

$$\begin{bmatrix} .13 & .02 & -.01 \\ .41 & .07 & -.03 \\ .55 & .09 & -.04 \\ .68 & .11 & -.05 \\ .15 & -.59 & .65 \\ .07 & -.73 & -.67 \\ .07 & -.29 & .32 \end{bmatrix} \begin{bmatrix} 12.4 & 0 & 0 \\ 0 & 9.5 & 0 \\ 0 & 0 & 1.3 \end{bmatrix} \begin{bmatrix} .56 & .59 & .56 & .09 & .09 \\ .12 & -.02 & .12 & -.69 & -.69 \\ .40 & -.80 & .40 & .09 & .09 \end{bmatrix}$$

$$\qquad U \qquad\qquad\qquad \Sigma \qquad\qquad\qquad\qquad V^{\mathrm{T}}$$

Figure 11.9 SVD for the matrix M' of Fig. 11.8

of rank three. The columns of U and V still correspond to concepts. The first is still "science fiction" and the second is "romance." It is harder to explain the third column's concept, but it doesn't matter all that much, because its weight, as given by the third nonzero entry in Σ, is very low compared with the weights of the first two concepts. □

In the next section, we consider eliminating some of the least important concepts. For instance, we might want to eliminate the third concept in Example 11.9, since it really doesn't tell us much, and the fact that its associated singular value is so small confirms its unimportance.

11.3.3   Dimensionality Reduction Using SVD

Suppose we want to represent a very large matrix M by its SVD components U, Σ, and V, but these matrices are also too large to store conveniently. The best way to reduce the dimensionality of the three matrices is to set the smallest of the singular values to zero. If we set the s smallest singular values to 0, then we can also eliminate the corresponding s columns of U and V.

EXAMPLE 11.10   The decomposition of Example 11.9 has three singular values. Suppose we want to reduce the number of dimensions to two. Then we set the smallest of the singular values, which is 1.3, to zero. The effect on the expression in Fig. 11.9 is that the third column of U and the third row of V^{T} are multiplied only by 0s when we perform the multiplication, so this row and this column may as well not be there. That is, the approximation to M' obtained by using only the two largest singular values is that shown in Fig. 11.10.

$$
\begin{bmatrix}
.13 & .02 \\
.41 & .07 \\
.55 & .09 \\
.68 & .11 \\
.15 & -.59 \\
.07 & -.73 \\
.07 & -.29
\end{bmatrix}
\begin{bmatrix}
12.4 & 0 \\
0 & 9.5
\end{bmatrix}
\begin{bmatrix}
.56 & .59 & .56 & .09 & .09 \\
.12 & -.02 & .12 & -.69 & -.69
\end{bmatrix}
$$

$$
=
\begin{bmatrix}
0.93 & 0.95 & 0.93 & .014 & .014 \\
2.93 & 2.99 & 2.93 & .000 & .000 \\
3.92 & 4.01 & 3.92 & .026 & .026 \\
4.84 & 4.96 & 4.84 & .040 & .040 \\
0.37 & 1.21 & 0.37 & 4.04 & 4.04 \\
0.35 & 0.65 & 0.35 & 4.87 & 4.87 \\
0.16 & 0.57 & 0.16 & 1.98 & 1.98
\end{bmatrix}
$$

Figure 11.10 Dropping the lowest singular value from the decomposition of Fig. 11.7

The resulting matrix is quite close to the matrix M' of Fig. 11.8. Ideally, the entire difference is the result of making the last singular value be 0. However, in this simple example, much of the difference is due to rounding error caused by the fact that the decomposition of M' was only correct to two significant digits. □

11.3.4   Why Zeroing Low Singular Values Works

The choice of the lowest singular values to drop when we reduce the number of dimensions can be shown to minimize the root-mean-square error between the original matrix M and its approximation. Since the number of entries is fixed, and the square root is a monotone operation, we can simplify and compare the Frobenius norms of the matrices involved. Recall that the *Frobenius norm*

How Many Singular Values Should We Retain?

A useful rule of thumb is to retain enough singular values to make up 90% of the *energy* in Σ. That is, the sum of the squares of the retained singular values should be at least 90% of the sum of the squares of all the singular values. In Example 11.10, the total energy is $(12.4)^2 + (9.5)^2 + (1.3)^2 = 245.70$, while the retained energy is $(12.4)^2 + (9.5)^2 = 244.01$. Thus, we have retained over 99% of the energy. However, were we to eliminate the second singular value, 9.5, the retained energy would be only $(12.4)^2/245.70$ or about 63%.

of a matrix M, denoted $\|M\|$, is the square root of the sum of the squares of the elements of M. Note that if M is the difference between one matrix and its approximation, then $\|M\|$ is proportional to the RMSE (root-mean-square error) between the matrices.

To explain why choosing the smallest singular values to set to 0 minimizes the RMSE or Frobenius norm of the difference between M and its approximation, let us begin with a little matrix algebra. Suppose M is the product of three matrices $M = PQR$. Let m_{ij}, p_{ij}, q_{ij}, and r_{ij} be the elements in row i and column j of M, P, Q, and R, respectively. Then the definition of matrix multiplication tells us

$$m_{ij} = \sum_k \sum_\ell p_{ik} q_{k\ell} r_{\ell j}$$

Then

$$\|M\|^2 = \sum_i \sum_j (m_{ij})^2 = \sum_i \sum_j \left(\sum_k \sum_\ell p_{ik} q_{k\ell} r_{\ell j} \right)^2 \tag{11.1}$$

When we square a sum of terms, as we do on the right side of Equation 11.1, we effectively create two copies of the sum (with different indices of summation) and multiply each term of the first sum by each term of the second sum. That is,

$$\left(\sum_k \sum_\ell p_{ik} q_{k\ell} r_{\ell j} \right)^2 = \sum_k \sum_\ell \sum_m \sum_n p_{ik} q_{k\ell} r_{\ell j} p_{in} q_{nm} r_{mj}$$

we can thus rewrite Equation 11.1 as

$$\|M\|^2 = \sum_i \sum_j \sum_k \sum_\ell \sum_n \sum_m p_{ik} q_{k\ell} r_{\ell j} p_{in} q_{nm} r_{mj} \tag{11.2}$$

Now, let us examine the case where P, Q, and R are really the SVD of M. That is, P is a column-orthonormal matrix, Q is a diagonal matrix, and R is the transpose of a column-orthonormal matrix. That is, R is *row-orthonormal*; its rows are unit vectors and the dot product of any two different rows is 0. To begin, since Q is a diagonal matrix, $q_{k\ell}$ and q_{nm} will be zero unless $k = \ell$ and $n = m$. We can thus drop the summations for ℓ and m in Equation 11.2 and set

$k = \ell$ and $n = m$. That is, Equation 11.2 becomes

$$\|M\|^2 = \sum_i \sum_j \sum_k \sum_n p_{ik} q_{kk} r_{kj} p_{in} q_{nn} r_{nj} \tag{11.3}$$

Next, reorder the summation, so i is the innermost sum. Equation 11.3 has only two factors p_{ik} and p_{in} that involve i; all other factors are constants as far as summation over i is concerned. Since P is column-orthonormal, We know that $\sum_i p_{ik} p_{in}$ is 1 if $k = n$ and 0 otherwise. That is, in Equation 11.3 we can set $k = n$, drop the factors p_{ik} and p_{in}, and eliminate the sums over i and n, yielding

$$\|M\|^2 = \sum_j \sum_k q_{kk} r_{kj} q_{kk} r_{kj} \tag{11.4}$$

Since R is row-orthonormal, $\sum_j r_{kj} r_{kj}$ is 1. Thus, we can eliminate the terms r_{kj} and the sum over j, leaving a very simple formula for the Frobenius norm:

$$\|M\|^2 = \sum_k (q_{kk})^2 \tag{11.5}$$

Next, let us apply this formula to a matrix M whose SVD is $M = U\Sigma V^{\mathrm{T}}$. Let the ith diagonal element of Σ be σ_i, and suppose we preserve the first n of the r diagonal elements of Σ, setting the rest to 0. Let Σ' be the resulting diagonal matrix. Let $M' = U\Sigma' V^{\mathrm{T}}$ be the resulting approximation to M. Then $M - M' = U(\Sigma - \Sigma')V^{\mathrm{T}}$ is the matrix giving the errors that result from our approximation.

If we apply Equation 11.5 to the matrix $M - M'$, we see that $\|M - M'\|^2$ equals the sum of the squares of the diagonal elements of $\Sigma - \Sigma'$. But $\Sigma - \Sigma'$ has 0 for the first n diagonal elements and σ_i for the ith diagonal element, where $n < i \leq r$. That is, $\|M - M'\|^2$ is the sum of the squares of the elements of Σ that were set to 0. To minimize $\|M - M'\|^2$, pick those elements to be the smallest in Σ. Doing so gives the least possible value of $\|M - M'\|^2$ under the constraint that we preserve n of the diagonal elements, and it therefore minimizes the RMSE under the same constraint.

11.3.5 Querying Using Concepts

In this section we shall look at how SVD can help us answer certain queries efficiently, with good accuracy. Let us assume for example that we have decomposed our original movie-rating data (the rank-2 data of Fig. 11.6) into the SVD form of Fig. 11.7. Quincy is not one of the people represented by the original matrix, but he wants to use the system to know what movies he would like. He has only seen one movie, *The Matrix*, and rated it 4. Thus, we can represent Quincy by the vector $\mathbf{q} = [4, 0, 0, 0, 0]$, as if this were one of the rows of the original matrix.

If we used a collaborative-filtering approach, we would try to compare Quincy with the other users represented in the original matrix M. Instead, we can map

Quincy into "concept space" by multiplying him by the matrix V of the decomposition. We find $qV = [2.32, 0]$.[3] That is to say, Quincy is high in science-fiction interest, and not at all interested in romance.

We now have a representation of Quincy in concept space, derived from, but different from his representation in the original "movie space." One useful thing we can do is to map his representation back into movie space by multiplying $[2.32, 0]$ by V^T. This product is $[1.35, 1.35, 1.35, 0, 0]$. It suggests that Quincy would like *Alien* and *Star Wars*, but not *Casablanca* or *Titanic*.

Another sort of query we can perform in concept space is to find users similar to Quincy. We can use V to map all users into concept space. For example, Joe maps to $[1.74, 0]$, and Jill maps to $[0, 5.68]$. Notice that in this simple example, all users are either 100% science-fiction fans or 100% romance fans, so each vector has a zero in one component. In reality, people are more complex, and they will have different, but nonzero, levels of interest in various concepts. In general, we can measure the similarity of users by their cosine distance in concept space.

EXAMPLE 11.11   For the case introduced above, note that the concept vectors for Quincy and Joe, which are $[2.32, 0]$ and $[1.74, 0]$, respectively, are not the same, but they have exactly the same direction. That is, their cosine distance is 0. On the other hand, the vectors for Quincy and Jill, which are $[2.32, 0]$ and $[0, 5.68]$, respectively, have a dot product of 0, and therefore their angle is 90 degrees. That is, their cosine distance is 1, the maximum possible.   □

11.3.6   Computing the SVD of a Matrix

The SVD of a matrix M is strongly connected to the eigenvalues of the symmetric matrices $M^T M$ and MM^T. This relationship allows us to obtain the SVD of M from the eigenpairs of the latter two matrices. To begin the explanation, start with $M = U\Sigma V^T$, the expression for the SVD of M. Then

$$M^T = (U\Sigma V^T)^T = (V^T)^T \Sigma^T U^T = V\Sigma^T U^T$$

Since Σ is a diagonal matrix, transposing it has no effect. Thus, $M^T = V\Sigma U^T$.

Now, $M^T M = V\Sigma U^T U\Sigma V^T$. Remember that U is an orthonormal matrix, so $U^T U$ is the identity matrix of the appropriate size. That is,

$$M^T M = V\Sigma^2 V^T$$

Multiply both sides of this equation on the right by V to get

$$M^T MV = V\Sigma^2 V^T V$$

Since V is also an orthonormal matrix, we know that $V^T V$ is the identity. Thus

$$M^T MV = V\Sigma^2 \tag{11.6}$$

Since Σ is a diagonal matrix, Σ^2 is also a diagonal matrix whose entry in the

---

[3] Note that Fig. 11.7 shows V^T, while this multiplication requires V.

*i*th row and column is the square of the entry in the same position of Σ. Now, Equation (11.6) should be familiar. It says that V is the matrix of eigenvectors of $M^{\mathrm{T}}M$ and Σ^2 is the diagonal matrix whose entries are the corresponding eigenvalues.

Thus, the same algorithm that computes the eigenpairs for $M^{\mathrm{T}}M$ gives us the matrix V for the SVD of M itself. It also gives us the singular values for this SVD; just take the square roots of the eigenvalues for $M^{\mathrm{T}}M$.

Only U remains to be computed, but it can be found in the same way we found V. Start with

$$MM^{\mathrm{T}} = U\Sigma V^{\mathrm{T}}(U\Sigma V^{\mathrm{T}})^{\mathrm{T}} = U\Sigma V^{\mathrm{T}}V\Sigma U^{\mathrm{T}} = U\Sigma^2 U^{\mathrm{T}}$$

Then by a series of manipulations analogous to the above, we learn that

$$MM^{\mathrm{T}}U = U\Sigma^2$$

That is, U is the matrix of eigenvectors of MM^{T}.

A small detail needs to be explained concerning U and V. Each of these matrices have r columns, while $M^{\mathrm{T}}M$ is an $n \times n$ matrix and MM^{T} is an $m \times m$ matrix. Both n and m are at least as large as r. Thus, $M^{\mathrm{T}}M$ and MM^{T} should have an additional $n - r$ and $m - r$ eigenpairs, respectively, and these pairs do not show up in U, V, and Σ. Since the rank of M is r, all other eigenvalues will be 0, and these are not useful.

11.3.7 Exercises for Section 11.3

EXERCISE 11.3.1   In Fig. 11.11 is a matrix M. It has rank 2, as you can see by observing that the first column plus the third column minus twice the second column equals **z**.

$$\begin{bmatrix} 1 & 2 & 3 \\ 3 & 4 & 5 \\ 5 & 4 & 3 \\ 0 & 2 & 4 \\ 1 & 3 & 5 \end{bmatrix}$$

Figure 11.11 Matrix M for Exercise 11.3.1

(a) Compute the matrices $M^{\mathrm{T}}M$ and MM^{T}.
! (b) Find the eigenvalues for your matrices of part (a).
(c) Find the eigenvectors for the matrices of part (a).
(d) Find the SVD for the original matrix M from parts (b) and (c). Note that there are only two nonzero eigenvalues, so your matrix Σ should have only two singular values, while U and V have only two columns.
(e) Set your smaller singular value to 0 and compute the one-dimensional approximation to the matrix M from Fig. 11.11.

(f) How much of the energy of the original singular values is retained by the one-dimensional approximation?

EXERCISE 11.3.2   Use the SVD from Fig. 11.7. Suppose Leslie assigns rating 3 to Alien and rating 4 to Titanic, giving us a representation of Leslie in "movie space" of $[0, 3, 0, 0, 4]$. Find the representation of Leslie in concept space. What does that representation predict about how well Leslie would like the other movies appearing in our example data?

! EXERCISE 11.3.3   Demonstrate that the rank of the matrix in Fig. 11.8 is 3.

! EXERCISE 11.3.4   Section 11.3.5 showed how to guess the movies a person would most like. How would you use a similar technique to guess the people that would most like a given movie, if all you had were the ratings of that movie by a few people?

11.4   CUR Decomposition

There is a problem with SVD that does not show up in the running example of Section 11.3. In large-data applications, it is normal for the matrix M being decomposed to be very sparse; that is, most entries are 0. For example, a matrix representing many documents (as rows) and the words they contain (as columns) will be sparse, because most words are not present in most documents. Similarly, a matrix of customers and products will be sparse because most people do not buy most products.

We cannot deal with dense matrices that have millions or billions of rows and/or columns. However, with SVD, even if M is sparse, U and V will be dense.[4] Since Σ is diagonal, it will be sparse, but Σ is usually much smaller than U and V, so its sparseness does not help.

In this section, we shall consider another approach to decomposition, called CUR-decomposition. The merit of this approach lies in the fact that if M is sparse, then the two large matrices (called C and R for "columns" and "rows") analogous to U and V in SVD are also sparse. Only the matrix in the middle (analogous to Σ in SVD) is dense, but this matrix is small so the density does not hurt too much.

Unlike SVD, which gives an exact decomposition as long as the parameter r is taken to be at least as great as the rank of the matrix M, CUR-decomposition is an approximation no matter how large we make r. There is a theory that guarantees convergence to M as r gets larger, but typically you have to make r so large to get, say within 1% that the method becomes impractical. Nevertheless, a decomposition with a relatively small value of r has a good probability of being a useful and accurate decomposition.

---

[4] In Fig. 11.7, it happens that U and V have a significant number of 0s. However, that is an artifact of the very regular nature of our example matrix M and is not the case in general.

Why the Pseudoinverse Works

In general suppose a matrix M is equal to a product of matrices XZY. If all the inverses exist, then the rule for inverse of a product tell us $M^{-1} = Y^{-1}Z^{-1}X^{-1}$. Since in the case we are interested in, XZY is an SVD, we know X is column-orthonormal and Y is row-orthonormal. In either of these cases, the inverse and the transpose are the same. That is, XX^{T} is an identity matrix of the appropriate size, and so is YY^{T}. Thus, $M^{-1} = Y^{\mathrm{T}}Z^{-1}X^{\mathrm{T}}$.

We also know Z is a diagonal matrix. If there are no 0s along the diagonal, then Z^{-1} is formed from Z by taking the numerical inverse of each diagonal element. It is only when there are 0s along the diagonal of Z that we are unable to find an element for the same position in the inverse such that we can get an identity matrix when we multiply Z by its inverse. That is why we resort to a "pseudoinverse," accepting the fact that the product ZZ^{+} will not be an identity matrix, but rather a diagonal matrix where the ith diagonal entry is 1 if the ith element of Z is nonzero and 0 if the ith element of Z is 0.

11.4.1   Definition of CUR

Let M be a matrix of m rows and n columns. Pick a target number of "concepts" r to be used in the decomposition. A *CUR-decomposition* of M is a randomly chosen set of r columns of M, which form the $m \times r$ matrix C, and a randomly chosen set of r rows of M, which form the $r \times n$ matrix R. There is also an $r \times r$ matrix U that is constructed from C and R as follows:

(1) Let W be the $r \times r$ matrix that is the intersection of the chosen columns of C and the chosen rows of R. That is, the element in row i and column j of W is the element of M whose column is the jth column of C and whose row is the ith row of R.

(2) Compute the SVD of W; say $W = X\Sigma Y^{\mathrm{T}}$.

(3) Compute Σ^{+}, the *Moore–Penrose pseudoinverse* of the diagonal matrix Σ. That is, if the ith diagonal element of Σ is $\sigma \neq 0$, then replace it by $1/\sigma$. But if the ith element is 0, leave it as 0.

(4) Let $U = Y(\Sigma^{+})^2 X^{\mathrm{T}}$.

We shall defer to Section 11.4.3 an example where we illustrate the entire CUR process, including the important matter of how the matrices C and R should be chosen to make the approximation to M have a small expected value.

11.4.2   Choosing Rows and Columns Properly

Recall that the choice of rows and columns is random. However, this choice must be biased so that the more important rows and columns have a better chance of being picked. The measure of importance we must use is the square of the Frobenius norm, that is, the sum of the squares of the elements of the row or column. Let $f = \sum_{i,j} m_{ij}^2$, the square of the Frobenius norm of M. Then each time we select a row, the probability p_i with which we select row i is $\sum_j m_{ij}^2/f$. Each time we select a column, the probability q_j with which we select column j is $\sum_i m_{ij}^2/f$.

	Matrix	Alien	Star Wars	Casablanca	Titanic
Joe	1	1	1	0	0
Jim	3	3	3	0	0
John	4	4	4	0	0
Jack	5	5	5	0	0
Jill	0	0	0	4	4
Jenny	0	0	0	5	5
Jane	0	0	0	2	2

Figure 11.12 Matrix M, repeated from Fig. 11.6

EXAMPLE 11.12   Let us reconsider the matrix M from Fig. 11.6, which we repeat here as Fig. 11.12. The sum of the squares of the elements of M is 243. The three columns for the science-fiction movies *The Matrix*, *Alien*, and *Star Wars* each have a squared Frobenius norm of $1^2 + 3^2 + 4^2 + 5^2 = 51$, so their probabilities are each $51/243 = .210$. The remaining two columns each have a squared Frobenius norm of $4^2 + 5^2 + 2^2 = 45$, and therefore their probabilities are each $45/243 = .185$.

The seven rows of M have squared Frobenius norms of 3, 27, 48, 75, 32, 50, and 8, respectively. Thus, their respective probabilities are .012, .111, .198, .309, .132, .206, and .033.   □

Now, let us select r columns for the matrix C. For each column, we choose randomly from the columns of M. However, the selection is not with uniform probability; rather, the jth column is selected with probability q_j. Recall that probability is the sum of the squares of the elements in that column divided by the sum of the squares of all the elements of the matrix. Each column of C is chosen independently from the columns of M, so there is some chance that a column will be selected more than once. We shall discuss how to deal with this situation after explaining the basics of CUR-decomposition.

Having selected each of the columns of M, we scale each column by dividing its elements by the square root of the expected number of times this column would be picked. That is, we divide the elements of the jth column of M, if it is selected, by $\sqrt{rq_j}$. The scaled column of M becomes a column of C.

Rows of M are selected for R in the analogous way. For each row of R we select from the rows of M, choosing row i with probability p_i. Recall p_i is the sum of the squares of the elements of the ith row divided by the sum of the squares of all the elements of M. We then scale each chosen row by dividing by $\sqrt{rp_i}$ if it is the ith row of M that was chosen.

EXAMPLE 11.13 Let $r = 2$ for our CUR-decomposition. Suppose that our random selection of columns from matrix M of Fig. 11.12 is first *Alien* (the second column) and then *Casablanca* (the fourth column). The column for *Alien* is $[1, 3, 4, 5, 0, 0, 0]^\mathrm{T}$, and we must scale this column by dividing by $\sqrt{rq_2}$. Recall from Example 11.12 that the probability associated with the *Alien* column is .210, so the division is by $\sqrt{2 \times 0.210} = 0.648$. To two decimal places, the scaled column for *Alien* is $[1.54, 4.63, 6.17, 7.72, 0, 0, 0]^\mathrm{T}$. This column becomes the first column of C.

The second column of C is constructed by taking the column of M for *Casablanca*, which is $[0, 0, 0, 0, 4, 5, 2]^\mathrm{T}$, and dividing it by $\sqrt{rp_4} = \sqrt{2 \times 0.185} = 0.608$. Thus, the second column of C is $[0, 0, 0, 0, 6.58, 8.22, 3.29]^\mathrm{T}$ to two decimal places.

Now, let us choose the rows for R. The most likely rows to be chosen are those for Jenny and Jack, so let's suppose these rows are indeed chosen, Jenny first. The unscaled rows for R are thus

$$\begin{bmatrix} 0 & 0 & 0 & 5 & 5 \\ 5 & 5 & 5 & 0 & 0 \end{bmatrix}$$

To scale the row for Jenny, we note that its associated probability is 0.206, so we divide by $\sqrt{2 \times 0.206} = 0.642$. To scale the row for Jack, whose associated probability is 0.309, we divide by $\sqrt{2 \times 0.309} = 0.786$. Thus, the matrix R is

$$\begin{bmatrix} 0 & 0 & 0 & 7.79 & 7.79 \\ 6.36 & 6.36 & 6.36 & 0 & 0 \end{bmatrix}$$

□

11.4.3 Constructing the Middle Matrix

Finally, we must construct the matrix U that connects C and R in the decomposition. Recall that U is an $r \times r$ matrix. We start the construction of U with another matrix of the same size, which we call W. The entry in row i and column j of W is the entry of M whose row is the one from which we selected the ith row of R and whose column is the one from which we selected the jth column of C.

EXAMPLE 11.14 Let us follow the selections of rows and columns made in Example 11.13. We claim

$$W = \begin{bmatrix} 0 & 5 \\ 5 & 0 \end{bmatrix}$$

The first row of W corresponds to the first row of R, which is the row for Jenny in the matrix M of Fig. 11.12. The 0 in the first column is there because that is the entry in the row of M for Jenny and the column for *Alien*; recall that the first column of C was constructed from the column of M for *Alien*. The 5 in the second column reflects the 5 in M's row for Jenny and column for *Casablanca*;

the latter is the column of M from which the second column of C was derived. Similarly, the second row of W is the entries in the row for Jack and columns for *Alien* and *Casablanca*, respectively. □

The matrix U is constructed from W by the Moore–Penrose pseudoinverse described in Section 11.4.1. It consists of taking the SVD of W, say $W = X\Sigma Y^{\mathrm{T}}$, and replacing all nonzero elements in the matrix Σ of singular values by their numerical inverses, to obtain the pseudoinverse Σ^{+}. Then $U = Y(\Sigma^{+})^{2}X^{\mathrm{T}}$.

EXAMPLE 11.15   Let us construct U from the matrix W that we constructed in Example 11.14. First, here is the SVD for W:

$$
W = \begin{bmatrix} 0 & 5 \\ 5 & 0 \end{bmatrix} = \begin{bmatrix} 0 & 1 \\ 1 & 0 \end{bmatrix} \begin{bmatrix} 5 & 0 \\ 0 & 5 \end{bmatrix} \begin{bmatrix} 1 & 0 \\ 0 & 1 \end{bmatrix}
$$

That is, the three matrices on the right are X, Σ, and Y^{T}, respectively. The matrix Σ has no zeros along the diagonal, so each element is replaced by its numerical inverse to get its Moore–Penrose pseudoinverse:

$$
\Sigma^{+} = \begin{bmatrix} 1/5 & 0 \\ 0 & 1/5 \end{bmatrix}
$$

Now X and Y are symmetric, so they are their own transposes. Thus,

$$
U = Y(\Sigma^{+})^{2}X^{\mathrm{T}} = \begin{bmatrix} 1 & 0 \\ 0 & 1 \end{bmatrix} \begin{bmatrix} 1/5 & 0 \\ 0 & 1/5 \end{bmatrix}^{2} \begin{bmatrix} 0 & 1 \\ 1 & 0 \end{bmatrix} = \begin{bmatrix} 0 & 1/25 \\ 1/25 & 0 \end{bmatrix} \quad □
$$

11.4.4   The Complete CUR Decomposition

We now have a method to select randomly the three component matrices C, U, and R. Their product will approximate the original matrix M. As we mentioned at the beginning of the discussion, the approximation is only formally guaranteed to be close when very large numbers of rows and columns are selected. However, the intuition is that by selecting rows and columns that tend to have high "importance" (i.e., high Frobenius norm), we are extracting the most significant parts of the original matrix, even with a small number of rows and columns. As an example, let us see how well we do with the running example of this section.

EXAMPLE 11.16   For our running example, the decomposition is shown in Fig. 11.13. While there is considerable difference between this result and the original matrix M, especially in the science-fiction numbers, the values are in proportion to their originals. This example is much too small, and the selection of the small numbers of rows and columns was arbitrary rather than random, for us to expect close convergence of the CUR decomposition to the exact values. □

$$CUR = \begin{bmatrix} 1.54 & 0 \\ 4.63 & 0 \\ 6.17 & 0 \\ 7.72 & 0 \\ 0 & 9.30 \\ 0 & 11.63 \\ 0 & 4.65 \end{bmatrix} \begin{bmatrix} 0 & 1/25 \\ 1/25 & 0 \end{bmatrix} \begin{bmatrix} 0 & 0 & 0 & 11.01 & 11.01 \\ 8.99 & 8.99 & 8.99 & 0 & 0 \end{bmatrix}$$

$$= \begin{bmatrix} 0.55 & 0.55 & 0.55 & 0 & 0 \\ 1.67 & 1.67 & 1.67 & 0 & 0 \\ 2.22 & 2.22 & 2.22 & 0 & 0 \\ 2.78 & 2.78 & 2.78 & 0 & 0 \\ 0 & 0 & 0 & 4.10 & 4.10 \\ 0 & 0 & 0 & 5.12 & 5.12 \\ 0 & 0 & 0 & 2.05 & 2.05 \end{bmatrix}$$

Figure 11.13 CUR-decomposition of the matrix of Fig. 11.12

11.4.5 Eliminating Duplicate Rows and Columns

It is quite possible that a single row or column is selected more than once. There is no great harm in using the same row twice, although the rank of the matrices of the decomposition will be less than the number of row and column choices made. However, it is also possible to combine k rows of R that are each the same row of the matrix M into a single row of R, thus leaving R with fewer rows. Likewise, k columns of C that each come from the same column of M can be combined into one column of C. However, for either rows or columns, the remaining vector should have each of its elements multiplied by $\sqrt{k}$.

When we merge some rows and/or columns, it is possible that R has fewer rows than C has columns, or vice versa. As a consequence, W will not be a square matrix. However, we can still take its pseudoinverse by decomposing it into $W = X\Sigma Y^{\mathrm{T}}$, where Σ is now a diagonal matrix with some all-0 rows or columns, whichever it has more of. To take the pseudoinverse of such a diagonal matrix, we treat each element on the diagonal as usual (invert nonzero elements and leave 0 as it is), but then we must transpose the result.

EXAMPLE 11.17 Suppose

$$\Sigma = \begin{bmatrix} 2 & 0 & 0 & 0 \\ 0 & 0 & 0 & 0 \\ 0 & 0 & 3 & 0 \end{bmatrix}$$

Then

$$\Sigma^+ = \begin{bmatrix} 1/2 & 0 & 0 \\ 0 & 0 & 0 \\ 0 & 0 & 1/3 \\ 0 & 0 & 0 \end{bmatrix} \qquad \square$$

11.4.6   Exercises for Section 11.4

EXERCISE 11.4.1   The SVD for the matrix

$$M = \begin{bmatrix} 48 & 14 \\ 14 & -48 \end{bmatrix}$$

is

$$\begin{bmatrix} 48 & 14 \\ 14 & -48 \end{bmatrix} = \begin{bmatrix} 3/5 & 4/5 \\ 4/5 & -3/5 \end{bmatrix} \begin{bmatrix} 50 & 0 \\ 0 & 25 \end{bmatrix} \begin{bmatrix} 4/5 & -3/5 \\ 3/5 & 4/5 \end{bmatrix}$$

Find the Moore–Penrose pseudoinverse of M.

! EXERCISE 11.4.2   Find the CUR-decomposition of the matrix of Fig. 11.12 when we pick two "random" rows and columns as follows:

(a) The columns for *The Matrix* and *Alien* and the rows for Jim and John.
(b) The columns for *Alien* and *Star Wars* and the rows for Jack and Jill.
(c) The columns for *The Matrix* and *Titanic* and the rows for Joe and Jane.

! EXERCISE 11.4.3   Find the CUR-decomposition of the matrix of Fig. 11.12 if the two "random" rows are both Jack and the two columns are *Star Wars* and *Casablanca*.

11.5   Summary of Chapter 11

✦ *Dimensionality Reduction*: The goal of dimensionality reduction is to re-place a large matrix by two or more other matrices whose sizes are much smaller than the original, but from which the original can be approximately reconstructed, usually by taking their product.

✦ *Eigenvalues and Eigenvectors*: A matrix may have several eigenvectors such that when the matrix multiplies the eigenvector, the result is a constant multiple of the eigenvector. That constant is the eigenvalue associated with this eigenvector. Together the eigenvector and its eigenvalue are called an eigenpair.

✦ *Finding Eigenpairs by Power Iteration*: We can find the principal eigenvector (eigenvector with the largest eigenvalue) by starting with any vector and repeatedly multiplying the current vector by the matrix to get a new vector. When the changes to the vector become small, we can treat the result as a close approximation to the principal eigenvector. By modifying the matrix, we can then use the same iteration to get the second eigenpair (that with the second-largest eigenvalue), and similarly get each of the eigenpairs in turn, in order of decreasing value of the eigenvalue.

✦ *Principal-Component Analysis*: This technique for dimensionality reduction views data consisting of a collection of points in a multidimensional space as a matrix, with rows corresponding to the points and columns to the dimensions. The product of this matrix and its transpose has eigenpairs, and the principal eigenvector can be viewed as the direction in the space along which the points best line up. The second eigenvector represents the direction in which deviations from the principal eigenvector are the greatest, and so on.

✦ *Dimensionality Reduction by PCA*: By representing the matrix of points by a small number of its eigenvectors, we can approximate the data in a way that minimizes the root-mean-square error for the given number of columns in the representing matrix.

✦ *Singular-Value Decomposition*: The singular-value decomposition of a matrix consists of three matrices, U, Σ, and V. The matrices U and V are column-orthonormal, meaning that as vectors, the columns are orthogonal, and their lengths are 1. The matrix Σ is a diagonal matrix, and the values along its diagonal are called singular values. The product of U, Σ, and the transpose of V equals the original matrix.

✦ *Concepts*: SVD is useful when there are a small number of concepts that connect the rows and columns of the original matrix. For example, if the original matrix represents the ratings given by movie viewers (rows) to movies (columns), the concepts might be the genres of the movies. The matrix U connects rows to concepts, Σ represents the strengths of the concepts, and V connects the concepts to columns.

✦ *Queries Using the Singular-Value Decomposition*: We can use the decomposition to relate new or hypothetical rows of the original matrix to the concepts represented by the decomposition. Multiply a row by the matrix V of the decomposition to get a vector indicating the extent to which that row matches each of the concepts.

✦ *Using SVD for Dimensionality Reduction*: In a complete SVD for a matrix, U and V are typically as large as the original. To use fewer columns for U and V, delete the columns corresponding to the smallest singular values from U, V, and Σ. This choice minimizes the error in reconstructing the original matrix from the modified U, Σ, and V.

✦ *Decomposing Sparse Matrices*: Even in the common case where the given matrix is sparse, the matrices constructed by SVD are dense. The CUR decomposition seeks to decompose a sparse matrix into sparse, smaller matrices whose product approximates the original matrix.

✦ *CUR Decomposition*: This method chooses from a given sparse matrix a set of columns C and a set of rows R, which play the role of U and V^{T} in SVD; the user can pick any number of rows and columns. The choice of rows and columns is made randomly with a distribution that depends on the Frobenius norm, or the square root of the sum of the squares of the elements. Between C and R is a square matrix called U that is constructed by a pseudoinverse of the intersection of the chosen rows and columns.

11.6   References for Chapter 11

A well-regarded text on matrix algebra is [4].

Principal component analysis was first discussed over a century ago, in [6].

SVD is from [3]. There have been many applications of this idea. Two worth mentioning are [1] dealing with document analysis and [8] dealing with applications in Biology.

The CUR decomposition is from [2] and [5]. Our description follows a later work [7].

[1] S. Deerwester, S.T. Dumais, G.W. Furnas, T.K. Landauer, and R. Harshman, "Indexing by latent semantic analysis," *J. American Society for Information Science* **41**:6 (1990).

[2] P. Drineas, R. Kannan, and M.W. Mahoney, "Fast Monte Carlo algorithms for matrices III: Computing a compressed approximate matrix decomposition," *SIAM J. Computing* **36**:1 (2006), pp. 184–206.

[3] G.H. Golub and W. Kahan, "Calculating the singular values and pseudo-inverse of a matrix," *J. SIAM Series B* **2**:2 (1965), pp. 205–224.

[4] G.H. Golub and C.F. Van Loan, *Matrix Computations*, JHU Press, 1996.

[5] M.W. Mahoney, M. Maggioni, and P. Drineas, Tensor-CUR decompositions For tensor-based data, *SIGKDD*, pp. 327–336, 2006.

[6] K. Pearson, "On lines and planes of closest fit to systems of points in space," *Philosophical Magazine* **2**:11 (1901), pp. 559–572.

[7] J. Sun, Y. Xie, H. Zhang, and C. Faloutsos, "Less is more: compact matrix decomposition for large sparse graphs," *Proc. SIAM Intl. Conf. on Data Mining*, 2007.

[8] M.E. Wall, A. Reichtsteiner and L.M. Rocha, "Singular value decomposition and principal component analysis," in *A Practical Approach to Microarray Data Analysis* (D.P. Berrar, W. Dubitzky, and M. Granzow eds.), pp. 91–109, Kluwer, 2003.

12 Large-Scale Machine Learning

Many algorithms are today classified as "machine learning." These algorithms share, with the other algorithms studied in this book, the goal of extracting information from data. All algorithms for analysis of data are designed to produce a useful summary of the data, from which decisions are made. Among many examples, the frequent-itemset analysis that we did in Chapter 6 produces information like association rules, which can then be used for planning a sales strategy or for many other purposes.

However, algorithms called "machine learning" not only summarize our data; they are perceived as learning a model or classifier from the data, and thus discover something about data that will be seen in the future. For instance, the clustering algorithms discussed in Chapter 7 produce clusters that not only tell us something about the data being analyzed (the training set), but they allow us to classify future data into one of the clusters that result from the clustering algorithm. Thus, machine-learning enthusiasts often speak of clustering with the neologism "unsupervised learning"; the term *unsupervised* refers to the fact that the input data does not tell the clustering algorithm what the clusters should be. In *supervised* machine learning, which is the subject of this chapter, the available data includes information about the correct way to classify at least some of the data. The data already classified is called the *training set*.

This chapter is not intended to be a complete discussion of machine learning. We concentrate on a small number of ideas, and emphasize how to deal with very large data sets. Especially important is how we exploit parallelism to build models of the data. We consider the classical "perceptron" approach to learning a data classifier, where a hyperplane that separates two classes is sought. Then, we look at more modern techniques involving support-vector machines. Similar to perceptrons, these methods look for hyperplanes that best divide the classes, so that few, if any, members of the training set lie close to the hyperplane. We next consider nearest-neighbor techniques, where data is classified according to the class(es) of their nearest neighbors in some space. We end with a discussion of decision trees, which are branching programs for predicting the class of an example.

12.1   The Machine-Learning Model

In this section we introduce the framework for machine-learning algorithms and give the basic definitions.

12.1.1   Training Sets

The data to which a machine-learning (often abbreviated ML) algorithm is applied is called a training set. A *training set* consists of a set of pairs $(\mathbf{x}, y)$, called *training examples*, where

- $\mathbf{x}$ is a vector of values, often called a *feature vector*, or simply an *input*. Each value, or feature, can be *categorical* (values are taken from a set of discrete values, such as {red, blue, green}) or *numerical* (values are integers or real numbers).
- y is the *class label*, or simply *output*, the classification value for $\mathbf{x}$.

The objective of the ML process is to discover a function $y = f(\mathbf{x})$ that best predicts the value of y associated with each value of $\mathbf{x}$. The type of y is in principle arbitrary, but there are several common and important cases.

(1) y is a real number. In this case, the ML problem is called *regression*.
(2) y is a Boolean value: true-or-false, more commonly written as $+1$ and -1, respectively. In this class the problem is *binary classification*.
(3) y is a member of some finite set. The members of this set can be thought of as "classes," and each member represents one class. The problem is *multiclass classification*.
(4) y is a member of some potentially infinite set, for example, a parse tree for x, which is interpreted as a sentence.

12.1.2   Some Illustrative Examples

EXAMPLE 12.1   Recall Fig. 7.1, repeated as Fig. 12.1, where we plotted the height and weight of dogs in three classes: Beagles, Chihuahuas, and Dachshunds. We can think of this data as a training set, provided the data includes the variety of the dog along with each height–weight pair. Each pair $(\mathbf{x}, y)$ in the training set consists of a feature vector $\mathbf{x}$ of the form [height, weight]. The associated label y is the variety of the dog. An example of a training-set pair would be ([5 inches, 2 pounds], Chihuahua).

An appropriate way to implement the decision function f would be to imagine two lines, shown dashed in Fig. 12.1. The horizontal line represents a height of 7 inches and separates Beagles from Chihuahuas and Dachshunds. The vertical line represents a weight of 3 pounds and separates Chihuahuas from Beagles and Dachshunds. The algorithm that implements f is:

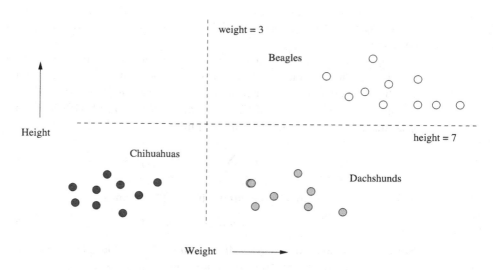

Figure 12.1 Repeat of Fig. 7.1, indicating the heights and weights of certain dogs

```
if (height > 7) print Beagle
else if (weight < 3) print Chihuahua
else print Dachshund;
```

Recall that the original intent of Fig. 7.1 was to cluster points without knowing which variety of dog they represented. That is, the label associated with a given height–weight vector was not available. Here, we are performing supervised learning with the same data augmented by classifications for the training data. □

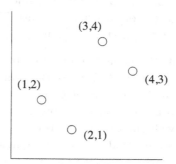

Figure 12.2 Repeat of Fig. 11.1, to be used as a training set

EXAMPLE 12.2   As an example of supervised learning, the four points $(1, 2)$, $(2, 1)$, $(3, 4)$, and $(4, 3)$ from Fig.11.1 (repeated here as Fig. 12.2), can be thought of as a training set, where the vectors are one-dimensional. That is, the point $(1, 2)$ can be thought of as a pair $([1], 2)$, where $[1]$ is the one-dimensional feature vector $\mathbf{x}$, and 2 is the associated label y; the other points can be interpreted similarly.

Suppose we want to "learn" the best model for the full set of points, from which these four points are taken as examples. A simple form of model, the one we shall consider, is a linear function $f(x) = ax + b$. A natural interpretation of "best" is that the RMSE of the value of $f(x)$ compared with the given value of y is minimized. That is, we want to minimize

$$\sum_{x=1}^{4}(ax + b - y_x)^2$$

where y_x is the y-value associated with x. This sum is

$$(a + b - 2)^2 + (2a + b - 1)^2 + (3a + b - 4)^2 + (4a + b - 3)^2$$

Simplifying, the sum is $30a^2 + 4b^2 + 20ab - 56a - 20b + 30$. If we then take the derivatives with respect to a and b and set them to 0, we get

$$60a + 20b - 56 \quad = \quad 0$$
$$20a + 8b - 20 \quad = \quad 0$$

The solution to these equations is $a = 3/5$ and $b = 1$. For these values the RMSE is 3.2.

Note that the learned straight line is not the principal axis that was discovered for these points in Section 11.2.1. That axis was the line with slope 1, going through the origin, i.e., the line $y = x$. For this line, the RMSE is 4. The difference is that PCA discussed in Section 11.2.1 minimizes the sum of the squares of the lengths of the projections onto the chosen axis, which is constrained to go through the origin. Here, we are minimizing the sum of the squares of the vertical distances between the points and the line. In fact, even had we tried to learn the line through the origin with the least RMSE, we would not choose the line $y = x$. You can check that $y = \frac{14}{15}x$ has a lower RMSE than 4. □

EXAMPLE 12.3   A common application of machine learning involves a training set where the feature vectors $\mathbf{x}$ are Boolean-valued and of very high dimension. We shall focus on data consisting of documents, e.g., emails, Web pages, or newspaper articles. Each component represents a word in some large dictionary. We would probably eliminate stop words (very common words) from this dictionary, because these words tend not to tell us much about the subject matter of the document. Similarly, we might also restrict the dictionary to words with high TF.IDF scores (see Section 1.3.1) so the words considered would tend to reflect the topic or substance of the document.

The training set consists of pairs, where the vector $\mathbf{x}$ represents the presence or absence of each dictionary word in document. The label y could be $+1$ or -1, with $+1$ representing that the document (an email, e.g.) is spam. Our goal would be to train a classifier to examine future emails and decide whether or not they are spam. We shall illustrate this use of machine learning in Example 12.4.

Alternatively, y could be chosen from some finite set of topics, e.g., "sports," "politics," and so on. Again, $\mathbf{x}$ could represent a document, perhaps a Web page. The goal would be to create a classifier for Web pages that assigned a topic to each. □

12.1.3 Approaches to Machine Learning

There are many forms of ML algorithms, and we shall not cover them all here. Here are the major classes of such algorithms, each of which is distinguished by the form by which the function f is represented.

(1) *Decision trees* were discussed briefly in Section 9.2.7 and will be covered more extensively in Section 12.5. The form of f is a tree, and each node of the tree has a function of $\mathbf{x}$ that determines to which child or children the search must proceed. Decision trees are suitable for binary and multiclass classification, especially when the dimension of the feature vector is not too large (large numbers of features can lead to overfitting).

(2) *Perceptrons* are threshold functions applied to the components of the vector $\mathbf{x} = [x_1, x_2, \ldots, x_n]$. A weight w_i is associated with the ith component, for each $i = 1, 2, \ldots, n$, and there is a threshold θ. The output is $+1$ if

$$\sum_{i=1}^{n} w_i x_i > \theta$$

and the output is -1 if that sum is less than θ. A perceptron is suitable for binary classification, even when the number of features is very large, e.g., the presence or absence of words in a document. Perceptrons are the topic of Section 12.2.

(3) *Neural nets* are acyclic networks of perceptrons, with the outputs of some perceptrons used as inputs to others. These are suitable for binary or multiclass classification, since there can be several perceptrons used as output, with one or more indicating each class.

(4) *Instance-based learning* uses the entire training set to represent the function f. The calculation of the label y associated with a new feature vector $\mathbf{x}$ can involve examination of the entire training set, although usually some preprocessing of the training set enables the computation of $f(\mathbf{x})$ to proceed efficiently. We shall consider an important kind of instance-based learning, k-nearest-neighbor, in Section 12.4. For example, 1-nearest-neighbor classifies data by giving it the same class as that of its nearest training example. There are k-nearest-neighbor algorithms that are appropriate for any kind of classification, although we shall concentrate on the case where y and the components of $\mathbf{x}$ are real numbers.

(5) *Support-vector machines* are an advance over the algorithms traditionally used to select the weights and threshold. The result is a classifier that tends to be more accurate on unseen data. We discuss support-vector machines in Section 12.3.

12.1.4   Machine-Learning Architecture

Machine-learning algorithms can be classified not only by their general algorithmic approach as we discussed in Section 12.1.3, but also by their underlying architecture – the way data is handled and the way it is used to build the model.

Training, Validating, and Testing

One general issue regarding the handling of data is that there is a good reason to withhold some of the available data from the training set. The remaining data is called the *test set*. In some cases, we withhold two sets of training examples, a *validation set* (sometimes called a *development set*), as well as the test set. The difference is that the validation set is used to help design the model, while the test set is used only to determine how good the model is. The problem addressed by a validation set is that many machine-learning algorithms tend to *overfit* the data; they pick up on artifacts that occur in the training set but that are atypical of the larger population of possible data. By using the validation set, and seeing how well the classifier works on that, we can tell if the classifier is overfitting the data. If so, we can restrict the machine-learning algorithm in some way. For instance, if we are constructing a decision tree, we can limit the number of levels of the tree.

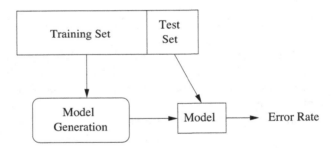

Figure 12.3 The training set helps build the model, and the test set validates it

Figure 12.3 illustrates the train-and-test architecture. We assume all the data is suitable for training (i.e., the class information is attached to the data), but we separate out a small fraction of the available data as the test set. We use the remaining data to build a suitable model or classifier. Then we feed the test data to this model. Since we know the class of each element of the test data, we can tell how well the model does on the test data. If the error rate on the test data is not much worse than the error rate of the model on the training data itself, then we expect there is little, if any, overfitting, and the model can be used. On the other hand, if the classifier performs much worse on the test data than on the training data, we expect there is overfitting and need to rethink the way we construct the classifier.

There is nothing special about the selection of the test data. In fact, we can repeat the train-then-test process several times using the same data, if we divide

---

Generalization

We should remember that the purpose of creating a model or classifier is not to classify the training set, but to classify the data whose class we do not know. We want that data to be classified correctly, but often we have no way of knowing whether or not the model does so. If the nature of the data changes over time – for instance, if we are trying to detect spam emails – then we need to measure the performance over time as best we can. For example, in the case of spam emails, we can note the rate of reports of spam emails that were not classified as spam.

---

the data into k equal-sized chunks. In turn, we let each chunk be the test data, and use the remaining $k-1$ chunks as the training data. This training architecture is called *cross-validation*.

Batch Versus On-Line Learning

Often, as in Examples 12.1 and 12.2, we use a *batch learning* architecture. That is, the entire training set is available at the beginning of the process, and it is all used in whatever way the algorithm requires to produce a model once and for all. The alternative is *on-line learning*, where the training set arrives in a stream and, like any stream, cannot be revisited after it is processed. In on-line learning, we maintain a model at all times. As new training examples arrive, we may choose to modify the model to account for the new examples. On-line learning has the advantages that it can

(1) Deal with very large training sets, because it does not access more than one training example at a time.
(2) Adapt to changes in the population of training examples as time goes on. For instance, Google trains its spam-email classifier this way, adapting the classifier for spam as new kinds of spam email are sent by spammers and indicated to be spam by the recipients.

An enhancement of on-line learning, suitable in some cases, is *active learning*. Here, the classifier may receive some training examples, but it primarily receives unclassified data, which it must classify. If the classifier is unsure of the classification (e.g., the newly arrived example is very close to the boundary), then the classifier can ask for ground truth at some significant cost. For instance, it could send the example to Mechanical Turk and gather opinions of real people. In this way, examples near the boundary become training examples and can be used to modify the classifier.

Feature Selection

Sometimes, the hardest part of designing a good model or classifier is figuring out what features to use as input to the learning algorithm. Let us reconsider Example 12.3, where we suggested that we could classify emails as spam or not spam by looking at the words contained in the email. In fact, we explore in detail such a classifier in Example 12.4. As discussed in Example 12.3, it may make sense to focus on certain words and not others; e.g., we should eliminate stop words.

But we should also ask whether there is other information available that would help us make a better decision about spam. For example, spam is often generated by particular hosts, either those belonging to the spammers, or hosts that have been coopted into a "botnet" for the purpose of generating spam. Thus, including the originating host or originating email address into the feature vector describing an email might enable us to design a better classifier and lower the error rate.

Creating a Training Set

It is reasonable to ask where the label information that turns data into a training set comes from. The obvious method is to create the labels by hand, having an expert look at each feature vector and classify it properly. Recently, crowdsourcing techniques have been used to label data. For example, in many applications it is possible to use Mechanical Turk to label data. Since the "Turkers" are not necessarily reliable, it is wise to use a system that allows the question to be asked of several different people, until a clear majority is in favor of one label.

One often can find data on the Web that is implicitly labeled. For example, the Open Directory (DMOZ) has millions of pages labeled by topic. That data, used as a training set, can enable one to classify other pages or documents according to their topic, based on the frequency of word occurrence. Another approach to classifying by topic is to look at the Wikipedia page for a topic and see what pages it links to. Those pages can safely be assumed to be relevant to the given topic.

In some applications we can use the stars that people use to rate products or services on sites like Amazon or Yelp. For example, we might want to estimate the number of stars that would be assigned to reviews or tweets about a product, even if those reviews or tweets do not themselves have star ratings. If we use star-labeled reviews as a training set, we can deduce the words that are most commonly associated with positive and negative reviews (called *sentiment analysis*). The presence of these words in other reviews can tell us the sentiment of those reviews.

12.1.5   Exercises for Section 12.1

EXERCISE 12.1.1   Redo Example 12.2 for the following different forms of $f(x)$.

(a) Require $f(x) = ax$; i.e., a straight line through the origin. Is the line $y = \frac{14}{15}x$ that we discussed in the example optimal?

(b) Allow $f(x)$ to be a quadratic, i.e., $f(x) = ax^2 + bx + c$.

12.2   Perceptrons

A *perceptron* is a linear binary classifier. Its input is a vector $\mathbf{x} = [x_1, x_2, \ldots, x_d]$ with real-valued components. Associated with the perceptron is a vector of *weights* $\mathbf{w} = [w_1, w_2, \ldots, w_d]$, also with real-valued components. Each perceptron has a *threshold* θ. The output of the perceptron is $+1$ if $\mathbf{w}.\mathbf{x} > \theta$, and the output is -1 if $\mathbf{w}.\mathbf{x} < \theta$. The special case where $\mathbf{w}.\mathbf{x} = \theta$ will always be regarded as "wrong," in the sense that we shall describe in detail when we get to Section 12.2.1.

The weight vector $\mathbf{w}$ defines a hyperplane of dimension $d - 1$ – the set of all points $\mathbf{x}$ such that $\mathbf{w}.\mathbf{x} = \theta$, as suggested in Fig. 12.4. Points on the positive side of the hyperplane are classified $+1$ and those on the negative side are classified -1. A perceptron classifier works only for data that is *linearly separable*, in the sense that there is some hyperplane that separates all the positive points from all the negative points. If there are many such hyperplanes, the perceptron will converge to one of them, and thus will correctly classify all the training points. If no such hyperplane exists, then the perceptron cannot converge to any hyperplane. In the next section, we discuss support-vector machines, which do not have this limitation; they will converge to some separator that, although not a perfect classifier, will do as well as possible under the metric to be described in Section 12.3.

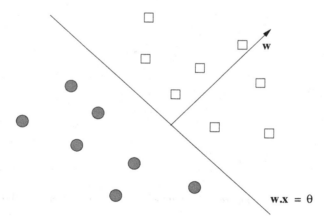

Figure 12.4 A perceptron divides a space by a hyperplane into two half-spaces

12.2.1   Training a Perceptron with Zero Threshold

To train a perceptron, we examine the training set and try to find a weight vector $\mathbf{w}$ and threshold θ such that all the feature vectors with $y = +1$ (the *positive examples*) are on the positive side of the hyperplane and all those with $y = -1$ (the *negative examples*) are on the negative side. It may or may not be

possible to do so, since there is no guarantee that *any* hyperplane separates all
the positive and negative examples in the training set.

We begin by assuming the threshold is 0; the simple augmentation needed
to handle an unknown threshold is discussed in Section 12.2.4. The following
method will converge to some hyperplane that separates the positive and negative
examples, provided one exists.

(1) Initialize the weight vector $\mathbf{w}$ to all 0s.
(2) Pick a *learning-rate* parameter η, which is a small, positive real number. The
    choice of η affects the convergence of the perceptron. If η is too small, then
    convergence is slow; if it is too big, then the decision boundary will "dance
    around" and again will converge slowly, if at all.
(3) Consider each training example $t = (\mathbf{x}, y)$ in turn.
    (a) Let $y' = \mathbf{w}.\mathbf{x}$.
    (b) If y' and y have the same sign, then do nothing; t is properly classified.
    (c) However, if y' and y have different signs, or $y' = 0$, replace $\mathbf{w}$ by $\mathbf{w} + \eta y \mathbf{x}$.
        That is, adjust $\mathbf{w}$ slightly in the direction of $\mathbf{x}$.

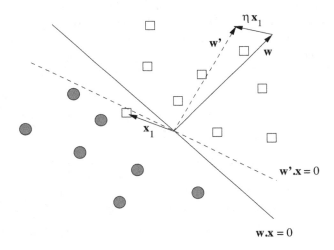

Figure 12.5 A misclassified point $\mathbf{x}_1$ moves the vector $\mathbf{w}$

The two-dimensional case of this transformation on $\mathbf{w}$ is suggested in Fig.
12.5. Notice how moving $\mathbf{w}$ in the direction of $\mathbf{x}$ moves the hyperplane that is
perpendicular to $\mathbf{w}$ in such a direction that it makes it more likely that $\mathbf{x}$ will
be on the correct side of the hyperplane, although it does not guarantee that $\mathbf{x}$
will then be correctly classified.

EXAMPLE 12.4   Let us consider training a perceptron to recognize spam email.
The training set consists of pairs $(\mathbf{x}, y)$ where $\mathbf{x}$ is a vector of 0s and 1s, with
each component x_i corresponding to the presence $(x_i = 1)$ or absence $(x_i = 0)$ of
a particular word in the email. The value of y is +1 if the email is known to be

spam and -1 if it is known not to be spam. While the number of words found in the training set of emails is very large, we shall use a simplified example where there are only five words: "and," "viagra," "the," "of," and "nigeria." Figure 12.6 gives the training set of six vectors and their corresponding classes.

	and	viagra	the	of	nigeria	y
a	1	1	0	1	1	$+1$
b	0	0	1	1	0	-1
c	0	1	1	0	0	$+1$
d	1	0	0	1	0	-1
e	1	0	1	0	1	$+1$
f	1	0	1	1	0	-1

Figure 12.6 Training data for spam emails

In this example, we shall use learning rate $\eta = 1/2$, and we shall visit each training example once, in the order shown in Fig. 12.6. We begin with $\mathbf{w} = [0,0,0,0,0]$ and compute $\mathbf{w}.\mathbf{a} = 0$. Since 0 is not positive, we move $\mathbf{w}$ in the direction of $\mathbf{a}$ by performing $\mathbf{w} := \mathbf{w} + (1/2)(+1)\mathbf{a}$. The new value of $\mathbf{w}$ is thus

$$\mathbf{w} = [0,0,0,0,0] + \left[\frac{1}{2},\frac{1}{2},0,\frac{1}{2},\frac{1}{2}\right] = \left[\frac{1}{2},\frac{1}{2},0,\frac{1}{2},\frac{1}{2}\right]$$

Next, consider $\mathbf{b}$. $\mathbf{w}.\mathbf{b} = [\frac{1}{2},\frac{1}{2},0,\frac{1}{2},\frac{1}{2}].[0,0,1,1,0] = \frac{1}{2}$. Since the associated y for $\mathbf{b}$ is -1, $\mathbf{b}$ is misclassified. We thus assign

$$\mathbf{w} := \mathbf{w} + (1/2)(-1)\mathbf{b} = \left[\frac{1}{2},\frac{1}{2},0,\frac{1}{2},\frac{1}{2}\right] - \left[0,0,\frac{1}{2},\frac{1}{2},0\right] = \left[\frac{1}{2},\frac{1}{2},-\frac{1}{2},0,\frac{1}{2}\right]$$

Training example $\mathbf{c}$ is next. We compute

$$\mathbf{w}.\mathbf{c} = \left[\frac{1}{2},\frac{1}{2},-\frac{1}{2},0,\frac{1}{2}\right].[0,1,1,0,0] = 0$$

Since the associated y for $\mathbf{c}$ is $+1$, $\mathbf{c}$ is also misclassified. We thus assign

$$\mathbf{w} := \mathbf{w} + (1/2)(+1)\mathbf{c} = \left[\frac{1}{2},\frac{1}{2},-\frac{1}{2},0,\frac{1}{2}\right] + \left[0,\frac{1}{2},\frac{1}{2},0,0\right] = \left[\frac{1}{2},1,0,0,\frac{1}{2}\right]$$

Training example $\mathbf{d}$ is next to be considered:

$$\mathbf{w}.\mathbf{d} = \left[\frac{1}{2},1,0,0,\frac{1}{2}\right].[1,0,0,1,0] = 1$$

Since the associated y for $\mathbf{d}$ is -1, $\mathbf{d}$ is misclassified as well. We thus assign

$$\mathbf{w} := \mathbf{w} + (1/2)(-1)\mathbf{d} = \left[\frac{1}{2},1,0,0,\frac{1}{2}\right] - \left[\frac{1}{2},0,0,\frac{1}{2},0\right] = \left[0,1,0,-\frac{1}{2},\frac{1}{2}\right]$$

For training example $\mathbf{e}$ we compute $\mathbf{w}.\mathbf{e} = [0,1,0,-\frac{1}{2},\frac{1}{2}].[1,0,1,0,1] = \frac{1}{2}$. Since the associated y for $\mathbf{e}$ is $+1$, $\mathbf{e}$ is classified correctly, and no change to $\mathbf{w}$ is made. Similarly, for $\mathbf{f}$ we compute

$$\mathbf{w}.\mathbf{f} = \left[0,1,0,-\frac{1}{2},\frac{1}{2}\right].[1,0,1,1,0] = -\frac{1}{2}$$

Pragmatics of Training on Emails

When we represent emails or other large documents as training examples, we would not really want to construct the vector of 0s and 1s with a component for every word that appears even once in the collection of emails. Doing so would typically give us sparse vectors with millions of components. Rather, create a table in which all the words appearing in the emails are assigned integers $1, 2, \ldots$, indicating their component. When we process an email in the training set, make a list of the components in which the vector has 1; i.e., use the standard sparse representation for the vector. If we eliminate stop words from the representation, or even eliminate words with a low TF.IDF score, then we make the vectors representing emails significantly sparser and thus compress the data even more. Only the vector $\mathbf{w}$ needs to have all its components listed, since it will not be sparse after a small number of training examples have been processed.

---

so $\mathbf{f}$ is correctly classified. If we check $\mathbf{a}$ through $\mathbf{d}$, we find that this $\mathbf{w}$ correctly classifies them as well. Thus, we have converged to a perceptron that classifies all the training set examples correctly. It also makes a certain amount of sense: it says that "viagra" and "nigeria" are indicative of spam, while "of" is indicative of nonspam. It considers "and" and "the" neutral," although we would probably prefer to give "and," "of," and "the" the same weight. □

12.2.2 Convergence of Perceptrons

As we mentioned at the beginning of this section, if the data points are linearly separable, then the perceptron algorithm will converge to a separator. However, if the data is not linearly separable, then the algorithm will eventually repeat a weight vector and loop infinitely. Unfortunately, it is often hard to tell, during the running of the algorithm, which of these two cases applies. When the data is large, it is not feasible to remember all previous weight vectors to see whether we are repeating a vector, and even if we could, the period of repetition would most likely be so large that we would want to terminate the algorithm long before we repeated.

A second issue regarding termination is that even if the training data is linearly separable, the entire dataset might not be linearly separable. The consequence is that there might not be any value in running the algorithm for a very large number of rounds, in the hope of converging to a separator. We therefore need a strategy for deciding when to terminate the perceptron algorithm, assuming convergence has not occurred. Here are some common tests for termination.

(1) Terminate after a fixed number of rounds.
(2) Terminate when the number of misclassified training points stops changing.
(3) Withhold a test set from the training data, and after each round, run the perceptron on the test data. Terminate the algorithm when the number of errors on the test set stops changing.

Another technique that will aid convergence is to lower the training rate as the number of rounds increases. For example, we could allow the training rate η to start at some initial η_0 and lower it to $\eta_0/(1+ct)$ after the tth round, where c is some small constant.

12.2.3 The Winnow Algorithm

There are many other rules one could use to adjust weights for a perceptron. Not all possible algorithms are guaranteed to converge, even if there is a hyperplane separating positive and negative examples. One that does converge is called *Winnow*, and that rule will be described here. Winnow assumes that the feature vectors consist of 0s and 1s, and the labels are $+1$ or -1. Unlike the basic perceptron algorithm, which can produce positive or negative components in the weight vector $\mathbf{w}$, Winnow produces only positive weights.

The general Winnow Algorithm allows for a variety of parameters to be selected, and we shall only consider one simple variant. However, all variants have in common the idea that there is a positive threshold θ. If $\mathbf{w}$ is the current weight vector, and $\mathbf{x}$ is the feature vector in the training set that we are currently considering, we compute $\mathbf{w}.\mathbf{x}$ and compare it with θ. If $\mathbf{w}.\mathbf{x} \leq \theta$, and the class for $\mathbf{x}$ is $+1$, then we have to raise the weights of $\mathbf{w}$ in those components where $\mathbf{x}$ has 1. We multiply these weights by a number greater than 1. The larger this number, the greater the training rate, so we want to pick a number that is not too close to 1 (or convergence will be too slow) but also not too large (or the weight vector may oscillate). Similarly, if $\mathbf{w}.\mathbf{x} \geq \theta$, but the class of $\mathbf{x}$ is -1, then we want to lower the weights of $\mathbf{w}$ in those components where $\mathbf{x}$ is 1. We multiply those weights by a number greater than 0 but less than 1. Again, we want to pick a number that is not too close to 1 but also not too small, to avoid slow convergence or oscillation.

We shall give the details of the algorithm using the factors 2 and $1/2$, for the cases where we want to raise weights and lower weights, respectively. Start the Winnow Algorithm with a weight vector $\mathbf{w} = [w_1, w_2, \ldots, w_d]$ all of whose components are 1, and let the threshold θ equal d, the number of dimensions of the vectors in the training examples. Let $(\mathbf{x}, y)$ be the next training example to be considered, where $\mathbf{x} = [x_1, x_2, \ldots, x_d]$.

(1) If $\mathbf{w}.\mathbf{x} > \theta$ and $y = +1$, or $\mathbf{w}.\mathbf{x} < \theta$ and $y = -1$, then the example is correctly classified, so no change to $\mathbf{w}$ is made.

(2) If $\mathbf{w}.\mathbf{x} \leq \theta$, but $y = +1$, then the weights for the components where $\mathbf{x}$ has 1 are too low as a group. Double each of the corresponding components of $\mathbf{w}$. That is, if $x_i = 1$ then set $w_i := 2w_i$.

(3) If $\mathbf{w}.\mathbf{x} \geq \theta$, but $y = -1$, then the weights for the components where $\mathbf{x}$ has 1 are too high as a group. Halve each of the corresponding components of $\mathbf{w}$. That is, if $x_i = 1$ then set $w_i := w_i/2$.

EXAMPLE 12.5 Let us reconsider the training data from Fig. 12.6. Initialize

$\mathbf{w} = [1, 1, 1, 1, 1]$ and let $\theta = 5$. First, consider feature vector $\mathbf{a} = [1, 1, 0, 1, 1]$. $\mathbf{w}.\mathbf{a} = 4$, which is less than θ. Since the associated label for $\mathbf{a}$ is $+1$, this example is misclassified. When a $+1$-labeled example is misclassified, we must double all the components where the example has 1; in this case, all but the third component of $\mathbf{a}$ is 1. Thus, the new value of $\mathbf{w}$ is $[2, 2, 1, 2, 2]$.

Next, we consider training example $\mathbf{b} = [0, 0, 1, 1, 0]$. $\mathbf{w}.\mathbf{b} = 3$, which is less than θ. However, the associated label for $\mathbf{b}$ is -1, so no change to $\mathbf{w}$ is needed.

For $\mathbf{c} = [0, 1, 1, 0, 0]$ we find $\mathbf{w}.\mathbf{c} = 3 < \theta$, while the associated label is $+1$. Thus, we double the components of $\mathbf{w}$ where the corresponding components of $\mathbf{c}$ are 1. These components are the second and third, so the new value of $\mathbf{w}$ is $[2, 4, 2, 2, 2]$.

The next two training examples, $\mathbf{d}$ and $\mathbf{e}$, require no change, since they are correctly classified. However, there is a problem with $\mathbf{f} = [1, 0, 1, 1, 0]$, since $\mathbf{w}.\mathbf{f} = 6 > \theta$, while the associated label for $\mathbf{f}$ is -1. Thus, we must divide the first, third, and fourth components of $\mathbf{w}$ by 2, since these are the components where $\mathbf{f}$ has 1. The new value of $\mathbf{w}$ is $[1, 4, 1, 1, 2]$.

$\mathbf{x}$	y	$\mathbf{w.x}$	OK?	and	viagra	the	of	nigeria
				1	1	1	1	1
$\mathbf{a}$	$+1$	4	no	2	2	1	2	2
$\mathbf{b}$	-1	3	yes					
$\mathbf{c}$	$+1$	3	no	2	4	2	2	2
$\mathbf{d}$	-1	4	yes					
$\mathbf{e}$	$+1$	6	yes					
$\mathbf{f}$	-1	6	no	1	4	1	1	2
$\mathbf{a}$	$+1$	8	yes					
$\mathbf{b}$	-1	2	yes					
$\mathbf{c}$	$+1$	5	no	1	8	2	1	2
$\mathbf{d}$	-1	2	yes					
$\mathbf{e}$	$+1$	5	no	2	8	4	1	4
$\mathbf{f}$	-1	7	no	1	8	2	$\frac{1}{2}$	4

Figure 12.7 Sequence of updates to $\mathbf{w}$ performed by the Winnow Algorithm on the training set of Fig. 12.6

We still have not converged. It turns out we must consider each of the training examples $\mathbf{a}$ through $\mathbf{f}$ again. At the end of this process, the algorithm has converged to a weight vector $\mathbf{w} = [1, 8, 2, \frac{1}{2}, 4]$, which with threshold $\theta = 5$ correctly classifies all of the training examples in Fig. 12.6. The details of the twelve steps to convergence are shown in Fig. 12.7. This figure gives the associated label y and the computed dot product of $\mathbf{w}$ and the given feature vector. The last five columns are the five components of $\mathbf{w}$ after processing each training example. $\square$

12.2.4 Allowing the Threshold to Vary

Suppose now that the choice of threshold 0, as in Section 12.2.1, or threshold d, as in Section 12.2.3 is not desirable, or that we don't know the best threshold to use. At the cost of adding another dimension to the feature vectors, we can treat θ as one of the components of the weight vector $\mathbf{w}$. That is:

(1) Replace the vector of weights $\mathbf{w} = [w_1, w_2, \ldots, w_d]$ by

$$\mathbf{w}' = [w_1, w_2, \ldots, w_d, \theta]$$

(2) Replace every feature vector $\mathbf{x} = [x_1, x_2, \ldots, x_d]$ by

$$\mathbf{x}' = [x_1, x_2, \ldots, x_d, -1]$$

Then, for the new training set and weight vector, we can treat the threshold as 0 and use the algorithm of Section 12.2.1. The justification is that $\mathbf{w}'.\mathbf{x}' > 0$ is equivalent to $\sum_{i=1}^{d} w_i x_i + \theta \times -1 = \mathbf{w}.\mathbf{x} - \theta > 0$, which in turn is equivalent to $\mathbf{w}.\mathbf{x} > \theta$. The latter is the condition for a positive response from a perceptron with threshold θ.

We can also apply the Winnow Algorithm to the modified data. Winnow requires all feature vectors to have 0s and 1s, as components. However, we can allow a -1 in the feature vector component for θ if we treat it in the manner opposite to the way we treat components that are 1. That is, if the training example is positive, and we need to increase the other weights, we instead divide the component for the threshold by 2. And if the training example is negative, and we need to decrease the other weights, we multiply the threshold component by 2.

	and	viagra	the	of	nigeria	θ	y
a	1	1	0	1	1	-1	$+1$
b	0	0	1	1	0	-1	-1
c	0	1	1	0	0	-1	$+1$
d	1	0	0	1	0	-1	-1
e	1	0	1	0	1	-1	$+1$
f	1	0	1	1	0	-1	-1

Figure 12.8 Training data for spam emails, with a sixth component representing the negative of the threshold

EXAMPLE 12.6   Let us modify the training set of Fig. 12.6 to incorporate a sixth "word" that represents the negative $-\theta$ of the threshold. The new data is shown in Fig. 12.8.

We begin with a weight vector $\mathbf{w}$ with six 1s, as shown in the first line of Fig. 12.9. When we compute $\mathbf{w}.\mathbf{a} = 3$, using the first feature vector $\mathbf{a}$, we are happy because the training example is positive, and so is the dot product. However, for the second training example, we compute $\mathbf{w}.\mathbf{b} = 1$. Since the example

x	y	w.x	OK?	and	viagra	the	of	nigeria	θ
				1	1	1	1	1	1
a	+1	3	yes						
b	-1	1	no	1	1	$\frac{1}{2}$	$\frac{1}{2}$	1	2
c	+1	$-\frac{1}{2}$	no	1	2	1	$\frac{1}{4}$	1	1
d	-1	$\frac{1}{2}$	no	$\frac{1}{2}$	2	1	$\frac{1}{4}$	1	2

Figure 12.9 Sequence of updates to **w** performed by the Winnow Algorithm on the training set of Fig. 12.8

is negative and the dot product is positive, we must adjust the weights. Since **b** has 1s in the third and fourth components, the 1s in the corresponding components of **w** are replaced by $1/2$. The last component, corresponding to θ, must be doubled. These adjustments give the new weight vector $[1, 1, \frac{1}{2}, \frac{1}{2}, 1, 2]$ shown in the third line of Fig. 12.9.

The feature vector **c** is a positive example, but $\mathbf{w}.\mathbf{c} = -\frac{1}{2}$. Thus, we must double the second and third components of **w**, because **c** has 1 in the corresponding components, and we must halve the last component of **w**, which corresponds to θ. The resulting $\mathbf{w} = [1, 2, 1, \frac{1}{2}, 1, 1]$ is shown in the fourth line of Fig. 12.9. Next, **d** is a negative example. Since $\mathbf{w}.\mathbf{d} = \frac{1}{2}$, we must again adjust weights. We halve the weights in the first and fourth components and double the last component, yielding $\mathbf{w} = [\frac{1}{2}, 2, 1, \frac{1}{4}, 1, 2]$. Now, all positive examples have a positive dot product with the weight vector, and all negative examples have a negative dot product, so there are no further changes to the weights.

The designed perceptron has a threshold of 2. It has weights 2 and 1 for "viagra" and "nigeria" and smaller weights for "and" and "of." It also has weight 1 for "the," which suggests that "the" is as indicative of spam as "nigeria," something we doubt is true. Nevertheless, this perceptron does classify all examples correctly. $\square$

12.2.5 Multiclass Perceptrons

There are several ways in which the basic idea of the perceptron can be extended. We shall discuss transformations that enable hyperplanes to serve as nonlinear boundaries in the next section. Here, we look at how perceptrons can be used to classify data into many classes.

Suppose we are given a training set with labels in k different classes. Start by training a perceptron for each class; these perceptrons should each have the same threshold θ. That is, for class i treat a training example $(\mathbf{x}, i)$ as a positive example, and all examples $(\mathbf{x}, j)$, where $j \neq i$, as a negative example. Suppose that the weight vector of the perceptron for class i is determined to be $\mathbf{w}_i$ after training.

Given a new vector **x** to classify, we compute $\mathbf{w}_i.\mathbf{x}$ for all $i = 1, 2, \ldots, k$. We take the class of **x** to be the value of i for which $\mathbf{w}_i.\mathbf{x}$ is the maximum, provided that value is at least θ. Otherwise, $\mathbf{x}$ is assumed not to belong to any of the k classes.

For example, suppose we want to classify Web pages into a number of topics, such as sports, politics, medicine, and so on. We can represent Web pages by a vector with 1 for each word present in the page and 0 for words not present (of course we would only visualize the pages that way; we wouldn't construct the vectors in reality). Each topic has certain words that tend to indicate that topic. For instance, sports pages would be full of words like "win," "goal," "played," and so on. The weight vector for that topic would give higher weights to the words that characterize that topic.

A new page could be classified as belonging to the topic that gives the highest score when the dot product of the page's vector and the weight vectors for the topics are computed. An alternative interpretation of the situation is to classify a page as belonging to all those topics for which the dot product is above some threshold.

12.2.6   Transforming the Training Set

While a perceptron must use a linear function to separate two classes, it is possible to transform the vectors of a training set before applying a perceptron-based algorithm to separate the classes. It is, in principle, always possible to find such a transformation, as long as we are willing to transform to a higher-dimensional space. But if we understand enough about our data, we can often find a simple transformation that works. An example should give the basic idea.

EXAMPLE 12.7   In Fig. 12.10 we see a plot of places to visit from my home. The horizontal and vertical coordinates represent latitude and longitude of places. Some of the places have been classified into "day trips" – places close enough to visit in one day – and "excursions," which require more than a day to visit. These are the circles and squares, respectively. Evidently, there is no straight line that separates day trips from excursions. However, if we replace the Cartesian coordinates by polar coordinates, then in the transformed space of polar coordinates, the dashed circle shown in Fig. 12.10 becomes a hyperplane. Formally, we transform the vector $\mathbf{x} = [x_1, x_2]$ into $[\sqrt{x_1^2 + x_2^2}, \arctan(x_2/x_1)]$.

In fact, we can also do dimensionality reduction of the data. The angle of the point is irrelevant, and only the radius $\sqrt{x_1^2 + x_2^2}$ matters. Thus, we can turn the point vectors into one-component vectors giving the distance of the point from the origin. Associated with the small distances will be the class label "day trip," while the larger distances will all be associated with the label "excursion." Training the perceptron is extremely easy. $\square$

12.2.7   Problems With Perceptrons

Despite the extensions discussed above, there are some limitations to the ability of perceptrons to classify some data. The biggest problem is that sometimes

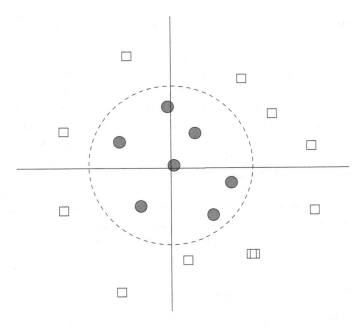

Figure 12.10 Transforming from rectangular to polar coordinates turns this training set into one with a separating hyperplane

the data is inherently not separable by a hyperplane. An example is shown in Fig. 12.11. In this example, points of the two classes mix near the boundary so that any line through the points will have points of both classes on at least one of the sides.

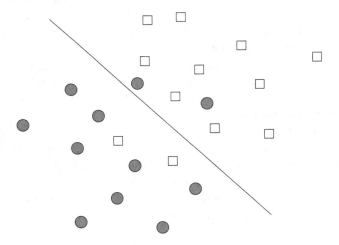

Figure 12.11 A training set may not allow the existence of any separating hyperplane

As mentioned in Section 12.2.6, it is, in principle, possible to find some function on the points that transforms them to another space where they are linearly separable. However, doing so could well lead to overfitting, the situation where the classifier works very well on the training set, because it has been carefully designed to handle each training example correctly. However, because the classifier is exploiting details of the training set that do not apply to other examples that must be classified in the future, the classifier will not perform well on new data.

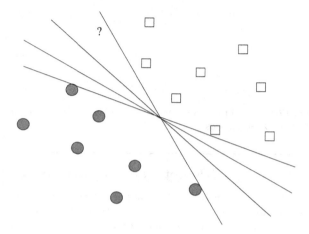

Figure 12.12 Generally, more that one hyperplane can separate the classes if they can be separated at all

Another problem is illustrated in Fig. 12.12. Usually, if classes can be separated by one hyperplane, then there are many different hyperplanes that will separate the points. However, not all hyperplanes are equally good. For instance, if we choose the hyperplane that is furthest clockwise, then the point indicated by "?" will be classified as a circle, even though we intuitively see it as closer to the squares. When we meet support-vector machines in Section 12.3, we shall see that there is a way to insist that the hyperplane chosen be the one that in a sense divides the space most fairly.

Yet another problem is illustrated by Fig. 12.13. Most rules for training a perceptron stop as soon as there are no misclassified points. As a result, the chosen hyperplane will be one that just manages to classify some of the points correctly. For instance, the upper line in Fig. 12.13 has just managed to accommodate two of the squares, and the lower line has just managed to accommodate two of the circles. If either of these lines represent the final weight vector, then the weights are biased toward one of the classes. That is, they correctly classify the points in the training set, but the upper line would classify new squares that are just below it as circles, while the lower line would classify circles just above it as squares. Again, a more equitable choice of separating hyperplane will be shown in Section 12.3.

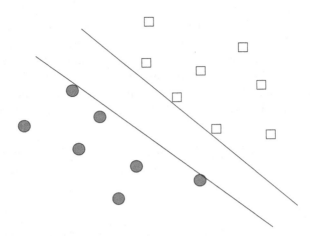

Figure 12.13 Perceptrons converge as soon as the separating hyperplane reaches the region between classes

---

Perceptrons on Streaming Data

While we have viewed the training set as stored data, available for repeated use on any number of passes, perceptrons can also be used in a stream setting. That is, we may suppose there is an infinite sequence of training examples, but that each may be used only once. Detecting email spam is a good example of a training stream. Users report spam emails and also report emails that were classified as spam but are not. Each email, as it arrives, is treated as a training example, and modifies the current weight vector, presumably by a very small amount.

  If the training set is a stream, we never really converge, and in fact the data points may well not be linearly separable. However, at all times, we have an approximation to the best possible separator. Moreover, if the examples in the stream evolve over time, as would be the case for email spam, then we have an approximation that values recent examples more than examples from the distant past, much like the exponentially decaying windows technique from Section 4.7.

12.2.8 Parallel Implementation of Perceptrons

The training of a perceptron is an inherently sequential process. If the number of dimensions of the vectors involved is huge, then we might obtain some parallelism by computing dot products in parallel. However, as we discussed in connection with Example 12.4, high-dimensional vectors are likely to be sparse and can be represented more succinctly than would be expected from their length.

  In order to get significant parallelism, we have to modify the perceptron algorithm slightly, so that many training examples (a "batch") are used with the same estimated weight vector $\mathbf{w}$. This modification changes slightly what the algorithm does, when compared with the sequential implementation where we

> ## A Key Trick for Obtaining Parallelism
>
> The method we used in Section 12.2.8 for turning an inherently serial process into a parallel one appears frequently when dealing with large datasets. In the serial version of the algorithm, there is a state that changes at every step. In this case, the state is the weight vector $\mathbf{w}$. As long as changes to the state tend to be small at every step, we can fix the state and calculate, in parallel, the changes to this exact state that would be caused by each of the serial steps. After the parallel step, combine the changes to make a new state, and repeat the parallel step until convergence.

change $\mathbf{w}$ after every misclassified training example. However, if the learning rate is small, as it normally is, then reusing a single $\mathbf{w}$ for many training examples makes little difference in the resulting value of $\mathbf{w}$ after the batch of training examples is considered. As an example, let us formulate the parallel algorithm as a MapReduce job.

The Map Function Each Map task is given a chunk of training examples, and each Map task knows the current weight vector $\mathbf{w}$. The Map task computes $\mathbf{w}.\mathbf{x}$ for each feature vector $\mathbf{x} = [x_1, x_2, \ldots, x_k]$ in its chunk and compares that dot product with the label y, which is $+1$ or -1, associated with $\mathbf{x}$. If the signs agree, no key-value pairs are produced for this training example. However, if the signs disagree, then for each nonzero component x_i of $\mathbf{x}$ the key-value pair $(i, \eta y x_i)$ is produced; here, η is the learning-rate constant used to train this perceptron. Notice that $\eta y x_i$ is the increment we would like to add to the current ith component of $\mathbf{w}$, and if $x_i = 0$, then there is no need to produce a key-value pair. In the interests of parallelism, we defer that change until we can accumulate many changes in the Reduce phase.

The Reduce Function For each key i, the Reduce task that handles key i adds all the associated increments and then adds that sum to the ith component of $\mathbf{w}$.

Probably, these changes will not be enough to train the perceptron. If any changes to $\mathbf{w}$ occur, then we need to start a new MapReduce job that does the same thing, perhaps with different chunks from the training set. However, even if the entire training set was used on the first round, it can be used again, since its effect on $\mathbf{w}$ will be different if $\mathbf{w}$ has changed.

12.2.9 Exercises for Section 12.2

EXERCISE 12.2.1   Modify the training set of Fig. 12.6 so that example **b** also includes the word "nigeria" (yet remains a negative example – perhaps someone telling about their trip to Nigeria). Find a weight vector that separates the positive and negative examples, using:

(a) The basic training method of Section 12.2.1.

(b) The Winnow method of Section 12.2.3.

(c) The basic method with a variable threshold, as suggested in Section 12.2.4.

(d) The Winnow method with a variable threshold, as suggested in Section 12.2.4.

! EXERCISE 12.2.2   For the following training set:

$$([1,2], +1) \quad ([2,1], +1)$$
$$([2,3], -1) \quad ([3,2], -1)$$

describe all the vectors $\mathbf{w}$ and thresholds θ such that the hyperplane (really a line) defined by $\mathbf{w}.\mathbf{x} - \theta = 0$ separates the points correctly.

! EXERCISE 12.2.3   Suppose the following four examples constitute a training set:

$$([1,2], -1) \quad ([2,3], +1)$$
$$([2,1], +1) \quad ([3,2], -1)$$

(a) What happens when you attempt to train a perceptron to classify these points using 0 as the threshold?

!! (b) Is it possible to change the threshold and obtain a perceptron that correctly classifies these points?

(c) Suggest a transformation using quadratic polynomials that will transform these points so they become linearly separable.

12.3   Support-Vector Machines

We can view a *support-vector machine*, or SVM, as an improvement on the perceptron that is designed to address the problems mentioned in Section 12.2.7. An SVM selects one particular hyperplane that not only separates the points in the two classes, but does so in a way that maximizes the *margin* – the distance between the hyperplane and the closest points of the training set.

In this section, we begin with a discussion of SVMs for training points that are separable, and we show how to maximize the margin in such a case. We then consider a more complex problem, where the points are not linearly separable. In that case, our goal is different. We need to find a hyperplane that does the best it can in separating the two classes. But "best" is a tricky notion. We shall develop a loss function that penalizes misclassified points, but also one that penalizes to a lesser extent points that are correctly classified but are too close to the separating hyperplane. This matter will be taken up in Section 12.3.3.

12.3.1   The Mechanics of an SVM

The goal of an SVM is to select a hyperplane $\mathbf{w}.\mathbf{x} + b = 0$ that maximizes the distance γ between the hyperplane and any point of the training set.[1] The idea is suggested by Fig. 12.14. There, we see the points of two classes and a hyperplane dividing them.

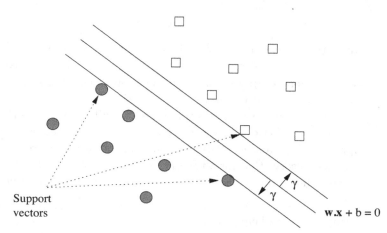

Figure 12.14 An SVM selects the hyperplane with the greatest possible margin γ between the hyperplane and the training points

Intuitively, we are more certain of the class of points that are far from the separating hyperplane than we are of points near to that hyperplane. Thus, it is desirable that all the training points be as far from the hyperplane as possible (but on the correct side of that hyperplane, of course). An added advantage of choosing the separating hyperplane to have as large a margin as possible is that there may be points closer to the hyperplane in the full data set but not in the training set. If so, we have a better chance that these points will be classified properly than if we chose a hyperplane that separated the training points but allowed some points to be very close to the hyperplane itself. In that case, there is a fair chance that a new point that was near a training point that was also near the hyperplane would be misclassified. This issue was discussed in Section 12.2.7 in connection with Fig. 12.13.

We also see in Fig. 12.14 two parallel hyperplanes at distance γ from the central hyperplane $\mathbf{w}.\mathbf{x} + b = 0$, and these each touch one or more of the *support vectors*. The latter are the points that actually constrain the dividing hyperplane, in the sense that they are all at distance γ from the hyperplane. In most cases, a d-dimensional set of points has $d+1$ support vectors, as is the case in Fig. 12.14. However, there can be more support vectors if too many points happen to lie on the parallel hyperplanes. We shall see an example based on the points of

---

[1] Constant b in this formulation of a hyperplane is the same as the negative of the threshold θ in our treatment of perceptrons in Section 12.2.

Fig. 11.1, where it turns out that all four points are support vectors, even though two-dimensional data normally has three.

A tentative statement of our goal is:

- Given a training set $(\mathbf{x}_1, y_1), (\mathbf{x}_2, y_2), \ldots, (\mathbf{x}_n, y_n)$, maximize γ (by varying $\mathbf{w}$ and b) subject to the constraint that for all $i = 1, 2, \ldots, n$,

$$y_i(\mathbf{w}.\mathbf{x}_i + b) \geq \gamma$$

Notice that y_i, which must be $+1$ or -1, determines which side of the hyperplane the point $\mathbf{x}_i$ must be on, so the $\geq$ relationship to γ is always correct. However, it may be easier to express this condition as two cases: if $y = +1$, then $\mathbf{w}.\mathbf{x}+b \geq \gamma$, and if $y = -1$, then $\mathbf{w}.\mathbf{x} + b \leq -\gamma$.

Unfortunately, this formulation doesn't really work properly. The problem is that by increasing $\mathbf{w}$ and b, we can always allow a larger value of γ. For example, suppose that $\mathbf{w}$ and b satisfy the constraint above. If we replace $\mathbf{w}$ by $2\mathbf{w}$ and b by $2b$, we observe that for all i, $y_i((2\mathbf{w}).\mathbf{x}_i + 2b) \geq 2\gamma$. Thus, $2\mathbf{w}$ and $2b$ is always a better choice that $\mathbf{w}$ and b, so there is no best choice and no maximum γ.

12.3.2 Normalizing the Hyperplane

The solution to the problem that we described intuitively above is to normalize the weight vector $\mathbf{w}$. That is, the unit of measure perpendicular to the separating hyperplane is the unit vector $\mathbf{w}/\|\mathbf{w}\|$. Recall that $\|\mathbf{w}\|$ is the Frobenius norm, or the square root of the sum of the squares of the components of $\mathbf{w}$. We shall require that $\mathbf{w}$ be such that the parallel hyperplanes that just touch the support vectors are described by the equations $\mathbf{w}.\mathbf{x} + b = +1$ and $\mathbf{w}.\mathbf{x} + b = -1$, as suggested by Fig. 12.15. We shall refer to the hyperplanes defined by these two equations as the *upper* and *lower* hyperplanes, respectively.

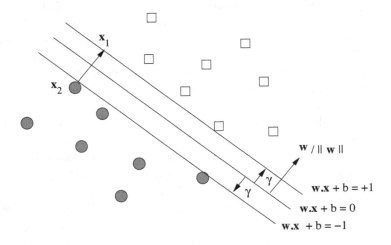

Figure 12.15 Normalizing the weight vector for an SVM

It looks like we have set $\gamma = 1$. But since we are using $\mathbf{w}$ as the unit vector, the margin γ is the number of "units;" that is, steps in the direction $\mathbf{w}$ needed to go between the separating hyperplane and the parallel hyperplanes. Our goal becomes to maximize γ, which is now the multiple of the unit vector $\mathbf{w}/\|\mathbf{w}\|$ between the separating hyperplane and the upper and lower hyperplanes.

Our first step is to demonstrate that maximizing γ is the same as minimizing $\|\mathbf{w}\|$. Consider one of the support vectors, say $\mathbf{x}_2$ shown in Fig. 12.15. Let $\mathbf{x}_1$ be the projection of $\mathbf{x}_2$ onto the upper hyperplane, also as suggested by Fig. 12.15. Note that $\mathbf{x}_1$ need not be a support vector or even a point of the training set. The distance from $\mathbf{x}_2$ to $\mathbf{x}_1$ in units of $\mathbf{w}/\|\mathbf{w}\|$ is 2γ. That is,

$$\mathbf{x}_1 = \mathbf{x}_2 + 2\gamma \frac{\mathbf{w}}{\|\mathbf{w}\|} \tag{12.1}$$

Since $\mathbf{x}_1$ is on the hyperplane defined by $\mathbf{w}.\mathbf{x}+b = +1$, we know that $\mathbf{w}.\mathbf{x}_1+b = 1$. If we substitute for $\mathbf{x}_1$ using Equation 12.1, we get

$$\mathbf{w}.\left(\mathbf{x}_2 + 2\gamma \frac{\mathbf{w}}{\|\mathbf{w}\|}\right) + b = 1$$

Regrouping terms, we see

$$\mathbf{w}.\mathbf{x}_2 + b + 2\gamma \frac{\mathbf{w}.\mathbf{w}}{\|\mathbf{w}\|} = 1 \tag{12.2}$$

But the first two terms of Equation 12.2, $\mathbf{w}.\mathbf{x}_2 + b$, sum to -1, since we know that $\mathbf{x}_2$ is on the lower hyperplane, $\mathbf{w}.\mathbf{x} + b = -1$. If we move this -1 from left to right in Equation 12.2 and then divide through by 2, we conclude that

$$\gamma \frac{\mathbf{w}.\mathbf{w}}{\|\mathbf{w}\|} = 1 \tag{12.3}$$

Notice also that $\mathbf{w}.\mathbf{w}$ is the sum of the squares of the components of $\mathbf{w}$. That is, $\mathbf{w}.\mathbf{w} = \|\mathbf{w}\|^2$. We conclude from Equation 12.3 that $\gamma = 1/\|\mathbf{w}\|$.

This equivalence gives us a way to reformulate the optimization problem originally stated in Section 12.3.1. Instead of maximizing γ, we want to minimize $\|\mathbf{w}\|$, which is the inverse of γ. That is:

- Given a training set $(\mathbf{x}_1, y_1), (\mathbf{x}_2, y_2), \ldots, (\mathbf{x}_n, y_n)$, minimize $\|\mathbf{w}\|$ (by varying $\mathbf{w}$ and b) subject to the constraint that for all $i = 1, 2, \ldots, n$,

$$y_i(\mathbf{w}.\mathbf{x}_i + b) \geq 1$$

EXAMPLE 12.8   Let us consider the four points of Fig. 11.1, supposing that they alternate as positive and negative examples. That is, the training set consists of

$$([1,2], +1) \quad ([2,1], -1)$$
$$([3,4], +1) \quad ([4,3], -1)$$

Let $\mathbf{w} = [u, v]$. Our goal is to minimize $\sqrt{u^2 + v^2}$ subject to the constraints we derive from the four training examples. For the first, where $\mathbf{x}_1 = [1, 2]$ and $y_1 = +1$, the constraint is $(+1)(u+2v+b) = u+2v+b \geq 1$. For the second, where $\mathbf{x}_2 = [2, 1]$ and $y_2 = -1$, the constraint is $(-1)(2u+v+b) \geq 1$, or $2u+v+b \leq -1$.

The last two points are analogously handled, and the four constraints we derive are:

$$u + 2v + b \geq 1 \qquad 2u + v + b \leq -1$$
$$3u + 4v + b \geq 1 \qquad 4u + 3v + b \leq -1$$

We shall cover in detail the subject of how one optimizes under constraints; the subject is broad and many packages are available for you to use. Section 12.3.4 discusses one method – gradient descent – in connection with a more general application of SVM, where there is no separating hyperplane. An illustration of how this method works will appear in Example 12.9.

In this simple example, the solution is easy to see: $b = 0$ and $\mathbf{w} = [u, v] = [-1, +1]$. It happens that all four constraints are satisfied exactly; i.e., each of the four points is a support vector. That case is unusual, since when the data is two-dimensional, we expect only three support vectors. However, the fact that the positive and negative examples lie on parallel lines allows all four constraints to be satisfied exactly. □

12.3.3   Finding Optimal Approximate Separators

We shall now consider finding an optimal hyperplane in the more general case, where no matter which hyperplane we choose, there will be some points on the wrong side, and perhaps some points that are on the correct side, but too close to the separating hyperplane itself, so the margin requirement is not met. A typical situation is shown in Fig. 12.16. We see two points that are misclassified; they are on the wrong side of the separating hyperplane $\mathbf{w}.\mathbf{x} + b = 0$. We also see two points that, while they are classified correctly, are too close to the separating hyperplane. We shall call all these points *bad* points.

Each bad point incurs a penalty when we evaluate a possible hyperplane. The amount of the penalty, in units to be determined as part of the optimization process, is shown by the arrow leading to the bad point from the hyperplane on the wrong side of which the bad point lies. That is, the arrows measure the distance from the hyperplane $\mathbf{w}.\mathbf{x} + b = 1$ or $\mathbf{w}.\mathbf{x} + b = -1$. The former is the baseline for training examples that are supposed to be above the separating hyperplane (because the label y is $+1$), and the latter is the baseline for points that are supposed to be below (because $y = -1$).

We have many options regarding the exact formula that we wish to minimize. Intuitively, we want $\|\mathbf{w}\|$ to be as small as possible, as we discussed in Section 12.3.2. But we also want the penalties associated with the bad points to be as small as possible. The most common form of a tradeoff is expressed by a formula that involves the term $\|\mathbf{w}\|^2/2$ and another term that involves a constant times the sum of the penalties.

To see why minimizing the term $\|\mathbf{w}\|^2/2$ makes sense, note that minimizing $\|\mathbf{w}\|$ is the same as minimizing any monotone function of $\|\mathbf{w}\|$, so it is at least an option to choose a formula in which we try to minimize $\|\mathbf{w}\|^2/2$. This expression is desirable because its derivative with respect to any component of $\mathbf{w}$ is that

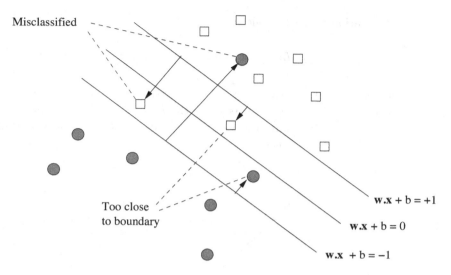

Figure 12.16 Points that are misclassified or are too close to the separating hyperplane incur a penalty; the amount of the penalty is proportional to the length of the arrow leading to that point

component. That is, if $\mathbf{w} = [w_1, w_2, \ldots, w_d]$, then $\|\mathbf{w}\|^2/2$ is $\frac{1}{2}\sum_{i=1}^{n} w_i^2$, so its partial derivative $\partial/\partial w_i$ is w_i. This situation makes sense because, as we shall see, the derivative of the penalty term with respect to w_i is a constant times each x_i, the corresponding component of each feature vector whose training example incurs a penalty. That in turn means that the vector $\mathbf{w}$ and the vectors of the training set are commensurate in the units of their components.

Thus, we shall consider how to minimize the particular function

$$f(\mathbf{w}, b) = \frac{1}{2}\sum_{j=1}^{d} w_j^2 + C\sum_{i=1}^{n} \max\left\{0, \ 1 - y_i\left(\sum_{j=1}^{d} w_j x_{ij} + b\right)\right\} \qquad (12.4)$$

The first term encourages small $\|\mathbf{w}\|$, while the second term, involving the constant C that must be chosen properly, represents the penalty for bad points in a manner to be explained below. We assume there are n training examples $(\mathbf{x}_i, y_i)$ for $i = 1, 2, \ldots, n$, and $\mathbf{x}_i = [x_{i1}, x_{i2}, \ldots, x_{id}]$. Also, as before, $\mathbf{w} = [w_1, w_2, \ldots, w_d]$. Note that the two summations $\sum_{j=1}^{d}$ express the dot product of vectors.

The constant C, called the *regularization parameter*, reflects how important misclassification is. Pick a large C if you really do not want to misclassify points, but you would accept a narrow margin. Pick a small C if you are OK with some misclassified points, but want most of the points to be far away from the boundary (i.e., the margin is large).

We must explain the penalty function (second term) in Equation 12.4. The summation over i has one term

$$L(\mathbf{x}_i, y_i) = \max\left\{0, \ 1 - y_i\left(\sum_{j=1}^{d} w_j x_{ij} + b\right)\right\}$$

for each training example $\mathbf{x}_i$. The quantity L is the *hinge function*, suggested in Fig. 12.17, and we call its value the *hinge loss*. Let $z_i = y_i(\sum_{j=1}^{d} w_j x_{ij} + b)$. When z_i is 1 or more, the value of L is 0. But for smaller values of z_i, L rises linearly as z_i decreases.

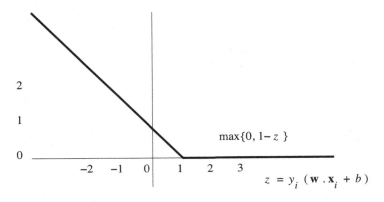

Figure 12.17 The hinge function decreases linearly for $z \leq 1$ and then remains 0

Since we shall have need to take the derivative with respect to each w_j of $L(\mathbf{x}_i, y_i)$, note that the derivative of the hinge function is discontinuous. It is $-y_i x_{ij}$ for $z_i < 1$ and 0 for $z_i > 1$. That is, if $y_i = +1$ (i.e., the ith training example is positive), then

$$\frac{\partial L}{\partial w_j} = \text{if } \sum_{j=1}^{d} w_j x_{ij} + b \geq 1 \text{ then } 0 \text{ else } - x_{ij}$$

Moreover, if $y_i = -1$ (i.e., the ith training example is negative), then

$$\frac{\partial L}{\partial w_j} = \text{if } \sum_{j=1}^{d} w_j x_{ij} + b \leq -1 \text{ then } 0 \text{ else } x_{ij}$$

The two cases can be summarized as one, if we involve the value of y_i, as:

$$\frac{\partial L}{\partial w_j} = \text{if } y_i\left(\sum_{j=1}^{d} w_j x_{ij} + b\right) \geq 1 \text{ then } 0 \text{ else } - y_i x_{ij} \qquad (12.5)$$

12.3.4   SVM Solutions by Gradient Descent

A common approach to solving Equation 12.4 is to use quadratic programming. For large-scale data, another approach, *gradient descent* has an advantage. We can allow the data to reside on disk, rather than keeping it all in memory, which is normally required for quadratic solvers. To implement gradient descent, we compute the derivative of the equation with respect to b and each component w_j of the vector $\mathbf{w}$. Since we want to minimize $f(\mathbf{w}, b)$, we move b and the components w_j in the direction opposite to the direction of the gradient. The amount we move each component is proportional to the derivative with respect to that component.

Our first step is to use the trick of Section 12.2.4 to make b part of the weight vector $\mathbf{w}$. Notice that b is really the negative of a threshold on the dot product $\mathbf{w}.\mathbf{x}$, so we can append a $(d+1)$st component b to $\mathbf{w}$ and append an extra component with value $+1$ to every feature vector in the training set (not -1 as we did in Section 12.2.4).

We must choose a constant η to be the fraction of the gradient that we move $\mathbf{w}$ in each round. That is, we assign

$$w_j := w_j - \eta \frac{\partial f}{\partial w_j}$$

for all $j = 1, 2, \ldots, d+1$.

The derivative $\frac{\partial f}{\partial w_j}$ of the first term in Equation 12.4, $\frac{1}{2}\sum_{j=1}^{d} w_i^2$, is easy; it is w_j. However, the second term involves the hinge function, so it is harder to express. We shall use an if–then expression to describe these derivatives, as in Equation 12.5. That is:

$$\frac{\partial f}{\partial w_j} = w_j + C \sum_{i=1}^{n} \left(\textbf{if } y_i(\sum_{j=1}^{d} w_j x_{ij} + b) \geq 1 \textbf{ then } 0 \textbf{ else } -y_i x_{ij} \right) \quad (12.6)$$

Note that this formula gives us a partial derivative with respect to each component of $\mathbf{w}$, including w_{d+1}, which is b, as well as to the weights $w_1, w_2, \ldots, w_d$. We continue to use b instead of the equivalent w_{d+1} in the if-then condition to remind us of the form in which the desired hyperplane is described.

To execute the gradient-descent algorithm on a training set, we pick:

(1) Values for the parameters C and η.
(2) Initial values for $\mathbf{w}$, including the $(d+1)$st component b.

Then, we repeatedly:

(a) Compute the partial derivatives of $f(\mathbf{w}, b)$ with respect to the w_j.
(b) Adjust the values of $\mathbf{w}$ by subtracting $\eta \frac{\partial f}{\partial w_j}$ from each w_j.

EXAMPLE 12.9 Figure 12.18 shows six points, three positive and three negative. We expect that the best separating line will be horizontal, and the only question is whether or not the separating hyperplane and the scale of $\mathbf{w}$ will cause the point $(2, 2)$ to be misclassified or to lie too close to the boundary. Initially, we shall choose $\mathbf{w} = [0, 1]$, a vertical vector with a scale of 1, and we shall choose $b = -2$. As a result, we see in Fig. 12.18 that the point $(2, 2)$ lies on the initial hyperplane and the three negative points are right at the margin. The parameter values we shall choose for gradient descent are $C = 0.1$, and $\eta = 0.2$.

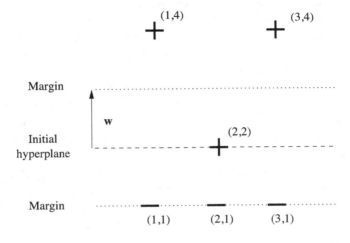

Figure 12.18 Six points for a gradient-descent example

We begin by incorporating b as the third component of $\mathbf{w}$, and for notational convenience, we shall use u and v as the first two components, rather than the customary w_1 and w_2. That is, we take $\mathbf{w} = [u, v, b]$. We also expand the two-dimensional points of the training set with a third component that is always 1. That is, the training set becomes

$$([1, 4, 1], +1) \quad ([2, 2, 1], +1) \quad ([3, 4, 1], +1)$$
$$([1, 1, 1], -1) \quad ([2, 1, 1], -1) \quad ([3, 1, 1], -1)$$

In Fig. 12.19 we tabulate the if–then conditions and the resulting contributions to the summations over i in Equation 12.6. The summation must be multiplied by C and added to u, v, or b, as appropriate, to implement Equation 12.6.

					for u	for v	for b
if	$u + 4v + b \geq +1$	then	0	else	-1	-4	-1
if	$2u + 2v + b \geq +1$	then	0	else	-2	-2	-1
if	$3u + 4v + b \geq +1$	then	0	else	-3	-4	-1
if	$u + v + b \leq -1$	then	0	else	$+1$	$+1$	$+1$
if	$2u + v + b \leq -1$	then	0	else	$+2$	$+1$	$+1$
if	$3u + v + b \leq -1$	then	0	else	$+3$	$+1$	$+1$

Figure 12.19 Sum each of these terms and multiply by C to get the contribution of bad points to the derivatives of f with respect to u, v, and b

The truth or falsehood of each of the six conditions in Fig. 12.19 determines the contribution of the terms in the summations over i in Equation 12.6. We shall represent the status of each condition by a sequence of instances of x and o, with x representing a condition that does not hold and o representing one that does. The first few iterations of gradient descent are shown in Fig. 12.20.

	$\mathbf{w} = [u, v]$	b	Bad	$\partial/\partial u$	$\partial/\partial v$	$\partial/\partial b$
(1)	$[0.000, 1.000]$	-2.000	oxooooo	-0.200	0.800	-2.100
(2)	$[0.040, 0.840]$	-1.580	oxoxxx	0.440	0.940	-1.380
(3)	$[-0.048, 0.652]$	-1.304	oxoxxx	0.352	0.752	-1.104
(4)	$[-0.118, 0.502]$	-1.083	xxxxxx	-0.118	-0.198	-1.083
(5)	$[-0.094, 0.542]$	-0.866	oxoxxx	0.306	0.642	-0.666
(6)	$[-0.155, 0.414]$	-0.733	xxxxxx			

Figure 12.20 Beginning of the process of gradient descent

Consider line (1). It shows the initial value of $\mathbf{w} = [0, 1]$, as we suggested in Fig. 12.18 was the initial value of $\mathbf{w}$. Recall that we use u and v for the components of $\mathbf{w}$, so $u = 0$ and $v = 1$. We also see the initial value of $b = -2$, which is the appropriate value for the initial hyperplane shown in Fig. 12.18. We must use these values of u, v, and b to evaluate the conditions in Fig. 12.19. The first of the conditions in Fig. 12.19 is $u + 4v + b \geq +1$. The left side is $0 + 4 + (-2) = 2$, so the condition is satisfied. However, the second condition, $2u + 2v + b \geq +1$ fails. The left side is $0 + 2 + (-2) = 0$. The fact that the sum is 0 means the second point $(2, 2)$ is exactly on the separating hyperplane, and not outside the margin. The third condition is satisfied, since $0 + 4 + (-2) = 2 \geq +1$. The last three conditions are also satisfied, and in fact are satisfied exactly. For instance, the fourth condition is $u + v + b \leq -1$. The left side is $0 + 1 + (-2) = -1$. Thus, the pattern oxoooo represents the outcome of these six conditions, as we see in the first line of Fig. 12.20.

We use these conditions to compute the partial derivatives. For $\partial f/\partial u$, we use u in place of w_j in Equation 12.6. This expression thus becomes

$$u + C\big(0 + (-2) + 0 + 0 + 0 + 0\big) = 0 + \frac{1}{10}(-2) = -0.2$$

The sum multiplying C can be explained this way. For each of the six conditions of Fig. 12.19, take 0 if the condition is satisfied, and take the value in the column labeled "for u" if it is not satisfied. Similarly, for v in place of w_j we get $\partial f/\partial v = 1 + \frac{1}{10}(0 + (-2) + 0 + 0 + 0 + 0) = 0.8$. Finally, for b we get $\partial f/\partial b = -2 + \frac{1}{10}(0 + (-1) + 0 + 0 + 0 + 0) = -2.1$.

We can now compute the new $\mathbf{w}$ and b that appear on line (2) of Fig. 12.20. Since we chose $\eta = 0.2$, the new value of u is $0 - \frac{1}{5}(-0.2) = -0.04$, the new value of v is $1 - \frac{1}{5}(0.8) = 0.84$, and the new value of b is $-2 - \frac{1}{5}(-2.1) = -1.58$.

To compute the derivatives shown in line (2) of Fig. 12.20 we must first check the conditions of Fig. 12.19. While the outcomes of the first three conditions have not changed, the last three are no longer satisfied. For example, the fourth condition is $u + v + b \leq -1$, but $0.04 + 0.84 + (-1.58) = -0.7$, which is not less than -1. Thus, the pattern of bad points becomes oxoxxx. We now have

more nonzero terms in the expressions for the derivatives. For example $\partial f / \partial u =$
$0.04 + \frac{1}{10}\left(0 + (-2) + 0 + 1 + 2 + 3\right) = 0.44$.

The values of $\mathbf{w}$ and b in line (3) are computed from the derivatives of line (2)
in the same way as they were computed in line (2). The new values do not change
the pattern of bad points; it is still oxoxxx. However, when we repeat the process
for line (4), we find that all six conditions are unsatisfied. For instance, the first
condition, $u + 4v + b \geq +1$ is not satisfied, because $(-0.118 + 4 \times 0.502 + (-1.083) =$
0.807, which is less than 1. In effect, the first point has become too close to the
separating hyperplane, even though it is properly classified.

We can see that in line (5) of Fig. 12.20, the problems with the first and third
points are corrected, and we go back to pattern oxoxxx of bad points. However,
at line (6), the points have again become too close to the separating hyperplane,
so we revert to the xxxxxx pattern of bad points. You are invited to continue
the sequence of updates to $\mathbf{w}$ and b for several more iterations.

One might wonder why the gradient-descent process seems to be converging
on a solution where at least some of the points are inside the margin, when there
is an obvious hyperplane (horizontal, at height 1.5) with a margin of $1/2$, that
separates the positive and negative points. The reason is that when we picked
$C = 0.1$ we were saying that we really don't care too much whether there are
points inside the margins, or even if points are misclassified. We were saying
also that what was important was a large margin (which corresponds to a small
$\|\mathbf{w}\|$), even if some points violated that same margin. □

12.3.5 Stochastic Gradient Descent

The gradient-descent algorithm described in Section 12.3.4 is often called *batch*
gradient descent, because at each round, all the training examples are considered
as a "batch." While it is effective on small datasets, it can be too time-consuming
to execute on a large dataset, where we must visit every training example, often
many times, before convergence.

An alternative, called *stochastic* gradient descent, considers one training example, or a few training examples at a time and adjusts the current estimate of
the error function ($\mathbf{w}$ in the SVM example) in the direction indicated by only the
small set of training examples considered. Additional rounds are possible, using
other sets of training examples; these can be selected randomly or according to
some fixed strategy. Note that it is normal that some members of the training
set are *never* used in a stochastic gradient descent algorithm.

EXAMPLE 12.10   Recall the UV-decomposition algorithm discussed in Section 9.4.3. This algorithm was described as an example of batch gradient descent.
We can regard each of the nonblank entries in the matrix M we are trying to
approximate by the product UV as a training example, and the error function is
the root-mean-square error between the product of the current matrices U and
V and the matrix M, considering only those elements where M is nonblank.

However, if M has a very large number of nonblank entries, as would be the case if M represented, say, purchases of items by Amazon customers or movies that Netflix customers had rated, then it is not practical to make repeated passes over the entire set of nonblank entries of M when adjusting the entries in U and V. A stochastic gradient descent implementation would look at a single nonblank entry of M and compute the change to each element of U and V that would make the product UV agree with that element of M. We would not make that change to the elements of U and V completely, but rather choose some learning rate η less than 1 and change each element of U and V by the fraction η of the amount that would be necessary to make UV equal M in the chosen entry. □

There is a compromise between batch and stochastic gradient descent called *minibatch* gradient descent. In the minibatch version, we partition the entire training set into "minibatches," of some chosen size, e.g., 1000 training examples. We work on one minibatch at a time, computing changes to $\mathbf{w}$ using Equation 12.4, but summing only over the selected training examples.

12.3.6 Parallel Implementation of SVM

The first observation is that stochastic gradient descent is inherently serial, since the state of the system – the vector $\mathbf{w}$ and the constant b – changes with every training example considered. On the other hand, batch gradient descent is most easily parallelized, since it uses each training example starting from the same state, and only combines the effects of these training examples at the end of a round.

Thus, we can parallelize SVM using gradient descent in a manner analogous to what we suggested for perceptrons in Section 12.2.8. You can start with the current $\mathbf{w}$ and b and divide the training examples into minibatches, creating one task for each minibatch. The tasks each apply Equation 12.4 to their minibatch, and the changes to the state, $\mathbf{w}$ and b, are summed after one parallel round. The new state is computed by summing all the changes, and the process can repeat with the new state distributed to all the tasks.

12.3.7 Exercises for Section 12.3

EXERCISE 12.3.1   Continue the iterations of Fig. 12.20 for three more iterations.

EXERCISE 12.3.2   The following training set obeys the rule that the positive examples all have vectors whose components sum to 10 or more, while the sum is less than 10 for the negative examples:

$$([3,4,5],+1) \quad ([2,7,2],+1) \quad ([5,5,5],+1)$$
$$([1,2,3],-1) \quad ([3,3,2],-1) \quad ([2,4,1],-1)$$

(a) Which of these six vectors are the support vectors?

! (b) Suggest a vector $\mathbf{w}$ and constant b such that the hyperplane defined by $\mathbf{w}.\mathbf{x} + b = 0$ is a good separator for the positive and negative examples.

Make sure that the scale of **w** is such that all points are outside the margin; that is, for each training example $(\mathbf{x}, y)$, you have $y(\mathbf{w}.\mathbf{x} + b) \geq +1$.

! (c) Starting with your answer to part (b), use gradient descent to find the optimum **w** and b. Note that if you start with a separating hyperplane, and you scale **w** properly, then the second term of Equation 12.4 will always be 0, which simplifies your work considerably.

! EXERCISE 12.3.3   The following training set obeys the rule that the positive examples all have vectors whose components have an odd sum, while the sum is even for the negative examples:

$$([1, 2], +1) \quad ([3, 4], +1) \quad ([5, 2], +1)$$
$$([2, 4], -1) \quad ([3, 1], -1) \quad ([7, 3], -1)$$

(a) Suggest a starting vector **w** and constant b that classifies at least three of the points correctly.

!! (b) Starting with your answer to (a), use gradient descent to find the optimum **w** and b.

12.4   Learning from Nearest Neighbors

In this section we consider several examples of "learning" where the entire training set is stored, perhaps preprocessed in some useful way, and then used to classify future examples or to compute the value of the label that is most likely associated with the example. The feature vector of each training example is treated as a data point in some space. When a new point arrives and must be classified, we find the training example or examples that are closest to the new point, according to the distance measure for that space. The estimated label is then computed by combining the closest examples in some way.

12.4.1   The Framework for Nearest-Neighbor Calculations

The training set is first preprocessed and stored. The decisions take place when a new example, called the *query example*, arrives and must be classified.

There are several decisions we must make in order to design a nearest-neighbor-based algorithm that will classify query examples. We enumerate them here:

(1) What distance measure do we use?
(2) How many of the nearest neighbors do we look at?
(3) How do we weight the nearest neighbors? Normally, we provide a function (the *kernel function*) of the distance between the query example and its nearest neighbors in the training set, and use this function to weight the neighbors. If there is no weighting, then the kernel function need not be specified.

(4) How do we define the label to associate with the query? This label is some function of the labels of the nearest neighbors, perhaps weighted by the kernel function, or perhaps not.

12.4.2   Learning with One Nearest Neighbor

The simplest cases of nearest-neighbor learning are when we choose only the one neighbor that is nearest the query example. In that case, there is no use for weighting the neighbors, so the kernel function is omitted. There is also typically only one possible choice for the labeling function: take the label of the query to be the same as the label of the nearest neighbor.

EXAMPLE 12.11   Figure 12.21 shows some of the examples of dogs that last appeared in Fig. 12.1. We have dropped most of the examples for simplicity, leaving only three Chihuahuas, two Dachshunds, and two Beagles. Since the height–weight vectors describing the dogs are two-dimensional, there is a simple and efficient way to construct a *Voronoi diagram* for the points, in which the perpendicular bisectors of the lines between each pair of points is constructed. Each point gets a region around it, containing all the points to which it is the nearest. These regions are always convex, although they may be open to infinity in one direction.[2] It is also a surprising fact that, even though there are $O(n^2)$ perpendicular bisectors for n points, the Voronoi diagram can be found in $O(n \log n)$ time.

In Fig. 12.21 we see the Voronoi diagram for the seven points. The boundaries that separate dogs of different breeds are shown solid, while the boundaries between dogs of the same breed are shown dashed. Suppose a query example q is provided. Note that q is a point in the space of Fig. 12.21. We find the region into which q falls, and give q the label of the training example to which that region belongs. Note that it is not too hard to find the region of q. We have to determine to which side of certain lines q falls. This process is the same as we used in Sections 12.2 and 12.3 to compare a vector $\mathbf{x}$ with a hyperplane perpendicular to a vector $\mathbf{w}$. In fact, if the lines that actually form parts of the Voronoi diagram are preprocessed properly, we can make the determination in $O(\log n)$ comparisons; it is not necessary to compare q with all of the $O(n \log n)$ lines that form part of the diagram. □

12.4.3   Learning One-Dimensional Functions

Another simple and useful case of nearest-neighbor learning has one-dimensional data. In this situation, the training examples are of the form $([x], y)$, and we

---

[2] While the region belonging to any one point is convex, the union of the regions for two or more points might not be convex. Thus, in Fig. 12.21 we see that the region for all Dachshunds and the region for all Beagles are not convex. That is, there are points p_1 and p_2 that are both classified Dachshunds, but the midpoint of the line between p_1 and p_2 is classified as a Beagle, and vice versa.

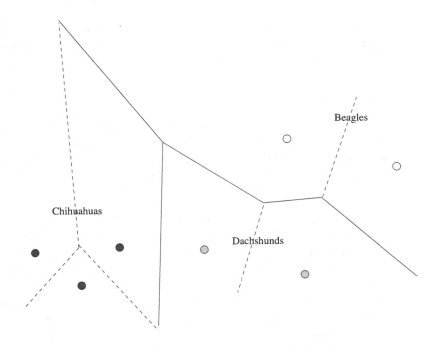

Figure 12.21 Voronoi diagram for the three breeds of dogs

shall write them as (x, y), identifying a one-dimensional vector with its lone component. In effect, the training set is a collection of samples of the value of a function $y = f(x)$ for certain values of x, and we must interpolate the function f at all points. There are many rules that could be used, and we shall only outline some of the popular approaches. As discussed in Section 12.4.1, the approaches vary in the number of neighbors they use, whether or not the neighbors are weighted, and if so, how the weight varies with distance.

Suppose we use a method with k nearest neighbors, and x is the query point. Let $x_1, x_2, \ldots, x_k$ be the k nearest neighbors of x, and let the weight associated with training point (x_i, y_i) be w_i. Then the estimate of the label y for x is $\sum_{i=1}^{k} w_i y_i / \sum_{i=1}^{k} w_i$. Note that this expression gives the weighted average of the labels of the k nearest neighbors.

EXAMPLE 12.12   We shall illustrate four simple rules, using the training set $(1, 1)$, $(2, 2)$, $(3, 4)$, $(4, 8)$, $(5, 4)$, $(6, 2)$, and $(7, 1)$. These points represent a function that has a peak at $x = 4$ and decays exponentially on both sides. Note that this training set has values of x that are evenly spaced. There is no requirement that the points be evenly spaced or have any other regular pattern. Some possible ways to interpolate values are:

(1) *Nearest Neighbor.* Use only the one nearest neighbor. There is no need for a weighting. Just take the value of any $f(x)$ to be the label y associated with

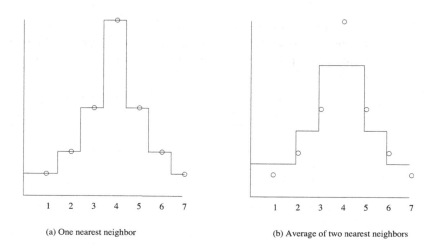

(a) One nearest neighbor   (b) Average of two nearest neighbors

Figure 12.22 Results of applying the first two rules in Example 12.12

the training-set point nearest to query point x. The result of using this rule on the example training set described above is shown in Fig. 12.22(a).

(2) *Average of the Two Nearest Neighbors.* Choose 2 as the number of nearest neighbors to use. The weights of these two are each $1/2$, regardless of how far they are from the query point x. The result of this rule on the example training set is in Fig. 12.22(b).

(3) *Weighted Average of the Two Nearest Neighbors.* We again choose two nearest neighbors, but we weight them in inverse proportion to their distance from the query point. Suppose the two neighbors nearest to query point x are x_1 and x_2. Suppose first that $x_1 < x < x_2$. Then the weight of x_1, the inverse of its distance from x, is $1/(x-x_1)$, and the weight of x_2 is $1/(x_2-x)$. The weighted average of the labels is

$$\left(\frac{y_1}{x - x_1} + \frac{y_2}{x_2 - x}\right) \Big/ \left(\frac{1}{x - x_1} + \frac{1}{x_2 - x}\right)$$

which, when we multiply numerator and denominator by $(x - x_1)(x_2 - x)$, simplifies to

$$\frac{y_1(x_2 - x) + y_2(x - x_1)}{x_2 - x_1}$$

This expression is the linear interpolation of the two nearest neighbors, as shown in Fig. 12.23(a). When both nearest neighbors are on the same side of the query x, the same weights make sense, and the resulting estimate is an *extrapolation*. We see extrapolation in Fig. 12.23(a) in the range $x = 0$ to $x = 1$. In general, when points are unevenly spaced, we can find query points in the interior where both neighbors are on one side.

(4) *Average of Three Nearest Neighbors.* We can average any number of the nearest neighbors to estimate the label of a query point. Figure 12.23(b)

shows what happens on our example training set when the three nearest neighbors are used, with no weighting. Weighting the three neighbors, such as in inverse proportion to their distances to the point in question, is another option.

☐

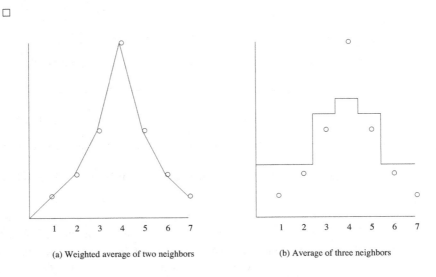

(a) Weighted average of two neighbors   (b) Average of three neighbors

Figure 12.23 Results of applying the last two rules in Example 12.12

12.4.4   Kernel Regression

A way to construct a continuous function that represents the data of a training set well is to consider all points in the training set, but weight the points using a kernel function that decays with distance. A popular choice is to use a normal distribution (or "bell curve"), so the weight of a training point x when the query is q is $e^{-(x-q)^2/\sigma^2}$. Here σ is the standard deviation of the distribution (a parameter you select) and the query q is the mean. Roughly, points within distance σ of q are heavily weighted, and those further away have little weight. There is an advantage to using a kernel function, such as the normal distribution, that is continuous and defined for all points in the training set; doing so assures that the resulting function learned from the data is itself continuous. (See Exercise 12.4.6 for a discussion of the problem when a simpler weighting is used.)

EXAMPLE 12.13   Let us use the seven training examples of Example 12.12. To make calculation simpler, we shall not use the normal distribution as the kernel function, but rather another continuous function of distance, namely $w = 1/(x-q)^2$. That is, weights decay as the square of the distance. Suppose the query q is 3.5. The weights $w_1, w_2, \ldots w_7$ of the seven training examples $(x_i, y_i) = (i, 8/2^{|i-4|})$ for $i = 1, 2, \ldots, 7$ are shown in Fig. 12.24.

Lines (1) and (2) of Fig. 12.24 give the seven training points. The weight of

(1)	x_i	1	2	3	4	5	6	7
(2)	y_i	1	2	4	8	4	2	1
(3)	w_i	4/25	4/9	4	4	4/9	4/25	4/49
(4)	$w_i y_i$	4/25	8/9	16	32	16/9	8/25	4/49

Figure 12.24 Weights of points when the query is $q = 3.5$

Problems in the Limit for Example 12.13

Suppose q is exactly equal to one of the training examples x. If we use the normal distribution as the kernel function, there is no problem with the weight of x: it is 1. However, with the kernel function discussed in Example 12.13, the weight of x is $1/(x - q)^2 = \infty$. Fortunately, this weight appears in both the numerator and denominator of the expression that estimates the label of q. It can be shown that in the limit as q approaches x, the label of x dominates all the other terms in both numerator and denominator, so the estimated label of q is the same as the label of x. That makes excellent sense, since $q = x$ in the limit.

---

each when the query is $q = 3.5$ is given in line (3). For instance, for $x_1 = 1$, the weight $w_1 = 1/(1 - 3.5)^2 = 1/(-2.5)^2 = 4/25$. Then, line (4) shows each y_i weighted by the weight from line (3). For instance, the column for x_2 has value $8/9$ because $w_2 y_2 = 2 \times (4/9)$.

To compute the label for the query $q = 3.5$ we sum the weighted values of the labels in the training set, as given by line (4) of Fig. 12.24; this sum is 51.23. We then divide by the sum of the weights in line (3). This sum is 9.29, so the ratio is $51.23/9.29 = 5.51$. That estimate of the value of the label for $q = 3.5$ seems intuitively reasonable, since q lies midway between two points with labels 4 and 8. □

12.4.5 Dealing with High-Dimensional Euclidean Data

We saw in Section 12.4.2 that the two-dimensional case of Euclidean data is fairly easy. There are several large-scale data structures that have been developed for finding near neighbors when the number of dimensions grows, and the training set is large. We shall not cover these structures here, because the subject could fill a book by itself, and there are many places available to learn about these techniques, collectively called *multidimensional index structures*. See the bibliographic notes for this chapter for information about such structures as *kd*-Trees, R-Trees, and Quad Trees.

Unfortunately, for high-dimensional data, there is little that can be done to avoid searching a large portion of the data. This fact is another manifestation of the "curse of dimensionality" from Section 7.1.3. Two ways to deal with the "curse" are the following:

(1) *VA Files.* Since we must look at a large fraction of the data anyway in order to find the nearest neighbors of a query point, we could avoid a complex data structure altogether. Accept that we must scan the entire file, but do so in a two-stage manner. First, a summary of the file is created, using only a small number of bits that approximate the values of each component of each training vector. For example, if we use only the high-order $(1/4)$th of the bits in numerical components, then we can create a file that is $(1/4)$th the size of the full dataset. However, by scanning this file we can construct a list of candidates that *might* be among the k nearest neighbors of the query q, and this list may be a small fraction of the entire dataset. We then look up only these candidates in the complete file, in order to determine which k are nearest to q.

(2) *Dimensionality Reduction.* We may treat the vectors of the training set as a matrix, where the rows are the vectors of the training example, and the columns correspond to the components of these vectors. Apply one of the dimensionality-reduction techniques of Chapter 11, to compress the vectors to a small number of dimensions, small enough that the techniques for multidimensional indexing can be used. Of course, when processing a query vector q, the same transformation must be applied to q before searching for q's nearest neighbors.

12.4.6   Dealing with Non-Euclidean Distances

To this point, we have assumed that the distance measure is Euclidean. However, most of the techniques can be adapted naturally to an arbitrary distance function d. For instance, in Section 12.4.4 we talked about using a normal distribution as a kernel function. Since we were thinking about a one-dimensional training set in a Euclidean space, we wrote the exponent as $-(x-q)^2$. However, for any distance function d, we can use as the weight of a point x at distance $d(x, q)$ from the query point q the value of

$$e^{-\left(d(x-q)\right)^2/\sigma^2}$$

Note that this expression makes sense if the data is in some high-dimensional Euclidean space and d is the usual Euclidean distance or Manhattan distance or any other distance discussed in Section 3.5.2. It also makes sense if d is Jaccard distance or any other distance measure.

However, for Jaccard distance and the other distance measures we considered in Section 3.5 we also have the option to use locality-sensitive hashing, the subject of Chapter 3. Recall these methods are only approximate, and they could yield false negatives – training examples that were near neighbors to a query but that do not show up in a search.

If we are willing to accept such errors occasionally, we can build the buckets for the training set and keep them as the representation of the training set. These buckets are designed so we can retrieve all (or almost all, since there can be false negatives) training-set points that are have a minimum similarity to a given query q. Equivalently, one of the buckets to which the query hashes will contain all those points within some maximum distance of q. We hope that as many nearest neighbors of q as our method requires will be found among those buckets.

Yet if different queries have radically different distances to their nearest neighbors, all is not lost. We can pick several distances $d_1 < d_2 < d_3 < \cdots$. Build the buckets for locality-sensitive hashing using each of these distances. For a query q, start with the buckets for distance d_1. If we find enough near neighbors, we are done. Otherwise, repeat the search using the buckets for d_2, and so on, until enough nearest neighbors are found.

12.4.7 Exercises for Section 12.4

EXERCISE 12.4.1 Suppose we modified Example 12.11 to look at the two nearest neighbors of a query point q. Classify q with the common label if those two neighbors have the same label, and leave q unclassified if the labels of the neighbors are different.

(a) Sketch the boundaries of the regions for the three dog breeds on Fig. 12.21.
! (b) Would the boundaries always consist of straight line segments for any training data?

EXERCISE 12.4.2 Suppose we have the following training set

$$([1,2],+1) \quad ([2,1],-1)$$
$$([3,4],-1) \quad ([4,3],+1)$$

which is the training set used in Example 12.9. If we use nearest-neighbor learning with the single nearest neighbor as the estimate of the label of a query point, which query points are labeled $+1$?

EXERCISE 12.4.3 Consider the one-dimensional training set

$$(1,1), (2,2), (4,3), (8,4), (16,5), (32,6)$$

Describe the function $f(q)$, the label that is returned in response to the query q, when the interpolation used is:

(a) The label of the nearest neighbor.
(b) The average of the labels of the two nearest neighbors.
! (c) The average, weighted by distance, of the two nearest neighbors.
(d) The (unweighted) average of the three nearest neighbors.

! EXERCISE 12.4.4 Apply the kernel function of Example 12.13 to the data of Exercise 12.4.3. For queries q in the range $2 < q < 4$, what is the label of q?

EXERCISE 12.4.5 What is the function that estimates the label of query points using the data of Example 12.12 and the average of the four nearest neighbors?

!! EXERCISE 12.4.6 Simple weighting functions such as those in Example 12.12 need not define a continuous function. We can see that the constructed functions in Fig. 12.22 and Fig. 12.23(b) are not continuous, but Fig. 12.23(a) is. Does the weighted average of two nearest neighbors always give a continuous function?

12.5   Decision Trees

A decision tree is a branching program that uses properties of a feature vector to produce the class to which that input belongs. We generally show the decisions made in the form of a tree. In this section, we shall discuss how to design trees that correctly classify training data. In a decision tree, each nonleaf node represents a test on the input. Its children are either tests (which we denote by ellipses) or a leaf that is a conclusion about the output (denoted by a rectangle). The children of a test node are labeled by the outcome of the test. Typically, there are only two outcomes – true or false (yes or no) – but there could be any number of outcomes of a test.

Also in this section, we examine ways to exploit parallelism while looking for the most efficient tree. As overfitting is a common problem, we shall also talk about how to simplify the tree by removing nodes, to reduce overfitting without losing too much accuracy.

12.5.1   Using a Decision Tree

Let us begin with an example of some training data and a tree that might be constructed from this data. The table in Fig. 12.25 gives 12 countries, their population (in millions), their continent, and their favorite sport. We shall treat Population and Continent as features of the input vector and the favorite sport as the class, or output. We assume the countries themselves are not known, and we want to predict the favorite sport just from the continent and population. In particular, we want to predict the favorite sport of countries other than these 12, from their continent and population only.

EXAMPLE 12.14 In Fig. 12.26 is a tree that correctly classifies the twelve countries of Fig. 12.25. To classify a country, given its population and continent, we start at the root and apply the test at the root. We go to the left child if the outcome of the test is true and to the right child if not. Whenever we are at a nonleaf node, we apply the test at that node and again move to the left or right child, depending on whether or not the test is satisfied. When we reach a leaf, we output the class at that leaf.

You can check that each of the twelve countries is correctly classified by this tree. For example, consider Spain. The continent of Spain is Europe, so the test at the root is satisfied. Thus, we go the the left child of the root, which asks us to test whether the population of Spain is between 60 and 70 million. It is not,

Country	Continent	Population	Sport
Argentina	SA	44	Soccer
Australia	Aus	34	Cricket
Brazil	SA	211	Soccer
Canada	NA	36	Hockey
Cuba	NA	11	Baseball
Germany	Eur	80	Soccer
India	Asia	1342	Cricket
Italy	Eur	59	Soccer
Russia	Asia	143	Hockey
Spain	Eur	46	Soccer
United Kingdom	Eur	65	Cricket
United States	NA	326	Baseball

Figure 12.25 Favorite sports of countries

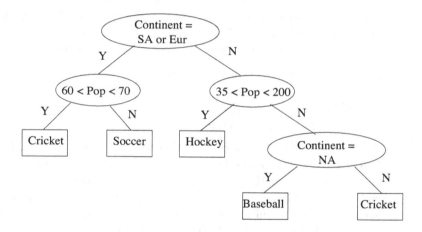

Figure 12.26 A decision tree for the favorite sports of countries

so we go to the right child, which is a leaf telling us correctly that the favorite sport of Spain is Soccer.

However, there are many countries not in the table of Fig. 12.25, and the decision tree does not do too well on these. For example, consider Pakistan, a country in Asia with a population of 182 million. Starting at the root, we find the condition there not satisfied, since Pakistan is not a European or South-American country. Thus, we go to the right child of the root. Since the population of Pakistan is in the range between 35 and 200 million, we move left, whereupon we are told that the favorite sport in Pakistan is Hockey.

The problem we face is overfitting. That is, the test at the root makes sense; Soccer is most popular in South America and Europe. But tests on population are probably useless, since it is unlikely that the size of a country has anything to do with what sport its people like. We have, in this example, simply used the population to distinguish among the small number of countries in Fig. 12.25 that reach a node of the tree. But unlike the root, the tests at the second level don't really say anything that applies to the larger, unseen set of countries. □

12.5.2   Impurity Measures

To design a decision tree, we need to choose good tests at the various nonleaf nodes of the tree. We would like to use as few levels as possible, so that new data points can be classified quickly, and we have a chance of avoiding the overfitting that we saw in Example 12.14. Ideally, we would like all the inputs that reach a certain node to have the same class, since then we can make that node a leaf and correctly classify all the training examples that reach the node.

We can formalize the property we would like for a node by the notion of *impurity*. There are many impurity measures we could use, but they all have the property that they are 0 for a node that is reached only by training examples with a single class. Here are three of the most common impurity measures. Each applies to a node reached by training examples with n classes, with p_i being the fraction of those training examples that belong the ith class, for $i = 1, 2, \ldots, n$.

(1) *Accuracy*: the fraction of the reaching inputs that are correctly classified, or $1 - \max(p_1, p_2, \ldots, p_n)$.
(2) *GINI Impurity*: $1 - \sum_{i=1}^{n}(p_i)^2$.
(3) *Entropy*: $\sum_{i=1}^{n} p_i \log_2(1/p_i)$.

EXAMPLE 12.15   Consider the impurity of the root of Fig. 12.26. There are four classes. Soccer is the favorite sport of $5/12$ of the countries in the training data. Baseball and Hockey are each the class of $1/6$ of the training examples, while Cricket is the class of $1/4$ of the training examples. The impurity of the root according to the accuracy measure is therefore $1 - 5/12 = 7/12 = .583$. The GINI impurity of the root is $1 - (1/6)^2 - (1/6)^2 - (1/4)^2 - (5/12)^2 = 103/144 = 0.715$. The entropy of the root is

$$\frac{1}{6}\log_2(6) + \frac{1}{6}\log_2(6) + \frac{1}{4}\log_2(4) + \frac{5}{12}\log_2(12/5) = 1.875$$

Note the fact that these impurity measures have rather different values is unimportant. Such measures have different ranges of possible values; see Exercise 12.5.2.

The left child of the root is much less impure. It is reached by the six countries in South America and Europe, of which five like Soccer and one likes Cricket. The impurity of this node according to the accuracy measure is thus $1 - 5/6 = 1/6 = .167$, while the GINI impurity is $1 - (1/6)^2 - (5/6)^2 = 5/18 = .278$. The entropy of the left child of the root is $\frac{1}{6}\log_2(6) + \frac{5}{6}\log_2(6/5) = .643$. □

12.5.3   Designing a Decision-Tree Node

The goal of node design is to produce children whose weighted average impurity is as small as possible, where the weighting of the children is proportional to the number of training examples that reach the node. In principle, the test at a node could be any function of the input. As this set of possibilities is essentially infinite, we need to restrict ourselves to simple tests at each node. In what follows, we will limit the possible tests to binary decisions based on one of two factors:

(1) The comparison of one numerical feature of the input vector with a constant.
(2) A test whether one categorical feature of the input vector is in a set of possible values.

EXAMPLE 12.16   Notice that the tests at the children of the root in Fig. 12.26 do not satisfy condition (1) for numerical features. For example, the right child of the root is the logical AND of two comparisons, population > 55 and population < 200. However, we could use both these conditions if we replaced the single node by two nodes, each testing one of the conditions. The root is a test for membership of the value of feature Continent in the set of two continents SA and Eur, so it does satisfy condition (2).   □

Suppose we are given a node of the decision tree that is reached by a subset of the training examples. If the node is pure, i.e., all these training examples have the same output, then we make the node a leaf with that output as value. However, if the impurity is greater than zero, we want to find the test that gives the greatest reduction in impurity. When selecting this test, we are free to choose any feature of the input vector. If we choose a numerical feature, we can choose any constant to divide the training examples into two sets, one going to the left child and the other going to the right child. Alternatively, if we choose a categorical feature, then we may choose any set of values for the membership test. We shall consider each of these cases in turn.

12.5.4 Selecting a Test Using a Numerical Feature

Suppose we want to split a set of training examples based on a numerical feature A. In our running example, A could only be Population, one of the two features – Population and Continent – that are components of feature vectors (recall we assume we do not see the country name; that name is used only to identify each training example). To select the best breakpoint, we

(1) Order the training examples according to their value of A. Let the values of A in this order be $a_1, a_2, \ldots, a_n$.
(2) For $j = 1, 2, \ldots, n$, compute the number of training examples in each class among $a_1, a_2, \ldots, a_j$. Note that these counts can be done incrementally, since the count for a class after the jth example is either the same as the count for $j-1$ (if the jth example in not in this class) or one more than the count for $j-1$ (if the jth example is in this class).
(3) From the counts computed in the previous step, compute the weighted-average impurity assuming the test sends the first j training examples to the left child and the remaining $n-j$ examples to the right node. Here, we

must assume the impurity can be computed from the counts for each class. That is surely the case for the three measures of impurity – accuracy, GINI, and entropy – that we discussed in Section 12.5.2.

(4) Select that value of j that minimizes the weighted-average impurity. However, note that not every possible value of j can be used at this step, since it is possible that $a_j = a_{j+1}$. We need to restrict our choice of j to those values such that $a_j < a_{j+1}$, so that we can use $A < (a_j + a_{j+1})/2$ as the comparison.

EXAMPLE 12.17   Suppose we use the root comparison from Fig. 12.26, which sends the six countries from Europe and South America to the left child, and the other six to the right. Now, we need to divide the six countries reaching the left child in such a way that the weighted impurity of the two children of the root's left child is as small as possible. We could use either the Continent or Population feature to do the division, and we must consider both in order to find the split that minimizes the impurity. Here, we shall consider only Population, since that is the only numerical feature. In Fig. 12.27 we see the six countries that reach the left child of the root, ordered by their population.

Ctry.	Pop.	Sp.	n_S	n_C	$p_S\leq$	$p_C\leq$	$p_S>$	$p_C>$	Im$\leq$	Im$>$	Wtd.
Arg.	44	S	1	0	1	0	4/5	1/5	0	8/25	4/15
Spain	46	S	2	0	1	0	3/4	1/4	0	3/8	1/4
Italy	59	S	3	0	1	0	2/3	1/3	0	4/9	2/9
UK	65	C	3	1	3/4	1/4	1	0	3/8	0	1/4
Ger.	80	S	4	1	4/5	1/5	1	0	8/25	0	4/15
Bra.	211	S	5	1	5/6	1/6	–	–	–	–	–

Figure 12.27 Computing the GINI index for each possible separation

The columns explain the calculation as follows. First, the column labeled "Sp" is the favorite sport, which for this set of countries is either Soccer (S) or Cricket (C). The columns n_S and n_C are the cumulative counts of the number of rows with sport Soccer and Cricket, respectively. For instance, in the row for Germany, we see $n_S = 4$, since four of the five rows from Argentina down to Germany have sport Soccer. In that row, we also have $n_C = 1$, since only one of the first five rows has sport Cricket.

The next two columns, labeled $p_S\leq$ and $p_C\leq$ are the fractions of the rows down to and including the row in question, that have sport Soccer and Cricket, respeectively. For example, in the row for Germany, four of the five rows from Argentina to Germany have sport Soccer, so $p_S\leq\ = 4/5$. The two columns after that, labeled $p_S>$ and $p_C>$, are the same fractions, but for the rows that are below the row in question. For example, in the row for Spain we see $p_S>\ = 3/4$, since three of the four rows from Italy down to Brazil have sport Soccer, and one of these rows has sport Cricket. Note that we do not have to do a cumulative count working up the rows. We can get the count 3 by subtracting $n_S = 2$ for Spain from the bottom value of n_S (that for Brazil), which is 5. Similarly we know there is one row below Spain with sport Cricket because 1 is the difference between n_C for Brazil and Spain.

Next, we see the columns for impurities, $\text{Im}\leq$ and $\text{Im}>$. These are the GINI impurities of the left and right children of the node we are designing, assuming that we use a comparison "population $< c$," for some c that lies between the populations for the row in question and the next row. Thus, in each row, we have $\text{Im}\leq = 1 - (p_S\leq)^2 - (p_C\leq)^2$ and $\text{Im}> = 1 - (p_S>)^2 - (p_C>)^2$. For instance, in the row for Spain, we have $\text{Im}\leq = 1 - 1^2 - 0^2 = 0$ and

$$\text{Im} >= 1 - (3/4)^2 - (1/4)^2 = 3/8$$

Finally, the last column is the weighted GINI impurity for the two children, weighted by the number of countries that reach each of these children. For example, in the row for Spain, if we divide between the populations of Spain and the next more populous country, Italy, then two countries go to the left child and four to the right child. Thus, the weighted impurity is $(2/6)0 + (4/6)(3/8) = 1/4$. Of the five rows after which a split is possible, we find the smallest weighted impurity to be $2/9$, which we get by splitting after Italy. That is, we would use a test like "Population < 60" to send Argentina, Spain, and Italy, all of whom like Soccer, to the left. The other three countries, two of which like Soccer and one Cricket, are sent to the right child. Since the left child is pure, it is a leaf declaring Soccer to be the sport, while the right child will need to be split again.

Technically, we also have to consider that the test at the left child of the root does not involve population at all, but rather is a test on the continent. However, we cannot do better by splitting Europe from South America; that gives a weighted GINI impurity of $1/4$. □

12.5.5 Selecting a Test Using a Categorical Feature

Now consider how we might split the training examples that reach a node, using the value of a categorical feature A. To avoid having to consider all possible subsets of the values of A, we shall only consider the case where there are two classes. In our running example, we might suppose that the two classes are Soccer (S) and anything but soccer (N). When there are two classes, we can order the values of A by the fraction of training examples with that value belonging to the first class.

Since there are only two classes, the partition of values with the lowest impurity will surely be based on a set of values that is a prefix of this order. That is, this set consists of the values of A whose fractions in the first class are above some threshold. Thus, the examples going to the left child will have many examples in the first class, while the examples going right will have many in the second class.

The process of finding the split in the ordered list of values that minimizes the weighted impurity is then essentially the same as for numerical features, which we explained in Section 12.5.4. The difference is that now we are going down a list of values of A, rather than down a list of training examples. We shall work an example, based on the categorical feature Continent from our running example.

EXAMPLE 12.18   Let us see how we might design the root of Fig. 12.26, assuming that we recognized only two classes: Soccer (S) and other sports (N). As before, we shall use GINI as the measure of impurity for nodes. Figure 12.28 summarizes our calculation. In the columns labeled S and N, we see the counts of training examples from Fig. 12.25 for which the favorite sport is Soccer and anything else. The continents are ordered by the fraction of their countries in the Soccer class. Thus, South America is first, because 100% of its training examples are in the class S. Then comes Europe, where 75% of its training examples are in class S. The remaining three continents have 0% in the Soccer class, and could have been ordered in any way.

Cont.	S	N	n_S	n_N	$p_S\leq$	$p_N\leq$	$p_S>$	$p_N>$	Im$\leq$	Im$>$	Wtd.
SA	2	0	2	0	1	0	3/10	7/10	0	21/50	7/20
Eur	3	1	5	1	5/6	1/6	0	1	5/18	0	5/36
NA	0	3	5	4	5/9	4/9	0	1	40/81	0	10/27
Asia	0	2	5	6	5/11	6/11	0	1	60/121	0	5/11
Aus	0	1	5	7	5/12	7/12	–	–	–	–	–

Figure 12.28 Computing the GINI index for sets of continents

The next columns in Fig. 12.28 are n_S and n_N. These are the cumulative sums of the number of examples in class S and not in class S, respectively, counting from the top. For instance, the row for North America has $n_S = 5$ and $n_N = 4$, because among the first three rows there are five examples in the class S and four in the class N. Note that, as for numerical features, we can compute the cumulative sum by a single pass from the top to the bottom. Also, we can get the numbers in each class among all the rows below by subtracting n_S or n_N from its corresponding value at the bottom row.

The next two columns are the fractions in each class for that row and above. That is, $p_S\leq = n_S/(n_S+n_N)$ and $p_N\leq = n_N/(n_S+n_N)$. After those come the two columns $p_S>$ amd $p_N>$ that give the fractions in the classes S and N among all the rows below. For example, in the row for NA, there are zero members of the class S below, which we can see because $n_S = 5$ in both the row for NA and the bottom row. Also, there are three members of the class N below, since the value of n_N for row NA is 4, while the value of n_N in the bottom row is 7.

The columns Im$\leq$ and Im$>$ follow. As in Example 12.17, these are the GINI impurities of the left and right children, assuming the row in question and all rows above are sent to the left child and all rows below are sent to the right child. Then, the last column gives the weighted GINI impurity of the children. For instance, consider the entries in the row for NA. If we use the test for whether the Continent is one of SA, Eur, and NA to send examples to the left child, then nine of the training examples will go left, and the remaining three will go right. Thus, the weighted GINI impurity for this split is $(9/12)(40/81) + (3/12)0 = 10/27$.

By far the best split comes after Eur, with a weighted impurity of $5/36$. That was the split we used in Fig. 12.26. □

12.5.6 Parallel Design of Decision Trees

The design of decision trees using the methods just described involves a serious amount of computation. The procedure must be applied to every node of the tree. Moreover, while we have described what to do with one feature of the input vector, the same must be done for every feature, after which we pick the best split among all features. If the feature is numerical, we need to sort all the training examples that reach the node. If the feature is categorical, we need to first group the training examples by the value of the feature, and then sort the values according to the fraction of examples that belong to the first class. Moreover, if there are really more than two classes, we need to consider all ways to divide the classes into two groups; these groups then play the role of the two classes in the discussion of Section 12.5.5.

However, to speed the process, there is a lot of easy parallelism available.

- At a node, we can find the best splits for all the features in parallel.
- All the nodes at one level can be designed in parallel. Moreover, each training example reaches at most one node at any level. A training example will reach exactly one node at a given level, unless it reaches a leaf at a higher level. Thus, even without parallelism, we expect the total work at each level to be about the same, rather than growing with the number of nodes.
- Grouping of training examples by value of a feature can be done efficiently in parallel. For example, we discussed how to do this task using MapReduce in Section 2.3.8.
- Parallelism can speed up sorting considerably. While we shall not discuss it here, there are known algorithms that can sort n items in parallel in $O(\log^2 n)$ parallel steps in the worst case, or $O(\log n)$ parallel steps on average.

Suppose now that we are working on the design of one node using one feature A, perhaps in parallel with many other node-feature pairs in parallel. After grouping (if A is nonnumeric) and sorting, we need to compute several accumulated sums. For instance, if A is numeric, then we need to compute for each training example and each class the number of training examples with that class, among this training example and all previous examples on the sorted list. The computation of accumulated sums appears to be inherently serial, but as we shall see, it can be parallelized quite well. Once we have the accumulated sums, we can compute the needed fractions and impurity values associated with each member of the list, in parallel. Notice that the row-by-row calculations suggested in Examples 12.17 and 12.18 are all independent and so open to a parallel implementation.

To complete the story of parallelization for decision trees, let us see how to compute accumulated sums in parallel. Formally, suppose we are given a list of numbers $a_1, a_2, \ldots, a_n$, and we wish to compute $x_i = \sum_{j=1}^{i} a_j$ for all $i = 1, 2, \ldots, n$. It might appear that we need n steps to compute all the x_i, and that could be time consuming when n is large; i.e., there is a large training set. However, there is a divide-and-conquer algorithm to calculate all the xs in $O(\log n)$ parallel steps, as follows:

BASIS: If $n = 1$, then $x_1 = a_1$. The basis requires one parallel step.

INDUCTION: If $n > 1$, divide the list of as into a left half and a right half, as evenly as possible. That is, if n is even, the left half is $a_1, a_2, \ldots, a_{n/2}$, and the right half is $a_{n/2+1}, a_{n/2+2}, \ldots, a_n$. If n is odd, then the left half ends with $a_{\lfloor n/2 \rfloor}$ and the right half begins with $a_{\lceil n/2 \rceil}$.

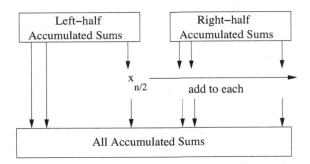

Figure 12.29 Recursive step in parallel computation of accumulated sums

The recursive step is suggested by Fig. 12.29. In parallel, we apply this algorithm to the left and right halves. Once we have done so, the last accumulated sum of the left half, shown as $x_{n/2}$, is then added in parallel to each of the accumulated sums of the right half. As a result, if the ith result in the right half is $\sum_{j=n/2+1}^{i} a_j$, we have, by adding $x_{n/2}$ to it, changed its value to the correct $\sum_{j=1}^{n/2+i} a_j$.

Each time we apply the recursive step, we require only one addition, done in parallel. If n is a power of 2, then each application of the recursive step divides the size of the lists we need to work on by 2, so the total number of parallel steps is $1 + \log_2 n$. If n is not a power of 2, the number of times we perform the recursive step is no greater than what we would have needed if n were the next higher power of 2. Thus, $1 + \lceil \log_2 n \rceil$ parallel steps suffices for any n.

12.5.7   Node Pruning

If we design a decision tree using as many levels as needed in order that each leaf is pure, we are likely to have overfit to the training data. If we can verify our design using other examples – either a test set that we have withheld from the training data or a set of new data – we have the opportunity to simplify the tree and at the same time limit the overfitting.

Find a node N that has only leaves as children. Build a new tree by replacing N and its children by a leaf, and give that leaf its majority class as its output. Then, compare the performance of the old and new trees on data that was not used as training examples when we designed the tree. If there is little difference between the error rates of the old and new trees, then the decision made at the node N probably contributed to overfitting and was not addressing a property of the entire set of examples for which the decision tree was intended. We can discard the old tree and replace it by the new, simpler tree. On the other hand, if the new tree has a significantly higher error rate than the old, then the decision made at node N really reflects a property of the data, and we need to retain the old tree and discard the new. In either case, we should continue looking at other nodes whose children are leaves, and see if these can be replaced by leaves without a significant increase in the error rate.

EXAMPLE 12.19   Let us consider the node in Fig. 12.26 with the test "Continent = NA." It has two leaves as children and so it can play the role of node N above. In the training data of Fig. 12.25 N is reached by three training examples, Cuba, the US, and Australia. As two of these three go to the leaf labeled "Baseball," we shall consider replacing N by a leaf labeled "Baseball."

Consider what happens if the old and new trees are applied to the entire set of countries of the world. First, note that to reach node N, a country has to be in one of the continents North America, Asia, Australia, or Africa. Moreover, it has to be either a small country (less than 35 million population) or a populous country (more than 200 million). There are many possible candidates, such as small countries in Africa, or large countries like China or Indonesia, none of which have either cricket or baseball as their favorite sport. If we consider the Carribean and Central American countries as belonging to North America, then N is reached by many more countries, only a few of which have baseball as their favorite sport.

The conclusion is that whether or not N is replaced by a "Baseball" leaf, the tree will have a significant error rate on these countries, and therefore the error rate of the two trees applied to all countries will be about the same. We conclude that this node N reflects only artifacts of the small and atypical set of twelve training examples that we chose. Thus, N can safely be replaced by a leaf without much increase in the error rate on the full set of countries.   □

12.5.8   Decision Forests

Because a single decision tree with many levels is likely to have many nodes at the lower levels that represent overfitting, there is another approach to the use of decision trees that has proven quite useful in practice. It is common to use *decision forests* of many trees that vote on the class to which a given data point

---

Ensemble Methods

Decision forests are but one example of an important strategy for making good decisions. We can use several different algorithms to make the same decision. Then, we combine the opinions of the different algorithms in some way, perhaps by learning the best weights as we suggested in Section 12.5.8. In the case of a decision forest, all the contributing algorithms are of the same type: a decision tree. However, the decision algorithms can also be of different kinds. For example, the winning solution to the Netflix challenge (see Section 9.5) was of this type, where several different machine-learning techniques were each applied, and their movie-rating estimates combined to make a better decision.

---

belongs. Each tree in the forest is designed using randomly or systematically chosen features, and is restricted to only a small number of levels, often one or two. Thus, each tree has a high impurity at each of its leaves, but collectively they often do much better on test data than any one tree, however many levels it has. Further, we can design each of the trees in the forest in parallel, so it can be even faster to design a large collection of shallow trees than to design one deep tree.

The obvious way to combine the outcomes from all the trees in a decision forest is to take a majority vote. If there are more than two classes, then we only expect a plurality of votes for one of the classes, while no class may be the choice of more than half the trees. However, more complex ways of combining the trees' results may yield a more accurate answer than straightforward voting. We can often "learn" the proper weights to apply to the opinions of each tree.

For example, suppose we have a training set $(\mathbf{x}_1, y_1), (\mathbf{x}_2, y_2), \ldots, (\mathbf{x}_n, y_n)$ and a collection of decision trees $T_1, T_2, \ldots, T_k$ that constitute our decision forest. When we apply the decision forest to one of the training examples $(\mathbf{x}_i, y_i)$, we get a vector of classes $\mathbf{c}_i = [c_{i1}, c_{i2}, \ldots, c_{ik}]$, where c_{ij} is the outcome of tree T_j applied to input $\mathbf{x}_i$. We know the correct class for the input $\mathbf{x}_i$; it is y_i. Thus, we have a new training set $(\mathbf{c}_1, y_1), (\mathbf{c}_2, y_2), \ldots, (\mathbf{c}_n, y_n)$, that we can use to predict the true class from the opinions of all the trees in the forest. For instance, we could use this training set to train a perceptron or SVM. By doing so, we place the right weights on the opinion of each of the trees, in order to combine their opinions optimally.

12.5.9   Exercises for Section 12.5

EXERCISE 12.5.1   Suppose a training set has examples in four classes, and the fractions of examples in these classes are $1/2$, $1/3$, $1/8$, and $1/24$. What is the impurity of the root of a decision tree designed for this training set, if the measure of impurity is: (a) Accuracy; (b) GINI; (c) Entropy?

EXERCISE 12.5.2   If a dataset consists of examples belonging to n different classes, what is the maximum impurity if the measure of impurity is: (a) Accuracy; (b) GINI; (c) Entropy?

! EXERCISE 12.5.3 An important property of a function f is *convexity*, meaning that if $x < z < y$, then

$$f(z) > \frac{z - x}{y - x} f(x) + \frac{y - z}{y - x} f(y)$$

Less formally, the curve of f between x and y lies above the straight line between the points $(x, f(x))$ and $(y, f(y))$. In the following, assume there are two classes, and $f(x)$ is the impurity when x is the fraction of examples in the first class.

(a) Prove that the GINI impurity is convex.
(b) Prove that the Entropy measure of impurity is convex.
(c) Give an example to show that the Accuracy measure of impurity is not always convex. Hint: Note that convexity requires strict inequality; a straight line is not convex.

EXERCISE 12.5.4 To see why convexity is important, repeat the calculation of Fig. 12.27, but using Accuracy as the impurity measure. What goes wrong?

EXERCISE 12.5.5 Continuing Example 12.19, suppose we have replaced the node labeled "Continent = NA" by a leaf labeled "Baseball." Which other interior nodes do you think can be replaced by leaves without a significant increase to the error rate when the tree is applied to all countries of the world?

12.6 Comparison of Learning Methods

Each of the methods discussed in this chapter and elsewhere has its advantages. In this closing section, we shall consider:

- Does the method deal with categorical features or only with numerical features?
- Does the method deal effectively with high-dimensional feature vectors?
- Is the model that the method constructs intuitively understandable?

Perceptrons and Support-Vector Machines These methods can handle millions of features, but they only make sense if the features are numerical. They only are effective if there is a linear separator, or at least a hyperplane that approximately separates the classes. However, we can separate points by a nonlinear boundary if we first transform the points to make the separator be linear. The model is expressed by a vector, the normal to the separating hyperplane. Since this vector is often of very high dimension, it can be very hard to interpret the model.

Nearest-Neighbor Classification and Regression Here, the model is the training set itself, so we expect it to be intuitively understandable. The approach can deal with multidimensional data, although the larger the number of dimensions, the sparser the training set will be, and therefore the less likely it is that we shall find a training point very close to the point we need to classify. That is, the "curse of dimensionality" makes nearest-neighbor methods questionable in high dimensions. These methods are really only useful for numerical features, although one could allow categorical features with a small number of values. For instance, a binary categorical feature like {male, female} could have the values replaced by 0 and 1, so there was no distance in this dimension between individuals of the same gender and distance 1 between other pairs of individuals. However, three or more values cannot be assigned numbers that are equidistant. Finally, nearest-neighbor methods have many parameters to set, including the distance measure we use (e.g., cosine or Euclidean), the number of neighbors to choose, and the kernel function to use. Different choices result in different classification, and in many cases it is not obvious which choices yield the best results.

Decision Trees Unlike the other methods discussed in this chapter, Decision trees are useful for both categorical and numerical features. The models produced are generally quite understandable, since each decision is represented by one node of the tree. However, this approach is most useful for low-dimension feature vectors. As discussed in Section 12.5.7, building decision trees with many levels often leads to overfitting. But if a decision tree has few levels, then it cannot even mention more than a small number of features. As a result, the best use of decision trees is often to create a decision forest of many, low-depth trees and combine their decision in some way.

12.7   Summary of Chapter 12

◆ *Training Sets*: A training set consists of a feature vector, each component of which is a feature, and a label indicating the class to which the object represented by the feature vector belongs. Features can be categorical – belonging to an enumerated list of values – or numerical.

◆ *Test Sets and Overfitting*: When training some classifier on a training set, it is useful to remove some of the training set and use the removed data as a test set. After producing a model or classifier without using the test set, we can run the classifier on the test set to see how well it does. If the classifier does not perform as well on the test set as on the training set used, then we have overfit the training set by conforming to peculiarities of the training-set data which is not present in the data as a whole.

✦ *Batch Versus On-Line Learning*: In batch learning, the training set is available at any time and can be used in repeated passes. On-line learning uses a stream of training examples, each of which can be used only once.

✦ *Perceptrons*: This machine-learning method assumes the training set has only two class labels, positive and negative. Perceptrons work when there is a hyperplane that separates the feature vectors of the positive examples from those of the negative examples. We converge to that hyperplane by adjusting our estimate of the hyperplane by a fraction – the learning rate – of the direction that is the average of the currently misclassified points.

✦ *The Winnow Algorithm*: This algorithm is a variant of the perceptron algorithm that requires components of the feature vectors to be 0 or 1. Training examples are examined in a round-robin fashion, and if the current classification of a training example is incorrect, the components of the estimated separator where the feature vector has 1 are adjusted up or down, in the direction that will make it more likely this training example is correctly classified in the next round.

✦ *Nonlinear Separators*: When the training points do not have a linear function that separates two classes, it may still be possible to use a perceptron to classify them. We must find a function we can use to transform the points so that in the transformed space, the separator is a hyperplane.

✦ *Support-Vector Machines*: The SVM improves upon perceptrons by finding a separating hyperplane that not only separates the positive and negative points, but does so in a way that maximizes the margin – the distance perpendicular to the hyperplane to the nearest points. The points that lie exactly at this minimum distance are the support vectors. Alternatively, the SVM can be designed to allow points that are too close to the hyperplane, or even on the wrong side of the hyperplane, but minimize the error due to such misplaced points.

✦ *Solving the SVM Equations*: We can set up a function of the vector that is normal to the hyperplane, the length of the vector (which determines the margin), and the penalty for points on the wrong side of the margins. The regularization parameter determines the relative importance of a wide margin and a small penalty. The equations can be solved by several methods, including gradient descent and quadratic programming.

✦ *Gradient Descent*: This is a method for minimizing a loss function that depends on many variables and a training example, by repeatedly finding the (derivative) of the loss function with respect to each variable when given a training example, and moving the value of each variable in the direction that lowers the loss. The change in variables can either be an accumulation of the changes suggested by each training example (batch gradient descent), the result of one training example (stochastic gradient descent), or the result of using a small subset of the training examples (minibatch gradient descent).

✦ *Nearest-Neighbor Learning*: In this approach to machine learning, the entire training set is used as the model. For each ("query") point to be classified, we search for its k nearest neighbors in the training set. The classification of the query point is some function of the labels of these k neighbors. The simplest case is when $k = 1$, in which case we can take the label of the query point to be the label of the nearest neighbor.

✦ *Regression*: A common case of nearest-neighbor learning, called regression, occurs when the there is only one feature vector, and it, as well as the label, are real numbers; i.e., the data defines a real-valued function of one variable. To estimate the label, i.e., the value of the function, for an unlabeled data point, we can perform some computation involving the k nearest neighbors. Examples include averaging the neighbors or taking a weighted average, where the weight of a neighbor is some decreasing function of its distance from the point whose label we are trying to determine.

✦ *Decision Trees*: This learning method constructs a tree where each interior node holds a test about the input and sends us to one of its children depending on the outcome of the test. Each leaf gives a decision about the class to which the input belongs.

✦ *Impurity Measures*: To help design a decision tree, we need a measure of how pure, i.e., close to a single class, is the set of training examples that reach a particular node of the decision tree. Possible measures of impurity include Accuracy (fraction of training examples with the wrong class), GINI (1 minus the squares of the fractions of examples in each of the classes), and Entropy (sum of the fractions of training examples in each class times the logarithm of the inverse of that fraction).

✦ *Designing a Decision-Tree Node*: We must consider each possible feature to use for the test at a node, and we must break the set of training examples that reach the node in a way that minimizes the average impurity of its children. For a numerical feature, we can order the traning examples by the value of that feature and use a test that breaks this list in a way that minimizes average impurity. For a categorical feature we order the values of that feature by the fraction of training examples with that value that belong to one particular class, and break the list to minimize average impurity.

12.8   References for Chapter 12

The perceptron was introduced in [14]. [8] introduces the idea of maximizing the margin around the separating hyperplane. A well-known book on the subject is [12].

The Winnow algorithm is from [11]. Also see the analysis in [2].

Support-vector machines appeared in [7]. [6] and [5] are useful surveys. [10] talks about a more efficient algorithm for the case of sparse features (most components of the feature vectors are zero). The use of gradient-descent methods is found in [3], [4].

For information about high-dimensional index structures for nearest-neighbor learning, see Chapter 14 of [9].

The original work on construction of decision trees is [13]. [1] is a popular paper describing the methodology used in this chapter.

[1] H. Blockeel and L. De Raedt, "Top-down induction of first-order logical decision trees," *Artificial intelligence* **101**:1–2 (1998), pp. 285–297.

[2] A. Blum, "Empirical support for winnow and weighted-majority algorithms: results on a calendar scheduling domain," *Machine Learning* **26** (1997), pp. 5–23.

[3] L. Bottou, "Large-scale machine learning with stochastic gradient descent," *Proc. 19th Intl. Conf. on Computational Statistics* (2010), pp. 177–187, Springer.

[4] L. Bottou, "Stochastic gradient tricks, neural networks," in *Tricks of the Trade, Reloaded*, pp. 430–445, edited by G. Montavon, G.B. Orr and K.-R. Mueller, Lecture Notes in Computer Science (LNCS 7700), Springer, 2012.

[5] C.J.C. Burges, "A tutorial on support vector machines for pattern recognition," *Data Mining and Knowledge Discovery* **2** (1998), pp. 121–167.

[6] N. Cristianini and J. Shawe-Taylor, *An Introduction to Support Vector Machines and Other Kernel-Based Learning Methods*, Cambridge University Press, 2000.

[7] C. Cortes and V.N. Vapnik, "Support-vector networks," *Machine Learning* **20** (1995), pp. 273–297.

[8] Y. Freund and R.E. Schapire, "Large margin classification using the perceptron algorithm," *Machine Learning* **37** (1999), pp. 277–296.

[9] H. Garcia-Molina, J.D. Ullman, and J. Widom, *Database Systems: the Complete Book*, Prentice Hall, Upper Saddle River NJ, 2009.

[10] T. Joachims, "Training linear SVMs in linear time." *Proc. 12th ACM SIGKDD* (2006), pp. 217–226.

[11] N. Littlestone, "Learning quickly when irrelevant attributes abound: a new linear-threshold algorithm," *Machine Learning* **2** (1988), pp. 285–318.

[12] M. Minsky and S. Papert, *Perceptrons: An Introduction to Computational Geometry* (2nd edition), MIT Press, Cambridge MA, 1972.

[13] J. R. Quinlan, "Induction of decision trees," *Machine Learning* **1** (1986), pp. 81–106.

[14] F. Rosenblatt, "The perceptron: a probabilistic model for information storage and organization in the brain," *Psychological Review* **65**:6 (1958), pp. 386–408.

13 Neural Nets and Deep Learning

In Sections 12.2 and 12.3 we discussed the design of single "neurons" (perceptrons). These take a collection of inputs and, based on weights associated with those inputs, compute a number that, compared with a threshold, determines whether to output "yes" or "no." These methods allow us to separate inputs into two classes, as long as the classes are linearly separable. However, most problems of interest and importance are not linearly separable. In this chapter, we shall consider the design of *neural nets*, which are collections of perceptrons, or *nodes*, where the outputs of one rank (or *layer* of nodes becomes the inputs to nodes at the next layer. The last layer of nodes produces the outputs of the entire neural net. The training of neural nets with many layers requires enormous numbers of training examples, but has proven to be an extremely powerful technique, referred to as *deep learning*, when it can be used.

We also consider several specialized forms of neural nets that have proved useful for special kinds of data. These forms are characterized by requiring that certain sets of nodes in the network share the same weights. Since learning all the weights on all the inputs to all the nodes of the network is in general a hard and time-consuming task, these special forms of network greatly simplify the process of training the network to recognize the desired class or classes of inputs. We shall study convolutional neural networks (CNNs), which are specially designed to recognize classes of images. We shall also study recurrent neural networks (RNNs) and long short-term memory networks (LSTMs), which are designed to recognize classes of sequences, such as sentences (sequences of words).

13.1 Introduction to Neural Nets

We begin the discussion of neural nets with an extended example. After that, we introduce the general plan of a neural net and some important terminology.

EXAMPLE 13.1 The problem we discuss is to learn the concept that "good" bit-vectors are those that have two consecutive 1s. Since we want to deal with only tiny example instances, we shall assume bit-vectors have length four. Our training examples will thus have the form $([x_1, x_2, x_3, x_4], y)$, where each of the x_i are bits, 0 or 1. There are 16 possible training examples, and we shall assume we are given some subset of these as our training set. Notice that eight of the possible bit vectors are good – they do have consecutive 1s, and there are also eight "bad" examples. For instance, 0111 and 1100 are good; 1001 and 0100 are bad.[1]

To start, let us look at a neural net that solves this simple problem exactly. How we might design this net from training examples is the true subject for discussion, but this net will serve as an example of what we would like to achieve. The net is shown in Fig. 13.1.

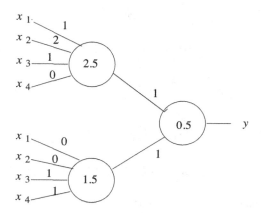

Figure 13.1 A neural net that tells whether a bit-vector has consecutive 1s

The net has two layers, the first consisting of two nodes, and the second with a single node that produces the output y. Each node is a perceptron, exactly as was described in Section 12.2. In the first layer, the first node is characterized by weight vector $[w_1, w_2, w_3, w_4] = [1, 2, 1, 0]$ and threshold 2.5. Since each input x_i is either 0 or 1, we note that the only way to reach a sum $\sum_{i=1}^{4} x_i w_i$ as high as 2.5 is if $x_2 = 1$ and at least one of x_1 and x_3 is also 1. The output of this node is 1 if and only if the input is one of 1100, 1101, 1110, 1111, 0110, or 0111. That is, it recognizes those bit-vectors that either begin with two 1s or have two 1s in the middle. The only good inputs it does not recognize are those that end with 11 but do not have 11 elsewhere. these are 0011 and 1011.

Fortunately, the second node in the first layer, with weights $[0, 0, 1, 1]$ and threshold 1.5 gives output 1 whenever $x_3 = x_4 = 1$, and not otherwise. This node thus recognizes the inputs 0011 and 1011, as well as some other good inputs that are also recognized by the first node.

Now let us turn to the second layer, with a single node; that node has weights $[1, 1]$ and threshold 0.5. It therefore behaves as an "OR-gate." It gives output $y = 1$ whenever either or both of the nodes in the first layer have output 1, but gives output $y = 0$ if both of the first-layer nodes give output 0. Consequently,

---

[1] We shall show bit vectors as bit strings in what follows, so we can avoid the commas between components, each of which is 0 or 1.

the neural net of Fig. 13.1 gives output 1 for all the good inputs but none of the bad inputs. □

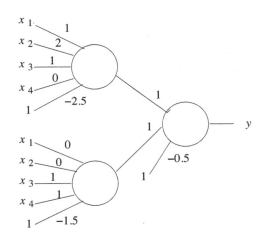

Figure 13.2 Making the threshold 0 for all nodes

It is useful in many situations to assume that nodes have a threshold of 0. Recall from Section 12.2.4 that we can always convert a perceptron with a nonzero threshold t to one with a 0 threshold if we add an additional input. That input always has value 1 and a weight equal to $-t$. For example, we can convert the net of Fig. 13.1 to that in Fig. 13.2.

13.1.1   Neural Nets, in General

Example 13.1 and its net of Fig. 13.1 is much simpler than anything that would be a useful application of neural nets. The general case is suggested by Fig. 13.3. The first, or *input layer*, is the input, which is presumed to be a vector of some length n. Each component of the vector $[x_1, x_2, \ldots, x_n]$ is an input to the net. There are one or more *hidden layers* and finally, at the end, an *output layer*, which gives the result of the net. Each of the layers can have a different number of nodes, and in fact, choosing the right number of nodes at each layer is an important part of the design process for neural nets. Especially, note that the output layer can have many nodes. For instance, the neural net could classify inputs into many different classes, with one output node for each class.

Each layer, except for the input layer, consists of one or more nodes, which we arrange in the column that represents that layer. We can think of each node as a perceptron. The inputs to a node are outputs of some or all of the nodes in the previous layer. So that we can assume the threshold for each node is zero, we can also allow a node to have an input that is a constant, typically 1, as we suggested in Fig. 13.2. Associated with each input to each node is a *weight*. The output of the node depends on $\sum x_i w_i$, where the sum is over all the inputs x_i,

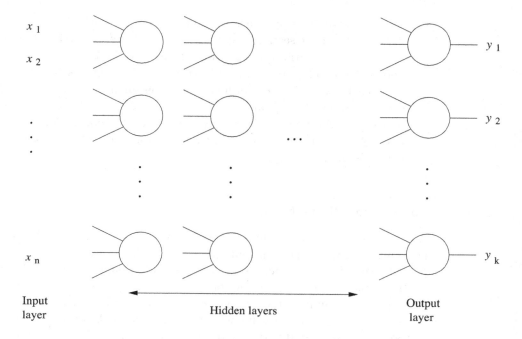

x_1

x_2

$\cdot$
$\cdot$
$\cdot$

x_n

$\cdots$

y_1

y_2

$\cdot$
$\cdot$
$\cdot$

y_k

Input
layer

Hidden layers

Output
layer

Figure 13.3 The general case of a neural network

and w_i is the weight of that input. Sometimes, the output is either 0 or 1; the output is 1 if that sum is positive and 0 otherwise. However, as we shall see in Section 13.2, it is often convenient, when trying to learn the weights for a neural net that solves some problem, to have outputs that are almost always close to 0 or 1, but may be slightly different. The reason, intuitively, is that it is then possible for the output of a node to be a continuous function of its inputs. We can then use gradient descent to converge to the ideal values of all the weights in the net.

13.1.2 Interconnections Among Nodes

Neural nets can differ in how the nodes at one layer are connected to nodes at the layer to its right. The most general case is when each node receives as inputs the outputs of every node of the previous layer. A layer that receives all outputs from the previous layer is said to be *fully connected*. Some other options for choosing interconnections are:

(1) *Random.* For some m, we pick for each node m nodes from the previous layer and make those, and only those, be inputs to this node.
(2) *Pooled.* Partition the nodes of one layer into some number of clusters. In the next layer, which is called a *pooling layer*, there is one node for each cluster, and this node has all and only the member of its cluster as inputs.

(3) *Convolutional.* This approach to interconnection, which we discuss in more detail in the next section and Section 13.4, views the nodes of each layer as arranged in a grid, typically two-dimensional. In a convolutional layer, a node corresponding to coordinates (i, j) receive as inputs the nodes of the previous layer that have coordinates in some small region around (i, j). For example, the node (i, j) at one convolutional layer may have as inputs those nodes from the previous layer that correspond to coordinates (p, q), where $i \leq p \leq i + 2$ and $j \leq q \leq j + 2$ (i.e., the square of side 3 whose lower-left corner is the point (i, j).

13.1.3   Convolutional Neural Networks

A *convolutional neural network*, or *CNN*, contains one or more convolutional layers. There can also be nonconvolutional layers, such as fully connected layers and pooled layers. However, there is an important additional constraint: the weights on the inputs must be the same for all nodes of a single convolutional layer. More precisely, suppose that each node (i, j) in a convolutional layer recieves $(i + u, j + v)$ as one of its inputs, where u and v are small constants. Then there is a weight w associated with u and v (but not with i and j). For any i and j, the weight on the input to the node for (i, j) coming from the output of the node $i + u, j + v)$ from the previous layer must be w.

This restriction makes training a CNN much more efficient than training a general neural net. The reason is that there are many fewer parameters at each layer, and therefore, many fewer training examples can be used, than if each node or each layer has its own weights for the training process to discover.

CNNs have been found extremely useful for tasks such as image recognition. In fact, the CNN draws inspiration from the way the human eye processes images. The neurons of the eye are arranged in layers, similarly to the layers of a neural net. The first layer takes inputs that are essentially pixels of the image, each pixel the result of a sensor in the retina. The nodes of the first layer recognize very simple features, such as edges between light and dark. Notice that a small square of pixels, say 3×3, might exhibit an edge at a particular angle, e.g., if the upper left corner is light and the other eight pixels dark. Moreover, the algorithm for recognizing an edge of a certain type is the same, regardless of where in the field of vision this little square appears. That observation justifies the CNN constraint that all the nodes of a layer use the same weights. In the eye, additional layers combine results from the previous layers to recognize more and more complex structures: long boundaries, regions of similar color, and finally faces and all the familiar objects that we see daily.

We shall have more to say about convolutional neural networks in Section 13.4. Moreover, CNNs are only one example of a kind of neural network where certain families of nodes are constrained to have the same weights. For example, in Section 13.5, we shall consider recurrent neural networks and long short-term memory networks, which are specially adapted to recognizing properties of sequences, such as sentences (sequences of words).

13.1.4 Design Issues for Neural Nets

Building a neural net to solve a given problem is partially art and partially science. Before we can begin to train a net by finding the weights on the inputs that serve our goals best, we need to make a number of design decisions. These include answering the following questions:

(1) How many hidden layers should we use?
(2) How many nodes will there be in each of the hidden layers?
(3) In what manner will we interconnect the outputs of one layer to the inputs of the next layer?

Further, in later sections we shall see that there are other decisions that need to be made when we train the neural net. These include:

(1) What cost function should we minimize to express what weights are best?
(2) How should we compute the outputs of each gate as a function of the inputs? We have suggested that the normal way to compute output is to take a weighted sum of inputs and compare it to 0. But there are other computations that serve better in common circumstances.
(3) What algorithm do we use to exploit the training examples in order to optimize the weights?

13.1.5 Exercises for Section 13.1

!! EXERCISE 13.1.1 Prove that the problem of Example 13.1 cannot be solved by a perceptron; i.e., the good and bad points are not linearly separable.

! EXERCISE 13.1.2 Consider the general problem of identifying bit-vectors of length n having two consecutive 1s. Assume a single hidden layer with some number of gates. What is the smallest number of gates you can have in the hidden layer if (a) $n = 5$? (b) $n = 6$?

! EXERCISE 13.1.3 Design a neural net that functions as an *exclusive-or* gate; that is, it takes two inputs and gives output 1 if exactly one of the inputs is 1 gives output 0 otherwise. *Hint*: remember that both weights and thresholds can be negative.

! EXERCISE 13.1.4 Prove that there is no single perceptron that behaves like an exclusive-or gate.

! EXERCISE 13.1.5 Design a neural net to compute the exclusive-or of three inputs; that is, output 1 if an odd number of the three inputs is 1 and output 0 if an even number of the inputs are 1.

13.2   Dense Feedforward Networks

In the previous section, we simply exhibited a neural net that worked for the "consecutive 1s" problem. However, the true value of neural nets comes from our ability to design them given training data. To design a net, there are many choices that must be made, such as the number of layers and the number of nodes for each layer, as was discussed in Section 13.1.4. These choices can be more art than science. The computational part of training, which is more science than art, is primarily the choice of weights for the inputs to each node.

The techniques for selecting weights usually involve convergence using gradient descent. But gradient descent requires a cost function, which must be a continuous function of the weights. The nets discussed in Section 13.1.4, on the other hand, use perceptrons whose output is either 0 or 1, so the outputs are not normally continuous functions of the inputs. In this section, we shall discuss the various ways one can modify the behavior of the nodes in a net so the outputs become continuous functions of the inputs, and therefore a reasonable cost function applied to the outputs will also be continuous.

13.2.1   Linear Algebra Notation

We can succinctly describe the neural network we used for the consecutive 1s problem using notation from linear algebra. The input nodes form a vector[2] $\mathbf{x} = [x_1, x_2, x_3, x_4]$, while the hidden nodes form a vector $\mathbf{h} = [h_1, h_2]$. The four edges connecting the input to hidden node 1 form a weight vector $\mathbf{w_1} = [w_{11}, w_{12}, w_{13}, w_{14}]$, and similarly we have weight vector $\mathbf{w_2}$ for hidden node 2. The threshold inputs to the hidden layer nodes (i.e., the negatives of the thresholds) form a 2-vector $\mathbf{b} = [b_1, b_2]$, often called the *bias vector*. The perceptron applies the nonlinear *step function* to produce its output, defined as:

$$\text{step}(z) = \begin{cases} 1 & \text{when } z > 0 \\ 0 & \text{otherwise} \end{cases}$$

Each hidden node h_i can now be described using the expression:

$$h_i = \text{step}(\mathbf{w}_i^\mathsf{T} \mathbf{x} + b_i) \text{ for } i = 1, 2$$

We could organize the weight vectors $\mathbf{w_1}$ and $\mathbf{w_2}$ into a 2×4 weight matrix W, where the ith row of W is $\mathbf{w}_i^\mathsf{T}$. The hidden nodes can thus be described using the expression:

$$\mathbf{h} = \text{step}(W\mathbf{x} + \mathbf{b})$$

In the case of a vector input, the step function just operates element-wise on the vector to produce an output vector of the same length. We can use a similar

---

[2] We assume all vectors are column vectors by default. However, it is often more convenient to write row vectors, and we shall do so in the text. But in formulas, we shall use the transpose operator when we actually want to use the vector as a row rather than a column.

> ## Why Use Linear Algebra?
>
> Notational brevity is one reason to use linear algebra notation for neural networks. Another is performance. It turns out that graphics processing units (GPUs) have circuitry that allows for highly parallelized linear-algebra operations. Mutiplying a matrix and a vector using a single linear algebra operator is much faster than coding the same operator using nested loops. Modern deep-learning frameworks (e.g., TensorFlow, PyTorch, Caffe) harness the power of GPUs to dramatically speed up neural network computations.

arrangement to describe the transformation that produces the final output from the hidden layer. In this case, the final output is a scalar y, so instead of a weight matrix W we need only a weight vector $\boldsymbol{u} = [u_1, u_2]$ and a single bias c. We thus have:

$$y = \text{step}(\boldsymbol{u}^\mathsf{T}\mathbf{h} + c)$$

Linear algebra notation works just as well when we have larger inputs and many more nodes in one hidden layer. We just need to scale the weight matrix and bias vector appropriately. That is, the matrix W has one row for each node in the layer and one column for each output from the previous layer (or for each input, if this is the first layer); the bias vector has one component for each node. It is also easy to handle the case where there is more than one node in the output layer. For example, in a multiclass classification problem, we might have an output node y_i corresponding to target class i. For a given input, the outputs specify the probability that the input belongs to the corresponding class. This arrangement results in an output vector $\mathbf{y} = [y_1, y_2, \ldots, y_n]$, where n is number of classes. The simple network from the prior section had a Boolean output, corresponding to two output classes (true and false), so we could have modeled the output equally well as a 2-vector. In the case of a vector output, we connect the hidden and output layers by a weight matrix of appropriate dimensions in place of the weight vector we used for the example.

The perceptrons in our example used a nonlinear step function. More generally, we can use any other nonlinear function, called the *activation function*, following the linear transformation. We describe commonly used activation functions starting in Section 13.2.2.

Our simple example used a single hidden layer of nodes between the input and output layers. In general, we can have many hidden layers, as was sugested in Fig. 13.3. Each hidden layer introduces an additional matrix of weights and vector of biases, as well as its own activation function. This kind of network is called a *feedforward network*, since all edges are oriented "forward," from input to output, without cycles.

Suppose there are ℓ hidden layers and an additional output layer, numbered $\ell + 1$. Let the weight matrix for the ith layer be W_i and let the bias vector for that layer be $\mathbf{b}_i$. The weights $W_1, W_2, \ldots, W_{l+1}$ and biases $\mathbf{b}_1, \mathbf{b}_2, \ldots, \mathbf{b}_{l+1}$ constitute the *parameters* of the model. Our objective is to learn the best values for these parameters to achieve the task at hand. We will soon describe how to go about learning the model parameters.

13.2.2   Activation Functions

A node (perceptron) in a neural net is designed to give a 0 or 1 (yes or no) output. Often, we want to modify that output is one of several ways, so we apply an *activation function* to the output of a node. In some cases, the activation function takes all the outputs of a layer and modifies them as a group. the reason we need an activation function is as follows. The approach we shall use to learn good parameter values for the network is gradient descent. Thus, we need activation functions that "play well" with gradient descent. In particular, we look for activation functions with the following properties:

(1) The function is continuous and differentiable everywhere (or almost everywhere).
(2) The derivative of the function does not *saturate* (i.e., become very small, tending towards zero) over its expected input range. Very small derivatives tend to stall out the learning process.
(3) The derivative does not *explode* (i.e., become very large, tending towards infinity), since this would lead to issues of numerical instability.

The step function does not satisfy conditions (2) and (3). Its derivative explodes at 0 and is 0 everywhere else. Thus the step function does not play well with gradient descent and is not a good choice for a deep neural network.

13.2.3   The Sigmoid

Given that we cannot use the step function, we look for alternatives in the class of *sigmoid functions* – so called because of the S-shaped curve that these functions exhibit. The most commonly used sigmoid function is the *logistic sigmoid*:

$$\sigma(x) = \frac{1}{1 + e^{-x}} = \frac{e^x}{1 + e^x}$$

Notice that the sigmoid has the value $1/2$ at $x = 0$. For large x, the sigmoid approaches 1, and for large, negtive x, the sigmoid approaches 0.

The logistic sigmoid, like all the functions we shall discuss, are applied to vectors element-wise, so if $\mathbf{x} = [x_1, x_2, \ldots, x_n]$ then

$$\sigma(\mathbf{x}) = [\sigma(x_1), \sigma(x_2), \ldots, \sigma(x_n)]$$

The logistic sigmoid has several advantages over the step function as a way to define the output of a perceptron. The logistic sigmoid is continuous and differentiable, so it enables us to use gradient descent to discover the best weights. Since its value is in the range $[0, 1]$, it is possible to interpret the outputs of the network as a probability. However, the logistic sigmoid saturates very quickly as we move away from the "critical region" around 0. So the derivative goes towards zero and gradient-based learning can stall out. That is, weights almost stop changing, once they get away from 0.

In Section 13.3.3, when we describe the backpropagation algorithm, we shall see that we need the derivatives of activation functions and loss functions. As an exercise, you can verify that if $y = \sigma(x)$, then

$$\frac{dy}{dx} = y(1 - y)$$

13.2.4 The Hyperbolic Tangent

Closely related to sigmoid is the *hyperbolic tangent* function, defined by:

$$\tanh(x) = \frac{e^x - e^{-x}}{e^x + e^{-x}}$$

Simple algebraic manipulation yields:

$$\tanh(x) = 2\sigma(2x) - 1$$

So the hyperbolic tangent is just a scaled and shifted version of the sigmoid. It has two desirable properties that make it attractive in some situations: its output is in the range $[-1, 1]$ and is symmetric around 0. It also shares the good properties and the saturation problem of the sigmoid. You may show that if $y = \tanh(x)$ then

$$\frac{dy}{dx} = 1 - y^2$$

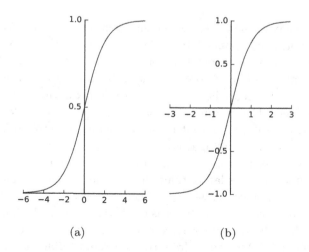

(a)   (b)

Figure 13.4 The logistic sigmoid (a) and hyperbolic tangent (b) functions

---

Accuracy of Softmax Calculations

The denominator of the softmax function involves computing a sum of the form $\sum_j e^{x_j}$. When the x_j take a wide range of values, their exponents e^{x_j} take on an even wider range of values – some tiny and some very large. Adding very large and very small floating point numbers leads to numerical inaccuracy issues in fixed-width floating point representations (such as 32-bit or 64-bit). Fortunately, there is a trick to avoid this problem. We observe that

$$\mu(x_i) = \frac{e^{x_i}}{\sum_j e^{x_j}} = \frac{e^{x_i - c}}{\sum_j e^{x_j - c}}$$

for any constant c. We pick $c = \max_j x_j$, so that $x_j - c \leq 0$ for all j. This ensures that $e^{x_j - c}$ is always between 0 and 1, and leads to a more accurate calculation. Most deep learning frameworks will take care to compute softmax in this manner.

Figure 13.4 shows the logistic sigmoid and hyperbolic tangent functions. Note the difference in scale along the x-axis between the two charts. It is easy to see that the functions are identical after shifting and scaling.

13.2.5   Softmax

The *softmax* function differs from sigmoid functions in that it does not operate element-wise on a vector. Rather, the softmax function applies to an entire vector. If $\mathbf{x} = [x_1, x_2, \ldots, x_n]$, then its softmax $\mu(\mathbf{x}) = [\mu(x_1), \mu(x_2), \ldots, \mu(x_n)]$ where

$$\mu(x_i) = \frac{e^{x_i}}{\sum_j e^{x_j}}$$

Softmax pushes the largest component of the vector towards 1 while pushing all the other components towards zero. Also, all the outputs sum to 1, regardless of the sum of the components of the input vector. Thus, the output of the softmax function can be intepreted as a probability distribution.

A common application is to use softmax in the output layer for a classification problem. The output vector has a component corresponding to each target class, and the softmax output is interpreted as the probability of the input belonging to the corresponding class.

Softmax has the same saturation problem as the sigmoid function, since one component gets larger than all the others. There is a simple workaround to this problem, however, when softmax is used at the output layer. In this case, it is usual to pick *cross entropy* as the loss function, which undoes the exponentiation in the definition of softmax and avoids saturation. Cross entropy is explained in Section 13.2.9. We address the problem of differentiating the softmax function in Section 13.3.3.

13.2.6   Recified Linear Unit

The *rectified linear unit*, or ReLU, is defined as:

$$f(x) = \max(0, x) = \begin{cases} x, & \text{for } x \geq 0 \\ 0, & \text{for } x < 0 \end{cases}$$

The name of this function derives from the analogy to *half-wave rectification* in electrical engineering. The function is not differentiable at 0 but is differentiable everywhere else, including at points arbitrarily close to 0. In practice, we "set" the derivative at 0 to be either 0 (the left derivative) or 1 (the right derivative).

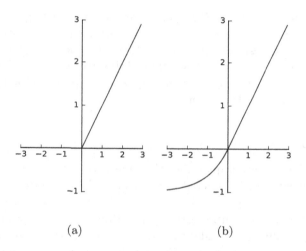

(a)   (b)

Figure 13.5 The ReLU (a) and ELU (b), with $\alpha = 1$ functions

In modern neural nets, a version of ReLU has replaced sigmoid as the default choice of activation function. The popularity of ReLU derives from two properties:

(1) The gradient of ReLU remains constant and never saturates for positive x, speeding up training. It has been found in practice that networks that use ReLU offer a significant speedup in training compared to sigmoid activation.

(2) Both the function and its derivative can be computed using elementary and efficient mathematical operations (no exponentiation).

ReLU does suffer from a problem related to the saturation of its derivative when $x < 0$. Once a node's input values become negative, it is possible that the node's output get "stuck" at 0 through the rest of the training. This is called the *dying ReLU* problem.

The *Leaky ReLU* attempts to fix this problem by defining the activation function as follows:

$$f(x) = \begin{cases} x, & \text{for } x \geq 0 \\ \alpha x, & \text{for } x < 0 \end{cases}$$

where α is typically a small positive value such as 0.01. The *Parametric ReLU* (PReLU) makes α a parameter to be optimized as part of the learning process.

An improvement on both the original and leaky ReLU functions is *Exponential Linear Unit*, or ELU. This function is defined as:

$$f(x) = \begin{cases} x, & \text{for } x \geq 0 \\ \alpha(e^x - 1), & \text{for } x < 0 \end{cases}$$

where $\alpha \geq 0$ is a *hyperparameter*. That is, α is held fixed during the learning process, but we can repeat the learning process with different values of α to find the best value for our problem. The node's value saturates to $-\alpha$ for large negative values of x, and a typical choice is $\alpha = 1$. ELUs drive the mean activation of nodes towards zero, which appears to speed up the learning process compared to other ReLU variants.

13.2.7   Loss Functions

A loss function quantifies the difference between a model's predictions and the output values observed in the real world (i.e., in the training set). Suppose the observed output corresponding to input $\mathbf{x}$ is $\hat{\mathbf{y}}$ and the predicted output is $\mathbf{y}$. Then a loss fucntion $L(\mathbf{y}, \hat{\mathbf{y}})$ quantifies the prediction error for this single input. Typically, we consider the loss over a large set of observations, such as the entire training set. In that case, we usually average the losses over all training examples.

We shall consider separately two cases. In the first, there is a single output node, and it produces a real value. In this case we study "regression loss." In the second case, there are several output nodes, each of which indicates that the input is a member of a particular class; we study this matter under "classification loss" in Section 13.2.9.

13.2.8   Regression Loss

Suppose the model has a single continuous-valued output, and $(\mathbf{x}, \hat{y})$ is a training example. For the same input $\mathbf{x}$, suppose the predicted output of the neural net is y. Then the *squared error* loss $L(y, \hat{y})$ of this prediction is:

$$L(y, \hat{y}) = (y - \hat{y})^2$$

In general, we compute the loss for a set of predictions. Suppose the observed (i.e., training set) input-output pairs are $T = \{(\mathbf{x}_1, \hat{y}_1), (\mathbf{x}_2, \hat{y}_2), \ldots, (\mathbf{x}_n, \hat{y}_n)\}$, while the corresponding input–output pairs predicted by the model are $P =$

$\{(\mathbf{x}_1, y_1), (\mathbf{x}_2, y_2), \ldots, (\mathbf{x}_n, y_n)\}$. The *mean squared error* (MSE) for the set is:

$$L(P, T) = \frac{1}{n} \sum_{i=1}^{n} (y_i - \hat{y}_i)^2$$

Note that the mean squared error is just square of the RMSE. It is convenient to omit the square root to simplify the derivative of the function, which we shall use during training. In any case, when we minimize MSE we also automatically minimize RMSE.

One problem with MSE is that it is very sensitive to outliers due the squared term. A few outliers can contribute very highly to the loss and swamp out the effect of other points, making the training process susceptible to wild swings. One way to deal with this issue is to use the *Huber loss*. Suppose $z = y - \hat{y}$, and δ is a constant. The Huber loss L_δ is given by:

$$L_\delta(z) = \begin{cases} z^2 & \text{if } |z| \le \delta \\ 2\delta(|z| - \frac{1}{2}\delta) & \text{otherwise} \end{cases}$$

Figure 13.6 contrasts the squared error and Huber loss functions.

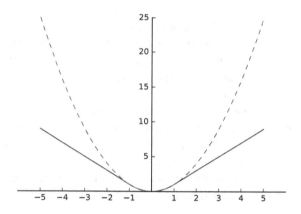

Figure 13.6 Huber loss (solid line, $\delta = 1$) and squared error (dotted line) as functions of $z = y - \hat{y}$

In the case where we have a vector $\mathbf{y}$ of outputs rather than a single output, we use $\|\mathbf{y} - \hat{\mathbf{y}}\|$ in place of $|y - \hat{y}|$ in the definitions of mean squared error and Huber loss.

13.2.9 Classification Loss

Consider a multiclass classification problem with target classes $C_1, C_2, \ldots, C_n$. Suppose each point in the training set is of the form $(\mathbf{x}, \mathbf{p})$ where $\mathbf{x}$ is the input and $\mathbf{p} = [p_1, p_2, \ldots, p_n]$ is the output. Here p_i gives the probability that the input $\mathbf{x}$ belongs to class C_i, with $\sum_i p_i = 1$. In many cases, we are certain that an input belongs to a particular class C_i; in this case $p_i = 1$ and $p_j = 0$ for $i \neq j$. In general, we may interpret p_i as our level of certainty that input $\mathbf{x}$ belongs to class C_i, and $\mathbf{p}$ as a *probability distribution* over the target classes.

We design our neural network to produce as output a vector

$$\mathbf{q} = [q_1, q_2, \ldots, q_n]$$

of probabilities, with $\sum_i q_i = 1$. As before, we interpret $\mathbf{q}$ as a probability distribution over the target classes, with q_i denoting the model's probability that input $\mathbf{x}$ belongs to target class C_i. In Section 13.2.5 we described a simple method to produce such a probability vector as output: use the softmax activation function in the output layer of the network.

Since both the labeled output and the model's output are probability distributions, it is natural to look for a loss function that quantifies the distance between two probability distributions. Recall the definition of entropy from Section 12.5.2. That is, $H(\mathbf{p})$, the entropy of a discrete probability distribution $\mathbf{p}$ is

$$H(\mathbf{p}) = -\sum_{i=1}^{n} p_i \log p_i$$

Imagine an alphabet of n symbols, and messages using these symbols. Suppose at each location in the message, the probability that symbol i appears is p_i. Then a key result from information theory is that if we encode messages using an optimal binary code, the average number of bits per symbol needed to encode messages is $H(\mathbf{p})$.

Suppose we did not know the symbol probability distribution $\mathbf{p}$ when we design the coding scheme. Instead, we believe that symbols appear following a different probability distribution $\mathbf{q}$. We might ask what the average number of bits per symbol will be if we use this suboptimal encoding scheme. A well-known result from information theory states that the average number of bits in this case is the *cross entropy* $H(\mathbf{p}, \mathbf{q})$, defined as:

$$H(\mathbf{p}, \mathbf{q}) = -\sum_{i=1}^{n} p_i \log q_i$$

Note that $H(\mathbf{p}, \mathbf{p}) = H(\mathbf{p})$, and in general $H(\mathbf{p}, \mathbf{q}) \geq H(\mathbf{p})$. The difference between the cross entropy and the entropy is the average number of additional bits needed per symbol. It is a reasonable measure of the distance between the distributions $\mathbf{p}$ and $\mathbf{q}$, called the *Kullback–Liebler divergence* (KL-divergence) and denoted $D(\mathbf{p}\|\mathbf{q})$:

$$D(\mathbf{p}\|\mathbf{q}) = H(\mathbf{p}, \mathbf{q}) - H(\mathbf{p}) = \sum_{i=1}^{n} p_i \log \frac{p_i}{q_i}$$

Even though KL-divergence is often regarded as a distance, it is not truly a distance measure because it is not commutative. However, it is perfectly adequate as a loss function for our purposes, since there is in fact an inherent assymmetry in the situation: $\mathbf{p}$ is the ground truth while $\mathbf{q}$ is the predicted output. Notice that minimizing the KL-divergence loss of a model is equivalent to minimizing the cross-entropy loss, since the term $H(\mathbf{p})$ depends only on the input and is independent of the model that is learned.

In practice, cross entropy is the most commonly used loss function for classification problems. Networks designed for classification often use a softmax activation function in the output layer. These choices are so common that many implementations, such as TensorFlow, offer a single function that combines softmax with cross entropy. In addition to convenience, one reason to do so is that the combined function is more stable numerically, and its derivative also takes a simple form, as we show in Section 13.3.3.

13.2.10 Exercises for Section 13.2

EXERCISE 13.2.1 Show that for the logistic sigmoid σ, if $y = \sigma(x)$, then
$$\frac{dy}{dx} = y(1 - y)$$

EXERCISE 13.2.2 Show that if $y = \tanh(x)$ then
$$\frac{dy}{dx} = 1 - y^2$$

EXERCISE 13.2.3 Show that $\tanh(x) = 2\sigma(2x) - 1$.

EXERCISE 13.2.4 Show that $\sigma(x) = 1 - \sigma(-x)$.

EXERCISE 13.2.5 Show that for any vector $[v_1, v_2, \ldots, v_k]$, $\sum_{i=1}^{k} \mu(v_i) = 1$.

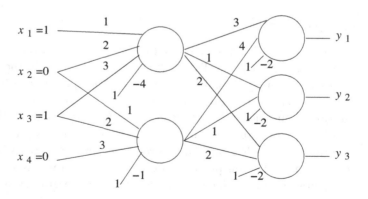

Figure 13.7 Neural net for Exercise 13.2.6

EXERCISE 13.2.6 In Fig. 13.7 is a neural net with particular values shown for all the weights and inputs. Suppose that we use the sigmoid function to compute outputs of nodes at the first layer, and we use softmax to compute the outputs of the nodes in the output layer.

(a) Compute the values of the outputs for each of the five nodes.

! (b) Assuming each of the weights and each of the x_i is a variable, express the output of the first (top) output node in terms of the weights and the x_i,

! (c) Find the derivative of your function from part (b) with respect to the weight on the first (top) input to the first (top) node in the first layer.

13.3   Backpropagation and Gradient Descent

We now turn to the problem of training a deep network. Training a network means finding good values for the parameters (weights and thresholds) of the network. Usually, we shall have access to a training set of labeled input/output pairs. The training process tries to find parameter values that minimize the average loss on the training set. The hope is that the training set is representative of the data the model will encounter in the future, and therefore, the average loss on the training set is a good measure of the average error on all possible inputs. We must be careful, however; since deep networks have many parameters, it is possible to find parameters that yield low training loss but nevertheless perform poorly in the real world. This phenomenon is called overfitting, a problem we have mentioned several times, starting in Section 9.4.4.

For the moment, we assume that our goal is to find parameters that minimize the expected loss on the training set. This goal is achieved by gradient descent. There is an elegant algorithm called *backpropagation* that allows us to compute these gradients efficiently. Before we describe backpropagation, we need a few preliminaries.

13.3.1   Compute Graphs

A compute graph captures the data flow of a deep network. Formally, a compute graph is a directed, acyclic graph (DAG). Each node in the compute graph has an operand and, optionally, an operator. The operand can be a scalar, a vector, or a matrix. The operator is a linear algebra operator (such as + or ×), an activation function (such as σ) or a loss function (such as MSE). When a node has both an operand and an operator, the operator is written above the operand.

When a node has only an operand, its output is the value associated with the operand. The output of a node with an operator is the result of applying its operator to its immediate predecessors in the graph and then assigning the result to the operand. In general, the operator can be an arbitrary expression that uses its inputs to produce an output.[3]

EXAMPLE 13.2   Figure 13.8 shows the compute graph for a single-layer dense network described by $\mathbf{y} = \sigma(W\mathbf{x} + \mathbf{b})$ where $\mathbf{x}$ is the input and $\mathbf{y}$ is the output.

---

[3] Sometimes the order of operands to the operator matters. We shall ignore that detail here and assume it is understood from the context.

We then compute an MSE loss against the training-set output $\hat{\mathbf{y}}$. That is, we have a single layer of n nodes. The vector $\mathbf{y}$ is of length n and represents the outputs of each of these nodes. There are k inputs, and $(\mathbf{x}, \hat{\mathbf{y}})$ represents one training example. Matrix W represents the weights on the inputs of the nodes; that is, W_{ij} is the weight for input j at the ith node. Finally, $\mathbf{b}$ represents the n biases, so its ith element is the negative of the threshold of the ith node.

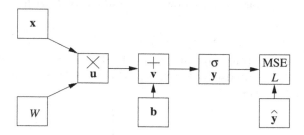

Figure 13.8 Compute graph for a single-layer dense network

For the graph in Fig. 13.8, we have:

$$\mathbf{u} = W\mathbf{x}$$
$$\mathbf{v} = \mathbf{u} + \mathbf{b}$$
$$\mathbf{y} = \sigma(\mathbf{v})$$
$$L = \text{MSE}(\mathbf{y}, \hat{\mathbf{y}})$$

Each of these steps corresponds to one of the four nodes in the middle row, in order from the left. The first step corresponds to the node with operand $\mathbf{u}$ and operator $\times$. Here is an example where it must be understood that the node labeled W is the first argument. If necessary, we could label each incoming edge with a number to indicate its order, but in this case the order should be obvious, since a column vector $\mathbf{x}$ could not multiply a matrix W unless the matrix happened to have only one row. The second step corresponds to the node with operator $+$ and operand $\mathbf{v}$. Here, the order of arguments does not matter, since $+$ on vectors is commutative. □

13.3.2 Gradients, Jacobians, and the Chain Rule

The goal of the backpropagation algorithm is to compute the gradient of the loss function with respect to the parameters of the network. Then, we can adjust the parameters slightly in the directions that will reduce the loss, and repeat the process until we reach a selection of parameter values for which little improvement in the loss is possible. Recall the definition of the gradient: given a function $f : \mathbb{R}^N \to \mathbb{R}$ from a real-valued vector to a scalar, if $\mathbf{x} = [x_1, x_2, \dots, x_n]$ and $y = f(\mathbf{x})$ then the gradient of y with respect to x, denoted by $\nabla_{\mathbf{x}} y$ is given by

$$\nabla_{\mathbf{x}} y = \left[\frac{\partial y}{\partial x_1}, \frac{\partial y}{\partial x_2}, \dots, \frac{\partial y}{\partial x_n} \right]$$

EXAMPLE 13.3   We could let function f be the loss function, e.g., the squared-error loss, which we denote L. This loss is a scalar-valued function of the output $\mathbf{y}$:

$$L(\mathbf{y}) = \|\mathbf{y} - \hat{\mathbf{y}}\|^2 = \sum_{i=1}^{n} (y_i - \hat{y}_i)^2$$

So we can easily write down the gradient of L with respect to $\mathbf{y}$:

$$\nabla_{\mathbf{y}} L = [2(y_1 - \hat{y}_1), (y_2 - \hat{y}_2), \ldots, 2(y_n - \hat{y}_n)] = 2(\mathbf{y} - \hat{\mathbf{y}}) \qquad \square$$

The generalization of the gradient to vector-valued functions is called the *Jacobian*. Suppose we have a function $f : \mathbb{R}^m \to \mathbb{R}^n$ and $\mathbf{y} = f(\mathbf{x})$. The Jacobian $J_{\mathbf{x}}(\mathbf{y})$ is given by:[4]

$$J_{\mathbf{x}}(\mathbf{y}) = \begin{bmatrix} \frac{\partial y_1}{\partial x_1} & \cdots & \frac{\partial y_n}{\partial x_1} \\ \vdots & \ddots & \vdots \\ \frac{\partial y_1}{\partial x_m} & \cdots & \frac{\partial y_n}{\partial x_m} \end{bmatrix}$$

We shall make use of the *chain rule* for derivatives from calculus. If $y = g(x)$ and $z = f(y) = f(g(x))$, then the chain rule says:

$$\frac{dz}{dx} = \frac{dz}{dy}\frac{dy}{dx}$$

Also, if $z = f(u, v)$ where $u = g(x)$ and $v = h(x)$, then

$$\frac{dz}{dx} = \frac{\partial z}{\partial u}\frac{du}{dx} + \frac{\partial z}{\partial v}\frac{dv}{dx}$$

For functions of vectors, we can restate the chain rule in terms of gradients and Jacobians. Suppose $\mathbf{y} = g(\mathbf{x})$ and $z = f(\mathbf{y}) = f(g(\mathbf{x}))$ then:

$$\nabla_{\mathbf{x}} z = J_{\mathbf{x}}(\mathbf{y}) \nabla_{\mathbf{y}} z$$

If $z = f(\mathbf{u}, \mathbf{v})$ where $\mathbf{u} = g(\mathbf{x})$ and $\mathbf{v} = h(\mathbf{x})$, then

$$\nabla_{\mathbf{x}} z = J_{\mathbf{x}}(\mathbf{u}) \nabla_{\mathbf{u}} z + J_{\mathbf{x}}(\mathbf{v}) \nabla_{\mathbf{v}} z$$

13.3.3   The Backpropagation Algorithm

The goal of the backpropagation algorithm is to compute the gradient of the loss function with respect to the parameters of the network. Consider the compute graph from Fig. 13.8. Here the loss function L is the MSE function. We shall use the notation $g(\mathbf{z})$ to stand for $\nabla_{\mathbf{z}}(L)$; that is, the gradient of the the loss

[4] The Jacobian is sometimes defined as the transpose of our definition. The formulations are equivalent. Recall that we are assuming all vectors are column vectors unless transposed, but we show them as row vectors so they can be written in-line.

function L with respect to some vector $\mathbf{z}$. We already know the gradient of L with respect to the output $\mathbf{y}$:

$$g(\mathbf{y}) = \nabla_{\mathbf{y}}(L) = 2(\mathbf{y} - \hat{\mathbf{y}})$$

We work backwards through the compute graph, applying the chain rule at each stage. At each point we pick a node all of whose successors have already been processed. Suppose $\mathbf{a}$ is such a node, and suppose it has just one immediate successor $\mathbf{b}$ in the graph (note that in the simple compute graph of Fig. 13.8, each node has just one immediate successor). Since we have already processed node $\mathbf{b}$, we have already computed $g(\mathbf{b})$. We can now compute $g(\mathbf{a})$ using the chain rule:

$$g(\mathbf{a}) = J_{\mathbf{a}}(\mathbf{b})g(\mathbf{b})$$

In the case where node $\mathbf{a}$ has more than one successor node, we use the more general sum version of the chain rule. That is, $g(\mathbf{a})$ would be the sum of the above terms for each successor $\mathbf{b}$ of $\mathbf{a}$.

Since we shall need to compute these gradients several times, once for each iteration of gradient descent, we can avoid repeated computation by adding additional nodes to the compute graph for backpropagation: one node for each gradient computation. In general, the Jacobian $J_{\mathbf{a}}(\mathbf{b})$ is a function of both $\mathbf{a}$ and $\mathbf{b}$, and so the node for $g(\mathbf{a})$ will have arcs to it from the nodes for $\mathbf{a}$, $\mathbf{b}$ and $g(\mathbf{b})$. Popular frameworks for deep learning (e.g., TensorFlow) know how to compute the functional expression for the Jacobians and gradients of commonly used operators such as those that appear in Fig. 13.8. In that case, the developer needs only to provide the compute graph and the framework will add the new nodes for backpropagation. Figure 13.9 shows the resulting compute graph with added gradient nodes.

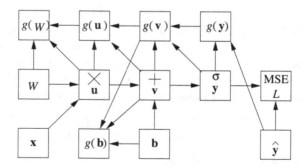

Figure 13.9 Compute graph with gradient nodes

EXAMPLE 13.4   We shall work out the functional expressions for the gradients of all the nodes in Fig. 13.8. We already know $g(\mathbf{y})$. So the next node we choose to process is $\mathbf{v}$:

$$g(\mathbf{v}) = \nabla_{\mathbf{v}}(L) = J_{\mathbf{v}}(\mathbf{y})\nabla_{\mathbf{y}}(L) = J_{\mathbf{v}}(\mathbf{y})g(\mathbf{y})$$

We know that $\mathbf{y} = \sigma(\mathbf{v})$. Since σ is an element-wise operator, the Jacobian $J_\mathbf{v}(\mathbf{y})$ takes a particularly simple form. Using the derivative for the logistic sigmoid function from Section 13.2.2, we see that

$$\frac{\partial y_i}{\partial v_j} = \begin{cases} y_i(1 - y_i) & \text{if } i = j \\ 0 & \text{otherwise} \end{cases}$$

The Jacobian is therefore a diagonal matrix:

$$J_\mathbf{v}(\mathbf{y}) = \begin{bmatrix} y_1(1-y_1) & 0 & \cdots & 0 \\ 0 & y_2(1-y_2) & \cdots & 0 \\ \vdots & \vdots & \ddots & \vdots \\ 0 & 0 & \cdots & y_n(1-y_n) \end{bmatrix}$$

Suppose $\mathbf{s} = [s_1, s_2, \dots, s_n]$ is a vector defined by $s_i = y_i(1-y_i)$ (i.e., the diagonal of the Jacobian matrix). We can express $g(\mathbf{v})$ simply as

$$g(\mathbf{v}) = \mathbf{s} \circ g(\mathbf{y})$$

where $\mathbf{a} \circ \mathbf{b}$ is the vector resulting from the element-wise product of $\mathbf{a}$ and $\mathbf{b}$.[5]

Now that we have $g(\mathbf{v})$, we can compute $g(\mathbf{b})$ and $g(\mathbf{u})$. We have $g(\mathbf{b}) = J_\mathbf{b}(\mathbf{v})g(\mathbf{v})$ and $g(\mathbf{u}) = J_\mathbf{u}(\mathbf{v})g(\mathbf{v})$. Since

$$\mathbf{v} = \mathbf{u} + \mathbf{b}$$

it is straightforward to verify that

$$J_\mathbf{b}(\mathbf{v}) = J_\mathbf{u}(\mathbf{v}) = I_n$$

where I_n is the $n \times n$ identity matrix. So we have

$$g(\mathbf{b}) = g(\mathbf{u}) = g(\mathbf{v})$$

We finally come to the matrix W. Recall that $\mathbf{u} = W\mathbf{x}$. There is a potential problem here, because all the machinery we have set up works for vectors, while W is a matrix. But recall from Section 13.2.1 that we assembled the matrix W from a set of vectors $\mathbf{w}_1, \mathbf{w}_2, \dots, \mathbf{w}_n$, where $\mathbf{w}_i^\mathsf{T}$ is the ith row of W. The trick is to consider each of these vectors separately and compute its gradient using the usual formula.

$$g(\mathbf{w}_i) = J_{\mathbf{w}_i}(\mathbf{u})g(\mathbf{u})$$

We know that $u_i = \mathbf{w}_i^\mathsf{T}\mathbf{x}$ and none of the other u_j have any dependency on $\mathbf{w}_i$ for $i \neq j$. Therefore, the Jacobian $J_{\mathbf{w}_i}(\mathbf{u})$ is zero everywhere except the ith column, which is equal to $\mathbf{x}$. Thus we have

$$g(\mathbf{w}_i) = g(u_i)\mathbf{x}$$

□

[5] This operation sometimes called the *Hadamard product*, so as not to confuse it with the more usual dot product, which is the sum of the components of the Hadamard product.

EXAMPLE 13.5   As we mentioned, neural networks for classification often use a softmax activation in the final layer followed by a cross-entropy loss. We will now compute the gradient of the combined operator.

Suppose the input to the combined operator is $\mathbf{y}$; let $\mathbf{q} = \mu(\mathbf{y})$, and let $l = H(\mathbf{p}, \mathbf{q})$, where $\mathbf{p}$ represents the true probability vector for the corresponding training example. We have:

$$\log(q_i) = \log\left(\frac{e^{y_i}}{\sum_j e^{y_j}}\right) = y_i - \log\left(\sum_j e^{y_j}\right)$$

Therefore, noting that $\sum_i p_i = 1$, we have:

$$l = H(\mathbf{p}, \mathbf{q}) = -\sum_i p_i \log q_i$$

$$= -\sum_i p_i \left(y_i - \log\left(\sum_j e^{y_j}\right)\right)$$

$$= -\sum_i p_i y_i - \log\left(\sum_j e^{y_j}\right)\sum_i p_i$$

$$= -\sum_i p_i y_i - \log\left(\sum_j e^{y_j}\right)$$

Differentiating, we get:

$$\frac{\partial l}{\partial y_k} = -p_k + \frac{e^{y_k}}{\sum_j e^{y_j}}$$

$$= -p_k + \mu(y_k)$$

$$= q_k - p_k$$

Therefore, we end up with the rather neat result:

$$\nabla_y l = \mathbf{q} - \mathbf{p}$$

This combined gradient does not saturate or explode, and leads to good learning behavior. That observation explains why softmax and cross entropy loss work so well together in practice.   □

13.3.4   Iterating Gradient Descent

Given a set of training examples, we run the compute graph in both directions for each example: forward (to compute the loss) and backwards (to compute the gradients). We average the loss and gradients across the training set to compute the average loss and the average gradient for each parameter vector.

At each iteration we update each parameter vector in the direction opposite to its gradient, so the loss will tend to decrease. Suppose $\mathbf{z}$ is a parameter vector. We set:

$$\mathbf{z} \leftarrow \mathbf{z} - \eta g(\mathbf{z})$$

Here η is a hyperparameter, the learning rate. We stop gradient descent either when the loss between successive iterations changes by only a tiny amount (i.e., we have reached a local minimum) or after a fixed number of iterations.

It is important to pick the learning rate carefully. Too small a value means gradient descent might take a very large number of iterations to converge. Too large a value might cause large oscillations in the parameter values and never lead to convergence. Usually picking the right learning rate is a matter of trial and error. It is also possible and common to vary the learning rate. Start with an initial learning rate η_0. Then, at each iteration, multiply the learning rate by a factor β, for $0 < \beta < 1$, until the learning rate reaches a sufficiently low value.

When we have a large training set, we may not want to use the entire training set for each iteration, as it might be too time-consuming. So for each iteration we randomly sample a "minibatch" of training examples. This variant is called stochastic gradient descent," as was discussed in Section 12.3.5, since we estimate the gradients using a different sample of the training set at each iteration.

We have left open the question of how the parameter values are initialized before we start gradient descent. The usual approach is to choose them at random. Popular approachaes include sampling each entry uniformly at random in $[-1, 1]$, or choosing randomly using a normal distribution. Notice that initializing all the weights to the same value would cause all nodes in a layer to behave the same way, and thus we would never reap the benefit of having different nodes in a layer recognize different features of the input.

13.3.5 Tensors

Previously, we have imagined that the inputs to a neural net are one-dimensional vectors. But there is no reason why we cannot view the input as having a higher dimension.

EXAMPLE 13.6   A grey-scale photo might be represented by a two-dimensional array of real numbers, corresponding to the intensity of each pixel. Each pixel of a color image typically requires 3 dimensions. That is, each pixel itself is a vector with three components, say for the intensity of the pixel in the red, green, and blue colors. One useful way to view a color image as input to a neural net is to think of each training example as a two-dimensional array of pixels, where the value of each pixel is not a real number, as we have heretofore imagined, but a vector with three dimensions, one for each of the three colors.   □

Similarly, we have viewed each layer of a neural net as a column of nodes. But there is no reason we cannot imagine the nodes in a layer to be organized as a two-dimensional array or even an array of dimension greater than two. Finally, we have viewed the input values as real numbers and similarly viewed the values produced by each node as a real number. But we could also think of the values attached to each input or output of a node as a vector or a higher-dimensional structure. The natural generalization of vectors and matrices is the *tensor*, which is an n-dimensional array of scalars.

Unfortunately, the backpropagation algorithm we described works for vectors, not higher-dimensional tensors. In such cases, we resort to the same trick we used in Section 13.3.3, where we unrolled the matrix W into collection of vectors. Just as we regard an $m \times n$ matrix as a set of m n-vectors, we can regard a 3-dimensional tensor of dimensionality $l \times m \times n$ as a set of lm n-vectors, and similarly for tensors of higher dimension.

EXAMPLE 13.7   This example is based on the *MNIST dataset*.[6] This dataset consists of 28×28 monochrome images, each represented by a two-dimensional square bit array whose sides are of length 28. Our goal is to build a neural net that determines whether an image corresponds to a handwritten digit (0–9) and if so which one. Consider a single image X, which is a 28×28 matrix. Suppose the first layer of our network is a dense layer[7] consisting of 49 hidden nodes, which we shall imagine is arranged in a 7×7 array. We model the hidden layer as a 7×7 matrix H, where the output of the node in row i and column j is h_{ij}.

We can model the weights for each of the 28×28 inputs and each of the 7×7 nodes as a *weight tensor* W with dimensions $7 \times 7 \times 28 \times 28$. That is, W_{ijkl} represents the weight for the input pixel in row i and column j of the image to the node whose position in the array of nodes is row k and column l. Then:

$$h_{ij} = \sum_{k=1}^{28} \sum_{l=1}^{28} w_{ijkl} x_{kl} \text{ for } 1 \le i, j \le 7$$

where we omit the bias term for simplicity (i.e., we assume all thresholds of all nodes are 0.

An equivalent way of thinking about this structure to *flatten* the input X into a vector $\mathbf{x}$ of length 784 (since $28 \times 28 = 784$) and the hidden layer H into a vector $\mathbf{h}$ of length 49. We flatten the weight tensor W as follows: the last two dimensions are flattened into a single dimension to match $\mathbf{x}$, and its first two dimensions are flattened into a single dimension to match the hidden vector $\mathbf{h}$, resulting in a 49×784 weight matrix. Suppose as in Section 13.2.1, we have $\mathbf{w}_i^\mathsf{T}$ denote the ith row of this new weight matrix. We can now write:

$$h_i = \mathbf{w}_i^\mathsf{T} \mathbf{x} \text{ for } 1 \le i \le 49$$

It's straightforward to see that there is a 1-to-1 mapping between the hidden nodes in the old and new arrangements. Moreover, the output of each hidden node is determined by a dot product, just as in Section 13.2.1. Thus the tensor notation is just a convenient way to group vectors. □

Thus the tensors used in neural networks have little in common with the tensors used in Physics and other mathematical sciences. A tensor in our context

---

[6] See yann.lecun.com/exdb/mnist/.
[7] In reality, the first network layer for this problem is likely to be a convolutional layer. See Section 13.4

is just a nested collection of vectors. The only tensor operation we shall need is the *flattening* of a tensor by merging dimensions as in Example 13.7. We can use the backpropagation algorithm described in Section 13.3.3 for tensors once we have flattened them approriately.

13.3.6   Exercises for Section 13.3

EXERCISE 13.3.1   This exercise uses the neural net from Fig. 13.7. However, assume that the weights on all inputs are variables rather than the constants shown. Note, however, that some inputs do not feed one of the nodes in the first layer, so these weights are fixed at 0. Assume that the input vector is $\mathbf{x}$, the output vector is $\mathbf{y}$, and the output of the two nodes in the hidden layer is the vector $\mathbf{z}$. Also, let the matrix and bias vector connecting $\mathbf{x}$ to $\mathbf{z}$ be W_1 and $\mathbf{b}_1$, while the matrix and bias vector connecting $\mathbf{z}$ to $\mathbf{y}$ are W_2 and $\mathbf{b}_2$. Assume that the activation function at the hidden layer is the hyperbolic tangent, and the activation function at the output is the identity function (i.e., no change to the outputs is made). Finally, assume the loss function is mean-squared error, where $\hat{y}$ is the true output vector for a given input vector $\mathbf{x}$. Draw the compute graph that shows how $\mathbf{y}$ is computed from $\mathbf{x}$.

EXERCISE 13.3.2   For the network described in Exercise 13.3.1:

(a) What is $J_{\mathbf{y}}(\mathbf{z})$?
(b) What is $J_{\mathbf{z}}(\mathbf{x})$?
(c) Express $g(\mathbf{x})$ in terms of $g(\tanh(\mathbf{z}))$.
(d) Express $g(\mathbf{x})$ in terms of the loss function.
(e) Draw the compute graph with gradient computation for the entire network.

13.4   Convolutional Neural Networks

Consider a fully-connected network layer for processing 224×224 images, with each pixel encoded using 3 color values (often called *channels* – the values of intensity for red, green, and blue)).[8] The number of weight parameters in the connection layer for each output node is $224 \times 224 \times 3 = 150,528$. Suppose we had 224 nodes in the output layer. We would end up with a total of over 33 million parameters! Given that our training set of images is usually of the order of tens or hundreds of thousands of images, the huge number of parameters would quickly lead to overfitting even using just a single layer.

A Convolutional Neural Network (CNN) greatly reduces the number of parameters by taking advantage of the properties of image data. CNNs introduce two new varieties of network layers: convolutional layers and pooling layers.

---

[8] This is the size of most of the images on ImageNet, for example.

13.4.1 Convolutional Layers

Convolutional layers make use of the fact that image features often are described by small contiguous areas in the image. For example, at the first convolutional layer, we might recognize small sections of edges in the image. At later layers, more complex structures, such as features that look like flower petals or eyes might be recognized. The idea that simplifies the calculation is the fact that the recognition of features such as edges does not depend on where in the image the edge is. Thus, we can train a single node to recognize a small section of edge, say an edge through a 5×5 region of pixels. This idea benefits us in two ways.

(1) The node in question needs only inputs from 25 pixels corresponding to any 5×5 square, not inputs from all 224×224 pixels. That saves us a lot in the representation of the trained CNN.

(2) The number of weights that we need to learn in the training process is greatly reduced. For each node in the layer, we require only one weight for each input to that node – say 75 weights if a pixel is represented by RGB values, not the 150,528 weights that we suggested above would be needed for an ordinary, fully connected layer.

We shall think of the nodes in a convolutional layer as *filters* for learning features. A filter examines a small spatially contiguous area of the image – traditionally, a small square area such as a 5×5 square of pixels. Moreover, since many features of interest may occur anywhere in the input image (and possibly in more than one location), we apply the same filter at many locations on the input.

To keep things simple, suppose the input consists of monochromatic images, that is, grey-scale images whose pixels are each a single value. Each image is thus encoded by a 2-dimensional pixel array of size 224×224. A 5×5 filter F is encoded by a 5×5 weight matrix W and single bias parameter b. When the filter is applied on a similarly-sized square region of input image X with the top left corner of the filter aligned with the image pixel x_{ij}, the *response* of the filter at this position, denoted r_{ij}, is given by:

$$r_{ij} = \sum_{k=0}^{4} \sum_{l=0}^{4} x_{i+k,j+l} w_{kl} + b \tag{13.1}$$

We now slide the filter along the length and width of the input image, applying the filter at each position, so that we capture every possible 5×5 square region of pixels in the image. Notice that we can apply the filter at input locations $1 \le i \le 220$ and $1 \le j \le 220$, although it does not "fit" at positions with a higher i or j. The resulting set of responses r_{ij} are then passed through an activation function to form the *activation map* R of the filter. In most cases, the activation function is ReLU or one of its variants. When trained, i.e., the weights w_{ij} of the filter are determined, the filter will recognize some feature of

the image, and the activation map tells whether (or to what degree) this feaure
is present at each position of the image.

EXAMPLE 13.8   In Fig. 13.10(b), we see a 2×2 filter, which is to be applied
to the 4×4 image in Fig. 13.10(b). To do so, we lay the filter over all nine of
the 2×2 squares of the image. In the figure, we suggest the filter being placed
over the 2×2 square in the upper-right corner. After overlaying the filter, we
multiply each of the filter elements by the corresponding image element and then
take the sum of the products. In principle, we then need to add in a bias term,
but in this example, we shall assume the bias is 0.

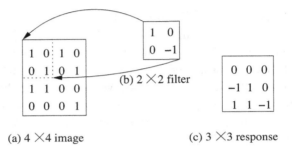

(a) 4×4 image   (c) 3×3 response

Figure 13.10 Applying a filter to an image

Another way to look at this process is that we turn the filter into a vector
by concatenating its rows, in order, and we do the same to the square of the
image. Then, we take the dot product of the vectors. For instance, the filter can
be thought of as the vector $[1, 0, 0, -1]$, and the square in the upper-left corner
of the image can be thought of as the vector $[1, 0, 0, 1]$. The dot product of these
vectors is $1 \times 1 + 0 \times 0 + 0 \times 0 + (-1) \times 1 = 0$. Thus, the result, shown in
Fig. 13.10(c), has a 0 for its upper-left entry.

For another example, if we slide the filter down one row, the dot product of
the filter as a vector and the vector formed from the first two elements of the
second and third rows of the image is $1 \times 0 + 0 \times 1 + 0 \times 1 + (-1) \times 1 = -1$.
Thus, the first element of the second row of the convolution is -1.   □

When we deal with color images, the input has three channels. That is, each
pixel is represented by three values, one for each color. Suppose we have a color
image of size $224 \times 224 \times 3$. The filter's output will also have three channels,
and so the filter is now encoded by a $5 \times 5 \times 3$ weight matrix W and single bias
parameter b. The activation map R still remains 5×5, with each response given
by:

$$r_{ij} = \sum_{k=0}^{4} \sum_{l=0}^{4} \sum_{d=1}^{3} x_{i+k,j+l,d} w_{kld} + b \tag{13.2}$$

In our example, we imagined a filter of size 5. In general, the size of the filter is
a hyperparameter of the convolutional layer. Filters of size 3, 4, or 5 are most

commonly used. Note that the filter size specifies only the width and height of the filter; the number of channels of the filter always matches the number of channels of the input.

The activation map in our example is slightly smaller than the input. In many cases, it is convenient to have the activation map be of the same size as the input. We can expand the repsonse by using *zero padding*: adding additional rows and columns of zeros to pad out the input. A zero padding of p corresponds to adding p rows of zeros each to the top and bottom, and p columns to the left and right, increasing the dimensionality of the input by $2p$ along both width and height. A zero padding of 2 in our example would augment the input size to 228×228 and result in an activation map of size 224×224, the same size as the original input image.

The third hyperparameter of interest is *stride*. In our example, we assumed that we apply the filter at every possible point in the input image. We could think instead of sliding the filter one pixel at a time along the width and height of the input, corresponding to a stride $s = 1$. Instead, we could slide the filter along the width and the height of image two or three pixels at a time, corresponding to a stride s of 2 or 3. The larger the stride, the smaller the activation map compared to the input.

Suppose the input is an $m \times m$ square of pixels, the output an $n \times n$ square, filter size is f, stride is s, and zero padding is p. It is easily seen that:

$$n = (m - f + 2p)/s + 1 \tag{13.3}$$

In particular, we must be careful to pick hyperparameters such that s evenly divides $m - f + 2p$; else we would have an invalid arrangement for the convolutional layer, and most software implementations would throw an exception.

We can intuitively think of a filter as looking for an image feature, such as a splotch of color or an edge. Classifying an image usually requires identifying many features. We therefore use many filters, ideally one for each useful feature. During the training of the CNN, we hope that each filter will learn to identify one of these features. Suppose we use k filters; to keep things simple, we constrain all filters to use same size, stride, and zero padding. Then the output contains k activation maps. The dimensionality of the output layer is therefore $n \times n \times k$, where n is given by Equation 13.3.

The set of k filters together constitute a *convolutional layer*. Given input with d channels, a filter of size f requires $df^2 + 1$ parameters (df^2 weight parameters and 1 bias parameter). Therefore, a convolutional layer of k such filters uses $k(df^2 + 1)$ parameters.

EXAMPLE 13.9   Continuing the ImageNet example, suppose the input consists of $224 \times 224 \times 3$ images, and we use a convolutional layer of 64 filters, each of size 5, stride 1, and zero padding 2. The size of the output layer is $224 \times 224 \times 64$. Each filter needs $3 \times 5 \times 5 + 1 = 76$ parameters (including one for the threshold) and the convolutional layer contains $64 \times 76 = 4864$ parameters – orders of magnitude smaller than the number of parameters for a fully connected layer with the same input and output sizes. □

13.4.2   Convolution and Cross-Correlation

This subsection is a short detour to explain why Convolutional Neural Networks are so named. It is not a pre-requisite for any of the other material in this chapter.

The convolutional layer is named because of the resemblance it bears to the convolution operation from functional analysis, which is often used in signal processing and probability theory. Given functions f and g, usually defined over the time domain, their convolution $(f * g)(t)$ is defined as:

$$(f * g)(t) = \int_{-\infty}^{\infty} f(\tau)g(t - \tau)d\tau = \int_{-\infty}^{\infty} f(t - \tau)g(\tau)d\tau$$

Here we are interested in the discrete version of convolution, where f and g are defined over the integers:

$$(f * g)(i) = \sum_{k=-\infty}^{\infty} f(k)g(i - k) = \sum_{k=-\infty}^{\infty} f(i - k)g(k)$$

Often convolution is viewed as using function g to transform function f. In this context, the function g is sometimes called the *kernel*. When the kernel is finite, so $g(k)$ is only defined for $k = 0, 1, \ldots, m - 1$, the definition simplifies to:

$$(f * g)(i) = \sum_{k=0}^{m-1} f(i - k)g(k)$$

We can extend the definition to 2-dimensional functions:

$$(f * g)(i, j) = \sum_{k=0}^{m-1}\sum_{l=0}^{m-1} f(i - k, j - l)g(k, l)$$

Let us define h to be the kernel obtained by *flipping* g, i.e., $h(i, j) = g(-i, -j)$ for $i, j \in \{0, \ldots, m - 1\}$. It can verified that the convolution $f * h$ of f with the flipped kernel h is given by:

$$(f * h)(i, j) = \sum_{k=0}^{m-1}\sum_{l=0}^{m-1} f(i + k, j + l)g(k, l) \tag{13.4}$$

Note the similarity of Equation 13.4 to Equation 13.1, ignoring the bias term b. The operation of the convolutional layer can be thought of as the convolution of the input with a flipped kernel. This similarity is the reason why convolutional layers are so named, and filters are sometimes called kernels.

The *cross-correlation* $f \star g$ is defined by $(f \star g)(x, y) = (f * h)(x, y)$ where h is the flipped version of g. Thus the operation of the convolutional layer can also be seen as the cross-correlation of the input with the filter.

13.4.3 Pooling Layers

A pooling layer takes as input the output of a convolutional layer and produces an output with smaller spatial extent. The size reduction is accomplished by using a *pooling function* to compute aggregates over small contiguous regions of the input. For example we might use *max pooling* over nonoverlapping 2 × 2 regions of the input; in this case there is an output node corresponding to every nonoverlapping 2 × 2 region of the input, with the output value being the maximum value among the four inputs in the region. The aggregation operates independently on each channel of the input. The resulting output layer is 25% the size of the input layer. There are three elements in defining a pooling layer:

(1) The *pooling function*, which is most commonly the max function but could in theory be any aggregate function, such as average.
(2) The *size f* of each pool, which specifies that each pool uses an $f \times f$ square of inputs.
(3) The stride s between pools, analogous to the stride used in the convolutional layer.

The most common use cases in practice are $f = 2$ and $s = 2$, which specifies nonoverlapping 2×2 regions, and $f = 3$, $s = 2$, which specifies 3×3 regions with some overlap. Higher values of f lead to too much loss of information in practice. Note that the pooling operation shrinks the height and width of the input layer, but preserves the number of channels. It operates independently on each channel of its input. Note that unlike the convolution layer, it is not common practice to use zero padding for the max pooling layer.

Pooling is appropriate if we we believe that features are approximately invariant to small translations. For example, we might care about the relative locations of features such as legs or wings and not their exact locations. In such cases pooling can greatly reduce the size of the hidden layer that forms the input to the subsequent layers of the network.

EXAMPLE 13.10 Suppose we apply max pooling with size = 2 and stride = 2 to the $224 \times 224 \times 64$ output of the convolutional layer from Example 13.9. The resulting output is of size $112 \times 112 \times 64$. □

13.4.4 CNN Architecture

Now that we have seen the building blocks of Convolutional Neural Networks, we can put them together to build deep networks. A typical CNN alternates convolutional and pooling layers, ending with one or more fully-connected layers that produce the final output.

EXAMPLE 13.11 For instance, Fig. 13.11 is a simple network architecture for classifying ImageNet images into one of 1000 image classes, loosely inspired by

VGGnet.[9] This simple network strictly alternates convolutional and pooling layers. In practice, high-performing networks are finely tuned to their task, and may stack convolutional layers directly on top of one another with the occasional pooling layer in between. Moreover, there is often more than one fully-connected layer before the final output. The input to the first layer is the 224×224, three-channel image. The input to each subsequent layer is the output of the previous layer.

Layer Type	Size	Stride	Pad	Filter Count	Output Size
Convolution	3	1	1	64	$224 \times 224 \times 64$
Max Pool	2	2	0	64	$112 \times 112 \times 64$
Convolution	3	1	1	128	$112 \times 112 \times 128$
Max Pool	2	2	0	128	$56 \times 56 \times 128$
Convolution	3	1	1	256	$56 \times 56 \times 256$
Max Pool	2	2	0	256	$28 \times 28 \times 256$
Convolution	3	1	1	512	$14 \times 14 \times 512$
Max Pool	2	2	0	512	$14 \times 14 \times 512$
Convolution	3	1	1	1024	$14 \times 14 \times 1024$
Max Pool	2	2	0	1024	$7 \times 7 \times 1024$
Fully Connected					$1 \times 1 \times 1000$

Figure 13.11 Layers of a Convolutional Neural Network

The first layer is a convolutional layer, consisting of 64 filters, each with three channels, as would be the case for any color-image processor. The filters are 3×3, and the stride is 1, so every 3×3 square of the image is an input to the filter. There is one unit of zero-padding, so the number of outputs of this layer equals the number of inputs. Further, notice that we can view the output as another 224×224 array. Each element of this array consists of 64 filters, each of which is a three-channel pixel.

The output of the first layer is fed to a max-pool layer, in which we divide the 224×224 array into 2×2 squares (because both the size and stride are 2). Thus, the 224×224 array has become a 112×112 array, and there are still the same 64 filters.

At the third layer, which is again convolutional, we take the 112×112 array of pixels from the second layer as input. This layer has more filters than the first layer – 128 to be exact. The intuitive reason for the increase is that the first layer recognizes very simple structures, like edges, and there are not too many different simple structures. However, the third layer should be recognizing somewhat more complex features, and these features can involve a 6×6 square of the input image, because of the pooling done at the second layer. Similarly, each subsequent convolutional layer takes inputs from the previous pooling layer and

9 K. Simonyan and A. Zussman, "Very Deep Convolutional Networks for Large-Scale Image Recognition," arXiv:1409–1556v6.

How Many Nodes in a Convolutional Layer?

We have referred to a node of a convolutional layer as a "filter." That filter may be a single node, or as in Example 13.11, a set of several nodes, one for each channel. When we train the CNN, we determine weights for each filter, so there are relatively few nodes. For instance, in the first layer in Example 13.11, there are 192 nodes, three for each of the 64 filters. However, when we apply the trained CNN to an input, we apply each filter to every pixel in the input. Thus, in Example 13.11, each of the 64 filters of the first layer is applied to $224 \times 224 = 50,176$ pixels. The key point to remember is that although a CNN has a succinct representation, the application of the represented neural net to data requires a significant amount of computation. The same, by the way, can be said for the other specialized forms of neural net that we discuss in Section 13.5.

---

its filters can represent structures of progressively larger sizes and complexities. Thus, the number of filters has been chosen to double at each convolution layer.

Finally, the eleventh, and last, layer is a fully connected layer. It has 1000 nodes, corresponding to the 1000 images classes we are trying to learn how to recognize. Being fully connected, each of these 1000 nodes takes all $7 \times 7 \times 3 = 147$ outputs from the 10th layer; the factor 3 is from the fact that all filters of the previous layers have three channels. □

Designing CNNs and other deep network architectures is still more art than science. Over the past few years, however, some rules of thumb have emerged that are worth keeping in mind:

(1) Deep networks that use many convolutional layers, each using many small filters, are better than shallow networks that use large filters.
(2) A simple pattern is to use convolutional layers that preserve the spatial extent of their input by zero padding, and have size reduction done exclusively by pooling layers.
(3) Smaller strides work better in practice than larger strides.
(4) It's very useful to have the input size evenly divisible by 2 many times.

13.4.5 Implementation and Training

An examination of Equation 13.1 (generalized so the filter is $f \times f$ rather than 5×5) suggests that we can express each entry in the output of the convolution as the dot product of vectors, followed by a scalar sum. To do so, we must flatten the filter $\boldsymbol{F}$ and the corresponding region in the input into vectors. Consider the convolution of an $m \times m \times 1$ tensor $\boldsymbol{X}$ (i.e., $\boldsymbol{X}$ is actually an $m \times m$ matrix) with an $f \times f$ filter $\boldsymbol{F}$ and bias b, to produce as output the $n \times n$ matrix $\boldsymbol{Z}$. We now explain how to implement the convolution operation using a single vector-matrix multiplication.

We first flatten the filter $\boldsymbol{F}$ into a $f^2 \times 1$ vector $\boldsymbol{g}$. We then create matrix $\boldsymbol{Y}$

from X as follows: each square $f \times f$ region of X is flattened into a $f^2 \times 1$ vector, and all these vectors are lined up as columns to form a single $f^2 \times n^2$ matrix Y. Construct the $n^2 \times 1$ vector b so that all its entries are equal to the bias b. Then

$$z = Y^\mathsf{T} g + b$$

yields a $n^2 \times 1$ vector z. Moreover, each element of z is a single element in the convolution. Therefore, we can rearrange the entries in z into an $n \times n$ matrix Z that gives the output of the convolution.

Notice that the matrix Y is larger than the input X (approximately by a factor of f^2), because each entry of X is repeated many times in Y. Thus, this implementation uses a lot of memory. However, multiplying a matrix and a vector is extremely fast on modern hardware such as Graphics Processing Units (GPUs), and so it is the method used in practice.

This approach to computing convolutions can easily be extended to the case of inputs with more than one channel. Moreover, we can also handle the case where we have k filters rather than just 1. We then need to replace the vector g with a $df^2 \times k$ matrix G and use a larger matrix Y $(df^2 \times n^2)$. We also need to use an $n^2 \times k$ bias matrix B, where each column repeats the bias term of the corresponding filter. Finally, the output of the convolution is expressed by an $n^2 \times k$ matrix C, with a column for the output of each filter, where:

$$C = Y^\mathsf{T} F + B$$

We have explained how to perform the forward pass through the convolutional layer. During training, we shall need to backpropagate through the layer. Since each entry in the output of convolution is a dot product of vectors followed by a sum, we can use the techniques from Section 13.3.3 to compute derivatives. It turns out that the derivative of a convolution can also be expressed as a convolution, but we shall not go into the details here.

13.4.6   Exercises for Section 13.4

EXERCISE 13.4.1   Suppose images are 512×512, and we use a filter that is 3×3.

(a) How many responses will be computed for this layer of a CNN?
(b) How much zero padding is necessary to produce an output of size equal to the input?
(c) Suppose we do not do any zero padding. If the output of one layer is input to the next layer, after how many layers will there be no output at all?

EXERCISE 13.4.2   Repeat Exercise 13.4.1(a) and (c) for the case when there is a stride of three.

EXERCISE 13.4.3   Suppose we have the output of an $m \times m$ convolutional layer with k filters, each having d channels. These outputs are fed to a pooling layer with size f and stride s. How many output values does the pooling layer produce?

EXERCISE 13.4.4   For this exercise, assume that inputs are single bits 0 (white) and 1 (black). Consider a 3×3 filter, whose weights are w_{ij}, for $0 \leq i \leq 2$ and $0 \leq j \leq 2$, and whose bias is b. Suggest wieghts and bias so that the output of this filter would detect the following simple features:

(a) A vertical boundary, where the left column is 0, and the other two columns are 1.
(b) A diagonal boundary, where only the triangle of three pixels in the upper right corner are 1.
(c) A corner, in which the 2×2 square in the lower right is 0 and the other pixels are 1.

13.5   Recurrent Neural Networks

Just as CNNs are a specialized family of neural networks for processing 2-dimensional image data, recurrent neural networks (RNNs) are networks specially designed for processing sequential data. Sequential data naturally arises in many settings: a sentence is a sequence of words; a video is a sequence of images; a stock market ticker is a sequence of prices.

Consider a simple example from the field of language processing. Each input is a sentence, modeled as a sequence of words. After processing each prefix of the sequence, we would like to predict the next word in the sentence; the output at each step is a probability vector across words. Our example suggests two key design considerations:

(1) The output at each point depends on the entire prefix of the sentence until that point, and not just the last word. The network needs to retain some "memory" of the past.
(2) The underlying language model does not change across positions in the sequence, so we should use the same parameters (weights for each of the nodes) at each position.

These considerations lead naturally to a *recurrent* network model, where we perform the same operation at each step, with the input to each step being dependent upon the output from prior steps. Figure 13.12 shows the structure of a typical recurrent neural network. The input is a sequence $x_1, x_2, \ldots, x_n$, and the output is also a sequence $y_1, y_2, \ldots, y_n$. In our example, each input x_i represents a word, and each output y_i is a probability vector for the next word in the seentence. The input x_i is typically encoded as a *1-hot vector* – a vector of length equal to the number of possible words,[10] with a 1 in the position

---

[10] Since there could in principle be an infinite number of words, we might in practice devote components of the vector only to the most common words or the words that are most important in the application at hand. Other words would all be represented by a single additional component of the vector.

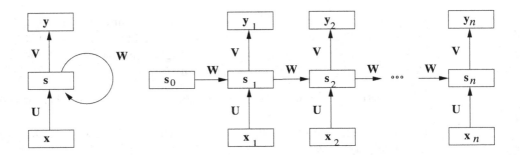

(a) The basic unit of an RNN.   (b) The unrolled RNN of length n.

Figure 13.12 RNN architecture

corresponding to the input word and a 0 in all other positions. There are two important difference between a general neural network and the RNN:

(1) The RNN has inputs at all (or almost all) layers, and not just at the first layer.
(2) The weights at each of the first n layers are constrained to be the same; these weights are the matrices U and W in Equation 13.5 below. Thus, each of the first n layers has the same set of nodes, and corresponding nodes from each of the layers share weights (and are thus really the same node), just as nodes of a CNN representing different locations share weights and are thus really the same node.

At each step t, we have a hidden state vector s_t that functions as the memory in which the network encodes information about the prefix of the sequence it has seen. The hidden state at time t is a function of the input at time t and the hidden state at time $t - 1$:

$$s_t = f(U x_t + W s_{t-1} + b) \tag{13.5}$$

Here f is a nonlinear activation function such as tanh or sigmoid. U and W are matrices of weights, and b is a vector of biases. We define s_0 to be a vector of all zeros. The output at time t is a function of the hidden state at time t, after being transformed by a parameter matrix V and an activation function g:

$$y_t = g(V s_t + c)$$

In our example, g might be the softmax function to ensure that the output is a valid probability vector.

The RNN in Figure 13.12 has an output at each time step. In some applications, such as machine translation, we need just a single output at the end of each sentence. In such cases, the RNN's single output is further processed by one or more fully-connected layers to generate the final output.

It is simplest to assume that our RNN's inputs are fixed-length sequences of length n. In this case, we simply unroll the RNN to contain n time steps. In practice, many applications have to deal with variable-length sequences e.g., sentences of varying lengths. There are two approaches to dealing with this situation:

(1) *Zero-padding.* Fix n to be the longest sequence we process, and pad out shorter sequences to be length n.

(2) *Bucketing.* Group sequences according to length, and build a separate RNN for each length.

A combination of these two approaches is used. We can create a bucket for a small number of different lengths, and assign a sequence to the bucket of the shortest length that is at least as long as the sequence. Then, within a bucket we use padding for sequences that are shorter than the maximum length for that bucket.

13.5.1   Training RNNs

We use backpropagation to train an RNN, just as we would any neural network. Let us work through an example. Suppose our input consists of sequences of length n. Our network uses the activation function tanh for the state update, softmax for the output, and the loss function is cross-entropy. Since the network has several outputs, one at each time-step, we seek to minimize the total error e, defined as the sum of the losses e_i at each time step i:

$$e = \sum_{i=1}^{n} e_i$$

To simplify notation, we use the following conventions. Suppose $\boldsymbol{x}$ and $\boldsymbol{y}$ are vectors, and z is a scalar. We define

$$\frac{dz}{d\boldsymbol{x}} = \nabla_{\boldsymbol{x}} z$$
$$\frac{d\boldsymbol{y}}{d\boldsymbol{x}} = J_{\boldsymbol{x}}(\boldsymbol{y})$$

Moreover, suppose W is a matrix, and $\boldsymbol{w}$ is the vector obtained by concatenating the rows of W. Then

$$\frac{dz}{dW} = \frac{dz}{d\boldsymbol{w}}$$
$$\frac{d\boldsymbol{y}}{dW} = \frac{d\boldsymbol{y}}{d\boldsymbol{w}}$$

These conventions also extend naturally to partial derivatives.

We use backpropagation to compute the gradients of the error with respect to the network parameters. We focus on $\frac{de}{dW}$; the gradients for U and V are similar, and left as exercises for the reader. It is clear that

$$\frac{de}{dW} = \sum_{t=1}^{n} \frac{de_t}{dW}$$

Focusing on step t, we have

$$\frac{de_t}{dW} = \frac{ds_t}{dW}\frac{de_t}{ds_t}$$

We leave it as an exercise to verify that

$$\frac{de_t}{ds_t} = V^{\mathsf{T}}(y_t - \hat{y}_t) \tag{13.6}$$

Setting $R_t = \frac{ds_t}{dW}$, we note that $s_t = \tanh(z_t)$, where $z_t = Ws_{t-1} + Ux_t + b$, we have:

$$R_t = \frac{ds_t}{dz_t}\frac{dz_t}{dW}$$

It is straightforward to verify that $\frac{ds_t}{dz_t}$ is the diagonal matrix A defined by:

$$a_{ij} = \begin{cases} 1 - s_{t_i}^2 & \text{when } i = j \\ 0 & \text{otherwise} \end{cases}$$

We should to be careful to note that z_t is a function of W both directly and indirectly, since s_{t-1} also depends on W. So we must express $\frac{dz_t}{dW}$ as a sum of two terms:

$$\frac{dz_t}{dW} = \frac{\partial z_t}{\partial W} + \frac{\partial z_t}{\partial s_{t-1}}\frac{ds_{t-1}}{dW}$$

It is easily verified that

$$\frac{\partial z_t}{\partial s_{t-1}} = W^{\mathsf{T}}$$

The form of $\frac{\partial z_t}{\partial W}$ is a little trickier. It is a matrix B with mostly zero entries, the nonzero elements being entries from s_{t-1}. We leave the computation of B as an exercise for the reader. Now, noting that $\frac{ds_{t-1}}{dW}$ is just R_{t-1}, we have the recurrence

$$R_t = A(B + W^{\mathsf{T}}R_{t-1})$$

Setting $P_t = AB$ and $Q_t = AW^{\mathsf{T}}$, we end up with

$$R_t = P_t + Q_t R_{t-1} \tag{13.7}$$

We can use this recurrence to set up an iterative evaluation of R_t, and thence $\frac{de}{dW}$. We initialize the iteration by setting R_0 to the matrix with all zeros. This iterative method for computing the gradients of an RNN is called *Backpropagation Through Time* (BPTT), since it reveals the effects of earlier time-steps on later time-steps.

13.5.2 Vanishing and Exploding Gradients

RNNs are a simple and appealing model for learning from sequences, and the BPTT algorithm is straightforward to implement. Unfortunately, RNNs have a fatal flaw that limits their use in many practical applications. They are effective only at learning short-term connections between nearby elements in the sequence and ineffective at learning long-distance connections. These are crucial in many applications; for example, there can be an arbitrary number of words or clauses separating a verb or a pronoun from the subject with which it is associated.

In order to understand the cause of this limitation, let us unroll Equation 13.7:

$$
\begin{aligned}
R_t &= P_t + Q_t R_{t-1} \\
&= P_t + Q_t(P_{t-1} + Q_{t-1}R_{t-2}) \\
&= P_t + Q_t P_{t-1} + Q_t Q_{t-1} R_{t-2}
\end{aligned}
$$
$$\cdots$$

ultimately yielding

$$
R_t = P_t + \sum_{j=0}^{t-1} P_j \prod_{k=j+1}^{t} Q_k \tag{13.8}
$$

From Equation 13.8, it is clear that the contribution of step i to R_t is given by

$$
R_t^i = P_i \prod_{k=i+1}^{t} Q_k \tag{13.9}
$$

Equation 13.9 includes the product of several matrices that look like diagonal matrix A. Each entry in A is strictly less than 1. Just as the product of many numbers, each strictly less than 1, approaches zero as we add more multiplicands, the term $\prod_{k=i+1}^{t} Q_k$ approaches zero for $i \ll t$. In other words, the gradient at step t is determined entirely by the preceding few time steps, with very little contribution from much earlier time steps. This phenomenon is called the problem of *vanishing gradients*.

Equation 13.9 results in vanishing gradients because we used the tanh activation function for state update. If instead we use other activation functions such as ReLU, we end up with the product of many matrices with large entries, resulting in the problem of *exploding gradients*. Exploding gradients are easier to handle than vanishing gradients, because we can *clip* the gradient at each step to lie within a fixed range. However, the resulting RNNs still have trouble learning long-distance associations.

13.5.3 Long Short-Term Memory (LSTM)

The LSTM model is a refinement of the basic RNN model to address the problem of learning long-distance associations. In the past few years, LSTM has become popular as the de facto sequence-learning model, and has been used with success in many applications. Let us understand the intuition behind the LSTM model before we describe it formally. The main elements of the LSTM model are:

(1) The ability to *forget* information by purging it from memory. For example, when analyzing a text we might want to discard information about a sentence when it ends. Or when analyzing a the sequence of frames in a movie, we might want to forget about the location of a scene when the next scene begins.

(2) The ability to *save* selected information into memory. For example, when we process product reviews, we might want to save only words expressing opinions (e.g., excellent, terrible) and ignore other words.

(3) The ability to *focus* only on the aspects of memory that are immediately relevant. For example, focus only on information about the characters of the current movie scene, or only on the subject of the sentence currently being analyzed. We can implement this focus by using a 2-tier architecture: a long-term memory that retains information about the entire processed prefix of the sequence, and a working memory that is restricted to the items of immediate relevance.

The RNN model has a single hidden state vector s_t at time t. The LSTM model adds an additional state vector c_t, called the *cell state*, for each time t. Intuitively, the hidden state corresponds to working memory and the cell state corresponds to long-term memory. Both state vectors are of the same length, and both have entries in the range $[-1, 1]$. We may imagine the working memory having most of its entries near zero with only the relevant entries turned "on."

The architectural ingredient that enables the ability to forget, save, and focus is the *gate*. A gate g is just a vector of the same length as a state vector s; each of the gate's entries is between 0 and 1. The Hadamard product[11] $s \circ g$ allows us to selectively pass through certain parts of the state while filtering out others. Usually, a gate vector is created by a linear combination of the hidden state and the current input. We then apply a sigmoid function to "squash" its entries to lie between 0 and 1. In general, an LSTM may use several different kinds of gate vectors, each for a different purpose. At time t, we can create a gate g as follows:

$$g = \sigma(W s_{t-1} + U x_t + b)$$

Here W and U are weight matrices and b is a bias vector.

At time t, we first compute a candidate state update vector h_t based on the previous hidden state and the current input:

$$h_t = \tanh(W_h s_{t-1} + U_h x_t + b_h) \tag{13.10}$$

---

[11] The *Hadamard product* of vectors $[x_1, x_2, \ldots, x_n]$ and $[y_q, y_2, \ldots, y_n]$ is the vector whose components are the products of the corresponding components of the two argument vectors; that is, $[x_1 y_1, x_2 y_2, \ldots, x_n y_n]$. The same operation may be applied to any matrices that have the same dimensions.

Note that W, U, and b with subscript h are two weight matrices and a bias vector that we learn and use for just the purpose of computing h_t for each t.

We also compute two gates, the *forget gate* f_t and the *input gate* i_t. The forget gate determines which aspects of the long-term memory we retain. The input gate determines which parts of the candidate state update to save into the long-term memory. These gates are computed using different weight matrices and bias vectors, which also must be learned. We indicate these matrices and vector with subscripts f and i, respectively:

$$f_t = \sigma(W_f s_{t-1} + U_f x_t + b_f) \tag{13.11}$$

$$i_t = \sigma(W_i s_{t-1} + U_i x_t + b_i) \tag{13.12}$$

We update the long-term memory using the gates and the candidate update vector as follows:[12]

$$c_t = c_{t-1} \circ f_t + h_t \circ i_t \tag{13.13}$$

Now that we have updated the long-term memory, we need to update the working memory. We do this in two steps. The first step is to create an *output gate* o_t. The second step is to apply this gate to the long-term memory, followed by a tanh activation:[13]

$$o_t = \sigma(W_u s_{t-1} + U_u x_t + b_u) \tag{13.14}$$

$$s_t = \tanh(c_t \circ o_t) \tag{13.15}$$

Here, we use subscript u to indicate two additional weight matrices and a bias vector – those concerning the output – that must be learned.

Finally, the output at time t is computed in exactly the same manner as the RNN output:

$$y_t = g(V s_t + d) \tag{13.16}$$

where g is an activation function, V is a weight matrix and d is a bias vector.

Equations 13.10 through 13.16 describe the state update operations at a single time step t of an LSTM. We can think of plain RNN as a special case of LSTM. When we set the forget gate to all 0s (so we throw away all prior long-term memory) and the input gate to all 1s (save the entire candidate state update), and the output gate to all 1s (working memory is same as long-term memory), we get something that looks very close to an RNN, the only difference being an extra tanh factor.

The ability to selectively forget allows LSTMs to avoid the vanishing-gradient problem at the expense of introducing many more parameters than vanilla RNNs.

---

[12] Technically, an entry of 1 in the forget gate results in retaining the corresponding memory entry; so the forget gate should really be called the *remember gate*. Similarly, the input gate might be better named the *save gate*. Here we follow the naming convention commonly used in the literature.

[13] Once again, the output gate might be better named the *focus gate* since it focuses the working memory on certain aspects of the long-term memory.

While we will not provide a rigorous proof here, we note that the key to avoiding vanishing gradients is the long-term memory update in Equation 13.13. Several variations of the basic LSTM model have been proposed; the most common variant is the *gated recurrent Unit* (GRU) model, which uses a single state vector instead of two state vectors (long-term and short-term). A GRU has fewer parameters than an LSTM and might be suitable in some situations with smaller data sets.

and state size s (use actual numbers). Calculate the number of parameters to be learned.

13.5.4   Exercises for Section 13.5

EXERCISE 13.5.1   In this exercise, you are asked to design the input weights for one or more nodes of the hidden state of an RNN. The input is a sequence of bits, 0 or 1 only.[14] Note that you can use other nodes to help with the node requested. Also note that you can apply a transformation to the output of the node so a "yes" answer has one value and a "no" answer has another.

(a) A node to signal when the input is 1 and the previous input is 0.

! (b) A node to signal when the last three inputs have all been 1.

!! (c) A node to signal when the input is the same as the previous input.

! EXERCISE 13.5.2   Verify Equation 13.6.

! EXERCISE 13.5.3   Give the formulas for the gradients $\frac{de}{dU}$ and $\frac{de}{dV}$ for the general RNN of Fig. 13.12.

13.6   Regularization

Thus far, we have presented our goal as one of minimizing loss (i.e., prediction error) on the training set. Gradient descent and stochastic gradient descent help us achieve this objective. In practice, the real objective of training is to minimize the loss on new and hitherto unseen inputs. Our hope is that our training set is representative of unknown future inputs, so a low loss on the training set translates into good performance on new inputs. Unfortunately, the trained model sometimes learns idiosyncrasies of the training data that allow it have low training loss, but not generalize well to new inputs – the familiar problem of overfitting.

How can we tell if a model has overfit? In general, we split the available data into a training set and a test set. We train the model using only the training-set data, withholding the test set. We then evaluate the performance of the model on the test set. If the model performs much worse on the test set than

---

[14] We should understand that RNNs, like any neural network, is to be learned from data, not designed as we are suggesting you do here.

on the training set, we know the model has overfit. Assuming data points are independent of one another, we can pick a fraction of the available data points at random to form the test set. A common ratio for the training:test split is 80:20. i.e, 80% of the data for training and 20% for test. We have to be careful, however: in sequence-learning problems (e.g., modeling time series), the state of the sequence at any point in time encodes information about the past. In such cases the final piece of the sequence is a better test set.

Overfitting is a general problem that affects all machine-learning models. However, deep neural networks are particularly susceptible to overfitting, because they use many more parameters (weights and biases) than other kinds of models. Several techniques have been developed to reduce overfitting in deep networks, usually by trading higher training error for better generalization. The process is referred to as *model regularization*. In this section we describe some of the most important regularization methods for deep learning.

13.6.1   Norm Penalties

Gradient descent is not guaranteed to learn parameters (weights and biases) that reduce the training loss to an absolute minimum. In practice, the procedure learns parameters that correspond to a *local minimum* in the training loss. There are usually many local minima, and some might lead to better generalization than others. In practice, it has been observed that solutions where the learned weights have low absolute values tend to generalize better than solutions with large weights.

We can force gradient descent to favor solutions with low weight values by adding a term to the loss function. Suppose w is the vector of all the weight values in the model, and L_0 is loss function used by our model. We define a new loss function L as follows:

$$L = L_0 + \alpha \|w\|^2 \tag{13.17}$$

The loss function L penalizes large weight values. Here α is a hyperparameter that trades off between minimizing the original loss function L_0 and the penalty associated with the L_2-norm of the weights. Instead of the L_2-norm, we could penalize the L_1-norm of the weights:

$$L = L_0 + \alpha \sum_i |w_i| \tag{13.18}$$

In practice, it is observed that the L_2-norm penalty works best for most applications. The L_1-norm penalty is useful in some situations calling for model compression, because it tends to produce models where many of the weights are zero.

13.6.2   Dropout

Dropout is a technique that reduces overfitting by making random changes to the underlying deep neural network. Recall that when we train using stochastic gradient descent, at each step we sample at random a minibatch of inputs to process. When using dropout, we also select at random a certain fraction (say half) of all the hidden nodes from the network and delete them, along with any edges connected to them. We then perform forward propagation and back-propagation for the minibatch using this modified network, and update the weights and biases. After processing the minibatch, we restore all the deleted nodes and edges. When we sample the next minibatch, we delete a different random subset of nodes and repeat the training process.

The fraction of hidden nodes deleted each time is a hyperparameter called the *dropout rate*. When training is complete, and we actually use the full network, we need to take into account that the full network contains a larger number of hidden nodes than the networks used for training. We therefore need to scale the weight on each outgoing edge from a hidden node by the dropout rate.

Why does dropout reduce overfitting? Several hypotheses have been put forward, but perhaps the most convincing argument is that dropout allows a single neural network to behave effectively as a collection of neural networks. Imagine that we have a collection of neural networks, each with a different network topology. Suppose we trained each network independently using the training data, and used some kind of voting or averaging scheme to create a higher-level model. Such a scheme would perform better than any of the individual networks. The dropout technique simulates this setup without explicitly creating a collection of neural networks.

13.6.3   Early Stopping

In Section 13.6.1 we suggested iterating through training examples (or minibatches) until we reach a local minimum in the loss function. In practice, this approach leads to overfitting. It has been observed that while the loss on the training set (the *training loss*) decreases through the training process, the loss on the test set (the *test loss*) often behaves differently. The test loss falls during the initial part of the training, and then many hit a minimum and actually increase after a large number of training iterations, even as the training loss keeps falling.

Intuitively, the point at when the test loss starts to increase is the point at which the training process has started learning idiosyncrasies of the training data rather than a generalizable model. A simple approach to avoiding this problem is to stop the training when the test loss stops falling. There is, however, a subtle problem with this approach: we might inadvertently overfit to the test data (rather than to the training data) by stopping training at the point of minimum test loss. Therefore, the test error no longer is a reliable measure of the true performance of the model on hitherto unseen inputs.

The usual solution is to use a third subset of inputs, the validation set, to determine the point at which we stop training. We split the data not just into training and test sets, but into three groups: training, validation, and test. Both the validation and test sets are withheld from the training process. When the loss on the validation set stops decreasing, we stop the training process. Since the test set has played no role at all in the training process, the test error remains a reliable indicator of the true performance of the model.

13.6.4   Dataset Augmentation

The accuracy of most machine-learning models increases when we provide additional training data. Usually, larger training sets also lead to less overfitting. When the actual training data available is limited, we can often create additional synthetic training examples by applying transformations or adding noise.

For example, consider the digit-classification problem we encountered in Example 13.7. It is clear that if we rotate an image corresponding to a digit by a few degrees, it still remains an image of the same digit. We can augment the training data by systematically applying transformations of this kind. One way to think of this process is as a way to encode additional domain knowledge (e.g., a slightly distorted image of a cat is still an image of a cat).

13.7   Summary of Chapter 13

◆ *Neural Nets*: A neural net is a collection of perceptrons (nodes), usually organized in layers, where the outputs from one layer provide inputs to the next layers. The first (inout) layer takes external inputs, and the last (output) layer indicates the class of the input. Other layers in the middle are called hidden layers and generally are trained to recognize intermediate concepts needed to determine the output.

◆ *Types of Layers*: Many layers are fully connected, meaning that each node in the layer has all the nodes of the previous layer as inputs. Other layers are pooled, meaning that the nodes of the previous layer are partitioned, and each node of this layer takes as input only the nodes of one block of the partition. Convolutional layers are also used, especially in image processing applications.

◆ *Convolutional Layers*: Convolutional layers can be viewed as if their nodes were organized into a two-dimensional array of pixels, with each pixel represented by the same collection of nodes. The weights on corresponding nodes from different pixels must be the same, so they are in effect the same node, and we need learn only one set of weights for each family of nodes, one from each pixel.

◆ *Activation Functions*: The output of a node in a neural net is determined by first taking the weighted sum of its inputs, using the weights that are learned during the process of training the net. An activation function is then applied to this sum. Common activation functions include the sigmoid function, the hyperbolic tangent, softmax, and various forms of linear recified unit functions.

✦ *Loss Functions*: These measure the difference between the output of the net and the correct output according to the training set. Commonly used loss functions include squared-error loss, Huber loss, classification loss, and cross-entropy loss.

✦ *Training a Neural Net*: We train a neural net by repeatedly computing the output of the net on training examples and computing the average loss on the training examples. Weights on the nodes are then adjusted by propagating the loss backward through the net, using the backpropagation algorithm.

✦ *Backpropagation*: By choosing our activation functions and loss functions to be differentiable, we can compute a deriative of the loss function with respect to every weight in the network. Thus, we can determine the direction in which to adjust each weight to reduce the loss. Using the chain rule, these directions can be computed layer-by-layer, from the output to the input.

✦ *Convolutional Neural Networks*: These typically consist of a large number of convolutional layers, along with pooled layers and fully connected layers. They are well suited to processing images, where the first convolutional layers recognize simple features, such as boundries, and later layers recognize progressively more complex features.

✦ *Recurrent Neural Networks*: These are designed to recognize sequences, such as sentences (sequences of words). There is one layer for each position in the sequence, and the nodes are divided into families, which each have one node at each layer. The nodes of a family are constrained to have the same weights, so the training process therefore needs to deal with a relatively small number of weights.

✦ *Long Short-Term Memory Networks*: These improve on RNNs by adding a second state vector – the cell state – to enable some information about the sequence to be retained, while most information is forgotten after a while. In addition, we learn gate vectors that control what information is retained from the input, the state, and the output.

✦ *Avoiding Overfitting*: There are a number of specialized techniques designed to avoid overfitting a deep network. These include penalizing large weights, randomly dropping some nodes each time we apply a step of gradient descent, and use of a validation set to enable us to stop training when the loss on the validation set bottoms out.

13.8   References for Chapter 13

For information on TensorFlow, see [12]. You can learn about PyTorch at [10] and about Caffe at [1]. The MNIST database is described in [9].

Backpropagation as the way to train deep neural nets is from [11].

The idea of convolutional neural networks begins with [2], which defined convolutional layers and pooling layers. However, it was [13] that introduced the idea of requiring nodes in one convolutional layer to share weights. The application of these networks to character recognition and other important tasks is from [8] and [7]. Also see [6] for the application to ImageNet of CNNs. ImageNet is available from [5].

Recurrent neural networks first appeared in [4]. Long short-term memory is from [3].

[1] http://caffe2.ai

[2] Fukushima, K., "Neocognitron, a self-organizing neural network model for a mechanism of pattern recognition unaffected by shift of position," *Biological Cybernetics* **36**:1 (1980), pp. 193–202.

[3] Hochreiter, S. and J. Schmidhuber, "Long Short-Term Memory," *Neural Computation* **9**:8 (1997), pp. 1735–1780.

[4] J.J. Hopfield, "Neural networks and physical systems with emergent collective computational abilities," *Proceedings of the National Academy of Sciences* **79**:8 (1982), pp. 2554–2558.

[5] http://www.image-net.org.

[6] Krizhevsky, A, I. Sutskever, and G.E. Hinton, "Image classification with deep convolutional neural networks," *Advances in Neural Information Processing Systems,* **25**, 1097–1105, (2012).

[7] LeCun, Y. and Y. Bengio, "Convolutional networks for images, speech, and time series," n *The Handbook of Brain Theory and Neural Networks* (M. Arbib, ed.), MIT Press, (1995).

[8] LeCun, Y., B. Boser, J.S. Denker, D. Henderson, R.E. Howard, and W. Hubbard, "Backpropagation applied to handwritten zip code recognition," *Neural Computation* **1**:4 (1989) pp. 541–551.

[9] LeCun, Y., C. Cortes, and C.J.C. Burges, "The MNIST database of handwritten digits," http://http://yann.lecun.com/exdb/mnist/

[10] http://pytorch.org

[11] Rumelhart, D.E., G.E. Hinton, and R.J. Williams, "Learning representations by back-propagating errors, *Nature* **323** (1986), pp. 533–536.

[12] http://www.tensorflow.org

[13] Waibel, A., T. Hanazawa, G.E. Hinton, K. Shikano, and K.J. Lang, "Phoneme recognition using time-delay neural networks," *IEEE Transactions on Acoustics, Speech, and Signal Processing* **37**:3 (1989), pp. 328–339.

Index

Printed in the United States
by Baker & Taylor Publisher Services